t
!

H
ir   # America's
b·
‾Lε Growing Inequality

Baiⁱᵉ
D

—

D1340364

OTHER BOOKS WRITTEN/CO-AUTHORED/EDITED/ CO-EDITED BY CHESTER HARTMAN

From Foreclosure to Fair Lending: Advocacy, Organizing, Occupy, and the Pursuit of Equitable Access to Credit—with Gregory Squires (New Village Press, 2013)

The Integration Debate: Competing Futures for American Cities—with Gregory Squires (Routledge, 2010)

Mandate for Change: Policies and Leadership for 2009 and Beyond (Lexington Books, 2009)

There's No Such Thing as a Natural Disaster: Race, Poverty and Hurricane Katrina—with Gregory Squires (Routledge, 2006)

Poverty and Race in America: The Emerging Agendas (Lexington Books, 2006)

A Right to Housing: Foundation of a New Social Agenda—with Rachel Bratt & Michael Stone (Temple Univ. Press, 2006)

City for Sale: The Transformation of San Francisco (Univ. of California Press, 2002)

Between Eminence & Notoriety: Four Decades of Radical Urban Planning (Rutgers Univ. Center for Urban Policy Research, 2002)

Challenges to Equality: Poverty and Race in America (M.E. Sharpe, 2001)

Double Exposure: Poverty and Race in America (M.E. Sharpe, 1997)

Paradigms Lost: The Post Cold War Era—with Pedro Vilanova (Pluto, 1992)

Housing Issues of the 1990s—with Sara Rosenberry (Praeger, 1989)

Winning America: Ideas and Leadership for the 1990s—with Marcus Raskin (South End Press, 1988)

Critical Perspectives on Housing—with Rachel Bratt & Ann Meyerson (Temple Univ. Press, 1986)

The Transformation of San Francisco (Rowman & Allanheld, 1984)

America's Housing Crisis: What Is To Be Done? (Routledge & Kegan Paul, 1983)

Displacement: How to Fight It—with Dennis Keating & Richard LeGates (National Housing Law Project, 1982)

Housing and Social Policy (Prentice-Hall, 1975)

Yerba Buena: Land Grab and Community Resistance in San Francisco (Glide Publications, 1974)

The World of the Urban Working Class—with Marc Fried & others (Harvard Univ. Press, 1973)

Housing Urban America—with Jon Pynoos & Robert Schafer (Aldine, 1973; Revised edition, 1980)

America's Growing Inequality

The Impact of Poverty and Race

Edited by Chester Hartman

Foreword by Chicago Congressman
Luis V. Gutiérrez

LEXINGTON BOOKS
Lanham • Boulder • New York • Toronto • Plymouth, UK

Published by Lexington Books
A wholly owned subsidiary of Rowman & Littlefield
4501 Forbes Boulevard, Suite 200, Lanham, Maryland 20706
www.rowman.com

10 Thornbury Road, Plymouth PL6 7PP, United Kingdom

British Library Cataloguing in Publication Information Available

Library of Congress Cataloging-in-Publication Data

America's growing inequality : the impact of poverty and race / edited by Chester W.
Hartman ; foreword by Chicago Congressman Luis Gutierrez.
    pages cm
  ISBN 978-0-7391-9171-2 (cloth : alk. paper) — ISBN 978-0-7391-9172-9 (ebook) 1.
Equality—United States. 2. Social stratification—United States. 3. Poverty—United States.
4. United States—Race relations. 5. United States—Social conditions. 6. United States—
Economic conditions. I. Hartman, Chester W.
  HN90.S6A55 2014
  305.800973—dc23
  ISBN 978-1-4985-2111-6 (pbk : alk, paper)   2013048981

∞™ The paper used in this publication meets the minimum requirements of
American National Standard for Information Sciences—Permanence of Paper
for Printed Library Materials, ANSI/NISO Z39.48-1992.

Printed in the United States of America

Contents

Foreword

Rep. Luis V. Gutiérrez (D-IL)

America remains iconic among nations as the "land of opportunity" and a destination for immigrants, entrepreneurs and dreamers seeking freedom and fortune. What drew my parents to the Chicago area from rural Puerto Rico in the early 1950s still draws people from all over the world to this country. Amid the optimism and self-sacrifice of my parents' generation, there were also tremendous obstacles of poverty, race, gender, education, language, discrimination and violence.

Today, many of those same obstacles to opportunity persist but have taken on different forms, sometimes subtler, but often just as real. Compared to the rest of the world, the promise of freedom and fortune remains alive in the United States, but the reality of increased economic inequality in American society has set in, making us more and more like the rest of the world; and increasingly so, as we enter the second decade of the 21st century, in a prolonged period of economic stagnation or decline. Economic inequality, and the uneven distribution of economic inequality across gender, race and ethnicity, has intensified.

The Great Recession, which followed the financial crisis of 2007–2008, has thrown into sharp relief trends in inequality that have been growing since the early 1980s.[1] Wealth and income have increasingly been concentrated at the top, with the share of income earned by the wealthiest 10 percent of households increasing from 34.6 percent in 1980 to 48.2 percent in 2008, and the share of income earned by the wealthiest 1 percent of households increasing from 10.0 percent in 1980 to 21.0 percent in 2010. Remarkably, inequality has only increased since the onset of our slow recovery; Pew Research Center analysis indicates the mean net worth of households in the top 7 percent of wealth distribution has increased by an estimated 28 percent during the first two years of recovery, while the mean net worth of the remaining 93 percent of households dropped by 4 percent during the same period.

While there is a significant racial gap in terms of income, the wealth gap may be an even more significant indicator of inequality, with White families on average owning approximately six times the wealth that Black and Latino families own. The Great Recession had a disparate racial impact, resulting in Latino families losing 40 percent of their wealth, Black families losing 31 percent of their wealth, and White families losing only 11 percent of their wealth. Additionally, while mid-wage jobs accounted for the bulk of jobs lost during the Great Recession, low-wage jobs have accounted for the majority of jobs created during the recovery. Minorities, Latinos in particular, are overrepresented in low-wage employment at a time when the federal minimum wage has seen a decline in terms of purchasing power (the federal minimum wage is currently pegged at $7.25 per hour, while it would be $10.67 per hour if it had kept pace with inflation since its creation in 1938). This continued rise in inequality and concentrated wealth illustrates the need for forward-thinking policy solutions, making this publication, and the ideas contained therein, all the more timely and valuable.

NOTES

1. Even before the recession, wages for American workers were on a multidecade decline. What Yale political scientist Jacob Hacker describes as "the breaking of the historical connection between 'growing economic output on the one hand and middle-class wages and income on the other'" has resulted in widening income inequality. http://www.nclr.org/images/uploads/publications/NCLR_Minimum_Wage_Fact_Sheet_April_2013.pdf

Introduction

Chester Hartman

PRRAC began publishing *Poverty & Race* shortly after its establishment in 1990, originally as a quarterly, a few years later expanded into a bi-monthly, its present form.

The upside of frequent publication of a popularly written periodical is how quickly, compared to books and most academic journals, research results, opinion pieces, etc. get out to the relevant audiences (not only our regular readership—a diverse group of academics, researchers, activists, legislators and other public officials, the media, foundations, etc.—but more recently via various web and Internet links).

The downside is that materials in this form often are soon discarded, have no longer life, which is something appropriate for much of what we publish.

Therefore, we've published three "best of *Poverty & Race*" volumes (some still available), each containing what, in my judgment, are the articles with more lasting relevance and appeal. These are:

> *Double Exposure: Poverty & Race in America* (M.E. Sharpe, 1997), Forewords by Julian Bond and by Bill Bradley

> *Challenges to Equality: Poverty and Race in America* (M.E. Sharpe, 2001), Foreword by Rep. John Lewis

> *Poverty & Race in America: The Emerging Agendas* (Lexington Books, 2006), Foreword by Rep. Jesse L. Jackson, Jr.

And so this is our fourth such book—and hopefully not the last. As with all such, the contributors—some well-known, others newish writers/voices—represent a wide and impressive range of researchers and activists (see the contributors section at end the book). This volume covers *Poverty & Race* issues from 2006 through most of 2013. Let me add one orthographic note: We have tried our best to produce a consistent style throughout and to not alter what's in quoted material—not the easiest task, given the varied style forms used by well over 100 authors. The one intentional inconsistency is whether the first letter of racial terms is capitalized or lower-case ("black" or "Black"—e.g.), since such usage, for many, has levels of meaning well beyond mere style.

We hope this volume will reach lots and lots of people and organizations concerned with our society's shameful record and current manifestation of poverty and racism—and will be used as course texts in many disciplines, as has been the case with the earlier books. We encourage feedback from readers as to the book's content, organization and use (send to chartman@prrac.org). And we hope readers will advance needed research and advocacy on the various topics the book's chapter cover.

Finally, some appropriate acknowledgments. Shanti Prasad proved an excellent assistant for the final stages of the book, supplemented by Jeremy Hartman—making up for this editor's limited technological capabilities. Similarly, Teri Grimwood provided related assistance, including preparing the index, in the manner she and I have been working together for a great many years, laying out each issue of *Poverty & Race* and doing the same indexing work for several of my earlier books. At my publisher, Lexington Books, Associate Editor Justin Race, Assistant Editor Alissa Parra, Associate Editor Kelly Shefferly, and proofreader Sue Draper have been most helpful working with me to put this volume together. PRRAC's Board member Don Nakanishi offered a useful suggestion for identifying the book's foreword writer. PRRAC Executive Director Philip Teleger has been of considerable assistance. And a number of PRRAC's former Interns and Fellows were helpful with specific tasks: Cara Brumfield, Greg Groves, Brittany Henry, Lauren Hill, Jasmine Jeffers, Joyce Leighton, Michele Vinson, and especially Brittney Calloway.

Chester Hartman
chartman@prrac.org

I

RACISM AND POVERTY: THE STRUCTURAL UNDERPINNINGS

Toward a Structural Racism Framework

Andrew Grant-Thomas & john a. powell

For many people, the term "structural racism" mystifies rather than clarifies. Popular confusion around what is meant by the term hampers our collective ability to build on the real gains made by two generations of anti-racism activism. With the end of Jim Crow laws and a clear decline in the most blatant forms of interpersonal racial discrimination, critical race projects often lack the explanatory clarity needed to effectively ground the ongoing struggle against racial inequity in the 21st century. As a result, anti-racist efforts can prove ineffective, even counterproductive. The absence of a clear understanding of structural racism also supports the cynicism of people who regard as "whining" any analysis that departs from strict individualist interpretations of racial inequality today.

The discussion of structural racism we present in this chapter and employ in the work of the Structural Racism Caucus emphasizes the powerful impact of inter-institutional dynamics, institutional resource inequities and historical legacies on racial inequalities today. These factors do not alone determine the depth or scope of racial inequality. In arenas from employment to housing to healthcare, interpersonal racial bias remains an active and powerful contributor to racial inequality. Economic booms and recessions, globalization, and technological and medical innovation certainly matter. Insofar as group "culture" is an adaptation to restrictive (or expansive) opportunity structures, cultural factors may also play a role. On the other hand, the social structures we emphasize promote racially inequitable distributions of social, political and economic goods and services even in the absence of avowed "racists," even absent self-sabotaging behavior by racial minorities, and notwithstanding the play of macroeconomic, cultural and other large-scale factors. Any promising attempt to dismantle the underpinning of durable racial inequality must account for the structural dynamics we highlight here.

TRADITIONAL APPROACHES
TO THINKING ABOUT RACISM

In terms of our understanding of racism, the last 50 years of activism and theorizing around race and racial inequality seem to have left us back where we started. Today, both popular and scholarly definitions of racism similarly refer most often to beliefs and belief systems, to feelings, or to behaviors based on race. Several features of this common sense about the nature of racism deserve mention:

On the one hand, because we associate feelings, beliefs and behaviors primarily with individuals, most accounts imply that racism is first and foremost a matter of individual agency. According to this conception, racism is lodged in the hearts and minds of individuals and made manifest by the words they speak, the actions they perform and the thoughts they harbor. The essentialist tinge of this construction is clear: One is or is not racist, all the time or never. As a rule, people's words and actions also are interpreted as racist only if they are intentionally enacted to produce outcomes that injure some or benefit others. Finally, for many, racism requires that the offending word or act be race-targeted.

Although the individualist, essentialist, intentionalist and race-targeted model of racism reflects our present common sense about the nature of racism, anti-racism efforts have long recognized the model's weaknesses as a general or inclusive account of racism. "Institutional racism" was the designation given in the late 1960s to the recognition that, at very least, racism need not be individualist, essentialist or intentional. Institutional racism can be prescribed by formal rules but depends, minimally, on organizational cultures that tolerate such behaviors. Racist institutional decisions neither require nor preclude the participation of racist individuals. In Jim Crow laws and anti-miscegenation statutes, many observers saw that the law, the institutions it governed and even the broader culture itself related differently to African Americans than to whites. Those institutional and cultural practices generated a dynamic only partly dependent on the racial attitudes of the people engaged in them. This suggested that while racist individuals had to be monitored and possibly reformed, rehabilitating our key social, political and cultural institutions was even more critical to the achievement of racial justice.

The institutional racism framework reflects a broader recognition of the forms through which racialized power is deployed, dispersed and entrenched. However, while elucidating ways in which racism is often nonindividualist, nonessentialist and nonintentionalist by focusing on intra-institutional dynamics, this framework fails to account for the ways in which the joint operations of social institutions produce important outcomes. This is a crucial gap, for it is often the interaction between institutions, rather than the operation of each in isolation, that generates racial group disparities. Whereas both the individual and institutional racism frameworks emphasize dynamics triggered immediately by race, racism and racial inequality often originate in treatment inspired by nonrace factors (e.g., class status, religious belief, language) that interact with race in patterned ways. This kind of secondary racism, a function of inter-institutional relations, forms the leading edge of structural racism.

THE STRUCTURAL RACISM FRAMEWORK

We review and critique the theoretical frameworks of individual racism and of institutional racism, not to suggest that they are irrelevant to understanding racial inequality today, but rather to underline their incompleteness. This is not merely a matter of semantics. Each framework represents vastly different ways of understanding the contemporary production of racial inequality. Each identifies different causes and implications, and points to different strategic responses. We present the structural racism framework as one that offers important additional insight into the nature of racism today and as a model for effective social praxis.

One's capacity to flourish, or "to lead a life one has reason to value," as Nobel Laureate Amartya Sen describes it, is contingent on access to opportunity. Opportunities, as we define them here, are resources and services that contribute to stability and advancement. Access to opportunity is not equally available to all. In American society, opportunity is produced and regulated by institutions, institutional interactions and individuals, jointly and differentially providing and denying access along lines of race, gender, class and other markers of social difference.

From both the individual and institutional racism perspectives, racist treatment attaches directly to the victim's race; the difference lies in the degree to which each sees racism as institutionally constrained. Where the individual racism view focuses on race-targeted, discretionary treatment, institutional racism speaks to the race-targeted and procedural (i.e., rule-based) dimension of racism. As institutional racism shifts our focus from the motives and actions of individual people to the practices and procedures within an institution, structural racism shifts attention from the single, intra-institutional setting to inter-institutional arrangements and interactions. "Inter-institutional arrangements and interactions" are what we mean by "structures." We turn away from the internal dynamics of institutions, not because those dynamics are incidental to the production of racial inequality, but because we want to highlight the degree to which (and means by which) inter-institutional arrangements themselves shape very important results.

Because Americans often take individual people to be the main vehicles of racism, we fail to appreciate the work done by racially inequitable structures. But, in fact, all complex societies feature institutional arrangements that help to create and distribute the society's benefits, burdens and interests. These structures are neither natural nor neutral, as Harvard law professor Roberto Unger argues. And just as we cannot account for or address the impact of institutional racism by only considering a given individual's actions or psychological state, we cannot adequately understand the work structures do simply by looking at the practices and procedures of a single institution, as political philosopher John Rawls underscores. Iris M. Young uses

Marilyn Frye's bird-in-the-birdcage metaphor for illustrating the works of structures. If we approach the problem of durable racial inequality one "bar" at a time, it is hard to appreciate the fullness of the bird's entrapment, much less formulate a suitable response to it. Explaining the bird's inability to take flight requires that we recognize the connectedness of multiple bars, each reinforcing the rigidity of the others. In confronting racism, we must similarly account for multiple, intersecting and often mutually reinforcing disadvantages, and develop corresponding response strategies.

We can describe a social system as structurally racist to the degree that it is configured to promote racially unequal outcomes. For example, a society marked by highly interdependent opportunity structures and large inter-institutional resource disparities will likely be very unequal with respect to the outcomes governed by those institutions and opportunity structures. Whether that inequality assumes a racial caste will depend, in part, on the racial conditions in place when the current structural configuration came into being, conditions that will have been shaped in turn partly by the previous structural configuration. The dynamic established by initial conditions can be very durable indeed. In a society that features structural inequalities with respect to opportunities and institutional resources, initial racial inequality in motion will likely stay in motion. But, again, actual outcomes, including the depth of inequality, will depend substantially on nonstructural factors, dynamics at the individual and intra-institutional levels not least among them. A thorough analysis of a given racial disparity will look to all three levels.

SOCIAL OPPORTUNITY AS A FUNCTION OF INTER-INSTITUTIONAL DYNAMICS

Institutional actors matter, not only because of the social goods under their immediate purview (schools and education, hospitals and medical care, faith-based organizations and spiritual guidance, among others), but also for the variable terms of access they offer to other institutions and to social networks. The operation of different institutional actors within and across domains such as education, employment, healthcare and criminal justice jointly produce social opportunities and outcomes. This interdependence has profound implications for transmitting inequality across domains and for remedying inequality. But how is racial inequality, in particular, introduced into the system in the first place? Part of the answer lies at the level of interpersonal and intra-institutional processes, which is why we underline the insights of the individual and institutional racism perspectives. Another important part of the answer is given by history.

THE SEDIMENT OF HISTORY

We argue that there are powerful causal links between historically grounded arrangements and conditions and present inequalities. The general failure to recognize them owes to several factors. For one, many people, especially white Americans, mistakenly believe that racial equality has already been achieved, not only in terms of the law and popular sensibilities, but in terms of group outcomes as well. Six in ten white respondents to a 2001 national survey by the *Washington Post,* the Kaiser Family Foundation and Harvard University believed that blacks had equal or better access to healthcare than whites do. Half thought blacks and whites had similar levels of education, and half thought blacks enjoyed comparable job status.

Perhaps the most important reason for past-present myopia in this context is the one highlighted by the structural racism framework—the inappropriately narrow construction of racism that sets the terms of the racial inequality debate in the United States. If we insist that racism can only take recognizably individualist, essentialist, intentionalist and race-targeted forms, then, indeed, with the demise of Jim Crow laws the connections between the past and present are relatively few and largely symbolic. But what if we relaxed the assumption that racism attaches only to people, policies and practices that intentionally discriminate on the basis of race? What if we agreed that racism is best defined with respect to the outcome it produces (racial inequality), rather than with reference to its specific content or intent? From this conceptual vantage point it becomes clear that the legacies of the past remain deeply implicated in the production and reproduction of racial and ethnic inequality in a variety of ways.

For example, the roots of contemporary wealth disparities between whites and nonwhites lie mainly in historical public and private sector practices that allowed millions of white, but not black, families to buy homes and build equity in the 1940s, 1950s and 1960s. The FHA funded sales in racially homogeneous white neighborhoods and favored the purchase of homes in the suburbs. The underwriting manual for home mortgage insurance disseminated by the federal government was forthrightly racist.

The federal government also pushed home buyers to adopt covenants that precluded the sale of subsidized homes to nonwhites. While both racial covenants and racist mortgage insurance policies were declared unconstitutional in 1948, their legacy prompted private companies to engage in redlining practices that continue to shape housing market outcomes. The effects of those policies play out in the huge contemporary gaps in the intergenerational transfers of wealth.

CONCLUSION

We believe that interpersonal and institutional racisms remain potent contributors to the persistence of racial and ethnic inequalities. We also acknowledge the likelihood that a range of other factors not discussed here also play important roles. But we also insist that any approach to remedying inequality that does not account for the role of inter-institutional arrangements and interactions and historical legacies is likely to fail or, at best, enjoy only partial success.

Borrowing from sociology professor Eduardo Bonilla-Silva, we can list four ways in which a structural racism approach troubles and refigures more conventional frameworks, with important implications for analysis and policy intervention. First, in contrast to the individualist discourse, a structural understanding conceives of racism as a societal outcome. Second, while traditional conceptualizations of racism understand it as a static phenomenon, a structural understanding sees racism as a dynamic force recognized more for its effects than for any particular content. Third, while traditional approaches identify only race-targeted treatment as possibly racist, a structural understanding underlines the significance of both overt and covert modes. Fourth, traditional understandings of racism conceive of it as a historical phenomenon whose presence in 21st century America can only be regarded as anomalous. The structural perspective understands contemporary disparities as partly derivative from norms and conditions established long ago, including some established without racial intent.

Structural Racism: Focusing on the Cause

Cliff Schrupp

Thanks to *Poverty & Race* (Nov./Dec., 2006) [available on PRRAC's website, www. prrac.org] for the detailed discussion on "Structural Racism." There are some perspectives advanced in the various articles that can be useful for practitioners, like myself, who need to keep ourselves informed about the theoretical dimensions of "racism" as it is practiced by white individuals and by white-controlled organizations and institutions. The following is being written from the perspective of one white male individual who has spent his adult life attempting to positively affect both the behavior and attitudes of white persons and white-dominated organizations and institutions on the issue of race. The intent of this chapter is to help focus some of the actions being taken to address the issue of racism on the basic cause of the problem, actions that are based on the myth of white racial superiority.

THE MYTH OF WHITE RACIAL SUPERIORITY

There has been a tendency among some social and civil rights theorists to properly identify "white racism" as the problem in race relations, and then focus most of their analysis and recommendations on remedying the symptoms of the problem in African-American communities. While such discussions and actions are often appropriate and necessary, they do little to address and change the root cause of the problem within the white community: actions that are based on the myth of white racial superiority. This chapter will attempt to offer some suggestions, primarily based on my own experiences, on ways to challenge, confront and change behaviors in the white community based on that myth.

This venture into addressing the cause of the problem is taken with knowledge of, and great appreciation for, the position taken by many African Americans that attempting to change white folks is a waste of time and resources. (Randall Robinson, in *Quitting America*, asserted: "America will always be a society of antagonistically opposed racial awareness. We will always be the majority's afterthought, modified Americans, parentheticals.") However, I am a white person, and I am responsible for the racist actions and behavior of myself and other white persons, organizations and institutions. My efforts, and the efforts of other persons of all races and nationalities, to challenge, confront and change the racist behavior in the white community may prove to be inadequate and futile, but without these efforts, the certainty of continued actions based on the myth of white racial superiority is assured.

The very helpful "structural racism" analyses included in *Poverty & Race* are part of the effort to change the racially based behavior of white-dominated institutions and social structures in the United States. There were some very practical suggestions made in the articles concerning institutional policies and behavioral changes that, if implemented, can help produce more equitable results, but little new insight concerning how to obtain the racially directed changes from white-dominated institutions that have consistently resisted racially directed corrective actions. This chapter is intended to add to the "structural racism" discussion some thoughts on ways to generate positive changes on the issue of race from white individuals and white-dominated institutions.

In the 1960s, when civil rights activists began using the phrase "institutional racism," one of the ways we used to help participants in seminars and action projects understand the subject matter was to define "institution" as "an organized social structure that makes decisions for which no one takes personal responsibility." Without thinking about the issue of race, many people were, and still are, acquainted with the jello-like responses of many social structures to complaints about policies or procedures. In an effort to achieve the desired change, we are left with the often futile task of identifying someone, or some group, in charge who will authorize the desired change. The lesson: Institutions, or social structures, do not change themselves. They change because someone, or a group of someones, has decided, for whatever reason, that change is necessary and they are in a position to effectuate that change. The implication for the discussion of structural racism is that there is a clear and crucial relationship between a structural racism analysis and an analysis of how we move individuals to the point where they make, or assist in making, those decisions that will positively change policies and practices of institutions and social structures in relation to the issue of race. The following discussion points to one of the ways that has worked, and is still working, to prompt individuals and groups of individuals in the housing industry to make positive institutional and social structure changes in relation to the issue of race.

FAIR HOUSING EDUCATION/ LAW ENFORCEMENT

When the Fair Housing Center of Metropolitan Detroit (FHC-Detroit) was organized in 1977, the organizers recognized that there were two models for addressing and changing the racially discriminatory practices of members of the housing industry: fair housing education and fair housing law enforcement. FHC-Detroit, and most of the 90+ other private, nonprofit fair housing organizations in the U.S., concluded that their first priority was assisting in effective fair housing law enforcement, with the expectation that strong enforcement of fair housing laws will prompt an environment in the housing industry that will make fair housing educational efforts desirable and effective. The strategy proved effective and continues to be the primary operating strategy of most of the fair housing groups in the U.S.

A few examples of the effectiveness of the "enforcement" strategy of FHC-Detroit may be helpful. Other private fair housing groups in the U.S. report similar positive examples.

- When FHC-Detroit was organized in 1977, virtually no rental, sales or mortgage-lending firm felt the need to provide fair housing training because "there have been no complaints or lawsuits against us." Today, after over 390 FHC-Detroit-assisted housing discrimination lawsuits have produced in excess of $9,000,000 in awards and settlements for the plaintiffs in those lawsuits, virtually every major rental management and real estate sales firm in the metropolitan Detroit area employs persons to be in charge of their fair housing employee education programs. FHC-Detroit staff have been hired by over 30 such firms to train in excess of 3,000 housing industry employees on fair housing laws. Some of the persons trained now take those laws seriously and attempt to follow those laws.

- In 1998, FHC-Detroit began to annually present "Fair Housing Leadership Awards" to members of the housing industry who have taken important and often courageous actions in support of fair housing practices. Included among the award recipients have been African-American agents and brokers who have openly and publicly challenged the racially discriminatory practices of white members and institutions in the industry; white real estate agents who have informed FHC-Detroit and the FBI of threats to the life and safety of themselves and their African-American buyers by white neighbors who objected to the possibility of having African-American neighbors; a white sales agent who refused a request by a retired state of Michigan district court judge to disclose the race of the buyer of his $64,000 residential property. The seller took the house off of the market and the agent informed the buyer and FHC-Detroit of the unlawful actions of the judge. The buyer, an African-American Gulf War veteran, filed a federal lawsuit that was settled with a $35,000 payment to the plaintiff.

- The Michigan Association of Realtors, prior to 1977, had opposed both state and federal fair housing legislation and had attempted to ignore fair housing issues. Since 1977, it has encouraged fair housing educational programs and requirements for sales agents and brokers; has publicly praised and presented awards to some of the real estate sales agents who have received FHC-Detroit Fair Housing Leadership Awards; has become the first statewide Realtor

Association in the U.S. to contract with a private nonprofit fair housing group to conduct fair housing tests of Association members.

- Top officials of three rental management companies, each of which were defendants in previous FHC-Detroit-assisted litigations, have come forward with critical evidence of racial discrimination by the owner of a multifamily housing complex in Livonia, Michigan. Their evidence has prompted a major racial discrimination lawsuit filed by FHC-Detroit and the U.S. Department of Justice (*FHC and U.S. v. General Properties Company*, Case #05-71426, U.S. District Court, Eastern District of Michigan, Southern Division).

There is little reason to believe that the still far-too-few positive fair housing actions of the real estate professionals and the firms that employed them would have occurred absent the motivation provided by 30 years of fair housing enforcement and litigation activities. Effective housing discrimination investigations and litigation activities have become the major tool for prompting behavior changes in the housing industry, especially changes by industry leaders who make key policies and practices decisions that can positively impact the behavior of employees and other members of the industry. When an employer who had previously not even talked with his/her employees about fair housing now says that following fair housing laws is a condition of employment, employees tend to listen.

What this suggests in relation to the issue of structural racism is the importance of improving and developing effective ways to positively impact choices and decisions made in relation to the issue of race by white individuals who control the institutions and structural arrangements in the U.S. We already know many strategies that have not worked particularly well: focusing on class distinctions and glossing over racial inequities; hoping that lower- and middle-class whites will identify more with their similarly situated African-American brothers and sisters than they do with the white-dominated institutions that employ them; waiting for the next generation of whites to be better than the previous one; informing white folks of the negative impact of our decisions on African Americans, with the naive expectation that increased knowledge of inequities will produce positive behavioral changes in the white community; promoting "diversity" as a goal without dealing with the past and continuing reality of white racism and white-skin privilege; holding Human Relations Day luncheons and dinners.

We also know that there have been very few actions that have been effective tools to positively change the decisions and choices made by white persons. Legal actions, where possible, have been helpful—especially in relation to voting rights, public accommodations, employment discrimination and housing discrimination. The argument that "diversity" and "fair and equal" practices are "good business practices" that positively impact the "bottom line" has been cited by some, but not very many, business executives as reasons for improved racial behavior. Actions by units of government, especially the U.S. military, to train personnel on human relations issues and to enforce equal opportunity requirements have had positive impacts both within and outside of the military. Informal "affirmative actions," long practiced by white folks to help ensure that other white folks receive the benefits of white-skin privilege, have been reluctantly extended to include some African Americans, but when "affirmative action" policies are incorporated into public policy by units of government or educational institutions they face much public, and an increasing degree of judicial, opposition.

NEEDED: CHANGING WHITE ATTITUDES AND DECISIONS

Other than noting the positive impact of some corrective actions in the housing industry, this chapter is simply a call for increased attention to the issue of changing the racial attitudes and decisions of white individuals as a necessary part of effecting positive institutional and structural changes in relation to the issue of race. To repeat: Institutions do not change themselves. Lawsuits that expose unlawful practices have had a positive impact on white behavior in the housing industry. We know how to open up the housing industry to examination and, with the assistance of laws and the courts, produce positive changes. What else is working in other institutions? This chapter is a call for social scientists, and other academics, to continue efforts to expose the negative impacts of white behavior on African-American persons, and help us focus some efforts toward addressing the basic cause of our racial problems in the U.S.: actions that are based on the myth of white racial superiority.

American Indian Tribes and Structural Racism

Sherry Salway Black

American Indian tribes and people face circumstances unique to any other racial or ethnic group in the United States. No other racial or ethnic group has as the basis of its relationship with the U.S. a legal framework of treaties, executive orders, judicial rulings and laws spanning centuries. This legal framework, developed over the past 300 years, has resulted in a system that was supposed to protect the rights and trust assets of tribes and Indian people, but in reality has created structures and systems that thwart self-determination and diminish the value of Native assets. These constraints, coupled with social and economic inequities, are the root cause of the severe problems that tribal governments face in providing the infrastructure, services and conditions necessary for healthy community development.

Analysis of the socioeconomic conditions confronting tribes and Indian people today typically focuses on this unique federal Indian history and relationship. It is not often described in terms of racially based policies and inequities, but rather a direct [federal] nation-to-[tribal] nation relationship, from which the federal trust responsibility is derived. Yet one cannot overlook or undermine the racial basis of many policies of colonialism and paternalism that are the hallmarks of federal-Indian relations and are reflected in present-day policies.

Historically and continuing into the modern era, the Indian policies of the federal government have been aimed either at dismantling tribal governments and assimilating Native people or at paternalistically isolating tribes to misappropriate their assets. By all accounts, these mixed and often misguided efforts resulted in the devastating social conditions found on many reservation communities today. Moreover, these policies left tribal governments facing a host of structural impediments that hamper their ability to fulfill their governmental responsibilities to their citizens.

At various times, the federal government has forcibly removed Native people from their homelands to reservations; divested Native people of millions of acres of valuable land filled with natural resources; required generations of Indian children to attend residential boarding schools far from their homes; passed legislation authorizing the termination of more than 100 tribal governments; forced tribal governments to adopt unfamiliar and inappropriate governance structures; and initiated a large-scale effort to relocate Native people from their tribal communities to urban areas. These policies had, as their basis, a prevailing view of the inferiority and incapability of Indian people in managing their own affairs and economic assets, and a goal of assimilation into the dominant, or white, Anglo-Christian culture. The lasting impact of these federal policies on tribal communities cannot be overstated.

Given these structural barriers and the resultant devastating conditions, it would be easy to let a sense of hopelessness overwhelm efforts for positive change in Native communities. Yet starting in the new era of self-determination in the 1960s and growing to the present day, tribal leaders are forging a new path to break down the pillars of structural racism that diminish opportunities for their peoples. Building strong foundations of tribal governance through systemic reform, leadership development and citizen engagement is a growing movement in American Indian communities today. Overcoming centuries of colonialism and paternalism will not be easy or quick, but the alternative cannot be considered.

Structural Racism and Rebuilding New Orleans

Maya Wiley

How do we rebuild an entire region, rebuild our country, and make it healthier, increasing the economic, social and political well-being of all its residents? And why does it matter for the nation? These are questions posed by the story of Gulf Coast rebuilding and of the fight to recover New Orleans. To answer them, we must look at race, particularly the way it has driven our structural arrangements–multiinstitutional interactions–which have created conditions for scarcity of resources instead of opportunities. We must also look at how to use race to transform the structural arrangements. Race has built an unsound house. The foundation is cracked, and the basement is filling with water. Those in the basement, largely people of color, thanks to generations of race discrimination, will drown first. But the upper floors will eventually fill with water too.

Consider that, nationally, from 2000 to 2005, housing costs rose 52 percent while incomes rose but 2 percent. Then consider that the U.S. Department of Housing and Urban Development's programs reach only 25 percent of those eligible. Our increasing insecurity across communities is a national issue brought into sharp relief in the Gulf Coast. Fifty-three percent of New Orleans' units were rental units. Yet rebuilding policies barely address that reality. Rental housing costs have risen almost 40 percent in New Orleans since the levees failed, thanks to the destruction of much of the rental housing stock. Rebuilding the Gulf Coast provides an opportunity to adopt policies to fix our local and national problems. If we pay attention to the basement, pour a better, stronger foundation and make sure no one is relegated to the basement, our national house would provide a place of community and comfort, as well as a reliable shelter from the storms we must weather.

The structural racism analysis, a diagnostic as well as strategic tool, helps us identify and target the national investments and national, state and local policies and practices that will both build a stronger New Orleans and a stronger nation. Struc-

16

tural racism looks to the relationship and interaction between our public and private institutions which produce barriers for people-of-color communities and, therefore, everyone. Schools, colleges and universities, employers, banks, housing, transportation systems and news media do not operate in isolation. They work together and affect each other. Employers want to be near transportation hubs. We look for housing near good schools. Schools are locally funded, so they tend to be better where housing is expensive. Thanks to a history of race discrimination that both created and disinvested in poor communities of color and poor communities in general, these relationships do not impact communities in a race-neutral way.

Consider, for example, that the federal government invested in the creation of a white middle class with both New Deal and post-World War II programs, giving those who received those investments opportunities to improve their lives. These programs were critically important, but also largely discriminated against people of color. The Federal Housing Administration (FHA), created in 1934, subsidized mortgages and insured private mortgages, but often required new owners to add racially restrictive covenants to their deeds, ensuring all-White neighborhoods. By the 1950s, federal money insured half the mortgages in the United States, but only in segregated White neighborhoods. The FHA urged developers, bankers and local governments to use zoning ordinances and physical barriers to protect racial segregation. The post-World War II GI Bill fueled a massive movement of White men into high-paying professional and managerial jobs. Blacks, many of whom were denied entry to the armed services because of the color of their skin, were less likely to get GI Bill benefits. Black veterans who did qualify did not get the good-paying jobs. In addition to job discrimination, the United States Employment Service funneled many Black veterans into low-skilled, lower-paying jobs than their White comrades in arms. These policies resulted in the creation of White suburbs and the shrinking of urban tax bases around the country, increasing racial segregation and concentrated poverty.

If your grandparents had an eighth-grade education, could not get a mortgage loan and were not eligible for any government mortgage assistance programs because of their race, they had no house to refinance to pay for a child's college tuition. They had no house to leave to next generations. They had no retirement benefits. White people, even poor ones, often had more educational opportunities, got more government help to buy homes and were able to buy them in areas where their homes would appreciate in value. This meant they could build asset wealth even if their incomes were low, and help their children and grandchildren. Racial disparities—high rates of poverty, unemployment, illnesses, etc.—are symptoms of structural arrangements that produced, directly or indirectly, disinvestment in communities of color.

This is an important point because while White poverty is unacceptable, White poverty and Black and Latino poverty nationally do not look the same. For example, 34 percent of poor Blacks and 22 percent of poor Latinos live in high-poverty neighborhoods (where at least 25 percent of the residents are poor), compared to only 6 percent of poor Whites. In fact, a low-income White family earning $15,000 per year has about $10,000 in asset wealth, while the same low-income Black family has zero asset wealth. In New Orleans, these disparities may explain why, as the Brookings Institution has reported, 32.7 percent of Black New Orleanians had no car to escape the flood waters, while more than 90 percent of Whites did. Again, White and Black poverty did not look the same, since 52 percent of poor Black New Orleanians lacked access to a car, compared to only 17 percent of poor Whites.

New Orleans exemplifies the multi-institutional historic policies and practices that produced White suburbs and nonwhite concentrated poverty. New Orleans has become more segregated and poverty more concentrated over the last 40 years. An important Brookings Institution report noted that as recently as 1976, there were no New Orleans neighborhoods with a concentration of Blacks. In 1970, although New Orleans was a poor city, its poor were not highly concentrated in hyper-segregated neighborhoods. Between 1970 and 2000, the poverty rates in the city didn't change, but there were 66 percent more neighborhoods of concentrated poverty (here defined as 40 percent or more of the residents living at or below the poverty level). This means that poor people had fewer choices about where to live and were living in communities with few jobs, inadequate transit to jobs and underfunded, poor-performing schools. In 1970, 54 percent of the region's population lived in the central city, but by 2000 New Orleans had only 36 percent of the region's population. This loss of population also meant the loss of jobs. In 1970, the city had two-thirds of the region's jobs. By 2000, the city's share of jobs sank to less than half (42 percent) of the region's jobs. The city lost jobs and tax revenues to the suburbs. Suburbs often do not thrive when the urban centers they are built around are struggling. The Census Bureau estimates that, in 2004, no population growth occurred in the New Orleans metropolitan region as a whole, and between 2000 and 2005 the city lost almost 29,000 residents.

Given that opportunity has not been spread evenly or fairly, it is not surprising that New Orleans' people-of-color communities were both more vulnerable to the flooding and, while incredibly resilient under the circumstances, are struggling to rebuild. Sixty-seven percent of the city was Black before the levees gave way to a Category 3 Hurricane Katrina (compared to 42 percent in 1970). Almost one-third (28 percent) of New Orleanians were poor, and 84 percent of those poor were Black. Poor Blacks were four times more likely than poor Whites to live in extremely poor areas (43 percent compared to 11 percent) and, according to the Louisiana Department of Education, during the 2004–2005 school year, the state considered 63 percent of New Orleans' public schools "academically unacceptable." Public education in New Orleans was 93 percent Black and only 4 percent White, and 74 percent of its black students were poor. Crime rates were high, and the city's criminal justice system contributed about 16 percent of the state's prison population.

Generally, those most significantly impacted by the current state of New Orleans, with the notable exceptions of the wealthy and predominantly White Lakeview neighborhood and the largely White working-class St. Bernard Parish, are poor communities of color. In the city of New Orleans, communities of color made up nearly

80 percent of the population in flooded neighborhoods. Over 20 percent of people hit hard by the flood waters from the broken levees were living at or below the poverty line, and another 30 percent were living just above the poverty line. Almost half (44 percent) of those harmed by the broken levees were Black. Nearly 70 percent of poor people impacted by the storm were Black.

The Center for Social Inclusion's (CSI) new report, "The Race to Rebuild: The Color of Opportunity and the Future of New Orleans," examines how rebuilding is progressing in planning districts across New Orleans. According to CSI's analysis contained in the study's Report Card, rebuilding is not making the grade. Rebuilding is far from robust in any community, but communities of color, regardless of middle-class status, are having a harder time rebuilding. Previous residents of neighborhoods such as the Lower Ninth Ward (97 percent African-American), Bywater (88 percent people of color) and Village de l'Est (96 percent people of color) face the greatest challenges to rebuilding. This is, in part, because of the length of time to get utilities like water and electricity working in these communities; reliance on public transit and public schools; and the lack of flood insurance.

Wealthier districts with large White populations, such as Lakeview, also face adversity, and their residents have suffered tremendous loss. Relatively speaking, however, Lakeview residents have more opportunities to rebound from catastrophe because they had greater financial assets and relied less on systems likely to be disrupted by these horrible events, such as public schools and transportation. The impact of destroyed housing, an economy struggling to recover, inadequate healthcare options, a limited public education system, and a hurricane protection system that may not be sufficient to withstand another assault do not offer many New Orleanians sufficient opportunities to return.

So some have rationalized the exclusion of a traumatized population with arguments that they are better off in Houston, Atlanta and other cities struggling to absorb unprecedented numbers of displaced people. The argument is that schools are better and there are more jobs. Maybe, but that depends. The structural arrangements may not be sufficiently different in displaced communities to allow more opportunity. It depends on whether people are able to get housing near job centers. It depends on whether they are able to get mental health and other health services. It depends on whether they are actually in high-performing schools. We know little about how displaced persons are faring, except in Houston, where the city has produced some survey results suggesting that 59 percent of displaced New Orleanians remain unemployed one year later. It also ignores the importance of social networks in helping people rebuild their lives. Whether or not they are able to maintain or recreate important social networks is unclear.

What we do know is that the fates and well-being of Whites, Blacks, Latinos, Asian Americans and Native Americans are linked. White communities may be farther along in rebuilding than communities of color, but are hardly thriving. We also know that to help all communities thrive, we must address the structures blocking opportunity. To do this, we look to the most vulnerable and excluded, identify how the structures are excluding them, and develop policy and practice interventions. Research by economist Manuel Pastor and others finds that when we invest in poor communities of color, whole regions become wealthier and regional poverty rates decrease. We also know that policy strategies like inclusionary zoning, transit that connects poor communities to job centers, and revising education financing formulas to increase resources to public schools help to connect people to opportunity and build more opportunity. The structural race lens points us to the importance of all of these strategies, across institutions, coordinated in implementation and impact.

Government investment created the White middle class. It can create and rebuild a stronger and expanded middle class that includes people of color. We can start in the Gulf Coast and in the communities asked to absorb tens of thousands of displaced people. We will learn there how to build our new national house and make that house a home.

Race vis-à-vis Class in the U.S.?

john a. powell & Stephen Menendian

In his groundbreaking 1903 treatise, *The Souls of Black Folk*, W.E.B. Du Bois wrote, "for the problem of the 20th Century is the problem of the color-line." A century later, and a full generation removed from the battles of the Civil Rights era, many now suggest that class, not race, is the greatest cleavage in American society. They fear that talk of race and the evils of racism obscure the more powerful politics of class and divide those sharing a common economic interest. Such claims hinge upon what is meant by race and class, and assume that the two are separable, conceptually and strategically.

In truth, neither race nor class is well understood. Perhaps the most critical flaw in our formulations of race and class is that they are assumed to be phenotypical markers or economic locations ahistorically derived and acontextually applied. Our current understanding of race and class did not arrive as the culmination of inevitable objective, historical logic. Race and class acquired meaning over time and are not comprehensible outside of that development.

HISTORY LESSONS

From the American Revolution to the Industrial Revolution and Civil War, race and class were uncertain markers in a struggle that ultimately shaped many of the institutional arrangements under which we live today. Through the ideology of the American Revolution, the indentured European servant became a free white laborer while black slavery remained firmly intact and protected by powerful economic interests and guarded by our Constitution. To reconcile the love for liberty with the reality of slavery, Americans adopted an uncomfortable narrative of black inferiority and racial otherness. These developments ensured that the newly emergent industrial working class clearly identified as white.

Immigrants arriving in this country forcibly negotiated a color line protected by law, custom and ideology. The first Immigration and Naturalization Act, unanimously passed by the first Congress, restricted immigration to free whites. The ways in which the Irish, for example, competed for work and adjusted to industrial morality in America made it all but certain that they would adopt and extend the politics of white unity. From this nation's inception, the race line was used to demarcate and patrol the divide between those who constituted the "We" in "We The People." It was no surprise when, in March of 1857, the United States Supreme Court, led by Chief Justice Roger B. Taney, declared in the *Dred Scott* case that all blacks—slaves as well as free—were not and could never become citizens of the United States.

Even when freed blacks were brought into the political community after the Civil War and granted citizenship, a now well-imbedded narrative of black inferiority and legacy of separation ensured that whites did not see themselves as having commonalities with blacks. According to economists Alberto Alesina and Edward Glaeser, much of the difference between American and European welfare systems can be explained by racial heterogeneity. In a pattern that persists today, opponents of welfare programs deploy racialized narratives to rouse a majority in opposition. In contrast to the generous Civil War pensions, provisions to the Freedmen's Bureau were short-lived, meager and stigmatizing. Many believed that welfare provisions to freed slaves were undeserved, and the Bureau was characterized as an immense bureaucracy whose programs were likely to make blacks lazy, dependent and prone to live off of "handouts." Racism contributed to the undoing of Reconstruction, but the failure of Reconstruction to secure blacks' rights as citizens and free laborers accelerated racism's spread until, by the early 20th century, it had fully pervaded the nation's culture and politics with profound class consequences, complicating the efforts of reformers for generations.

Not only were blacks excluded from the bevy of New Deal programs, race was carefully used to narrow these programs, limit their applicability and ultimately to reverse their trajectory to the detriment of similarly situated whites. New Deal programs could not survive the Southern voting block unless they were carefully restricted to leave the region's racial patterns undisturbed. As a consequence of our racialized past, Americans live with a comparatively thin social welfare system.

The phenomenal economic growth of the post-WWII period was shaped by racially inscribed New Deal programs and policies to produce the economic reality and new identity of the middle class, from which blacks were substantially excluded. The racism that influenced the New Deal programs and excluded blacks institutionalized racial disparities and imprinted the emergent middle class as white. The invisibility of the racial imprint on middle-class consciousness and institutions makes it possible for rejuvenated narratives of black otherness and unworthiness, conceived in the antebellum period, to persist, now explained in cultural rather than biological terms. The narrative of the American Dream—hard work and fair play—is the primary explanation for social mobility. Race is a critical part of the construction of class-as-merit. It is this individualistic ideology that helps to defeat class solidarity.

TODAY'S TASKS

Race is so intimately intertwined with our class understandings that a politics of class will ultimately be split asunder by the subterranean use of race. Today, the race issue undergirds messages on taxes, government spending, poverty, immigration, crime, rights, values and even urban development. The racial mythology of the welfare state has become so entrenched in party politics that it constrains the policy choices for progressive change that would benefit all Americans, whatever their color or class. Race was critical to the development of arrangements that prevent class solidarity and of a political movement hostile to helping citizens in need.

American exceptionalism, characterized by a weak labor movement, a thin social welfare apparatus and a stronger states' rights institutional framework, cannot be understood without seeing the role that race has played as our formative institutions were developed. Class identity and class consciousness itself has been thoroughly shaped and limited by our racialized arrangements. Because class is understood as an individual position, it is an empty vessel for building up a progressive movement. All but the most destitute and wealthiest Americans consider themselves middle-class.

As we move toward a majority-minority nation, the need to develop and sustain multiracial, multiclass coalitions will become increasingly important. The challenge is to link—to integrate—the interests of people of color with those of the white working and middle classes without losing sight of race. Race and class inequalities are inextricably linked, and collective solidarity across races can be achieved only by fleshing out their intersections, not by ignoring them. The most successful multiracial, multiclass progressive movements in the United States tackled race directly. Multiracial coalitions were critical to Abolition movement, the Civil Rights Movement and even the New Deal coalition. The key to whether progressive movements will obtain widespread support or be vulnerable to the negative use of race, implicitly or explicitly deployed, has been their commitment to interracial solidarity.

SUMMING UP

Long-standing institutional arrangements and deeply imbedded social narratives were disrupted by the transformation following the Civil War. As freed slaves were incorporated into the body politic of the nation, white workers and farmers glimpsed the possibility of solidarity along class lines unencumbered by racial division. The Populist movement sought to harness this possibility into a broad-based, multiracial alliance of white farmers, trade workers and freed slaves. Southern planters, fearing an alliance between white and blacks, used race to split the movement. Fifty years later, union efforts were similarly stymied because of the fear of disrupting the racial order of the South. The CIO's de-emphasizing race and failing to make strong appeals to black workers made it virtually impossible to generate the grassroots support necessary to combat the exclusions and weaknesses of New Deal labor legislation. Indeed, Southern fears of returning black soldiers joining the union movement were part of the impetus for the Taft-Hartley Act. In the late 1970s Cleveland Mayor Dennis Kucinich tried to build a progressive movement by emphasizing economic issues, since these united various city constituencies, but downplaying social issues, the most important of which was race. In doing so, race-baiting crept into the election and destroyed his chances of uniting the city's black and white working-class neighborhoods.

A closer look at the evolution and interplay of race and class in America illustrates the limitations of a race-neutral politics of class. Progressives who call for universalist programs that focus on class in lieu of race offer no mechanism for instilling the social solidarity necessary to propel a progressive agenda forward. Targeted universalism is a strategy that recognizes the need for a platform that is universal and also responsive to the needs of the particular. Leadership can also make a difference. Both Harold Washington in Chicago and Los Angeles Mayor Antonio Villaraigosa built broad-based multiracial, multiclass coalitions and succeeded by keeping both race and class issues in focus. There has never been—at least in 20th century American— a progressive political movement built solely on class. To inoculate such efforts from divisive race-baiting, there must be discourse to inspire whites to link their fates to nonwhites. This cannot be done by ignoring race, but by finding a way to speak to a multiracial, multiclass audience with ideas like targeted universalism and with language that unashamedly embraces American values of justice.

More Than Just Race: Being Black and Poor in the Inner City

William Julius Wilson

In *More than Just Race*, I hope to further our understanding of the complex and interrelated factors that continue to contribute to racial inequality in the United States. In the process, I call for re-examining the way social scientists discuss two important factors associated with racial inequality—social structure and culture. Although the book highlights the experiences of inner-city African Americans, it should be emphasized that the complexities of understanding race and racial inequality in America are not limited to research on blacks. Formal and informal aspects of inequality have also victimized Latinos, Asian Americans and Native Americans. In this book, however, I use the research on inner-city African Americans to elaborate my analytic framework because they have been the central focus of the structure-versus-culture dispute.

TAKING CULTURE SERIOUSLY

The book will likely generate controversy in some circles because I dare to take culture seriously as one of the explanatory variables in the study of race and urban poverty—a topic that is typically considered off-limits in academic discourse because of a fear that such analysis can be construed as "blaming the victim." Indeed, I develop a framework that integrates structural forces—ranging from those that are racial, such as segregation and discrimination, to those that are nonracial, such as changes in the economy—and cultural forces to not only show how the two are inextricably linked, but also to explain why structural forces should receive far more attention than cultural factors in accounting for the social outcomes of poor African Americans and in framing public policies to address racial inequality.

That said, my book examines two types of cultural forces: (1) national views and beliefs on race, and (2) cultural traits—shared outlooks, modes of behavior, traditions, belief systems, worldviews, values, skills, preferences, styles of self-presentation, etiquette, and linguistic patterns—that emerge from patterns of intra-group interaction in settings created by discrimination and segregation, and that reflect collective experiences within those settings.

I want to avoid limited conceptions of culture defined in the simple and traditional terms of group norms, values and attitudes toward family and work, and also consider cultural repertoires (habits, styles and skills) and the micro-level processes of meaning-making and decision-making—that is, the way that individuals in particular groups, communities or societies develop an understanding of how the world works and make decisions based on that understanding. The processes of meaning-making and decision-making are reflected in cultural frames (shared group constructions of reality).

Racism has historically been one of the most prominent American cultural frames and has played a major role in determining how whites perceive and act toward blacks. In the United States today, there is no question that the more categorical forms of racist ideology—in particular, those that assert the biogenetic inferiority of blacks—have declined significantly, even though they still may be embedded in institutional norms and practices.

The vast majority of social scientists agree that as a national cultural frame, racism, in its various forms, has had harmful effects on African Americans as a group. Indeed, considerable research has been devoted to the effects of racism in American society. However, there is little research and far less awareness of the impact of emerging cultural frames in the inner city on the social and economic outcomes of poor blacks.

HOW CULTURAL FRAMES ARE SHAPED

Note that distinct cultural frames in the inner city have not only been shaped by race and poverty, but in turn often shape responses to poverty, including responses that may contribute to the perpetuation of poverty. Indeed, one of the effects of living in racially segregated neighborhoods is exposure to group-specific cultural traits (orientations, habits and worldviews as well as styles of behavior and particular skills) that emerged from patterns of racial exclusion and that may not be conducive to factors that facilitate social mobility.

However, many liberal scholars are reluctant to discuss or research the role that culture plays in the negative outcomes found in the inner city. It is possible that they fear being criticized for reinforcing the popular view that the negative social outcomes—poverty, unemployment, drug addiction and crime—of many poor people in the inner city are due to the shortcomings of the people themselves. Harvard University sociologist Orlando Patterson maintains that there is "a deep-seated dogma that has prevailed in social science and policy circles since the mid-1960s: the rejection of any explanation that invokes a group's cultural attributes—its distinctive attitudes, values and tendencies, and the resulting behavior of its members—and the relentless preference for relying on structural factors like low incomes, joblessness, poor schools and bad housing."

Patterson claims that social scientists have shied away from cultural explanations of race and poverty because of the widespread belief, referred to above, that such explanations are tantamount to blaming the victim; that is, they support the conclusion that the poor themselves, and not the social environment, are responsible for their own poverty and negative social outcomes. He colorfully contends that it is "utterly bogus" to argue, as do many academics, that cultural explanations necessarily blame the victim for poor social outcomes.

Patterson argues that to hold an individual responsible for his behavior is not to rule out any consideration of the environmental factors that may have evoked the questionable behavior to begin with. "Many victims of child abuse end up behaving in self-destructive ways," he states. "To point out the link between their behavior and the destructive acts is in no way to deny the causal role of their earlier victimization and the need to address it." Patterson also contends that a cultural explanation of human behavior not only examines the immediate relationship between attitudes and behavior, but it also looks at the past to investigate the origins and changing nature of these attitudes.

THE PERILS OF THE CULTURAL ARGUMENT

The use of a cultural argument, however, is not without peril. Anyone who wishes to understand American society must be aware that explanations focusing on the cultural traits of inner-city residents are likely to draw far more attention from policymakers and the general public than structural explanations will. It is an unavoidable fact that Americans tend to de-emphasize the structural origins and social significance of poverty and welfare.

In other words, the popular view is that people are poor or on welfare because of their own personal shortcomings. A 2007 Pew Research Center survey revealed that "fully two-thirds of all Americans believe personal factors, rather than racial discrimination, explain why many African Americans have difficulty getting ahead in life; just 19 percent blame discrimination." Nearly three-fourths of U.S. whites (71 percent), a majority of Hispanics (59 percent), and even a slight majority of blacks (53 percent) "believe that blacks who have not gotten ahead in life are mainly responsible for their own situation."

The strength of American cultural sentiment that individuals are primarily responsible for poverty presents a dilemma for anyone who seeks the most comprehensive explanation of outcomes for poor black Americans. Why? Simply because, as noted above, cultural arguments that focus on individual traits and behavior invariably draw more attention than do structural explanations in the United States. Accordingly, I feel that a social scientist has an obligation to try to make sure that the explanatory power of his or her structural argument is not lost to the reader and to provide a context for understanding cultural responses to chronic economic and racial subordination.

THE CAUSAL FLOW BETWEEN STRUCTURE AND CULTURE

Consider, for example, the complex causal flow between structure and culture. In an impressive study that analyzes data from a national longitudinal survey, with methods designed to measure intergenerational economic mobility, the sociologist Patrick Sharkey of New York University found that "more than 70 percent of black children who are raised in the poorest quarter of American neighborhoods, the bottom 25 percent in terms of average neighborhood income, will continue to live in the poorest quarter of neighborhoods as adults."

He also found that since the 1970s, a majority of black families have resided in the poorest quarter of neighborhoods in consecutive generations, compared to only 7 percent of white families. Thus he concludes that the disadvantages of living in poor black neighborhoods, like the advantages of living in affluent white neighborhoods, are in large measure inherited.

We should also consider another path-breaking study that Sharkey co-authored with senior investigator Robert Sampson, a Harvard University sociologist, and another colleague, Steven Raudenbush, that examined the durable effects of concentrated poverty on black children's verbal ability. They studied a representative sample of 750 African-American children, ages 6–12, who were growing up in the city of Chicago in 1995, and followed them anywhere they moved in the United States for up to 7 years. The children were given a reading examination and vocabulary test at three different periods. Their study shows "that residing in a severely disadvantaged neighborhood cumulatively impedes the development of academically relevant verbal ability in children."

Their results reveal: (1) that the neighborhood environment "is an important developmental context for trajectories of verbal cognitive ability"; (2) that young African-American children who had earlier lived in a severely disadvantaged neighborhood had fallen behind their counterparts or peers who had not resided previously in disadvantaged areas by up to 6 IQ points, a magnitude estimated to be equivalent to "missing a year or more of schooling"; and (3) "that the strongest effects appear several years after children live in areas of concentrated disadvantage." This research raises important questions "about ways in which neighborhoods may alter growth in verbal ability, producing effects that linger on even if a child leaves a severely disadvantaged neighborhood."

The studies by Sharkey and Sampson and his colleagues both suggest that neighborhood effects are not solely structural. Among the effects of living in segregated neighborhoods over extended periods is repeated exposure to cultural traits—and this would include linguistic patterns, the focus of Sampson et al.'s study—that emanate from or are the products of racial exclusion, traits, such as verbal skills, that may impede successful maneuvering in the larger society.

As Sharkey points out, "when we consider that the vast majority of black families living in America's poorest neighborhoods come from families that have lived in similar environments for generations . . . continuity of the neighborhood environment, in addition to continuity of individual economic status, may be especially relevant to the study of cultural patterns among disadvantaged populations." Unfortunately, very little research attention has been given to these cumulative cultural experiences.

Thus, in addition to structural influences, exposure to different cultural influences in the neighborhood environment over time has to be taken into account if one is to really appreciate and explain the divergent social outcomes of human groups. But, to repeat, in delivering this message we must make sure that the powerful influence of structural factors does not recede into the background.

THE RELATIVE IMPORTANCE OF CULTURE AND STRUCTURE

Indeed, a fundamental question remains: What is the relative importance of these two dimensions in accounting for the formation and persistence of the inner-city ghetto, the plight of black males and the breakdown of the black family—three subjects that I focused on in my book. Culture matters, but I would have to say it does not matter nearly as much as social structure.

From a historical perspective, it is hard to overstate the importance of racialist structural factors that Dr. Martin Luther King, Jr. fought so hard against. Aside from the enduring effects of slavery, Jim Crow segregation, public school segregation, legalized discrimination, residential segregation, the FHA's redlining of black neighborhoods in the 1940s and 1950s, the construction of public housing projects in poor black neighborhoods, employer discrimination and other racial acts and processes, there is the impact of political, economic and policy decisions that were at least partly influenced by race.

In contrasting the combined impact of the structural factors with cultural factors, it would be very hard to argue that the cultural factors in the black community are equally as important in determining life chances or creating racial group outcomes. For example, if one attempts to explain rapid changes in social and economic outcomes in the inner city, there is little evidence that cultural forces have the power of changes in the economy. We only need to consider the impact of the economic boom on the reduction of concentrated racial poverty in the 1990s to illustrate this point.

Policymakers who are dedicated to combating the problems of race and poverty and who recognize the importance of structural inequities face an important challenge—namely, how to generate political support from Americans who tend to place far more emphasis on cultural factors and individual behavior than on structural impediments in explaining social and economic outcomes. After all, beliefs that attribute joblessness and poverty to individual shortcomings do not engender strong support for social programs to end inequality. Nonetheless, in addressing the problem of structural inequities it would not be wise to leave the impression in public discussions that cultural problems do not matter. Indeed, proposals to address racial inequality should reflect awareness of the inextricable link between aspects of structure and culture.

FRAMING PUBLIC POLICY DISCUSSION

For all of these reasons, it is extremely important to discuss how the issues of race and poverty are framed in public policy discussions. How we situate social issues in the larger context of society says a lot about our commitment to change. A useful example of how this works comes to me from Robert Asen, a professor in the Department of Communication Arts at the University of Wisconsin. He has reminded me that the political framing of poverty—that is, the way in which political leaders formulate arguments about how we as a nation should talk about and address issues of poverty—in the New Deal era was quite different from the political framing of poverty today.

During the New Deal era, the emphasis was on structure—namely, the devastating impact of the economic crisis. Americans clearly recognized that hundreds of thousands of citizens were poor or unemployed mainly because of a severe and prolonged job shortage. In the public arena today, poverty tends to be discussed in reference to individual initiative. This distinction, he points out, reveals how larger shifts in society have influenced our understanding of the nature of poverty.

Therefore, we ought to consider the contingency of political frames at particular moments in time. These "deliberative frames" not only orient our debates on public policy, but they can also be shifted through debate. So, just because cultural explanations resonate with policymakers and the public today does not mean that structural explanations cannot resonate with them tomorrow. To shift political frames, however, and hopefully provide a more balanced discussion, requires parallel efforts among politicians, engaged citizens and scholars.

In my previous writings, I called for the framing of issues designed to appeal to broad segments of the population. Key to this framing, I argued, would be an emphasis on policies that would directly benefit all groups, not just people of color. My thinking was that, given American views about poverty and race, a color-blind agenda would be the most realistic way to generate the broad political support that would be necessary to enact the required legislation. I no longer hold to this view.

The question is not whether the policy should be race-neutral or universal, the question is whether the policy is framed to facilitate a frank discussion of the problems that ought to be addressed and to generate broad political support to alleviate them. So now my position has changed: In framing public policy, we should not shy away from an explicit discussion of the specific issues of race and poverty; on the contrary, we should highlight them in our attempt to convince the nation that these problems should be seriously confronted and that there is an urgent need to address them. The issues of race and poverty should be framed in such a way that not only a sense of fairness and justice to combat inequality is generated, but also people are made aware that our country would be better off if these problems were seriously addressed and eradicated.

BARACK OBAMA'S SPEECH

In considering this change of frame—indeed, a change of mindset on race and poverty—I am drawn to then-Senator Barack Obama's speech on race given March 18, 2008. His oratory provides a model for the type of framing I have in mind. In taking on the tough topic of race in America, Obama spoke to the issue of structure and culture, as well as their interaction. He drew America's attention to the many disparities that exist between the "African-American community and the larger American community today"—disparities that "can be traced to inequalities passed on from an earlier generation that suffered under the brutal legacy of slavery and Jim Crow." He also discussed the lack of economic opportunity among black men, and how "the shame and frustration that came from not being able to provide for one's family contributed to the erosion of black families."

However, Obama did not restrict his speech to addressing structural inequities; he also focused on problematic cultural and behavioral responses to these inequities, including a cycle of violence among black men, and a "legacy of defeat" that has been passed on to future generations. And he urged those in the African-American community to take full responsibility for their lives by demanding more from their fathers, and spending more time with their children "reading to them, and teaching them that while they may face challenges and discrimination in their own lives, they must never succumb to despair or cynicism; they must always believe that they can write their own destiny."

By combining a powerful discussion of structural inequities with an emphasis on personal responsibility, Barack Obama did not isolate the latter from the former, as is so often the case in the remarks of talk show hosts, journalists, and conservative politicians and commentators. Obama's speech gave an honest appraisal of structural racial inequality as he called for all Americans to support blacks in their struggle to help themselves. To repeat, I feel that this speech could serve as a model for the kind of careful political framing of the issues of race and poverty that we need in this country in order to move forward.

Tensions Among Minority Groups

Symposium with S.M. Miller, Wade Henderson,
Don T. Nakanishi, john a. powell, Maria Blanco,
Howard Winant

Last December [2007], New America Media (NAM) released the results of a major
national poll, "Deep Divisions, Shared Destiny: A Poll of African Americans, Hispanics
and Asian Americans on Race Relations Sponsored by New America Media and Nine
Founding Ethnic Partners." A total of 1,105 African American, Asian American and
Hispanic adults were polled (as noted below, Native Americans were not included), us-
ing sophisticated methodology, "designed to be representative of the adult population of
the three major racial and ethnic minorities in the United States." A typical newspaper
headline reporting the story was "Survey Points to Tensions Among Chief Minorities"
(New York Times, 12/13/07).

Yet the results—covering attitudes about a wide range of issues—are far more complex,
and less one-sidedly conflictful, than these headlines suggested. We therefore asked several
of PRRAC's close associates to comment on the results.

* * * * *

RACIAL-ETHNIC DESTINIES

S.M. MILLER

Polls, such as this one on "Deep Divisions, Shared Destiny," report the low (5 percent) margin of error of their study. Like many other polls, they neglect to point out
that this error margin applies to the study as a whole. The margin of error for each
of the three racial-ethnic groups, the sub-samples, may be larger than the overall error margin. Some lowering of confidence in the reports for each group is necessary.

A second concern is that polling is affected by contexts—political, economic, cultural—that occur around the time of the question-asking. Would the respondents have the same response in today's reeling economy as they had in August–September, 2007 before the economy's faltering became disturbingly evident? Better times breed optimism. As the report declares, the racial-ethnic landscape is in flux. The landscape will be made by events, circumstances, actions and responses by each group and by the broader society. In a few months and certainly years from now, new outlooks may appear.

Despite these and other doubts about the confidence we should place in polling reports, it is useful to examine convergence and differences among the three racial-ethnic groups. The great positive report is that people of color have positive attitudes about American society and each other. That provides the potential of their becoming a (somewhat) unified political force. Many pressures, particularly competition for jobs and political space, operate against that potential.

Unfortunately, America needs scapegoats, especially in difficult days. Over the years, Blacks, Irish, Jews, Italians, leftists, gays, etc. have been isolated, demeaned and discriminated against. One of the three racial-ethnic groups may be offered as economic villains or illegal workers (Hispanics) or as authors of their own economic difficulties (Blacks), undeserving of attention, because they are not motivated to produce the social capital that would provide them easy access to the higher reaches of the economic ladder. A common front against the scapegoating of any of the three groups may not emerge.

The immigration issue affects Black attitudes toward Hispanics who compete for jobs and are willing to work for low wages. Blacks are much more pessimistic about full inclusion in American society than the other two groups (two-thirds of Blacks do not believe that equal opportunity occurs) and may engage in actions that disturb the others. In some localities, Hispanics may be moved to issues and confrontations that bother the other two groups. Asians may decide that their economic and social integration in the USA is secure and avoid working with the other two groups. Both Hispanics and Asians fear crime by Blacks and may reject collaborating with them.

How to surmount these possible obstacles? One important approach has developed. Leaders of national organizations of the three groups are meeting. Perhaps over time some public remarks on political and other issues will emerge from the joint sessions as common purposes and actions occur. A national day calling attention to the difficulties and achievements of the three, and Native Americans, might be useful. The prospects of working together will be affected by the state of the economy (which group, Black or Hispanics, gains more political attention). A particular issue that needs a common position is immigration, which is of great importance for Hispanics. If a common position has emerged among the national leaders, it has not had wide publicity.

At least as important as national coordination is the coming together of the three groups at local levels. Local variations are not highlighted by national politics. As the report declares, "high levels of ethnic isolation exist among the groups which may underlie and reinforce racial tensions." Discussions among local leaders and organizations could diminish antagonisms and differences among the groups. The goal would be to move toward joint action, although the early stage is likely to be mutual aid where the other two groups support the third group on its particular issue. Over time, this mutual aid might grow into an on-going coalition with a common agenda.

The common local program would emphasize one or another of such issues as unemployment, low wages, job upgrading, affirmative action, housing inadequacies, police and criminal justice treatment, access to health facilities, neighborhood amenities, educational issues. Focusing on a very limited set of issues—my mantra is that if you have more than three goals or issues at a time, you don't have any goal—is important. Big goals and limited means lead to disillusioning failure (unless limited compromises are acceptable).

The report concludes optimistically that the three groups "will *ultimately* work out ways to relate to each other for their mutual benefit over the long term" because they share important values. The assumption is that attitudes about values and conditions as depicted in a poll will have an enduring trajectory. Looking to a nearer-term future, consultation, collaboration, mutual aid, positive joint experiences and good economic and political times may reduce the time needed for ultimate change based on common core values. Today's fields of action are important.

* * * * *

GREAT CAUSE FOR OPTIMISM

WADE HENDERSON

The survey gives me great cause for optimism. Throughout history, people have drawn boundaries based on differences of race and ethnicity, and untold conflicts have resulted. America—and in particular, our Civil Rights Movement—changed that by enshrining the principle of equality under law and by promising tolerance and respect for all people. Distrust isn't completely absent (and the survey reflects some of that distrust)—but what is remarkable is the degree to which today's African Americans, Latinos and Asian Americans are bonded by friendship and a commitment to working together to make America a more just and equal society.

Strikingly, all three groups view the Civil Rights Movement as establishing a template for equality which benefits all Americans. Until the Civil Rights Movement in the 1950s and 1960s, America lived a contradiction, denying African Americans its foundational ideal of equality. As a result, African Americans, but Latinos and Asians as well, were stigmatized and denied opportunities solely because of race.

The fully realized American promise now benefits African Americans, but also Latinos and Asian Americans. Indeed, Title VII established protections against discrimination not only for African Americans, but for those of any race or national origin; *Brown v. Board of Education* banned the separate-but-equal doctrine for all minorities. So it's not surprising that nearly 70 percent of Latinos and Asian Americans believe that the Civil Rights Movement helped them and almost 90 percent of the three groups believe they should work together for their collective good.

The Rev. Martin Luther King, Jr. and the Civil Rights Movement left an indelible imprint on our national fabric, so that America would never again betray our founding principles by excluding minorities. Today, anti-immigrant sentiments test these principles. But the legal tenets and the tolerance the Civil Rights Movement established continue to turn Americans toward equality.

* * * * *

ACHIEVING RACIAL CONVERGENCE: A LEADERSHIP CHALLENGE

DON T. NAKANISHI

The "Deep Divisions, Shared Destiny" poll provides credence for a continuum of competing views on the interracial and interethnic relations and perceptions among African Americans, Asian Americans and Latino Americans. The results, for example, underscore the familiar themes of mistrust, tensions, competition and lack of social relations that have often characterized the interactions among these groups. The findings, however, also demonstrate a number of common experiences and shared views of being people of color in 21st century American society, as well as mutual appreciation for the contributions and strengths of each group.

There were two findings which I found to be particularly noteworthy and far from obvious. First, I was very pleased to see that the vast majority of Latino-American (73 percent) and Asian-American (65 percent) respondents agreed with the statement, "African Americans have helped all racial and ethnic groups by leading the fight for civil rights and against discrimination." I found this positive recognition to be significant because most of these respondents—55 percent of the Latino Americans and 80 percent of the Asian Americans in the survey—were immigrants, who are oftentimes described as lacking knowledge, appreciation, as well as a sense of linked fate with the leadership and contributions that African Americans have provided in expanding civil rights for all Americans, especially those from racial and ethnic communities. Moreover, Latino and Asian immigrants, be they workers or small business owners, have been viewed largely as competitors, antagonists or worse in many highly publicized urban conflicts with African Americans in recent years.

For both political organizing and political research purposes, it would be revealing to build on this survey and to understand the extent to which these positive sentiments are widespread, how they were acquired, and whether they can be leveraged for future collective action. For example, Asian immigrants are oftentimes described as having acquired negative stereotypes of African Americans in their Asian home countries prior to migrating to the United States, and continuing to adhere to them during their adjustment and acculturation to this country. If that is the case, then how do they come to believe that they have benefited from the struggles of African Americans? And do they or can they, in turn, develop a sense of reciprocity towards African Americans? Future research efforts might also be undertaken to see if the efforts and achievements of Latino-American and Asian-American civil rights and progressive groups and leaders in the past, as well as the present, are also positively recognized and shared by members of all three populations.

The second somewhat unexpected, but welcomed finding was that the three groups of respondents, despite their many differences, expressed their highest level of agreement in the entire survey for the following statement: "African Americans, Latinos, and Asians have many similar problems. They should put aside their differences and work together on issues that affect their communities." 92 percent of Latino Americans, 89 percent of African Americans and 86 percent of Asian Americans agreed with the statement. Since this poll was undertaken by ethnic media organizations, the respondents were asked whether the ethnic media had a responsibility for bringing the three communities "closer together." 78 percent of Latino-American, 69 percent of African-American and 73 percent of Asian-American respondents believed that the ethnic media had such a responsibility.

However, if they had been asked, I am fairly certain that the respondents would have expressed the same expectation of other leaders, sectors and groups of these three communities to seek common ground and undertake more collective action. I believe they are understandably tired and angry about many divisive aspects of the current state of relationships among the three groups, and challenge all of us to work towards achieving greater racial convergence.

* * * * *

"MINORITY" IS A PROBLEM CONCEPT

JOHN A. POWELL

The New America Media poll on racial and ethnic attitudes between Blacks, Hispanics and Asian Americans is both very important and subject to many of the limitations that we have experienced in the past when striving to talk openly about the attitudes and positions of different racial and ethnic groups in the United States. There are problems with the poll. The poll continues the troubling practice of leaving out Native Americans; there may be a good reason for this, but it is not offered. Polls tend to only capture what a respondent is consciously thinking at the time. They are generally not sensitive to implicit attitudes, nor do they capture how attitudes are impacted and shift by structural arrangement. But this poll, though important, suffers from additional problems (discussed below) which are more closely related to the subject matter of race. This poll is important because there has been far too little attention paid to salient differences in attitudes and perceptions between racial and ethnic populations in this country. Typically, the focus is on European Americans in relationship to other groups, particularly African Americans. Consequently, there is a need to better understand the dynamic interactions between African Americans, Latinos and Asian Americans.

For some time, there has been a call for a more inclusive and nuanced approach to looking at racial and ethnic issues in the United States. And while this is somewhat easier said than done, this poll begins to move us in the right direction even as it exposes some of the difficulties. In looking at the issue of race in America, it is easy to overfocus or underfocus on European Americans when thinking about race. This poll suffers from the latter. We have to recognize the dominant role European Americans have played and continue to play in many ways, but we must also broaden our gaze, to work for a more textured, multirelational perspective. Indeed, we should be interested not only in perspective, but also in conditions and situatedness. Again, not an easy task.

This poll includes Blacks, Hispanics, and Asians as the three largest ethnic and racial minority groups in the U.S. There are a number of problems even at this level. "Minority" is a problem concept. Do they mean a numeric minority? If so, then what does majority-minority mean? If they just mean numbers, why don't we refer to men in the U.S. as minorities? What is the difference between racial groups and ethnic groups? Blacks, for example, are clearly more than one ethnic group, and Hispanics are clearly more than one race.

The problems go beyond nomenclature. I believe that it is important for groups to gain mutual understanding and work together. But what are the conditions and assumptions that can support these collaborations? Is there some similar experience—immigration, exclusion, income level, education, culture or history—that might help to bring these groups together and reduce the tension between them? Are there institutional or structural issues that make cooperation—or competition—more likely, such as competing in a school system? It is not surprising that people who voluntarily immigrate to the U.S. from great distances are more likely to believe in the American Dream than those living here historically denied the dream. Asians are disaggregated, while other groups are not. This might make sense, but it needs some explanation. Ten percent of Blacks are foreign-born. Does this impact how they answer the questions in the poll? We do not know. One might think that Africans who come to the U.S. as immigrants, not refugees, might have similar opinions about the American Dream as other immigrants.

There are some surprises in this poll. For example, Blacks and Hispanics both indicate experiencing a high degree of discrimination, 92 percent and 85 percent, respectively. Asians report discrimination at much lower levels. Yet Hispanics were the most likely to believe that every American has an equal opportunity to succeed. It might be useful to point out where there is significant tension between what a group believes and what it experiences.

Finally, there were a few questions that stand out as odd, if not problematic. For example, why are groups being asked about their fear of Blacks and no other populations or Hispanics taking jobs?

While there are a number of issues with this poll that need attention, the poll is a move in the right direction toward a deeper nuanced understanding of how different racial and ethnic groups understand each other. New American Media and its partners should be congratulated for this undertaking. But more work is needed.

* * * * *

UNDERSTANDING COMMONALITIES

MARIA BLANCO

In December 2007, New American Media released the results of a poll of African-American, Asian-American and Latino adults on race relations between these groups. In a long overdue method to obtain clear and in-depth polling results, the respondents were interviewed in English, Spanish, Mandarin, Cantonese, Korean, Vietnamese or Tagalog, as needed.

Much of the media coverage that followed release of the poll focused on the poll's findings that tensions and stereotypes existed between the groups. For the most part, this was not news to anyone who lives and works in these communities and is familiar with ethnic relations in cities where "minorities" have become the majority. The 1990 Census revealed that racial and ethnic minorities constitute a majority in seven of the country's ten largest cities. The demographic changes that brought Latinos and Asian Americans into traditionally African-American neighborhoods have occurred in a period of increasing economic stratification and deterioration of urban housing and infrastructure. The intergroup tensions produced by diminishing opportunities and resources in large cities are as predictable as the existence of tensions and stereotypes between whites and African Americans, Asian Americans and Latinos during this period.

Unfortunately and predictably, the media said little about arguably the most novel and important poll finding: All the groups expressed optimism and a strong belief that relations between the groups will improve significantly over the next decade. Not only did they expect relations to improve, they strongly (80–92 percent) indicated that they needed to put aside their differences and work together on problems they believe they share with each other. These findings are important not only because they anticipate a much-desired reduction in tensions. They presage an understanding that to move beyond conflict, communities must identify the shared policies and politics needed to address the deterioration of neighborhoods and schools in cities and suburbs that are increasingly segregated and left behind. This understanding of commonalities can also be the basis for an analysis of work competition that identifies the origin of that competition in employer practices and government inattention that have supported a race to the bottom in wages and working conditions.

The failure to report this insight underscores another hidden nugget in the survey: Large numbers of respondents across groups indicated that mainstream media were irresponsible in their coverage of racial tensions. Hopefully, the New American Media survey points to a more responsible way to report on the issues of communities of color.

* * * * *

THE SURVEY BLUES

HOWARD WINANT

This New America Media Poll appears to be state-of-the-art stuff, although I haven't been able to examine the data. That's on one level. Yet, looked at in another way, in terms of what these results *mean* about racial/ethnic identity in the U.S., about interracial conflict, belief in "the American dream," or just about anything else, the jury is still out.

For all the professionalism of the survey design, the questions leave a lot to be desired. Essentially, respondents are asked to comment on a series of cliches about race in the United States. Such topics as social mobility by race, patterns of discrimination, fear of blacks (they "commit most of the crime," you know . . .), intergroup competition, and so on have been extensively studied. Therefore, we have very good data on, say, patterns of discrimination in housing, arrest and sentencing practices, and many other similar issues. To conduct a survey on attitudes toward these topics both repeats other works and in many ways doesn't live up to them. Indeed, so many surveys of racial attitudes have been carried out in recent years that it would require a whole bibliographic essay just to list them all with any evaluative criteria in view. Let's just cite some important practitioners: Larry Bobo (Harvard), Howard Schuman (Univ. Michigan), Michael Dawson (Univ. Chicago), Reynolds Farley (Univ. Michigan), Jennifer Hochschild (Harvard), Joe Feagin (Texas A&M).

I'm generally suspicious of the concerns and wordings of questions. I have doubts about "construct validity" throughout this and at least some other inquiries. I wonder about the experiential dimensions and effects of interviewing people about their racial attitudes. And I am annoyed by the repeated trumpeting of "new findings" and the general pattern of publicity-seeking that the completion and publication of the most recent, and usually lavishly subsidized, survey receives. It is striking that, in the case of the NAM poll, all this fanfare is accompanied by quite wishy-washy and impressionistic statements by central figures in the project: In some ways things are better, in some ways they are worse.

Richard Rodriguez, now a major figure at NAM, makes some valuable comments and some fanciful ones in his interview about the survey. Although Latin American groups of various national origins now see themselves as "Hispanic," he shares the U.S. Census position that " . . . we [Latinos/Hispanics] are not a racial group." He adopts "the remarkable idea" that, despite interracial conflict, "the Hispanic new-comer and the Asian newcomer would see in the African American the future for themselves." That these are hardly obvious conclusions from this or other compa-rable surveys goes without saying. It's just riffing on the mainstream (or let us say left-liberal) party line.

Attitude surveys, especially in the "post-civil rights" era, will of course split the dif-ference between narratives of "remarkable progress" and "ongoing despair," between "inclusion" and "isolation." Surveys at their best are snapshots of "collective subjec-tivities," as Durkheim might say. They are limited to an artificially constructed here and now, even when they ask much better questions than the NAM survey appar-ently did, like those about the black public sphere that Dawson explored in his 2001 book, *Black Visions: The Roots of Contemporary African-American Political Ideologies.*

So what drops out of the picture is in many ways the most important informa-tion: questions about racial democracy and racial despotism, questions about the social structure of race, questions about what the U.S. will look like when, by 2050 or so, it becomes a "majority-minority" society, questions about the vast legacy of racial exploitation that continues unchecked today. Are there any questions about incarceration, about the racial dimensions of the wars in Iraq and Afghanistan, the subprime lending meltdown, neoliberalism at home and abroad, the reliability of elections, racial profiling, Katrina, the meaning of whiteness? Are there breakdowns of results along gender and class lines? Maybe there are; I didn't get to see the data. But these are not the topics reported in the *NY Times* or highlighted at their press conference held at the National Press Club.

Don't get me wrong. We learn something from these studies. They are the meat-and-potatoes of my field, and of many others. We gotta have them. But at the same time they are necessarily lame efforts to make sense of conflict, violence and the waste of human potential (with a little "progress" thrown in too, the result of endless outpourings of blood, sweat and tears). They are "racial formation projects" in their own right, attempts to reconcile in official and academic (and sometimes progres-sive) discourse opposing forces that can only be resolved though politics.

Indigenous Peoples: Response to the Periodic Report of the United States to the United Nations Committee on the Elimination of Racial Discrimination

Prepared by: U.S. Human Rights Network CERD Working Group on Indigenous Peoples, Alberto Saldamando, Working Group Co-coordinator; International Indian Treaty Council, Julie Fishel, Working Group Co-coordinator; Western Shoshone Defense Project; Indian Law Resource Center; Hope Clark, Candidate for Masters in Intercultural Service, Leadership, and Management from the School for International Training; Manuel Pino; Josh Clark; Tom Goldtooth, Indigenous Environmental Network; Jaime Arsenault; Roxanne Ornelas, University of Minnesota; Sakura Saunders, CorpWatch.

* * * * *

EXECUTIVE SUMMARY OF THE REPORT OF THE WORKING GROUP ON INDIGENOUS PEOPLES

The International Convention on the Elimination of All Forms of Racial Discrimination provides numerous protections for indigenous peoples. Article 1 addresses freedom from discrimination based on race, color, descent or national or ethnic origin. Article 2 requires States to refrain from practicing racial discrimination. Article 5(a) guarantees the right to equal treatment before the tribunals and all other organs administering justice, and Article 5(b) guarantees the right to security of person and protection by the State against violence or bodily harm. . . . Article 5(c) guarantees equality in the enjoyment of political rights. Articles 5(d)(v) and (d)(vii) provide that signatory States must guarantee the right of everyone to equality before the law, particularly with regard to the right to own property alone as well as in association with others and the right to freedom of thought, conscience and religion. Articles

41

5(e)(iv), (e)(v) and (e)(vi) provide that signatory States must guarantee the right of everyone to equality before the law, particularly with regard to the right to public health, medical care, social security and social services, the right to education and training, and the right to equal participation in cultural activities.

Despite these protections and obligations, by every measure, indigenous peoples in the United States continue to rank at the bottom of every scale of economic and social well-being, in and of itself powerful evidence of the existence of racial discrimination in the US. Moreover, the domestic laws and policies of the United States perpetuate a legal system that has blatant and significant discriminatory impacts on indigenous peoples, particularly with regard to rights to property, religious freedom, cultural activities, health, education and political rights. The federal government, acting through Congress and the executive branch, continues to take tribal lands and resources, in many cases without payment and without any legal remedy for the tribes. Congress frequently responds to Indian property and Indian claims by enacting legislation that would be forbidden by the Constitution if addressed to any other group's property or claims. Because the federal government asserts essentially limitless power over Indians, and engages in constant intrusion in the affairs of indigenous peoples under the plenary power doctrine, Indian governments cannot effectively govern their lands or carry out much-needed economic development. This denial of simple justice has long served to deprive Indian nations of a fair opportunity to advance the interests of their communities. The untenable and insecure position of indigenous peoples vis-á-vis the federal government in the U.S. is unique, and gives rise to multiple violations of the rights of indigenous peoples under the Convention.

The federal court system of the United States has affirmed that the federal government is under an obligation to conform its laws as much as possible to international law. Despite this obligation, the United States continues to flagrantly violate many of its legal obligations under the Convention when developing and implementing domestic policy relating to indigenous peoples. . . .

Tribal Self-Government in the United States

John Dossett

More than 560 federally recognized Indian Nations (variously called tribes, nations, bands, pueblos, communities, native villages) exist in the United States. Some 226 of these are located in Alaska; the rest are located in 34 other states. Indian Nations are ethnically, culturally and linguistically diverse.

Sovereignty is a legal word for an ordinary concept—local self-government. The United States Constitution recognizes that Indian Nations are sovereign governments, just like Canada and California. Hundreds of treaties, the Supreme Court, the president and the Congress have repeatedly affirmed that Indian Nations retain their inherent powers of self-government. These treaties and laws have created a fundamental contract between Indian Nations and the United States. Indian Nations ceded millions of acres of land that made the United States what it is today, and in return received the guarantee of self-government on their own lands. The treaties and laws also provide for federal assistance in ensuring the success of tribal governments, much as the federal government assists state governments.

Tribal self-government serves the same purpose today as it always has. It empowers Indian Nations to remain viable as distinct groups of people. Tribal cultures enrich American life, and tribal economies provide opportunities where few would otherwise exist. Tribal governments provide a broad range of governmental services on tribal lands, including education, law enforcement, justice systems and environmental protection, and provide basic infrastructure such as roads, bridges and public buildings. Tribal governments and state governments have a great deal in common, and there is often far more cooperation at the local level than there is conflict.

The status of Indian Nations as a form of government is at the heart of nearly every issue that touches Indian Country. Self-government is essential if tribal communities are to continue to protect their unique cultures and identities. However, too few people are aware of the history and purpose of tribal self-government. The great challenge for Indian Nations, as it is for all of the allies in the fight against racism and poverty, is to build understanding of history and legal rights as we address economic and social problems.

When Affirmative Action Was White

Ira Katznelson

Hurricane Katrina's violent winds and waters tore away the shrouds that ordinarily mask the country's racial pattern of poverty and neglect. Understandably, most commentators focused on the woeful federal response. Others, taking a longer view, yearned for a burst of activism patterned on the New Deal. But that nostalgia requires a heavy dose of historical amnesia. It also misses the chance to come to terms with how the federal government in the 1930s and 1940s contributed to the persistence of two Americas.

In "To Fulfull These Rights," a June 1965 graduation address at Howard University, President Lyndon Johnson asked why the black population of the United States had fallen even further behind the country's white majority during the two decades since the end of the Second World War, despite the era's sustained national prosperity. Conceding that "we are not completely sure why this is," he stressed the need to adopt bold new policies of affirmative action to remedy the disabilities following from two centuries of oppression.

Johnson missed the chance to assay how the major policies of the New Deal and Fair Deal of the 1930s and 1940s, inflected by the preferences of the Southern wing of the Democratic Party, had massively advantaged American whites while often excluding African Americans, especially the majority who still lived in the 17 states that mandated de jure racial segregation. Southern members of Congress used occupational exclusions and took advantage of American federalism to insure that their region's racial order would not be disturbed by national policies. Farmworkers and maids, the jobs held by most Southern blacks, were denied Social Security pensions and access to labor unions. Benefits for veterans were administered locally. The famous GI Bill adapted to "the Southern way of life" by accommodating to segregation in higher education, to the job ceilings local officials imposed on returning black soldiers who came home from a segregated Army, and to an unwillingness to offer loans to blacks even when they were insured by the federal government. Of the 3,229 GI Bill-guaranteed home, business and farm loans made in 1947 in Mississippi, for example, only 2 went to black veterans.

Together, these policies transferred more than $100 billion to create a modern middle class during the first decade after the Second World War, a sum more than six times the amount spent on Marshall Plan aid in war-torn Europe. Without attention to this history, the ambition to create affirmative action for the black poor and the dispossessed was made difficult. Without attention to this history today, it is hard to know how to proceed.

Affirmative action, as it came to operate, focused mainly on opportunities for middle-class blacks seeking access to higher education and top-tier jobs. This affirmative action has worked to great effect, creating a more racially just and diverse society than otherwise would have been the case. But the black affirmative action programs instituted since 1965 in fact were paltry in their scope and scale compared to the massive governmental transfers that disproportionately aided whites in the previous three decades, 1935–1965.

QUESTIONING AFFIRMATIVE ACTION

Presently, many U.S. politicians and much of the wider public are questioning the effectiveness of any kind of affirmative action in the face of continuing black disadvantage and the wider impact of globalization on the population as a whole. Many view affirmative action as an expensive exercise that violates principles of merit and equal opportunity and that, in any event, has not achieved its original goals as enunciated by President Johnson in 1965. Further, there is no agreement or clarity about what, if anything, should be put in its place.

Current policy possibilities become clearer when we take into account not just the affirmative action policies that have been called by that name, but the full range of affirmative action—including affirmative action for whites—that marked much of American social policy in the key formative period that preceded the civil rights revolution.

The almost exclusively white-targeted nature of this extensive federal legislation has largely been ignored by policy analysts, just as it was by Lyndon Johnson.

Thus, often without realizing it, the United States has practiced what, in effect, was white affirmative action on a highly generous and widespread basis, followed by a much more modest program of black affirmative action. By understanding this history, we can come to terms with the widening gap between blacks and whites noted by Lyndon Johnson and with the incapacity of many blacks to be able to make good this gap in the following four decades.

The policy implications of a full appreciation of these features of modern U.S. history, in short, are the opposite of currently popular views. Properly designed and funded, affirmative action policies can work very effectively, but the ingrained bias in a white direction has to be acknowledged and transcended. If American politicians and public opinion are serious about racial equality, this history indicates the need to implement an affirmative action program as ambitious as that delivered to whites during the three decades before President Johnson spoke out in 1965. It is important to consider both the principles that could animate such an effort and to imagine the form it might take.

THE ROOSEVELT AND TRUMAN ADMINISTRATIONS

Although no single period can account for why race and class continue to be so closely entwined today, such a critical moment lies just behind us, during the Administrations of Franklin Roosevelt and Harry Truman, when such great progressive national policies as Social Security, protective labor laws and the GI Bill generated what I have called "affirmative action for whites." As a historian, I have tried to set this record straight. As a political scientist, I have sought to understand the mechanisms that made this history possible. As a citizen, I have sought to comprehend the implications of these past policies for possibilities today.

During Jim Crow's last hurrah in the 1930s and 1940s, when Southern members of Congress controlled the gateways to legislation, policy decisions dealing with welfare, work and war excluded or differentially treated the vast majority of African Americans. Between 1945 and 1955, the federal government transferred unprecedented sums to support retirement and fashion opportunities for job skills, education, homeownership and small business formation. Together, these domestic programs dramatically reshaped the country's social structure by creating a modern, well-schooled, homeowning middle class. At no other time in American history had so much money and so many resources been targeted at the generation completing education, entering the workforce and forming families.

Imagine two countries, one the richest in the world, the other among its most destitute. Then suppose a global program of foreign aid transferred well over $100 billion, but to the rich nation, not the poor. This is exactly what happened as a result of the cumulative impact of the most important domestic policies of the 1930s and 1940s. Social Security began to pay old age pensions in 1939. By the end of the 1940s, its original provisions had been impressively improved. The GI Bill was the largest targeted fully national program of support in American history. The country passed new labor laws that promoted unions and protected people as they worked. The Army was a great engine of skill-training and mobility during the Second World War. None of these was a marginal or secondary program. To the contrary, individually and collectively they organized a revolution in the role of government that remade the country's social structure in dramatic, positive ways.

But most blacks were left out. The damage to racial equity caused by each program was immense. Taken together, the effects of these public laws were devastating. Social Security, from which the majority of blacks were excluded until well into the

1950s, quickly became the country's most important social legislation. The labor laws of the New Deal and Fair Deal created a framework of protection for tens of millions of workers who secured minimum wages, maximum hours and the right to join industrial as well as craft unions. African Americans who worked on the land or as domestics—the great majority—lacked these protections. When unions made inroads in the South, where most blacks lived, moreover, Congress changed the rules of the game to make organizing much more difficult. Perhaps most surprising and most important, the treatment of veterans after the war, despite the universal eligibility for the benefits offered by the GI Bill, perpetuated the blatant racism that had marked the affairs of a still-segregated military during the war itself. Comparatively little of this largesse was available to black veterans. With these policies, the Gordian Knot binding race to class tightened.

This is an unsettling history, especially for those of us who keenly admire the New Deal and Fair Deal. At the very moment a wide array of public policies were providing most white Americans with valuable tools to insure their old age, get good jobs, acquire economic security, build assets and gain middle-class status, black Americans were mainly left to fend on their own. Ever since, American society has been confronted with the results of this twisted and unstated form of affirmative action.

Despite the prosperity of post-war capitalism's golden age, an already immense gap between white and black Americans widened. Even today, after the great achievements of civil rights and affirmative action, wealth for the typical white family, mainly in homeownership, is ten times the average net worth for blacks, and a majority of African-American children in our cities subsist below the federal poverty line.

RETRIEVING LBJ'S AMBITIOUS PROJECT

By contrast, Lyndon Johnson depicted policies for racial equity that would target "the poor, the unemployed, the uprooted, and the dispossessed." He famously noted that "freedom is not enough," because "you do not take a person who, for years, has been hobbled by chains and liberate him, bring him to the starting line of a race and then say, 'you are free to compete with all the others,' and still justly believe you have been completely fair." The past four decades have not been kind to this vision. It is important now, in the early 21st century, to retrieve Johnson's ambitious project by connecting the goals and precepts he enunciated to the history of racial bias that was deeply embedded in American social policy.

Johnson had in mind the kind of comprehensive effort the GI Bill had provided to most returning soldiers but without its exclusionary pattern of implementation. But that form of assertive, mass-oriented affirmative action never happened. By sustaining and advancing a growing African-American middle class, the affirmative action we did get has done more to advance fair treatment across racial lines than any other recent public policy, and thus demands our respect and support. But as the scenes from New Orleans vividly displayed, so many who were left out before have been left out yet again.

Rather than yearn for New Deal policies that were tainted by racism, we would do better in present circumstances to return to the ambitious plans President Johnson announced but never realized in order to close massive gaps between blacks and whites, and between more and less prosperous blacks.

THE *BAKKE*/JUSTICE POWELL STANDARDS

In the 1978 Supreme Court case, *Regents of the University of California v. Bakke*, Justice Lewis Powell, a quite conservative Republican, offered clear and strict standards for racial rectification. These guidelines can help guide such a program. Powell argued that modifications to color-blind policies could be undertaken to remedy race-based disadvantages when two conditions are met. There must be a clear and tight link connecting affirmative action's remedies to specific historical harms based on race. This tie between past action and present policy has to be strong and precise. More general claims about racism in the country's past are not enough. Neither can the goal to be pursued by affirmative action be vague or only of moderate importance. It must be sufficiently valuable as a social good to justify suspending rules that ordinarily must be blind to race. Further, if there is a nonracial way to pursue a given goal, that course should always be preferred. Powell insisted on these two principles—that racial injuries be specific and clear; and that a compelling public purpose must be identified when racial remedies are applied—because a color-blind society is desirable and color-coding is inherently susceptible to misuse.

Building on these principles has significant advantages. First, Powell's demand for strict scrutiny appropriately sets the bar high, but not beyond reach. It balances a widely shared desire to make color-neutrality the dominant norm with the cheerless recognition that this goal cannot be achieved if the role race has played in American life is downplayed or, worse, ignored. As settled law, Powell's deeply historical approach has been applied to the type of affirmative action developed during the Johnson and Nixon administrations, but it also can shape and motivate a considerably broader effort that might target affirmative action at those who are less well-off.

Powell's distinctions placed the onus of proof on the character of the historical evidence that is deployed to justify rectification. A focus on the policies about welfare and work, as well as war and post-war, which the Southern wing of the Democratic Party successfully imposed during the New Deal and Fair Deal, is consistent with this requirement. They provide the content Powell requires to justify acts of official rectification.

Retrospectively, we can also see how Johnson's 1965 speech anticipated Powell's standards. The President's analysis of how the racial gap had widened, though deficient, sought to clarify the facts regarding the present status of blacks in American society. He provided a model of justification for affirmative action by summarizing the racial gap, arguing about causes and spelling out why the divide distinguishing racial groups constitutes a major public concern. By taking these steps, he fulfilled Justice Powell's second stipulation. He also sought to connect his remedies to the causes he had identified. In this approach, he followed Justice Powell's first requirement.

Combining Powell's principles and Johnson's ambitions can push us forward to a framework for public policies that can respond to the injuries inflicted by officially sanctioned racism. Though motivated by a desire to protect Jim Crow, many of the methods and instruments those programs used were adopted on a nonracial basis. A renewed and extended program of affirmative action could offer a reciprocal possibility. Responding to non-racial racism, affirmative action could be established in ways that at least partially transcend race, even while primarily rectifying racial injustice.

Beneficiaries must be targeted with clarity and care. The color-blind critique argues that race, as a group category, is morally unacceptable even when it is used to counter discrimination. But there is an important distinction this view misses. African-American individuals have been discriminated against because they were black, and for no other reason. Obviously, this violates basic norms of fairness. But under affirmative action, they are compensated not for being black, but only because they were subject to unfair treatment at an earlier moment because they were black. If, for others, the policies also were unjust, they, too, must be included in the remedies. When national policy kept out farmworkers and maids, the injury was not limited to African Americans. Nor should the remedy.

On this understanding, it is important to identify the recipients of affirmative compensation who have a direct relationship to the harm being remedied. This does not mean that they necessarily had to experience a specific act of discrimination directly. To qualify, however, it needs to be shown how discriminatory institutions, decisions, actions and practices have negatively affected their circumstances. This approach does not limit remedies to individuals who have faced injustice directly, one at a time; neither does it justify remedies for African Americans as a unitary or exclusive group that has shared in a history of racism except when the harm, as in military segregation, was created with unambiguously racist categories.

NEEDED: CORRECTIVE JUSTICE

Popular and political support for corrective justice, in short, as well as judicial legitimacy, will depend on the clarity and persuasiveness of the association between harms and remedies. One of two approaches is possible. A closely targeted program of rectification would search for identifiable individuals who have been harmed, even at the distance of one or two generations, by the pattern of exclusions and local administration documented in my book (see below). This policy could yield both tangible and symbolic compensation. As examples:

- For the lag in entering the Social Security system, the excluded could be identified and they, or their heirs, could be offered one-time grants that would have to be paid into designated retirement funds.
- For the absence of access to the minimum wage, tax credits equivalent to the average loss could be tendered.
- For the lack of access to key programs under the GI Bill, programs of subsidized mortgages, small business loans and educational grants could now be put in place.

These measures could be targeted to those who stand in a direct line to those who were harmed, but both to keep their costs in check and target spending on those most in need, they would also be available only up to a particular level before being taxed back.

Alternatively, a less administratively burdensome but still exacting approach could be crafted. With this design, the broad target group for assertive federal policies would be poor Americans who face conditions produced by the constellation of the patterns of eligibility and administration the South placed inside the most important New Deal and Fair Deal programs. Although less exact at the individual and family level, this approach would authorize a major assault on inequality and poverty that would be justified by these historical patterns and remedied by policy interventions offering boosts into middle-class status. The major instruments would be the same as those the federal government utilized in the GI Bill: subsidized mortgages, generous grants for education and training, small business loans, and active job-searching and placement. This line of attack on the legacies of exclusion also could deploy an expanded Earned Income Tax Credit, assure generous childcare and guarantee basic health insurance.

Either way, it is not only the persons, or group of people, who have to be identified, but the specific qualities of racial discrimination. There is something of a hierarchy. Individual private acts of prejudice and discrimination count for less than more pervasive institutional ones. Injuries dealt by government count for more than private patterns of institutional racism. When government is directly involved, claims for systemic compensation to match systemic harm become most compelling. Public policies, after all, have been the most decisive instruments dividing Americans into different racial groups with vastly different life circumstances and possibilities.

Speaking from the French Quarter in New Orleans last September [2005], President George W. Bush recognized that Hurricane Katrina has revealed "deep, persistent poverty" with "roots in a history of racial discrimination." Any serious search for what he called "bold policies" might begin by taking both the history of affirmative action for whites and Lyndon Johnson's urgency and prescriptions to heart. For without an unsentimental historical understanding of the policy roots of black isolation and dispossession, the response to the disaster in the Gulf states will remain no more than a gesture.

The Importance
of Targeted Universalism

john a. powell, Stephen Menendian & Jason Reece

The impulse to craft universal rather than targeted public policies is natural for a democratically elected leader, accountable to a broad electorate. The conventional wisdom suggests that particular or targeted policies will not garner the same level of support as universal policies. Targeted policies and programs (poorhouses in the 19th century, mothers' pensions in 1910, the War on Poverty in the 1960s) are likely to be viewed through the prism of zero-sum politics. At a time of perceived scarcity and contracting government budgets, targeted policies may be viewed as favoring some constituent group rather than the public good. If the target group is historically disfavored or considered "undeserving," targeted policies risk being labeled "preferences" for "special interests." In order to avoid alienating voters, policies are often packaged for broad appeal.

As the default alternative to targeted policies, universal policies suffer from a conceptual defect. Universal policies assume a universal norm. Universal programs begin with some conception of what is universal. The Social Security Act, often described as the quintessential universal policy, was universal only insofar as the universal was a white, male, able-bodied worker. In its early years, the elderly were excluded, since they had not been in the workforce or in it long enough to qualify. The definition of work excluded women. Under the cultural norms of the era, men were the primary wage-earner, and women typically worked in the home. As a consequence of discriminatory patterns, they were often kept out of most areas of the labor force. Unpaid household labor and child-rearing responsibilities are not counted toward Social Security earnings. Even today, women who take time off to raise children or select careers with more flexible working hours will earn less, on average, than their male counterparts and will therefore have lower Social Security benefits upon retirement. And because of exclusions of agricultural and domestic workers, since rescinded, exclusions built in to appease Southern resistance to the Act, 65 percent of African Americans were denied its protections.

As troubling as is the conceptual problem of defining what exactly is meant by "universal," broadly conceived universal programs are very likely to exacerbate inequality rather than reduce it. Defined as one of this country's greatest accomplishments, the Interstate Highway Act of 1956 used federal dollars to subsidize the creation of the suburbs. This was the largest public works project in American history at the time. It gave impetus to waves of migrating middle- and upper-class families to abandon the central cities for the suburbs. At the same time, many downtown regions were surrounded or demolished by massive highway construction, and the revenue generated by these projects did not return to the communities that were losing their churches, schools and homes. The ensuing arrangement of racially isolated urban dwellers and equally racially isolated suburban residents, hastened by the white flight that followed *Brown v. Board of Education*'s integration mandate, is a pattern we live with today. Simply put, ostensibly universal programs have no less potential to exacerbate inequality than ameliorate it. Treating people who are situated differently as if they were the same can result in much greater inequities.

FALSE CHOICES

Universal and targeted approaches are false choices. There is a third possibility. An alternative to either a straight universal program or a solely particularistic program is to pursue what we call "targeted universalism." This is an approach that supports the needs of the particular while reminding us that we are all part of the same social fabric. Targeted universalism rejects a blanket universal which is likely to be indifferent to the reality that different groups are situated differently relative to the institutions and resources of society. It also rejects the claim of formal equality that would treat all people the same as a way of denying difference.

Targeting within universalism means identifying a problem, particularly one suffered by marginalized people, proposing a solution, and then broadening its scope to cover as many people as possible. It sees marginalized populations in American society as the canary in the coal mine, to borrow a metaphor developed by Lani Guinier and Gerald Torres. It recognizes that problems faced by particular segments of American society are problems that could spill over into the lives of everyone, just as the Lower Ninth Ward was not the only part of New Orleans to suffer in the wake of Katrina. Likewise, the subprime credit crisis did not end in poor, urban communities, but has spread far beyond and has been felt throughout the global economy.

Targeting within universalism means being proactive and goal-oriented about achievable outcomes. As an initial step, an Opportunity Impact Statement could be employed to gauge how a universal policy would impact particular groups. But an impact assessment alone, although a move in the right direction, is not enough. At times, the impact will not be predictable. In a complex real-world setting, policies have unintended consequences and resistance that thwart policy intentions. It is critical that targeted universal policies set clear goals and use mechanisms to closely monitor and correct for negative feedback loops and other resistance to achieve those goals.

AN APPROACH TO INFRASTRUCTURE INVESTMENT

President Obama's $787 billion infrastructure stimulus plan will fundamentally reshape our nation, as the Highway Act and other public works projects of the last century did for the baby boomer generation. If the infrastructure rebuilding merely follows the same patterns of resource allocation, it will make things worse, not better. A program to build large-scale broadband networks will not reduce the digital divide unless access is cost-inexpensive so that low-income families can afford the service. In addition, there must be support for these new users to educate them on how to take advantage of this technology. Affluent students and parents from wealthy districts often have access to the Internet and computer technology as a matter of everyday life.

Many of the current proposals for spending the infrastructure funds look to divert much of the funding to existing road proposals across states. This broad and regressive use of the infrastructure stimulus funds may produce jobs in the short term, but it is just a replication of existing models of public investment that have produced inequitable and unsustainable growth. What are truly needed are strategic investments that produce economic development at a broad scale while strategically transforming communities and cities. Road investments spread widely will not reach this goal. Instead of spreading infrastructure funds broadly, we need to use funds to invest in our most investment-deprived communities in our cities. By making these communities more functional, we increase the economic competitiveness of our cities and region, which are the economic growth engines for our economy.

In addition, we must think more strategically about who benefits from investments in new technologies. Instead of investing billions in wind power infrastructure which would be capital-intensive and produce few jobs, would it be better to target funds to energy-efficient home improvements? This labor-intensive investment could train and employ underemployed workers to recondition homes with energy-efficient measures (like insulation and heating/cooling improvements) while subsidizing these home improvements in low-income communities, where the energy efficiency gains will impact our most economically vulnerable households. In essence, this approach would produce universal environmental gains (energy conservation), while targeting many of the benefits to our most vulnerable households (through energy savings and employment opportunities).

Similar critiques could be made of the initial response to the credit and foreclosure crisis. The initial response provided no widespread comprehensive policies which were goal-oriented (keeping more people in their homes). The response in Fall of 2008 gave massive financial support to Wall Street but limited relief for vacant property reform and weak support for foreclosure prevention. But, even the $4 billion in vacant property support was problematic. Neighborhood stabilization funds targeted toward cities to address the impact of the foreclosure crisis only address the outcome of foreclosure (vacant properties), and cities have been given little incentive to target funds to holistic approaches (foreclosure prevention, counseling, and negotiating loan workouts with lenders) or to specific neighborhoods (such as the communities of color most impacted by the crisis). The initial housing plans from the Obama Administration look more promising, with multiple policy mechanisms to prevent future foreclosures, such as incentives for workouts, providing some flexibility for judges to modify loan terms in bankruptcy and refinancing offered for those loans affiliated with Fannie Mae and Freddie Mac. Although these new initiatives are untested, these new policies appear promising, but the response cannot end with these initiatives. We still must comprehensively look at the impact of vacant properties on neighborhoods must devastated by the crisis and look at the longer-term goal of providing sustainable credit and housing to highly impacted communities in the future. These new goals must guide future policy and be responsive to the concentrated racial footprint of bad loans and foreclosures, targeting resources and initiatives to assure sustainable credit and stable housing for the future of these communities.

The manifold crisis of our fundamental institutions, from our system of healthcare provision to the regulatory apparatus of our banking system, has produced a once-a-century opportunity for institutional change. The opportunities to transform our present institutional and regulatory arrangements are now open. The policies we promulgate will set the course of development for generations to come, just as the post-New Deal and post-WWII arrangements laid the groundwork for generations that followed them. This window of opportunity will remain open for only so long, and the chance for dramatic change will diminish. In this moment, we can work towards building a more equitable future or repeat the mistakes of the past. It is critical that we meet these opportunities with the proper solutions now. If we fail at this, we will be trying to correct our missteps for years to come.

Implicit Bias: A Forum

The insight that we are all, in different ways, subject to "unconscious" or "implicit" bias is a continuing theme in modern anti-discrimination theory, even though it is still largely ignored in civil rights legal jurisprudence. Tracing back at least to Charles Lawrence's path-breaking 1987 article "The Id, the Ego, and Equal Protection: Reckoning with Unconscious Racism," the concept has gained momentum in recent years with research results from the "Implicit Association Test" and the increasingly sophisticated use of racial images in political advertising. For proponents of using the research in legal advocacy (political and litigation), it offers a possible strategy to garner support from those who are skeptical that racial bias continues to exist. The theory is also thought by some to allow for a more open and less defensive discussion about race. At the same time, there are those who believe that placing too much emphasis on implicit bias undermines the more important project of addressing structural discrimination and its outcomes; that it lets people off the hook for their conscious racist views; and that it is a potential trap for anti-discrimination law. The Forum that follows presents several aspects of this debate from some of the leading proponents and critics of the implicit bias approach. We hope that the discussion will shed some light on this important issue.

* * * * *

DOES UNCONSCIOUS BIAS MATTER?

RALPH RICHARD BANKS & RICHARD THOMPSON FORD

During the past several years, psychological research on unconscious racial bias has grabbed headlines, as well as the attention of legal scholars. The most well-known test of unconscious bias is the Implicit Association Test (IAT), a sophisticated and methodologically rigorous computer-administered measure available over the Internet that has been taken by millions of people. Its proponents contend that the IAT reveals widespread unconscious bias against African Americans, even among individuals who believe themselves to be free of racial bias.

The IAT is a compelling interactive experience, and featured in print and broadcast media. The IAT measures the strength of the association between social categories (e.g., blacks or whites) and positive and negative attributes (e.g., "joy" and "love" versus "agony" and "evil"). Akin to a computer game for grownups, the IAT requires momentary immersion into the interactive medium. In a series of trials, the participant categorizes images or words that appear on the computer screen by pressing particular computer keyboard keys as quickly as possible. At the end of the exercise, the computer calculates a score that reflects the nature and magnitude of one's implicit bias. Most participants are found to have an implicit bias against African Americans. The overt racism of the Jim Crow era, the psychological research suggests, has given way to racial bias that is predominantly unconscious.

In fact, the findings of the IAT are ambiguous. The characterization of the IAT as a measure of implicit bias depends on being able to distinguish implicit bias from conscious bias. Yet it is extraordinarily difficult to disentangle the two because, since the disavowal of racism during the civil rights era, research participants have become increasingly unwilling to openly express views that may be condemned as racist. Thus, the IAT could defensibly be viewed as a subtle measure of conscious psychological processes, of attitudes and beliefs that are known to oneself yet intentionally concealed from researchers. This empirical ambiguity has been practically eclipsed by the unconscious bias account. Why?

Scholars may focus on unconscious bias because they think it poses unique challenges for anti-discrimination doctrine. This explanation for the ascendance of the unconscious bias discourse is intuitively appealing and widely embraced. But it is wrong. Anti-discrimination law grapples as well, or as poorly, with unconscious bias as with covert bias. Neither statutory nor constitutional anti-discrimination law turns on the distinction between the two. While the research cannot distinguish between conscious and unconscious bias, the law (fortunately) does not require courts to do so.

The better explanation for the prominence of the unconscious bias discourse relates to the comforting narrative it offers about our nation's progress in overcoming its racist history. Assertions of widespread unconscious bias are more palatable than parallel claims about covert bias. The invocation of unconscious bias levels neither accusation nor blame so much as it identifies a quasi-medical problem buried deep within us all, an ailment that distorts our thinking and behavior. People may be willing to accept that unconscious bias influences their behavior, even if they would vigorously deny harboring conscious bias. Assertions of conscious bias would open a constellation of vexing issues—for example, whether racial disparities reflect discrimination or group differences, whether discrimination may be rational, and if so whether it should be prohibited. The discussion of such matters would be uncomfortable for many and, in any event, would be unlikely to yield any quick consensus. The unconscious bias discourse promotes a (superficial) consensus that the race problem persists precisely by bypassing potential sources of disagreement.

Despite its ostensible political benefits, the unconscious bias discourse may disserve the cause of racial justice. Just as it misdescribes the IAT by eclipsing the ambiguity of its findings, the unconscious bias approach prompts people to acknowledge the persistence of the race problem by misdescribing it. The unconscious bias approach not only discounts the persistence of knowing discrimination, it elides the substantive inequalities that fuel conscious and unconscious bias alike. While we do not doubt the existence of unconscious bias, we do doubt that contemporary racial bias accounts for all, or even most, of the racial injustice that bedevils our society. The racial injustices that most trouble us are substantive—educational failure, large-scale incarceration, segregated and impoverished communities—and stem from a complex interplay of economic, historical, political and social influences. While historical bias has certainly played a role in producing these inequalities, it is fanciful to attribute their persistence to contemporary bias, unconscious or otherwise. The goal of racial justice efforts should be the alleviation of substantive inequalities, not the eradication of unconscious bias.

The unconscious bias discourse is as likely to subvert as to further the goal of substantive racial justice. A narrow focus on the IAT may fail as its empirical claims receive greater scrutiny, which would make it difficult for scholars who have linked their policy positions to the IAT to maintain the impartiality that is the hallmark of the scholar's commitment to truth. But even emphasizing unconscious bias more generally would be a mistake.

The most fundamental problems with the unconscious bias discourse are that it reinforces a misguided preoccupation with mental state, and perpetuates an obsession with anti-discrimination law, rather than policy reform, as a means of realizing racial justice goals. If the goal is to eliminate substantive inequalities, then the task of racial justice advocates should be to say why those inequalities are objectionable and how to address them. Not every claim for racial justice needs to be addressed to a court applying anti-discrimination doctrine. The best political approach, over the long term, is to straightforwardly define and defend policy goals, and then figure out how to achieve them.

* * * * *

IMPLICIT BIAS INSIGHTS AS PRECONDITIONS TO STRUCTURAL CHANGE

JOHN A. POWELL & RACHEL GODSIL

We generally assume that we "control" our behavior most of the time—particularly when an issue is important. This assumption, like many assumptions, is wrong.

Scientists estimate that we have conscious access to only 2 percent of our brain's emotional and cognitive process. Neuroscientists have also determined that we process 11 million bits of information at a time but have the capacity only to be aware at best of 40 bits. In other words, the vast majority of our behavior is dictated by the 98 percent of our brain that works without our express cognition. This startling fact, social psychologists contend, is crucial to our ability to understand an array of seeming inconsistencies between our conscious attitudes and our behavior. Lawyers, law professors and activists have begun to look to this body of research to address our nation's otherwise baffling contradictions surrounding race.

Professors Banks and Ford—able scholars who have devoted much of their academic writing to issues of racial justice—argue that the move to embrace this research may disserve this cause. We disagree—and instead are convinced that scholars, as well as racial justice activists and advocates, need the insights into human behavior available from the mind sciences for our work to advance our nation toward social justice goals.

The argument that other scholars' use of implicit bias research is somehow an impediment to progress is surprising coming from Banks and Ford—both of whom have written in complex and thoughtful ways about race. In this context, however, their argument seems to presume that but for the improvident attempt to use implicit bias insights, our country would be open to a discussion of the role race plays in limiting life opportunities for many people of color. It also appears to be undergirded by the presumption that following this frank discussion about race, our polity will support policies intended to eliminate these structural barriers. As Banks and Ford have discussed in other work, the evidence does not support these assumptions.

What the Evidence Shows

First, the Right has successfully co-opted the concept of "color-blindness" to suggest that any attention paid to race is itself racist—and therefore created a strong presumption against any conversations about race. Richard Ford's 2008 book, *The Race Card: How Bluffing About Race Makes Racial Bias Worse*, describes this phenomenon brilliantly. Second, the reasons progressives seek to address issues of race follow from the extraordinary racial disparities found in virtually every aspect of life. However, the fact of racial disparities does not suffice to prompt a constructive discussion about race. And the insights from the implicit bias research help explain why not. If we have bias toward members of a particular group, even when structures are clearly shown to be the cause of disparity, we are likely to attribute the cause to personal behavior. Scholars have termed this tendency the "the attribution error." The combination of the rhetorical success of the "color-blindness" frame and attribution error is crucial to understanding why cold hard facts about significant racial disparities do not result in any moral urgency to address these disparities.

In our view, Americans' cognitive dissonance regarding race is on the rise. We can boast that we have elected a Black man as our President and confirmed another Black man as Attorney General, while our prisons house a shockingly large number of Black men. Black and Latino men and women serve as executives at Fortune 500 companies and as presidents of our finest universities, yet Black and Latino children are 3 times as likely to live in poverty and 20 percent less likely to graduate from high school than White children.

The challenge of addressing these opposing racial realities has never been more difficult. Many Whites see the continuing string of racial firsts along with the broad acceptance of intermarriage and support for anti-discrimination laws as signs that, as a nation, we have finally moved beyond our origins in slavery and the dark years of Jim Crow. If a person in public life uses a racial epithet or other language suggesting a disagreement with the prevailing anti-discrimination norm, that person is immediately condemned by people across the political spectrum. The combination of these factors makes a powerful case to most Whites that issues of class and individual initiative explain how different individuals and families are situated.

Many people of color and racial justice advocates of all races see an additional set of facts that complicate the picture. Despite the progress our nation has experienced on issues of race, dramatic racial disparities in imprisonment, wealth, academic achievement, rates of housing foreclosure, and environmental protection, along with housing and educational segregation, continue to create harsh obstacles to the full inclusion of people of color into American life. People of color regularly experience micro-aggressions in workplaces, schools, stores and restaurants. For racial justice advocates, the combination of the data and lived experience are seen as proof that we have far to go before we can truly claim the mantle of racial equality.

How to Move Past This Impasse

The political challenge is how to move past this impasse. To address these polarized points of view, we must create a political space in which it is possible to first have a constructive dialogue about the continuing salience of race, then generate support for the policies necessary to address the role race continues to play, and finally, and as importantly, develop implementation measures that will allow these policies to achieve the sought-after outcomes. Contrary to Banks and Ford, we think the insights from social psychologists about how the human brain functions—and how humans see themselves and their environment—have great promise to make these steps possible.

Social psychologists, with a scientific sophistication Freud would have found unimaginable, have developed the ability to test and measure biases we hold implicitly. These implicit biases are important because they can determine our behavior—even if we consciously hold a different set of values. Implicit attitudes flow from our brain's natural tendency to categorize stimuli—to create schemas. As our brains develop, we create schemas for objects we encounter (tables, cars, cell phones), which rarely have political salience, but instead are helpful in allowing us to function in a complex world. Not surprisingly, we also create schemas for humans (men, women, old, young). These schemas need not be problematic if the categories within a society are considered worthy of equal respect. However, if categories applied to humans are subject to negative stereotypes or otherwise determine "out-groups," these schemas can result in bias. A wide array of data, from political opinion surveys to marked disparities, support the idea that race continues to be salient. Yet, as we note above, it is now a deeply held American value to reject racial stereotypes. Those people who seek to subscribe to the egalitarian ideal, but whose brains schematize people on the basis of race, then, are said to hold an implicit bias.

Banks and Ford argue against the use of this research in law reform on two primary grounds. First, that it fails to distinguish with complete confidence between implicit (or unconscious) bias and covert bias. Second, they suggest that accepting the conclusions from this research with respect to race may disserve the goals of racial justice. Implicit bias research, they contend, will result in a diversion of energies away from addressing the substantive inequalities that form the most destructive aspects of our country's racial hierarchy and instead will result in a move to the diversity training room or the therapists' couch rather than the legislative table.

Critiquing Banks and Ford

We will begin with the latter critique. First, implicit bias researchers reject the reductionist trap that concludes that the study of how information operates in individuals necessarily entails ignoring the connection between individual and society. Indeed, the vast majority of those who study implicit social cognition are "social" psychologists. And the research concludes that bias in our society is social rather than individual and that our material conditions can act as primes. Implicit bias is the result of the pervasive stereotypical images (of Blacks as unequal and criminal, of Latinos as "other" and illegal, of women as passive—the list goes on) in our society—not individual views and ideas.

Implicit bias researchers are also not so naïve as to think that implicit bias will be "cured" by diversity training. This is a straw argument. Social psychologists are acutely aware of the challenges of addressing bias. And it is notable that, though relatively nascent, the research suggests that truly to overcome those biases, broad societal change will be required. People will need to experience sustained intergroup contact, the presence of racial exemplars, interactions with people of color in positions of authority, and an end to the cultural barrage of negative images. In addition, changes in the material environment will be important in disturbing the negative associations. For those conditions to be present, we will have to address the overincarceration of young Black men, racial isolation in education from K to higher education, the paucity of people of color in positions of authority throughout our society—this list is also long. In other words, our unconscious minds are highly cognizant of current inequalities even if our conscious selves try to ignore them so that we can consider our society to be fair and our own positions to be earned. Our unconscious minds are not so easily fooled.

We agree with Ford and Banks that bias (implicit or explicit) does not account for many of the most troubling racial injustices. As co-author powell has argued in many other settings, individual racial attitudes are only one form of how race affects human interactions; to achieve reform, we must focus our efforts on structural racialization. Racialization refers to the set of practices, cultural norms and institutional arrangements that both are reflective of and simultaneously help create and maintain racialized outcomes in society.

However, implicit bias insights are crucial to addressing the substantive inequalities that result from structural racialization in two respects. First, they will allow us to enter into the political discourse effectively rather than being heard only by those (fairly few) who already agree with us. Second, these insights, along with other insights from social psychology about the effects of racial anxiety, will be necessary for successful implementation of any political victories. If we achieve substantive victories either through legislation or litigation, any remedial scheme will likely require human implementation. So long as humans are guided by their implicit biases, conditions of inequality will continue to be present.

Some might argue that if Banks and Ford are correct that a significant percent of Americans are in fact consciously hiding their bias rather than holding egalitarian values but still possessing implicit bias, then our view that people will choose to overcome or correct for their bias is naïve. A large body of social science data, however, shows that people go to considerable lengths to correct for any potential racial bias if the potential for such bias is evident—even if there is no reason to think that their bias will be made public. Jury studies, for example, demonstrate that when race is made explicitly relevant, White jurors will treat a Black and a White defendant identically. However, when race is present as a factor but not highlighted, White jurors tend to treat Black defendants more harshly.

Nonetheless, we agree with Banks and Ford that the line between implicit (literally unknown) and conscious but hidden bias may not be stark. It can be argued that people are perhaps choosing to ignore their biases so that their sense of themselves as "good" people with egalitarian values can be maintained. Yet people's desire to maintain their self-concept is powerful—and can induce changes in behavior when they are aware that their actions conflict with their self-concept. So even if we accept that implicit social cognition and the measures of bias such as the Implicit Association Test (IAT) cannot perfectly distinguish between implicit bias and deliberately hidden bias, the value of the tool for measurement is clear. In contrast with self-reporting (which, as Banks and Ford acknowledge, is unlikely to unearth honest results), the IAT provides a window into the bias that would otherwise be effectively hidden. And it serves as a more objective mechanism to measure the degree to which that bias continues to be present.

The final argument Banks and Ford's chapter seems to raise is that using the language of implicit bias—if it is possible that hidden bias is in fact at play—is somehow a form of political pandering that lets racists off the hook. We disagree. The fact that our nation has adopted such a powerful sense that anti-discrimination and equality of race are necessary attributes of our fundamental values is deeply important. To allow people to maintain a self-concept as egalitarian—but to challenge behavior and structural conditions that are inconsistent with those values—is the only route to progress. Saying bias is implicit does not rob us of our moral obligation to act—just as structures that unintentionally create racialized outcomes require a social response. Continuing to argue about "hidden" racism will keep us locked in a polarized debate that is ultimately impossible to win.

* * * * *

LITIGATING IMPLICIT BIAS

EVA PATERSON

If you find yourself applying for a job, you may want to make sure your name is Emily or Greg rather than Lakisha or Jamal. A recent study found candidates with more "white-sounding" names received 50 percent more callbacks for jobs than those with "African-American sounding" names, even when the resumes were otherwise nearly identical. This is not because employers are necessarily weeding out African-American candidates because of overt racism, but because implicit racial biases still affect everyday decisions and behavior.

Racial justice advocates must engage in multipronged strategies that include pushing the courts to seek remedies for rights violations. After years of forward momentum in racial justice litigation, the Supreme Court retrenched anti-discrimination jurisprudence in one fell swoop—*Washington v. Davis*. 426 U.S. 229 (1976). In that case, the Court created a new evidentiary standard for victims of discrimination: Plaintiffs needed to establish a perpetrator's *intent to discriminate*. The "Intent Doctrine," as it is now known, places a heavy burden on plaintiffs who are alleging discrimination in violation of the Equal Protection Clause of the Fourteenth Amendment. It requires them to prove that the discriminating actor or agency "selected or reaffirmed a particular course of action at least in part 'because of,' not merely 'in spite of,' its adverse effects upon an identifiable [racial] group" under the Equal Protection Clause. *Personnel Adm'r of Mass. v. Feeney*, 442 U.S. 256, 279 (1979). But in contemporary society, much racial bias is not overt. Rather, racial stereotypes often infect people's decision-making processes in a subconscious way. Consequently, the courts need to "catch up" to modern forms of racism and allow plaintiffs to prove that race discrimination exists beyond the intentional racial animus that plaintiffs currently have to prove under the Intent Doctrine. Requiring proof of discriminatory intent essentially closes the courthouse doors to victims of racial bias. If there has ever been a law worth the struggle to change in modern society, this is it.

The Intent Doctrine needs to be overturned for anti-discrimination law to actually be successful in overcoming racial injustice. After all, the Court has long recognized that the Equal Protection Clause is meant to protect individuals from discrimination. Yet a growing body of research confirms that racism is not an isolated, unconnected, and intentional act, but a process that is influenced and internalized as a subconscious process. In fact, the subconscious processes or implicit biases influence the way in which we perceive and make determinations about other people.

Less than a decade after *Washington v. Davis*, Professor Charles Lawrence wrote a seminal article that addressed the limitations and shortcomings of the Intent Doctrine. Lawrence utilized social psychology to demonstrate that "requiring proof of conscious or intentional motivation as a prerequisite to constitutional recognition that a decision is race-dependent ignores much of what we understand about how the human mind works." Lawrence's critique of the intent standard centered on the idea that unconscious racism is a modern form of discrimination that the courts fail to understand and subsequently remedy: "By insisting that a blameworthy perpetrator be found before the existence of racial discrimination can be acknowledged, the Court creates an imaginary world where discrimination does not exist unless it was consciously intended." "The Id, the Ego, and Equal Protection," 39 *Stan. L. Rev* 317, 324-25 (1987). As Judge Charles Breyer recognized in *Chin v. Runnels,* unconscious racial stereotyping and group bias are pervasive, and "these unconscious processes can lead to biased perceptions and decision-making even in the absence of conscious animus or prejudice against any particular group." 343 F. Supp. 2d 891, 906 (N.D. Cal. 2004) (citing law review articles by scholars).

Since the publication of Lawrence's article, psychological and social science research has made great strides in providing a broader understanding of how we all possess subconscious or implicit biases—beliefs, attitudes and expectations that are based on stereotypes about specific discrete categories (i.e., race, gender, age, etc.) to which an individual belongs. There is "increasing recognition of the natural human tendency to categorize information and engage in generalizations, of which stereotyping is a part, as a means of processing the huge amount of information confronting individuals on a daily basis." *Chin*, 343 F. Supp. 2d at 906.

In fact, implicit bias and unconscious racism received mainstream attention through Malcolm Gladwell's bestseller, *Blink*. In *Blink*, Gladwell discussed the way in which people engage in rapid cognition based on "instantaneous impressions" which can result in significant—albeit sometimes unintended—harms. As an example of the pernicious impact that may result from acting on instantaneous impressions, Gladwell discusses the 1999 killing of Guinean immigrant Amadou Diallo and the racial prejudices that led to his death. While the New York City police were attempting to question him, Diallo, scared and confused, reached for his wallet. Based largely on racial prejudices, the police assumed the wallet to be a gun and shot Diallo 41 times.

In light of our present inability to find adequate redress for racism and racial injustices through the courts because of the impossible (and unrealistic) standard of the Intent Doctrine, we need a new doctrinal paradigm to advance racial justice through Equal Protection jurisprudence. This approach must include psychological and social science research to prove that discrimination exists even when it may not be tied to an overt act. Since our society has become somewhat hostile to people holding racial biases, social scientists and psychologists have developed increasingly subtle mechanisms that detect implicit racial biases. Through methods like the Implicit Association Test, litigators have made great strides in marshaling psychological and social scientific research on implicit bias to prove instances of discrimination. It is critical that we find ways to present this evidence in court to establish that implicit bias is the catalyst of discriminatory injustices in this day and age.

Using social science in litigation is not a new phenomenon, nor would it be the first time that the Supreme Court would rely on social science evidence to address historical grievances. Charles Hamilton Houston developed a strategic litigation plan in the 1930s that combined impact litigation, innovative use of social science and collaboration with civil rights organizations across the political spectrum to challenge *Plessy v. Ferguson*'s principle of "separate but equal" from the ground up. The Houston Plan (as it has come to be known) led to overturning *Plessy* in the landmark decision *Brown v. Board of Education*. As part of the Houston Plan, litigators in *Brown* from the NAACP Legal Defense Fund introduced social science data from the "doll test," which illustrated the devastating impact of segregation on the emotions and psyches of black children. As part of the test, children were shown two dolls, one white and the other black, and asked a series of questions to determine which doll was associated with positive attributes and which was associated with negative attributes. The results overwhelmingly showed that the majority of children—both black and white—attributed positive aspects to the white dolls and negative aspects to the black dolls. The Supreme Court relied upon this study along with six others to support its conclusion that "separate but equal" violated the Equal Protection Clause. *Brown v. Bd. of Educ. of Topeka*, 347 U.S. 483, 494-95n.11 (1954)

Social science research and data coupled with legal arguments have more recently been used in the fight for marriage equality in the courts. This is striking, considering the evolution of perspectives and attitudes towards homosexuality in the United States from just 17 years prior in *Bowers v. Hardwick*, 478 U.S. 186 (1986); *Perry v. Schwarzenegger*, 704 F. Supp. 2d 921, 941-44 (N.D. Cal. 2010); *Lawrence v. Texas*, 539 U.S. 558, 568-71 (2003). As an example of changing attitudes, in August 2011 the American Psychological Association unanimously approved a resolution supporting same-sex marriage, citing numerous social science studies. These studies provide the courts with evidence of discriminatory actions, effects and implications.

While we must continue to address conscious bias, that task is made difficult in a society where few are willing to admit to holding such beliefs. An implicit bias discourse, as opposed to a strict intentional racism approach, allows for a more open societal conversation about racism than could otherwise happen. Implicit bias discourse focuses the attention on the creation of structural inequality and internalized biased actions that entrench such inequality. My organization, The Equal Justice Society (EJS), has accomplished important groundwork through the introduction of the social science (e.g., implicit bias cognitive theory) of race and racism to judges, racial justice litigators, employment litigators and federal civil rights agencies charged with upholding anti-discrimination laws. Judges are a necessary part of the target group. Training judges on implicit bias can have tremendous results for open-mindedness in the courtroom and helps to cement a deeper understanding of how the reality of race discrimination today conflicts with current legal doctrine.

The judiciary is often concerned about how wide-sweeping their decisions will be and what policy ramifications will result. In particular, trial judges are concerned about making decisions without a strong factual basis, even though they might be sympathetic to plaintiffs. In his dissent in *McCleskey v. Kemp*, Justice Brennan attributed the majority's concern that a ruling for McCleskey would lead to increased litigation as a fear of "too much justice." 481 U.S. 279, 339 (1987). Yet this is exactly why litigators need to continue raising implicit bias in the courts and presenting strong social science data to judges. The law should reflect real-life experiences, serve to counter discrimination, and substantively address structural and implicit bias' effects. Our role as litigators is to keep pressing and educating judges both in court and outside of chambers.

Judges do listen and implement techniques to prevent bias from entering their courtrooms. There are also judges who believe that we now live in post-racial America. Recently, Judge Noonan denied relief to transit riders of color, writing: "What is true of the young is already characteristic of the Bay Area where social change has been fostered by liberal political attitudes, and a culture of tolerance. An individual bigot may be found, perhaps even a pocket of racists. The notion of a Bay Area board bent on racist goals is a specter that only desperate litigation could entertain." *Darensburg v. Metropolitan Transp. Com'n*, 636 F.3d 511, 523-24 (9th Cir. 2011). We strongly disagree with Judge Noonan's assertion that the Bay Area has purged itself of all racial bias.

As racial justice advocates, we understand that racism, bias and discrimination are alive and well. Our focus is to develop remedies for victims of discrimination by providing as many tools as possible to victims and their attorneys, while pushing the courts to be creative in providing solutions. Although in many parts of the country race discrimination has become increasingly subtle over time, the effects of discrimination on victims and society remain as powerful as ever. It is thus crucial to lead a multifaceted approach to remedying such injustice. Through our work in these areas, there are three lessons we have learned as litigators: (1) implicit bias is a tool that addresses acts of racism that are not overt but still pernicious in impact; (2) the use of implicit bias is part of a long-standing tradition of using social science research to provide the courts with evidence of discriminatory actions and effects; and (3) implicit bias provides an entry-point for people to discuss race.

Accordingly, EJS has met with experienced public interest litigators and our own legal staff to discuss the many areas in which the Intent Doctrine acts as a barrier to achieving racial justice. Litigation in these areas already exists.

EJS's role is to raise legal arguments based on implicit bias and, as appropriate, structural racism. We have established new relationships and fortified existing ones with key legal advocates. Together, we are addressing some fundamental questions to best position ourselves to litigate: how best to use social science, what the structure of the arguments should be, and where we can obtain the necessary resources, including legal support and funding, to bolster our litigation. We are focusing on racial disparities in the criminal justice system that could also affect death penalty litigation and municipal disparities in delivering governmental services.

If the goal of racial justice is to acknowledge and ameliorate substantive inequalities, we can never get there by solely focusing on conscious bias. We absolutely must fight the battle against racial injustice on every front: tackling conscious discrimination and unconscious discrimination together; educating the public; advocating in the legislatures for policy reform; and litigating implicit bias in the courts to overturn the regressive Intent Doctrine. Each step takes us closer to having a judiciary that may once again serve as a bastion of justice for victims of race discrimination.

* * * * *

IMPLICIT BIAS, RACIAL INEQUALITY AND OUR MULTIVARIATE WORLD

ANDREW GRANT-THOMAS

Richard Banks and Richard Thompson Ford make a number of potentially important arguments. I focus here on two: first, their assertion that the Implicit Association Test may measure conscious-but-concealed bias rather than implicit bias; and, second, their claim that attention to unconscious or implicit bias deflects attention from "substantive inequalities" and the policies needed to remedy them. Like Banks and Ford, I refer here almost exclusively to IAT-based work, but note that evidence for the prevalence and impact of implicit bias extends well beyond results garnered through use of the IAT and well beyond the domain of racial attitudes.

What Does the IAT Measure?

In addition to the possibility that the IAT taps concealed-but-conscious bias, some research psychologists have argued that the IAT may tap other kinds of mental content as well, including the subject's awareness of biases in the culture, anxiety about being labeled a racist, and sympathy with, or guilt regarding, disadvantaged populations. Some critics also protest the inference, drawn largely from IAT test results reported at the Project Implicit demonstration site, that most Americans harbor "racist" attitudes against Black people. Both criticisms underline the need for greater clarity about the meaning of implicit, and wider appreciation of the contingency of our racial attitudes and related behaviors. I take these points in turn.

On the one hand, Banks and Ford are doubtless right to note that some testers will deliberately misreport their explicit attitudes. On the other, they are wrong to believe that that fact poses a problem for the IAT. The main purpose of the IAT, after all, is to probe attitudes people may be unable or unwilling to report. Myriad studies offer strong support for the notion that implicit attitudes, as gauged by the IAT, and explicit attitudes, as inventoried through self-reports, are related but distinct. Self-reported attitudes, and those probed by the IAT, have been found to be associated with different kinds of brain activity.

Leaving aside the details of the highly technical, largely methodological grounds on which researchers in the cognitive sciences wage their wars of interpretation, one would have to be awfully cynical to suppose that most people who express surprise at their IAT results, including the lead researchers behind Project Implicit, are simply being disingenuous. We have very little reason to believe this. The likelier explanation is that self-reports reflect attitudes of which subjects are aware, IAT results reflect attitudes of which they are not, and sometimes there is a dismaying difference between the two.

In any case, for those of us concerned with the role that implicit racial biases may play in the world, their critical feature is not that they operate outside our awareness, but that they operate automatically—without need for intentionality or reflection. Someone taking the IAT, knowing it is meant to reveal "hidden bias," may well try to manage the expression of those biases. (Whether they are able to do so is another matter.) The same person looking to hire a new employee, sit next to one person or another on the bus ride home, decide whether to call 911 about a late-night scuffle outside her home is apt to be less vigilant. In these cases, automatic biases may well influence her actions and help trigger the consequences that flow from them.

What about the broader criticism, that IAT results may reflect mental factors other than personal bias? John Jost, Laurie Rudman and their co-authors offer a compelling response in their 2009 review: "If IAT scores were [sic] measured nothing more than familiarity or sympathy (or any of the other artifacts proposed by critics), then there is no way that such scores would predict discriminatory attitudes and behaviors in the manner and to the extent that they do." Here we get to a question arguably more fundamental than the one about precisely what the IAT assesses: Does it provide information that reliably helps us anticipate behaviors we care about? Yes, it does.

A Nation of Racists?

Researchers have accumulated significant evidence that implicit bias, as measured on the IAT or in other ways, correlates with discriminatory behavior. Employment recruiters with large implicit biases in favor of native Swedes were much more likely to invite applicants with male Swedish names for interviews than they were to invite equally qualified applicants with male Arab names. White students with high implicit bias scores were more likely to report having directed verbal abuse or physical violence against racial others. Many studies have shown that police officers and civilians alike are more likely to shoot unarmed Blacks than unarmed Whites, and to shoot armed Blacks but not armed Whites in video simulations.

More broadly, Anthony Greenwald and his collaborators found in their meta-analysis of relevant research studies that IAT results did much better than self-reported attitudes in predicting Black-White and other intergroup behaviors—including hiring and salary decisions, sentencing decisions and intention to vote for John McCain in 2008. The reverse was true in the seven other behavioral domains examined. The researchers also found that IAT and self-report measures offered the best behavioral predictions when used in tandem than either did when used alone.

While the power of the IAT to predict interracial behavior has often been impressive by the standards of behavioral science, its predictive capacity nonetheless must be considered modest by real-world standards. As a rule, cultural information, social setting, recent experience, explicit attitudes and other factors together influence individual behaviors much more than implicit attitudes alone do. And, again, having implicit bias is not the same as embracing that bias, and people can be differently alert about whether, when and how they express their biases. As a result, "low-bias" people will act in discriminatory ways sometimes and "high-bias" people will often refrain from doing so.

Where does this leave us? On the one hand, according to the Project Implicit website, "75–80 percent of self-identified Whites and Asians show an implicit preference for racial White relative to Black" and a large and growing body of empirical work indicates that such preferences help predict many race-related behaviors and judgments, doing so better than self-reported data on racial attitudes. On the other hand, implicit biases usually account for modest amounts of the variation in such behaviors and, as Jost, Rudman and their colleagues note, implicit bias researchers warn repeatedly against using the IAT to diagnose individual prejudice.

This is shades-of-gray stuff, and as such very much in tension with the American inclination to reduce matters of race to stark, either-or binaries. Thus, in the United States, a person is either Black or not-Black. The degree to which many of us are invested in the distinction, in particular, is evident in the back-and-forth about Barack Obama's racial identity. Either George W. Bush's leaden response to Hurricane Katrina betrayed his racism or his diverse cabinet showed that he was not-racist. Either Obama's election confirmed what the *Wall Street Journal* called the "myth of racism" or it is completely anomalous. When it comes to race, we are often blind to shades of gray.

Racial Bias and Inequality

Suppose we suspected that many people in the United States, especially members of its White-identified majority, harbored readily activated biases, implicit or explicit, against people of color and especially against Black Americans. (In 2009, public opinion scholars Lawrence Bobo and Camille Charles concluded that "between half and three-quarters of whites in the United States still express some degree of negative stereotyping of blacks and Latinos.") Suppose we knew that these biases sometimes manifest in discriminatory behaviors. Suppose we recognized the substantial role that human discretion plays in the distribution of societal benefits, burdens and resources in such opportunity arenas as housing, education, employment and criminal justice. And what if we also recognized that the power to distribute benefits and burdens was vested overwhelmingly in the hands of White Americans?

Under this set of assumptions, that three in four African Americans are confined to 16 percent of the nation's census block groups would not surprise us. The gross overrepresentation of Latinos and African Americans in our country's prisons would not shock us. It might not even shock us to learn that the only two states that allow prisoners to vote, Maine and Vermont, are also the two "whitest" states in the country. An argument like that proposed by Alberto Alesina and Edward Glaeser, that the United States' greater racial and ethnic diversity accounts for half the difference between this country's public welfare spending and Europe's more generous support for its poor, would seem quite plausible on its face.

The point, of course, is that interpersonal bias has very practical implications for our work on race. Let's consider the case of racial segregation in some detail. With reference to the pronounced residential segregation of African Americans, I suggest that racial preferences might enforce segregation in the United States today in at least four ways.

Historical sediment. Many people have elaborated on the ways that White racial attitudes, especially in the North, fueled a range of "fight" and "flight" responses directed mainly against African Americans through much of the 20th century. I propose two ongoing effects. First, history has bequeathed us patterns of segregation in many metro areas of the Northeast and Midwest that would require time to disrupt even if racial attitudes, policies and housing market practices today presented no further obstacles to doing so. Absent strong remedial action, segregation in motion tends to stay in motion. Second, in some areas, historical antagonisms and discriminatory public policies have entrenched entitlements to "racialized space" that residents regard as invariable.

Policy preferences. We know that public support for policies depends substantially on the explicit racial preferences people bring to their considerations. We know much less about how implicit attitudes affect policy choices, though one recent study concluded that the IAT captures automatic attitudes that shape individual preferences for immigration policy.

Current policy struggles with implications for racial segregation abound. In Milwaukee, then-County Executive Scott Walker (same guy) successfully championed a fight against developing public transportation that would have connected mostly Black city residents to jobs in mostly White suburban areas. To similar effect, Westchester County's (NY) executive so far has defied federal orders to dismantle exclusionary zoning ordinances that have limited the availability of affordable housing throughout much of the county. It is quite likely that racial attitudes drive much of the dynamic in these cases and many comparable ones across the country.

Private actions. Any hope we have to generate much greater neighborhood integration will depend largely on modifying people's automatic associations about race. A video experiment by Maria Krysan and three collaborators found that Whites in Chicago and Detroit regard all-Black and racially mixed neighborhoods as much less attractive than literally identical neighborhoods with White residents alone. We see the corresponding dynamics in places like Cincinnati, St. Louis and Philadelphia, where African-American and, in some cases, Latino movement to older suburbs have been echoed by the movement of Whites to the exurbs.

One of the most notable findings of the literature on residential segregation has been the status of African Americans as both the least-favored neighbors and the group most disposed toward integration. Bobo and Charles report that "[a]ctive racial prejudice—negative racial stereotypes, feelings of social distance, and perceptions of racial group competition—is the primary factor driving preferences for neighborhood racial integration, and prejudice is therefore implicated in the persistence of racially segregated communities." A more recent trend finds more middle-class African Americans wanting to settle in predominantly "Black" neighborhoods, possibly presenting yet another attitudinal barrier to greater integration.

System justification. System justification theory highlights the tendency, shared by advantaged and subordinate groups alike, to legitimate the status quo. The professed beliefs of many Whites that residential segregation is fed mainly by the wish of African Americans and Latinos to "be with their own," by their reluctance to do the hard work required to succeed, or simply by (legitimate) socioeconomic differences rather than (illegitimate) racial aversions can all be construed as supportive of the theory.

So too, arguably, do results from a 2007 Pew Research Center survey showing majorities of African Americans agreeing that Blacks were mainly "responsible for their own condition" (53 percent) and that the "values held by middle-class blacks and poor blacks have become more different" (61 percent). Almost 4 in 10 respondents believe that "because of diversity within their community, blacks can no longer be thought of as a single race." How same-group racial attitudes, inflected by notions of deservingness, condition the wish of Black Americans to live among same-race peers across class lines, and our willingness to remain invested in the broader struggle to upturn the racial status quo—these are issues that would reward additional study.

Our Multivariate World

Of course, the persistence of segregation and most other features of racial inequity cannot be due entirely to the persistence of implicit or explicit biases. For one thing, unless we believe that racial biases have actually worsened over time, even pervasive bias cannot account for the rapidly increasing resort to incarceration over the last three decades, the resegregation of public schools in the South, the recent widening of the racial wealth divide, or the bifurcation of fortunes within the African-American population, among other trends.

For another, we know that personal biases are not required to maintain some inequalities, though pervasive biases surely exacerbate them. An appallingly high number of Black and Latino children attend high-poverty schools with too few qualified teachers, crumbling buildings and classes that prepare them poorly for college. In 2000, one in four Black children and one in eight Latino children (but only one in 100 White children) lived in a severely distressed neighborhood. These kinds of institutional and structural inequalities have terrible, self-reinforcing consequences for the people of color who suffer them, regardless of the play of biases within them.

We are complex creatures living in a multivariate social world largely of our creation. Making substantial progress in remedying racial injustice and inequality will require a multipronged, insistently integrated approach that engages issues of bias, culture, ideology, institutional and structural inequities, and power. The lag with respect to progressive policy reform that Banks and Ford lament is about the ascension of color-blindness as a norm in public life; about who controls the policy levers, and who does not; about the cultural models to which those decision-makers and most of their constituents subscribe with respect to racial inequality; and so on. An unhealthy preoccupation that racially progressive people have with anti-discrimination law has very little to do with it.

Implicit Bias and Racial Justice—Next Steps

In terms of research, and even more in terms of vision and strategy, we have much to learn and much to do. With respect to the implicit bias agenda in particular, we have a range of pressing needs.

We need a deeper understanding of the factors that shape the initial development of implicit bias in young people and on a communitywide scale; better processes and tools for demystifying the idea of implicit bias with lay audiences; wider acceptance of the need to engage implicit bias among racial progressives and moderates; better tools for measuring implicit bias and its behavioral effects across contexts; much greater headway in fashioning policy and practical remedies to bias; and more insights into the ways implicit bias shapes our social structures and vice versa. By what mechanisms do our biases shape the institutional structures we create and allow to persist? How do we reconcile that premise with the systems perspective that draws attention to unintended consequences? How do the structures we create impact the way we think about people?

Time to get back to work.

* * * * *

BEYOND BIAS

OLATI JOHNSON

Professors Banks and Ford are correct to highlight the dangers of the current preoccupation with implicit bias among academics and civil rights advocates. The central problem is not an empirical ambiguity in the Implicit Association Test (IAT). And, notwithstanding the Court's recent decision in *Walmart v. Dukes* questioning expert testimony that relied in part on the science of implicit bias, I am more hopeful than Professors Banks and Ford about the utility of implicit bias research for law and policy. Yet I agree with their essential observation that implicit bias is too thin an account of the forces that maintain contemporary racial inequality.

Of course, I understand the appeal of the implicit bias research. The findings of the IAT and other research on unconscious bias appear to provide an empirical account for continuing racial inequality, potentially countering narratives that focus on individual attributes. Also, the unconscious bias account centers not on historic discrimination, but on contemporary discrimination in which we are all complicit. But in presenting implicit bias as universal, something that we all harbor and experience, this account obscures the extent and multiplicity of barriers facing the most disadvantaged groups in our society. Moreover, an emphasis on individual-level behavior—whether covert or explicit—fails to show how individual processes are reinforced or produced by private and public institutions. In short, it omits what we have typically called the "structural" aspects of inequality.

In my view, our challenge as scholars and advocates concerned about inequality should be to provide rich empirical accounts of the contemporary forces that sustain inequality. Just terming these inequalities "structural" will not go far enough. The term conjures up racial discrimination that is too pervasive and amorphous to be quantified or remedied. Instead, to capture the appeal of empirical accounts of bias, we need to similarly document how the structural aspects of racial inequality are maintained today—for instance, by showing how racialized geographic spaces operate to limit economic and social advancement or how race-specific networks and poor social capital contribute to racial disparities in employment. In addition, rather than simply concentrating on the individual, we need to show the symbiotic relationship that exists between individual-level bias and the macro-level forces that sustain inequality.

Rich accounts are manifest in research showing how race-neutral policies interact with individual-level bias to produce racial disparities in juvenile justice confinement; in Deidre Royster's account of how segregated job networks exclude African Americans from blue-collar jobs; and in Devah Pager's work showing how employer attitudes, discrimination and the racialized consequences of mass incarceration affect labor market outcomes for African Americans. Lawyers and advocates should build on this research to promote better understanding of contemporary racial inequality, and to alter the policies and institutional practices that produce it.

At the end of their piece, Professors Banks and Ford argue that the contemporary problems of racial inequality are better addressed by "policy," not law. Their suggestion is that law is best suited to eradicating bias, and has little purchase in addressing more systemic barriers. Here I would disagree. Law, after all, is about litigation and regulation, advocacy and problem-solving, about legislatures and policymaking bodies. I see promise in litigation and policy advocacy that promotes spatial integration and regional equity in housing, challenges disparities in the criminal and juvenile justice system, furthers transportation equity, and battles occupational segregation and pay inequities in low-wage jobs. These efforts combat not just discrimination, but what Glenn Loury calls "development bias"—the policies and practices that lead to "unequal chances to realize one's productive potential." These interventions understand that civil rights lawyering is more than anti-discrimination practice, it is challenging the multitude, complex and enduring forces that sustain racial inequality.

* * * * *

BANKS & FORD RESPONSE

We are grateful that so many scholars and civil rights activists took the time to consider our arguments and to reply to them. We cannot address to all of the important issues that the commentators raise, so we have decided to respond to what we see as their major themes. One set of issues is substantive: What does the research show? How do we conceptualize racial inequality? The other set of issues is pragmatic and political: What are the most promising avenues of reform?

Substantive Concerns

Many commentators remarked that the implicit bias research is more nuanced than we acknowledged. We are very familiar with the empirical research and we agree that the primary research is remarkably nuanced and careful. But any fair reading of that research would have to acknowledge the difficulty that we discuss: that of disentangling covert bias from unconscious bias. Andrew Grant-Thomas notes that the purpose of the IAT is to "probe attitudes that people may be unable or unwilling to report." That characterization both highlights and elides precisely our point:

the distinction between covert and unconscious attitudes. We view the IAT more as a useful and subtle measure of covert racial attitudes than as a measure of wholly unconscious attitudes.

The thrust of our critique, though, is not simply to quibble with the research. We think that the research exemplifies a widely shared view: that the problem of racial inequality is in large part a problem of individuals' biased attitudes. We do not embrace that characterization. We think that in contemporary society the problem of racial inequality is not primarily one of people having "biased" thoughts or acting on such biased thoughts. Pervasive racial inequalities persist, to be sure, and race remains salient largely because of those inequalities. But we think that the "problem" is those inequalities, not some supposedly biased mental state that has led to them.

This is not to say that racial bias doesn't exist or that people are color-blind. They most certainly are not. It is to say that many racial attitudes and stereotypes are in part a reflection of the social world that we all inhabit, a world in which racial disparities are pervasive, and in which prevailing contemporary racial attitudes are as much a symptom of inequality as its cause. Our view is perfectly consistent with the IAT research, if it is understood as a psychological reflection of substantive inequalities, but it is inconsistent with the use to which that research is often put, which is to unearth the hidden causes of biased decisions.

We are convinced that the now-dominant civil rights focus on mental state is misguided and that implicit bias analysis is just another way to focus on mental state. We think mental state has always been too elusive to serve as the basis for liability and remediation in specific disputes, and it has very little to do with today's social injustices, and so we question the wisdom of a new focus on mental state.

Political and Pragmatic Concerns

Typically, of course, the IAT is not portrayed as a measure of how substantive inequalities shape people's views. Nor do advocates highlight the difficulty of disentangling covert and unconscious attitudes. Rather, the research is often characterized in the media and by racial justice advocates in ways that eclipse the subtlety and limitations of the empirical findings. Commentators have suggested, for example, that the research links implicit bias to a wide range of discriminatory behaviors even when, in fact, the evidence was quite sparse.

Racial justice advocates are all too eager to link implicit bias to all manner of race-related disparities. For example, the commentaries on our chapter suggest that the findings of Devah Pager's excellent work on race and incarceration in the job-seeking process and of Marianne Bertrand and Sendhil Mullainathan's well-known resume studies as evidence of implicit bias. In fact, neither study measured implicit bias—both were consistent with a range of explanations, including consciously concealed racial biases and more complex reactions to social familiarity and acculturation.

While some advocates genuinely have come to believe that implicit bias does account for some substantial portion of contemporary racial disparities, we suspect that others deploy implicit bias, either knowingly or not(!), in response to the political pressures with which all racial justice advocates must contend. We suspect that deep down, even many proponents of the implicit bias research sense that the findings are being stretched and deployed in ways that are not supported by the actual research. Yet they feel they have little choice.

As many of the commentators remarked, racial justice advocates face a political quandary: Many people don't want to talk about race; they would prefer to believe, especially after having elected a black president, that our nation's racial problems are behind us. And under no circumstances will people talk about race if there is a risk they will be labeled a racist. To this political impasse, implicit bias seems to come to the rescue. It seems to offer a way of encouraging people to talk about race, without fear of being labeled a racist. (After all, even many blacks, the research tells us, are implicitly biased against African Americans.)

We agree that it may be beneficial to have people talk more honestly about race, but we are less sanguine about whether the implicit bias framework will produce that conversation. But we worry that the prominence of the implicit bias framework depends in part on the exaggerated claims that so often are thrown around in the media and by some advocates. We suspect that if advocates consistently limited themselves to what rigorous social science research has actually demonstrated, much of the rhetorical punch of implicit bias would be lost and it would be one of the thousands of sound and useful social science theories that few outside the field are interested in. But the strong claims are speculative at best and reckless at worst. For example, some in the popular press have proposed that we could use the IAT to disqualify racist jurors. No respectable social psychologist would embrace this proposal, but it's just this kind of thinking that has made the IAT so popular.

Another problem arises if the implicit bias framework is successful in capturing the attention of policymakers. As the stakes become greater, the research and the claims made on its behalf will be subject to greater scrutiny. And as people begin to look more closely, many will conclude that implicit bias is not in fact the primary cause of racial differences in incarceration, employment or education, to name a few. Having relied so heavily on implicit bias, advocates will then be at a loss when people can reasonably disagree about whether implicit bias is the source of some particular social problem. Implicit bias will become yet another in a long line of tactical arguments used in the now depressingly repetitive debates about race and racism.

We suspect—and many of the comments confirm this suspicion—that many scholars and advocates know that implicit bias is not the real problem, but embrace it as a politically effective means of getting people to focus on the substantive racial disparities with which we are all concerned. If it weren't for the pressure to frame racial problems in terms of bias—as a result of the court-centric disparate treatment framework that animates the legal and political approach to racial inequality—we suspect that many researchers would be freer to acknowledge the ambiguity of the findings, and not to attempt so relentlessly to force a set of various and complex social problems into the narrow box labeled "unconscious bias."

Implicit bias is unlikely to cause people to focus on the substantive disparities; in fact, it is more likely, in the long run, to reinforce the view that a situation is not racially unjust unless a "biased" decision-maker can be identified and blamed. If no biased decision-maker is available, or the decision-maker is found not to be biased, then, according to this logic, there is no injustice. Although many of the commentators hope that a focus on implicit bias will expand our focus beyond isolated acts of discrimination, we think that the implicit bias approach is more likely to reinforce the misguided idea that malignant mental state is the crux of racial injustice.

This strikes us as another case in which liberals and progressives have been politically out-maneuvered by conservatives. Once progressives focused directly on substantive inequalities and the importance of policy reform, while conservatives preferred the piecemeal and inevitably incomplete approach of courts focused on individual acts of discrimination. Ironically, today many progressive advocates have embraced a framework that tends to eclipse the structural and substantive inequalities that generate contemporary racial problems. We believe that individual psychology is simply the wrong focus for civil rights law. The Left knew this in the 1970s, when it was less true than it is today. But after decades of conservative insistence that individual animus is the sine qua non of a civil rights violation, the Left, having basically accepted this bad premise, is frantically trying to gin up new forms of "bias" to attack.

The political payoff of the implicit bias approach is uncertain and the substantive focus misplaced, so why not turn our sights directly on the real problems? Why not zero in unapologetically on the complicated historical and contemporary forces that sustain and promote harmful racial inequalities? This would not guarantee results, as many of the commentators note, nor would it magically surmount all the obstacles to sustained and serious conversation about racial injustice, but it would at least direct our own analytic energies in the right direction. It would direct attention to real problems, rather than politically expedient measures, and it would move us closer to practical solutions and away from futile conceptual puzzles (can a person be biased and not know it?).

Of course the implicit bias framework is not the primary impediment to a more substantive and fruitful analysis of racial inequality (and we have never suggested otherwise), but it certainly doesn't help matters. The current focus on implicit bias is grossly out of proportion to its utility or capacity to advance our understanding of social injustice and law reform. As such, it threatens to both divert energies better spent on more practical solutions and to reinforce the dangerous belief that mental state is the central issue in civil rights law. The obsession with implicit bias strikes us as an act of desperation by advocates and scholars who have watched civil rights law undermined, dismantled or turned against itself year after year. We sympathize: Desperation is an understandable response in the era of the Roberts Court, and implicit bias seems to offer at least a modest response to a growing hostility to civil rights claims: any port in a storm. Still, we believe the implicit bias "solution" to the unraveling of civil rights law is a false hope, and we hope to discourage those we see as our allies from mistaking shallow and rocky shoals for a safe harbor.

Tax Aversion: The Legacy of Slavery

Robin Einhorn

The evidence is clear, especially around April 15: With a passion, Americans hate everything about taxation. We sometimes tell pollsters we are willing to pay higher taxes to get better public services from our governments (schools, roads, and so on), but, in a "read my lips" political culture, no campaign promise works better than the promise to cut taxes.

Americans are easily persuaded of our desperate need for "tax relief," but the fact is that our taxes are low relative to other nations. According to the Organization for Economic Cooperation and Development (OECD), American governments (federal, state, local) take less of our incomes in taxes than the governments of other countries with comparable economies. In 2002, American taxes amounted to 26 percent of GDP. This was only half the burden in the true high-tax countries, Sweden (50 percent) and Denmark (49 percent), and well below the average for the 30 OECD member countries (36 percent).

Most Americans would probably agree that our hatred for taxes has something to do with a more profound aversion to government in general, an aversion with deep roots in our history. A nation founded in a tax revolt, we are told, is true to itself only when it is "starving the beast." Yet the original revolutionary objection was never to taxes in general, much less to government in general. It was to taxation without representation [shades of DC—ed.] and government by a faraway empire.

Nevertheless, Americans are right to think that our antitax and antigovernment attitudes have deep historical roots. Our mistake is to dig for them in Boston. We should be digging in Virginia and South Carolina rather than in Massachusetts or Pennsylvania, because the origins of these attitudes have more to do with the history of American slavery than the history of American freedom. They have more to do with protections for entrenched wealth than with promises of opportunity, and more to do with the demands of privileged elites than with the strivings of the common

78

man. Instead of reflecting a heritage that valued liberty over all other concerns, they are part of the poisonous legacy we have inherited from the slaveholders who forged much of our political tradition.

THE ROLE OF SLAVERY

Slavery was a major institution in the American economy, slaveholders major players in American politics, and major political decisions, such as tax decisions, always had to take these facts into account. To tell a story about early American political history that ignores slavery is to miss what often was the very heart of that story.

It might seem strange to trace our antitax and antigovernment ideas to slavery instead of to liberty and democracy. Isn't it obvious that a democratic society where "the people" make the basic political decisions will choose lower taxes and smaller governments? The short answer is no. In this democratic society, the people might decide to pool their resources to buy good roads, excellent schools, convenient courthouses and an effective military establishment. But slaveholders had different priorities than other people and special reasons to be afraid of taxes. Slaveholders had little need for transportation improvements (since their land was often already on good transportation links such as rivers) and hardly any interest in an educated workforce (it was illegal to teach slaves to read and write because slaveholders thought education would help African Americans seize their freedom). Slaveholders wanted the military, not least to promote the westward expansion of slavery, and they also wanted local police forces ("slave patrols") to protect them against rebellious slaves. They wanted all manner of government action to protect slavery, while they tended to dismiss everything else as wasteful government spending.

But the crucial thing was the fear. Slaveholders could not allow majorities to decide how to tax them, even when the majorities consisted solely of white men. Slaveholders occasionally supported lavish government spending, but they would never yield the decisionmaking power to nonslaveholding majorities. Recognizing that the power to tax was "the power to destroy," they could not risk the possibility that nonslaveholding majorities would try to destroy slavery, even when the nonslaveholders insisted on their loyalty to the "peculiar institution." As a Virginia planter phrased it in 1829, opposing a reform that would have granted a nonslaveholding majority its fair share of seats in the state legislature, this was a flat-out rejection of anything that "put the power of controlling the wealth of the State into hands different from those which hold the wealth." It was a flat-out rejection of democracy.

Before the Civil War, slaveholding "masters" often dominated the political terrain. It was no accident that the first Southern representative to issue a secession threat was a signer of the Declaration of Independence. On July 30, 1776, less than a month after adoption of the Declaration, Thomas Lynch of South Carolina issued an ultimatum: "If it is debated, whether their Slaves are their Property," Lynch warned, "there is an End of the Confederation." Unless Congress agreed to stop talking about slavery, Lynch was saying, the United States would survive for a total of only three weeks!

Congress was not talking about slavery in July, 1776 because its members were abolitionists who wanted to act on the promise of the Declaration. That was not the problem at all. Congress was talking about slavery because its members were framing a national government for the new nation what would become the Articles of Confederation. Trying to figure out how to count the population to distribute tax burdens to the various states, the members inevitably faced the problem of whether to count the population of enslaved African Americans. Since slaves were 4 percent of the population in the North (New Hampshire to Pennsylvania) and 37 percent of the population in the South (Delaware to Georgia), this decision would have a huge impact on the tax burdens of the white taxpayers of the Northern and Southern states. Predictably, Northerners wanted to count the total population (including slaves) while Southerners wanted to count only the white population. As the members jostled with each other over this basic conflict of interest, they began to justify their positions by making claims about whether slavery was profitable and therefore made a state able to pay higher taxes (Northerners said yes, Southerners said no). The important point, however, is that once this issue had been opened, it was impossible to prevent discussions of the injustice of slavery itself in a Congress that had just declared that "all men are created equal." When Congress finally held this debate in 1783 (by which time the Confederation was all but bankrupt), it hammered out the infamous fraction that later entered the Constitution as the three-fifths rule for apportioning "representatives and direct taxes."

Variations on this problem would recur over and over again. Every time Northerners and Southerners had to make a national decision together, they found themselves forced to talk about the practical implications of a sectionalized institution of slavery. These were debates about the implications of slavery for whites rather than about the liberation of African Americans. The problem was institutional rather than ideological, built into the very structure of the nation itself because the United States was half slave and half free. Every time a discussion of this kind began, slaveholders worried that nonslaveholders would try to abolish the institution of slavery by imposing prohibitive taxes on slaves. Thus, at the Virginia convention that debated the ratification of the U.S. Constitution in 1788, Patrick Henry worried about a federal slave tax hefty enough to "compel the Southern States to liberate their negroes."

Whether they were worrying about the federal government or about the governments of their own states, slaveholders developed three solutions to this general problem. First, they tried to guarantee that they dominated the legislative process by manipulating the representation rules. Second, they demanded weak governments that would make few of the decisions that provoked discussions of slavery. Third, they insisted on constraining the tax power through constitutional limitations on its use. Regardless of which of these strategies they were pursuing at a particular moment, slaveholders were always trying to prevent nonslaveholding whites from talking about how the institution of slavery harmed them. The goal was always to prevent situations in which the nonslaveholders would think about taxing the institution of slavery out of existence.

THE SLAVEHOLDERS' REAL VICTORY

Yet the real slaveholder victory lay in a fourth strategy: persuading the nonslaveholding majorities that the weak government and constitutionally restrained tax power actually were in the interests of the nonslaveholders themselves. Proslavery representation rules—the three-fifths clause of the U.S. Constitution and similar devices within Southern states—became necessary compromises with slavery, but the other two solutions to the slaveholders' political problem became protections for the "common man." Majorities voluntarily renounced the right to regulate their society by majority rule. Giving up the essence of democratic self-government, they celebrated the outcome as democracy. The consequences would outlive the slaveholders who played such a large role in establishing this attitude toward government and taxation. Long after slavery was gone, a regime forged around preferential treatment for the slaveholding elite came to favor very different elites: commercial and industrial elites who shared little with their slaveholding predecessors except a demand that majorities renounce their right to govern what ostensibly was a democratic society.

The irony is that the slaveholding elites of early American history have come down to us as the champions of liberty and democracy. In a political campaign whose audacity we can only admire, charismatic slaveholders persuaded many of their contemporaries, and then generations of historians looking back, that the elites who threatened American liberty in their era were the nonslaveholders! Today, this brand of politics looks eerily familiar. We have experience with political parties that attack "elites" in order to rally voters behind policies that benefit elites. This is what the slaveholders did in early American history, and they did it very well. Expansions of slavery became expansions of "liberty"; constitutional limitations on democratic self-government became defenses of "equal rights"; and the power of slaveholding elites became the power of the "common man." In the topsyturvy political world we have inherited from the age of slavery, the power of the majority to decide how to tax became the power of an alien "government" to oppress "the people."

Tax Aversion: The Sequel

Robin Einhorn

Since publishing "Tax Aversion: The Legacy of Slavery," by Robin Einhorn, in the March/
April 2008 Poverty and Race, *PRRAC has learned of an innovative new lawsuit that*
attacks the constitutional property tax provisions of the State of Alabama on the basis of
their discriminatory origins.

In *P&R*, Prof. Einhorn argues that the United States' anti-taxation tendencies
stem not from the radical artisans of the Boston Tea Party, but from the oligarchic
slaveholding elites of the South. The provisions of the Alabama Constitution pertaining to ad valorem ("according to value") taxes place limits on the amount of
taxation municipalities, counties and referenda can raise. By "persuading the nonslaveholding majorities that the weak government and constitutionally restrained
tax power were actually in the interests of the nonslaveholders themselves," Prof.
Einhorn wrote, " . . . .[m]ajorities voluntarily renounced the right to regulate their
society by majority rule. Giving up the essence of self-government, they celebrated
the outcome as democracy."

In *India Lynch et al. v. The State of Alabama*, CV-08-S-0450-NE, plaintiffs are
seeking a declaratory judgment from a federal court that the property tax restrictions
in the Alabama Constitution violate Title VI of the Civil Rights Act, 42 U.S.C. §
200d et seq., and the United States Constitution. This novel approach derives from
the U.S. District Court for Northern District of Alabama's reasoning in a recent Alabama higher education case, *Knight and Sims v. Alabama*, 458 F.Supp2d 1273 (N.D.
Ala. 2004). *Knight* was brought by long-time civil rights attorney James Blacksher
in 1981, claiming that Alabama's policies governing higher education tended to
perpetuate its formerly de jure segregated university system. Although the court in
Knight did not find a continuing connection between the discriminatory property
taxes and the current higher education system, the court observed: "the current ad
valorem [property] tax structure is a vestige of discrimination inasmuch as the [state]

82

constitutional provisions governing the taxation of property are traceable to, rooted in, and have their antecedents in an original segregative, discriminatory policy."

In nonlegal terms, *Knight* states that Alabama's response to Reconstruction, *Brown v. Board of Education* and other attempts to provide equal access to Blacks in education were met with hostility from the white establishment. To ensure that the Black population would continue to be undereducated and disenfranchised, Alabama placed constitutional limits on how much money could be raised by property taxes for education within the state. This ensured that black schools would be underfunded, even if many white students also suffered. Such tax provisions are still in place today. The plaintiffs wanted the tax structure to be held as having a segregative effect on Alabama's colleges and universities. Although, as noted above, they were denied because the court found no nexus between the higher education system and the tax structure, the current lawsuit seeks a declaratory judgment affirming the findings in *Knight* about the underlying property tax system, thereby helping to eliminate an excuse to keep taxes low and schools underperforming.

Scapegoating Blacks for the Economic Crisis

Gregory D. Squires

A simple, yet likely powerful, explanation has now been offered for the subprime mortgage-lending and foreclosure problems that have helped trigger the nation's gravest economic crisis since the Depression. The beauty and simplicity of this explanation makes one wonder why it took so long for us to see it. According to this view, it was the fault of black people! The federal government, another favorite whipping boy, also played a hand in this by trying to increase homeownership among minorities and other undeserving poor. The combination of big government and blacks simply could not be resisted any longer. As Fox News' Neil Cavuto concluded, "Loaning to minorities and risky borrowers is a disaster."

According to many conservative commentators, including Cavuto, Charles Krauthammer (*Washington Post*), Lou Dobbs (CNN) and editorial writers at the *Wall Street Journal*, it is the federal Community Reinvestment Act, basically a ban on redlining, that forced lenders to make bad loans to African Americans, other minorities and other unworthy recipients in poor neighborhoods around the nation, leading to the challenges that are now plaguing the nation's economy. The argument is gaining traction. And it is utterly false.

Under the Community Reinvestment Act (CRA), passed in 1977, Congress concluded that "regulated financial institutions have a continuing and affirmative obligation to help meet the credit needs of the local communities in which they are chartered." This included all communities in a lender's service area, and federal financial regulatory agencies were charged with the responsibility to "assess the institution's record of meeting the credit needs of its entire community, including low- and moderate-income neighborhoods, consistent with the safe and sound operation of such institution." The goal was to put an end to redlining and to increase access to credit for qualified borrowers in areas that had long been underserved. But, again, only consistent with safe and sound lending practices. And the law has worked.

Prior to the CRA, government policy, particularly federal policy, complemented private industry practices to deny credit in minority neighborhoods, undercut minority homeownership and perpetuate racial segregation. As is now well known, for at least the first 30 years of its existence, the Federal Housing Administration insured mortgage loans almost exclusively in white, suburban communities. Urban renewal and the concentration of public housing in central city neighborhoods reinforced traditional patterns of segregation. And the federally financed highway system enabled white suburbanites to commute to their downtown jobs without coming into contact with racial minorities and predominantly minority communities. Exclusionary zoning ordinances in virtually every suburb to this day keep housing prices artificially high, discouraging low-income families, disproportionately people of color, from moving into the more prosperous and predominantly white neighborhoods outside of central cities.

But government has hardly acted alone. Overt redlining, along with more subtle practices by mortgage lenders (e.g., refusing to finance, or providing loans only on more onerous terms, for older and lower-priced homes), steering by real estate agents, fraudulent appraisals and other practices reinforced racial segregation throughout U.S. metropolitan areas.

The CRA was enacted as part of an effort to undo the effects of such public policies and private practices. and it is succeeding. According to studies by the Treasury, the Federal Reserve, Harvard Joint Center for Housing Studies and others, the CRA has led to increasing homeownership in precisely those economically distressed markets where the law intended to do so; it has nurtured integration by increasing homeownership for racial minorities in predominantly white neighborhoods that have traditionally been closed to them; and CRA-related lending has been found to be profitable. If any lender made a loan to a black applicant (or anyone else) who was not qualified, that lender simply did not understand the law. If such lending institution was told it had to do so, it was by a compliance officer who did not understand the law.

Timing alone demonstrates the erroneous nature of the CRA critique. The law was strongest in the 1990s, before the statute was watered down and before the surge in subprime lending. Not coincidentally, the CRA was weakened by the Phil Gramm-led Financial Modernization Act of 1999 and subsequent regulatory "reforms." As a result, fewer mortgage lenders were covered by the law, and the rules that did apply to many institutions were less stringent. So the CRA was strongest when families were able to buy and stay in their homes at record levels. The law was weakened just as the subprime lending craze took off, with the foreclosure and related economic crises that immediately followed.

More importantly, it is essential to understand that CRA-covered lenders did not make the loans that went bad. When the law was passed in 1977, approximately three-quarters of all mortgage loans were made by depository institutions covered by the CRA. Today, approximately three-quarters of all loans are made by independent mortgage brokers and bankers that have never been covered by the law. And as the National Community Reinvestment Coalition reported, CRA lenders have originated less than one-quarter of subprime loans, with the overwhelming number of those loans—the loans that have led to the mortgage meltdown—being made by institutions that had no CRA responsibilities. In 2005, the Federal Reserve reported that just 5 percent of loans made by CRA institutions were high-cost loans, compared to 34 percent for non-CRA lenders.

With the federal government about to spend as much as $700 billion to "invest" in troubled financial institutions, CRA and related fair lending laws should be even more rigorously enforced. Here is an opportunity for the federal government to significantly advance the cause of fair lending, fair housing and equitable community development generally. As Janet L. Yellen, President and CEO of the San Francisco Federal Reserve Bank [and the newly appointed Chair of The Federal Reserve Board], stated last March:

> There has been a tendency to conflate the current problems in the subprime market with CRA-motivated lending, or with lending to low-income families in general. I believe it is very important to make a distinction between the two. Most of the loans made by depository institutions examined under the CRA have not been higher-priced loans, and studies have shown that the CRA has increased the volume of responsible lending to low- and moderate-income households. We should not view the current foreclosure trends as justification to abandon the goal of expanding access to credit among low-income households, since access to credit, and the subsequent ability to buy a home, remains one of the most important mechanisms we have to help low-income families build wealth over the long term.

Unfortunately, there is no magic bullet for what ails the nation's economy. Apparently this does not undermine the appeal of simple solutions, particularly when they buy into long-standing stereotypes. Among the many responsibilities now confronting policymakers, as the public is about to make its multibillion dollar investment, is to resist the racist, anti-government rants that have all too often fueled public policy and private practice throughout our nation's history.

Speculators, Not CRA, Behind Foreclosures in Black Neighborhoods

John I. Gilderbloom & Gregory D. Squires

Foreclosures continue to decimate communities around the nation, with black neighborhoods being the hardest hit. Some pundits and politicians point to federal policies that encouraged homeownership in low- and moderate-income communities, coupled with reckless behavior on the part of greedy homeowners, as the crux of the problem. One example is the statement by Fox News reporter Neil Cavuto that "loaning to minorities and risky borrowers is a disaster." To the contrary, our recent research demonstrates that it is outside investors living in other, predominantly white neighborhoods, not local homeowners, who account for the adverse impact on our nation's black communities.

Observers ranging from Credit Suisse to the Center for Responsible Lending estimate that about 6 million families have lost their homes to foreclosure and project that 12 to 15 million families altogether will lose their homes before the crisis is over. According to the U.S. Department of the Treasury, $17 trillion in household wealth was eliminated between 2007 and 2009 and more losses are sure to come. Such losses reduce property taxes, cut consumer buying power for local businesses, and weaken the ability of municipalities to provide vital services. In the end, all households, businesses and nonprofits suffer if they or their neighbors are foreclosed and lose their homes.

Recent foreclosure activity and the subsequent costs are not race-neutral. According to the Center for Responsible Lending, approximately 8 percent of African-American and Latino families have lost their homes to foreclosure, compared to 4.5 percent of white families. United for a Fair Economy has estimated that a third of black households and 40 percent of Latinos are at risk of falling out of the middle class and into poverty as a result of the foreclosure and related economic crises.

So what accounts for the concentration of subprime lending and foreclosures in minority neighborhoods? The culprit, at least in Louisville [where co-author

Gilderbloom teaches], is investors, primarily white investors who do not reside in the affected communities. In our research we found that in 2007 and 2008 there were approximately 2,000 foreclosure sales each year in Louisville. There were 39 per census tract (a rough approximation of a neighborhood) in black communities compared to 20 in white tracts. More telling is the fact that in black communities there were 15 foreclosures on properties owned by investors rather than owner-occupants, compared to 2 foreclosures in white areas. A close examination of foreclosed properties in black neighborhoods found most owners were white and often living miles away in suburbs.

It is investors seeking a quick profit, not homeowners, who are the real problem in black neighborhoods. We suspect Louisville's story is not unique. Louisville is right in the middle of this pack, ranking 103 out of 203 metropolitan regions in the rate of foreclosures in recent years.

Several factors account for why a property goes into foreclosure and why foreclosure rates are higher in some neighborhoods than others. Race is certainly not the only factor, and may not even be a consideration when other variables are taken into consideration.

We controlled on a range of variables that contribute to foreclosures—crime rates, housing values, household income, employment levels, vacancies, number of high-cost loans—and found that the rate of foreclosures for owner-occupants was no different in black and white Louisville neighborhoods. That is, race was not a factor in accounting for differences in the rate of owner-occupied foreclosures among Louisville neighborhoods.

But when we examined investor foreclosures, neighborhood racial composition was the primary predictor. Not only was race a significant factor in accounting for different levels of investor foreclosures among Louisville neighborhoods, race was the single most important factor, even more important than the rate of high-priced or subprime lending.

So black communities have been hardest hit, but not because of the federal policies pointed to by Cavuto and other conservative observers like Lou Dobbs, Charles Krauthammer and editorial writers from the *Wall Street Journal* and a range of other newspapers. Their prime target is the federal Community Reinvestment Act that prohibits redlining. Yet as researchers with the Federal Reserve, National Community Reinvestment Coalition, and several other government, nonprofit and academic institutions have demonstrated, this is simply nonsense.

The CRA does require federally regulated depository institutions (banks and thrifts) to affirmatively ascertain and be responsive to the credit needs of all neighborhoods in their service areas, including low- and moderate-income communities. But the law also explicitly states they must do so consistent with safe and sound lending practices. The Federal Reserve reported that only 6 percent of high-cost subprime loans made to low- and moderate-income borrowers were originated by lenders covered by the CRA. The overwhelming majority were made by mortgage bankers and brokers not covered by the law. And while all households in a community suffer when foreclosures mount, our research indicates it is investors, generally white investors, not owner-occupants, whose properties in black neighborhoods are lost to foreclosure, again to the detriment of all who live and work in those communities.

Foreclosures continue to devastate millions of families and the communities in which they live. But it is not reckless or greedy homeowners who are the problem. Likewise, federal policies that have increased responsible lending in low-income and minority communities are not the culprits either. It is investors who do not live in, understand or appreciate the black communities they are tearing apart, who are at the heart of the problem.

The Missing Class: The Near Poor

Victor Tan Chen & Katherine S. Newman

Wearing an ankle-length black skirt and a matching jacket with gold trim, her hair wrapped tightly in a bun beneath her black scarf, Danielle shuttles over to her desk at the New York City Human Resources Administration office. She trades pleasantries with her boss, helps a co-worker complete a claim form and joins another officemate in complaining about all the "crazy" people who work there. It's a typical day for Danielle—a typical day for any other administrative assistant in America—but just a few years ago, it was more than Danielle Wayne would have dreamed possible.

Back then, Danielle was sitting on the other side of her desk: an African-American single mother of three young children, unemployed and unskilled, a recipient of welfare checks for more years than she cared to remember. Her job experience was limited to stints packing food trays for airlines and cleaning bed pans in a mental hospital. The father of her children had physically and emotionally abused her during their tumultuous years together, and though he was now gone, she still suffered from clinical depression and a stifling lack of self-esteem.

But then President Clinton signed a bill to "end welfare as we know it," and Danielle was pushed—like hundreds of thousands of other women—into the workforce. Fortunately, the late 1990s were a time of booming stock markets, quiescent inflation and surging wages, when employers were so desperate for help that they were turning to neglected groups—the poorly educated and chronically unemployed among them—to staff their stores and agencies and offices. Danielle was fortunate enough to be drafted into the city's welfare bureaucracy as a clerical assistant. It was her first office job, and she immediately impressed the higher-ups with her dedication. Learning she could play the part of a professional—and play it convincingly—gave Danielle a much-needed boost of self-confidence. She actually enjoyed getting up every morning, dressing for work and joining the throngs of commuters on the subway—it made her proud to be part of working America, all those hurried masses yearning to make a buck.

Unfortunately, Danielle's gain was in some ways her children's loss. Before she started working, she was volunteering most days at her children's elementary school, where she clocked in countless hours as a hall monitor and PTA officer. Spending so much time at the school meant she got ample face time with her kids' teachers. "There ain't nobody here that don't know me," she boasted. But since she began her new job, Danielle has been too busy to volunteer. What's more, she can't afford private daycare, so she has to put her youngest child under the care of her mother-in-law, who lives in a housing project where drug addicts routinely walk in and out. It's no surprise that, growing up under these less-than-enriching conditions, Safiya is more reluctant to engage adults than most other two-year-olds. She has a vocabulary of only two words—"NO! SHUDDUP!"—shouted with the kind of vehemence that makes you wonder whom she might be imitating.

WHO ARE THE NEAR POOR?

Danielle Wayne is no longer poor, but she is not truly middle-class. She is part of a group that is often invisible in our national debates—ignored by social scientists and social policy, which focus on those living below the poverty line, but neglected by politicians, who, at the very least, heap adulation upon the middle class in their speeches and campaign platforms. In our new book, *The Missing Class: Portraits of the Near Poor in America*, we describe in detail the challenges faced by people like Danielle. These hard-working Americans struggle to support their families with little help from the government, even while their incomes fail to pay for adequate childcare, healthcare, housing and other foundations of a middle-class lifestyle.

As we define it, the "Missing Class"—also known as the "near poor"—live on incomes between one and two times the poverty line. A household of four that brings in $20,000- $40,000 a year falls into this category.

The near poor are a much larger group than the poor. More than 50 million Americans fall into this category, compared to 37 million who are poor. That means that nearly one out of three Americans is poor or near-poor.

As we know, America's poor households are disproportionately comprised of racial and ethnic minorities, and for the near poor, these ratios are fairly similar. The near poor are 54 percent non-Hispanic white, 15 percent non-Hispanic black, 4 percent Asian and 24 percent Hispanic, according to 2006 Census data. (Among poor households, the proportions are 46 percent white, 23 percent black, 4 percent Asian and 24 percent Hispanic.)

Race complicates the situation of near-poor households in predictable ways. For example, many Missing Class families live in urban areas or inner-ring suburbs segregated along racial, ethnic and socioeconomic lines, the product of the exodus of middle-class families and raging epidemics of crime and drug use. When the economy soared in the late 1990s, employment trickled back into these neighbor-hoods. Improved policing tactics helped clean the corners and offered hope for neighborhood change. Meanwhile, high real estate prices elsewhere in the city sent young white professionals in search of more affordable rents—eventually luring them into near-poor neighborhoods.

For the families who were already living there, the results are mixed. On the one hand, gentrification means a higher quality of life for all, thanks to reduced crime, better schools, and greater investment in transportation and other services. On the other hand, it raises the rents for near-poor families already struggling to make do, and likewise pushes out the low-margin pharmacies and stores and eateries that catered to their needs. Those old-timers who don't leave may wonder if their newly integrated, newly Yuppified neighborhood is still home.

Of course, upwardly mobile workers like Danielle who previously knew poverty may have more difficulty dealing with this sort of neighborhood upheaval than an-other segment of the Missing Class: once middle-class households that have fallen down the economic ladder. The latter group includes people like Rita Gervais, a single mother who supports herself, her mother and her young daughter on a $20,000 annual income, the profits of a daycare business housed in her northern Manhattan apartment. Rita found herself instantly in the Missing Class after her husband divorced her several years ago. Suddenly, she was toiling nonstop to stay a month ahead of the bill collectors, racking up huge credit card debts and drafting her mother to help keep her fledgling business alive.

SHIFTS IN THE ECONOMY

Unfortunately, the situation of the Gervais family is becoming all too familiar to many American households. The economy's shifting center of gravity—from the manufac-turing sector to the service sector—has meant a sharp reduction in union power (with its wage-lifting pressures) and a dearth of high-paying jobs (with benefits) for those without education. Meanwhile, the broad-based integration of markets that goes under the name of globalization—most noticeable in offshoring and outsourcing trends—has led to an intense international competition that keeps wages low.

The result is that a growing economy has not translated into significant wage in-creases for middle-class workers. (For racial and ethnic minorities, who suffer from higher rates of unemployment than their white counterparts, the situation is even more grim.) Median household income went up in the past year, but this was largely because people were working more, rather than being paid more. A recent report sponsored by the Pew Charitable Trusts, for instance, noted that men in their 30s now make 12 percent less than their fathers did at their age; the main reason family incomes are rising is because more women are going to work.

The trade-off of relying on more hours than higher wages, of course, is that middle-class incomes have become increasingly precarious. When a household loses a worker for whatever reason—in Rita's case, divorce—the result can be a quick descent into poverty or near poverty. As for the rest of the Missing Class, their financial situation may be stable or even improving. Like Danielle Wayne, many used to be poor and lived off welfare. Looking back, they are grateful for the progress they have made, which means not having to submit to invasive questions from caseworkers about their lifestyle, not having to plow through bewildering government paperwork and not being as concerned about when the next paycheck will come.

LOSS OF GOVERNMENT BENEFITS

At the same time, their more-than-minimum wages place them above the government thresholds for many important benefits. For example, Medicaid covers poor households; the State Children's Health Insurance Program (SCHIP) does cover near-poor children, but currently in the vast majority of states adults—childless or not—are left uninsured.

The lack of public insurance may account for the disproportionate number of poor and near-poor families who go without insurance: The ratio is 25 percent among people in households that make less than $25,000 a year, and 21 percent among those in households just one income bracket above. That means that 29 million of the 47 million Americans who are uninsured have household incomes of less than $50,000 a year, which includes the poor and near-poor.

In terms of income support, too, the near poor are neglected. The Earned Income Tax Credit, a government subsidy for low-wage workers, pays out its maximum benefit of $4,500 when a family with two or more children makes between roughly $11,000 and $15,000 a year ($17,000 for married couples filing jointly); the benefit lessens with more income and phases out completely at a household income of a little more than $36,000 ($38,000 for married couples). That means that many near-poor households get no or little help from this crucial income-support program.

This situation is even worse for workers without dependent kids. Take Tomas Linares. A divorced father of two adult children, Tomas works two jobs at centers for people with disabilities. He makes $20,000 a year by toiling seven days a week. Officially, he no longer has dependents (tell that to his daughters, though, who keep hounding him for cash), so he does not qualify for the Earned Income Tax Credit, which for childless workers phases out at an annual income of $12,000 ($14,000 for married couples).

LACK OF HEALTH COVERAGE

When they lack health coverage or high wages, just one crisis—a divorce, lay-off or illness—can send Missing Class families hurtling into poverty. Gloria Hall, a divorced mother of two young children, worked in law enforcement and enjoyed a decent salary with benefits. But then she was diagnosed with a rare cancer, which quickly spread from a gland behind her breastbone to her diaphragm, requiring the removal of part of her lungs.

Gloria believes that the cancer would have been detected earlier if her HMO had been willing to pay for a test her doctor had recommended. Then, when Gloria's situation became dire, the HMO refused to cover treatment at Memorial Sloan-Kettering Cancer Center, a world-class cancer treatment and research facility just a borough away from Gloria's Brooklyn home. In any case, once Gloria stopped working, she was able to apply for Medicaid, which did cover her treatment.

In Gloria's case, the problem was not being uninsured, but underinsured: She didn't have the kind of extensive, no-nonsense coverage that wealthier families, paying higher premiums, can obtain. In this, she is hardly alone. The Kaiser Family Foundation estimates that a fifth of insured Americans are underinsured, making do with sharply limited coverage or significant out-of-pocket medical expenses when faced with illness.

EDUCATION IMPACTS

If our government gives short shrift to the near poor in regards to health insurance and income support, it has intervened quite intensively—but not always for the better—in the domain of education. The No Child Left Behind Act demands that today's children pass a battery of standardized tests in order to progress, but with teachers and school administrators already overburdened in our public schools, the responsibility for meeting the new requirements has largely fallen on parents, who are expected to supply their kids with the extra help in reading and math that they need to prevail.

High-stakes testing in effect requires an auxiliary teaching force of parents, but in near-poor households, the parents are working too hard to be of any use, and can't afford to pay for professional tutoring. For the Guerras, another family profiled in our book, the fact that the two parents were always away working contributed to some very unfortunate outcomes for their sons. The middle son—once praised by his teacher as one of the two "most brilliant kids" in the class—started receiving reprimands for subpar performance in his third-grade subjects. The oldest son skipped classes regularly, failed his classes and eventually got arrested for sexual assault.

The children's decline occurred around the time that the mother, Tamar, started working at a New Jersey factory an hour away. Before, Tamar had been a regular presence at home, but she needed a job to pay off the family's growing pile of unpaid bills.

LACK OF FINANCIAL KNOWLEDGE

Another major problem facing the near poor is their lack of basic financial knowledge—how credit cards work, how to get a home mortgage, how to spot predatory lenders. Poor households are also vulnerable, but because they have less money they often won't contemplate getting a credit card or home mortgage to begin with. For example, six out of ten near-poor households own credit cards, about double the rate among the poor.

Missing Class families are cash cows for the credit card industry because they tend to use their credit cards less judiciously than their wealthier counterparts. Rather than paying off their balances every month, they are more likely to drag out their payments, subjecting themselves to exorbitant interest rates. Julia Coronado, one of the near-poor workers profiled in our book, has found herself caught in this limbo of revolving balances and crushing debt. At one point she had 17 credit cards and had accumulated $9,000 in unpaid charges. The minimum payments alone amounted to $300 a month.

Julia is the first to blame herself, and clearly she is responsible for the wanton spending sprees that in large part brought about her financial crisis. At the same time, it's also obvious that Julia was woefully ignorant of how credit cards worked. While the credit card companies tacked finance charge after finance charge onto her unpaid balance, Julia was actually putting away money every week into an informal savings arrangement run by members of the Dominican community—money that could have gone to paying off her high-interest debt. Especially for immigrants like Julia, who often do not have much exposure to banks and other financial institutions in their home countries, the ways of credit can be arcane.

On the other hand, native-born Americans show a worrisome lack of financial literacy, too. John and Sondra Floyd—a near-poor couple who are raising seven grandchildren—used to be the proud owners of their own home. But then an unscrupulous contractor convinced them that they needed to have repairs done. They signed paperwork they didn't understand, and when the contractor came back with a bill for $92,000—almost twice what the work was supposed to cost—the Floyds suddenly found themselves in a legal struggle over ownership of their one asset, their home. They eventually lost their fight, and since then they have sorely missed the financial stability provided by homeownership, which would have allowed them to borrow money and build savings for retirement.

WHAT CAN BE DONE?

What can be done to help the Missing Class? In our book, we offer some proposals. The first is expanding educational opportunities. It can take many years for adults in this class to complete their education, in part because our financial-aid system was never designed to support the kind of intermittent learning that fits their schedules and needs. We could do more to help these workers get the training and credentials they need. Supporting community colleges and expanding financial aid for low-income students are sensible first steps. For the nearly one out of six Americans over 25 without a high-school degree, we also need to promote so-called second-chance high schools that offer intensive tutoring and flexible scheduling.

For young children, we need to establish a comprehensive, public-supported network of daycare and kindergartens, so that working parents like Danielle Wayne don't have to worry about what happens to their kids during the workday. For the older children, we need to improve public schools through not only higher teacher pay and smaller class sizes, but also a greater degree of public-school choice, including charter schools that receive greater control over teacher hiring and curriculum in exchange for more accountability and oftentimes less funding. Though evaluations of the performance of charter schools vis-à-vis traditional public schools have so far been mixed, greater competition and choice will spur needed reforms across all schools while preserving the public character of the system.

Beyond education, we need a serious attempt to establish universal health coverage in this country, so that families are not at risk of falling into poverty or near poverty because of preventable or treatable illnesses. We also should do more to make work pay, by making it easier for workers to form unions and raising subsidies for low-wage work.

In the neighborhoods where near-poor families live, we need to establish public-private partnerships to entice stores with affordable prices to stay or locate there. In particular, near-poor workers would benefit from having more banks nearby; major banks have shunned these neighborhoods in recent years, meaning that these families have to resort to check-cashing outlets, loan sharks and other unsavory financial options.

Helping the near poor to save would also make a huge difference, given that they—unlike the truly poor—are in a position to sock away some money every month. We can provide them with incentives to do this—and thus make it less likely they'll have to turn to public support when times get tough—by expanding programs that provide matching government contributions to low-income families who save toward retirement, education and other long-term goals.

Finally, we need to do more to help near-poor families get—and keep—title to their own homes. The possibilities here include stiffer penalties and tougher enforcement of laws against predatory lending; housing vouchers that cover not just rent but also home purchases; and property-tax rebates for low-income families as well as homeowners who make improvements on their properties. We also need to support initiatives to assist first-time home buyers with mortgage financing.

Are these proposals feasible? They entail more spending, but the kind of spending that is a long-term investment in our country's future—an investment that will eventually pay huge dividends. For example, an Economic Policy Institute study finds that the benefits of universal early-childhood education would outweigh the costs by $31 billion by 2030 if we factor in the expected returns on lifetime earnings and decreased criminal behavior alone.

As we consider the prospects of the near poor, we might find it helpful to look back to another group in American history that also struggled, at times in obscurity: the generation who survived the Great Depression and fought in World War II.

Intelligent investments in the form of the GI Bill and related legislation sent these veterans to college and provided them with low-interest home loans.

From that foundation of equal opportunity, this country created a strong middle class. Today, facing as we are an uncertain economy that has eroded the gains won by past generations, we would be wise to make similar investments in the promise of the hardest-working Americans among us, our modern Missing Class.

Criminalization of Poverty: UN Report

In August of last year [2011], the U.N. Special Rapporteur on Extreme Poverty and Human Rights issued her report to the U.N. General Assembly on the criminalization of poverty. We were struck by how many of the U.N. report's findings are echoed in recent critiques of policy here in the U.S. Below, we present excerpts from the Special Rapporteur's report, along with excerpts of recent studies by the National Law Center on Homelessness & Poverty and Professor Kaaryn Gustafson's work on criminalization in the welfare system.

Selected Excerpts from the U.N. Report of the Special Rapporteur on Extreme Poverty and Human Rights.

Report prepared by Magdalena Sepúlveda Carmona, Special Rapporteur; transmitted 11 August 2011 by the Secretary General to the U.N. General Assembly.

The full report is available at http://www.ohchr.org/EN/Issues/Poverty/Pages/PenalizationOfPoverty.aspx.

* * * * *

SUMMARY

In the present report, the Special Rapporteur on Extreme Poverty and Human Rights analyses several laws, regulations and practices that punish, segregate, control and undermine the autonomy of persons living in poverty. Such measures have been adopted with increasing frequency over the past three decades, intensifying in recent years owing to the economic and financial crises, and now represent a serious threat to the enjoyment of human rights by persons living in poverty.

The ways in which States and social forces penalize those living in poverty are interconnected and multidimensional, and cannot be analysed in isolation. For the purpose of this report, the Special Rapporteur identifies the following four areas of concern: (a) laws, regulations and practices which unduly restrict the performance of life-sustaining behaviours in public spaces by persons living in poverty; (b) urban planning regulations and measures related to the gentrification and privatization of public spaces that disproportionately impact persons living in poverty; (c) requirements and conditions imposed on access to public services and social benefits which interfere with the autonomy, privacy and family life of persons living in poverty; and (d) excessive and arbitrary use of detention and incarceration that threatens the liberty and personal security of persons living in poverty.

* * * * *

10. In every country, developed or developing, historical social divisions and power structures ensure that the poorest and most excluded are at a constant disadvantage in their relations with State authorities. Asymmetries of power mean that persons living in poverty are unable to claim rights or protest their violation.

29. Increasingly, States are implementing laws, regulations and practices limiting the behaviour, actions and movements of people in public space, which greatly impede the lives and livelihoods of those living in poverty. These measures vary considerably across and within States, with the common denominator being the penalization of actions and behaviours which are considered "undesirable" or a "nuisance" in public spaces. States justify these measures by classifying the prohibited behaviours as dangerous, conflicting with the demands of public safety or order, disturbing the normal activities for which public spaces are intended, or contrary to the images and preconceptions that authorities want to associate with such places.

36. These laws are being implemented in a context in which the economic and financial crises have resulted in an unprecedented increase in foreclosures and evictions, forcing a growing number of families to live on the streets. Instead of using public funds to assist these families, States are instead carrying out costly operations to penalize them for their behaviour. Where there is insufficient public infrastructure and services to provide families with alternative places to perform such behaviours, persons living in poverty and homelessness are left with no viable place to sleep, sit, eat or drink. These measures can thus have serious adverse physical and psychological effects on persons living in poverty, undermining their right to an adequate standard of physical and mental health and even amounting to cruel, inhuman or degrading treatment.

49. It is becoming increasingly common for States to impose strict requirements and conditions on access to public services and social benefits. By imposing excessive

requirements and conditions on access to services and benefits, and severe sanctions for noncompliance. States punish, humiliate and undermine the autonomy of persons living in poverty, exacerbating the challenges they face in overcoming their situation. Moreover, beneficiaries are kept in a state of uncertainty about their future and are unable to plan for the long term.

57. To ensure that beneficiaries comply with conditions and requirements, States often subject them to intensive examinations and intrusive investigations. Social benefit administrators are empowered to interrogate beneficiaries about a wide range of personal issues and to search their homes for evidence of fraudulent activity. Beneficiaries are required to report regularly and disclose excessive amounts of information whenever it is demanded of them. In some countries, they must even submit to mandatory screening for drug use. They must also give their consent to authorities to scrutinize every aspect of their lives and to question their friends, colleagues and acquaintances. Beneficiaries are encouraged to watch each other and report abuses to programme administrators through anonymous channels. These intrusive measures undermine beneficiaries' personal independence, seriously interfere in their right to privacy and family life, make them vulnerable to abuse and harassment, and weaken community solidarity.

61. Being excluded from social benefit assistance has an especially harsh effect on women, who make up the majority of social benefit beneficiaries, and who generally hold primary responsibility for the care of children and maintenance of the household. If women are denied access to social benefits, it will generally have implications for the whole family. Furthermore, there is an increased likelihood that women will remain in or return to abusive relationships, or be forced to live in other vulnerable situations, if they are unable to access social benefits.

68. The economic and social costs of detention and incarceration can be devastating for persons living in poverty. Detention not only means a temporary loss of income, but also often leads to the loss of employment, particularly where individuals are employed in the informal sector. The imposition of a criminal record creates an additional obstacle to finding employment. Detention and incarceration, even for minor nonviolent offences, will often result in the temporary or permanent withdrawal of social benefits or the denial of access to social housing, for both the detainee and his or her family.

* * * * *

In many cases, the cost of employing reactive penalization measures greatly outweighs the costs that would be incurred in addressing the root causes of poverty and exclusion. If resources dedicated to policing, surveillance and detention were instead invested in addressing the causes of poverty and improving access to public services, including social housing, States could drastically improve the lives of persons living in poverty and ensure that the maximum available resources are dedicated to increasing the levels of enjoyment of economic, social and cultural rights.

75. Measures that result in the penalization of those living in poverty do nothing to tackle the root causes of poverty and social exclusion. They serve only to entrench further the multiple deprivations faced by those living in poverty and create barriers to poverty reduction and social inclusion. Consequently, they greatly undermine the ability of States to comply with their obligations to respect, protect and fulfill human rights.

Can We Think about Poverty without Thinking about Criminality?

Kaaryn Gustafson

Every September, the Census Bureau releases updated statistics on the poverty rate in the United States. For a day or two, I will read media reports about poverty, and then poverty disappears from the news until the next September. The poverty rate varies a bit from year to year but remains consistently—and shamefully—high.

According to a 2009 study drawing upon data from the Luxembourg Income Study, a project that gathers comparative economic information from various nations, the only upper-income countries with child poverty rates equal to or higher than United States (22 percent) were Russia (also 22 percent) and Mexico (27 percent). Some level of economic inequality within a population may be inevitable, but poverty—and the stress, hunger, homelessness, and daily chaos that go with it—is not. How much attention a country gives poverty, how a country tolerates poverty, and how a country allocates the resources targeted for the poor are political decisions. The United States has become poverty-tolerant and, increasingly, tax dollars are going to police the poor rather than to address poverty.

There have been moments in American history when poverty has been an issue of public and political concern, but those moments are distant memories. Since the War on Poverty in the 1960s, the public and politicians have become complacent about ameliorating poverty. Political concern about the poor has, indeed, remained, but it has taken a new form. Over the last few decades, federal and state governments have instituted a host of policies and practices that equate receipt of certain public benefits with criminality, that police the everyday lives of the poor, and that weave the criminal justice system into the fabric of the welfare system.

The first few chapters of my recently released book, *Cheating Welfare: Public Assistance and The Criminalization of Poverty*, trace the ways that tactics for crime control have crept into welfare administration in the United States. From fingerprinting and mug shots to suspicionless home searches, from welfare bans on adults with drug convictions to aggressive prosecutions of welfare recipients who underreport income, and from increased access of law enforcement officials to welfare records to a flurry of new legislative proposals to drug-test welfare recipients, we can see government policies that increasingly treat the poor as criminals.

The central chapters of my book, which draw upon interviews with welfare recipients in Northern California, examine the thoughts and experiences of adults who use public benefits. Their stories revealed that these parents needed the benefits they received but could not survive on welfare benefits alone. Many of them broke the rules—some of them knowingly, some of them unknowingly. They struggled to understand and follow the complicated welfare rules and requirements and also struggled to juggle family caretaking, job searches, employment obligations and unmet financial needs. What became clear during the study was that the federal welfare reforms instituted in 1996 were not serving to transition these parents from welfare to work. Moreover, some of the punitive aspects of the policies were making life for these parents and their children more difficult rather than providing a minimal level of security.

Surprisingly, most of the welfare recipients I interviewed, even while breaking the welfare rules themselves, embraced popular beliefs about "welfare queens" and the need to have punitive welfare rules to police the poor. Rather than translating their own difficult experiences with the welfare system into critiques of the system, they instead neutralized their own rule-breaking and lodged their support for get-tough policies aimed at the poor. In short, even the poor could not talk about poverty without shifting the discussion to issues of criminality and punishment.

One of the questions the book raises is whether it is possible to disentangle criminalization, which includes latent assumptions of criminality among the poor and efforts to police them, from the issue of poverty. To have meaningful public conversations about how to address poverty and its effects, rather than discussions about how to punish the poor, would mark a dramatic shift in discourse. It is my hope that readers will avoid the distractions of the rhetoric of criminalization and become part of a new public conversation about poverty.

The Criminalization of Homelessness

National Law Center on Homelessness & Poverty

The following is an excerpt from the National Law Center on Homelessness & Poverty's June 2011 report, "Simply Unacceptable: Homelessness & the Human Right to Housing in the United States 2011," available at http://nlchp.org/view_report.cfm?id=357. The excerpt, prepared by Eric Tars of the Center, had in its original submission nearly two dozen footnotes supporting the text; as P&R eschews footnotes, readers who want to obtain that can contact Tars at 202/638-2535, etars@nlchp.org, who will provide a copy of his original submission. Post-dating this report, the Law Center also organized a ground-breaking meeting with the U.N. Rapporteur and officials from the Departments of Housing & Urban Development, Justice, and State to discuss the Rapportuer's report and actions the U.S. can take domestically and abroad to implement its recommendations.

* * * * *

THE CRIMINALIZATION OF HOMELESSNESS

Despite our nation's treaty commitments and obligations to uphold the basic human dignity of every person, many states have enacted laws or ordinances that target homeless individuals by making it illegal to sleep or sit on the sidewalk, ask for money or "camp" outside. These ordinances are being enacted even though nationally, as well as in cities enacting them, there is a severe shortage of shelter space to meet even the emergency needs of the homeless population. Other ways that cities have criminalized homelessness include: sweeps of areas in which homeless people sleep, laws that restrict their freedom of movement, search and seizure of their personal property, selective enforcement of general provisions, and anti-panhandling laws.

In Orlando, Florida, for example, an anti-camping law prohibits camping on all public property without authorization. "Camping" is defined as "sleeping or otherwise being in a temporary shelter out-of-doors, sleeping out-of-doors, or cooking over an open flame or fire out-of-doors." Similarly, police in Fresno, California engaged in targeted sweeps of areas in which homeless individuals were known to congregate. In the sweeps, police destroyed homeless people's property, including medicine, identification documents, and clothing.

Many of the individual laws targeting homeless individuals have faced constitutional challenges. In *Pottinger v. City of Miami*, for instance, homeless individuals brought a class action suit against the City of Miami, Florida, claiming that police were harassing them for performing life-sustaining activities in public when no alternative shelter or location was available. They argued in part that such harassment was unconstitutional under the Eighth Amendment bar against cruel and unusual punishment and a violation of the Equal Protection Clause of the Fourteenth Amendment, and the City of Miami was ordered to provide redress. The decision of the district court survived on appeal.

Similarly, in *Jones v. City of Los Angeles*, the Ninth Circuit Court of Appeals struck down as unconstitutional a Los Angeles city ordinance, which prohibited sleeping, sitting or lying on the street at any time of day and was selectively enforced in the downtown area of Los Angeles known as "Skid Row." The Ninth Circuit held that the ordinance violated the Eighth Amendment's prohibition on cruel and unusual punishment for criminalizing conduct that is unavoidable.

Despite the decision in *Jones*, Los Angeles has continued its trend of criminalization of homelessness through the so-called "Safer Cities Initiative." This policy has sent hundreds more police officers to Skid Row, but rather than addressing violent crime, the officers have been targeting homeless and poor African Americans for minor violations such as jaywalking and littering. This program has drawn the attention of both the UN Special Rapporteur on Racism and the Special Rapporteur on Housing, prompting recommendations to cease the disparate enforcement and allow homeless persons to shelter themselves in public when there is inadequate shelter space.

During a mission in March, 2011, the UN Independent Expert on the Right to Water & Sanitation heard testimony from the Law Center and visited a homeless encampment in Sacramento, CA. The independent expert released her preliminary report on March 4. She noted the increase in criminalization of homelessness and detailed the story of Tim, a homeless man who facilitates the removal of hundreds of pounds of human wastes from the homeless encampment each week. The expert stated: "The fact that Tim is left to do this is unacceptable, an affront to human dignity and a violation of human rights that may amount to cruel, inhuman or degrading treatment. An immediate, interim solution is to ensure access to restrooms facilities in public places, including during the night." This is the strongest, clearest statement by a UN expert to date on the issue of criminalization, and given its condemnation in terms similar to our own Eighth Amendment's protection from cruel and unusual treatment, one that may lend itself to protecting homeless persons' rights in the courts.

In 2009, Congress passed the HEARTH Act, which required the Federal Interagency Council on Homelessness to produce a plan to end and prevent homelessness; that plan was published in June, 2010. The plan includes the following quote from Maria Foscarinis, executive director of NLCHP: "Criminally punishing people for living in public when they have no alternative violates human rights norms, wastes precious resources, and ultimately does not work." In a separate provision, the Act requires the Interagency Council to promote alternatives to the criminalization of homelessness. Although the council has to date held a national summit, bringing together cities, providers and advocates to discuss constructive alternatives to criminalization of homelessness, it has to date not taken concrete steps to prevent their enactment.

Several cities have had great success in combating homelessness by finding creative alternatives to criminalization. "A Key Not a Card program," enacted by the City of Portland, Oregon, enables outreach workers at various city-funded agencies to offer permanent housing immediately to people living on the street. The funding is flexible and can be used to pay rent, back rent and security deposits. From the program's inception in 2005 through Spring 2009, 936 individuals in 451 households have been housed, including 216 households placed directly from the street. At twelve months after placement, at least 74 percent of households remain housed.

Puyallup, Washington responded positively to a national trend of "tent cities" by passing an ordinance that provides permits to religious organizations for the specific purpose of hosting tent encampments for homeless individuals. The ordinance is part of a comprehensive plan drawn up by the Puyallup City Council describing various objectives for eliminating homelessness in Puyallup. The ordinance provides a critical first step because it offers religious organizations the ability to host one encampment for up to 40 people at any given time. However, there are numerous areas for improvement, such as granting this right to nonreligious organizations as well as religious ones and expanding the size and number of the camps, given that one encampment of 40 individuals is insufficient to meet the needs of the hundreds of homeless individuals in Puyallup. Moreover, as advocates and the comprehensive plan make clear, legalized tent cities are not a long-term solution to homelessness—that is something only adequate, affordable housing can provide.

Can We Organize for Economic Justice Beyond Capitalism?

LeeAnn Hall & Danny HoSang

In October 2008, former Federal Reserve chairman Alan Greenspan shocked many observers when he acknowledged that the economic crisis had forced him to rethink his long-standing faith in the tenets of free markets. With the global economy in a tailspin, one of the most prominent advocates of unregulated markets publicly questioned the governing ideology of 21st century capitalism.

Ironically, Greenspan broached two topics that community organizers in the U.S. often take pains to avoid: ideology and capitalism. A long tradition of "pragmatic" issue-based organizing has admonished organizers to be wary of all matters ideological. In *Rules for Radicals* (1971), Saul Alinsky explained that "no ideology should be more specific than that of America's founding fathers: "For the general welfare," Alinsky instead advised "real radicals" to focus on immediate, winnable issues that created concrete changes and built lasting organization; pragmatism was the only ideology that should concern organizers.

In an October 2012 essay in the *Boston Review*, Michael Gecan of the Industrial Areas Foundation reiterated this ethos in extolling an organizing approach that is "nonideological, focused, flexible, and short-term," and rooted in "an effective freedom at odds with ideology."

This approach—as practiced by the Industrial Areas Foundation and many other organizing formations—has produced countless improvements in cities and communities across the country, and engaged a broad group of people often excluded from traditional politics in the governance of their lives. Both of us were largely trained in this tradition and have spent many years attempting to build organizations around these principles.

At the same time, a growing segment of organizing groups are questioning whether pragmatism and competent organizing practice alone is capable of responding to the crises that are now a permanent feature of the contemporary economy: the collapse of the housing market, structural unemployment, massive incarceration, rising student and household debt, and deepening race and gender disparities.

The imperative to recreate and transform our economy comes from three fundamental dangers that we face today: the crisis of global inequity that thrives on racial hierarchies and bias; threats to democracy from increased militarization and corporate control; and the global environmental crisis. Ignoring the confluence of these crises is not an option; we need to lay claim to innovation, ingenuity and inventiveness to advance new solutions.

In the face of large-scale migration, permanent war and an unprecedented concentration of wealth, how must organizing practice respond and evolve? Is it possible to imagine, articulate and implement new visions of economic life beyond capitalism? How can pragmatic, issue-based organizations engage such ideologically driven challenges?

LEARNING FROM THE MOVEMENT

The Alliance for a Just Society (AJS, formerly the Northwest Federation of Community Organizations), a national network of state and local organizing groups focused on economic, social and racial justice, has begun a long-term initiative to grapple with these questions. Part of this effort includes an effort to engage and learn from other social justice organizers, thinkers and activists around such challenges.

To this end, in September 2012, AJS convened a two-day gathering in Los Angeles titled "Our Economy: Envisioning and Organizing for Economic Justice Beyond Capitalism." The meeting brought together organizers, trainers, academics and grassroots leaders to consider the alternative policies, practices, theories and worldviews that might create more ethical, equitable and sustainable economies.

Michael Leon Guerrero, who recently completed an eight-year tenure as national coordinator of the Grassroots Global Justice Alliance (GGJA), opened the meeting with a talk describing lessons organizers in the U.S. might learn from contemporary social movements in Latin America. In most Latin American countries, Guerrero explained, broad sectors of the population are regularly engaged in discussions about neoliberal policy and ideology. Similarly, discussions of "21st century socialism" adapted to the conditions, history and culture of individual nations often reside at the center of national political debates.

Guerrero discussed the range of forces and conditions that gave rise to this consciousness and political engagement: a long history of struggle against structural adjustment and other neoliberal policies; traditions of liberation theology; the influence of socialism and communism on the region's political culture; and the incorporation of anti-capitalist ideas and frameworks within electoral politics and the state. Guerrero concluded by explaining how organizations in the U.S., including GGJA and groups participating in the U.S. Social Forum, were working to frame economic justice campaigns in the U.S. in the larger context of neoliberalism and global justice.

Francis Calpotura, executive director of the Transnational Institute for Grassroots Research and Action (TIGRA), which focuses on winning fairness, equity and accountability in the global remittance (money transfer) industry, explained on a later panel that organizers should remain alert for the everyday ways that people can reconsider the legitimacy of capitalism and free markets. Rather than trying to imagine the wholesale transformation of global capitalism, Calpotura suggested that we can build from a variety of existing practices and habits—including co-ops, community credit systems, alternative remittance systems and even Craig's List—to legitimate and make visible forms of economic activity not solely based on profit maximization and wealth accumulation.

On a panel examining the ways critiques of capitalism could be incorporated into everyday organizing campaigns, Dylan Rodriguez, a professor of ethnic studies at UC Riverside, argued that organizers must acknowledge and confront the deeply conservative orientation of Alinskyism. *Rules for Radicals*, Rodriguez maintained, was deeply dismissive of the mass-based anti-colonial and economic justice movements vying for legitimacy at the time, and this anti-radical underpinning continues to prevent many community organizers from discussing the impact of capitalism and genocide that many people can identify in their daily lives.

Steve Williams, co-founder of People Organized to Win Employment Rights (POWER) in San Francisco, reflected on his visits to South Africa in the 1990s to raise the importance of political education and discussion as an everyday practice within social justice organizations. Grassroots leaders, members and organizers must afford themselves the resources and space to understand the complexity of the economic and political structures they face in order to develop effective long-term campaigns.

Tammy Bang Luu of the Labor Community Strategy Center and Bus Riders Union (BRU) in Los Angeles described the uncertain ground on which their work for transformative organizing around mass transit takes place. On some days, she explained, the BRU's work has the feeling of a mass-based social movement rooted in widely felt anti-racist principles and politics. At other times, they feel like modest efforts to simply win more buses. Luu argues that organizers must be comfortable with this contradiction, so that they can recognize and have the capacity to respond to opportunities for broader political transformation when they arise.

IDEAS INTO ACTION

These insights, and the comments raised during other panels and workshops at the meeting, affirmed for the leadership of the Alliance for a Just Society that we must develop a capacity to imagine a world beyond capitalism that can be advanced in our campaigns for economic, racial and social justice. Creating this shift will not be easy—it will require a cultural, power and policy shift—to move in waves across our country and the world, resulting in the re-imagining and transformation of our economy and society.

Such a transformation depends less on a change in rhetoric and more on an examination of the way all of us interact with profit-generating practices and institutions in our lives. For example, most organizing groups now have a well-developed critique of the role the banking industry has played in producing the current economic crisis, yet many families and communities are absolutely dependent on this same system to meet their daily needs. Retailers like Wal-Mart decimate wage standards and destabilize local economies, but also furnish a large portion of the (meager) jobs and access to goods on which many people depend.

This is the deep contradiction and challenge of our moment. In order to address the current crisis, we are often forced to rely on the very structures, institutions and ideas that wreaked havoc on so many families and communities in the first place. How can we reframe our existing campaign fights to advance alternative economic perspectives? What new forms of political education, leadership development and approaches to campaign strategy are necessary to support such a transformation?

We see at least three short-term imperatives. First, we must continue to ratchet up direct action campaigns that directly confront corporations and challenge and limit their growing power. For example, AJS affiliates joined a wave of actions against big banks in 2012 designed to further highlight their role in the foreclosure crisis and the economic collapse. The next phase of the campaign involves winning support for partnership banks, modeled after the North Dakota State Bank, that ensure public funds are invested and controlled for the public good. These campaigns have the potential to challenge the financial and political capital of big banks by redirecting state funds to more accountable institutions. The efforts have required both compromise and partnership—including with small businesses, community banks and the local agricultural sector—to help build support for the proposition that the interests of big banks often run counter to the economic development and job creation needs of local communities.

Second, we must build our power by investing in building strong active civic and political organizations and creating a truly participatory democracy. For AJS, this means continuing to challenge the claim that "corporations are persons" and that corporate interests are compatible with a robust and active citizenry. Campaigns that highlight the corrupting influence of corporate money in politics, highlight the connection between corporate formations like the American Legislative Exchange Council (ALEC) and voter suppression efforts, and invest in long-term voter education and mobilization are critical.

Finally, we must push out an alternative and broad-based worldview, sharing bold ideas and constructing a new foundation for an economy that functions in the public interest and does more than simply ameliorate the worst of market excesses. This cannot be an exercise in doctrinaire thinking, nor simply focus-group tested turns of phrase. Instead, we have to engage one another in a process of specifying the practices, values and outcomes within the dominant system that we reject, and in generating (and re-generating) the characteristics of the one we imagine.

AJS has developed a working document, "Building a Movement for a Constructive Commonwealth," (http://allianceforajustsociety.org/wp-content/uploads/2013/01/Building-a-Movement-for-a-Constructive-Commonwealth1.pdf) that seeks to highlight some attributes of this worldview—clear limitations on the political, economic and cultural authority of corporations; an exploration of the value of public ownership of resources; and a particular commitment to analyzing the role of race and racism in structuring and legitimating inequalities—as an initial step in this process.

In short, capitalism and ideology can no longer be taboo topics in the world of issue-based community organizing. They affect every aspect of our lives, and we do a disservice to our constituencies and our politics if we refuse to engage them, even if we don't always know the best way to do it.

Beyond Public/Private: Understanding Corporate Power

john a. powell & Stephen Menendian

Who inhabits the circle of human concern? Who counts as a person or a member of the community, and what rights accompany that status? In a democratic society, there is nothing more vital than membership. Those who inhabit the circle of human concern, who count as full members, may rightfully demand such concern and expect full regards. It is they who design and give meaning to that society's very structures and institutions; they have voice. This is the ideal of democracy. But there is an important question: Who inhabits this circle?

In our history, there have been varying answers to these questions. In *Dred Scott*, our nation's highest Court announced that persons of African descent were not and could never become members of the political community, and enjoyed "no rights which the white man was bound to respect." Yet the same Court carefully carved space in the circle for corporations, extending quasi-citizenship rights, and eventually full personhood. Consequently, corporations today enjoy never intended constitutional rights and protections. They exercise authority, power and influence that threaten not just democratic accountability, environmental safety and the rights of workers, but individual freedom, personal privacy, and civil and human rights.

OCCUPY WALL STREET

The Occupy Wall Street Movement is a grassroots challenge to this power. The Movement harkens back to the 1870s Populist and farmers' rebellion against unchecked financial speculation which regularly set off Wall Street panics that sent families ever deeper into debt. The Occupy Movement highlights the contemporary predatory practices of companies like Goldman Sachs, one of the engineers of the great 2008 financial meltdown. On the other hand, the anti-statist Tea Party

112

would insulate and secure corporate power, leaving individuals defenseless against unchecked corporate avarice. Its most basic tenets are market fundamentalism and governmental noninterference in the economy: Roll back regulations, reduce taxes and privatize government. These ideas are offered as the best, last defense of individual liberty in what is commonly perceived as an enduring contest between the public and private spheres.

Yet the debate over public versus private misses the point. In fact, it hides the real issue. The debate over public versus private, the size of government, the tax rate, the stimulus, the jobs bill, public worker benefits and so much more draws attention away from the behemoth in the boardroom: corporate power. By framing the issue as public versus private, government versus the individual, we blind ourselves to the ways in which corporations distort our democracy. The Occupy Wall Street Movement senses this, but cannot name it as such.

The public/private distinction papers over meaningful differences between real human beings and corporations. Entrepreneurs, small business owners, farmers, workers and enormous corporations are all swept up into the "private" sphere. In turn, the public sphere is seen as a threat to the private, and any growth in government as harmful to all "private" persons. From this perspective, regulations intended to curb the excesses of corporate behavior seem equally hostile to the small business owner or homeowner. For example, the Dodd-Frank Wall Street Reform and Consumer Protection Act, which was designed to protect consumers and homeowners from the kind of predatory lending practices that resulted in the meltdown of 2008, is attacked as an unnecessary regulation that strangles local banks, small businesses and start-ups.

How have we gotten to the point where any regulation that constrains major corporations is viewed as an attack on individual liberty, small farmers and business owners? We must know that neither corporations nor markets can exist without enabling and constraining regulations. There never has been or will be an unregulated market. The architects of this nation and its citizens understood that concentrated power in either government or the economy may threaten freedom. But those on the right miss this reality in current debates, in large part because the public/private dichotomy uncomfortably sorts everyone into one of these two categories. The result is a blind spot in which corporations dwell as merely "private" persons like everyone else. In essence, the public/private distinction has grounded the expansion and protection of corporate power.

A BRIEF HISTORY OF CORPORATE POWER

Corporations were never intended to be persons or citizens. In our republic's early years, corporations were public institutions, chartered to serve public purposes: build roads, facilitate commerce and educate the public. In exchange for the benefits of corporate form, including perpetual life, corporations were expected to serve the nation. Early Americans were as wary of concentrated economic power in corporate form as they were of concentrated political power in monarchal form. But 19th century lawyers and judges, often in the service of corporate entities, began to free corporations from state control.

Corporations were traditionally understood to be creatures of the state—artificial entities that could enter into contracts, sue and be sued, and enjoy perpetual life. By the 1840's, the Taney Court decided that corporations counted as citizens under the Constitution for the purpose of suing in federal court. Passage of the 14th Amendment, designed to protect the rights of freed slaves after the Civil War, became an even firmer basis for protecting corporate prerogative. The equal protection and due process protections therein were quickly extended to corporations. And, in *Santa Clara v. Southern RR* (1886), the Court asserted, without argument or explanation, that corporations were considered "persons" under the Constitution that enjoyed many of the rights it afforded.

Just as the Court extended standing rights to corporations, it denied those rights to blacks. This inverse connection between limited rights for blacks and other marginalized groups and the concomitant expansion of corporate power persists. Between 1890 and 1910, just 19 cases brought under the 14th Amendment dealt with the rights of descendants of slaves, whereas 288 dealt with the rights of corporations. Justice Hugo Black pointed out that by 1938, of the cases that applied the 14th Amendment since the *Santa Clara* decision, "less than one-half of 1 percent invoked in it protection of the Negro race, and more than 50 percent asked that its benefits be extended to corporations." This period is well-known as the Jim Crow era, and in legal circles as the infamous *Lochner* era, named for Supreme Court decisions that struck down state labor and minimum wage laws, and economic regulations. The Tea Party's anti-statism is reminiscent of this era, which severely curtailed the power of the federal government and states to regulate the economy.

This period came to a crashing halt with the New Deal and FDR's Court-packing plan to stop the Court from overturning it. The Court reversed course on both race and economic regulations in a series of cases epitomized by *Carolene Products*. In that case, the Court announced a rule that economic regulations were presumptively constitutional rather than presumptively unconstitutional, and that courts would defer to legislatures to fashion reasonable labor and wage laws in the public interest. At the same time, the Court announced that laws that reflect prejudice against "discrete and insular minorities" would be more carefully scrutinized by courts. As the law constrained corporate and economic prerogative, it conversely protected the rights of "minorities."

Even as this approach helped spur the Civil Rights Movement, a massive resistance emerged in the South, followed by a backlash in the North. The country and courts again moved away from protecting, first minorities, then all people, in favor of expanding corporate discretion. It was Justice Powell, a former lawyer in the firm that opposed *Brown*, who secured renewed corporate power that had been limited by civil rights and labor. He simultaneously rejected the claim that the 14th Amendment protected "discrete and insular minorities," and revived the spirit of corporations as deserving of protection as persons and citizens.

In the 1970s, Justice Powell authored a series of decisions arguing that commercial speech did not lose First Amendment protections because of the corporate actor. Even the conservative Justice Rehnquist foresaw the danger of protecting the free speech rights of entities that control vast amounts of economic power and enjoy the "blessings of potentially perpetual life and limited liability." In particular, the dissenting Justices warned of the potentially distorting influence of corporate campaign contributions—protected as speech—in a democracy. These fears have now been realized and the full logic of corporate personhood exposed. In *Citizens United v. FEC* in 2010, the Court held that corporations enjoy unbridled First Amendment rights to spend independent money on political campaigns.

We are currently living out Powell's dream, not Dr. King's. It is Justice Powell's vision which Chief Justice Roberts and his Court have embraced, along with the Tea Party. Speaking less in terms of the 14th Amendment and its purposes, they frame this dream in terms of "public" and "private," with some acknowledgment that we may need to cut back on civil rights, unions and environmental protection in order to secure these liberties for corporations.

BEYOND PUBLIC/PRIVATE

We do not mean to suggest, however, that the exercise of excessive corporate power is simply a byproduct of errant Court decisions rendered over the past 125 years. While removing corporate personhood and limiting corporate speech rights within our jurisprudence would be a step in the right direction, the manifold bases of corporate power are much broader. It is the public/private distinction that distorts our legal and political culture into thinking that corporations are just like everyone else. The case against corporations is not anti-capital. Rather, it is an indictment of the pernicious influence of corporate power to influence our political system, manipulate our democracy and even reverse legislative decisions.

We suggest that a more appropriate schema for understanding corporate power and observing the dangers posed by it is to think in terms of four domains rather than two: public, private, nonpublic/nonprivate, and corporate. The conflation of the corporate and private spheres confuses small business owners and ordinary citizens with powerful corporate actors. It also makes any legislative act that curbs corporate power appear to infringe the liberties of ordinary people. Critical legal scholars have long criticized the public/private dichotomy as a meaningless and misleading legal distinction. Historically, corporations were both quasi-public and quasi-private entities, but the conflation of corporations and their confirmed personhood with private space became a source of corporate power, and continues to generate unintended corporate constitutional protections, rights, powers and authority.

The idea of public or private spheres is also misleading for certain marginalized groups that enjoy, historically and today, neither the rights and freedoms of the public in public space, nor those of individuals in private space. The public/private distinction not only makes it more difficult to appreciate how corporations threaten individual freedom and privacy, but to understand the exclusion of marginalized groups from both public benefits and private rights. Historically, women and slaves inhabited the nonpublic/nonprivate sphere. Today, immigrants, the incarcerated and formerly incarcerated, and to some extent the disabled, also inhabit this space, which is sometimes abusive.

PRIVATIZATION AS CORPORATIZATION

The expansion of corporate power represents a threat, not only to the public, but to the private and nonpublic/nonprivate spheres as well. In *Kelo v. City of New London*, the Supreme Court upheld the condemnation of a stretch of riverfront homes when the sole purpose of the taking was to enable private redevelopment by pharmaceutical giant Pfizer, Inc. Although not a privatization case, this decision suggests the true function of privatization. The privatization of public entities or property is not simply a shift from public to private control; it is a shift from public to corporate. As a heuristic, the public/private dichotomy fails to capture these shifts in power or account for the consequences.

Not only may corporations collect and store personal information (Google's "street view project" being one example), individual privacy and speech rights are often sharply circumscribed in corporate space. Consider the context of a commercial shopping mall. We may think of that space as public space, but it is not. Not only are there limited privacy rights free from surveillance, but First Amendment rights are limited, and there is virtually no right to organize or petition.

Meanwhile, the Tea Party would shield and protect the discretion of corporate prerogatives from the government under the banner of free markets, while remaining silent regarding the exclusion and oppression of the "private sector." The unbridled exercise of corporate rights and prerogatives threatens our democratic process as well as "discrete and insular minorities." It is our view that the market, banks and corporations should exist to serve people, as they were originally intended to do, not the other way around. Neither Adam Smith nor the founders of the nation subscribed to a faith in the intrinsic beneficence of corporate interests for the nation. Quite the contrary, they feared the concentration of economic power just as they feared the concentration of political power.

Who inhabits the circle of human concern? Some might argue that the poor, unemployed, gays, immigrants or Muslims do not belong as full members of our democracy. On the other hand, many, such as those in the Tea Party movement or jurists like Chief Justice Taney, would argue that corporations do belong, and enjoy constitutional privileges and rights. Along with the Occupy Wall Street Movement, we reject this position. We could draw the circle of inclusion and belonging liberally, but it would not include corporations. The public/private dichotomy is a false one that obscures what is at stake and blinds us to the separate corporate sphere. Despite the position of the Court and well-known politicians, corporations are neither people nor citizens. They do not belong in either the traditional public or private space, but rather inhabit their own space. Our position is not anti-corporate. Rather, we call for a proper alignment of corporations in a liberal democracy. Corporations make good servants, but bad masters. To realize this realignment will require a transformative wave of individual, judicial and legislative actors. Our goal is not to eliminate corporations, but to build an inclusive democracy with a sustainable economy of shared responsibility and prosperity. This is the unfinished dream of America.

The Help

Ida E Jones, Daina Ramey Berry, Tiffany M. Gill, Kali Nicole Gross & Janice Sumler-Edmond

On behalf of the Association of Black Women Historians (ABWH), this statement provides historical context to address widespread stereotyping presented in both the film and novel version of *The Help*. The book has sold over three million copies, and heavy promotion of the movie will ensure its success at the box office. Despite efforts to market the book and the film as a progressive story of triumph over racial injustice, *The Help* distorts, ignores and trivializes the experiences of black domestic workers. We are specifically concerned about the representations of black life and the lack of attention given to sexual harassment and civil rights activism.

During the 1960s, the era covered in *The Help*, legal segregation and economic inequalities limited black women's employment opportunities. Up to 90 percent of working black women in the South labored as domestic servants in white homes. *The Help*'s representation of these women is a disappointing resurrection of Mammy—a mythical stereotype of black women who were compelled, either by slavery or seg-regation, to serve white families. Portrayed as asexual, loyal and contented caretak-ers of whites, the caricature of Mammy allowed mainstream America to ignore the systemic racism that bound black women to back-breaking, low-paying jobs where employers routinely exploited them. The popularity of this most recent iteration is troubling because it reveals a contemporary nostalgia for the days when a black woman could only hope to clean the White House rather than reside in it.

Both versions of *The Help* also misrepresent African-American speech and culture. Set in the South, the appropriate regional accent gives way to a child-like, overexag-gerated "black" dialect. In the film, for example, the primary character, Aibileen, re-assures a young white child that, "You is smat, you is kind, you is important." In the book, black women refer to the Lord as the "Law," an irreverent depiction of black vernacular. For centuries, black women and men have drawn strength from their community institutions. The black family in particular provided support and the

118

validation of personhood necessary to stand against adversity. We do not recognize the black community described in *The Help*, where most of the black male characters are depicted as drunkards, abusive or absent. Such distorted images are misleading and do not represent the historical realities of black masculinity and manhood.

Furthermore, African-American domestic workers often suffered sexual harassment as well as physical and verbal abuse in the homes of white employers. For example, a recently discovered letter written by civil rights activist Rosa Parks indicates that she, like many black domestic workers, lived under the threat and sometimes reality of sexual assault. The film, on the other hand, makes light of black women's fears and vulnerabilities, turning them into moments of comic relief.

Similarly, the film is woefully silent on the rich and vibrant history of black civil rights activists in Mississippi. Granted, the assassination of Medgar Evers, the first Mississippi-based field secretary of the NAACP, gets some attention. However, Evers' assassination sends Jackson's black community frantically scurrying into the streets in utter chaos and disorganized confusion—a far cry from the courage demonstrated by the black men and women who continued his fight. Portraying the most dangerous racists in 1960s Mississippi as a group of attractive, well-dressed society women, while ignoring the reign of terror perpetuated by the Ku Klux Klan and the White Citizens Council, limits racial injustice to individual acts of meanness.

We respect the stellar performances of the African-American actresses in this film. Indeed, this statement is in no way a criticism of their talent. It is, however, an attempt to provide context for this popular rendition of black life in the Jim Crow South. In the end, *The Help* is not a story about the millions of hard-working and dignified black women who labored in white homes to support their families and communities. Rather, it is the coming-of-age story of a white protagonist who uses myths about the lives of black women to make sense of her own. The Association of Black Women Historians finds it unacceptable for either this book or this film to strip black women's lives of historical accuracy for the sake of entertainment.

Reshaping the Social Contract: Demographic Distance and Our Fiscal Future

Manuel Pastor & Vanessa Carter

The 2010 Census brought some startling news: a 43 percent increase in the number of Latinos since 2000, a 43 percent increase in those of Asian and Pacific Islander heritage over the same period, an 11 percent increase in the African-American population, and a barely perceptible increase of 1 percent in the number of non-Hispanic whites. With that, two days of reckoning have come closer: the moment in which we become a "majority-minority" nation and the moment in which we align our tax and fiscal decisions with our real American tomorrow.

The two are related. While the future always seems a long way off, it is usually right here right now. While most have focused on the growth rates noted above, the really important news is the difference between the median age of various racial/ethnic groups: For non-Hispanic whites, the median age is 42; for Asian Pacific Islanders, it is 35; for African Americans, it is 32; and for Latinos, it is 27. That's a 15-year gap—and the relational gulf between those with whiter hairs (and lighter skin) and the younger and browner future workforce will eventually come back to hurt us all.

After all, the Census Bureau estimates that we will cross over the "majority-minority" line sometime around 2042; the year has been moving forward steadily in the estimates, despite a fall in immigration projections due to declining birth rates in sending countries and the effects of a faltering economy on the attraction to job-seekers. By 2050, 45 percent of us will be non-Hispanic white, 12 percent black, 31 percent Latino, 8 percent Asian, and 4 percent some other race. And it's clear from where the growth is emanating: In the past decade, a full 92 percent of population growth came from people of color.

For our youth, this demographic reality has more or less already arrived. Nearly half (46.5 percent) of those under 18 are children of color. Between 2000 and 2010, the number of non-Hispanic white children dropped by more than 4.3 million while the number of Latino children rose by nearly 5 million. Asian/Pacific Islander children also saw more modest gains (near 1 million), as did Others (including Native Americans and those classified as multiracial). Meanwhile, the number of black children actually dropped slightly (by about 250,000).

THE WIDENING GENERATIONAL GAP

All this action on the young side has widened the racial generation gap. In the 2010 Census, 80 percent of those who were 65 years and older were non-Hispanic white, compared to a 54 percent figure for those below the age of 18. That's a gap between seniors and youth of 26 percent, up from 12 percent in 1975. It was increasing just as public investment was retrenching, and this is one reason why that famous Tea Party sign, "Keep your government hands off my Medicare," is interpreted by some not just as a sign of silliness (after all, Medicare is a government program) but also as a signal that some want to lift the drawbridge as new generations are arriving.

While this might seem like an aggressive interpretation of a time trend, the impact of the racial generation gap holds in cross-section analysis as well. Those states with the largest generation gaps (the whitest old and the brownest young) also tend to have less state-level capital outlays per capita, as well as less education spending per student (with both figures adjusted for the state's per capita income to control for ability and thus focus on political will). While the causality is still to be determined, one possibility is that when the old do not see themselves in the young, underinvestment in physical and human capital results.

Consider Arizona, a state of (mostly white) snowbirds and (mostly Mexican) immigrants. Here, 82 percent of those 65 and over are non-Hispanic white, while 58 percent of youth are people of color. This racial demographic gap is the largest of any state, using 2009 American Community Survey data. The Grand Canyon state also came in 49th (of 51, including DC) in terms of public school expenditures per pupil, according to data from 2007–2008. Wracked by political conflicts over undocumented immigrants and ethnic studies, and distressed by foreclosures and a weakened economy, Arizona has become a poster child for a larger trend of racial disconnection resulting in more tension, less spending and diminished futures for everyone.

After all, the nation's economy relies on young workers becoming as productive as possible. However, in pooled 2008–2011 data, 37 percent of black children, 32 percent of Latino children and 14 percent of Asian children were below the poverty level—a conservative estimate of well-being in some places—compared to 12 percent for non-Hispanic white children. This could be turned around with proper investments in education, social services and health. Yet schools in poor neighborhoods are typically of the worst quality—lacking funding because of modest property values, operating under harmful zero tolerance policies, and, as a result, failing to graduate many. Six of every 10 black, Latino and Native-American high-school students graduate, compared with 8 of 10 non-Hispanic white students.

OUR FUTURE WORKFORCE

Partly as a result, while youth of color make up 40 percent of youth ages 16 to 24, they comprise 51 percent of disconnected youth—neither working nor in school. Lacking a successful work or educational experience by the age of 25 increases the risk of lifelong poverty and reduces the probability of making a positive contribution to the nation's wealth. Nationally, of those who are working age (25 to 64 years old), 34 percent of non-Hispanic whites, 19 percent of blacks, 18 percent of U.S.-born Latinos and 10 percent of immigrant Latinos have Bachelor's degrees—and this is happening just as the need for an educated workforce is on the rise. By 2020, the share of adults with some advanced education is projected to decline in all but six states, while the population of dropouts will swell well beyond the pool of jobs for people without a high-school education; the Educational Testing Service calls this a "perfect storm of demographic, labor market, and educational trends that threatens the American dream."

We don't expect these data to be shocking, or even particularly new to this audience. What we think is new is the argument: What has been a racial divide is now a generational divide, and this divide is weakening us all. Current retirees and the baby boomers quickly on their heels will rely on the strength of the nation's economy— read, current and future generations of workers. They will need nurses and doctors to care for their bodies—sure to ail with age. They will need workers in good jobs to pay into the Social Security coffers. And as Dowell Myers has insisted in *Immigrants and Boomers: Forging a New Social Contract for the Future of America* (Russell Sage Foundation, 2007), they will need families with some amount of wealth to buy their excessively large homes, now empty of children.

A NEW SOCIAL CONTRACT

But crossing the divide is not just a matter of issuing a bland call for a unified America. William Julius Wilson, once a proponent of universalist, race-neutral strategies, suggested in his most recent book and related writing that to really get to solutions, we will need to engage in conversations that expose the gravity of race in America. It may be our mutual self-interest that will keep us at the table when these conversations approach a breaking point, but a new and deeper social consensus will have to deal with the taboo reality of race, since it is the undercurrent of our disconnection.

Dealing honestly with race may help us secure new revenues and new expenditures. But it will also help us get the policies right. john a. powell and his colleagues, for example, have called for "targeted universalism," an approach that would stresses common goals but nuanced strategies (*P&R*, March/April 2009). Workforce development, for example, should address both joblessness (important to the African-American community) as well as paying livable wages (important to immigrant Latinos who are often working but at the bottom of the labor market).

Such an approach would also emphasize the importance of cradle-to-career pathways to reverse the school-to-prison pipeline, as well as the centrality of the DREAM Act as both a signal and a reality to immigrant youth. Because race, place and poverty (i.e., underinvestment) are so highly correlated, coordinated place-based efforts like the Neighborhood Revitalization Initiative, the Sustainable Communities Initiative, and Promise Neighborhoods are part of any race-sensitive policy package, as well.

But stepping back from the specifics to the bigger picture, a simple point is clear: With the benefits for an older generation, such as Social Security and Medicare, seemingly shielded by strong lobbies and the Boomer generation resisting any increase in taxes while in their prime earning years, it feels like the ladder of opportunity is being pulled up just as a new generation, disproportionately of color, is entering the labor market and coming to social and political influence. This might seem viable in the short run, but it cannot last.

Those who have pulled up the ladder may find themselves temporarily protected on the house roof as the floodwaters rise—but we've seen this picture before and we know how it turns out. Eventually, the foundation erodes and the house comes tumbling down. It's time to invest in the next generation, building new bridges across race, place and age that can help meet our demographic, economic and fiscal future with confidence and cohesion.

Social Justice Movements in a Liminal Age

Deepak Bhargava

Liminal—1. relating to a transitional or initial stage of a process; 2. occupying a position at, or on both sides of, a boundary or threshold

INTRODUCTION

The brief, ecstatic Obama-centered period of 2008–2010 seems to resist all of the stories that have since been spun about it, from triumphant narratives of transformation, to angry jeremiads of betrayal of the progressive cause, to the apocalyptic stories of national ruin that animate the Right. In sober hindsight, it looks more like an opening chapter than a climax: a period in which a few major, hard-fought breakthroughs that will tangibly improve people's lives were won; many opportunities were squandered, and many crises were left unaddressed; no grand ideological re-alignment occurred; and the social justice movement overall did honorable work, but struggled to make the most of an extraordinary moment.

I remember vividly now a moment in the heady days after the 2008 election, when some heralded the triumphant return of a Rainbow Coalition that might produce a lasting progressive governing majority. A close aide and friend to the president said to me that in his view nothing fundamental about American politics and society had changed, other than that there would be a new occupant at 1600 Pennsylvania Avenue, and that it would be a mistake to over-read the election results, as many were doing. The balance of power among contending social forces in America was not essentially altered. Most Americans who voted for and against Obama, contrary to what ideologues of both left and right like to believe, subscribe to no coherent doctrine of any kind and are capable of holding utterly contradictory opinions without discomfort. There had been no tectonic shift in ideological underpinnings. And whatever one chooses to believe about the underlying commitments of the president, it is indisputable that he was elected by himself, not with legions of members of Congress sworn to his or any agenda. In other words, we have gotten pretty much what might be expected, given the prevailing social conditions, political institutions and ideological contours of the country.

The achievements of this period—the largest expansion of anti-poverty programs and the largest expansion of the New Deal state in 40 years—were far from trivial in policy terms. They were achieved largely through disciplined, hard-fought ground campaigns which have not received the appreciation or recognition they deserve, perhaps understandably so, given the period of backlash that followed. It is notable that what was achieved in policy terms was in no way accompanied by a story that has stuck—and if there is a great failure of both the Obama Administration and the Left in this period, it has been (until Occupy!) a failure of story-telling.

That this period was brought to an abrupt end by the Tea Party, virulent right-wing populism and its electoral expression in 2010 also raises the questions about whether the country is now in for a lasting period of backlash and whether the hopes raised in 2008 were altogether unjustified.

It may be that the arc of the story is hard to decipher because we are still in the opening chapters. We are, I would argue, in a liminal period—a confusing, contradictory and highly unstable period of transition in which many futures are now possible—and aspects of those very different futures are manifest in our present. The confluence of the economic crisis, demographic change, and the radicalization of the Right have created a highly volatile situation, and we are probably not done lurching back and forth between the futures presaged by the elections of 2008 and 2010. Neither the hope for an inclusive, just world nor the prospect of a brutally unequal and racialized one are fantastical—they are both here, right now.

Perhaps what is most striking about the present moment is the extent to which, after such wild swings in the public debate, nothing definitive about our country's trajectory is yet decided. Not even the highly consequential election of 2012 alone is likely to decide the question. What we do now and in the coming years matters a great deal.

If it is true that we are in a historically significant period of transition, it may be helpful to take a step back from the maelstrom of events and ask some grounding questions. What are the forces and factors at play in this current period that will shape the trajectory of our future? What are the key strategic tasks that those concerned with social justice must tackle in order to win the day, particularly those areas in which we need more than incremental progress, where we need major breakthroughs?

This chapter is not a roadmap to the future, but more an inventory of some of the key questions that face us in hopes that it may facilitate the focusing of our discussions.

Though the questions are closely interrelated, for purposes of this chapter I will lift up four areas of particular strategic concern where we have urgent needs:

- A cogent progressive approach to the economy, particularly with respect to the questions of mass unemployment and the future of work, that is grounded in a coherent theory not only of re-distribution but also of wealth creation.
- A practical approach to addressing structural racism that can work at the levels of hearts and minds, policy and constituency-building all at once. The highly racialized discourse of the national political environment has raised the stakes on getting this right.
- A deep reckoning with the cultural and moral force of radical individualism, which stands at this stage as an enormous obstacle to advancing a social justice agenda in the U.S.
- A clear-eyed understanding of the nature of our conservative opposition, in order that we might more strategically and effectively resist, and more effectively speak to the center.

I'll conclude with a brief inventory of some of the assets and liabilities that our movement carries into this critical period.

THE ECONOMY

The depth of the crisis we face is evident to all in the catastrophe of unemployment, increasing poverty and foreclosures that has gripped the United States. What has perhaps been less well understood is how deep the roots of that crisis are. While the crisis was precipitated by the financial collapse, the source of our problems is deeper than the invention of toxic financial instruments. We will therefore need a transformational program for the "real" economy as the foundation for a social justice agenda in this decade.

Joseph Stiglitz and others have argued that, much as the Great Depression had its roots in the transition from agriculture to manufacturing and the difficulty of absorbing a massive new labor force, so too today's crisis has its roots in the transition from an industrial economy to a service economy and the resulting displacement of vast numbers of workers. This has been compounded in a vicious circle, as Robert Reich and others have pointed out, by levels of inequality that actually retard growth and by an aggressive and concerted attack by corporations and the Right on the social consensus that had kept inequality within bounds in the post-war period. The debate about the role of globalization in the current economic crisis is unsettled, but what does seem clear is that multinational companies can make record profits while radically shrinking employment levels in the U.S. That development makes working people extremely vulnerable.

I never thought I would quote Larry Summers approvingly, but his take in the Jan. 8, 2012 *Financial Times* captures the dilemma well:

"The spread of stagnation and abnormal unemployment from Japan to the rest of the industrialized world does raise doubts about capitalism's efficacy as a promoter of employment and rising living standards for a broad middle class. The problem is genuine. Serious questions about the fairness of capitalism are being raised. These are driven by sharp increases in unemployment beyond the business cycle—one in six American men is likely to be out of work even after the economy recovers—combined with dramatic rises in the share of income going to the top 1 percent (and even the top .01 percent) of the population and declining social mobility. The problem is real and profound and seems very unlikely to correct itself untended."

If this line of thinking is correct, the problem is not just how to get back at the banks, but how to transform an economy that at the level of production will no longer generate reliable or steady employment for millions of people. Barring massive intervention by the government to increase demand in labor markets, we will be living with a massive rate of unemployment for a decade at least. This will not only create misery for millions of unemployed people but also depress wages and working conditions for people with jobs throughout the West, make austerity the ruling paradigm, create fertile ground for nativism and viable far-right political parties (as we are seeing in Europe), and stifle efforts at worker organization. This is why chronic joblessness is the central political problem for the Left in the West today.

Unfortunately, the Left has, with many notable exceptions, been better at answering questions of redistribution than in posing coherent alternatives with respect to wealth creation and job creation. A coherent and vicious program of austerity will not be defeated without a credible alternative. In the short run, it is critical that we be prepared with a cogent program for the post-election period in which the Bush tax cuts are slated to expire and "sequestration" of domestic and defense spending will begin. This is an enormous opportunity to demand a set of affirmative, creative interventions to address persistent joblessness through government action, coupled with a traditional redistributionist approach anchored in tax policy, and to begin to lay the foundations for a progressive story about the economy. One can imagine, for example, a strategy to tie the expiration of the Bush tax cuts to a massive, sectorally focused jobs program (targeted to communities most in need) in areas such as care work, infrastructure, education and the green economy. There is no reason in principle that we could not create 10 or 15 million new jobs, using the revenue of the expiring Bush tax cuts to do so—and such a demand should and can be made by a broad alliance.

Over the long term, we urgently need more robust discussions among and between the various camps and thinkers on the Left about what the shape of a new economy should or could be. Is our highest aspiration a version of Scandinavian social democracy with strong safety nets? A German- or Chinese-inspired statist approach with strong intervention in labor markets and sectors of the economy? What role for local economies, cooperatives and sustainability concerns, which many argue should be central to a new economic vision? Until we have a clearer picture of the economic system we seek to build, it will be extremely difficult to organize the kind of movement needed to shake us loose from the grip of market fundamentalism.

STRUCTURAL RACISM

One of the great accomplishments of the past decades has been the articulation by many thinkers and the embrace by significant parts (though not yet a majority) of the progressive movement of an analytic framework called "structural racism." One of the great failures of this same period has been the inability to put the analysis into action in a large-scale way at the level of consciousness, campaigns or policy.

The stakes on this are getting higher. Heightened and overt racist appeals in the national political discourse, evident in the Republican Presidential primary but not only there, are obviously fed by animus to an African-American president and by deep unease about the demographic change that is gripping the country. Manuel Pastor and Vanessa Carter are right that the conflict between an aging, fearful, shrinking white population and a growing, more hopeful younger brown and black population is the axis on which our politics now turns. (See their "Reshaping the Social Contract" in this volume.) It lies at the heart of nasty anti-immigrant attacks, but also attacks on voting rights, financing for public education and the role of government itself. We can easily imagine a future in which full citizenship is effectively denied to large numbers of people of color (because of mass incarceration, immigration policies that foster a large undocumented population, and the restriction of the franchise by means of 21st century poll taxes)—and an angry, older white minority holds on to power for a generation at the expense of the common good. The failure to offer a bold, affirmative and specific program on race around which constituencies can be mobilized and public debate conducted leaves the field clear for a dangerous, racist paradigm to take root.

Changing demography is, of course, the single greatest potential asset for progressives in the 21st century, if we can build a real coalition among African Americans, Latinos and Asian Americans. Doing so will require the articulation of a clear proactive racial justice agenda and aggressive coalition-building strategies. There are promising seeds of this all over the country—and I'm particularly moved by the way in which the debate over the country's worst anti-immigrant law in Alabama has sparked a multiracial coalition with great promise.

I do not know the answers to the questions I am posing, but here offer some thoughts to get the discussion started. In the realm of policy, I think the related crises of mass incarceration and mass unemployment, both of which are devastating in their impact, may offer the two strongest entry points to building a stronger racial justice movement in the country. In terms of consciousness, we need to develop a popular language around racial justice with great moral force that can be applied across a range of issues and problems. One of the main negative effects of the culture of individualism discussed below is that racism is seen nearly exclusively by the public in terms of questions of intent and individual behavior—structures and interlocking systems are invisible to most, and we therefore need a moral language that can break through this pervasive way of understanding race. And in terms of movement-building, strengthening movement infrastructure in African-American communities, and deliberate building of relationships—particularly between African Americans and Latinos—are the critical and obvious, but not necessarily easy, tasks in front of us.

A CULTURE OF INDIVIDUALISM

A thoughtful recent analysis by Ron Brownstein of polling since the economic crisis began by the *National Journal* found the following:

"One theme consistently winding through the polls is the emergence of what could be called a 'reluctant self-reliance,' as Americans look increasingly to reconstruct economic security from their own efforts, in part because they don't trust outside institutions to provide it for them. The surveys suggest that the battered economy has crystallized a gestating crisis of confidence in virtually all of the nation's public and private leadership class—from elected officials to the captains of business and labor. Taken together, the results render a stark judgment: At a time when they believe they are navigating much more turbulent economic waters than earlier generations, most Americans feel they are paddling alone. Shawn Kurt, an unemployed lumber-mill worker in Molalla, Ore., who responded to one survey, spoke for many when he plaintively declared, 'I myself don't see no one trying to help me.' The Heartland Monitor surveys document pervasive dissatisfaction with the nation's direction; deep apprehension about the opportunity for future generations (particularly among whites); a collapse of faith in the public and private leadership class; intense political polarization that largely tracks racial lines; and the absence of a reliable majority for either side's vision of government's role in society, all leavened only by individual Americans' reluctant self-reliance and their tenacious faith in their own ability to manage the mounting financial risks they see confronting them. Those attitudes cumulatively resemble the sentiments a poll might find in a Third World country before a coup."

Notably, when people are asked whether their financial well-being depends mostly on their own actions or on factors out of their control, even in the face of striking evidence to the contrary, nearly 60 percent cite their own actions, compared to less than 40 percent who cite factors beyond their control. Interestingly, people of color are more likely to say that their financial well-being rests on their own efforts than are whites.

This radical individualism shows up everywhere in the culture—from the cult of Ron Paul to the near hegemonic penetration of a therapeutic language of self-realization and self-expression in our everyday conversation. And it is coupled with a deep distrust of all institutions—banks and corporations to be sure, but government and labor unions just as much so.

The consequences of this phenomenon for progressive politics are enormous. Efforts to target corporations and banks are important and mine a deep vein of public sympathy, but unless the fundamental conviction of the efficacy of collective enterprise is restored, it will reinforce solipsism and skepticism rather than leverage major structural change. There has been no progressive project in human history that has not relied on the centrality of community—a shared sense of what we owe to each other. The vernaculars of the moral language that nourished that core conviction are in deep decline.

I am very unclear how to tackle this problem, because its roots are so deep and profound. We at the Center for Community Change have tried to lift up "community values" in a variety of campaigns, and I'm encouraged that transformational campaigns like Caring Across Generations are leading explicitly with interdependence as a core value. (CAG is led by Domestic Workers United and Jobs With Justice—www.caringacrossgenerations.org) Still more is needed to nourish the taproots of solidarity and community in the culture. Ilyse Hogue has intriguing ideas about renewing the connection between service, mutual aid and progressive politics (see her article, "Why the Right Attacked Unions, ACORN and Planned Parenthood" in the March 21, 2100 edition of *The Nation*)—and it may be that some robust experiments in a variety of fields are needed to develop a path forward. There is not likely to be a shortcut to developing structures, institutions, habits and practices that embody values of interdependence and community in an experiential way. Caring circles for mutual aid, cooperatives, the revival and reconstruction of community fabric in particular neighborhoods or places, and even spiritual practices and rituals may be part of the path forward.

UNDERSTANDING THE RIGHT, SPEAKING TO THE CENTER

It has become commonplace now on the left to trace a lineage for modern-day conservatism—back to Goldwater, Buckley, Oakeshott, Hayek and all the way back to Burke. But it is the discontinuities between today's Right and the conservatism of previous eras that are striking. Mark Lilla put this well in an insightful article "Republicans for Revolution," in the Jan. 12, 2012 *NY Review of Books*:

"What we have not seen much of, except on the fringes of American politics, are redemptive reactionaries who think the only way forward is to destroy what history has given us and wait for a new order to emerge out of the chaos. At least until now. The real news on the American right is the mainstreaming of political apocalypticism. This has been brewing among intellectuals since the Nineties, but in the past four years, thanks to the right-wing media establishment and economic collapse, it has reached a wider public and transformed the Republican Party. . . All this is new—and it has little to do with the principles of conservatism . . . No, there is something darker and dystopic at work here. People who know what kind of new world they want to create through revolution are trouble enough; those who only know what they want to destroy are a curse."

There is an increasingly dominant part of the conservative movement in America that is playing for keeps—to roll back the 20th century and blow up the current social order and most of what we take for granted in it—from the existence of safety nets to voting rights. The combination of this apocalyptic temperament with vast sums of corporate money hell-bent on using power to acquire more power (and destroy the power centers of the Left, particularly labor, but also Planned Parenthood and others) is a very dangerous stew.

Its implications for us are three-fold. First, that for a weak and besieged Left a "united front" approach that attempts to engage with centrist groups and constituencies to marginalize the Right is imperative. This is not a period where the vanity of small differences or sectarianism will serve us well. Second, that we must not delude ourselves, as I fear some have done in the wake of the disappointments (real or perceived) of the Obama administration, that electoral politics do not matter. In liminal moments where multiple futures are possible, who controls the state matters a great deal—as Scott Walker has convincingly demonstrated in Wisconsin. Third, we must resist the siren song of magical thinking, particularly the trope that the vast majority of Americans already agree with us and that we are one militant action away from our own Arab Spring. Recruitment and engagement of the millions of people who do not already agree with us about everything is at least as important a task as mobilizing the already converted for action.

Learning to speak effectively to the center of American politics from our core values about this central troika of issues—the economy, race, and community—may be the fundamental challenge for the Left in the 21st century. This is not mainly a matter of "messaging" or polling and focus groups – it will require reconstructing and refreshing our core ideas, at the roots, which will put us in a much better position to speak to the vast majority of Americans.

CONCLUSION: CAN OUR MOVEMENTS MEET THE MOMENT?

We bring many assets to the fights ahead of us. New and inspiring leadership in many key institutions. A real resistance movement in many states against the excesses of the Right that have in many cases turned the tide. Bold attempts to do fresh thinking on the issues laid out above, some of which are finding their way into innovative practice. New approaches to organizing that move the locus of recruitment, strategy and action away from paid organizers to unpaid activists moved by big ideas. An Occupy Movement that, whatever it does next, has opened up political space. Some parts our movement are growing, especially the LGBT and immigrant rights movements, and they are having a real impact on public consciousness and culture even through the ups and downs of particular policy battles. And while demography is not destiny, the growth of constituencies of color is an enormous advantage for us in the 21st century.

And we also face some daunting challenges: the extraordinary dominance of money in politics and corporate power; chronic underinvestment in African-American organizing capacity; a lack of organizing to scale in nearly any constituency, with limited exceptions; continued and exacerbated instability in the sources of financing for social justice work; the continued existential threat to the labor movement in the U.S., without which a progressive movement is difficult to conceive; a culture of individualism that is deeply hostile to the notions of community upon which our politics fundamentally depend; and major ideological lacunae, particularly in the field of economics.

Yet I see encouraging signs that our movements can meet the moment. In 2011, we were called to defend some of the great gains of the 20th century, from voting rights to collective bargaining, the New Deal and Great Society social insurance programs that are our heritage. Progressives showed up to fight—from Wisconsin to Wall Street, and in many other less well- noticed and some unlikely battlegrounds—in Ohio, Maine, North Carolina, Arizona, Montana and Alabama. The question that now faces us is whether, having weathered the onslaught, we can go from opposing to proposing—whether we can build an independent mass movement that is durable, resilient and grounded in big, transformative ideas about economics, race and community and is willing to engage with the vast majority of Americans who are not yet progressives.

The future is very much within our grasp.

II

DECONSTRUCTING POVERTY AND RACIAL INEQUALITY

The Spirit Level: Why Greater Equality Makes Societies Stronger

Richard Wilkinson & Kate Pickett

The belief that inequality is divisive and socially corrosive goes back several hundred years. But now we have comparable measures of the scale of income inequality in different societies and we can actually see what effect it has. The new evidence shows that inequality is much the most important explanation of why, despite their extraordinary material success, some of the most affluent societies seem to be social failures.

WHAT GREATER EQUALITY BRINGS

In societies where income differences between rich and poor are smaller, the statistics show that community life is stronger and more people feel they can trust others. There is also less violence—including lower homicide rates; health tends to be better and life expectancy is higher. In fact, most of the problems related to relative deprivation are reduced: Prison populations are smaller, teenage birth rates are lower, math and literacy scores tend to be higher, and there is less obesity.

That is a lot to attribute to inequality, but all these relationships have been demonstrated in at least two independent settings: among the richest developed societies, and among the 50 states of the USA. In both cases, places with smaller income differences do better and the relationships cannot be dismissed as chance findings. Some of them have already been shown in large numbers of studies—there are over 200 looking at the tendency for health to be better in more equal societies and something like 40 looking at the relation between violence and inequality. As you might expect, inequality makes a larger contribution to some problems than to others, and it is of course far from being the only cause of social ills. But it does look as if the scale of inequality is the most important single explanation for the huge differences in the prevalence of social problems between societies. The relationships tend to be strongest among problems that show the sharpest class differences and are most closely related to relative deprivation.

The most obvious explanation for these patterns is the suggestion that more unequal societies have more social problems because they have more poor people. But this is not the main explanation. Most of the effect of inequality is the result of worse outcomes across the vast majority of the population. In a more unequal society, even middle-class people on good incomes are likely to be less healthy, less likely to be involved in community life, more likely to be obese, and more likely to be victims of violence. Similarly, their children are likely to do less well at school, are more likely to use drugs and more likely to become teenage parents.

REDISTRIBUTION, NOT GROWTH

The first thing to recognize is that we are dealing with the effects of relative rather than absolute deprivation and poverty. Violence, poor health or school failure are not problems that can be solved by economic growth. Everyone getting richer without redistribution doesn't help. Although economic growth remains important in poorer countries, across the richest 25 or 30 countries, there is no tendency whatsoever for health to be better among the most affluent rather than the least affluent of these rich countries. The same is true of levels of violence, teenage pregnancy rates, literacy and math scores among school children, and even obesity rates. In poorer countries, both inequality and economic growth are important to outcomes such as health, but rich countries have reached a level of development beyond which further rises in material living standards do not help reduce health or social problems. While greater equality is important at all levels of economic development, the connection between life expectancy and Gross National Income per head weakens as countries get richer until, among the very richest countries, the connection disappears entirely.

However, within each country, ill health and social problems are closely associated with income. The more deprived areas in our societies have more of most problems. So what does it mean if the differences in income within rich societies matter, but income differences between them do not? It tells us that what matters is where we stand in relation to others in our own society. The issue is social status and relative income. So for example, why the USA has the highest homicide rates, the highest teenage pregnancy rates, the highest rates of imprisonment, and, based on information from WHO sources, it also has the biggest income differences, comes somewhere between 25th and 40th in the international league table of life expectancy. In contrast, countries like Japan, Sweden and Norway, although not as rich as the U.S., all have smaller income differences and do well on all these measures. Even among the 50 states of the USA, those with smaller income differences perform as well as more egalitarian countries on most of these measures.

CHRONIC STRESS

But how can social status differences affect health? There is a health gradient running right across society, from the bottom to the top. Even the comfortably off middle classes tend to have shorter lives than those who are very well off. Having a house with a smaller lawn to mow, or one less car, is not a plausible explanation for these differences. Research has now shown the importance to health of psychological and social factors. Friendship, sense of control and good early childhood experience are all highly protective of health, while things like hostility, anxiety and major difficulties are damaging. The many pathways through which chronic stress makes us more vulnerable to disease are becoming clearer. Stress compromises the immune and cardiovascular systems and increases our vulnerability to so many diseases that it has been likened to more rapid ageing.

We now know that a major contribution to health inequalities comes from the psychological and emotional impact of people's social status. This picture received powerful confirmation from studies of nonhuman primates. Although among humans you cannot unambiguously separate out the effects of social status from better material conditions, among animals you can. Studies in which social status among macaque monkeys was experimentally manipulated by moving animals between groups, while ensuring material conditions and diets were kept the same, showed that the stress of low social status can produce physiological effects similar to those associated with low status in humans. Since then, studies of other nonhuman primates species have shown that the stress effects of social status vary according to the nature of the dominance hierarchy and the quality of social relations.

SOCIAL RELATIONS AND HIERARCHY

The growing awareness of the importance of the social environment to health raised the question of whether the quality of social relations differed between more, and less, equal societies. The data left no room for doubt: People in more unequal societies trust each other less, they are less likely to be involved in community life, and rates of violence are higher. All suggest that inequality damages the quality of social relations. Indeed, this must be one of the most important ways inequality affects the quality of life. In the most unequal of the 50 states of the USA, 35 or 40 percent of the population feel they cannot trust other people, compared to perhaps only 10 percent in the more equal states. The international differences are at least as large. Measures of "social capital" and the extent to which people are involved in local community life also confirm the socially corrosive effects of inequality.

Americans often ask whether these patterns reflect ethnic divisions. The answer is that they do and they don't. The same patterns are found in international analyses and within other countries where they cannot be explained by ethnic divisions. In addition, some analyses have controlled for the proportion of minority group members in different societies. However, insofar as skin color or, in different contexts, language or religious group membership become markers of social status, then they are stigmatized like any other marker of low class or social status. These issues are centrally about social status differentiation: Its effects explain why people in lower classes feel they are treated as a different race and people of a different race feel they are treated as second-class citizens. But the effects of inequality are far too large to be attributed to racial discrimination. Inequality is associated with worse outcomes among the vast majority of the population, though discrimination can intensify inequality. Worse outcomes are seen even when comparisons are restricted to just the white populations in more and less equal societies.

Income inequality tells us something about how hierarchical societies are and about the scale of class differentiation within them. The limited comparable data on social mobility in different countries suggest that more unequal countries have less social mobility. Rather than being the "land of opportunity," the United States has unusually low rates of social mobility which seem to match its unusually large income differences. And it also looks as if increased income inequality has led, in both Britain and the U.S., to greater residential segregation of rich and poor. Bigger differences seem to mean less mixing—both socially and geographically.

With such profound effects on society and health, it would be surprising if inequality did not also exacerbate most of the problems associated with relative deprivation, so giving rise to the relationships we found between greater inequality and higher rates of imprisonment, poorer literacy and math scores, increased obesity, more violence, higher teenage pregnancies rates and poorer mental health. It seems likely that the bigger the income and status differences, the more important social position and social status competition becomes.

INEQUALITY AND SOCIAL ANXIETY

But why are we so sensitive to inequality? Why does it affect us so much? Some pointers to the mechanisms involved are provided by the psychosocial risk factors for poor health. Foremost amongst these, as we saw earlier, are three intensely social factors: low social status, weak friendship networks, and poor quality of early childhood experience. Given that we know these work through chronic stress, the research seems to be telling us that these are the most pervasive sources of chronic stress in affluent societies.

Thinking more about these three sources of chronic stress, we can see that they may all be indicators of underlying social anxieties. The insecurities we may carry with us from a difficult early childhood are not unlike the insecurities associated with low social status, and one may make us more vulnerable to the other. Friendship fits into this picture because friends provide positive feedback: They enjoy your company, laugh at your jokes, seek your advice, etc.—you feel valued. In contrast, not having friends, feeling excluded, people choosing not to sit next to you fills most of us with self-doubt. We worry about being unattractive, boring, unintelligent, socially inept, and so on.

There is now a large body of experimental evidence which shows that the kinds of stress which have the greatest effect on people's levels of stress hormones are "social evaluative threats," such as threats to self-esteem or social status, in which others can negatively judge performance. It seems then that the most widespread and potent kind of stress in modern societies centers on our anxieties about how others see us, on our self-doubts and social insecurities. As social beings, we monitor how others respond to us, so much so that it is sometimes as if we experienced ourselves through each other's eyes. Shame and embarrassment have been called the social emotions: They shape our behavior so that we conform to acceptable norms and spare us from the stomach-tightening we feel when we have made fools of ourselves in front of others. Several of the great sociological thinkers have suggested that this is the gateway through which we are socialized, and it now looks as if it is also how society gets under the skin to affect health.

Given that the social hierarchy is seen as a hierarchy from the most valued at the top, to the least valued at the bottom, it is easy to see how bigger status differences increase the evaluative threat and add to status competition and status insecurity. This perspective also explains why violence increases with greater inequality. The literature on violence points out how often issues of respect, loss of face and humiliation are the triggers to violence. Violence is more common where there is more inequality, not only because inequality increases status competition, but also because people deprived of the markers of status (incomes, jobs, houses, cars, etc.) become particularly sensitive to how they are seen. What hurts about having second-rate possessions is being seen as a second-rate person.

Similar processes are involved in the social gradient in children's educational performance. A 2004 study for the World Bank (K. Hoff & P. Pandey, "Belief Systems and Durable Inequalities," Research Working Paper 3351) showed that while high- and low-caste children in rural India were unaware of the caste differences between them, they performed equally well when asked to solve a series of puzzles; but when made aware of the differences, the performance of children from low castes was substantially reduced.

Increased social hierarchy and inequality substantially raises the stakes and anxieties about personal worth throughout society. We all want to feel valued and appreciated, but a society that makes large numbers of people feel they are looked down upon, regarded as inferior, stupid and failures, not only causes suffering and wastage, but also incurs the costs of anti-social reactions to the structures that demean them.

INEQUALITY, CONSUMPTION AND THE ENVIRONMENT

For thousands of years, the best way of improving the quality of human life has been to raise material living standards. We are the first generation to have got to the end of that process. No longer does economic growth improve health, happiness or well-being. If we are to improve the real quality of life further, we have to direct our attention to the social environment and the quality of social relations. But rather than continuing to tackle each problem separately, by spending more on medical care, more on police, social workers and drug rehabilitation units, we now know that it is possible to improve the psychosocial well-being and social functioning of whole societies. The quality of social relations is built on material foundations—on the scale of the material inequalities between us.

During the next few decades politics is likely to be dominated by the necessity of reducing carbon emissions. There are three ways in which greater equality is crucial to achieving sustainability. The greatest threat to reining in carbon emissions is consumerism. Several economists (see, for instance, Robert Frank, *Luxury Fever: Why Money Fails to Satisfy in an Era of Success*, Free Press, 1999) have shown that consumerism is driven by status competition. Status competition is, in turn, intensified by greater inequality. Consumerism reflects social neuroses and insecurities fanned by inequality and increased competition for status. Advertisers play on these insecurities, suggesting their products enhance attractiveness, sophistication and exclusivity. Rather than a sign of our innate materialism, consumerism is an indication of our need for emotional comfort—as in "retail therapy" or "eating for comfort"—to provide a sense of well-being that we fail to get from society. By improving the quality of social relations, narrow income differences make us less vulnerable to these pressures.

The second important contribution that greater equality can make to achieving sustainability is that it increases public spiritedness. Less exposed to status competition, people in more equal societies are less out for themselves. Higher levels of trust and involvement in community life mean that people are more likely to think in terms of the greater good. Confirming this, we found that more equal societies give more in overseas aid and score better on the Global Peace Index. An international survey of business leaders showed that those in more equal countries think it more important that their governments abide by international environmental agreements. Reducing carbon emissions and achieving sustainability depend, like nothing else, on our ability to act for the common good.

Finally, the changes needed to cope with global warming are unlikely to command public support unless they are seen to be fair. If people are to cooperate in the effort to reduce carbon emissions, the burden must be fairly shared. Policies that penalize the poor while allowing the rich to continue with much more environmentally damaging lifestyles will not be acceptable.

Why Racial Integration Remains an Imperative

Elizabeth Anderson

In 1988, I needed to move from Ann Arbor to the Detroit area to spare my partner, a sleep-deprived resident at Henry Ford Hospital, a significant commute to work. As I searched for housing, I observed stark patterns of racial segregation, openly enforced by landlords who assured me, a white woman then in her late twenties, that I had no reason to worry about renting there since "we're holding the line against blacks at 10 Mile Road." One of them showed me a home with a pile of cockroaches in the kitchen. Landlords in the metro area were confident that whites would rather live with cockroaches as housemates than with blacks as neighbors. We decided to rent a house in South Rosedale Park, a stable working-class Detroit neighborhood that was about 80 percent black. It was a model of cordial race relations. Matters were different in my place of employment, the University of Michigan in Ann Arbor. At the time, a rash of racially hostile incidents targeting black, Latino, Native American and Asian students was raising alarms. Although overtly racist incidents got the most publicity, they did not constitute either the dominant or, in aggregate effect, the most damaging mode of undesirable racial interactions on campus. More pervasive, insidious and cumulatively damaging were subtler patterns of racial discomfort, alienation, and ignorant and cloddish interaction, such as classroom dynamics in which white students focused on problems and grievances peculiar to them, ignored what black students were saying, or expressed insulting assumptions about them. I wondered whether there was a connection between the extreme residential racial segregation in Michigan and the toxic patterns of interracial interaction I observed at the university, where many students were functioning in a multiracial setting for the first time.

My investigations led me to write my book, *The Imperative of Integration*, which focuses primarily (but not exclusively) on black-white segregation. Since the end of concerted efforts to enforce *Brown v. Board of Education* in the 1980s, activists, politicians, pundits, scholars and the American public have advocated nonintegrative paths to racial justice. Racial justice, we are told, can be achieved through multiculturalist celebrations of racial diversity; or equal economic investments in de facto segregated schools and neighborhoods; or a focus on poverty rather than race; or more rigorous enforcement of anti-discrimination law; or color-blindness; or welfare reform; or a determined effort within minority communities to change dysfunctional social norms associated with the "culture of poverty." As this list demonstrates, avoidance of integration is found across the whole American political spectrum. *The Imperative of Integration* argues that all of these purported remedies for racial injustice rest on the illusion that racial justice can be achieved without racial integration.

Readers of *Poverty & Race* are familiar with the deep and pervasive racial segregation in the U.S., especially of blacks from whites, which was caused and is currently maintained by public policies such as zoning, massive housing discrimination and white flight, and which generates profound economic inequalities. Segregation isolates blacks from access to job opportunities, retail outlets, and commercial and professional services. It deprives them of access to public goods, including decent public schools and adequate law enforcement, while subjecting them to higher tax burdens, concentrated poverty, urban blight, pollution and crime. This depresses housing values and impedes blacks' ability to accumulate financial and human capital. If the effects of segregation were confined to such material outcomes, we could imagine that some combination of nonintegrative left-liberal remedies—color-blind anti-poverty programs, economic investment in disadvantaged neighborhoods, vigorous enforcement of anti-discrimination law, and multiculturalist remedies to remaining discrimination—could overcome racial inequality.

NONINTEGRATIONIST REMEDIES ARE INSUFFICIENT

Such nonintegrationist remedies are insufficient because they fail to address the full range of effects of segregation on group inequality. *The Imperative of Integration* documents three additional effects that can only be undone through integration: social/cultural capital inequality, racial stigmatization, and anti-democratic effects. These effects recognize that segregation isn't only geographic, and so can't be undone simply by redistributing material goods across space. More fundamentally, segregation consists of the whole range of social practices that groups with privileged access to important goods use to close ranks to maintain their privileges. This includes role segregation, where different groups interact, but on terms of domination and subordination.

Everyone knows that who you know is as important as what you know in getting access to opportunities. This idea captures the social capital effects of racial segregation. In segregated societies, news about and referrals to educational and job opportunities preferentially circulate within the groups that already predominate in a given institution, keeping disadvantaged groups off or at the back of the queue. Cultural capital also matters: Even when the gatekeepers to important opportunities do not intentionally practice racial discrimination, they often select applicants by their "fit" with the informal, unspoken and untaught norms of speech, bodily comportment, dress, personal style and cultural interests that already prevail in an institution. Mutually isolated communities tend to drift apart culturally, and thereby undermine disadvantaged groups' accumulation of the cultural capital needed for advancement. Integration is needed to remedy these inequalities.

Segregation also stigmatizes the disadvantaged. When social groups diverge in material and social advantages, people form corresponding group stereotypes and tell stories to explain these differences. These stories add insult to injury, because people tend to attribute a group's disadvantages to supposedly intrinsic deficits in its abilities, character or culture rather than to its external circumstances. Spatial segregation reinforces these demeaning stories. Ethnocentrism, or favoritism towards those with whom one associates, induces self-segregated groups to draw invidious comparisons between themselves and the groups from which they are isolated. They create worldviews that are impervious to counter-evidence held by members of out-groups with whom they have little contact. They tend to view extreme and deviant behaviors of out-group members, such as violent crimes, as representative of the out-group. Role segregation also creates stereotypes that reinforce out-group disadvantage. People's stereotypes of who is suited to privileged positions incorporate the social identities of those who already occupy them. Occupation of dominant positions also tends to make people prone to stereotype their subordinates, because dominant players can afford to be ignorant of the ways their subordinates deviate from stereotype. Popular understandings of racial stigma and how it works lead people to drastically underestimate its extent and harmful effects. We imagine racially stigmatizing ideas as consciously located in the minds of extreme racists. Think of the KKK member who claims that blacks are biologically inferior and threatening to whites, proclaims his hatred of them, and discriminates against them out of sheer prejudice. Most Americans despise such extremists, disavow explicitly racist ideas, and sincerely think of themselves as not racist. Most say that racial discrimination is wrong. It is tempting to conclude that negative images of blacks are no longer a potent force in American life.

Tempting, but wrong. While the old racist images of black biological inferiority may have faded, they have been replaced by new ones. Now many whites tend to see blacks as choosing badly, as undermining themselves with culturally dysfunctional norms of single parenthood, welfare dependency, criminality, and poor attachment to school and work. Since, on this view, blacks are perfectly capable of solving their own problems if they would only try, neither whites nor the government owe them anything.

These ideas don't have to be believed, or even conscious, for them to influence behavior. Mere familiarity with derogatory stereotypes, even without belief, can cause unwitting discrimination. No wonder that even people who consciously reject anti-black stereotypes have been found to discriminate against blacks. This is because stereotypes typically operate automatically, behind our backs. In addition, we need to multiply our models of how racially stigmatizing ideas cause discrimination. Pure prejudicial discrimination, as in the KKK case, offers just one model. Economists stress statistical discrimination, in which decision-makers use race as a proxy for undesirable traits such as laziness or criminal tendencies. But often stereotypes work by altering perceptions. For some white observers, that rambunctious black youth shooting hoops in the park looks aggressive and hostile, although if he were white, he would be perceived as harmlessly horsing around. Other times they work by making well-meaning people anxious. Nervous about appearing racist, whites may avoid blacks, or act stiffly and formally toward them. The very desire to avoid discrimination can cause it.

Racial stigmatization also harms blacks through paths other than discrimination. This is why *The Imperative of Integration* argues that the standard discrimination account of racial inequality needs to be replaced by a broader account, based on the joint effects of segregation and stigmatization. Negative effects of stigmatization not mediated by discrimination include "stereotype threat"—anxiety caused by the fear that one's behavior will confirm negative stereotypes about oneself—which depresses blacks' performance on standardized tests. In addition, stigmatizing images of blacks are not just in people's heads; they are in our culture and public discourse. TV news and police dramas disproportionately depict criminals as black and exaggerate the extent of black-on-white crimes. Such taken-for-granted stigmatizing public images of blacks amount to a massive assault on the reputation of blacks, a harm in itself. They also generate public support for policies that have a disproportionately negative impact on blacks. White support for the death penalty jumps when whites are told that more blacks than whites are executed. White hostility to welfare is tied to the public image of the welfare recipient as a single black mother, even though most recipients are white.

Such impacts of racial stigmatization on democratic policy formation reinforce the anti-democratic effects of spatial and role segregation. Democracy isn't only about the universal franchise. It requires a trained elite, institutional structure, and culture that is systematically responsive to the interests and voices of people from all walks of life. This requires that people from all walks of life have effective access to channels of communication to elites, and that they be able to hold them accountable for their decisions. Segregation blocks both communication and accountability. There is nothing like face-to-face confrontation to force people to listen and respond to one's complaints. Out of sight, out of mind: Segregated elites are clubby, insular, ignorant, unaccountable and irresponsible. The history of the Civil Rights Movement demonstrates how mass disruptive protests were needed to teach segregated elites, and whites at large, fundamental lessons about democracy and justice that they were incapable of learning on their own.

RACIAL SEGREGATION:
A FUNDAMENTAL CAUSE OF RACIAL INJUSTICE

So racial segregation is a fundamental cause of racial injustice in three ways: It blocks blacks' access to economic opportunities, it causes racial stigmatization and discrimination, and it undermines democracy. It stands to reason that racial integration would help dismantle these injustices. We can think of integration as taking place by stages. We start with formal desegregation: ending laws and policies that turned blacks into an untouchable caste by forcing them into separate and inferior public spaces. This is an essential step toward destigmatization.

While stigma still exists, blacks' public standing is better now that they can no longer be forced to the back of the bus. Next comes spatial integration, in which racial groups actually share common public spaces and facilities. This enables blacks to get access to many of the public goods—notably, safe, unblighted, relatively unpolluted neighborhoods with decent schools and public services—that most whites enjoy. Studies of integration experiments involving low-income families, from *Gautreaux* to Moving to Opportunity, show that spatial integration yields important material and psychic benefits to formerly segregated blacks, notably better housing, lower stress and greater freedom for children to play outdoors.

The next step is formal social integration: cooperation on terms of equality in institutions such as schools, workplaces, juries and the military. This is where some of the biggest payoffs of integration occur. Extensive interracial cooperation on equal terms expands blacks' social and cultural capital, leading to better education and job opportunities. Sustained formal social integration under moderately favorable conditions, including institutional support and cooperative interaction, also reduces prejudice, stigma and discrimination, often to the point of promoting informal social integration—interracial friendship and intimate relations.

Formal social integration also improves the responsiveness of democratic institutions to all social groups. Racially integrated police forces are less violent toward blacks and more responsive to community concerns than racially homogeneous ones. Integrated teaching staffs are less punitive toward black students and less likely to consign them to lower educational tracks. Integrated juries deliberate longer, take into account more evidence, make fewer factual mistakes, and are more alert to racial discrimination in the criminal justice process than all-white juries. Part of the greater intelligence of integrated juries is due to the diverse information provided by blacks, who are more likely to raise critical questions, such as the reliability of whites' eyewitness identification of blacks. Deliberation in an integrated setting also makes whites deliberate more intelligently and responsibly: They are less likely to rush to a guilty judgment, and more likely to raise and take seriously concerns about discrimination in the criminal justice process, than in all-white juries. The need to justify oneself face-to-face before diverse others motivates people to be responsive to the interests of a wider diversity of people. In public opinion polling, too, whites express more racially conciliatory positions when they think they are talking to a black pollster.

The Imperative of Integration argues that the evidence on the positive effects of racial integration, combined with theory and evidence that these effects cannot be achieved in other ways, provide a powerful case for re-instituting racial integration as a policy goal. Integration needs to be pursued on multiple fronts, including housing vouchers to promote low-income black mobility into integrated middle-class neighborhoods, abolition of class-segregative zoning regulations, adoption of integrative programs by school districts, extension and aggressive enforcement of differential impact standards of illegal discrimination to state action, and deliberate selection for racially integrated juries. I also argue that voting districts should be integrated in such a way that politicians cannot be elected without running on platforms with multiracial appeal. This will correct a serious downside of majority-minority districting, which is that remaining districts tend to favor race-baiting politicians running on a politics of white racial resentment. In many parts of the U.S., race relations have relaxed enough to enable blacks, even when a minority in their district, to elect their preferred candidate in coalition with a critical mass of racially tolerant whites, Latinos, Asian Americans and Native Americans.

The Imperative of Integration also argues for alternative models of affirmative action. Right now, discussion of affirmative action is dominated by two models: diversity and compensation. The diversity model stresses the supposed connections between racial diversity and diversity of cultures and ideas. It doesn't do much to support affirmative action in industries such as construction and manufacturing, where the culture and ideas of most employees make little difference. Nor does it explain why selective schools should preferentially admit African Americans and Latinos, as opposed to foreign students. The compensatory model portrays affirmative action as making up for past discrimination. This encourages people to believe that racial inequalities are due to long-past deeds, overlooking the powerful continuing causes of racial injustice rooted in current segregation and stigmatization. It also supports public impatience with affirmative action. No wonder the Supreme Court, even while upholding affirmative action in *Grutter v. Bollinger*, expressed the view that affirmative action will no longer be needed in 25 years.

Once we understand that current racial inequality is rooted in current racial stigmatization and segregation, affirmative action can be understood differently. De facto segregation creates referral networks that exclude blacks from information and recommendations to job openings in firms that employ few blacks. Role segregation within firms creates stereotypes of qualified workers that mirror the identities of those who already occupy those roles. Nonstereotypical workers are therefore perceived to be unqualified for such roles even when they could fill them successfully, and so are excluded even when managers believe they are hiring on merit. Affirmative action within firms serves to block these and other racially exclusionary practices. This is discrimination-blocking affirmative action. Integrative affirmative action explicitly adopts racial integration as an institutional goal, in the name of promoting democratic responsiveness to the full diversity of people whom the institution is supposed to serve, overcoming racial inequalities in social and cultural capital, and breaking down racial anxieties, prejudices and stereotypes through integrated, cooperative work teams.

Any argument for restoring racial integration to a central place in the public policy agenda must address three objections. Conservatives oppose integrative policies on grounds of color-blindness. In *The Imperative of Integration*, I argue that the color-blind principle is conceptually confused, because it conflates different meanings of race and different kinds of racial discrimination. It is one thing to discriminate out of pure prejudice against a group with a different appearance or ancestry, or to treat race as a proxy for intelligence or other merits; quite another to take race-conscious steps to counteract racial discrimination and undo the continuing causes of racial-based injustice. Affirmative action, properly administered, does not compromise but rather promotes meritocratic selection. Some on the left oppose integrative policies because they fear the destruction of autonomous black institutions and cultural practices in the name of assimilation and object to the psychic costs of integration on blacks. I argue that integration is distinct from assimilation, since its aim is not to erect white practices as the norm, but rather to abolish white exclusionary practices and replace them with practices inclusive of all. And, while integration is stressful, as people learn to cooperate across racial lines the psychic costs of integration decline. Finally, readers of *Poverty & Race* will be familiar with the argument that integration is an unrealistic fantasy. We know, however, that the experience of integration is self-reinforcing: people of all races who grew up in more integrated settings tend to choose more integrated settings later in life. So we should not foreclose all hope. After all, only a few years ago the idea of a black President was regarded by many Americans to be an unrealizable dream.

Building a National Museum

Lonnie G. Bunch, III

BEGINNINGS

When construction started on the new National Museum of African American History and Culture in the Fall of 2012, it signaled a beginning for some. For those of us who have been involved with the museum's development, however, the groundbreaking was more like rounding the clubhouse turn on a long, fast and furious race to the building's opening on the National Mall in 2015.

Calls for a national museum recognizing the contributions of African Americans to the building and defense of the nation date back to the early 1900s. Two World Wars, a Depression and political opposition, however, prevented any progress until 1988, when Rep. John Lewis of Georgia, an icon of the Civil Rights Movement, introduced a bill in Congress.

Still, it would be more than a decade before Congress created a Presidential Commission on the National Museum of African American History and Culture in 2002.

Finally, in 2003, nearly 100 years after the first appeals, President George W. Bush signed a bill establishing the National Museum of African American History and Culture as part of the Smithsonian Institution. The Smithsonian Board of Regents, the governing body of the Institution, voted in January 2006 to build the museum on a five-acre site on Constitution Avenue between 14th and 15th Streets NW. This site is between the Washington Monument and the Smithsonian's National Museum of American History. The new museum, the Smithsonian's 19th, will be the only national museum devoted exclusively to the documentation of African-American life, art, history and culture.

The enabling legislation also established a council for the museum to advise the Smithsonian regents on such museum matters as recommendations on the museum's planning, design and construction; the museum's administration; and acquisition of objects for the museum's collections. The museum's 25-member council, similar to a board of directors, is a veritable who's who of the corporate and business world, including American Express CEO Kenneth Chenault; former BET founder and CEO Robert Johnson; and music impresarios Quincy Jones and Oprah Winfrey, just to name a few. Recent additions to the council include former first lady Laura Bush and former secretary of state Gen. Colin Powell.

In early 2005, I was chosen to be the Museum's founding director. At the time, I was President of the Chicago Historical Society, one of America's oldest museums of history. Prior to that, I spent a number of years in various positions at the Smithsonian. From 1994 to 2000, I was Associate Director for Curatorial Affairs at the National Museum of American History. From 1978 to 1979, I was an education specialist at the National Air and Space Museum, where I developed multicultural instructional programs and researched and wrote the history of African Americans in aviation.

I knew returning to the Smithsonian as director of this new museum was an opportunity not to be missed. I realized that my job at the Chicago Historical Society fulfilled my soul, but helping to build the National Museum would nurture the souls of my ancestors.

A MUSEUM FOR ALL

As I go about the daunting task of building a museum and finding the objects that will fill it, my vision for the institution is that it will be one that speaks to all Americans, not just African Americans. This is not a museum that celebrates black history solely for black Americans. Rather, I see this history as America's history. We will use African-American history and culture as a lens into what it means to be an American.

Visitors don't have to wait for the museum to open in 2015. Exhibitions and events are going on right now. Through collaboration with IBM, the first phase of the museum on the Web was launched in September 2007. MOW offers interactive programs and educational resources for people of all ages. A prominent feature of the website is the Memory Book, which allows site visitors to share family stories, photographs and intergenerational conversations.

The museum opened its inaugural exhibition in May 2007 at the International Center of Photography in New York in a unique collaboration with that museum and the Smithsonian's National Portrait Gallery, from whose collection the exhibition images were drawn. The exhibition, "Let Your Motto Be Resistance: African American Photographs," was on a national tour through 2012.

In January 2009, the museum opened its own gallery in space provided by my friends at American History, which is being used to mount exhibitions until the new building is completed. The first exhibition presented in the gallery was "The Scurlock Studio and Black Washington: Picturing the Promise," featuring more than 100 photos taken by one of Washington, DC's preeminent African-American photographers.

The third exhibition organized by the Museum and the second opened in the NMAAHC Gallery in April 2010, "Ain't Nothing Like the Real Thing: How the Apollo Theater Shaped American Entertainment." It also made national tour stops in a number of U.S. cities, including New York, Detroit, Atlanta and Los Angeles.

The Museum recently opened its latest exhibition, "For All the World to See: Visual Culture and the Struggle for Civil Rights." The multimedia exhibition examines the role that images played in the fight for racial equality. It features photographs, TV and movie clips, magazines, newspapers, posters, books, pamphlets and other media.

One of my first priorities at the museum was to create "Save Our African American Treasures: A National Collections Initiative of Discovery and Preservation." In this series of daylong workshops, participants work with conservation specialists and historians to learn to identify and preserve items of historical value, ranging from photographs and jewelry to military uniforms and textiles. Instruction is offered through hands-on activities, audio-visual presentations and a 30-page guidebook developed by the museum. Launched in Chicago in January 2008, "Treasures" workshops have been held in cities around the country, including Atlanta, Charleston, SC, Los Angeles, New York, Detroit and Washington, DC.

MUSEUM DESIGN AND CONSTRUCTION

The Smithsonian held a design competition that attracted entries by architects from around the world. Six firms were chosen as finalists and asked to submit a formal proposal for the design of the new museum. In April 2009, I chaired a jury that selected Freelon Adjaye Bond/SmithGroup as the architectural team to design the Museum. The Tanzanian-born architect David Adjaye, who has offices in Berlin, London and New York, is the lead designer.

I am pleased to have the opportunity to work with this talented team. Their vision and spirit of collaboration moved all members of the design competition jury. I am confident that they will give us a building that will be an important addition to the National Mall and to the architecture of this city.

COLLECTIONS

Even as I was choosing an architect to build the museum, curators were already busy looking for the artifacts that will fill it. In addition to its central hall, the museum is slated to have galleries focusing on history, culture and community. Within the history galleries will be exhibitions on slavery; the period following Reconstruction into the 20th century and the civil rights era; and the years after 1968.

The culture galleries will include ones on music, sports, visual arts and one entitled the Center for African American Media Arts (CAAMA). CAAMA will be a specialized resource that will house extensive collections of various media, including photographs, films, recordings and other items relating to the African Diaspora. CAAMA will also provide on-site expertise and web access to images from other Smithsonian Institution collections, as well as important holdings housed at external institutions.

The community galleries will be titled "Power of Place," "Making a Way out of No Way" and "Military History." The "Power of Place" gallery will immerse visitors in the broad diversity of African-American life in different regions across the United States. Through interactive, multimedia technologies, visitors will explore the themes of place and region.

The "Making a Way . . . " gallery will feature themed stories that will show how African Americans crafted possibilities in a world that denied them opportunities.

I recently hired Ralph Appelbaum Associates, planners, designers and producers of award-winning museum exhibitions, visitor centers and educational environments, to design the galleries.

So far, the museum has acquired roughly 11,000 objects, including art, photographs, costumes and fashion accessories, musical instruments, sports-related objects and many others. Among objects recently acquired are The Mothership—the iconic stage prop made famous by legendary funk collective Parliament-Funkadelic; the set from Soul Train, the longest running syndicated program in American history; and we will soon accept delivery of a PT-13 Stearman bi-plane used to train the Tuskegee Airmen.

One of my favorite objects in the collection is a beautifully engraved powder horn with a stopper, with the inscription: "Prince Simbo his horn made at Glastonbury November 17th AD 1777." This powder horn was used during the American Revolution by a black soldier and former slave, Prince Simbo, a resident of Glastonbury, Connecticut. Simbo served as a private in the Seventh Regiment, Connecticut Line of the Continental Army. Related documents include a payment note to Prince Simbo; a manuscript document listing the cost of supplies for eleven soldiers, including Prince Simbo; and a manuscript document providing blankets for two black soldiers, Sampson Freeman and Prince Simbo. With this and other compelling material, the museum will present the rich history of African Americans who served in the U.S. military.

For some, the year 2015 may seem far away. But not for me and my staff at the National Museum of African American History and Culture. We still have a lot of work to do. We are in a race with time, and we can see the finish line in the distance.

How White Activists Embrace Racial Justice

Mark R. Warren

How can white Americans come to care enough about racism to take action to change the systems that produce and perpetuate racial inequality in this country? Communities of color have long organized to build the power to press for change. But that is not enough. Greater support among white Americans is necessary if our country is to make further progress in advancing the cause of racial justice. If the nature of racism 30 or 40 years ago was one of overt racism, in my view the problem today is largely one of white passivity in the face of continued racial inequality. Although intentional and overt racism is not always necessary for institutional racism to persist, positive action is required in order to change institutions and policies that create and perpetuate racial injustice.

However, if white people are not victims of racial discrimination themselves, and if their closest family and friends are not victims of discrimination, how can they come to care enough about racism to take action against it? I sought answers to that question by studying 50 white people who became committed activists for racial justice. I asked people how they first became aware of racism and this is one of the stories I heard:

Jim Capraro grew up in Marquette Park, Chicago, in the 1950s and early 1960s, a child of Italian Catholic immigrants. His neighbors, like his parents, were white working-class ethnics who had moved out of Chicago's inner city to this neighborhood of modest homes. Jim's family and the nuns and teachers at his Catholic high school taught him that the future was bright, that America was the land of opportunity, "the greatest country in the world." When Jim was sixteen, however, he experienced an incident that would alter his sense of the world profoundly. It was the Summer of 1966 and Jim's parents had just given him permission to use the family car for the first time on a date. This was going to be a big day for Jim, but not for the reason he had in mind.

Jim took a break from preparations for the date and walked out of his house—straight into the middle of an open housing demonstration in Marquette Park. He recounts what he saw:

I saw a huge crowd of white people, four or five deep, on the sidewalk going out into the street. There were policemen with batons holding them off away from the street. People were throwing beer bottles, just hurling them, at something. Across the street there's some big hubbub, and I could see black people. I could also see clergy who were not black. They all had signs, and the signs said things like End Slums, Open Housing. It was a demonstration. And it was going past the Marquette Park monument. . . . People are jeering and yelling, "Niggers go home," and it's terrible. It's ugly. And it was so strange, because literally twenty minutes before, I'm thinking, "got to gas up the car. I'm going on a date!"

At the intersection, a black couple came up in a car and got stopped at a stoplight. The crowd pushes past the police and surrounds this car. I remember this so vividly—it's a Corvair, Chevy Corvair. Crowd totally surrounds the car. The people inside the car are really afraid. I mean, they're just terrified. People start rocking this car back and forth. The people inside are literally huddled. The light is red. They're stopped. There's a crowd all around them. A girl about my age jumps up on the hood, screaming and yelling, and swearing at the people inside, and kicking at the windshield in front of the driver. I remember thinking she would have mangled their faces, if there wasn't this windshield in the way.

Jim returned to his house and this is what he said, reflecting on the day's events:

I don't know that I was there more than a half an hour, maybe forty minutes, but it was the longest half-hour in my life. And it changed my life forever. Kind of an epiphany, I guess. When I went home, that night I couldn't sleep. I had this never-ending stream of thoughts. Everything I thought I had learned or was led to believe, I thought was a lie. We're not the greatest country in the world. I was always taught that we were the greatest. Six years ago, John Kennedy was elected President. What happened? What just happened two blocks from my house? This can't be the best neighborhood. Look at what people do? Look at how they were behaving. Anybody could grow up to be President—I believed this, right? Well, I didn't think the people who were marching in the park that day had any shot at ever being President.

I got mad. How dare these people do this stuff? This is a democracy. People have a right to say things and march, and think of themselves as being equal with everybody else, and in fact be equal to everybody else.

Jim went on to college and heard Stokely Carmichael give a black power speech challenging whites who cared about racism to stop coming South to help African Americans and combat racism in their own communities. Jim took that charge seriously and stayed in Marquette Park where he helped found the Greater Southwest Development Corporation and has spent the last 40 years combating redlining and white flight, and working for economic development and stable racial integration in a neighborhood that had become a symbol of Northern racism.

[A useful companion piece to Warren's work is *Combined Destinies: Whites Sharing Grief about Racism*, eds. Ann Todd Jealous and Caroline T. Haskell, Potomac Books, 2013. It's an anthology of very personal and moving self-reports by many (unnamed) white contributors, organized into 8 sections (Guilt, Shame, Silence, Resistance and Freedom being some of them). The book includes a chapter-by-chapter Reader's Guide to Self-Reflection: Questions and Topics for Discussion.—*Ed.*]

SEMINAL EXPERIENCES AND THE MORAL IMPULSE TO ACT

Jim's story is a powerful one, and it's the kind of story I heard from almost everyone I interviewed. Jim had what I call a seminal experience where he directly witnessed racism. This direct experience generated an anger at injustice, but more so at the violation of deeply held values of fairness. This led Jim to what I call a moral impulse to act for racial justice. Although Jim and the other white activists I interviewed began their activism with this kind of moral stance, their commitment to racial justice grew and deepened as they began to take action with others to create change.

The 50 white Americans I interviewed were active in three fields: education, community organizing and development, and legal advocacy work, often around criminal justice issues. I selected the respondents by mapping the fields of racial justice activism and consulting with leaders of racial justice organizations in those fields. I looked for people who self-identified as white and who worked for institutional and policy change. I wanted to make clear that I was not studying people who saw themselves as "saviors" of people of color, but rather as serious collaborators with them. I interviewed people from a range of ages, both men and women, from across the country, including activists in the Bay Area, Los Angeles, Chicago, Milwaukee, Dallas, New Orleans, Greensboro and the Baltimore/Washington area. I conducted extensive interviews with each activist focused on their life histories and activist trajectories. I also asked them about their contemporary understandings of their experience working to build multiracial organizations, to influence the beliefs and behaviors of other whites, and their own understanding of their place as white people working for racial justice.

THE POWER OF RELATIONSHIPS WITH PEOPLE OF COLOR

I analyzed the interviews and constructed a model of the development of commitment by white people to racial justice. Activists start with a moral impulse but do not stop there. The second key process occurs as white activists build relationships with people of color. I found, first, that white Americans learned more deeply about the realities of racism and came to see their own experiences as white people in a different way through these relationships. The key informants ranged in age from 20 to 64. Most were women. They include interviewees who are Latino, Middle Eastern and African-American, respectively. The results of these interviews are included as "sidebars" in our full report.

Penda Hair is the co-director of the Advancement Project in Washington, DC, an organization that works with communities to advance racial justice through law, public policy and strategic communication. Penda had a seminal experience growing up in Knoxville, Tennessee, that helped shape her commitment to racial justice. She eventually went to college and law school and then got a job with the NAACP Legal Defense Fund, where she traveled the country fighting discrimination and voting rights cases. Penda built relationships with her black clients and with black colleagues at LDF through which she started learning more about the realities of racism. Here she describes an early experience (using pseudonyms):

My first case was a claim of promotion discrimination by the postal service in Jacksonville, Florida. My first client that I put on the witness stand was a person named James Douglas, who had applied for something like 25 or 30 promotions at the post office. He was a mail carrier, African-American. I went to his house, met his family, and talked to him about all these jobs.

He had been in the army in World War II. He had gotten a college degree and a master's degree, and the only job he could get was working as a mail carrier. It occurred to me that my father did not have a college degree or a master's degree, was roughly the same age as Mr. Douglas, had come out of the army and had gotten this nice job at Union Carbide. He worked his way up through the ranks. We always thought we were deserving because my father worked hard. He got up at 5:30 in the morning to make sure he was there on time. He worked the swing shift, which means that he worked one week 8 to 4 and the next week 4 to midnight, and the next week midnight to 8. That was a hard life for us, we thought. But when I saw Mr. Douglas's life, it was like, "Oh, I'm privileged." For the first time I understood in a different way that I was racially privileged. Because of my father's ability to get that job at Union Carbide, I got put in the best high school in the city where we lived and got the education that allowed me to go to Harvard. I could see that Mr. Douglas's kids probably didn't have as many of those opportunities. I saw the intergenerational effect in a personal way, but I also saw it in a structural way in all the promotions that he had been denied, and the way that other people in the class action case were kept back.

Penda built close relationship with colleagues, where she learned more:

One night we were in the car driving home from a class action meeting with a white man and black woman in the front seat, Sam and Barbara, and a white woman and black man in the back seat, me and an expert witness. We were stopped by a police car. I remember it was on a dark road and there didn't seem to be much around. We were driving by railroad tracks. Barbara and Sam freak out. We look like two interracial couples. The tension and fear became so palpable in that car immediately. "Oh my God, you know, this is lynching territory." At first I was totally oblivious. To me, policemen were benign. They give you speeding tickets every once in a while, but otherwise they protected you. I just remember that feeling of fear sweeping through that car and I became afraid also. We were sitting there in the dark, and these bright lights were shining from behind. Then at some point I hear Sam say from the front seat, "The police officer is a brother," which meant he was black. The police officer was black. Then of course the tension all goes away. He gave us some routine warning. We had a light missing or something. But everybody else in that car knew to be afraid. I didn't even know to be afraid. So it was one of the first times I started seeing victimization from the other side of the color line.

I found that relationships with people of color led to something more than understanding for the white activists I interviewed. Through these relationships, white activists began to care more personally about racism because it affected real people they knew and cared about. For example, Penda eventually became head of the LDF's office in Washington and was there when President Bill Clinton nominated Lani Guinier, a close friend and former African-American colleague at LDF, to be assistant attorney general for civil rights. The right wing immediately attacked her as a "quota queen," and Clinton abandoned her in what was widely seen as a humiliating dismissal.

Lani was attacked because of her views on voting rights, and so it was personal in the sense that, well, I'm a voting rights lawyer. I have the same views as Lani. If she can be attacked and humiliated publicly, then that's essentially saying the same thing about me. And then it was personal in the sense that Lani was staying at my house part of the time when she would come down to do her DC round of meetings. I remember I had just had a baby. At the time, when the newspapers throughout DC were writing all these things about how anti-white she was, I remember her sitting in my house in the rocking chair, holding my white, blond-headed baby. And it was just surreal. How can this happen? How can they paint a picture of her that is so beyond reality, and yet they get away with it?

MORAL PURPOSE AND MORAL VISION

If some whites start out with a moral impulse leading them to do "for" people of color, through relationships white activists start to work "with" people of color and care more deeply about racism. However, they have still not embraced the cause as their own. The third piece of the puzzle is what I call the development of a moral vision. I found two parts to this. First, the white activists I interviewed report that racial justice activism provides a meaningful life for them. For example, Josh Kern attended a Jewish high school that fostered social justice values. But after college, Josh pursued a career in business consulting. Disillusioned, he went to Georgetown Law School, was placed in a high school in Washington where he had a seminal experience that ignited his passion for educational justice. Josh went on to help found the Thurgood Marshall Academy, a civil rights-oriented public charter high school in Washington, DC. Josh reflects on the trajectory of his life in this way:

Those high school years were years that I really felt myself develop and become my own person. It took me ten years to get that back. This time in my life and that time in my life were the only two times where I really felt alive, good about what I was doing, connected in a way that felt like I'm a whole person. I find it very fulfilling, very meaningful. It gives my life purpose and it's something that I've come to feel passionate about as I've gotten immersed in it. I actually think this work has been incredibly beneficial for me, because it feeds me in some way. I believe in it in my core. I'm trying to articulate why I do it. It's not easy to say, but I know this: I wake up every morning and I'm excited about the day's work. In three years of consulting, I never woke up and was excited about what I was doing.

I found that activists gain this sense of moral purpose through working together with others. Bay Area organizer Ingrid Chapman stresses the sense of community she finds in her work:

I have been so inspired by the different work that people are doing. It gives me a sense of possibility and gives me inspiration to continue to struggle and continue to build my hope that another world is possible. For me that is really big. Lots of people that I know want to just disengage because they have no hope that another world is possible. They are disconnected from struggles for social justice and feel totally disempowered and have turned to drugs and alcohol to make it. That sense of community helps me keep going in a world that is really disempowering and really degrading in a lot of ways.

I asked people what kind of society are they working to create. I found and analyzed six components to what I call the visions that they articulated. What was striking was that almost everyone led with a notion of human community. Activists report that they are trying to build a new kind of multiracial society and community where people care about each other, treat each other with respect and where everyone's full potential can be developed. Indeed, activists say that this new kind of community is needed because racism undermines the humanity of whites as well as blacks. The Chicago community organizer Madeline Talbott put it powerfully and bluntly with an analogy to Noah's ark:

I think being white and privileged in a racist society, you feel like you're one of the family members of Noah on the ark. You hear all the people beating on the doors trying to get in and you've got to find a way to open the door. This work allows you to crack the door open, which otherwise you'd have to kill yourself. I mean that's the way it feels to me. You feel like that kind of privilege is killing you. It's one of the things that makes white society less connected and less welcoming and less warm because it's constantly protecting itself from the people and the flood on the outside. It's a terrible way to live.

Even though I probably started in order to help, I'm here for me now. I'm getting huge benefits out of this myself. There's no sacrifice. I'm doing what I want and I get to experience change and wins and transformations and be a part of personal relationships that you couldn't get in America any other way. It's a great opportunity. I feel that very deeply.

Activists, whether explicitly faith-based or not, express a moral vision very similar to Martin Luther King's Beloved Community. Z. Holler, a retired Presbyterian minister and one of the organizers of the Truth and Reconciliation Commission on racism in Greensboro, North Carolina, described it this way:

Where everyone is honored and respected for who they are, where the brokenness and the sins are recognized. We help one another see our weaknesses. Others help us see what we don't see. We help them see what they don't see. Together, if what we see in each other is grossly unjust, we call it by name. We try to come to grips with it. We forgive one another. We move ahead as best we can. And that means policy; that means the structures of government; it means what you do with the economy. The goals you pursue.

Milwaukee community leader Reverend Joseph Ellwanger put it this way:

It is practicing anti-racism and insisting that we work together across racial, ethnic, denominational lines. That in itself is a living out of what King describes as the Beloved Community. So we're not just working for the ultimate goal of social justice, which certainly is what we're working for. But we're also working at building community and in the process we have to dismantle some of the expectations and the fears and the structures that our society has built.

The people I interviewed are not primarily visionaries; nor are they moralists. They are practitioners who believe that racism blocks a more progressive social and political agenda that would materially benefit the vast majority of white people as well. But I found that what sustains them is not just the day-to-day practice, but rather working together in relationship to build a new kind of community. Indeed, their moral visions are worked out in the present through taking action with others across racial lines. Roxane Auer, a young labor organizer in Los Angeles, perhaps summed it up best:

It's not really about contributing to someone else's cause. I feel that I'm contributing to the world that I would rather want to live in. . . . I think extreme inequalities hurt everybody. For human beings to be very complete and really experience the full sense of community or a full, happy life there needs to be more equality in it. So I see it as serving myself. I see it as working for what I want, not just what they want or need. It's what we all need to be happier and more centered and fulfilled in this world.

HEART, HAND AND HEAD

My findings run counter to much conventional wisdom. Efforts to persuade white Americans typically focus on the cognitive dimension. If we can get whites to understand racism and discrimination, we believe they will oppose it. Or we make rational arguments for the interests of white Americans in racial justice. For example, it costs more to incarcerate a child than to educate him or her. However, I found little evidence from my research that knowledge alone moves many whites to caring and action. Hardly anyone I interviewed said anything like: "I read about racism in a book and decided to do something about it." Rather, I found knowledge to play a supportive role in the development of white people's commitment. Knowledge about racism is critically important for determining how to combat it. But it does not provide the motivation to do it in the first place. Numbers are "just" numbers if disconnected from real people whites know and care about. A more compelling approach places knowledge and interest-based arguments in alignment with the moral and relational processes that engage values and foster caring and commitment. I sum this up in the model of "heart, hand and head." Whites come to racial awareness and commitment when their values are engaged (heart) through action in which they build relationships (hand) that align with knowledge and interests (head).

Progress in moving larger numbers of white Americans toward racial justice will not come easy. We know that local community organizing efforts over many years built the foundation for the emergence of the Civil Rights Movement in the fifties and sixties. The activists I interviewed are working hard with people of color and other whites to build a new foundation for just such a movement to re-emerge in our era.

Ending/Reducing Poverty: A Forum

In April [2007], the Center for American Progress—"a nonpartisan research and educational institute dedicated to promoting a strong, just and free America that ensures opportunity for all"—released the final report of its Task Force on Poverty: From Poverty to Prosperity: A National Strategy to Cut Poverty in Half. The Task Force was co-chaired by Angela Glover Blackwell of PolicyLink and Peter B. Edelman, Prof. of Law at Georgetown Univ. Other Task Force members were: Rebecca Blank, Linda Chavez-Thompson, Rev. Dr. Floyd H. Flake, Wizipan Garriott, Maude Hurd, Charles E.M. Kolb, Meizhu Lui, Alice M. Rivlin, Barbara J. Robles, Robert Solow, Dorothy Stoneman and Wellington E. Webb. Mark Greenberg was Task Force Executive Director.

Below is the report's Executive Summary (the full report is available at the CAP website: www.americanprogress.org). We asked a range of policy experts and activists for their comments on the report and its recommendations, along with the Center's responses to those comments, by Task Force Co-Chairs Blackwell and Edelman, CAP Sr. VP for Domestic Policy Cassandra Butts and Task Force ED Mark Greenberg.

* * * * *

FROM POVERTY TO PROSPERITY: EXECUTIVE SUMMARY

CENTER FOR AMERICAN
PROGRESS TASK FORCE ON POVERTY

Thirty-seven million Americans live below the official poverty line. Millions more struggle each month to pay for basic necessities, or run out of savings when they lose their jobs or face health emergencies. Poverty imposes enormous costs on society.

The lost potential of children raised in poor households, the lower productivity and earnings of poor adults, the poor health, increased crime, and broken neighborhoods all hurt our nation. Persistent childhood poverty is estimated to cost our nation $500 billion each year, or about 4 percent of the nation's Gross Domestic Product. In a world of increasing global competition, we cannot afford to squander these human resources.

The Center for American Progress last year convened a diverse group of national experts and leaders to examine the causes and consequences of poverty in America and make recommendations for national action. In this report, our Task Force on Poverty calls for a national goal of cutting poverty in half in the next 10 years and proposes a strategy to reach the goal.

Our nation has seen periods of dramatic poverty reduction at times when near-full employment was combined with sound federal and state policies, motivated individual initiative, supportive civic involvement, and sustained national commitment. In the last six years, however, our nation has moved in the opposite direction. The number of poor Americans has grown by five million, while inequality has reached historic high levels.

Consider the following facts:

One in eight Americans now lives in poverty. A family of four is considered poor if the family's income is below $19,971—a bar far below what most people believe a family needs to get by.

Still, using this measure, 12.6 percent of all Americans were poor in 2005, and more than 90 million people (31 percent of all Americans) had incomes below 200 percent of federal poverty thresholds.

Millions of Americans will spend at least one year in poverty at some point in their lives. One-third of all Americans will experience poverty within a 13-year period. In that period, one in 10 Americans are poor for most of the time, and one in 20 are poor for 10 or more years.

Poverty in the United States is far higher than in many other developed nations. At the turn of the 21st century, the United States ranked 24th among 25 countries when measuring the share of the population below 50 percent of median income.

Inequality has reached record highs. The richest one percent of Americans in 2005 had the largest share of the nation's income (19 percent) since 1929. At the same time, the poorest 20 percent of Americans had only 3.4 percent of the nation's income.

It does not have to be this way. Our nation need not tolerate persistent poverty alongside great wealth.

The United States should set a national goal of cutting poverty in half over the next 10 years. A strategy to cut poverty in half should be guided by four principles:

Promote Decent Work. People should work and work should pay enough to ensure that workers and their families can avoid poverty, meet basic needs, and save for the future.

Provide Opportunity for All. Children should grow up in conditions that maximize their opportunities for success; adults should have opportunities throughout their lives to connect to work, get more education, live in a good neighborhood, and move up in the workforce.

Ensure Economic Security. Americans should not fall into poverty when they cannot work or work is unavailable, unstable, or pays so little that they cannot make ends meet.

Help People Build Wealth. All Americans should have the opportunity to build assets that allow them to weather periods of flux and volatility, and to have the resources that may be essential to advancement and upward mobility.

We recommend 12 key steps to cut poverty in half:

1. Raise and index the minimum wage to half the average hourly wage. At $5.15, the federal minimum wage is at its lowest level in real terms since 1956. The federal minimum wage was once 50 percent of the average wage but is now 30 percent of that wage. Congress should restore the minimum wage to 50 percent of the average wage, about $8.40 an hour in 2006. Doing so would help over 4.5 million poor workers and nearly nine million other low-income workers.

2. Expand the Earned Income Tax Credit and Child Tax Credit. As an earnings supplement for low-income working families, the EITC raises incomes and helps families build assets. EITC expansions during the 1990s helped increase employment and reduced poverty. But the current EITC does little to help workers without children. We recommend tripling the EITC for childless workers, and expanding help to larger working families. Doing so would cut the number of people in poverty by over 2 million. The Child Tax Credit provides a tax credit of up to $1,000 per child, but provides no help to the poorest families. We recommend making it available to all low- and moderate-income families. Doing so would move 2 million children and 1 million parents out of poverty.

3. Promote unionization by enacting the Employee Free Choice Act. The Employee Free Choice Act would require employers to recognize a union after a majority of workers signs cards authorizing union representation and establish stronger penalties for violation of employee rights. The increased union representation made possible by the Act would lead to better jobs and less poverty for American workers.

4. Guarantee childcare assistance to low-income families and promote early education for all. We propose that the federal and state governments guarantee childcare help to families with incomes below about $40,000 a year, and also expand the childcare tax credit. At the same time, states should be encouraged to improve the quality of early education and broaden access for all children. Our childcare expansion would raise employment among low-income parents and help nearly 3 million parents and children escape poverty.

5. Create 2 million new "opportunity" housing vouchers, and promote equitable development in and around central cities. Nearly 8 million Americans live in neighborhoods of concentrated poverty where at least 40 percent of residents are poor. Our nation should seek to end concentrated poverty and economic segregation, and promote regional equity and inner-city revitalization. We propose that over the next 10 years the federal government fund 2 million new "opportunity vouchers"

designed to help people live in opportunity-rich areas. New affordable housing should be in communities with employment opportunities and high-quality public services, or in gentrifying communities. These housing policies should be part of a broader effort to pursue equitable development strategies in regional and local planning efforts, including efforts to improve schools, create affordable housing, assure physical security, and enhance neighborhood amenities.

6. Connect disadvantaged and disconnected youth with school and work. About 1.7 million poor youth ages 16 to 24 were out of school and out of work in 2005. We recommend that the federal government restore Youth Opportunity Grants to help the most disadvantaged communities and expand funding for effective and promising youth programs—with the goal of reaching 600,000 poor disadvantaged youth through these efforts. We propose a new Upward Pathway program to offer low-income youth opportunities to participate in service and training in fields that are in high demand and provide needed public services.

7. Simplify and expand Pell Grants and make higher education accessible to residents of each state. Low-income youth are much less likely to attend college than their higher-income peers, even among those of comparable abilities. Pell Grants play a crucial role for lower-income students. We propose to simplify the Pell grant application process, gradually: raise Pell Grants to reach 70 percent of the average costs of attending a four-year public institution, and encourage institutions to do more to raise student completion rates. As the federal government does its part, states should develop strategies to make post-secondary education affordable for all residents, following promising models already underway in a number of states.

8. Help former prisoners find stable employment and reintegrate into their communities. The United States has the highest incarceration rate in the world. We urge all states to develop comprehensive re-entry services aimed at reintegrating former prisoners into their communities with full-time, consistent employment.

9. Ensure equity for low-wage workers in the Unemployment Insurance system. Only about 35 percent of the unemployed, and a smaller share of unemployed low-wage workers, receive unemployment insurance benefits. We recommend that states (with federal help) reform "monetary eligibility" rules that screen out low-wage workers, broaden eligibility for part-time workers and workers who have lost employment as a result of compelling family circumstances, and allow unemployed workers to use periods of unemployment as a time to upgrade their skills and qualifications.

10. Modernize means-tested benefits programs to develop a coordinated system that helps workers and families. A well-functioning safety net should help people get into or return to work and ensure a decent level of living for those who cannot work or are temporarily between jobs. Our current system fails to do so. We recommend that governments at all levels simplify and improve benefits access for working families and improve services to individuals with disabilities. The Food Stamp Program should be strengthened to improve benefits, eligibility, and access. And the

Temporary Assistance for Needy Families Program should be reformed to shift its focus from cutting caseloads to helping needy families find sustainable employment.

11. Reduce the high costs of being poor and increase access to financial services. Despite having less income, lower-income families often pay more than middle-and high-income families for the same consumer products. We recommend that the federal and state governments should address the foreclosure crisis through expanded mortgage assistance programs and by new federal legislation to curb unscrupulous practices. And we propose that the federal government establish a $50 million Financial Fairness Innovation Fund to support state efforts to broaden access to mainstream goods and financial services in predominantly low-income communities.

12. Expand and simplify the Saver's Credit to encourage saving for education, homeownership and retirement. For many families, saving for purposes such as education, a home, or a small business is key to making economic progress. We propose that the federal "Saver's Credit" be reformed to make it fully refundable. This credit should also be broadened to apply to other appropriate savings vehicles intended to foster asset accumulation, with consideration given to including individual development accounts, children's saving accounts, and college savings plans.

We believe our recommendations will cut poverty in half. The Urban Institute, which modeled the implementation of one set of our recommendations, estimates that four of our steps would reduce poverty by 26 percent, bringing us more than halfway toward our goal. Among their findings:

Taken together, our minimum wage, EITC, child credit, and childcare recommendations would reduce poverty by 26 percent. This would mean over 9 million fewer people in poverty and a national poverty rate of 9.1 percent—the lowest in recorded U.S. history.

The racial poverty gap would be narrowed. White poverty would fall from 8.7 percent to 7 percent. Poverty among African Americans would fall from 21.4 percent to 15.6 percent. Hispanic poverty would fall from 21.4 percent to 12.9 percent and poverty for all others would fall from 12.7 percent to 10.3 percent.

Child poverty and extreme poverty would both fall. Child poverty would drop by 41 percent. The number of people in extreme poverty would fall by over 2 million.

Millions of low- and moderate-income families would benefit. Almost half of the benefits would help low- and moderate-income families.

That these recommendations would reduce poverty by more than one quarter is powerful evidence that a 50 percent reduction can be reached within a decade.

The combined cost of our principal recommendations is in the range of $90 billion a year—a significant cost but one that is necessary and could be readily funded through a fairer tax system. An additional $90 billion in annual spending would represent about 0.8 percent of the nation's Gross Domestic Product, which is a small fraction of the money spent on tax changes that benefited primarily the wealthy in recent years. Consider that: The current annual costs of the tax cuts enacted by Congress in 2001 and 2003 are in the range of $400 billion a year.

In 2008 alone, the value of the tax cuts to households with incomes exceeding $200,000 a year is projected to be $100 billion.

Our recommendations could be fully paid for simply by bringing better balance to the federal tax system and recouping part of what has been lost by the excessive tax cuts of recent years. We recognize that serious action has serious costs, but the challenge before the nation is not whether we can afford to act, but rather that we must decide to act.

The Next Steps

In 2009, we will have a new president and a new Congress. Across the nation, there is a yearning for a shared national commitment to build a better, fairer, more prosperous country, with opportunity for all. In communities across the nation, policymakers, business people, people of faith, and concerned citizens are coming together. Our commitment to the common good compels us to move forward.

* * * * *

COMMENTARIES ON CAP REPORT

CHRISTOPHER HOWARD

From Poverty to Prosperity performs a valuable service by describing the poverty problem clearly and collecting many good ideas to remedy the problem. Now comes the hard part—figuring out how to translate these ideas into practice. Frankly, we have known for a while that more childcare assistance, a larger Earned Income Tax Credit (EITC) and many other recommendations in this report would reduce poverty. The main difficulty, now and throughout U.S. history, is convincing people in power to embrace these changes and fight for them. We need to think about politics as much as policy.

The authors of the report believe that the United States has an opportunity to do something significant about poverty. This opportunity is supposedly rooted in a national yearning for change (which is asserted but never proven) and upcoming elections. While I can see some positive signs, I also see trouble. As the authors note, poverty remains stubbornly high in the United States while inequality is growing. The report's recommendations, if enacted, would reduce both poverty and inequality. Nevertheless, the relationship between poverty and inequality has become more complicated in recent years, and it is possible to reduce inequality without doing much at all to relieve poverty. Politically, the temptation to do so is strong, which is why a report drawing attention to poverty is particularly important right now.

The missing piece here is the middle class. While inequality has worsened in recent decades, literally all the growth has occurred in the upper half of the income distribution. The gap between the rich and poor in this country has grown because the gap between the rich and the middle class has grown; the income gap between the poor and the middle class is virtually identical today to what it was 30 years ago. Thus, when you tax the affluent to pay for benefits targeted at the middle and upper-middle classes, you reduce inequality without reducing poverty. The U.S. government currently spends hundreds of billions of dollars each year doing just that. Major tax expenditures for homeowners and for workers with health and pension benefits are the best examples, but the Child Tax Credit qualifies as well. Some of our social regulations, such as the Family and Medical Leave Act, also help the haves more than the have-nots. This trend could easily continue. Many middle-class families are experiencing greater economic insecurity and having trouble affording health insurance, saving for their own retirement or saving for their child's education. Because political participation varies directly with income and education, and because fiscal constraints seem daunting, many elected officials will be inclined to focus on the middle class before they worry about the poor and the near-poor. Advocates who worry about poverty need to make sure that discussions about inequality do not leave out the most disadvantaged members of society. They should insist that any changes in policy address poverty *and* inequality.

As far as politics, the report is largely silent. The basic strategy consists of setting an ambitious goal, listing dozens of policy changes that would help achieve that goal, and arguing that the benefits of change would outweigh the costs. From *Poverty to Prosperity* is long on charts, tables, statistics and references to previous studies—the kind of evidence that policy experts and academics find persuasive. I'm just not sure that anyone else does. For instance, as Kent Weaver demonstrates in *Ending Welfare as We Know It* (Brookings, 2000), social scientific research did not have much impact on the 1996 welfare reform law. Instead, elected officials used such studies as ammunition to justify policy changes they already planned to support for personal, partisan or ideological reasons.

If part of the strategy is to attract more attention to poverty, my reading of recent history says to be careful. When issues surrounding poverty have been in the spotlight, the trend has been to retrench means-tested social programs; dramatic cuts in 1981 and 1996 are the best examples. On the other hand, when policymakers have worked a bit more behind the scenes, growth has been possible. During the 1980s and 1990s, eligibility for Medicaid and the EITC was expanded on several occasions, and EITC benefits increased substantially. In each case, there were few Congressional hearings and little media coverage. Advocates shrewdly attached their changes to much larger bills and watched while legislators debated other, more controversial provisions. Admittedly, "Be Quiet and Be Clever" may not be the most inspiring or most democratic strategy in the world. To win a truly public debate, however, the authors of this report may need to recast some of their recommendations in order to distribute benefits across a larger constituency, ranging from the poor to the middle class.

* * * * *

HERBERT J. GANS

In these dark days when almost no one in Washington talks about poverty, "A National Strategy to Cut Poverty in Half" is a welcome and comprehensive anti-poverty program. It also contains an implicit four-part strategy which is worth analyzing briefly because it is both a typical and an apolitical strategy.

It treats nonpoor Americans with *data-generating shock*, in order to impress them with the amount of poverty and inequality in the country and with *guilt-tripping*, in order to shame them for permitting these evils to exist. Then it advocates *economic rationality*, by proposing to spend $90 billion to save the country the $500 billion childhood poverty alone is said to cost, and it ends with *consensual rhetoric*, claiming a national "yearning for a shared national commitment to build a . . . fairer . . . country . . . with opportunity for all."

Many of us active in anti-poverty policy in the 1960s but outside politics used a similar strategy. Although it may have helped to prepare the substantive ground for the original War on Poverty, I do not think it accomplished its political goal, and I doubt it will work now.

Many nonpoor people are unmoved by inequality—in fact, many like to be slightly ahead of the Joneses. They are ambivalent about poverty, sympathizing with but also stigmatizing the poor, especially nonworking ones. While they want poverty ended, they oppose many specific anti-poverty policies, starting with welfare.

Consequently, policy must be complemented by an explicit political strategy, and let me suggest six parts of one that may be useful to activists and campaigning politicians.

1. Broaden the policy to cover the below-median-income population, the country's "working people," or target it mainly to the working poor but without excluding the politically less popular nonworking ones.
2. Wherever possible, add to the budgets and broaden the eligibility for already existing and thus politically accepted policies—e.g., EITC, the Child Tax Credit, etc. as well as other income and job programs known to get resources to the poor. Suggest realistic and politically feasible ways of funding them.
3. Demonstrate the policy's political virtues—e.g., how it might persuade its supporters and beneficiaries to vote and vote Democratic.
4. Participate in programs to increase voting among the poor, although they may wait until they have more reason to vote—i.e., the existence of an anti-poverty policy like this one.
5. Lobby for the policy with the Democratic frontrunners—unless the already-persuaded John Edwards is one. If funds and workers are limited, work instead in the congressional elections. A new anti-poverty policy requires a majority of liberal and center-left Democrats in both Houses.
6. Publicize the novel and long-range programs in order to place them on the political agenda and to familiarize people who will someday vote on and implement them.

*****

DAVID K. SHIPLER

This thoughtful report vividly illustrates the American contradiction: a society with the skills, but not the will, to alleviate poverty. Most of the problems addressed in this blueprint are susceptible to the enhancement of existing government programs and the addition of a few new, creative ideas. But the hardships afflicting poor families run across a broad spectrum. At one end are those easiest to overcome with more money, in the areas of housing, schooling, health, wages, childcare, asset building and the like. This is the part of the spectrum where the country has failed, as liberals rightly observe, in its public education, government services and private economy.

At the other end, more distant from ready solutions, stand the issues central to conservatives' arguments: the personal and family failures that become critical to a person's capacity in the competitive labor market. How to combat the bad parenting, teenage pregnancy, low graduation rates, inadequate skills, drug use, alienation, poor work ethics and other internal obstacles to success? Just as liberals are right to point to societal institutions, so conservatives are correct to aim at individual and family dysfunction. Both are part of the ecology of poverty.

It is easy for many conservatives to use individual disabilities to blame the victims and wash their hands of the issue. And many liberals find it convenient to blame societal institutions for creating the individual handicaps. At the extremes, these two ideologies freeze discussion. What we need is a multi-ideological approach that recognizes both ends of the spectrum and acknowledges the full sweep of the difficulties that burden families in destitution.

The recommendations here are dramatic, sensible and expensive investments with the likelihood of a handsome return. But they are only a step. They do not recognize fully that when a poor person in America presents her problem to an agency, she comes inside an invisible web of other problems that cannot be addressed unless we create gateways through which people can pass into multiple services. Imagine if a teacher with a hungry student could do more than toss the kid a Granola bar (as some have told me they do), but also had resources in school to check the family's eligibility for food stamps and refer them to a food bank or even to a malnutrition clinic if the child is underweight or developmentally delayed. Imagine if probation officers, pediatricians, job trainers, housing specialists and caseworkers of various kinds had the tools to address the issues backstage that jeopardize the performances of their clients. Solving poverty is a matter of connecting the dots, recognizing interactions among those in both the liberals' and the conservatives' favorite arenas, and then changing the ecological system.

*****

MTANGULIZI SANYIKA

The report's Executive Summary prescribes solutions that might have some impact on the protracted problem of poverty in the U.S. However, it raises more questions than it provides answers. The report sounds quite similar to other neoliberal ideas that have been proposed over the years on how to address the problems of poverty within the existing rules and structures. The report implies that poverty can be reduced while maintaining the existing race-class-gender relationships within the political economy. After years of observing the failed policy prescriptions that vacillate between government and market approaches, it is my conclusion that the types of "practical" recommendations in the report are limited as permanent solutions to the protracted problem of decades-old poverty. The issue of poverty elimination is linked to a variety of other social issues requiring a paradigm shift that transforms the social, political and economic relationships in American society. Problems such as globalization, wealth concentration, militarism, the environment, gentrification, healthcare, etc. are intrinsically linked to the problem of poverty. Poverty is not simply a problem of insufficient income; instead, it is also a problem of "opportunity deprivation" which is structural in nature as evidenced by the decades of systemic racism, sexism and wealth-income inequalities.

For instance, policy proposals to rebuild New Orleans—a low-income, predominantly Black city—must transcend the rhetoric of equitable intent, and instead develop models of a transformed nonracial, urban economic democracy. That is to say, a "new" New Orleans must eliminate all of the prior systemic inequalities based on race, class and gender, or we are simply recreating the "separate and unequal" status quo of the past. It is not enough to argue that 10 or 20 years from now poverty will be reduced by 50 percent. African Americans and poor people in New Orleans should not have to wait that long, especially the 40 percent who have lived in disgraceful poverty since the 1960s. As we watched billions of no-bid dollars and incentives flow through the hands of the established white elites, or observed the squandering of millions of taxpayer dollars on a sweetheart deal to mismanage the Road Home program, it is obvious that the rich keep getting richer at the people's expense. Radical solutions are required if poverty is to be eliminated in New Orleans. While I do not object to the proposed recommendations of the report, at best they are only transitional. Thus, I would argue that more systemic interventions are also required to eradicate both income inequality and opportunity deprivation.

The following five strategic approaches might move us closer to democracy by eradicating the race-class-gender inequalities and problems that existed in New Orleans and elsewhere for decades. Katrina simply exposed the magnitude of the problem that exists in all urban communities in the U.S. New Orleans will be a testing ground to develop an urban economic democracy that eliminates poverty.

First, reparations are due to African Americans and others who were exploited for centuries by the forces of government and capital in the building of this country. This is especially true for the resource-limited African Americans whose ancestors provided the free labor that built the agrarian South and laid the groundwork for industrialization of the North. The principle of reparations is a well-established international legal right that is due to Black Americans and others as well. Reparations could take many forms, including wealth and land transfers, cash payments, community development projects that address healthcare, housing, education, business development and other services that may equalize opportunity.

Secondly, there should be a victims' compensation fund established for the victims of Katrina, just as there was for the victims of 9/11, to compensate all victims of this disaster that resulted from human error. A legitimate claim can be made that levee failure and government neglect imposed unnecessary harm, loss of life and material belongings, and undue suffering on thousands of people, for which they should be compensated. A starting place might be $250,000 per household.

Thirdly, as the city is rebuilt, there should be specific provisions to enhance wealth-building opportunities for Black and poor people, such as access to homeownership for public housing residents, rental dwellers and Section 8 voucher holders. As the economy expands and diversifies, there should also be opportunities for asset-limited populations to develop partnerships with developers and asset-rich firms, in order to expand opportunity and wealth.

Fourthly, the 75,000 former Orleanian workers in the hospitality industry should be paid a "livable wage" with good benefits and working conditions. This alone would remove significant numbers of Orleanians from the income poverty rolls. A minimum wage will not eliminate poverty for the working poor. Locally based good jobs and employment training are also required.

Finally, there should be integrated federal, state and municipal policies that require schools to work, healthcare to be available, housing to remain affordable, public transit to work everywhere, public safety to be accountable, and deep taxation on intergenerational wealth transfers. Youth must be integrated into all aspects of poverty elimination, and illegal drugs and weapons *must* be eradicated from all communities.

Such a comprehensive approach is the only solution to the decades of systemic inequality and neglect. Transitional policies and programs are useful, but much more radically practical interventions are required to eliminate poverty, rather than to simply alleviate it.

* * * * *

WILLIAM E. SPRIGGS

The Center for American Progress put together a stellar team of experts on poverty. Their report is very comprehensive. A key component is to remind people that work must pay, and be able to lift people out of poverty. This truth ought to be self-evident; unfortunately, since the 1980s the discussion of fighting poverty has taken on the burden of fighting individual behavior.

The CAP recommendations on the minimum wage may appear to be silly to some, because of the degeneration in the debate. The report recommends raising the minimum wage and then indexing it to prevent the labor market from producing the oxymoron of working poor people.

People are poor because they do not make enough money. This limit could be because they cannot work. Laws prevent children from working, and not surprisingly, among Hispanics and African Americans huge shares of poor people are children. The elderly and the disabled, for the most part, also are unlikely to work, but are helped by Social Security. Children whose parents have died or are disabled are helped by Social Security as well, and now outnumber those children who are helped by Temporary Assistance to Needy Families (TANF), the reform of the previous entitlement, Aid to Families with Dependent Children (AFDC).

Among working-age adults, however, the problem of poverty is primarily the problem of needing higher wages and more opportunities to work. Of course, working-age women household heads in poverty are heavily affected by the need to earn enough for them and to support their nonworking dependent children (as opposed to their nonworking dependent parents who are helped by Social Security). In the 1990s, women were helped by previous increases in their human capital—thanks to lowering discriminatory barriers to women in education and in the labor market—and a re-cord- breaking increase in employment that helped pressure the easing of gender (and racial) discrimination in the labor market. The result was that the median earnings for women, for the first time, rose above the poverty threshold for a family of three. Childhood poverty dipped, accordingly. Similarly, in the 1960s, a then record labor market and measures to decrease racial discrimination pushed the median earnings of Black men above the poverty threshold for, first, a family of three, and then for a family of four. And, Black child poverty declined almost in half. Those are the only two periods of meaningful declines in American child poverty. And, both the 1960 and 1990 spurts were helped by increases in the federal minimum wage.

The hard reality of our economy is that it does generate bad jobs—those that pay low wages and lack benefits. And, in a competitive labor market, that means those who face the most hurdles—those created by society by discrimination and inequality, and those created by poor individual choice—end up losing the sprint for decent jobs. Clearly, poor individual choices alone cannot explain who ends up being poor—Scooter Libby, and his criminal record, Paris Hilton and Britney Spears, now a single mom, are evidence enough that poor choices are not the real issue. So, while it is true that poor choices can lead to poverty, not all mistakes land all people in poverty; and the deeper truth is that society's acceptance of low wages for the jobs we want done, and should value—child daycare worker, nursing home attendant—trap people below the poverty line, and because we need those jobs done, people who are virtuous, and people who have made mistakes, will end up in those jobs. The CAP report is important for putting that all in perspective.

* * * * *

MARGY WALLER

A review of The Center for American Progress' Task Force on Poverty report begins—and ends—with the report's title: *From Poverty to Prosperity: A National Strategy to Cut Poverty in Half.*

Others may have a detailed analysis of the task force policy recommendations. But because the report is premised on a goal to cut poverty, these recommendations will have little impact. If CAP had developed a different title and goal, there would be more payoff from the organizational endorsement of this set of proposals.

As it is, utilizing a goal to end poverty probably dooms the rest of the report, because it won't work.

A policy framework that slices and dices beneficiaries creates an "other," violating the big idea that we are all in this together. Rather than arguing to fix the economy for a distinct class—the poor—our narrative should describe an economy that works for all of us.

There are three problems with the poverty goal.

First, poverty is a flawed measure for assessing progress toward desired outcomes, including many of the report's proposals. As a result, a goal to "halve poverty" is both limited and limiting. CAP copied this initiative from the UK, where Tony Blair established a similar goal in 1999, but the definition and public understanding of poverty are vastly different in the UK than in the US, making the UK model difficult to transfer across the Atlantic.

Poverty in the UK is measured using absolute and relative measures of income and also by a material deprivation measure (added to ensure that families do not fall too far behind the rest in meeting material needs), all supporting an official national plan for social inclusion. In the US, the official poverty formula uses only an *absolute measure* of income deprivation based on household budgets in the 1950s. Since poverty signifies something quite narrow in our country, we need a new framework for the kind of multidimensional policy proposals in the CAP report.

Second, public understanding of the causes and remedies for poverty hinders adoption of the very policy solutions outlined in the CAP report. While advocates point to opinion surveys showing public support for "helping the needy," such arguments overlook the limitations of opinion polling. If the public support were indeed this strong, Congress would have acted accordingly long ago.

The limitations of the support identified by the polls are significant. Too many people believe that people are poor because of *bad decisions* or *personal moral failing.* While the percentage agreeing with such statements can shift depending on how the question is worded and where it falls in the survey, the agreement is so strong across surveys over time that it's folly to wrap policy proposals in a goal to reduce poverty.

In a recent Pew survey, 7 of 10 people agreed that the poor are too dependent on government assistance. And a review of the opinion surveys after the 1996 changes in federal welfare law finds as much as half the public is inclined to blame individual "lack of effort" for poverty, as many or more than before the law changed. It turns out that welfare changes didn't undermine conservative arguments after all.

Third, by defining the problem as "poverty," the CAP report opens the door to a losing scenario for policymaking. The media simplify these debates and portray them as two competing proposals. My crystal ball predicts proposals like these in any congressional debate over the best way to cut poverty in half:

1. The Law to Halve Poverty Over Ten Years with good schools, universal pre-K, financial education, expanded tax credits and Pell Grants, health coverage for all, expanded food stamps and childcare, indexed minimum wage, unions; and
2. Making Poverty History Act, stressing marriage and work.

Conservatives would demolish the first, comprehensive proposal because it goes far beyond the stated goal of raising income above the poverty line (about $20,000 for a family of 4), and the public won't support such spending proposals if they believe people are poor due to personal failures.

The CAP report and goal sets up a debate about "personal responsibility" that will feel sadly familiar to anyone who followed the evolution of welfare legislation in the last decade. We should develop policy goals by consulting the research evidence and anticipating the debate's impact on policy outcomes and public understanding.

Progressives have already lost on the issues of poverty and "personal responsibility." It's time to recast the goal as one of economic mobility and social inclusion. CAP missed an opportunity by sticking to an old—and failed—framework for this debate. The progressive agenda and political campaigns of the near and longer term will benefit greatly if CAP would expend its considerable expertise and resources on developing an alternative lens designed to build broad public support for these policy solutions.

* * * * *

JILL CUNNINGHAM

"In the fight to overcome extreme poverty, the poorest families are the first ones to take action. Make us your partners as you move forward on the agenda of peace, development and human rights for all. Let's pool our knowledge, yours and ours. Let's act now, no longer separately, but together."

Such was the call to partnership that Tita Villarosa, a grandmother who has lived in a cemetery in Manila for more than 15 years, delivered in a face-to-face meeting with then-UN secretary general Kofi Annan on October 17, 2005. She was part of a small delegation from impoverished communities in 8 countries (including the U.S.) who dialogued with Annan on that International Day for the Eradication of Poverty (www.oct17.org).

It is Tita's call for a partnership involving the experience, know-how and participation of people in poverty themselves that, in our view, is lacking in the CAP's nonetheless comprehensive report. To have seen people with a direct experience of persistent poverty as experts on the CAP Task Force on Poverty, and to more expressly acknowledge what struggling families do already to fight poverty, would, in our view, have strengthened the report's ambitious and far-reaching policy proposals.

In November of 2005, independent UN expert Arjun Sengupta followed this vital strategy, consulting with those hit hard by Hurricane Katrina and its aftermath, as well as people affected by long-term poverty in other communities. In his report on extreme poverty and human rights in the US, he emphasized that *"The full participation of people living in poverty should be ensured in the design, implementation, monitoring and assessment of programs for combating poverty. Such programs should build on poor people's own efforts, . . . responding to their actual needs. "* (http://www.ohchr.org/english/bodies/chr/docs/62chr/E.CN.4.2006.43. Add.1.pdf, p.2, my emphasis). We commend CAP's idea of an annual report on progress, but would like to see the expressed framework for people in poverty to be part of that evaluation.

Such a multivoiced partnership is not easy, nor automatic. Families and communities in extreme poverty have had sometimes generations of humiliations and failures. Very few initiatives in society have proven to them that they have an expertise to share. Thus, we need to create more opportunities that bring people from different social backgrounds together to work on common aspirations. Such initiatives create greater understanding of the obstacles faced by families in poverty, and can help generate greater social cohesion and solidarity.

Cutting poverty in half—whether in the U.S. or internationally—is insufficient. Tita and others like her, here and abroad, do not ask to halve poverty; they want to eradicate it. Our experience has shown that, unless anti-poverty strategies make special efforts, from the start, to reach those living in extreme poverty, the gap between them and the rest of the population simply increases, economically and in terms of social exclusion. Programs that effectively include the "hardest to reach," however, have proven to benefit all concerned. To this end, we appreciate CAP's "progressive universalism" approach and applaud the real goal: "to end American poverty in a generation." Or sooner. As Tita said, "Let's act now . . . together."

* * * * *

MICHAEL R. WENGER

I applaud The Center for American Progress for trying to put the elimination of poverty back on the public policy agenda. The report of its Task Force on Poverty is an important step in this direction.

But the report's failure to acknowledge the critical intersection of race and poverty is deeply disappointing:

1. Racism is never explicitly mentioned as a cause of poverty, which risks leaving the impression that the racial disparities the report enumerates have nothing to do with the legacy of our oppressive history or with persistent institutional racism today.

2. There is no mention of addressing racism as a way to reduce poverty, which guarantees that the report's recommendations will not level the playing field for people of color.

Failure to recognize that racism and poverty are inextricably intertwined has significant policy implications. For example, the report recommends ways in which to assist with prisoner re-entry, but it never mentions the mandatory sentencing policies that disproportionately and unjustly send people of color to prison in the first place. Similar examples of racist policies and practices must be addressed in education, employment, and access to homeownership and quality healthcare if we are to create equal opportunity for people of color. The preponderance of black faces in the gruesome post-Katrina pictures was no accident. Even President Bush acknowledged, at least verbally, that the legacy of our history of racism played a major role in the disproportionate impact of the disaster on African Americans.

We know the issue of race is fraught with emotion and is, thus, a difficult topic to discuss. And the report does make the point that its recommendations will narrow the racial poverty gap. Fair enough. However, unless we recognize racism as a root cause of poverty and propose specific steps to uproot it, we will treat only symptoms. The disease of racism will continue unchecked, and ending poverty will remain a distant dream.

Public officials shy away from the issue because they believe it alienates white voters. But a think tank like The Center for American Progress, by thoughtfully and forthrightly addressing the issue and providing data to demonstrate the continuing salience of race as a determinant of treatment in society, could educate the public that the civil rights legislation of the 1960s did not create racial equity. This could begin to change the racial climate, build a critical mass of support for directly confronting racism, and offer some political cover for public officials.

The Katrina disaster, by riveting the nation's attention, created a window of opportunity—still slightly ajar, though closing fast—to talk more openly about the interconnection of poverty and race. We should seize what remains of this window to advance the racial dialogue in a way that does not blame people for past wrongs or ascribe racial animus to current policies and practices, but reflects upon our collective community responsibility to address past wrongs, as well as current, often subconscious, racist practices that persist in our institutions. As Rabbi Abraham Heschel has told us: "We may not all be guilty, but we are all responsible."

* * * * *

CENTER FOR AMERICAN PROGRESS RESPONSE

ANGELA GLOVER BLACKWELL, PETER EDELMAN, CASSANDRA BUTTS & MARK GREENBERG

We thank PRRAC for encouraging discussion of and commentary on our report. We wrote the report to show that the nation has the capacity to dramatically reduce poverty and to help make the case for a national goal of cutting poverty in half in the next ten years. The report is one of a number of recent initiatives and efforts across the country—from the faith-based community, civil rights groups, mayors and others—seeking to elevate local, state and national attention to poverty. We are encouraged both by the growing momentum and by the number of people and groups who have found our report helpful. We recognized that our recommendations, while extensive, were not a comprehensive cataloging of a complete agenda for progressive social change in America. Addressing poverty is one part of a broader agenda, but we wrote the report to emphasize that it should be an essential part of that agenda.

We agree with a number of observations made by commenters. For example, we agree with Jill Cunningham about the importance of active involvement and participation of the poor, and with Herbert Gans about the importance of promoting higher voting turnout among low-income people, elevating attention to poverty in the 2008 elections, and building on successful and popular programs. We share David Shipler's view that a successful strategy needs to meld calls for social and personal responsibility.

We agree with Mtangulizi Sanyika that poverty is not simply a problem of insufficient income but is also a structural problem of "opportunity deprivation." That is why we propose a strategy combining the four themes of decent work, promoting opportunity, ensuring security and helping people build wealth. And we agree with Bill Spriggs, both about the critical role of adequate wages, and about the importance of not treating the failures of the labor market as failures of personal responsibility.

Our report includes twelve recommendations which we believe, taken together, would cut poverty in half. Several commenters point to areas that we didn't discuss or that they wished we had discussed in greater detail. In particular, Mike Wenger wishes we had spent more time discussing the role of and calling for efforts to bring an end to racism. We are very mindful of the central role that racism has played in American social policy, and a number of Task Force members have spent much of their lives addressing it. We think that an important contribution of this report is that, in addition to highlighting the role of racism, we call for measuring the extent to which policies reduce the racial poverty gap. Moreover, our proposals, if implemented, would result in the lowest African-American and Hispanic poverty rates in U.S. history and a dramatic reduction in the racial poverty gap. At the same time, a comprehensive agenda should include but must go beyond the report's recommendations—as we emphasize in the report.

Almost all of the commenters speak favorably of the need for a renewed national effort to address poverty. Several, however, raise questions about how to make the most effective case or about the political viability of focusing on poverty. Herbert Gans emphasizes the limits of "guilt-tripping" and "consensual rhetoric." Chris Howard suggests the importance of tying efforts to those that benefit the middle class, and working "behind the scenes" with a "be quiet and be clever strategy." Margy Waller asserts that it is folly to wrap policy proposals in a goal of reducing poverty.

We agree that guilt-tripping is not an effective strategy, but we think a broad consensus can be built, on moral and economic grounds, that sustained poverty is contrary to our national interest. The moral case is not that we should feel guilty about poverty but rather that it is wrong to tolerate it. The economic case cannot be limited to a call to narrow self-interest, because most Americans aren't poor and don't risk persistent poverty. But Americans respond to more than narrow self-interest— one compelling example is the success of the minimum wage movement; another is the increasing recognition of the importance of early education to the nation's future growth. Our nation needs a healthy, well-educated, capable workforce in order to be globally competitive in the 21st century. The research of Harry Holzer of Georgetown University and his colleagues found that poverty imposes a half trillion dollar cost on the economy each year.

For many issues, an effective approach can draw upon the shared interests of low- and moderate-income Americans. We urge a framework of progressive universalism—that when a problem or need is shared by many, the solution should provide help to all, with the most help to those who need it most. However, an effective long-run strategy cannot just talk publicly about the middle class while seeking to quietly slip provisions to help the poor into bills. If legislators don't see or hear a constituency urging them to do more than address middle-class needs, why would they do so? Further, some issues that are fundamental to addressing poverty—helping disconnected youth re-engage, prisoner re-entry, housing and development strategies to address concentrated poverty—are not likely to be prominent in a middle-class agenda. The agendas to address middle-class insecurity and to reduce poverty are overlapping and complementary, but limiting our public discussion to the middle class won't get us far enough.

Margy Waller essentially dismisses the relevance to the U.S. of the UK's commitment to end child poverty because the UK uses a broader set of measures of poverty. But advancing a commitment to a national goal could, and likely would, generate renewed discussions about how to better measure poverty. When Tony Blair in 1999 announced the goal of ending child poverty, there was no established official poverty measure in the UK for purposes of reaching the goal. The measures were announced in 2003, after a consultation process, and four years after the national goal was declared. Since 1998-99, absolute child poverty has fallen in the UK by more than half, relative poverty by 18 percent, and the Tory Party leadership now speaks favorably of the importance of reducing child poverty. UK policymakers urge the need for both poverty reduction and social inclusion, but it is highly unlikely that there would be the same pressure for efforts to reduce child poverty in the absence of a quantifiable, measurable goal.

Waller also contends that talking about poverty is doomed to fail because many people believe the poor are at fault for their conditions, and progressives have "lost" the personal responsibility issue. Polling data show that the public is pretty evenly divided on whether the biggest explanation for poverty is individual behavior or social conditions, but the data also show that most people believe it's a combination of the two. This isn't reason to avoid talking about poverty. Of course it's true that poverty is caused by both individual and social causes. We won't generate public support for policies that appear to reward bad behavior—whether we talk about "poverty" or another term or concept. Our report makes clear that the persistence of poverty cannot be reduced to individual failings, but it also shows how the nation can dramatically reduce poverty in ways that are entirely consistent with expecting and rewarding individual initiative and responsibility.

We are very encouraged by the increasing attention to poverty in Congress, among the public, and among presidential candidates. Such attention can and should grow in the coming months—a John Zogby poll recently found that most voters would be more likely (58 percent more likely, 8 percent less likely) to vote for a candidate committed to a goal of cutting poverty in half in ten years. This is a key moment in which to advance a national campaign to address poverty in America, and we look forward to working with a broad range of people and groups in such an effort.

Unions Make Us Strong

Julius G. Getman

My 2010 book *Restoring the Power of Unions: It Takes a Movement* (Yale Univ. Press) analyzes the current weakened state of organized labor and evaluates the prospect for union resurgence.

For organized labor to regain power, it must become again, as it was in the past, a social movement. Organized labor today is in the main a progressive interest group, but not a movement. To constitute a movement requires something more than money, members and economic power, significant though all these factors are. A movement entails developing and utilizing the passionate energies of workers. It means fostering solidarity across unions and occupations. It requires leaders who are willing to trust and who are committed to sharing power with the union's rank-and-file. The spirit of movement also requires a concern for issues such as environmental justice, racial equality and the rights of immigrants which transcend the economic well-being of the union members. The spirit necessary for a vital movement remains largely dormant, although never totally absent in most labor organizations. In some labor organizations, it is abundantly present. Those organizations are the model that shows the way to a broader union resurgence. They demonstrate that achieving and maintaining a spirit of movement is possible, but is never easy. In every case in which it has been accomplished, the spirit of movement has required internal struggle and leaders with faith in the rank-and-file membership.

HERE

The history of the Hotel Employees & Restaurant Employees International Union (HERE) from its early days to the mid-1980s demonstrates that along the way the union has faced virtually every problem that has confronted the labor movement

178

generally, including employer opposition, corruption, mob infiltration, weak internal leadership, fear of change, political divisions, racism, sexism, anti-immigrant prejudice and economic catastrophe. It has successfully overcome its internal problems through a dynamic collaboration between up-from-the-ranks working-class leadership and progressive, college-trained political activists with roots in student and civil-rights movements. The collaboration began when Vincent Sirabella, a long-time union dissident from an immigrant, working-class background who headed the union's local of maintenance workers at Yale, hired and trained John Wilhelm, a Yale graduate and long-time political activist. Together with a remarkable group of organizers and activists, they won a series of victories culminating with the successful organizing campaign and strike by Yale's clerical and technical workers. The Connecticut and Yale locals of HERE in the early 1980s represented a return to a model of collaboration between workers and intellectuals that had been absent from organized labor for many years. Its main architect was Sirabella. The struggle at Yale and the tutelage of Sirabella were crucial to the leadership development of John Wilhelm, who is today president of HERE's successor organization, UNITE HERE.

The history of the HERE is my focus because it has been transformed since the 1970s from a business union dedicated to the well-being of the staff to a workers' movement. This transformation is evident in its diverse and dedicated leadership and in the successes of its key locals in such cities as New York, San Francisco, Las Vegas, Los Angeles and Chicago. In each of these cities, the local unions have organized successfully, bargained effectively and allied themselves with progressive forces on major social issues. In all of these locations and others as well, HERE's success has been achieved despite the enmity of employers who have routinely resisted organization and have tried to use the bargaining process as a technique for weakening or destroying the union.

The greatest problem for unions generally is organizing workers in the face of determined employer resistance. Our current labor laws give an advantage to employers and make organizing difficult and often dangerous. Those unions that have had success in organizing in recent years have done so by obtaining agreement from employers to remain neutral and to grant recognition once a union was able to obtain authorization cards from a majority of workers in a mutually accepted unit. Obtaining such agreements has generally involved major struggles with employers who have rarely if ever accepted them without pressure. The success of the neutrality and card check agreements led organized labor to seek to have recognition through card check made a part of the National Labor Relations Act. This was the major provision of the Employee Free Choice Act (EFCA) which organized labor spent large sums of money on and devoted great resources to in the aftermath of Democratic Party victories in the 2008 elections. Organized labor's focus on EFCA was a mistake: Augmenting the right to strike, by outlawing an employer's ability to permanently replace striking workers, would be considerably more valuable in building a sense of movement.

Not all the obstacles to labor's advance come from outside. Internal divisions—some ideological, some political and others personal—have been a major obstacle to worker solidarity, as labor history, including that of HERE, demonstrates with depressing regularity.

WE NEED A STRONG, PROGRESSIVE MOVEMENT

A strong, vital and progressive labor movement is important for our society, both economically and politically. When unions were strong, the United States had the longest period of equitably shared prosperity in our nation's history—a sharp contrast with our current situation of a weak labor movement and growing economic discontent and gross disparities in wealth. The weakness of organized labor has had a negative impact on our political culture. It has made it relatively easy for right-wing demagogues to shamelessly appropriate the banner of populism and to turn to their own advantage the feelings of working-class people that they are not visible to those in power.

It is important to explain the decline of the labor movement, why it has failed to organize the unorganized, has lost strikes, and has become more professional but less militant and less inspiring. The role of law must be recognized in this, but there is also need to place emphasis on the problems inherent in the structure of the current union movement and the attitudes of its leaders. The labor movement bears more responsibility for its decline than most union leaders, liberal commentators and scholars have been willing to acknowledge. Understanding this complex issue requires focus on the law and the practice of organizing. The National Labor Relations Act (NLRA) has provided a system of representation elections for determining whether a group of workers is to be represented by a union. Management's advantage in the process comes mainly from its opportunity to assemble workers and argue that unionization would be a risk for them and not an advantage. Employers are permitted to reject union requests to similarly address the worker voters and state the case for unionization.

Because of his successes at Yale and elsewhere, Sirabella in the early 1980s was appointed HERE's director of organizing. Sirabella believed that the model he developed at Yale could transform the labor movement, and he began a national organizing campaign, which failed in immediate terms but which brought a new group of aggressive organizers into the unions. From that failure came the seeds of later success.

HERE's transformation into a movement came through a series of individual struggles: how Local 226, the Culinary, became a major force in Las Vegas after winning the Frontier strike, one of the longest and most bitter struggles in labor history, which grew out of the determination of the Frontier Hotel's new owners to reduce wages and rid themselves of the union; how Local 11 in Los Angeles was transformed from a bastion of Anglo supremacy to a diverse battler for immigrant rights; how Local 2 in San Francisco managed to unite radical activists with long-time rank-and-file workers to become a major force in California.

THE MERGER

HERE subsequently merged with UNITE, an amalgamation of garment industry unions. The merger made obvious sense to most observers and supporters of HERE. It was thought likely to strengthen both unions. HERE had a growing membership base but was sorely lacking in money to fund organizing and job actions. UNITE had great resources, including prime NY property and a successful bank, but a declining membership base. Each union had a long history of organizing immigrant workers. The leaders of the two unions spoke a common language and seemed committed to similar progressive values. Bruce Raynor of UNITE became general president and John Wilhelm was designated as co-president.

DIFFERING LEADERSHIP STYLES

However, behind the apparent similarities lay very different styles of leadership and different approaches to organizing. Wilhelm's style of leadership is notably collaborative, while Raynor's is notably top-down. Wilhelm and other leaders of HERE believed in organizing through worker committees. Raynor favored organizing through deals between himself and management officials. An open dispute erupted when it became apparent that Wilhelm and not Raynor would be elected general president at the union's 2009 convention. The dispute became open and increasingly ugly in the Winter of 2008. It involved several lawsuits, including one brought by Raynor to force dissolution of the merger. The battle was made far more bitter and potentially destructive by the involvement of Andy Stern, president of the Service Employees International Union (SEIU). Stern's goal was to incorporate both UNITE and HERE into SEIU. To achieve this goal, he supported Raynor's insistence that the merger be dissolved. When Wilhelm and his allies rejected Stern's proposal, Stern and Raynor created Workers United, composed of dissident elements in UNITE HERE. Bruce Raynor was promptly elected president of the new organization, which announced that it would raid UNITE HERE locals. A long, bitter battle ensued which, despite the Workers United advantages in money and staff, was won by UNITE HERE, which held fast and won the loyalty of its members and the support of key leaders of organized labor.

THE NLRA ELECTION PROCESS

The fact that the NLRA election process does not work well for unions is well recognized by commentators and union spokespeople, most of whom focus on unlawful employer resistance and the law's system of woefully inadequate remedies. It is partly with a view to avoiding the harmful impact of illegal employer behavior that unions made passage of the EFCA their major goal. Earlier field studies indicate that unions and academic commentators have exaggerated the impact of the threats and reprisals, and they have for too long limited themselves to what is called "hot-shop organizing," i.e., focusing on locations where worker discontent is evident.

The ability to strike is critical to the success of the labor movement. And the law, particularly the right of employers to hire permanent replacements, has turned out to be a significant hindrance to labor's effective use of the strike. The secondary-boycott laws are both harmful and unconstitutional, and the Racketeer Influenced and Corrupt Organizations Act (RICO) has a potentially devastating effect on the strength of the strike weapon.

PROPOSED CHANGES TO THE NLRA

EFCA was unlikely to provide the great boost to organizing that its proponents look forward to and its opponents dread. EFCA would not do away with organizing campaigns: The employer's advantage in terms of access to employees would remain a critical factor. Passage of the act would lead many employers to conduct anti-union campaigns earlier than they might otherwise. It is vital to amend the NLRA to prohibit employers from hiring permanent replacement workers in place of strikers. The regular use of permanent replacement workers during the 1980s has made organized labor fearful, with good reason, of striking. However, throughout labor history, successful strikes have been crucial to organizing success.

It is important to consider whether the NLRA, administered by a supposedly expert agency, is a worthwhile scheme or whether it should be scrapped and replaced by a different federal act or by state law. The NLRA is worth saving, but it needs a fundamental overhaul. Board members should be chosen from a limited pool of neutral experts, possibly from the National Academy of Arbitrators, and a special court should review its decisions. Among the needed amendments to the NLRA are the following:

- The board's remedial power needs to be increased.
- Injunctions against employers' unfair labor practices need to be regularly issued, just as they are currently issued against union secondary boycotts.
- Unions need to be given equal time to respond to employer speeches and meetings, and the election process should be accelerated.
- Employees unlawfully fired during an organizing campaign should be quickly reinstated.
- Most significantly, strikers who engage in no serious misconduct should not be risking their jobs when they lawfully walk out.

A frequently made suggestion is to permit minority bargaining, wherein unions which do not represent a majority of workers in a unit bargain contracts for their own members. Several prominent labor scholars believe that the NLRA, properly interpreted, permits minority bargaining. I disagree. Minority bargaining violates the law and permitting it would not do much to strengthen the labor movement.

SUMMARY

It is important to recognize the distinction between organized labor in its current state and a vital, democratic labor movement. Too often, union leaders have failed to take needed chances or to accept responsibility for their organizing and bargaining failures. It is possible to organize and increase worker power in the face of employer opposition and a hostile NLRB, as several unions—including HERE—have demonstrated. Fear of failure has made unions too cautious and unwilling to depart from the antiquated models. Taking chances is critical. Indeed, failed efforts, such as HERE's national organizing drive of the late 1980s, have provided the basis for later success. The success of the labor movement is critical to the goal of a just society. For all its flaws and weaknesses, organized labor provides the most effective voice for the workers, immigrants and progressive causes.

A Freedom Budget for All Americans

Chester Hartman

The incoming Obama administration, John Podesta's Center for American Progress and others seeking to vastly reduce or eliminate poverty in America—39 million of our fellow countrymen, -women and -children live in poverty, according to the obsolete government measure that understates the problem—would do well to look to and emulate a half-century-old model: A Freedom Budget for All Americans.

It was the work of economist Leon Keyserling and Bayard Rustin [see chapter on Bayard Rustin in this volume], the legendary civil rights and nonviolent resistance activist best known for his role as organizer-in-chief of the 1963 March on Washington, then-executive director of the A. Philip Randolph Institute, named to honor the equally legendary head of the Brotherhood of Sleeping Car Porters and who served as the Institute's president. The foreword is by Martin Luther King, Jr.

The Freedom Budget's seven basic objectives (details of the program of course are too long to be described here) were:

1. To provide full employment for all who are willing and able to work, including those who need education or training to make them willing and able.
2. To assure decent and adequate wages to all who work.
3. To assure a decent living standard to those who cannot or should not work.
4. To wipe out slum ghettos and provide decent homes for all Americans.
5. To provide decent medical care and adequate educational opportunities to all Americans, at a cost they can afford.
6. To purify our air and water and develop our transportation and natural resources on a scale suitable to our growing needs.
7. To unite sustained full employment with sustained full production and high economic growth.

184

The Freedom Budget proposed an outlay of $185 billion in 10 years which "sounds like a great deal of money, and it is a great deal of money." But it presumed, indeed called for, an expansion of the nation's economy, leading to increased federal revenues. And of course, even adjusting for 2009 dollars, that sum is dwarfed by what we now spend in bail-out and war funding. The document reported that 34 million Americans were then living in poverty, 28 million others "just on the edge." Almost one-third of our nation lives in poverty or want. (Shades of FDR . . .)

The 211 signers of the document represented a who's who of late 1960s progressive thinking and activism: Walter Reuther, I.W. Abel, David Dubinsky, Albert Shanker et al. from the labor movement; academics Kenneth Clark, John Kenneth Galbraith, Gunnar Myrdal, Hylan Lewis, C. Vann Woodward, David Riesman et al.; civil rights leaders Dorothy Height, Roy Wilkins, Floyd McKissick, Whitney Young, Jr., John Lewis, Vernon Jordan; Ralph Bunche, Ossie Davis, Ruby Dee, Jules Feiffer, Father Robert Drinan, Burke Marshall, Benjamin Spock . . . [Truth in advertising: I was one of the signers, in my then-position at the MIT-Harvard Joint Center for Urban Studies—something I had forgotten about until retrieving a copy of the document from the NY Public Library's wonderful Schomberg Center for Research in Black Culture.]

Randolph's introduction eloquently speaks in a voice that could well be Barack Obama's, characterizing America 2009:

"[In] the richest and most productive society ever known to man, the scourge of poverty and racism must be abolished—not in some distant future, not in this generation, but within the next ten years! . . . The tragedy is that the workings of our economy so often pit the white poor and the black poor against each other at the bottom of society . . . [A]ll Americans are the victims of our failure as a nation to distribute democratically the fruits of our abundance. For, directly or indirectly, not one of us is untouched by the steady spread of slums, the decay of our cities, the segregation and overcrowding of our public schools, the shocking deterioration of our hospitals, the violence and chaos in our streets, the idleness of able-bodied men deprived of work, and the anguished demoralization of our youth . . . [T]he "Freedom Budget" is not visionary or utopian, It is feasible. It is concrete. It is specific. It talks dollars and sense. It sets goals and priorities. It tells how these can be achieved. And it places responsibility for leadership with the Federal Government, which alone has the resources equal to the task."

Yes, we can . . .

The Kerner Commission: Remembering, Forgetting and Truth-Telling

Bruce R. Thomas

The National Advisory Commission on Civil Disorders (NACCD) released its report 40 years ago—on March 1, 1968. The NACCD was popularly known as the Kerner Commission, after its chair, Governor Otto Kerner of Illinois. The vice-chair was New York City Mayor John Lindsay. Kerner was a Democrat, Lindsay a Republican. The other nine members reflected the standard political arithmetic of such commissions:

Four Members of Congress: Senator Edward Brooke (R-MA), Senator Fred Harris (D-OK), Congressman James Corman (D-CA), Congressman William McCulloch (R-OH).

One corporate executive: Charles Thornton, CEO, Litton Industries.

One labor leader: I.W. Abel, President, United Steelworkers of America.

One state government executive: Katherine Peden, Commissioner of Commerce, State of Kentucky.

One law enforcement official: Herbert Jenkins, Chief of Police, Atlanta, GA.

One civil rights leader: Roy Wilkins, Executive Director, National Association for the Advancement of Colored People.

Nine Commissioners were white, two African-American; ten were male, one female. Of the eleven members, two are alive: Edward Brooke and Fred Harris.

I worked on the Kerner Commission staff. What follows are reflections on the meaning of the Kerner Commission Report (KCR) as a matter of remembering, forgetting and truth-telling.

* * * * *

The French philosopher and critic Ernest Renan argued that a country's unifying sense of self entails both forgetting and remembering. The French envelop the St. Bartholomew's Day massacre in amnesia. America has done much the same in the matter of race and racism. The KCR assembled a remarkable brief in support not only of remembering our nation's racist past but also of acknowledging the multiple ways in which the consequences of that past are written into the nation's present. Two key paragraphs in the KCR summary told the truth in plain, blunt terms:

- (Paragraph One)
  This is our basic conclusion: Our nation is moving toward two societies, one black, one white—separate and unequal.
- (Paragraph Two)
  What white Americans have never fully understood—but what the Negro can never forget—is that white society is deeply implicated in the ghetto. White institutions created it, white institutions maintain it, and white society condones it.

The two paragraphs are markedly different in their relationship to the text of the report.

Paragraph one brings forward to the beginning of the KCR key phrases and concepts from the conclusions to chapter 16 ("The Future of the Cities") :

- *The nation is rapidly moving toward two increasingly separate Americas. Within two decades, this division could be so deep that it would be almost impossible to unite:*
  - *a white society principally located in suburbs, in smaller central cities and in the peripheral parts of large central cities; and*
  - *a Negro society largely concentrated within large central cities.*

Paragraph two does not preview subsequent narrative language. It performs two purposes. One is to state in a few carefully crafted words the racist theme and argument of the KCR. The actual language of the narrative comes at the opening of chapter 4, "The Basic Causes." Acknowledging that the causes of racial disorders are "a massive tangle of issues and circumstances," the report goes on to say:

- *Despite these complexities, certain fundamental matters are clear. Of these, the most fundamental is the racial attitude and behavior of white Americans toward black Americans. Race prejudice has shaped our history decisively in the past; it now threatens to do so again. White racism is essentially responsible for the explosive mixture which has been accumulating in our cities since the end of World War II.*

The second purpose or function of paragraph two is to place in the reader's mind a summary explanatory category for the myriad of concrete details about the black experience in America that suffuse the 265 pages of the main narrative text. From a host of candidates, here are two such details:

- *[D]ifferential food prices constitute another factor convincing urban Negroes in low-income neighborhoods that whites discriminate against them. (p.141)*
- *Most Negroes distrust what they refer to as the "white press." As one interviewer reported:*
  - *The average black person couldn't give less of a damn about what the media say. The intelligent black person is resentful at what he considers to be a totally false portrayal of what goes on in the ghetto. Most black people see the newspapers as mouthpieces of the "power structure." (p. 206)*

With hindsight, we can today say that paragraph two unwittingly served a third purpose: as a preview of one of the three reports that make up the largely unknown second volume of the KCR: "Supplemental Studies for The National Advisory Commission on Civil Disorders." Released in July 1968, "Supplemental Studies" presented the results of inquiries commissioned (but not endorsed) by the NACCD: "Racial Attitudes in Fifteen American Cities"; "Between Black and White—The Faces of American Institutions in the Ghetto"; and "Who Riots? A Study of Participation in the 1967 Riots."

The "Between Black and White" study generally supports paragraph two, but in a more nuanced way. This study, done by a team led by Peter Rossi from Johns Hopkins University, sought to understand "the interface between central community institutions and urban ghettos. . . ." It focused on police, teachers, social workers, merchants, employers and political workers. Two of the study's four principal findings were:

1. "Although our respondents were aware that their cities faced severe problems of housing, education, poverty, crime and unemployment, *their views can be characterized as optimistic denials of the full seriousness of the position of urban Negroes in their cities.*"
2. "Our respondents' explanations of why civil disorders were occurring showed a contradictory pattern of reasons. On the one hand, they were very willing to concede that important sources of civil disorders lay in the basic conditions of ghetto life—poverty, unemployment, poor housing. On the other hand, they gave a much more important role to militants and 'agitation' than the Commission's Report was able to find was actually the case."

(Italics in the original)

So: How do we explain this rare instance of remembering and truth-telling in a nation's public discourse?

At the July 29, 1967 press conference announcing his creation of the NACCD, President Lyndon Johnson laid out the questions the commission was to answer (What happened? Why? How to prevent recurrences in the future?) and also issued a truth-telling charge: "As best you can, find the truth and express it in your report."

But presidential exhortation was no guarantee of commission execution. How did the commission find its way toward remembering and truth-telling?

Five explanations come to mind. First, one might say that truth-telling possibilities are unleashed when history explodes. So it did in the first nine months of 1967 in the United States; there were, in this period, some 164 separate incidents of urban rioting. Two were momentous: Newark and Detroit. The images in the nation's media were staggering, almost beyond comprehension. This domestic explosion of violence took the country out of the realm of business as usual—and then, as if the domestic events were insufficient, came a second eruption of illusion-shattering violence, in February 1968: the Tet offensive in Vietnam.

The second explanation has to do with the nature of the beast. Commissions like Kerner are born of a political act that creates a nonpolitical space. For both commission members and staff, the work is a career parenthetical. Involvement with the commission entailed no negative personal or political consequences. The voice of the commission was a collective (this is *our* conclusion) in which no single voice could be singled out for criticism or retribution. The self-editing that is a constituent part of the political mind was largely checked in at the commission's cloakroom.

Third is the commission experience itself. For both commission members and staff, producing the report was an education, as much affective as cognitive. A number of commissioners traveled to cities where riots had occurred. The commissioners had homework and, to a remarkable degree, did it, as, for example, in reading staff papers. Particularly notable among those papers was the "Harvest of Racism" document prepared by research director Bob Shellow and his team. Though never publicly released, it exercised considerable internal influence.

Fourth, there were the witnesses, the men and women who appeared in person before the commission to give testimony. Over months of time, the commissioners listened to an array of voices that sketched out a portrait of America that became as undeniable as it was uncomfortable. The cumulative impact of this chorus is revealed on the final page of the KCR narrative, the stunningly brief conclusion built around the words of one witness whose testimony came early in the life of the commission. The speaker was Dr. Kenneth B. Clark, and the conclusion quoted his words:

- *I read that report . . . of the 1919 riot in Chicago, and it is as if I were reading the report of the investigating committee on the Harlem riot of 1935, the report of the investigating committee on the Harlem riot of 1943, the report of the McCone Commission on the Watts riot.*

- *I must again in candor say to you members of this Commission—it is a kind of Alice in Wonderland with the same moving picture reshown over and over again, the same analysis, the same recommendations and the same inaction.*

The fifth explanation rests upon the foundational four. It involved a dollop of artifice, a little procedural two-step that gave us the two memorable paragraphs in the Summary. I have one version of this artifice; I don't know definitively if it's wholly true, partly true or not true at all. But even if its specifics are not precisely true, the version is nonetheless valid as a representation of the human and political process that shaped the final version of the KCR, particularly the summary.

The version is this: The time came to finalize the report. The day before the final vote approving the text, Mayor Lindsay said to the commissioners that no one would read the full report and it needed a few short prefatory paragraphs that would convey in just a few words the spirit and meaning of the report and the convictions of the commissioners. The commission agreed. Lindsay volunteered to draft those few short prefatory paragraphs that night and to present them at the final meeting the next day. Lindsay presented his draft the next day; the commission accepted it; and so the report opened with those memorable words.

In fact, Lindsay had several weeks earlier asked some of his mayoral staff who were active in assisting his commission work to start drafting those few short prefatory pages. Lindsay had the pages in his back pocket when he volunteered to draft them overnight. He had decided to choose the most propitious moment for the idea of their necessity that would optimize the likelihood of their acceptance.

Accepted they were—and, in the minds of millions of Americans, the two key paragraphs in the summary became the Kerner Commission Report. The two volumes of the complete report comprise some 650 pages, but it was these two paragraphs in the summary that carried the burden of truth-telling.

How Seattle and King County Are Tackling Institutional Inequities

Julie Nelson, Glenn Harris, Sandy Ciske & Matias Valenzuela

At PRRAC's May 2009 meeting in Seattle in conjunction with its latest round of research/advocacy grants, city and county representatives made fascinating presentations of their respective social justice initiatives. We asked them to describe these steps for *P&R* readers, in the hope that other cities and counties might replicate these important moves.

At first sight, the Seattle-King County area in the Pacific Northwest seems to be a land of wealth and good living. It is the epicenter of major industries such as Microsoft, Boeing and Starbucks. But take a closer look: The region's social inequities mirror national trends, and many communities are losing ground.

Two government entities in the Pacific Northwest are tackling the problem directly. The City of Seattle's Race and Social Justice Initiative (RSJI) seeks to end institutional racism in City government and to promote multiculturalism and full participation by all residents. King County's Equity and Social Justice Initiative seeks to create a place of opportunity, fairness, equity and social justice where all people thrive.

Seattle is the largest city in King County, which stretches from the shores of Puget Sound to the western slopes of the Cascade Mountains. The county's 1.9 million people are about 70 percent white. Asian communities comprise 13.4 percent of the total population, Latinos 6.8 percent, African Americans 5.3 percent and mixed-race 3.2 percent. The Seattle-King County area has a national reputation for being politically progressive and culturally diverse.

The history of the Pacific Northwest reflects the complexities of the nation's ongoing struggle to achieve racial and social equity. Early trading relationships between Northwest tribes and European settlers soon gave way to armed conflict, usurpation of land and establishment of tribal reservations. The Chinese, Japanese, Filipinos and other Asians succeeded in establishing strong communities, yet experienced periodic waves of repression, legal containment or expulsion. The most infamous of these was the forced relocation and internment of approximately 110,000 Japanese Americans in 1942 under Executive Order 9066. African Americans migrated to Seattle-King County to escape Jim Crow conditions in other parts of the country; once they arrived, they were forced to navigate a seldom-acknowledged system of restricted employment and segregated housing. Prior to the Civil Rights Movement, African Americans and other people of color in Seattle were systematically excluded from higher education and many professions and industries. The current racial makeup of Seattle neighborhoods is a legacy of restrictive, race-based covenants and redlining that were common in Seattle until the early 1950s. In 1964, the voters of Seattle rejected a local "Open Housing" initiative by a margin of two to one.

When it comes to racial and other systemic inequities, Seattle-King County in 2009 is no different than any other city in the United States. Race influences where we live, where we work, how well we do in school, how long we will live, and the likelihood of our involvement in the criminal justice system. To this day, people of color in Seattle-King County account for a disproportionate number of people living in poverty. In 2006, the poverty rate of Native Americans and African Americans was 30 percent. People of color also continue to experience discrimination in employment, housing, education and public places. Significant inequities exist in environmental justice, criminal justice, health and education.

Geography still plays a part in defining inequities. The north ends of both Seattle and King County, which historically were racially restricted areas, have better outcomes in health, education and other indicators.

The Seattle Race and Social Justice Initiative and the King County Equity and Social Justice Initiative were planned and introduced independently of one another. Seattle Mayor Greg Nickels called for a Race and Social Justice Initiative in 2001 at the start of his first term as mayor, after his own experiences on the campaign trail revealed a racial chasm in residents' perceptions of city government. Several city departments already had been working for years to address racial disparities and race-based barriers to the use of city services. Citywide diversity and cultural competency training had created a relatively diverse and civil workplace, but it had done little to address underlying systemic issues. In 2004, Seattle began to implement its initiative to address these issues throughout city government.

Among the various activities by King County that contributed to launching its Equity and Social Justice Initiative, two stand out. First, several years ago, Executive Ron Sims (2009–2011 the deputy secretary of the U.S. Department of Housing and Urban Development) convened a cross-departmental group to examine inequities for young men of color, based on the national Dellums Commission that looked at health, education, employment, child welfare, criminal/juvenile justice and media. Similarly, over the last three years, King County, along with about 16 other sites across the country, has been participating in an effort called Place Matters to identify and address root causes of inequities and the social determinants of health.

CITY OF SEATTLE RACE AND
SOCIAL JUSTICE INITIATIVE (RSJI)

Seattle's Race and Social Justice Initiative focuses on race because race has profoundly shaped all our institutions and public policies. Until now, government typically had responded to inequities—when it responded at all—by developing programs and services to ameliorate the effects of racism. The RSJI attempts to focus on root causes. Ending institutional racism involves more than simply developing programs to help people of color. The Race and Social Justice Initiative is the City of Seattle's effort to change the underlying system that creates and preserves inequities, rather than attempt to treat the symptoms.

Since 2005, all city departments are required to develop and implement annual RSJI work plans, whose key elements also are included in department directors' Accountability Agreements with the mayor. Each department has created its own Change Team to guide and support the department's work plan implementation and to support its RSJI activities. RSJI also requires departments to work on citywide issues:

- End racial disparities internal to the city—improve workforce equity, increase city employees' knowledge and tools, and increase contracting equity.
- Strengthen the way the city engages the community and provides services—improve outreach and public engagement, improve existing services using Race and Social Justice best practices, and improve immigrants' and refugees' access to city services.
- Eliminate race-based disparities in the broader community.

The Seattle Office for Civil Rights oversees the initiative, monitoring departments' progress and coordinating citywide employee training. An interdepartmental sub-cabinet monitors RSJI work and makes broad policy recommendations.

In 2007, the initiative underwent a thorough assessment to measure progress and make recommendations for the future. The next year, the city announced the next phase of RSJI. In addition to continuing to address racial disparities within Seattle city government, the Initiative also would begin to address fundamental race-based disparities in the larger community by developing partnerships with other key institutions—such as the King County Equity and Social Justice Initiative.

KING COUNTY EQUITY AND
SOCIAL JUSTICE INITIATIVE (ESJI)

The King County Equity and Social Justice Initiative is built on the premise that people of color, low-income residents and ethnic groups who have limited English proficiency are more likely to experience racism, underemployment, low education, poor health outcomes, incarceration and general loss of opportunity. In addition, they are more likely to have unsafe living conditions with less access to public goods and services, resources and life opportunities.

King County acknowledges that it needs to change the way it does business in order to address the root causes of inequities. Since there is no blueprint for a government to take on these issues, the county recognizes that it must create a new culture—one that promotes learning and provides spaces for groups and departments to attempt different approaches. The push is for departments and their employees to look beyond individual behaviors to the social, economic and physical factors in communities that shape behaviors. In other words, it is not about blaming the individual, but pushing "upstream" and addressing the root causes of inequities. And it is about looking at decisions, systems and policies that will create more equitable conditions. This means working across departments and side-by-side with communities and partners, especially historically marginalized communities, so they will influence decisions.

The Equity and Social Justice Initiative has prioritized three areas of work. First, it is working to incorporate an equity lens into countywide policy development and decision-making. Second, all executive departments make yearly commitments to address equity and social justice. And third, the county is engaging community groups that are the most impacted by inequities, as well as groups that hold institutional power, to raise the common understanding about equity and identify policies that will make a difference.

An Inter-Departmental Team is responsible for the initiative's accountability and oversight, and reports to both the executive and operations cabinets. This team, with the Public Health Department as the facilitator, includes high-level representation from all executive departments plus the executive's office and the office of strategic planning and performance measures. More recently, the Inter-Departmental Team has had participation from county departments headed by separately elected officials, such as district and superior courts.

RSJI and ESJI share several important similarities:

- Both Initiatives use community organizing models to move the work forward. In both Initiatives, teams are responsible for developing critical mass within a larger community—to "widen the circle" of participants who understand the theory behind the Initiatives and can begin to put it into practice by changing the institutions' policies, practices and procedures.
- Both Initiatives strive for systemic change; neither represents a program or "project." There are no quick fixes, only a long-term commitment to a new way of doing business through institutional change.

RSJI and ESJI do differ, however, in a number of critical areas:

- Seattle's RSJI focuses explicitly on institutional racism. Although the Initiative acknowledges other systemic inequities based on class, gender or heterosexism,

RSJI keeps its lens focused on racism because of its centrality within Seattle's experience.

- For its part, King County's ESJI aims to improve the conditions for people of color, low-income residents and ethnic groups who have limited English proficiency due to the barriers faced by these communities—ranging from racism to lack of opportunity. The work of the county focuses on 13 social, economic and physical environment factors that are also termed the social determinants of equity. (These factors include family-wage jobs/job training; community economic development; affordable, quality, healthy housing; quality early childhood development; quality education; healthy physical environment; community and public safety; neighborhood social cohesion; access to all modes of safe and efficient transportation; access to affordable food systems and affordable and healthy foods; access to parks and nature; access to affordable and culturally appropriate health and human services; and racial justice in organizational practices.)
- Seattle and King County also have taken different community organizing approaches. Seattle's Initiative began by focusing on the city's own programs and services, because the first priority was to "get its own house in order"—in other words, to address institutional racism within city government as a necessary first step before engaging the community more broadly. Only when the city felt the Initiative had gained some internal traction did it begin to tackle its "next phase"—to address race-based disparities in the external community.

Although King County has focused on its internal practices and policies from the start, it has also engaged communities since the launch of its initiative. The goal is to work closely with community partners who can both lead and support efforts that ensure fairness and opportunity for all King County residents. Also, the county seeks opportunities to participate in a community dialogue process with community members to increase collective understanding of equity and social justice and to spur action.

RSJI ACCOMPLISHMENTS

The RSJ Initiative has resulted in significant policy and program changes within Seattle city government:

- Translation and Interpretation Policy: A comprehensive Translation and Interpretation Policy was created in 2007 as part of strategies to improve immigrants' and refugees' access to services. All city departments now provide essential translation and interpretation services for non-English speaking customers.
- Outreach and Public Engagement Policy: To improve civic participation, departments are working together on new inclusive outreach and public engagement strategies. Department liaisons have received training in the new strategies, and are expected to train co-workers within their own departments.

- Contracting Equity: To provide more contracting opportunities for communities of color, the city has improved its process and increased opportunities to compete. From 2003 to 2007, the city doubled the percentage of contracting for nonconstruction goods and services with women and minority-owned businesses. The city exceeded its 2007 goal by more than 40 percent. Despite these increases, results were not uniformly positive: Use of African-American, Latino and Native-American business enterprises did not increase substantially, and have become a focus of current contracting efforts.

- Racial Equity Toolkit for Policies and Programs: City departments have begun to use this tool to analyze the race and social justice implications of all budget proposals, as well as departments' own programs and policies. Through use of the toolkit, programs and policies are being revamped to further racial justice.

- Capacity-Building: The initiative developed and implemented a quality basic training program for all city employees based on the PBS documentary, "Race: The Power of an Illusion." Managers, departmental Change Team members and other key stakeholders receive more in-depth training, including use of the Racial Equity Toolkit. By August 2009, two-thirds of all city employees had participated in RSJI training.

- Other significant changes to business operations: Under RSJI, departments have implemented significant changes to their business operations. For example, the Department of Neighborhoods created a new RSJI category as part of its Neighborhood Matching Grant program to support actions in the community geared towards achieving racial equity. The Human Services Department revised its funding process for nonprofit community agencies to make it more accessible for smaller organizations, including agencies that serve communities with limited English skills. Seattle Public Utilities created a new Environmental Justice and Service Equity division to ensure that all utility customers receive equitable services, as well as have access to SPU decision-making processes. As part of the region's Ten-Year Plan to End Homelessness, the Human Services and Housing Departments crafted a fundamental shift in the city's housing and shelter policies to acknowledge racial disproportionality in homelessness, and to focus efforts on people with the greatest housing needs.

Since its launch in early 2008, King County's ESJI has major accomplishments in its main areas of work:

- Policy development and decision-making: King County has committed to ensuring that promoting equity is intentionally considered across all departments, and developed an Equity Impact Review Tool to determine whether policies and programs advance a shared agenda of fairness, spread burdens fairly, and help address historic patterns of institutional bias and discrimination. A training curriculum was created for the Equity Impact Review Tool, and county staff is receiving training on how to use it. Several departments have used the tool. All departments described equity impacts of program reductions in their business plans.

- Department commitments and delivery of county services: In 2008, all executive departments committed to specific actions that promote equity and social justice. For example, Development and Environmental Services has begun to rewrite the zoning code to allow greater flexibility for developers and encourage more vibrant, mixed-use neighborhoods in return for providing public benefits such as mixed-income housing, walkability and sustainability. Natural Resources and Parks conducted a GIS-based equity assessment that mapped benefits (for example, proximity to a park or trail) and burdens (for example, proximity to a wastewater regulator facility) related to demographic variables such as race, income and language. This analysis helped to identify and promote action on potential areas of disproportionality in the department's facility locations and service delivery.

- Community partnerships: King County has committed to support capacity-building of local organizations and communities and to more effectively involve community members in creating solutions to inequities. The initiative's Community Engagement Team, comprised of county staff and community partners, has provided leadership to engage communities in dialogues and actions related to equity and social justice. Over 100 people have received training to facilitate community dialogues involving screening of the PBS documentary "Unnatural Causes: Is inequality making us sick?" Throughout the county, discussion and dialogues have already taken place with over 100 groups. These groups cross many sectors of the community, including education, criminal justice, human services, public health, youth and faith-based groups. Additionally, hundreds of county residents attended three town hall meetings in 2008—one led by King County Executive Ron Sims, a second hosted by the King County Council, and a third one focusing on neighborhoods and health.

Although the two initiatives began separately and have somewhat different focuses, staff teams from both government jurisdictions have begun meeting regularly to update each other and to discuss strategies and approaches. Each team is taking advantage of the other's expertise: King County staff are learning more about the challenges of large-scale employee training, and City of Seattle staff are absorbing lessons from the county's initial community work. The two teams also are actively looking for areas of collaboration. Last January, they co-sponsored a lecture in south King County by educator Dr. Jawanza Kunjufu that attracted hundreds of school teachers and administrators from throughout the region.

Seattle's Race and Social Justice Initiative and King County's Equity and Social Justice Initiative both remain works-in-progress with significant challenges ahead. For one thing, there are shifting political realities: In November 2009, both governments will elect new leaders who have had limited or no prior involvement in either Initiative's efforts. In addition, both initiatives recognize that the work thus far represents merely first steps down a long road. The initiatives have tried to incorporate some of the lessons learned from the many others who have labored for social justice; at the same time, Initiative organizers believe that their experiences might offer lessons for other governments and institutions that want to pursue a similar course.

Both the city and county have committed themselves to long-term systemic change, and both Initiatives hope to demonstrate that government can be a catalyst in the struggle to achieve real equity for the people who live and work in Seattle-King County.

One Nation Indivisible: Just Cause—Causa Justa: Multiracial Movement-Building for Housing Rights

Maria Poblet & Dawn Phillips

Causa Justa :: Just Cause (CJJC) is a multiracial, multigenerational grassroots organization building community leadership to achieve housing justice and immigrant rights for low-income San Francisco and Oakland residents.

In 2010, CJJC emerged from the strategic merger of two powerful organizations: St. Peter's Housing Committee and Just Cause Oakland. These two organizations represent more than 30 years of combined experience working toward housing and racial justice for African Americans and Latinos. The primary goal of the merger was to build a more powerful grassroots force for justice in San Francisco, Oakland and beyond.

We saw that as small organizations, often working in relative isolation, our community-based work was deep, but the scale of our impact was limited. We saw the need for a stronger organizational vehicle in order to make a lasting and strategic impact on the social, racial and economic justice problems facing our communities in this time of economic and housing crisis.

We believed that a larger, stronger organization that effectively combines service, organizing and electoral strategies across a broader geographic and demographic reach results in a more cohesive and strategic justice movement, with more wins for our communities. And we thought that by consolidating resources and streamlining systems we would be able to build a more sustainable and effective organization in the long run.

Prior to the merger, St. Peter's Housing Committee had been working for more than 25 years defending tenants' and immigrant rights and fighting gentrification in San Francisco's Mission District. Just Cause Oakland emerged from a successful 2002 campaign to pass a tenants' rights ballot initiative to restrict evictions and evolved into long-term organizing and policy advocacy to defend housing rights.

Both organizations also had in common an active base of community residents who played key roles in developing and directing the work of the organizations.

Over the years, the two organizations ran parallel campaigns around housing, anti-gentrification and community development in our respective cities. We engaged in numerous discussions about our organizational models and our analyses of the problems in our communities. Our members have participated in joint actions, and they have built relationships at countless conferences and meetings. Through those years of shared work, we have built an incredibly strong foundation; we have a high degree of shared values, a solid working relationship, strong personal relationships and complementary organizational models. This foundation put us in an ideal place to take our work to the next level in this crucial historical moment.

About four years ago, we began a deliberative process to examine the viability of merging into a single organization. We spent one year engaged in research and discussions with our staff, members and key stakeholders and allies to thoughtfully examine the potential benefits, risks, challenges and opportunities of a merger. We concluded that turning two organizations into one would lead to greater impact for low-income communities in San Francisco and Oakland. We also believed that our experience could provide guidance to other organizations considering structural convergence of this kind.

Implementation of the merger began in earnest in January 2010, with restructuring of staff roles, opening new offices, developing our board, joint fundraising and administration, and beginning the on-the-ground integration of our programs. On July 1, 2010 we legally became a single organization.

Based on our analysis of the political moment and our organizational potential, we hoped to achieve four key outcomes from the merger:

BUILD POWER AND SCALE

The enormity of the challenges that poor people face today—where injustices felt locally (e.g., the foreclosure crisis, cuts in critical social programs, etc.) are deeply connected to national and international dynamics—requires that progressives work in new and different ways, focused on building convergence and alignment, for greater impact. No longer can small organizations, working in isolation, have lasting and strategic impact on social, racial and economic justice issues that are degrading our communities. Not only does national and global interconnectedness demand that we become smarter, stronger organizers, but also that we collaborate to a degree we have not in the past in order to launch winning strategies for municipal, regional and even national change.

The merger allowed us to qualitatively scale up our work. We went from the original 500 members each previous organization had, to our current membership of 2,100. We now work with over 20 staff in 3 offices and in two languages (Spanish and English), and reach thousands more community members through our various programs and activities. Other aspects of our growing scale include adding foreclosure prevention and defense work with homeowners, engaging around municipal budget and revenue issues, and tripling the number of people we reach through our online and social media communications. As the crises facing our communities worsen, we want to ensure that the level of support we can provide grows proportionally.

While coalitions, alliances and networks have played an important role, yielded results and built strong relationships, they are often impermanent and subject to the unpredictable capacity and shifting priorities of member organizations. Most fall short of arriving at meaningful long-term agreements, political alignment, strategic allocation of resources, sharing of staff and claims of leadership. This limits our collective impact. In spite of good intentions and rhetoric, at the end of the day it is nearly impossible for groups to prioritize what is best for all the partners, and for the movement as a whole, rather than for their own organization.

The majority of today's generation of progressives have not seen a grassroots movement that can operate on a large scale and where sacrifices for the whole are readily made. Our vision is that this merger can be part of a larger trend towards convergence, alignment and greater impact among grassroots progressive organizations in the United States. Realizing this vision means that it will not be enough to just build up and advance the work of our individual organization. We have to actively participate and in fact lead the development of new formations that can create this type of national and international connections with our local work and programs. In the last few years, CJJC has committed heavily to building up the Right to the City alliance (RTTC) because we think that it has the potential to promote this type of dynamic movement convergence.

Right to the City is a national alliance of almost 40 racial, economic and environmental justice organizations located in 9 national urban centers. Through shared principles and a common analysis of gentrification, the alliance is providing local organizations like CJJC a way to engage in national work around housing, land use and anti-displacement issues. RTTC supports grassroots groups, who are deeply grounded in the frontline struggles and needs of working-class communities, to summarize and lift up visionary solutions and policy alternatives to address the various aspects of the housing and economic crisis. The alliance allows organizations like ours to come together with similar groups nationally, and fight at a scale much larger than we are individually able to. What is even more exciting is the ability to re-articulate the wisdom we have accumulated from deep, local work into viable national policy. A vibrant national housing movement needs formations like RTTC.

BUILD A STRONGER ORGANIZING MODEL

St. Peter's Housing Committee developed out of a service provision model into a model that brings together services and organizing. St. Peter's had been running a tenant counseling clinic helping tenants advocate for themselves around issues like rent increases, evictions and harassment. These counseling services served as a mechanism for building a membership organization that can, in turn, organize fighting campaigns around issues of gentrification and displacement. Just Cause Oakland, on the other hand, developed out of a more traditional community-organizing model that prioritized door-to-door outreach to recruit large numbers of members to participate in fighting campaigns. This organizational merger offered an exciting opportunity to build on the best capacities of both organizations.

Our merged model has also integrated an electoral organizing aspect focused on using election cycles and relevant ballot issues as a way to engage our membership and community base. We have dramatically increased our involvement in sweeping outreach to our neighborhoods to engage residents in crucial civic processes that impact their lives. We have developed the skills, team and technology to reach out to thousands of people in a matter of weeks, in both San Francisco and Oakland. Our civic engagement work is ensuring that our communities count and are counted around the key political issues and processes that affect their lives.

At its core however, community organizing is fundamentally about building relationships and developing leadership. Causa Justa :: Just Cause has invested deeply in developing resident leaders from the neighborhoods where we work. A large part of our work is about creating the spaces for members to engage with each other around political discussion, learn about issues affecting their communities, and support them in developing both the analytical and "hard" skills necessary to be effective organizers and political actors. Our members serve on committees that develop our campaigns, they support each other in fighting the banks and landlords, they raise funds for the organization, and they push themselves to be leaders of the organization, their communities and a broader movement for social, economic and racial justice.

BUILD MULTIRACIAL ALLIANCES

An important motivation for the merger was our shared commitment to building solidarity between Just Cause Oakland's African-American base and St. Peter's Housing Committee's large membership in San Francisco's Latino community. While systematic racism has created many divisions between these two groups, we believed, then as now, that an equally strong basis and need for unity exists. Building a multiracial organizing model is about answering the question of how to simultaneously build the strength and position of each group while advancing an agenda of mutual interest.

Both communities share a common experience of disenfranchisement, permanent second-class citizenship, racial discrimination and oppression, as well as having been deeply impacted by state violence and policing. Effective multiracial organizing has to just as accurately articulate the specific and unique ways in which these conditions are affecting each group. CJJC's work is about supporting African Americans and Latinos to name the specific conditions impacting their individual community, to understand the basis of their shared struggle, and to develop campaigns that speak both to specific community interests as well as the shared interests of both groups. This is challenging and complicated work that since the merger we have strived daily to be better at.

By bringing African Americans and Latinos together to address these conditions, we hope to contribute to building the foundation of a vibrant national grassroots movement. African-American and Latino unity is one part of a broader front, made up of other low-income and working-class communities of color, who have to be at the forefront of any successful effort to address inequity and injustice. Multiracial alliances are foundational to movement-building, and our experience has shown that unity can't be built in the abstract. It has to be forged through real relationships and shared work. Through our work, we are committed to building on and creating a truly multiracial organization and movement.

BUILD A MORE SUSTAINABLE ORGANIZATION

While increasing political impact and effectiveness was the core motivation for the merger, we did want to become better positioned to respond to the economic crisis threatening the viability of many social justice organizations. We also wanted to alleviate having two organizations duplicating the tedious work of fund-raising, administration and management, and instead put that time and resources into the direct organizing and movement-building work.

In the first phase, the merger allowed CJJC to develop a more efficient organization where we have been able to do more work with the same amount of financial resources. In the current phase, we have worked on growing and diversifying our organizational resource base. As of this year, we have grown our overall budget by approximately 20 percent, and among other successes, completed an inspiring effort that raised $100,000 from individual donor contributions alone.

The merger has allowed us to effectively use economies of scale to our organizational benefit. As a larger organization, we have been able to improve everything from our level of technology, to our financial management system, to increasing our organizational presence by expanding into more neighborhood offices. Growing our organizational infrastructure has boosted our organizing capacity. We can now more closely track the level of participation of our members in the work, improve the level of media coverage around our key issues, and provide community residents with more physical access to our work and services.

For small organizations such as we used to be, we strongly feel that considering a strategic restructuring creates the possibility of both realizing the potential for large-scale change and a creative approach for dealing with this challenging economic environment.

This process has not been easy or simple. We merged two organizations with very different practices, cultures (literally and figuratively), languages, histories and roots. It took a great deal of commitment for everyone involved to go from a place of comfortable familiarity with doing things a certain way and with folks we knew well, to diving into unknown territory with new and different people. While there was widely held belief in the strategic opportunities the merger presented, there were also serious challenges, including the departure of some who felt that their interests were no longer a fit with the organization's new direction.

As our experiment continues to evolve, we are committed to ensuring that being "bigger" is not just about increasing our size. That it is much more about growing the quality and impact of our work. That "more" actually means more justice for more people in more places. And that, fundamentally, we remain grounded in our core political commitments, even as we encounter more opportunities that could take us away from our roots and community base.

We want our work to contribute towards building a broad social justice movement that can wrestle our communities and this country back from big banks and corporations, corrupt politicians, and those that keep racism alive and well. As a growing regional organization, we will continue to anchor and advance key efforts around housing and immigration statewide and nationally. We will support sister organizations working on other issues, in other areas, so that the momentum of our collective efforts results in a just and equitable future for all people.

The change we want cannot be achieved through the passage of legislation, or by electing a new person into political office, or by becoming a better-funded organization. The change we want to see requires us to develop new political, economic and social relationships from the blocks in our neighborhoods, to cities across the country, and nations across the globe. The change we want to see requires us to build a real peoples' movement for justice, human rights and democracy.

The Opportunity Impact Statement

The Opportunity Agenda

The recent and ongoing investments in the nation's economic recovery have the potential to not only revitalize our economy, but also the American promise of opportunity itself. American opportunity is the idea that everyone should have a fair chance to achieve his or her full potential, and that ensuring this fair chance requires not only certain basic conditions, but also the fulfillment of specific core values: equal treatment, economic security and mobility, a voice in decisions that affect us, a chance to start over after misfortune or missteps, and a sense of shared responsibility for each other as members of a common society. Fulfilling those values is not merely good policy, but part of our fundamental human rights.

An important chance to promote opportunity arises each time a governmental body supports or controls a major public or private project. Taxpayers support, and governments initiate and regulate, a wide range of projects, from highways and mass transit lines, to schools and hospitals, to land use and economic development, to law enforcement and environmental protection. These projects, in turn, can improve or restrict access to quality jobs, housing, education, business opportunities and good health, among other opportunities. And, depending on their design and administration, they can serve all Americans fairly and effectively, or they can create and perpetuate unfairness and inequality based on race, gender or other aspects of who we are.

Despite the progress we have made as a nation, research shows that people of color, women, immigrants and low-income people continue to face unequal barriers to opportunity in a range of situations, including education, employment, healthcare, housing, economic development, asset-building, business opportunities, environmental protection and in the criminal justice system. In authorizing, funding and regulating projects, federal, state and local governments have a responsibility to keep the doors of opportunity equally open to everyone. And history shows that when they fulfill that role, we move forward together as a society.

205

The need for promoting opportunity is stronger than ever, given current efforts to revitalize the economy through the American Recovery and Reinvestment Act of 2009 and other recovery proposals under consideration by the president and Congress. These proposed plans involve unprecedented federal spending linking multiple sectors, and create an opportunity for extraordinary and lasting investment in communities throughout America that need assistance in moving forward toward a strong economic future. This chapter introduces a new and promising policy strategy designed to ensure that publicly supported and regulated projects provide equal and expanding opportunity to all the communities they serve: The Opportunity Impact Statement.

THE IDEA

The Opportunity Impact Statement (OIS) is a road map that public bodies, affected communities and the private sector can use to ensure that programs and projects offer equal and expanded opportunity for everyone in a community or region.

On both the federal and state levels, impact statements are a well-established practice, intended to ensure that policymakers have full awareness of the impact of proposed rules before taking major action. Fiscal impact statements from the nonpartisan Congressional Budget Office outline the costs and benefits of congressional legislation, and many states have adopted similar financial analyses for legislative action. Iowa, Connecticut and Minnesota have established impact statements that review proposed changes in criminal justice policy to determine whether such action will exacerbate or reduce racial disparities in sentencing and incarceration. Perhaps the most well-known impact statement is the federal Environmental Impact Statement (EIS) found in the National Environmental Policy Act (NEPA) that federal agencies must prepare when a major construction or other project is likely to have a significant effect on the environment. An EIS is prepared based on available data and investigation. It compares the proposed project to other alternative approaches, and invites public scrutiny and public comment. Ultimately, it aims to facilitate informed, sophisticated and democratic decision making that pursues sustainable development in service to the public interest.

The Opportunity Impact Statement seeks to pursue similar goals in the context of opportunity. Just as the EIS is designed to "force federal agencies to carefully consider significant environmental impacts arising from projects under agency jurisdiction" and to create a formal procedure in which "members of the public are afforded an opportunity for meaningful participation in the agency's consideration of the proposed action," the Opportunity Impact Statement will bring both the voice of affected communities and balanced analysis to the table in the context of opportunity.

Using empirical data as well as community input and investigation, the OIS will assess the extent to which a project will expand or contract opportunity for all (e.g., Would jobs be created or lost? Would affordable housing be created or destroyed?)

as well as the extent to which it will equitably serve residents and communities of different races, incomes and other diverse characteristics (e.g., Would displacement or environmental hazards be equitably shared by affected communities?)

These factors would be considered in the context of communities' differing assets, needs and characteristics. For example, will a construction project offer job-training opportunities to both women and men from communities with high unemployment rates, or will it bypass those communities? Will a new highway or light rail system connect distressed minority neighborhoods to quality jobs, hospitals and green markets, or will it further isolate those communities? Experience shows that simply asking these types of questions and requiring a thorough and public response will have a positive effect on the development of publicly subsidized or authorized projects.

The Opportunity Impact Statement would include four major elements:

1. Coverage of Projects Involving Public Funds or Governmental Engagement.

The mechanism applies to projects intertwined with taxpayer or government resources. It does not apply to wholly private activities.

2. Data Collection and Analysis.

The Opportunity Impact Statement will collect and analyze data regarding the characteristics of affected communities (e.g., employment rates and health status, socioeconomic and racial make-up, etc.), as well as the assets and opportunities currently available to those communities (e.g., access to hospitals, schools, banking, jobs, etc.), both independently and in comparison to surrounding communities. In some cases, historical patterns (e.g., patterns of hospital closings, housing segregation) will also be relevant. An important part of the analysis will be the consideration of alternative approaches to achieving the goals of the project that may be more effective in ensuring equal access to greater opportunity, as well as changes that could mitigate or remove negative implications. Also important will be consideration of the proposed project's compliance with equal opportunity laws and other applicable legal standards.

3. Public Comment and Participation.

Members of the public—especially communities that would be positively or negatively affected by the proposed project—will participate in the decision making process in two ways. In the initial fact-finding stage, input from civil society will help guide information-gathering regarding relevant impacts, potential alternatives and sources of additional information. Once a preliminary assessment has been created, the public will have the opportunity to comment on the conclusions, express concerns or support, and complement factual information with practical human experiences and interaction.

4. Transparency and Accountability.

The OIS process will result in a public, written report, as well as a record of the goals, data, analysis and public comments that led to the report's conclusions. The report will guide governmental and community decision-making regarding the proposed project while providing guidelines for the future development and regulation of projects that are ultimately approved.

LEGAL UNDERPINNINGS

A network of federal laws provides the underpinning for the Opportunity Impact Statement. Title VI of the Civil Rights Act of 1964 and the federal regulations that implement it prohibit policies that have a discriminatory intent or effect based on race or language ability in federally funded programs. Section 504 of the Rehabilitation Act prohibits discrimination in those programs based on disability. And Title IX of the Education Act prohibits gender discrimination in federally funded education programs. Each of these laws requires the analysis of data similar to that covered by the OIS.

Moreover, laws in particular areas like health, housing and the environment require information collection and analysis. The Environmental Impact Statement requirement in federal law covers impact on the human environment in ways that may overlap with the Opportunity Impact Statement. Medicaid law and other healthcare laws prohibit discrimination against low-income people and communities under certain circumstances.

In addition to these federal laws, international human rights laws support the use of the Opportunity Impact Statement. These include the Covenant on Civil and Political Rights, the Convention on the Elimination of Racial Discrimination, the Convention on the Rights of the Child, and the Convention on the Elimination of Discrimination Against Women (CEDAW). In a recent effort, the City of San Francisco adopted CEDAW as part of its municipal law, resulting in a gender audit that was similar in key aspects to the Opportunity Impact Statement.

The U.S. Supreme Court has increasingly relied on these standards in its interpretation of domestic legal obligations.

ADOPTION AND IMPLEMENTATION

Existing law supports the use of an OIS process in many instances. The web of federal laws and treaties described above support and, in some cases, require the collection, reporting and consideration of impact data based on race, ethnicity, gender, disability and language status. Laws in many sectors, such as healthcare and education, require inclusion and equitable treatment of low-income communities. And existing mechanisms, such as the Certificate of Need process that many states use to consider the distribution of healthcare resources, require only minor practical changes to fit within the Opportunity Impact Statement model. Indeed, Executive Order 12250 and a number of agency-implementing regulations under Title VI appear to require some affirmative mechanism of this kind.

HOW IT WILL WORK

As described above, the Opportunity Impact Statement draws from the lessons of the Environmental Impact Statement. Similar to the EIS, the Opportunity Impact Statement will seek to "provide a full and fair discussion of significant . . . impacts" and "inform decision makers and the public of the reasonable alternatives which would avoid or minimize adverse impacts." As with the EIS, agency implementation of Opportunity Impact Statements will balance both the need for efficiency in review of necessary government-funded projects with evidence-based evaluation and transparency. The process envisions that an agency will have approval authority over projects within its mandate, and will use the Opportunity Impact Statement to guide and strengthen its evaluation of proposals.

The OIS will take place in four stages:

1. Opportunity Assessment

The Opportunity Assessment is an initial agency evaluation of the impact a project may have on affected communities' opportunity. This assessment will be submitted by those proposing the project under review, and will serve as either a gateway to a complete and full Opportunity Impact Statement or, with a Finding of Equal and Expanded Opportunity, permit the proposed plan to move forward without changes.

2. Draft OIS

The Draft OIS should encourage both solid analysis and clear presentation of the alternatives, allowing the agency, the applicant and members of the affected communities to understand the opportunity implications of the proposed project.

3. Public Comment

The process provides for an open and substantive Public Comment Period, including proactive outreach to stakeholders.

4. Final OIS

The Final OIS will assess, consider and respond to all comments. In many cases, the Opportunity Assessment or OIS will reveal no cause for denial or modification, and the project will go forward. Data and public comments developed in the process, however, may be part of subsequent monitoring or complaint resolution.

CONCLUSION

The Opportunity Impact Statement carries the potential to expand opportunity greatly in communities around the country while encouraging public account-ability and civic engagement. Moreover, it is a flexible tool that can be applied to any number of projects, big or small. We believe that providing the Opportunity Impact Statement is an important step in realizing our society's promise as a land of opportunity.

The International Year for People of African Descent

Richard Clarke

During its 64th session, held in 2009, the United Nations General Assembly, in its resolution 64/169, proclaimed the year beginning on 1 January 2011 The International Year for People of African Descent. The stated purpose of the International Year was to strengthen national actions, and regional and international cooperation for the benefit of people of African descent in relation to their full enjoyment of economic, cultural, social, civil and political rights; their participation and integration in all political, economic, social and cultural aspects of society; and the promotion of a greater knowledge of and respect for their diverse heritage and culture.

The General Assembly encouraged Member States, the United Nations specialized agencies, within their respective mandates and existing resources, and civil society to make preparations for and identify possible initiatives that could contribute to the success of the Year. It also requested the Secretary-General to submit to the General Assembly, at its 65th session, a report containing a draft program of activities for the International Year, taking into account the views and recommendations of Member States, the United Nations High Commissioner for Human Rights, the Committee on the Elimination of Racial Discrimination, the Working Group of Experts on People of African Descent and other relevant United Nations agencies, funds and programs, as appropriate.

For over 50 years, the General Assembly has used International Years to draw attention to, and rally support around, issues of particular importance. Similar examples include the International Year for the World's Indigenous People (1993), the International Year of Mobilization against Racism, Racial Discrimination, Xenophobia and Related Intolerance (2001), and the International Year to Commemorate the Struggle against Slavery and its Abolition (2004). The Years offer an opportunity for Member States, civil society and all other stakeholders to reflect upon what they

211

can do to address the challenges related to the subject matter of the Year. The International Year for People of African Descent was officially launched on 10 December last year [2009], Human Rights Day, by the Secretary-General.

The General Assembly requested the secretary-general to establish a voluntary fund for the activities of the International Year and encouraged Member States and all relevant donors to contribute to this fund. It also requested the secretary-general to close the International Year with the convening of a High Level Thematic Debate on the achievements of the goals and objectives of the Year.

The Working Group of Experts on People of African Descent is the main UN entity charged with tackling the situation of this population group. It holds annual sessions to discuss the different challenges faced by Afro-descendants and makes recommendations on measures that should be taken to effectively address these challenges. It also carries out country visits to examine the situation of Afro-descendant populations in situ and makes recommendations to the host government on actions that should be taken to address any problems identified. Naturally, the Working Group will play an active role in the context of the International Year for People of African Descent and contributed suggestions to the Secretary-General's draft Programme of Activities that was presented to the General Assembly at its 65th session in November 2010.

Among other initiatives, the Working Group will be focusing its thematic discussions during its 2011 session (28 March to 2 April) on the contextualization of the International Year, including an overview of the present situation faced by people of African descent; the perspective of the Working Group on positive discrimination; the contribution made by people of African descent to global development; and the lack of knowledge of the culture, history and traditions of people of African descent, by themselves and others. Presentations by the members of the Working Group and invited expert panelists will help promote an understanding of the importance, and necessity, of the International Year for People of African Descent.

The International Year is an opportunity to give due recognition to the enormous contribution that people of African descent have made to the societies in which they live and redouble efforts to fight against racism and racial discrimination directed at them. It is hoped that Member States, civil society and all other stakeholders will become actively involved in the Year and ensure it is a success.

Count Them One by One: Black Mississippians Fighting for the Right to Vote

Gordon A. Martin, Jr.

In 1962 in Forrest County, Mississippi, only 12 of the 7,500 adult black citizens were permitted to register to vote. That year, I made my first trip to the Deep South as one of the trial lawyers of Robert Kennedy's Civil Rights Division. I was less than two years out of law school. The Justice Department was about to try its first major case against a Mississippi Registrar of Voters for discrimination against blacks.

Together with my section chief Bob Owen, I first interviewed prospective African-American witnesses. We had been prepared to present our case solely through their testimony. They were a diverse, impressive group, including five teachers, three men and two women, all with master's degrees awarded or in process from prestigious Northern universities.

Every one of the small group of lawyers who made up the Southern trial staff of the Civil Rights Division had experienced certain particularly memorable events. One of Jim Groh's was finding the man who would become our first witness, Jesse Stegall. Jim had worked on the Tennessee sharecropper cases with John Doar when John first became the division's first assistant in August 1960.

In September 1961, Jim, then 27, was, as he put it, "sent down to cruise Forrest County and make cold calls on possible sources/witnesses . . . We were still feeling our way around in Mississippi, having spent most of 1960 in Tennessee and then focusing on the Middle District of Alabama . . . with time out for the Freedom Riders for most of May 1961 . . ."

"Hattiesburg was obviously a gold mine, and Jesse was the key to the mine. By that time I had probably visited fifty or so counties full of frightened, intimidated, and often very marginally educated people. To find a school principal and other teachers—people with graduate degrees—who were willing to try to register and to testify was like finding the Holy Grail. I also believe that Hattiesburg was the largest

213

town we had tackled to date . . . Forrest County immediately became a hot prospect. I don't think it is any secret that the Kennedy administration at the time was interested in early, dramatic and successful results, and I suspect that is why Forrest was put on the front burner."

CHOOSING THE FIRST WITNESS

In any multiple witness trial, a significant strategic decision is choosing the first witness. The first witness will likely get the longest, toughest, possibly nastiest cross-examination. The first witness will set the tone of the case, impressing or not impressing opposing counsel and, more important, the judge.

You don't want a witness you must protect excessively with objections, sound or not. That will only annoy the judge. One of your tasks also is building the record for an appeal, here to the far more receptive arena of the United States Court of Appeals for the Fifth Circuit.

For us, the choice to lead off was not that hard. Jesse Stegall was an elementary school principal, married, a father, a man with a lot to lose in publicly seeking to vote in hostile Forrest County. What gave Stegall the necessary courage to step forward?

Jesse was the youngest of seven children born to the first Mrs. Stegall. Most of his siblings went in different directions—from Memphis to New York. The only other Mississippi voter applicant among them was Annie Kathryn, the only black registered nurse of her day at Hattiesburg's Forrest General Hospital.

Of the 54 in Jesse's graduating class at Laurel's Oak Park High School, over half went on to college. Besides working while a student at historically black Jackson State, Jesse was vice-president of the student council and business manager of the choir. He also managed his fraternity house. His fraternity was selective: a B average was required, as was persevering and helping those less fortunate. At a fraternity dance, Jesse won a membership to the NAACP.

Summer study was the only way he could later earn a master's degree. Jesse selected the University of Wisconsin, which offered tuition, room and board at a reasonable price. He studied in Madison summers from 1960 through 1963.

Jesse and his friends always wanted to vote. They didn't like paying the two dollars a year poll tax just to be eligible to vote, but blacks who applied were able to vote in Jones County where he had grown up, and Jesse hadn't thought he would have a problem—until he arrived in Hattiesburg. John Doar told Stegall: "I think I'll put you on first." Stegall replied: "Well, okay."

But we had more than the teachers. There were seven workers from Hercules Powder, Hattiesburg's major employer, some of whom had broken the employment color line by being selected for skilled jobs previously reserved for whites. The importance of labor unions is often ignored today, but the union shop steward at the Hercules plant could not have had greater impact for his black workers.

Raymond Ralph Dunagin, known to all as "Huck," was not given to calling meetings. He didn't have to. He always seemed to be everywhere as he walked the floor of the plant. Huck Dunagin was big and powerful, a former all-state lineman when in high school football. He was the steward the blacks had elected. And Huck Dunagin was white.

"I'm no integrationist," he told me years later. "If they wanted to keep the races separate in school, that was okay with me. But my men not be able to vote—my men not be able to hold any job they were capable of holding—I couldn't permit that." With Huck's encouragement and his commitment that their jobs were safe, the black Hercules workers went to Registrar Theron Lynd's office time after time, not deterred by delay or rejection.

Our black witnesses also included two full-time ministers, one Baptist and one Methodist; and two leaders of the county's tiny NAACP cell and of the county's black community as a whole, Vernon Dahmer and B.F. Bourn.

FORREST COUNTY WHITES

In a late decision, we sought to add to their testimony that of Forrest County whites, one for each general time period when one of our black witnesses was either rejected after completing the state's literacy test, or not even permitted to take it. We were not seeking converts to the cause of racial justice. We just wanted white people who would tell the truth: that, making only one visit to Registrar Lynd's office, they were assisted in filling out the application and given one of the easier sections of the Mississippi constitution to interpret or just permitted to sign the registration book without being required to fill out a form at all. Lynd had been elected in February 1959 in an election where candidates literally addressed their campaign "TO THE WHITE DEMOCRATIC VOTERS OF FORREST COUNTY."

Judge Harold Cox, nominated by President Kennedy at the insistence of a fellow Delta native, the powerful chairman of the Senate Judiciary Committee, James O. Eastland, had handled the case since its filing in July 1961, the month he was sworn in as a judge. Cox had barred our presenting any testimony dealing with voting discrimination prior to the day Theron Lynd took office. Thus we had to focus on recent applicants for registration, who would have just become 21, the then voting age.

Cox had also dismissed the August 1960 demand the attorney general had made for Forrest County's voting records pursuant to the 1960 Civil Rights Act, saying we had abandoned that action when we brought the basic voting rights discrimination suit under the 1957 Act eleven months later. There was no legal basis for his not having allowed our records demand, let alone having dismissed it. Nor was there any basis for his not allowing our standard discovery motion in the new case. We were confronted with what Appeals Court Chief Judge Elbert Tuttle would term the "well-nigh impossible task" of proving voting discrimination by the registrar without access to any of his records.

Judge Cox's barring testimony as to Lynd's predecessors had at least targeted the white population we had to reach. The yearbooks of Hattiesburg High School and of the county high school were obvious first steps. Testifying before the United States

Civil Rights Commission three years later, Assistant Attorney General Burke Marshall referred to Bob Owen's and my being "in Hattiesburg for almost three weeks sifting through newspapers, graduation yearbooks, city directories and other documents in order to identify and locate white persons who were placed on the rolls by the Mississippi registrars."

FBI ASSISTANCE

With names from the yearbooks, we were ready to bring on special agents from the New Orleans office of the FBI to interview them. It was a sensible division of labor. The FBI would get on better with white Southerners, and we certainly got on better with prospective black witnesses.

FBI reports needed direction, the dotting of every "i" and crossing of every "t". With Bureau Director J. Edgar Hoover no enthusiast for our work, that was the only way we could ensure that the work product of his agents would be what we wanted. We set forth in a lengthy memorandum to the bureau the exact language of every question we wanted asked, in the order we wanted them asked, from name and address to what was said to and by the women who serviced Theron Lynd's registration counter. Much of the New Orleans regional office of the bureau was soon working the white residents of Forrest County, asking those questions about their registration experience, in order, in our words.

After we reviewed the reports of the bureau interviews, we did some follow-up visits to whites we anticipated calling. About 7 pm, the father of a 25-year-old man I was trying to interview ordered me out of their house in no uncertain terms. I did not delay, but decided to make one final stop, driving to the outskirts of the city to see a young man another division lawyer had talked to briefly.

I was greeted by his angry parents, who accused four FBI agents, as well as my colleague, of having harassed their son, also 25, several times throughout the day. It took a long time, but finally they agreed with me that the agents had not intentionally ganged up on their son.

Bureau agents always worked in pairs (as we were also supposed to). It turned out that two agents had called on his brother in the morning, and two other agents had come back in the afternoon to see him. By the time I had agreed that they were all "100 percent Americans" and certainly not "outlaws," I had been invited to stay for dinner and to "come back and shoot a bird sometime," both of which I politely declined.

BLACK REGISTRATION DENIED

When a black person came into Theron Lynd's office to try to register, he or she was generally turned away. The women who worked in the outer office never even gave an application to a black man, claiming it made them uncomfortable to deal with them, so blacks had to return when Lynd was available. The application (uniform throughout the state) asked for various personal information, including one's precinct, had more than one line for a signature, and required a written section on the rights and duties of a citizen. Then the applicant was given a section of the state constitution and told to copy it out and explain in writing what it meant. Black applicants were given long and complicated sections, best dealt with by a lawyer, but they often did an excellent job despite this. Nevertheless, they were rejected. Sometimes the registrar gave as a reason for rejection an error such as having written the wrong precinct number. White applicants, if they had to fill out the application at all, were given such information on the spot.

Without Lynd's voting records, when we began the trial we had no knowledge of who had applied or what they had written, except for the FBI investigation and what our witnesses told us. Only when the witnesses testified did we get to see their applications.

The opposing lawyers, Justice's John Doar, Lynd's M. M. Roberts and Mississippi Assistant Attorney General Dugas Shands, were in many ways larger than life. When we all, lawyers and witnesses alike, reached Judge Cox's courtroom on March 5, 1962, it had not taken long for M. M. to paint for the court his picture of how we prepared our witnesses: "Swarms of federal government employees, they go in the nighttime to see them, everybody in the nighttime under cover of night, without a moon . . ." Actually, we generally worked from early morning to early evening. Nighttime was reserved for dinner and planning the next day.

THE TRIAL

Over a three-day period, our 16 courageous African-American witnesses who had been rejected for registration testified, along with the 16 contrasting white witnesses who had either been registered without being subjected to the literacy test or been asked to interpret a brief easy section of the Mississippi Constitution—typically, "There shall be no imprisonment for debt." When Judge Cox granted a 30-day continuance to the defendants, refusing to enter an injunction against Lynd, Doar immediately appealed to the Fifth Circuit Court of Appeals. Eisenhower appointees Elbert Tuttle, John Brown and John Minor Wisdom, along with Truman appointee Richard Rives, had changed the outlook of that court, which ruled against Lynd in a detailed opinion by Tuttle. It would be nice to say that resolved things, but Theron Lynd violated the order within days of its being served upon him.

It took three more trials, two for contempt, to deal just with Forrest County. It became painfully clear that with 82 counties in Mississippi, 128 in Georgia and the multiple parishes of Louisiana and counties of Alabama, the county-by-county, case-by-case approach would not work in our lifetimes. The radical answer, the Voting Rights Act of 1965, enacted by the 89th Congress and strongly supported by

President Lyndon Johnson, abolished the scam of the discriminatory literacy test and authorized federal registrars in place of county officials. There was some resistance, but before the end of the decade the shame of the caste system in Southern racial voting had ended.

REVISITING MISSISSIPPI

I returned home to be a federal prosecutor and then practice law in Boston and ultimately became a judge, but I never forgot the witnesses in *United States v. Lynd* and the courage they showed in attempting to register and testifying about their rejection. I returned to Mississippi and renewed my acquaintance with them, and also talked with the relatives of those who had died, including Vernon Dahmer, who had been murdered in an attack engineered by Sam Bowers, the Imperial Wizard of the White Knights of the Klan. In 1998, 32 years later, Bowers would be convicted of Dahmer's murder in a moving state prosecution.

For the first time, I met the white shop steward at the Hercules Powder plant, Huck Dunagin, who had stood behind the black workers who tried to vote, guaranteeing to them that their jobs would be safe. At a time when unions are under siege, it is important to recall his example of how much a union leader who cares about his workers can accomplish.

In the Mississippi State Archives and McCain Library of the University of Southern Mississippi, I found documents such as reports of the State Sovereignty Commission and incendiary letters from attorney Roberts, which further illuminated the tensions in the society the Civil Rights Division lawyers confronted. *Count Them One by One: Black Mississippians Fighting for the Right to Vote* (Univ. Press of Mississippi, 2010) is the account of those 16 African-American men and women who testified, of the trial that led to passage of the Voting Rights Act, and of how Mississippi has changed.

HATTIESBURG TODAY

Today, Hattiesburg has a black mayor who had enough clout on a statewide level to become the Democratic nominee for governor in 2011. In the racial polarization that exists between the parties in today's Deep South, he, of course, could not succeed. On a more personal level, I recently met Reggie Howze, the grandson of one of our witnesses and a graduate of the formerly all-white Hattiesburg High School. Learning that I was from Boston, he told me that his classmate and "best friend in the world" was also living in Boston. When I met his friend Jeremy, he repeated the same phrase about Reggie. Jeremy is white. Neither of them seemed to find this fact significant.

We cannot be complacent about the access achieved then. The ballot must be intelligible to all, particularly new citizens. Voter ID laws such as those in Georgia and Indiana, and proposed in Wisconsin and many other states since the 2010 election, must be scrutinized carefully. Felon disenfranchisement laws that are an impediment to meaningful re-entry to society should be eliminated. And each generation of new voters must recognize the efforts that had to be made by many of their forebears in order to be able to vote, and understand that their vote does count and may make a difference.

Why Are African Americans and Latinos Underrepresented Among Recipients of Unemployment Insurance and What Should We Do About It?

Andrew Grant-Thomas

While the Great Recession left no group or community unmarked, it marked some more than others. African Americans and Latinos, for example, have endured much higher rates of unemployment than have non-Hispanic Whites—16 percent, 12 percent and 8 percent, respectively, in January 2011. African Americans are also especially prominent among the long-term unemployed. According to the Current Population Survey, Black workers were 11 percent of the U.S. labor force but 22 percent of workers unemployed for 27 weeks or longer in 2009. Latinos fared better, but not well: 15 percent of the work force, they comprised 17 percent of the long-term unemployed.

How much of a safety net does unemployment insurance (UI) provide for jobless workers of color and their families? Data on the racial and ethnic identities of workers who apply for and get unemployment benefits are not reported fully or consistently by the states, each of which runs its own unemployment program under a broad set of federal guidelines. Using data from the Department of Labor Employment and Training Administration ("Characteristics of the Insured Unemployed"), we found 15 states that reported racial (Black, White, etc.) and ethnic identity data (Hispanic, non-Hispanic) for all, or nearly all, of their UI recipients. Specifically, in these states the sum of the percentages of recipients whose racial or ethnic identity was 10 percent or lower in 2009. These states are Alaska, Arkansas, Delaware, Georgia, Illinois, Louisiana, Maryland, Massachusetts, Mississippi, Montana, North Carolina, North Dakota, Ohio, Pennsylvania and Tennessee. Combined, those designated as unemployed in these states included 2.9 million White workers, 1.1 million African-American workers and 360,000 Latino workers. Although this sample is not as expansive as we might like, the findings it yields are suggestive.

A comparison between the racial and ethnic compositions of unemployed workers and UI recipients across all 15 states reveals that 43 percent of unemployed Whites,

39 percent of unemployed Blacks and only 32 percent of unemployed Latinos received UI benefits. This result is consistent with a National Urban League study finding that, in 2008, "17.5 percent of unemployed black workers received UI benefits as compared to 25.3 percent of white unemployed workers." Allowing for the limitations of the data, it appears that African Americans are underrepresented, and Latinos very underrepresented, among UI recipients relative to Whites. In addition, given that solid majorities of workers in all three groups do not collect UI benefits, it is likely that many White, Black and Latino workers are foregoing benefits for which they are eligible.

The implications of these unemployment and UI recipiency figures for the well-being of people of color are grim in light of what we know about the financial resources available to Black and Latino families. In a recent presentation entitled "Social Security at 75: Building Economic Security, Closing the Racial Wealth Gap," the Insight Center for Community and Economic Development provided data on racial differences in wealth that help put into relief the challenge many families of color face, especially when unemployment strikes.

Among married and cohabiting householders, the typical non-Hispanic White family ($193,400) had more than four times the wealth of its African-American counterpart ($46,900) and almost five times the wealth of its Latino counterpart ($39,100) in 2007. Among households led by single men and women, the disproportions were equally or more dramatic, but for our purposes what is perhaps more telling is the sheer wealth poverty of people of color. For example, whereas the median wealth of households led by single White women was $49,180 ($41,500 if we exclude the value of any vehicles owned), for single Black and Latino female-headed households those values were $5,000 and $2,680, respectively.

The underrepresentation of African Americans and Latinos among UI recipients is cause for alarm. This is so not simply because racial disparities in the distribution of important social benefits (and burdens) are in themselves suspect, but also because many African Americans and Latinos have little or no financial reserves with which to weather the storm of unemployment. No surprise then, that local welfare offices and homeless shelters have seen a surge in people seeking help. Or that more and more people are turning for shelter and aid to families and friends, many of whom are struggling themselves. The costs of prolonged unemployment include health and mortality declines, marital conflict, and a rise in violent crime, poverty and debt. Extending UI coverage to more people, especially to more people of color, can help mitigate some of these costs.

ARE RACIAL AND ETHNIC DISPARITIES IN UI RECEIPT DUE TO "PRE-EXISTING" CONDITIONS?

How can we account for the apparent underrepresentation of African Americans and Latinos among unemployment insurance beneficiaries? There are at least four possible answers, none of them exclusive of the others. First, it may be that Blacks and

Latinos are less likely than Whites to apply for unemployment insurance. I am not aware of any good data that would allow us to evaluate that possibility effectively.

Second, it may be that Blacks and Latinos, but not Whites, happen to be most numerous in those states with the most restrictive UI eligibility criteria. This explanation has merit. I divided the 50 states and the District of Columbia into three tiers of 17 territories each according to the proportions of their unemployed workers receiving UI at the end of 2009. I then compared the distributions of the White, Black and Latino populations across these territories and found that Blacks and Latinos are unfavorably distributed with respect to state recipiency rates when compared to Whites. Whereas 35 percent of Whites lived in territories that fell into the least-generous third of the coverage distribution, 36 percent of African Americans and a sizable 53 percent of Latinos lived in such states. At the high end, 33 percent of Whites but only 27 percent of African Americans and 27 percent of Latinos lived in the most generous third of states.

Third, it is also possible that African Americans and Latinos are more likely than Whites to fall into worker status categories that make them less likely to meet state UI eligibility criteria. This possibility also seems to bear some explanatory weight. Among the unemployed, African Americans were less likely than Whites to be "job losers" in fourth quarter, 2010: 58 percent of Blacks and 64 percent of Whites were "job losers." We know from previous research that job losers are more likely to meet UI eligibility criteria than other categories of unemployed, including "new entrants" and "reentrants" to the job market.

Blacks and Latinos are also disproportionately low-income workers. The Economic Policy Institute estimated, for example, that in 2009 Blacks were 11 percent of the workforce, but 18 percent of workers whose incomes were low enough to be affected by the minimum wage increase to \$7.25/hour in that year. Latinos were 14 percent of the workforce and 19 percent of workers affected. New entrants to the labor force, re-entrants, and low-income workers are all less likely to meet state monetary eligibility criteria for unemployment benefits.

ARE RACIAL AND ETHNIC DISPARITIES IN UI RECEIPT ALSO DUE TO DIRECT RACIAL BIAS IN THE UI SYSTEM?

A final possible reason for racial disparities in UI receipt is that the unemployment insurance program itself is racialized in ways that merit attention and redress. Of course, race and racial bias may actually play causal roles in the explanations outlined above as well.

It is possible that the original design of UI criteria was racialized and continues to do its racial work today. Note that the state-by-state distribution of the Black population has changed only moderately in the 75 years since passage of the Social Security Act that established the UI program. The same band of states and territories that had the largest shares of Black Americans and included many of the most restrictive

UI eligibility rules back in the 1930s—from the eastern half of Texas through the northern tip of Florida and up to the District of Columbia—still remain home to the country's largest shares of African Americans and many of its most restrictive UI criteria. Race is hardly the only plausible reason for this convergence of geography and rule-making. That said, from the exclusion of agricultural and domestic workers from the original provisions of the Social Security Act itself to the mid-19th Century establishment of felon disenfranchisement laws in some states that attached the sharpest penalties to crimes thought to be committed most often by Blacks, many scholars have argued that brute racial bias accounts for much of the contemporary racialized impact of some of our most important social policies.

On a second front, a large and growing research literature on implicit cognitive bias provides a strong prima facie case for the role of racial bias in the distribution of UI benefits. Implicit or hidden biases refer to the automatic beliefs, attitudes and stereotypes we hold about categories of people or things. As Jerry Kang notes in his "primer" on implicit bias for the National Center for State Courts, researchers have found that implicit bias predicts how much more readily players will "shoot" African Americans compared to Whites in a videogame simulation when given a split second to decide whether the target represents a danger to oneself or others. Greater levels of implicit bias have been linked to more negative assessments of ambiguous actions taken by African Americans. Researchers have documented a positive association between medical doctors' implicit racial attitudes and their unequal treatment for Latino and Black patients compared to White patients. More or less implicit bias corresponds to comfort level and body language in interracial interactions. And so on.

Especially at a time when the number of contested UI benefit claims have soared—56,000 in the year ending June 2010 in Maryland alone, according to the *Baltimore Sun*—the workings of the UI system rely substantially on human judgment. Does the evidence support the claimant's argument that she was fired rather than the employer's contention that she quit? Is ambiguity in this or that regulation best resolved in the claimant's favor or not? On the strength of the rapidly mounting evidence of the real-world effects of implicit bias, it is not cynical to suppose that bias, implicit and otherwise, might play a systematic role in how UI bureaucrats (i.e., human beings) answer these questions. Arguably, it would be naïve to suppose otherwise.

If racial and ethnic biases help produce racial and ethnic disparities in the receipt of unemployment benefits, one might expect, for example, a negative association between state recipiency rates and the proportion of the state population that is African-American or Latino. On the assumption that racial biases will most often operate against Blacks and Latinos, the logic here is that states with larger proportions—not numbers, but proportions—of Blacks or Latinos will also have lower recipiency rates. That is what we see: a negative association for African Americans (correlation coefficient of -.40) and Latinos (correlation coefficient of -.16), but a positive association for Whites (correlation coefficient of .22). This I take to be fairly compelling evidence for the bias claim.

By a similar logic, if bias were systematically skewing outcomes against Blacks and Latinos, we would expect to see an association between the proportion of cases in which UI benefits are denied in error and the proportion of claimants who are Black or Latino. Using data from the Department of Labor Employment and Training Administration's Benefit Accuracy Measurement Report for 2009, we found that states' shares of African Americans and Latinos were indeed positively associated with the rates of one kind of improper denial (improper monetary denial rates, correlation coefficient of .27), but not with either of the other two kinds (improper separation and nonseparation error rates).

IS IT TIME TO FULLY FEDERALIZE
THE UNEMPLOYMENT INSURANCE SYSTEM?

There are several compelling reasons to federalize unemployment insurance. Perhaps most compelling is the matter of funding, the "elephant in the room" with respect to UI. The huge number of unemployed workers receiving regular and extended federally funded benefits makes the program de facto a federal one already. As noted in a February 9, 2011 *New York Times* editorial ("Relief for States and Businesses"), UI trust funds in 32 states are currently insolvent; those states are $42 billion in debt to the federal government, with more states likely to follow suit in 2011. In the 1980s, a similar crisis led 44 states to reduce the extent and amount of their benefit coverage.

Given the limits of the states' ability or willingness to manage their trust funds effectively, it may make sense now to hand over the program entirely to the federal government. If the "modernization" reforms recently adopted by a majority of states are to be made permanent, federal control makes even more sense.

As of December 2010, 18 states had left unclaimed some or all of the federal funds available to them if they modernize their UI systems. The main thrust of the modernization reforms has been to extend coverage to previously excluded workers, including part-time and low-wage workers. As we have seen, people of color feature prominently among those too often left out before the recent wave of modernization. Governors and some legislators in the holdout states express concern about the conditions attached to the federal dollars. Some, like Texas Governor Rick Perry, worry that the demand for a more inclusive UI system will remain in place long after the federal funding to support it has dried up.

In light of such resistance, those concerned to see more vulnerable workers of color covered now and in the future, as needed, should hope to see the program federalized and modernization reforms extended to more states and made permanent. Our analyses show that for both Blacks and Latinos, modernization measures enacted in 2009 and 2010 mitigated the relationships between racial proportionality and recipiency rate at the state level. As recent work by Wayne Vroman and Jacob Benus demonstrates, because unemployment insurance dollars are typically spent, rather than saved, states with higher UI recipiency rates also provide greater boosts to their economies than states with lower recipiency rates. More extensive modernization efforts, then, would likely be a boon for the economies in affected states, as well as for unemployed workers of color in those states.

The key caveat to the claim that UI is effectively a federal program is this: The federal government can only "incentivize" certain state-level choices, as it did in the case of modernization. It lacks the authority to make efficient programmatic decisions. The federal government cannot easily make mandatory the collection of racial and ethnic identity data for UI claimants and recipients, though this would greatly improve our ability to assess the program's fairness. The federal government can conduct audit tests of bias in claims processing, and should do so, but how readily it could provide de-biasing training in those places showing evidence of bias is unclear.

Finally, placing the unemployment insurance system under federal control would make it much more possible to meet the challenge of creating greater equity across states, as well as within them. As discussed above, both African Americans and Latinos are substantially underrepresented, relative to White workers, in the least restrictive UI states. Relative to White workers, Latinos are also greatly overrepresented in the most restrictive states. These "horizontal" inequities extend to other important dimensions of the system, such as large state variation in the portion of the weekly paycheck replaced by the UI benefit and the degree to which unemployed workers have exhausted their benefits.

CONCLUSION

It was only a short while ago that unemployment insurance was national news. The occasion was President Obama's agreement with his political opponents to extend "tax cuts for the wealthy" as well as unemployment benefits. Little attention was paid then, before or since to questions of racial equity in the disbursement of UI benefits. The suggestive findings reported here regarding the underrepresentation of African Americans and Latinos receiving UI benefits, coupled with the undeniable social and economic vulnerability of many members of those two groups, make it imperative that much more attention be paid to the matter of UI equity.

Given the scarcity and other limitations of the data, some energy should be devoted to data-gathering and fact-finding. Not least, we need rigorous collection of racial data on who applies for and receives UI across all 50 states, the District of Columbia and Puerto Rico. We also need to understand why so many potential claimants do not file for UI benefits in the first place. Beyond this, the UI system needs higher levels of sustainable funding; greater "vertical" equity across worker status categories within states; and greater "horizontal" equity to bridge disparities in payment amounts, exhaustion rates and worker status treatment across states. In sum, from funding to operations, the unemployment system needs the resources and coordination capacity that only the federal government can provide.

The Cobell Trust Land Lawsuit

Justin Guilder

Cobell v. Kempthorne (Dirk Kempthorne, the current[2009] Secretary of the Interior) is one of the nation's more complex, long-running and important lawsuits, seeking justice for a class of American Indians who beneficially own allotted trust land. The trust assets include oil, natural gas, timber, minerals, land leases, grazing leases, etc. The geographical area covered by these trust revenues stretches all across the Western U.S., from Oklahoma to Montana to California to Arizona and everywhere in between. The land was the subject of the 1887 Dawes Act, which broke up reservations and gave individual Indians their own land in order to assimilate the Indians into white culture by destroying their sense of tribal (community) property and instilling a sense of self-(individual)-ownership.

THE BACKGROUND

In 1996, five Indians filed a complaint in the U.S. District Court for the District of Columbia on behalf of themselves and all other individual Indian trust beneficiaries (over 500,000 in all), alleging the federal government had breached its fiduciary obligations, claiming that the government destroyed critical records, failed to account to trust beneficiaries, and either lost trust assets or converted them to government use. Over the next three years, the District Court certified the case as a class action, issued many opinions and, after conducting a lengthy trial, concluded that the federal government had failed to discharge its fiduciary duties and was in breach of trust. In 2001, the Court of Appeals for the District of Columbia Circuit generally affirmed and recognized that the individual Indian trust that Congress created over 100 years ago had been mismanaged nearly as long.

Plaintiffs and defendants battled over many issues over the next five years. During these years, mediation occurred, yet the government never offered to settle the lawsuit at any price, rejecting every proposal to settle the case made by plaintiffs and by mediators. Extraordinarily, two previous Secretaries of the Interior have been held in contempt by the District Court.

On August 7, 2008, Judge James Robertson of the U.S. District Court for the District of Columbia issued the latest opinion in *Cobell v. Kempthorne* (*Cobell XXI*: there have been so many major decisions—and minor ones—in this case that the courts have begun numbering the major ones for identification purposes). This most recent decision, which follows on the heels of a January 30, 2008 decision in which the court concluded that the historical accounting of all individual Indian trust funds was impossible, awards the plaintiff class in restitution from defendants $455.6 million of undisbursed trust funds. Although the court in *Cobell XXI* determined that the plaintiff class is entitled to recover their own undisbursed trust funds, several significant legal errors exist; the plaintiff class is in the process of seeking appellate review of those issues.

APPELLATE REVIEW

Plaintiffs are challenging (at least) the following three paramount questions of law contained in *Cobell XXI*: (1) Although the government rendered impossible its declared accounting duty, the court held that it is unfair to hold the government accountable to the plaintiff class in accordance with traditional trust law, despite the absence of congressional limitations on either the government's accounting duty or its accountability for breach of such duty; (2) The court held that the government has not waived its immunity under 5 U.S.C. § 702 with respect to a claim for specific relief for interest that has accrued on plaintiffs' trust funds, notwithstanding an express statutory trust duty to pay such interest; and, (3) The court held that funds expressly held in trust by the government for the benefit of individual Osage Tribe members of the plaintiff class are not recoverable if held in an account not expressly designated as an individual Indian trust account.

First, the District Court concluded that it would be unfair to invoke traditional trust law presumptions and adverse inferences against the government as trustee that ordinarily apply where, as here, the trustee has destroyed, lost and compromised records essential to a complete and accurate accounting, because, in the District Court's opinion, unique characteristics of the Individual Indian Trust "temper the application of ordinary trust law." *Cobell XXI*, 2008 WL 3155157, at *24. The District Court's ruling that the government as trustee is not obligated to prove or justify disbursements that it claims it has made from the IIM (Individual Indian Money) Trust and that traditional presumptions and adverse inferences do not apply to the government is inconsistent and in conflict with controlling Supreme Court and Circuit law, as well as governing trust law. The government's trust duties are not diminished by the unique qualities of the IIM Trust, because Congress has enacted no legislation that expressly, or by necessary implication, limits such fiduciary duties and obligations. The District Court's expressed concern about fairness to the government when it rejected traditional trust law presumptions and inferences is unprecedented and in conflict with controlling law.

Indeed, Supreme Court and Circuit precedent make clear that traditional trust principles apply to the government's management of the IIM Trust notwithstanding its unique qualities. In *Mitchell v. United States*, 463 U.S. 206, 225 (1983), the Supreme Court held that traditional trust duties and ordinary incidents of trusteeship apply to the IIM Trust because the government exercises complete control over Individual Indian Trust lands and trust revenue solely for the benefit of the plaintiff class. District of Columbia Circuit law is in accord. A trustee must show how the trust assets and funds entrusted to them have been administered or applied. And if full and accurate accounts have not been kept, all presumptions are adversely indulged, and all obscurities and doubts are to be taken most strongly against them. Plaintiffs, therefore, are challenging the court's conclusion that the presumptions typically utilized in trust cases do not apply to this case because of the unique nature of the trust.

Second, the court held that enforcement of 25 U.S.C. § 4012—which requires the Secretary of the Interior to pay interest "to an individual Indian in full satisfaction of any claim . . . for interest on amounts deposited" where the claim is identified through 'a reconciliation process of individual Indian money accounts"—is not specific relief within the waiver of immunity in 5 U.S.C. § 702. This ruling not only conflicts directly with Supreme Court precedent, but with the law of the *Cobell* case; the D.C. Circuit has already explained that the plaintiff class is entitled to recovery of interest for any delay in payment. *Cobell v. Norton (Cobell XIII*, 392 F.3d 461, 468 (D.C. Cir. 2004). Plaintiffs are deeply troubled by the court's blatant disregard for such controlling precedent.

Third, the District Court rejected the arguments of both the plaintiffs and the Osage Tribe that individual Osage Indian trust funds collected by the government should be included in the calculation of individual Indian trust revenue, and thus in the calculation of a remedy to the extent the funds remain undisbursed. The court's sole basis for that conclusion is the fact that the government contends that individual Osage Indian trust revenue was deposited into a "tribal" rather than an IIM account. Plaintiffs contend that the particular Treasury account holding individual Indian trust moneys is irrelevant to whether it constitutes IIM funds for purposes of this action. The exclusion of the individual Osage revenue had a significant adverse impact on the restitution calculation.

NEXT PHASE

Plaintiffs recently filed briefs with the Court of Appeals for the District of Columbia Circuit seeking immediate appellate review of these three issues. It is important to resolve these legal issues regarding the exclusion of class members and trust revenue before significant time and money are expended on notice to beneficiaries and a plan for distribution. Plaintiffs hope that the Court of Appeals reverses the lower court's rulings and that this case may move forward to a fair and expeditious resolution. Individual Indians have faced significant problems throughout the 120-year history of this trust and, unfortunately, justice is still years away. That is, of course, if it can ever be attained.

Truth and Reconciliation in Greensboro, North Carolina: A Paradigm for Social Transformation

Marty Nathan & Signe Waller

Race and class oppression form the backdrop of everyday reality in the United States. Popular culture is blind to the endemic and systemic nature of racism in our political and economic institutions. Mostly, we tell ourselves comforting stories about who we are and what we have done. Told most often from the point of view of those whose power and fortunes depend on institutionalizing disunity and fragmentation, these stories rarely lay bare the social structures of domination that continue to perpetuate oppression for the vast majority.

The twin oppressions of race and class are implicitly denied or covered up with a veneer of normality. But reality is not to be denied: It continues to be and to influence all that is. Sometimes reality breaks through the veneer, as it did with the videotaped savage beating of Rodney King or as it did with the criminal neglect of the poor and people of color population of New Orleans following Katrina. When this happens, we are, momentarily at least, shocked out of our denial. A veil is removed, and society's structure stands exposed before us. We see what was there all along. We have a frightening glimpse into where we are heading. Thankfully, we are also offered a teachable moment with a window of opportunity for wholesale social transformation. Such a precious gift signifies no less than a way toward truth and wholeness, a possibility for healing, an opening to resist oppression, to liberate ourselves and to discover new forms of authentic democracy.

The city of Greensboro, North Carolina, is witnessing what may happen when the veil is removed, as a three-year-old truth and reconciliation process unfolds, flying a banner of truth, civic accountability, restorative justice, healing, and reconciliation. The mandate for Greensboro's Truth and Reconciliation Commission, charged with engaging one of the worst civil rights atrocities in U.S. history, reads in part: "The passage of time alone cannot bring closure, nor resolve feelings of guilt and lingering trauma for those impacted by the events of November 3rd, 1979. Nor can there be

230

any genuine healing for the city of Greensboro, unless the truth surrounding these events is honestly confronted, the suffering fully acknowledged, accountability established, and forgiveness and reconciliation facilitated."

What follows is a brief summary of the incident at the heart of the commission's investigation, as well as a description of the truth and reconciliation process. All who are dedicated to overcoming poverty and racism need to reflect on what is happening in Greensboro and its relevance to your own city, to our nation and to the world. After all, similar histories of race and class conflict and similar social structures to those in Greensboro are found in all regions of the country.

THE HISTORY

On November 3, 1979 in Greensboro, an anti-Klan march and educational conference was planned. However, neither occurred. On that day, just before the march was to begin, nine carloads of Ku Klux Klansmen and American Nazis drove into Morningside Homes, a Black housing project, and opened fire on a group of 100 Black, white and Latino men, women and children preparing to march. The attack took place in broad daylight in front of local TV cameras set to film the march. No police were visible.

The organizers of the march, local members of the Workers Viewpoint Organization, soon to be known as the Communist Workers Party, worked, organized and led unions in local textile mills and nearby hospitals. Jim Waller was president of his Amalgamated Clothing and Textile Workers Union local at the nearby Cone Mills Granite Finishing Plant and had led a strike there in 1978. Bill Sampson was a shop steward for his local at the Cone Mills White Oak plant in Greensboro, and Sandi Smith had been the co-chair of an organizing drive to unionize another Cone Mills plant in Greensboro and had recently moved to Kannapolis to take on organizing Cannon Mills.

All three were shot and killed by Klansmen and Nazis leisurely picking their targets and shooting fleeing demonstrators. Dr. Mike Nathan and Cesar Cauce, both labor activists in nearby Durham hospitals, also were killed. Ten others were injured.

When the shooting stopped, police appeared on the scene.

Later it would be revealed that police had surveilled the 40 KKK-ers and Nazis as they gathered on Greensboro's south side and that Detective Jerry Cooper had had phone contact with KKK leader Edward Dawson. Dawson, a paid informant for the Greensboro Police Department, had called Cooper, his control agent, twice that morning to report that the racists had gathered and were armed. That report was shared on the morning of November 3rd at a police briefing with the tactical squads charged with protecting the march. Yet, instead of warning the marchers, increasing march security or stopping the caravan as it was followed by an unmarked police car on its route across town for the attack, the tactical squad was sent to an early lunch. Later it would be discovered that a patrol car serendipitously in the neighborhood of the attack at that time had been told by police headquarters to "Clear the area," leaving the demonstrators completely unprotected by police. One of the attackers' vans was stopped leaving the murder scene by two officers who arrived there moments after the last shot. They were not ordered to go there.

Fourteen Klansmen and Nazis were ultimately indicted and, of those, six were brought to trial. In the Fall of 1980, an all-white jury found innocent the six shooters clearly seen on videotape firing their rifles and shotguns as they advanced on unarmed demonstrators.

Regional protest and outrage engendered by the acquittals forced the Civil Rights Division of a reluctant Reagan Justice Department to prosecute the Klan and Nazis on civil rights charges in 1984. However, the federal case was tainted. By then, it was well known that federal agencies were also implicated through the person of Bernard Butkovich, an agent of the Bureau of Alcohol, Tobacco and Firearms, who had infiltrated the Nazi Party prior to its participation in the attack. He had attended and participated in key meetings, egging on Klansmen and Nazis to violent acts; had reported to his superiors in the ATF, to local police and to the FBI; and yet had left town the day after the killings without making any arrests.

Unwilling to pursue official lawlessness, the U.S. Department of Justice chose to prosecute the KKK and Nazis using a Reconstruction-era federal civil rights law requiring that it be proved that the killings were racially motivated. Klansmen and Nazis said, no, we didn't kill them because they were Black; we killed them because they were communists. That made it all right to the all-white North Carolina jury that, once again, issued blanket acquittals.

THE CIVIL RIGHTS SUIT

In 1985, a civil rights suit, using federal civil rights laws and state wrongful death and assault laws, was filed on behalf of the victims. The result was a judgment, paid in total by the City of Greensboro, against six Klansmen and Nazis and two Greensboro police officers for the death of one demonstrator. The proceeds ($75,000) were used to create a foundation, the Greensboro Justice Fund, for the support of community-based organizations working against racism and the oppression of workers in the South. Although far from perfect justice, the verdict represented a tremendous victory for all justice- and truth-loving people: It was the first time in an American court of law that Klansmen, Nazis and police officers were found jointly liable.

But the civil suit was not sufficient. There was no public acknowledgment of wrong-doing, no involved police or federal agents were fired, demoted or even rebuked. Some officers involved were promoted! The commander of the Tactical Support unit, Lt. Daughtry, became Greensboro's chief of police a few years later. The city government's official position was that the incident had nothing to do with Greensboro: It happened in the city but was not of the city. The media portrayed the incident as one in which violence between two equally abhorrent and violent outsider groups simply erupted. Survivors, isolated from communities of support and treated as pariahs, protested that they had been targeted because their organizing work in the textile mills and in the community was perceived as a threat to the status quo. From business and governmental centers of power came the message to Greensboro citizens that we needed to put the whole affair behind us—in other words, sweep it under the rug and go about business as usual.

The effect in the aftermath was a quelling of dissent, particularly of labor and anti-racist dissent, and a deepened distrust between Black and white communities in this divided city. As stated by one leading Black activist at a gathering commemorating the 19th anniversary of the Massacre: "No matter what you try to do, it all comes back to the Morningside Homes incident. They think they can get away with anything and the people are still scared and distrustful."

CREATION OF THE TRUTH AND RECONCILIATION COMMISSION

Several of the surviving victims were the driving force for the movement that led to the Truth and Reconciliation Commission. Determined to "reinvestigate," to unearth the connections between local, state and federal police, textile mill officials, and the KKK and Nazis, they contacted the Andrus Family Foundation. Andrus' interests focus on "communities that are searching for a way forward that will bring real, just and sustainable change on these issues. We refer to that path forward very broadly as 'community reconciliation'." Andrus adopted the project, taking upon itself the funding of the first Truth and Reconciliation Commission in the United States. The entire process has been guided, and has unfolded, in such a way that its rich spiritual basis and profound implications for community-building and democratic renewal are daily manifested in Greensboro and beyond. A judicial model that promotes adversarial relationships, divisiveness and punishment is being superceded by one that promotes loving relationships, unity of purpose and healing of the whole community.

The Greensboro Truth and Community Reconciliation Project is based on the South African model of soliciting public and private "truth-telling" by victims, witnesses and perpetrators as a way of basing change, and community transformation, on a full and truthful understanding of the violent historical events. Since the first truth commission established in Uganda in 1974, this model has proven to be an effective method for addressing human and civil rights abuses. At the outset of the Greensboro project, the International Center for Transitional Justice (www.ictj.org), experienced with truth commissions in East Timor, Peru, Morocco, Ghana and many other lands where violence and injustice had destroyed lives and social fabric, became involved. The center has provided guidance and support for the at times beleaguered Greensboro Local Task Force, a large and diverse group of residents that helped bring into being the Truth and Reconciliation Commission (via another equally diverse and democratically constituted group of citizens that formed a Selection Panel).

The promotion of community dialogue and education has been and continues to be the essential work of the local task force of the project and other supporting groups in the city. Understandably, those doing this work encounter resistance and opposition, some of it from the same forces that were guardians of the status quo in 1979 and that feel a stake in preserving what they take to be their prerogatives today.

The history of November 3, 1979 is all too alive in the present. The same newspaper that had transformed an "ambush" into a "shootout" more than two decades ago has found it very difficult to fully appreciate the truth and reconciliation process without some major distortions and misrepresentations of what lies before its eyes. Perhaps it is not surprising, but some media sources from outside the city appear to have had less trouble in covering the process more accurately and grasping its amazing potential. An ultimate expression of official hostility came in the Greensboro City Council vote to oppose the truth and reconciliation process in April 2005, despite 5,000 residents' signatures on a petition asking for City Council support. The Council voted on strict racial lines—all white members against the commission, all Blacks supporting it. Yet Greensboro contends it has moved beyond racism! Current and ongoing is a recently breaking scandal that has resulted in the forced resignation of the police chief. As details of the lawless conduct of a "secret police" within the Greensboro Police Department surface, one of many trails leads to the nefarious role that some police officers played in 1979 in enabling the Klan and Nazi terrorist attack at Morningside Homes.

The Truth and Reconciliation Commission and the citywide project that spawned it were very solidly established over the past three years. Despite opposition, and with a fanfare worthy of a city and a movement steeped in civil rights history, the first Truth and Reconciliation Commission of its kind was sworn in on June 12, 2004. With District Court Judge Lawrence McSwain, Chair of the Selection Panel of the Truth and Community Reconciliation Project, United States Congressman Mel Watt and former Greensboro Mayor Carolyn Allen blessing the proceedings, seven Commissioners took a solemn oath to revisit an unresolved episode in the city's past by reviewing evidence, hearing testimony and issuing a report.

Five months later, over 1,000 people marched in Greensboro on the 25th anniversary of the massacre. They marched to continue the unfinished work of economic and racial justice for which five people gave their lives in 1979; to protect free speech and the right to public assembly and dissent—rights under siege today through the Patriot Act; and to support the Truth and Reconciliation Commission in carrying out its mandate to examine the "context, causes, sequence and consequence of the events of November 3, 1979."

2005 DEVELOPMENTS

In 2005, three public hearings were held in Greensboro, with scores of witnesses testifying, reading prepared statements and answering commissioners' questions.

Many more have spoken to the commission privately. Without government support, amnesty or subpoena power, why would perpetrators, their supporters and witnesses come forward?

The answer to that question has been one of the most interesting of all, opening political and philosophical gates to terrain most victims never even imagined.

At the start, the widows declared that they would not seek further indictment of those found responsible for the violence in the course of the commission's work. It was an attempt to shield those perpetrators willing to divest themselves of their guilty memories before the commission from the potential legal consequences and thus to maximize the possibility for truth to emerge.

One of the most dramatic events was the televised apology by of one of the shooters to the widows of the murdered. On November 2, 2005, 26 years after shooting down demonstrators, the previously flamboyant, now-ailing former Nazi Roland Wayne Wood spoke before cameras from his home in Winston-Salem, North Carolina, of the regret he felt for his actions. Since then, he has testified to the commission.

In addition to the moving testimonies of massacre survivors, others whose testimony had never been heard before included:

- A TV news editor speaking of the censorship of the media at that time.
- The prosecutors and the judge in the first trial, who let fly with their hostility to the anti-Klan demonstrators, illustrating the mindset that could have chosen that first all-white jury that acquitted the murderers.
- An eloquent African-American former co-worker at Bill Sampson's textile mill who spoke of the hope that the union activity of those years brought to workers.
- A member of the Morningside Homes community, where the attack took place. A child in 1979, she was told by her father who worked "downtown" at City Hall not to go out that day because the KKK was coming to Morningside.
- Police officers whose persistent staunch support of their department's actions in 1979 revealed its continued entrenchment in now-indefensible excuses.
- Community activists who placed the massacre in the context of decades of ongoing violent police and city attitudes toward those on the wrong side of the tracks.

For many of the victims, the process has been a chance to proclaim their humanity after years of vicious dehumanization. Most of them have found new strength in the opportunity to publicly air a history that had long been suppressed or distorted, and, for the first time, to be listened to.

WHAT IS TO COME? WHAT CAN WE HOPE FOR?

Already gained for victims, friends and present-day activists is the pride in a history of resistance to race and class oppression and the public acknowledgment of the viciousness of the attack on November 3, 1979 by the KKK and Nazis in complicity with lawless and politically motivated officials. We expect a report this spring that is, at the very least, critical of the lack of oversight of law enforcement in the city. Such a finding would support a civilian review of police, state and federal officials acting in the bounds of the city. Further, we would expect recommendations for injecting a truthful account of the events of 1979 into educational and cultural institutions as well as other creative ways to memorialize those who were killed and continue the struggle against racism and classism that their lives and deaths exemplified. Already gained too is a living example of what genuine democracy could look like on a community and municipal level when people, with a great deal of organization and compassion, are able to confront their history and speak honestly about it. When people are motivated by a desire to be responsible to each other for their collective destiny, through a process of truth and reconciliation, and when they are willing to do the hard work necessary to promote healing and unity in the civic body, what social problem would not yield? Greensboro is showing what is possible.

Necessary but less likely in this process would be a dissection of the power structure in Greensboro that led to the targeting of those seeking change in the then-dominant textile industry to the point that, it is charged, the police arranged a goon squad for the activists' demise. That is the alternate paradigm that makes most sense of the testimony so far. Yet it is not clear that the commissioners, most of them Greensboro residents, have the courage to address the underlying issues at such a deep level.

Whatever the outcome, citizens in communities with histories of civil and human rights abuses, such as Wilmington, North Carolina; Tulsa, Oklahoma; Birmingham, Alabama; Cincinnati, Ohio; and Miami, Florida, are turning their gaze toward Greensboro as providing a model for truth and healing in their own communities. Greensboro's unprecedented truth and reconciliation process has once again placed the city at the forefront of America's perennial and hard-fought struggle for civil and human rights.

Greensboro Truth & Reconciliation Commission

Marty Nathan & Signe Waller

A follow-up to our lead story in the Jan./Feb. [2006] *P&R*: The commission, culminating nearly two years of work by seven volunteer commissioners and the commission's paid staff, released its 300+-page final report on May 25 at a ceremony held at Bennett College for Women in Greensboro (whose president is Johnnetta Cole). Speaking at the ceremony was Dr. Peter Storey, former president of the South African Council of Churches and former prison chaplain to Nelson Mandela.

The report analyzed police performance; police/community relations; the history of Ku Klux Klan, the Communist Workers Party and federal law enforcement agencies; the history of the black power movement and multicultural organizing efforts in Greensboro; labor and labor organizing history; and judicial system issues. Included as well are recommendations for future implementation in areas including community acknowledgment and institutional reform.

The May 26 *NY Times* story was headed, "Report Blames Police for Deaths at a '79 Rally in North Carolina," and noted that "Despite having a paid informer among the Klansmen, the police 'showed a stunning lack of curiosity in planning for the safety of the event'."

At the ceremony, the commission ceased to exist, and the continuing community reconciliation work will fall to the Report Receivers—a variety of local and national religious, civic and other community groups—and to the Greensboro and Community Reconciliation Project. In keeping with the 2003 Declaration of Intent, the project will engage in 6–12 months of follow-up discussions in the community.

Other communities in the South and elsewhere have followed the GTRC's work. Success in Greensboro offers promise that the truth-seeking model previously used in South Africa, Peru and elsewhere can be effective in U.S. communities.

Apologies/Reparations, 2003–2011

- The Virginia House of Delegates unanimously approved a resolution express-ing "profound regret for the Commonwealth's role in sanctioning the immoral institution of human slavery . . . and . . . all other forms of discrimination and injustice that have been rooted in racial and cultural bias and misunderstand-ing"; the statement also condemns the "egregious wrongs" that European set-tlers inflicted on Native Americans. The action comes as the state is celebrating the 400th anniversary of the founding of Jamestown, the first settlement of Europeans. (*Wash. Post*, 2/3/07)
- Immediately thereafter, Maryland lawmakers heard testimony on a similar reso-lution "expressing regret" for that state's role in maintaining slavery and "for the discrimination that was slavery's legacy." The resolution says in part: "Maryland citizens trafficked in human flesh until the adoption of the Constitution of 1864. . . . Slavery's legacy has afflicted the citizens of our state down to the present." (*Wash. Post*, 3/2/07)
- The City Council of Maryland's capital city, Annapolis, has under consideration a resolution calling for an official apology for slavery, in the words of its sponsor, Alderman Sam Shropshire, "part of a healing process, a process that still needs to take place even today in 2007. . . for our municipal government's past sup-port and involvement in slavery and for our support of segregation for nearly 100 years." (*Wash. Post*, 3/23/07)
- Britain's lawmakers granted posthumous pardons to some 300 soldiers executed during World War I for failing to return to the front. (*Wash. Post*, 11/8/06)
- Topeka, Kansas officials have named a building after the first Topeka parent to sign on as a plaintiff in *Brown v. Board of Education*. The Lucinda Todd Educa-

tion Center houses administrative offices and an alternative school for students in danger of dropping out. Ms. Todd, who died in 1993, was secretary of the local NAACP chapter and helped recruit other plaintiffs. (*Wash. Post*, 11/19/06)

- The Montgomery, Alabama City Council voted unanimously to formally apologize to Rosa Parks and others mistreated in the 1955 bus boycott. (*Wash. Post*, 4/20/06)

- A federal judge approved a $35 million settlement in a class action against an Italian insurance company by Holocaust survivors and relatives of victims, adding to the $100 million the company already had agreed to pay. (*NY Times*, 2/28/07)

- A ceremony at the U.S. Capitol honored Oscar Marion, a slave owned by Revolutionary War Gen. Francis Marion (known as the "Swamp Fox" for his battle against the British in So. Carolina), who accompanied and served the general for 7 years during the War of Independence. Oscar Marion is depicted in many paintings (including one hanging in the Senate wing of the Capitol) and is described only as "the faithful Negro servant" in books written about Gen. Marion. A distant cousin, a genealogist, undertook to establish his identity. Rep. Albert R. Wynn (D-Md.), who helped arrange the ceremony, noted that "African Americans have been marginalized in so many different events in American history, as if they didn't exist. Whenever we can bring to light the name of a figure engaged in a historic event, it is good thing." (*Wash. Post*, 12/29/06)

- A bill approved by Congress calls for a federal study to better define the Trail of Tears route, when more than 15,000 members of the Cherokee, Creek and other tribes were forced from their homes in 1838 to make way for white settlement. Untold hundreds, perhaps thousands, of Native Americans died during the forced removal to Indian Territory—in what is now Oklahoma. The National Park Service oversees the Trail of Tears National Historic Trail, which winds through nine states. The study likely will also result in an education and research center. Rep. Zach Wamp (R-Tenn.), primary sponsor of the bill, who claims Cherokee ancestry, noted: "You have to recognize and acknowledge your mistakes for the white man to make this right. There has to be an acknowledgment that . . . slavery was a mistake, the Trail of Tears was a mistake." (*Wash. Post*, 11/24/06)

- The House and Senate passed a bill committing $38 million in National Park Service grants to restore and pay for research at 10 World War II internment camps for Japanese Americans, some 120,000 of whom were rounded up and imprisoned under a 1942 Executive Order signed by President Roosevelt, which also prohibited Japanese Americans from living on the West Coast. The Park Service already operates centers at two camps, the Manzanar National Historic Site in California and the Minidoka Internment National Monument in Idaho. The 10 camps specified in the new legislation are in Arizona, Arkansas, California, Colorado, Idaho, Utah and Wyoming. In 1988, President Reagan signed a presidential apology. (*NY Times*, 12/6/06)

- H.R. 662, the Commission on Wartime Relocation and Internment of Latin Americans of Japanese Descent Act, has been introduced by Reps. Xavier Becerra (D-Calif.) and Dan Lundgren (R-Calif.). During World War II, an estimated 2,300 people of Japanese descent from 13 Latin American countries were taken from their homes and forcibly transported to a government-run internment camp in Crystal City, Texas. Adding to this injustice, some 800 of them were then sent to Japan in exchange for American prisoners of war, the rest held in camps without due process until the war ended. The bill authorizes study of these events (via U.S. military and State Department records) and recommendation of appropriate remedies. The earlier Commission on Wartime Relocation of Civilians led to passage of the Civil Liberties Act of 1988, which provided an official apology and financial redress to most of the Japanese Americans who were subjected to wrongdoing and confined to camps during World War II.

- The Serbian entity of the government of Bosnia and Herzegovina officially apologized to the victims of the 1992–1995 civil war, 2 days after international judges in The Hague ruled that Bosnian Serb forces had committed genocide in the killing of nearly 8,000 Muslims in Srebrenica in 1995. (*NY Times*, 3/1/07)

- The Justice Department is partnering with civil rights organizations—the NAACP, National Urban League and Southern Poverty Law Center—to pursue the killers of scores of black men and women slain by white vigilantes in the South during the 1950s and 1960s. There are 40 unsolved murder cases that are of interest to the federal government (although the Southern Poverty Law Center has compiled a list of 76 unsolved cases, mainly in Mississippi, Alabama and Georgia), and the Department will re-open investigations in 12 cases.

And the not-so-good news:

- The Cherokee Nation members voted to revoke the tribal citizenship of the Freedmen, some 2,800 descendants of the people the Cherokee's once owned as slaves. A similar battle in 2003 involving the Seminole nation was won by the Freedmen. (*Wash. Post*, 3/3/07, *NY Times*, 3/3/07, 3/4/07)

- Indonesia's Constitutional Court ruled the country's truth and reconciliation commission illegal, casting doubt on whether victims of former dictator Suharto will ever see justice. (*Wash. Post*, 12/9/06)

- A grand jury in Leflore County, Mississippi, refused to issue new indictments in the Emmett Till case. While two men admitted to the killing in 1956 after being acquitted by an all-white jury, the Justice Dept. re-opened the case in 2004, seeking others who had been involved, including Carolyn Bryant, the white woman Till was supposed to have whistled at—which led to his murder. The 8,000+ page FBI report was turned over to the district attorney, who sought a manslaughter charge against Ms. Bryant, the last living suspect in the case. (*New York Times*, 2/28/07)

- Japanese Prime Minister Shinzo Abe has denied that Japan's military forced foreign women into sexual slavery during World War II, contradicting the Japanese government's long-time official position, issued in 1993, acknowledging the military's role in setting up brothels and directly or indirectly forcing women into sexual slavery—a declaration that also offered an apology to the euphemistically termed "comfort women." The U.S. House of Representatives has begun debating a resolution that would call on Tokyo to "apologize for and acknowledge" the military's role. Historians believe that some 200,000 women—Koreans, Chinese, Taiwanese, Filipinos, as well as Japanese, Dutch and other European women, served in such brothels. The government earlier established a private, nongovernmental fund to compensate the women (set to close down this month), but many former slaves refused to accept compensation from this fund, claiming it evaded direct official responsibility. (*NY Times*, 3/2/07, 3/6/07, 3/8/09)

- Rev. Bob Jones Univ., the fundamentalist Christian school in Greenville, South Carolina, issued an apology for past racist policies that included a ban until 2000 on interracial dating and its unwillingness until 1971 to admit blacks. (*NY Times*, 11/22/08)

- Pres. Bush signed a bill giving the Army authority to award back pay with interest to 28 black soldiers wrongly convicted of rioting—an Army board overturned the convictions, citing lack of due process—in one of the largest court-martials of World War II. Only one of the soldiers is known to survive. (*NY Times*, 10/15/08)

- A group of about 200 prominent Turkish intellectuals—academics, journalists, writers, artists—issued an apology on the Internet for the World War I-era massacre of more than a million Armenians in Turkey by the Ottoman Turk government. (*NY Times*, 12/16/08)

- A delegation of British Baptists apologized in Jamaica for Britain's role in the transatlantic slave trade. "We have heard God speaking to us. We repent of the hurt we have caused." (*Wash. Post*, 5/31/08)

- Canadian Prime Minister Stephen Harper, in an address to the House of Commons carried live across Canada, apologized to Canada's native people for the long-time government policy of forcing their children to attend state-funded schools designed to assimilate them. Phil Fontaine, national chief of the Assembly of First Nations, wearing a traditional native headdress, was allowed to speak from the floor in response. The government has offered those taken from their families compensation for the years they attended the residential schools, as part of a lawsuit settlement. Several months earlier, Australian Prime Minister Kevin Rudd made a similar gesture to the so-called Stolen Generations—thousands of aborigines forcibly taken from their families as children under assimilation policies that lasted from 1910 to 1970. (*San Francisco Chronicle*, 6/12/08).

- A church in St. Augustine, FL, in a "service of reconciliation," apologized for turning away blacks in 1964 and honored two women who, as child civil rights activists, accompanied by an elderly white woman, were barred admission. (*SFGate*, 6/14/04)

- Ellis Island is adding a new Peopling of America Center, to be completed in 2011, expanding its story of U.S. immigration history, adding for the first time Native Americans and African slaves. (*Wash. Post*, 9/25/08)

- The Spanish government, in a "law of historic memory," has offered citizenship to the descendants of those exiled from Spain during the Spanish Civil War and the fascist dictatorship of Gen. Francisco Franco. A half million people, many of them in Argentina, Venezuela, Cuba and elsewhere in Latin America, are expected to file for citizenship. The same law provides public financing to unearth the mass graves of thousands of Spaniards buried during the war. (*NY Times*, 12/29/08)

- Tens of thousands of Mexicans who toiled as railroad workers and farm laborers—braceros—in the U.S. from 1941–1946 will be allowed to collect back pay under the terms of a settlement of a long-fought class action lawsuit, originally filed in 2001. Under the program, 10 percent of their pay was deducted and transferred to the Mexican government, to be given to the workers when they returned to Mexico, but many said they never received the pay or even knew about the deduction. Each bracero, or surviving heirs, will receive $3,500. Many are living in California, Texas, Illinois and other parts of the U.S. (*NY Times*, 10/16/08)

- *The Magic of an Apology*, by Deborah Howard of Guiding Change, examines the potential for apologies to prevent rather than create litigation. http://guidingchange.org/ blog/2008/05/29/the-magic-of-an-apology/#more.64

- "Paid in Full? A Federal judge closes the door on a reparations suit," by Mick Dumke, appeared in the Winter 2005–2006 issue of *ColorLines*. The suit, brought by 19 plaintiffs from across the country, accused Aetna, CSX, JP Morgan Chase and 14 other companies of "unjust enrichment" and crimes against humanity, noting how the firms' predecessors had owned, traded, insured and transported enslaved Africans—and demanded disclosure of all such involvement and establishment of a trust fund to pay an unspecified amount of restitution.

- The Irish Republican Army apologized to relatives of about a dozen people it murdered and buried in hidden graves over the 30 years of Northern Ireland's sectarian conflict. (*NY Times*, 10/25/03)

- The Christian Brothers, a Roman Catholic order that ran many Irish schools throughout the 20th century, apologized for the actions of a brother convicted of sexually abusing boys from 1959–1974. (*NY Times*, 11/27/03)
- "The Reparations Bandwagon," by Salim Muwakkil, on the acceleration of the national movement to gain reparations for descendants of enslaved Africans, appeared in the Sept. 2006 issue of *In These Times.*
- New York City's Museum of Natural History, in a ceremony attended by nearly 4 dozen members of the Tseycum First Nation in British Columbia, in traditional dress at the end of a 3,000-mile journey, is repatriating the remains of 55 of their ancestors, guessed to be at least 2,000 years old and at the museum for about 100 years—ending a 7-year campaign. (*NY Times*, 6/18/08)
- The American Medical Association made a public address to the National Medical Association (the black physicians' group formed in 1895 in response to their exclusion from the AMA and its constituent societies), apologizing for a century of "past wrongs." (*NY Times*, 7/29/ 08)
- "Long March to an Apology," an op-ed by Mindy Kotler, on the justice due to American prisoners of war taken prior to the Dec. 7, 1941 Pearl Harbor attack (members now of the American Defenders of Bataan and Corregidor), appeared in the 5/28/08 *NY Times.*
- Two real estate developers in Stonewall, MS, having just purchased a shuttered cotton mill, discovered the edge of a buried swimming pool, learning that "in its heyday, the kids lived there all day long"—the white kids, that is. In the early 1970s, the mill owners filled the pool with dirt rather than integrate it. Now the (white) developers are spending about $250,000 to excavate and restore the pool and open it up to kids (and adults) of all races. (*AARP Bulletin*, Dec. 2006)
- A federal government formal Native American Apology Resolution passed Congress in 2010 as an attachment to the Dept. of Defense Appropriations Act [sic] and is now Public Law 111.118, detailed wording in HR3326.
- In November 2011, the City of Atlanta rededicated Fair St. SW (between Northside Dr. and Joseph E. Lowry Blvd.) as Atlanta Student Movement Boulevard SW.
- In November 2011, Liberty, Mississippi dedicated a historical marker commemorating Herbert Lee, a voting rights activist who in September 1961 was killed at a local cotton gin in broad daylight in front of some dozen witnesses, black and white. His killer, the late state Rep. E.H. Hurst, was exonerated that same day by a coroner's jury and never charged (and is not mentioned on the marker).
- France's state-run railroad has for the first time expressed "sorrow and regret" for its role in the deportation of Jews during World War II and is handing its station in Bobigny, a Paris suburb, to local authorities to create a memorial to the 20,000 Jews shipped from there to Nazi camps. (*NY Times*, 1/26/11)

- Barbara Smith Conrad was the focus of racist furor back in 1957 when, as a Univ. of Texas-Austin student, she was cast as Dido, the Queen of Carthage, in a production of Purcell's "Dido and Aeneas" opposite a white male lead—the Texas legislature threatened to withdraw state financing from the university if it did not replace her with a white Queen—which it did. In 1985, she returned to UT to receive a distinguished alumna award, and in 2009 she was honored by the Texas legislature for her distinguished later singing career, which included roles with the Metropolitan Opera and major symphony orchestras. Her story is the subject of a new documentary, "When I Rise" (OMDbPro.com) (*NY Times*, 2/8/11)
- "Japan Apologies to South Korea on Colonization" (*NY Times*, 8/11/11)
- "Australia Apologizes for Aborigines," along with call for bipartisan action to improve their lives. (*NY Times*, 11/3/08)
- "No-No Boy" was the title of a Dec. 28, 2010 *NY Times* short editorial in praise of Frank Emi, who died earlier that month at age 94. As a young man, he was sent to an internment camp in Wyoming after Pearl Harbor. After receiving draft notices in 1944, he and 6 others created the Fair Play Comm., signing a declaration challenging the internment policy and their conscription as affronts to the Constitution and American ideals, and refusing to serve. Originally mocked by other Japanese Americans and some of their organizations as "no-no boys," Emi spent 18 months in prison at Leavenworth. In the 1980s, he joined the fight for redress for Japanese Americans deprived of property and freedom, and in 1988 Congress issued a formal apology.
- A much more recent instance of reparations was reported in the *NY Times* on Oct. 20, 2013 "Caribbean Nations to Seek Reparations, Putting a Price on Decades of Slavery."
- Can't Win 'Em All Item: The Mississippi Div. of Sons of Confederate Veterans wants to sponsor a series of state-issued license plates to mark the 150th anniversary of the Civil War, one of which will honor Gen. Nathan Bedford Forrest, an early leader of the Ku Klux Klan.
- And of course the granddaddy of all recent positive events is President Obama's Dec. 2010 signing of a landmark $1.15 billion settlement (*Pigford II*) of a class action documenting extensive discrimination by the U.S. Dept. of Agriculture against black farmers, mainly in the form of loan denials (which in turn led to loss of farms) and access to agricultural subsidy programs. However, see "Black Farmers Still Losing Ground," which describes the work of the Black Farmers and Agriculturalists Association—bfaa.us.org—in the Jan. 2011 issue of *In These Times*. In addition, $3.4 billion is being given to Native Americans under a land trust claim (*Corbell v. Salazar*) for the Dept. of Interior's mishandling of water and mineral rights on reservation land. Interestingly, the settlement includes up to $60 million to fund scholarships to improve access to higher education for Indian youth. It still must be approved by the U.S. District Court, which is holding a hearing on June 20, 2011. Further inf. from www.

IndianTrust.com and John Boyd at www.blackfarmers.org. See also the Associated Press's series on black land loss: http://www. theauthenticvoice.org/ Torn_From_The_Land_ Intro.html. And the administration just announced it will offer at least $1.3 billion to settle similar complaints re USDA payment and other assistance discrimination against female and Hispanic farmers. (*Wash. Post*, 2/26/11)

Apology for Slavery (H.Res. 194)

On July 29, 2008 the House passed, by voice vote (with no nays), an apology for slavery. The resolution, introduced in February 2007 by Rep. Steve Cohen of Memphis, had 120 sponsors.

Full, eloquent text below:

H. Res. 194
In the House of Representatives, U.S.,
July 29, 2008.

Whereas millions of Africans and their descendants were enslaved in the United States and the 13 American colonies from 1619 through 1865;

Whereas slavery in America resembled no other form of involuntary servitude known in history, as Africans were captured and sold at auction like inanimate objects or animals;

Whereas Africans forced into slavery were brutalized, humiliated, dehumanized, and subjected to the indignity of being stripped of their names and heritage;

Whereas enslaved families were torn apart after having been sold separately from one another;

Whereas the system of slavery and the visceral racism against persons of African descent upon which it depended became entrenched in the Nation's social fabric;

Whereas slavery was not officially abolished until the passage of the 13th Amendment to the United States Constitution in 1865 after the end of the Civil War;

Whereas after emancipation from 246 years of slavery, African Americans soon saw the fleeting political, social, and economic gains they made during Reconstruction eviscerated by virulent racism, lynchings, disenfranchisement, Black Codes, and racial segregation laws that imposed a rigid system of officially sanctioned racial segregation in virtually all areas of life;

Whereas the system of de jure racial segregation known as 'Jim Crow,' which arose in certain parts of the Nation following the Civil War to create separate and unequal societies for whites and AfricanAmericans, was a direct result of the racism against persons of African descent engendered by slavery;

Whereas a century after the official end of slavery in America, Federal action was required during the 1960s to eliminate the de-jure and de-facto system of Jim Crow throughout parts of the Nation, though its vestiges still linger to this day;

Whereas AfricanAmericans continue to suffer from the complex interplay between slavery and Jim Crow—long after both systems were formally abolished—through enormous damage and loss, both tangible and intangible, including the loss of human dignity, the frustration of careers and professional lives, and the longterm loss of income and opportunity;

Whereas the story of the enslavement and de jure segregation of AfricanAmericans and the dehumanizing atrocities committed against them should not be purged from or minimized in the telling of American history;

Whereas on July 8, 2003, during a trip to Goree Island, Senegal, a former slave port, President George W. Bush acknowledged slavery's continuing legacy in American life and the need to confront that legacy when he stated that slavery "was . . . one of the greatest crimes of history . . . The racial bigotry fed by slavery did not end with slavery or with segregation. And many of the issues that still trouble America have roots in the bitter experience of other times. But however long the journey, our destiny is set: 'liberty and justice for all'";

Whereas President Bill Clinton also acknowledged the deepseated problems caused by the continuing legacy of racism against AfricanAmericans that began with slavery when he initiated a national dialogue about race;

Whereas a genuine apology is an important and necessary first step in the process of racial reconciliation;

Whereas an apology for centuries of brutal dehumanization and injustices cannot erase the past, but confession of the wrongs committed can speed racial healing and reconciliation and help Americans confront the ghosts of their past;

Whereas the legislature of the Commonwealth of Virginia has recently taken the lead in adopting a resolution officially expressing appropriate remorse for slavery and other State legislatures have adopted or are considering similar resolutions; and

Whereas it is important for this country, which legally recognized slavery through its Constitution and its laws, to make a formal apology for slavery and for its successor, Jim Crow, so that it can move forward and seek reconciliation, justice, and harmony for all of its citizens: Now, therefore, be it

Resolved, That the House of Representatives—
1. acknowledges that slavery is incompatible with the basic founding principles recognized in the Declaration of Independence that all men are created equal;
2. acknowledges the fundamental injustice, cruelty, brutality, and inhumanity of slavery and Jim Crow;
3. apologizes to African Americans on behalf of the people of the United States, for the wrongs committed against them and their ancestors who suffered under slavery and Jim Crow; and
4. expresses its commitment to rectify the lingering consequences of the misdeeds committed against African Americans under slavery and Jim Crow and to stop the occurrence of human rights violations in the future.

Joint Resolution of Apology to Native People

John Dossett

Over the past several sessions of Congress, several senators and representatives have introduced a congressional resolution "to acknowledge a long history of official depredations and ill-conceived policies by the United States Government regarding Indian tribes and offer an apology to all Native Peoples on behalf of the United States." Senator Sam Brownback, the conservative and strongly Christian Senator from Kansas, has been one of the most outspoken proponents of the apology resolution and introduced the first version (S. J. RES. 37) during the 108th Congress.

The apology resolution references the historical importance of tribes in the United States and acknowledges that Native people suffered cruelly as a result of the United States' reservation policy and military massacres. In particular, the resolution lists such events such as the Trail of Tears, The Long Walk, the Sand Creek Massacre in 1864 and the Wounded Knee Massacre in 1890. The resolution acknowledges the resilience and unique nature of Native Peoples' cultures; and that Native Peoples' creator has endowed Native People with certain inalienable rights.

The National Congress of American Indians has worked with congressional leadership to analyze the impact of the apology resolution. NCAI solicited responses to the proposed language and facilitated discussion among tribal leadership and Congress on the issue. Tribal leadership across Indian Country has offered a variety of responses to the apology resolution.

Some tribal leaders are in favor of the resolution, believing that an apology would begin a process for reconciliation for past injustices, offering a way to move past historical wrongs that linger in Native communities and refocus on the future. Other tribal leaders believe that an apology must be accompanied by actions to repair the wrongs. "Sorry we stole your land, but we are keeping the land" isn't much of an apology. The federal government continues to fiercely resist a settlement for mismanagement of Indian trust funds [see accompanying chapter on *Cobell* lawsuit]; contin-

249

ues to underfund tribal healthcare and education; and has done little to restore tribal lands or support economic development. Tribes are denied the ability to develop an equitable tax base necessary for infrastructure and services, similar to state and local governments, and the Supreme Court continues to chip away at tribal jurisdiction at every opportunity.

In late 2008, the Senate was considering a reauthorization of the Indian Health Care Improvement Act that would have done much to modernize reservation healthcare. The apology resolution was attached to the healthcare bill, but so was a meaningless and politically charged amendment on abortion. (All federal spending on abortion is already prohibited by the Hyde Amendment.) As intended, the abortion amendment became a flash point for election year politics, and the critical Indian healthcare bill and the apology resolution failed to move through the House of Representatives. In this environment, it is difficult for tribal leaders to see that an apology by a majority in Congress is sincerely intended.

III

(RE)EMERGING ISSUES

The Seattle/Louisville Decision and the Future of Race-Conscious Programs

Philip Tegeler

By now, most readers of *Poverty & Race* will have had the chance to absorb some of the commentary on the Supreme Court's recent decision in *Parents Involved in Community Schools v. Seattle School District No. 1* (the consolidated ruling in challenges to "voluntary" school integration programs in Louisville and Seattle)—and the important message that: a) the legal justifications for racial integration are still in place, b) school districts can still take a variety of steps to promote racial integration, and c) we are one Supreme Court Justice away from a radical rollback of state and local power to undertake race-conscious programs of any kind.

A DIVIDED COURT

The good news in this decision is that, despite the obviously adverse result and an extremely troubling plurality opinion (Justices Roberts, Alito, Thomas and Scalia), at the end of the day a narrow majority of five justices, including Justice Kennedy, supported the principle that reduction of racial isolation (also referred to as the interest in diversity or integration) constitutes a compelling governmental interest, and that government can take race-conscious steps to achieve these goals so long as they do not classify individuals on the basis of race in a way that allocates educational benefits.

The bad news is not so much the adverse result (or the new and stricter scrutiny of individual racial classifications dictated by Justice Kennedy's concurring opinion), but rather the plurality opinion's barely concealed hostility to any kind of remedial race-conscious measure, whether or not it includes an individual racial classification.

As Justice Breyer eloquently points out, the plurality opinion ignores the long-standing duality of equal protection jurisprudence—where much stricter scrutiny is applied to racial classifications that exclude members of racial minority groups than to those programs that seek to include them.

The plurality opinion's failure to observe this distinction between exclusion and inclusion is related to their rewriting of the history of the 14th Amendment not as a compensatory response to slavery but as a prescription for a color-blind society—and their re-reading of the arguments in *Brown v. Board of Education* to stand not for racial integration of formerly excluded Black students but for the elimination of all racial assignments in public schools (a re-reading that prompted protests from the advocates who argued *Brown—NY Times* 6/29/07).

And, in a willful misuse of precedent, the plurality opinion seeks to conflate what school districts may be required to do by the courts with what districts are permitted to do on their own: referring to the long-standing principle that court-ordered racial remedies under the 14th Amendment are permitted only in response to "de jure" (or intentional) segregation, the plurality conjures this same de jure principle as a necessary predicate to voluntary use of racial classifications by local districts—without acknowledging their judicial sleight-of-hand and without acknowledging the long-standing precedent permitting such voluntary measures.

The arguments raised by PRRAC and others in their "Amicus Brief of Housing Scholars and Research and Advocacy Organizations" were not directly cited by the court, but the underlying arguments of the amicus brief—regarding the government's role in creating and sustaining residential segregation, and the relationship between housing and school segregation (including the positive effect of school integration on stable integrated housing patterns)—were recognized in both the concurrence and the dissent.

Justice Kennedy, casting the crucial "ninth vote" (5-4) that will ultimately define the meaning and application of this decision, writes that "the decision today should not prevent school districts from continuing the important work of bringing together students of different racial, ethnic, and economic backgrounds. Due to a variety of factors—some influenced by government, some not—neighborhoods in our communities do not reflect the diversity of our Nation as a whole." And Justice Breyer observes: "Cities that have implemented successful school desegregation plans have witnessed increased interracial contact and neighborhoods that tend to become less racially segregated," and that school integration plans are "helpful in limiting the risk of 'white flight'," citing studies from Marvin Dawkins, Jomills Braddock and Gary Orfield (a member of PRRAC's Social Science Advisory Board).

RESPONDING TO THE COURT'S RULING

In response to the Court's ruling, there may be a temptation to abandon the goal of racial integration in favor of either separate-but-equal enhancements to racially isolated schools, or integration on socioeconomic grounds alone. The former approach is always an important and valuable goal, but can never stand alone—and while the latter is a promising approach, we cannot rely solely on economic integration to address the real educational harm that involves educational isolation on the basis of both race and poverty.

This is not the time to retreat. Justice Kennedy's concurrence—supported by four dissenting justices—authorizes new and creative efforts to reduce racial isolation in the public schools, and we should take advantage of this moment of opportunity to expand choice for racially isolated students. Advocates who have successfully advanced educational adequacy claims in a dozen or more states should consider the role of racial and economic isolation in the design of their remedial plans. Metropolitan, interdistrict public school choice programs in Boston, Hartford, St. Louis and Minneapolis should be replicated in other cities as a means of easing racial isolation. The federal government should expand its funding of interdistrict magnet schools in the most racially segregated regions of the country. New federal, state and local programs to "affirmatively further fair housing" should take a more prominent role in addressing racial isolation in the public schools, using expanded housing mobility programs, inclusionary zoning, regionally targeted use of housing trust fund expenditures, and site selection guidelines for assisted family housing that look explicitly at school performance and school racial and economic isolation.

Looking beyond the decision's immediate impact on public education, we must also consider the vulnerability of race-conscious programs in the areas of housing, health, environmental regulation, employment and criminal justice, and develop a plan to protect and expand programs designed to attack long-standing racial disparities in these areas.

There is an important research agenda here, which PRRAC has already begun, to identify work that is needed both to protect race-conscious programs by ensuring that they are narrowly tailored to achieve their goals, and to develop alternative approaches that take race into account but also weigh other factors (including alternative definitions of poverty and poverty concentration) in targeting persistent racial disparities.

THE COURT AND INTERNATIONAL LAW

Finally, it is ironic that *Parents Involved in Community Schools* has been issued while the United States is in the midst of a UN review of its compliance with the Convention on the Elimination of All Forms of Racial Disparities (see *P&R* 16:1, March/April 2007), a treaty that expects detailed internal assessments of racial segregation and racial disparities, and requires affirmative (and even race-conscious) measures by state parties to remedy both governmental discrimination and general societal discrimination and disparities. What will the CERD Committee think of the Court's plurality opinion—which can fairly be read as a rejection of the entire concept of the treaty? This will not be the first time that the United States is out of step with world opinion, but in the area of human rights and civil rights, the U.S. has sometimes prided itself on being in the lead. Perhaps one day soon the Court will return to the precedents and international obligations it is on the verge of rejecting. In the meantime, we need to keep moving forward in our organizing and advocacy, in the shadow of this fragile 5-4 ruling.

REAFFIRMING THE ROLE OF SCHOOL INTEGRATION IN K-12 EDUCATION POLICY

POST-CONFERENCE STATEMENT: AN URGENT NEED FOR FEDERAL SUPPORT

The November 13, 2009 Conference of the National Coalition on School Diversity brought together more than 300 people from across the nation. This included parents, teachers, school administrators, local and state elected leaders, long-time civil rights advocates, community organizers, and government officials. We engaged in a substantive, compelling dialogue with representatives from the U.S. Department of Education (USDOE), the Justice Department, the Department of Housing & Urban Development (HUD), Congressional staff, and the White House Domestic Policy Council. We expressed our collective concerns about the slow pace of support for voluntary school integration in the new administration. We feel that our concerns were heard. Now, we must work together to ensure that the new leadership at USDOE goes beyond a mere rejection of the prior administration's hostile approach toward racial and economic integration, affirmatively expanding support for policies that directly ensure that educational and social benefits reach all racial groups.

This statement summarizes the most important steps we believe the federal government must take in the next two years to support voluntary school integration in American public schools. It is not intended as an exhaustive recap of all the research and policy proposals presented.

1. Rescind the August 2008 Guidance Issued by the Previous Administration

The goals of promoting integration and avoiding racial isolation were recently reaffirmed as compelling government interests by five justices of the U.S. Supreme Court in *Parents Involved in Community Schools v. Seattle School District #1*. The decision did strike down specific elements of voluntary plans in Seattle and Louisville. However, a majority of the Court indicated support for a wide range of race-conscious measures to promote school integration that do not assign individual students based on their race.

In August 2008, the USDOE issued a misleading "Guidance" to local districts suggesting that race-conscious plans were no longer permissible, and advising districts to adopt "race-neutral" policies. Needless to say, the department's 2008 Guidance caused confusion among school administrators. We urge the USDOE, in consultation with the Department of Justice, to rescind the 2008 Guidance and replace it with an affirmative statement that accurately reflects the law.

2. Expand Funding for the Magnet Schools Assistance Act

The Magnet Schools Assistance Program (MSAP) is the primary source of federal funding for innovative school integration programs. As set out in the No Child Left Behind Act, "[i]t is in the best interests of the United States . . . to continue to desegregate and diversify schools by supporting magnet schools, recognizing that segregation exists between minority and nonminority students as well as among students of different minority groups." 20 U.S.C. § 7231(a)(4). However, as we heard at the conference, the President's FY 2010 budget for MSAP has been flat-funded since FY 08, and the number of school districts served has steadily decreased. The current budget level funds the program at $104.83 million, supporting approximately 41 MSAP grantees in 17 states. Without funding increases or adjustments for inflation, MSAP is unable to meet the demand for more magnet school programs. We urge the USDOE to double funding for the MSAP to at least $210 million in 2011–2012, and to include much stronger integration goals in the funding application process, along with other equity measures (including protection against within-school segregation and tracking).

3. Provide Support for Interdistrict Transfer Programs

Some of the most successful school integration programs now operating involve the voluntary transfer of students in high-poverty urban districts across district lines to attend higher-performing (and racially integrated) suburban public schools. These programs have been studied exhaustively, and it is clear that they provide important benefits to both city and suburban students. They need the full support of the federal government, and could serve as models for other highly segregated metropolitan areas. This should include support for parent education and organizing, and transportation costs, as well as staff development and training to ensure that incoming students receive the best possible education when they arrive. Additional efforts should be made to avoid in-school segregation and address the needs of low-income Latino students, students with disabilities, and students with limited English proficiency.

4. Open Up the New Stimulus Education Funds to Voluntary School Integration Programs

The "Race to the Top Fund" and the "Investing in Innovation Fund," adopted pursuant to the American Recovery and Reinvestment Act of 2009 (ARRA), both have the potential to expand quality, integrated educational options for low-income children in low-performing schools. We again urge the USDOE to consider its mandate to promote racial and economic integration in its administration of these funds.

5. Promote School Integration in the Reauthorization of the Elementary and Secondary Education Act (ESEA)

The upcoming reauthorization of the ESEA (which includes most of the current elements of "No Child Left Behind") is an important opportunity to restructure the delivery of Title I funding to states and local districts in a way that incentivizes integration. Specifically, the USDOE should consider strong incentives to states to require cross-district transfers to permit low-income students to move from high-poverty schools to lower-poverty schools, with funds appropriately following the students to their new districts. The USDOE should also support revisions in the basic Title I funding formula to more strongly encourage racial and economic integration, expansion of funding for parent involvement, and inclusion of a "private right of action" to permit parents to enforce their children's rights under the act.

6. Incorporate Civil Rights Requirements in the Charter School System

The growing charter school system should not be exempt from the obligation to promote racial and economic integration. These schools have great potential for diversity, because they are usually not restricted by school district boundaries. Yet in practice these schools tend to be more segregated than nearby conventional public schools. The USDOE should require all charter schools receiving federal funding to take affirmative steps to promote racial and economic integration—including active recruitment of children of color, lower-income families, English language learners and students with disabilities under the IDEA, as well as other appropriate prointegration measures consistent with the *Parents Involved* decision. Similarly, consistent with Title VI, the department should also refrain from funding new racially isolated schools unless such funding is necessary to prevent imminent educational harm.

7. Better Coordinate Housing and School Policy in Support of School Integration

HUD and the U.S. Department of Treasury, through their extensive low-income housing programs, exert significant control over where low-income families are permitted to live. However, in spite of a clear mandate to promote integration, these agencies have generally not considered the educational impacts of their policies—often steering children of low-income families and children of color into high-poverty, segregated schools. It is time for the USDOE to work collaboratively with HUD and Treasury to better link federal housing and school policy, including civil rights siting requirements for the Low Income Housing Tax Credit Program, strong affirmative marketing of all federally funded housing assets in high-performing school districts, and expansion of mobility counseling in the portable Housing Choice Voucher Program to allow families with young children to move into higher-performing schools.

8. Support Strong Civil Rights-Related Research
at the Department of Education

The federal government should engage in and fund research designed to assist racially integrated schools both to improve and sustain their diversity. Similarly, studies of successful, integrated schools need to be disseminated and understood. For example, teachers in diverse and racially changing schools could benefit from research on strategies that confront and resolve racial tension, teaching strategies that include and affirm children from a variety of cultural backgrounds and strategies that help educators devise effective and fair alternatives to "tracking" systems that often disproportionately place students of color in lower-level classes. The USDOE should also explore joint research efforts with HUD on combined housing and education strategies to reduce school segregation.

9. Increase Civil Rights Monitoring and Enforcement

The USDOE, through its Office of Civil Rights, should visibly increase its monitoring and enforcement of civil rights laws, including such issues as parental concerns of racially segregated students in re-established school boundaries and "neighborhood" schools, unnecessary clustering of English language learner students, access to special programs such as gifted and talented programs, and ongoing active review of existing enforcement agreements.

10. Use the Secretary's National Leadership Role to Endorse
Racial Integration in Schools and Inspire Integration Efforts

In speeches and other public comments, the secretary of education could emphasize that integrated public schools are important training grounds as our nation becomes more diverse. Such schools, the Secretary should emphasize, are critical elements in the health of our democracy. Visits to racially integrated magnet schools that are also high-performing, for example, would provide public examples of such models and further endorse the goal of racial integration in public schools. Officials can stress that prodiversity efforts are voluntary measures that provide families expanded educational choices.

Separate ≠ Equal: Mexican Americans Before *Brown v. Board*

Philippa Strum

It was September 1943, more than a decade before *Brown v. Board of Education* was decided by the Supreme Court, when Soledad Vidaurri walked up to a schoolhouse door with five little children in her wake. American soldiers were still fighting overseas—almost two more years of battles lay ahead before World War II would end—but Orange County, California, in the heart of citrus-growing country, was peaceful and bustling economically because of the wartime demand for agricultural products and war factory materiel. Mrs. Vidaurri had come to the Westminster Main School to enroll her two daughters—Alice and Virginia Vidaurri—and her niece and two nephews—Sylvia Méndez, Gonzalo Méndez, Jr,. and Jerome Méndez—in the neighborhood public school.

Mrs. Vidaurri was welcomed to the school and was told that her daughters could be registered. Their father had a French ancestor, and their last name sounded acceptably French or Belgian to the teacher in charge of admissions. Besides, the Vidaurri girls were light-skinned. The Méndez children, however, were visibly darker and, to the teacher, their last name was all too clearly Mexican. They would have to be taken to the "Mexican" school a few blocks away. Little Gonzalo Jr. would remember the teacher telling his aunt, "We'll take those," indicating the two Vidaurri girls, "but we won't take those three." "We were too dark," Gonzalo recalled.

"No way," an outraged Mrs. Vidaurri replied, and marched all the children home. Her equally outraged brother and sister-in-law, Gonzalo and Felícitas Méndez, simply refused to send their children to the "Mexican" school. Two years later, the Méndezes would lead a group of Mexican-American parents into federal court, challenging the segregation of their children, and *Mendez v. Westminster* would become the first case in which a federal court declared that "separate but equal" was not equal at all.

Mexicans had migrated to the United States in large numbers in the first decades of the 20th century, driven by Mexico's political and economic turmoil and the promise of jobs up north. Historians estimate that more than 1 million Mexicans—one-eighth to one-tenth of the Mexican population—arrived between 1910 and 1930. They settled primarily in the Southwest. By the 1940s, Mexicans and Mexican-Americans constituted the entire picking force for California agriculture, which produced a major share of the state's income.

Discrimination was endemic. Most of the workers and their families lived in wooden-shacked colonias on the outskirts of towns or farms, with no paved streets, sewers, toilets or refrigerators. Tuberculosis was a constant threat and affected the Mexican-American community at a rate three to five times that of the Anglo community. A survey of conditions in 1927 found that the average Mexican couple had buried two children, and many had buried three or more. Work was not always available. When it was, the average wage for men was 38¢ an hour; for women, 27¢. (The average wage for all male workers in the United States that year was 61¢; for women, 40¢.) Their wages, in other words, could not provide adequate food, shelter and clothing. There was no sick pay; no payment for injuries sustained on the job; no guarantee that even an underpaid job would be waiting for someone who had to stop working temporarily.

The children of the colonias were consigned to rundown schools that taught the boys gardening and woodworking and the girls sewing and housekeeping. The assumption of school authorities was that there was no point in grooming the students for anything other than low-paying jobs, and the curriculum followed in "Mexican" schools insured their being prepared for nothing else. One former Orange County student recalled the difference between the curriculum at the "white" Roosevelt School and that at the "Mexican" Lincoln School in the town of El Modena: "I remember math . . . a little bit of biology, science, we'd never really heard of that at Lincoln and I know they were being taught stuff like that at Roosevelt." Many of the "Mexican" schools opened at 7:30 in the morning and ended the day at 12:30, so the children could go to work in the citrus groves. Students were routinely permitted to miss school during the two weeks when the walnut harvest was in. The ostensible reason for the segregation was the children's lack of English language skills, but in fact school districts simply directed children with Hispanic surnames to the "Mexican" schools without giving them language tests. Instruction was in English, provided by teachers who spoke no Spanish. Many students were kept in each grade for two years.

In 1928, two University of Southern California professors were asked by the Santa Ana school district in Orange County to conduct a survey of all its schools. The professors concluded that Delhi, one of the "Mexican" schools, was a wooden fire hazard. They reported that another, the Artesia School, "has a low single roof with no air space, which makes the temperature in many of the rooms almost unbearable. Since no artificial light is provided in the building, it is impossible to do satisfactory reading without serious eye strain on many days of the year." Had they investigated Westminster, they would have found its "white" school surrounded by lawns and shrubs. The "Mexican" school was a simple building on bare earth next to a cow pasture, and the children sitting on the ground to eat their lunch (there was no lunchroom) would be covered by flies.

Discouraged, most Mexican-American students left school when they turned 16, bound for low-wage jobs. The Méndezes, like other Latino families in Southern California, knew nonetheless that education was the way out of the life of the colonias—but not the kind of inferior education provided by the "Mexican" schools. They had moved to Westminster to live and work on a farm leased from Japanese Americans who were interned in Arizona during the war, and assumed that their children would go to the nearby public school. That turned out to be the "white" school. Told that the children would have to go elsewhere, the Méndezes repeatedly petitioned school authorities, to no effect.

TURNING TO LITIGATION

The Méndezes then turned to attorney David C. Marcus, the Jewish-American son of immigrants who specialized in immigration and civil liberties law and was himself married to a Mexican American. Marcus had recently won an order from a federal court in nearby San Bernardino, admitting Mexican Americans to the city's only public park and swimming pool. He believed that the Méndezes' case would be stronger if they could document additional instances of educational discrimination in Orange County, and so for a year Gonzalo Méndez and Marcus drove from colonia to colonia, locating families in other school districts who had also tried to put their children into "white" schools.

Felícitas Méndez, who had migrated from Puerto Rico as a child and was insistent on her and her children's rights as Americans, ran the 40-acre farm for that year. "We always tell our children they are Americans," she would testify in court, "and we thought that they shouldn't be segregated like that, they shouldn't be treated the way they are. So we thought we were doing the right thing and just asking for the right thing, to put our children together with the rest of the children there." She initiated 151 meetings with parents and helped turn their enthusiasm into a group, the Asociación de Padres de Niños Mexico-Americanos, which provided moral support for the lawsuit. Marcus filed the case in federal court, arguing that segregated schools for Mexican Americans violated the Fourteenth Amendment's Equal Protection clause ("No State shall . . . deny to any person within its jurisdiction the equal protection of the laws").

As with many clauses of the Constitution, the meaning of "equal protection of the laws" was not immediately apparent. The Supreme Court had held in *Plessy v. Ferguson* (1896), however, that the demands of equal protection were met if states separated people on racial grounds but provided them with equal facilities. In 1945, when Marcus had to choose his strategy, it was so clear that the Supreme Court was not about to undo *Plessy* that the NAACP had adopted the approach of challenging segregated higher education on the grounds of unequal educational facilities. It hoped that if the South had to provide separate institutions that were truly equal, the additional cost would convince Southern legislatures that segregation was simply not worth the expense.

Marcus chose a different route. He could have emulated the NAACP strategy, or he could have focused on a California law that specifically permitted segregation of Asian-American and Indian students but made no mention of Mexican Americans. He was eager to attack segregation against Latinos frontally, however, and argued instead that the segregation itself resulted in an inferior education and therefore constituted a violation of equal protection. In carrying out a "common plan, design and purpose" to keep the children from specific schools solely because of their "Mexican or Latin descent or extraction," the four Orange County school districts named as defendants had caused the parents and their children "great and irreparable damage." Segregation was hurting the Mexican-American students' ability to improve their language skills and become more knowledgeable about and more familiar with the larger society in which they lived. Marcus differentiated the case from *Plessy* by saying that it was not about race, because Mexicans and Mexican Americans were white—as they had been labeled in the 1940 Census. Rather, he asserted, this was intra-race discrimination. The litigation, in his formulation, was about ethnicity rather than race.

The case was assigned to federal District Court Judge Paul J. McCormick, a prominent Los Angeles Irish Catholic Republican who had been appointed to the bench by President Calvin Coolidge in 1924. McCormick was initially skeptical about his court's jurisdiction over the case, as education was traditionally treated as a state matter rather than one appropriate for the intervention of federal officials and institutions. In addition, and bound by the Supreme Court's ruling in *Plessy* and subsequent cases, McCormick was far from certain that segregation was to be equated with discrimination and denial of equal protection of the laws.

At trial, Marcus had parents testify about the refusal of school authorities to move their children out of the "Mexican" schools and the officials' insistence that the children could not speak English and were dirty to boot. One of the mothers had tried to get her eight-year-old son into a Santa Ana "white" school. Denying her request, the school district's assistant superintendent had asked her why the Mexican people were so dirty. Joe, her oldest son, was in the U.S. Navy, stationed in the Philippines. "I told him that if our Mexican people were dirty, and all that," she testified, "why didn't they have all of our boys that are fighting overseas, and all that, why didn't they bring them back and let us have them home . . . I told him if Joe wasn't qualified, why didn't they let me have him and not take him overseas, as he is right now."

Marcus then called Orange County school officials to the stand. James L. Kent, the superintendent of one of the districts, was prominent among them. Kent had written a master's thesis asserting that Mexicans were "an alien race that should be segregated socially." He wrote, in a belief shared by many educators of the time, that

Mexican Americans were biologically distinct. "The schools are confronted with the problem of dealing with groups of children of different racial characteristics, with different intellects and different emotions," he declared. "Their racial language handicap seems to be a severe liability to their advancement in school. This fact, coupled with the fact that the test intelligence of the average Mexican is below that of the average white child, makes it seem probable that a separate curriculum adjusted to them is advisable." It was apparent from their testimony that other school officials agreed.

Marcus brought two students into court, demonstrating their facility in English. Finally, he presented the testimony of two educational experts who testified that, contrary to the Supreme Court's holding in *Plessy*, segregation did carry a stigma that affected the students' ability to learn. The Orange County counsel countered that the segregation was in the best interests of both "white" and "Mexican" students, because the great gap in the two groups' language abilities necessitated that they be taught differently. Segregation was not discrimination.

FOSTERING ANTAGONISMS, SUGGESTING INFERIORITY

Judge McCormick was unconvinced. In 1946, in a landmark opinion, he declared that "a paramount requisite in the American system of public education is social equality." He did not specifically cite the language of "separate but equal," but in effect he declared that separate could not possibly be equal. What segregation did, McCormick asserted, was "foster antagonisms in the children and suggest inferiority among them where none exists," and they were thereby deprived of an equal education.

The County appealed to the Ninth Circuit Court of Appeals, sitting in San Francisco. In New York, NAACP Assistant Special Counsel Robert Carter, Thurgood Marshall's second-in-command and later a federal District Court judge, expressed surprise that the NAACP had known nothing about the case. Marshall was ill, and Carter was temporarily in charge. He immediately understood that if the case reached the Supreme Court, it could be the one to attack segregated education on its face. He had come to believe that sociological evidence, illustrating the psychological and pedagogical effects of school segregation, could be a useful weapon in the litigation arsenal. Other lawyers who worked with the NAACP were less sanguine. The social sciences, they said, were not pure science, so their findings were too weak to use in court. Carter, however, considered the *Méndez* case too good an opportunity to ignore. The NAACP entered the case at the appeals level as an amicus curiae, and Carter drafted a brief that he later described as the NAACP's trial brief for *Brown v. Board of Education*.

The American Jewish Congress, the ACLU, the Japanese American Citizens League and Governor Earl Warren's Attorney General entered the case as well, all in support of the Méndezes. In 1947, the Ninth Circuit struck down the segregation based on California law, which, as noted above, permitted segregation of Indian and Asian-American children but made no mention of Mexican Americans. The California legislature decided that other children should not be segregated either. They and Governor Warren quickly repealed the law. Orange County decided not to take the case further. Within a few months, its schools were integrated. Mexican Americans throughout the state were enheartened, as were others elsewhere in the Southwest. Parents brought cases and the threat of litigation to school boards throughout California as well as Texas, New Mexico and Arizona, achieving integration.

Mexican Americans such as Gonzalo Méndez became politically active in the years during and following World War II, and found a society newly open to their claims. By the mid-1940s, there were more Mexican Americans—those born in the United States of immigrant parents or of parents themselves born in the United States—than Mexican noncitizens living in the United States. Many of them were ready to become politically involved. Hundreds of thousands of Mexican Americans fought in World War II, returning ready to battle the kind of injustice they had been fighting abroad. They and their compatriots at home reacted to *Méndez* by creating organizations that, among other activities, brought integration to schools throughout the Southwest.

The American legal elite's ideas had also been affected by the war, and it greeted Judge McCormick's ruling as a harbinger of things to come. His opinion, the *Yale Law Journal* wrote in June 1947, "has questioned the basic assumption of the *Plessy* case and may portend a complete reversal of the doctrine." Drawing on statistics in the NAACP's brief, the *Journal* declared that the facts that 34.5 percent of African Americans had failed to meet the 1943 minimum educational standards for military service, and that there were too few African-American physicians, dentists and lawyers, indicated that segregated education was counterproductive. The *Michigan Law Review* called the *Méndez* decision "a radical departure from the tacit assumption of the legality of racial segregation" and predicted that it, in concert with the education cases the NAACP had won in the Supreme Court, "may well force a reconsideration of the whole problem." The *Columbia Law Review* urged the Supreme Court to overturn *Plessy*, agreeing that "modern sociological investigation would appear to have conclusively demonstrated" that segregation implies inferiority. The *Southern California Law Review* called segregated education "anomalous" in "a nation priding itself on its solid foundation of basic tolerance and equality of opportunity."

INTERNATIONAL RELATIONS CONSIDERATIONS

The societal climate was also affected by considerations of international relations. The Truman Administration, seeking allies in the Cold War, was concerned about the image of the United States in Mexico and other developing nations. "Eager eyes and attentive ears North and South of our borders await the result" of the *Méndez* case, David Marcus had told Judge McCormick. One of the Ninth Circuit judges wrote to Governor Warren after the *Méndez* decision was handed down, saying that if segregation of Mexican Americans was not ended in California, the ambassadors of 20 Latin-American nations would technically be excluded from public facilities. Warren in turn wrote, "I personally do not see how we can carry out the spirit of the United Nations if we deny fundamental rights to our Latin American neighbors."

Méndez both reflected and influenced the new thinking. It nonetheless remains largely unknown, perhaps because it did not go to the Supreme Court, but in 1954 Judge McCormick's language would be echoed by Chief Justice Earl Warren in *Brown v. Board*. It was the plaintiffs in *Méndez*, however, who first got a federal court to declare that the doctrine of "separate but equal" ran counter to American law and American values.

Segregation and Exposure to High-Poverty Schools in Large Metropolitan Areas, 2008–2009

Nancy McArdle, Theresa Osypuk & Dolores Acevedo-García

Schools are a key environment influencing child development, and research has documented the negative effects of concentrated-poverty schools as well as the advantages of racially/ethnically diverse learning environments. Yet minority children continue to attend high-poverty, high-minority schools, separate from the vast majority of white children. A new report by diversitydata.org, "Segregation and Exposure to High-Poverty Schools in Large Metropolitan Areas: 2008–2009," describes patterns of school segregation and poverty concentration of 30,989 public primary schools in the 100 largest metropolitan areas for the 2008–2009 school year, drawing on the National Center for Education Statistics' Common Core of Data. In these schools overall, enrollment is already "majority minority," with Hispanics comprising over a quarter and blacks almost a fifth of enrollment. However, school composition differs greatly across the country, with enrollment in the West close to two-thirds minority. School composition also differs within metropolitan areas. High levels of neighborhood segregation fuel high levels of school segregation. As a result, white students attend schools that are disproportionately white and low-poverty, and black and Hispanic students attend schools that are disproportionately minority and high-poverty. Data on school segregation and differential exposure to high-poverty schools by student race/ethnicity and income level are available for all 362 metro areas at diversitydata.org.

In previous work, diversitydata.org has documented that racial/ethnic minority children are more likely than non-Hispanic white children to experience disadvantaged environments which compromise their chances of achieving positive developmental and health outcomes. For example, black and Hispanic children are about 20 times more likely than white children to experience double jeopardy—to live both in poor families and concentrated poverty neighborhoods.

267

In addition to families and neighborhoods, schools are a key context influencing child development. Currently, much media and policy attention is devoted to charter schools, despite the fact that charters enroll only about 2 percent of primary and secondary school students. The debate focusing on the charter school versus traditional public school models means that the issues of persistent high racial/ethnic segregation and high exposure of minority children to economic disadvantage at the school level remain largely unaddressed.

Among public primary schools in the 100 largest metro areas, the highest levels of school segregation from whites, as defined by the commonly used Dissimilarity Index, are experienced by black students, followed by Hispanics and then Asians. The most segregated metros for black students are located primarily in older, large Midwest and Northeast metros such as Chicago, Milwaukee, New York, Detroit and Cleveland. In these metros, at least 80 percent of black students would have to change schools in order for the metro area to be fully desegregated. The least segregated metros are primarily in the West but also in some Southeastern locations. This finding coincides with previous research that revealed higher levels of segregation in large metropolitan areas which are fragmented into many districts and which have large concentrations of minority students.

While Los Angeles tops the list of segregated metros for Hispanic students, the most segregated metros are generally found in the Northeast and Midwest, with a heavy representation in New England. Four out of the top ten most segregated metros for Hispanics are in New England (Springfield [MA], Boston, Hartford and Providence). The least segregated metros for Hispanics are located mostly in the Southeast. Baton Rouge, LA is the most segregated metro for Asian students.

Another useful measure of segregation is the extent to which minority students are exposed to other students of their own group (in other words, their degree of isolation) relative to the extent to which white students in the same metro area are exposed to students of that particular minority group. For example, in Chicago, the average black student attends a school that is 73.7 percent black, while the average white student attends a school that is 6.3 percent black. In other words, the average black student attends a school with a black share of enrollment that is 11.7 times that of the school attended by the average white student, the highest disparity of any large metro area. The average black student in Cincinnati attends a school with a black share over ten times that of the school attended by the average white student. In Detroit and Buffalo, the average Hispanic student attends a school with a Hispanic share over nine times that of the school attended by the average white student. In Baton Rouge, the average Asian student attends a school with an Asian share almost six times that of the school attended by the average white student.

Being educated in less isolated, more diverse environments is a benefit both to students and to the community, a benefit that becomes more important as our nation becomes increasingly diverse. Research has shown that "racially integrated schools prepare students to be effective citizens in our pluralistic society, further social cohesion, and reinforce democratic values. They promote cross-racial understanding, reduce prejudice, improve critical thinking skills and academic achievement, and enhance life opportunities for students of all races." [Brief of 553 Social Scientists as Amici Curiae Supporting Respondents, *Parents Involved in Community Schools v. Seattle School District No. 1*] Despite these benefits, high levels of school segregation and isolation persist.

HIGH-POVERTY SCHOOLS

Racially isolated minority schools are very often also high-poverty schools. Children in high-poverty schools face enormous challenges, with classmates who are generally less prepared, have lower aspirations and graduation rates, and have greater absences; parents who are less involved, with less political and financial clout; and teachers who tend to be less experienced and more commonly teach outside their fields of concentration.

In the vast majority of large metros (88 of 97 metros analyzed), the average black student attends a school where half or more of the students are poor. This is also the case in 83 metros for Hispanics. In only 11 metros for Asians and 8 metros for whites does the average Asian or white student attend a school where over half of the students are impoverished.

In some metro areas, students attend schools with fairly similar poverty levels regardless of their race/ethnicity, while in others there is great disparity in the extent to which students of various races/ethnicities attend high-poverty schools. With some exceptions, metros with the lowest levels of disparity in exposure to high-poverty schools tend to be in the South. There is a strong consistency among those metros showing the highest minority/white disparities for all racial/ethnic minority groups, with Bridgeport, Hartford, Milwaukee, Boston, New York, Philadelphia and San Francisco ranking in the top ten highest disparity metros for all three major racial/ethnic minority groups. In metro Bridgeport, the average black student attends a school with a poverty rate 5.2 times that of the school attended by the average white student, and the average Hispanic student attends a school with a poverty rate 4.7 times that of the school attended by the average white student. Overall across all the largest metros, black and Hispanic exposure to poverty in schools is 2.2 times that of whites, while Asian exposure to poverty is just 1.3 times that of whites. Close to 60 percent of black and Hispanic students are enrolled in metros where the average student of their group experiences both high-poverty schools (at least 50 percent poor) and attends a school with a poverty rate twice as high as that of the average white student in that metro. No Asian students live in a metro with similarly high rates of poverty and disparity.

MEASURES ATTACKING BOTH ARE USEFUL TOOLS

Residential segregation and the routine assignment of students to schools based on geographic proximity are the underlying causes of school segregation and differential exposure to high-poverty schools. Thus, measures that attack residential segregation, such as enforcement of fair housing laws, situating affordable housing in higher-opportunity areas, reducing zoning restrictions, and aiding in geographic mobility, are all useful tools in reducing racial and economic segregation in schools as well. Policies to boost school and neighborhood quality in lower-income minority areas, such as the new Promise Neighborhood Initiative, could also help by reducing poverty in those schools/neighborhoods and attracting more mixed-income and white families, producing more middle-income and diverse schools. At the same time, school mobility and assignment programs should not be overlooked. More should be done to allow students in failing schools to transfer to better schools, even if they are outside school district boundaries. Innovative school assignment plans, which take into consideration the composition of students' neighborhoods as well as other factors, should continue to be explored, perfected and utilized to break down segregation. Magnet schools that provide high-quality education and draw diverse students from diverse neighborhoods may be another important tool. Schools should prepare all students to excel. The fact that such gross levels of disparity continue must not be met with apathy or acceptance but rather confronted to ensure that our children and our nation can thrive in an increasingly diverse and challenging world.

The Social Science Evidence on the Effects of Diversity in K-12 Schools

Roslyn Arlin Mickelson

Racial segregation of students in public schools is increasing. Ironically, schools are resegregating just as the responsibility to provide high-quality, equitable education to all children is becoming more complicated because of the ongoing demographic transformation of our society. Findings from recent social science research are consistent and persuasive: Integrated schools are an important component of high-quality, equitable education. In the Supreme Court's recent Louisville and Seattle cases, the four-justice plurality opinion dismissed the social science evidence on the benefits of integration as insufficiently compelling to support race-conscious school integration practices. A majority of five justices, drawing upon the corpus of social science research that shows school racial composition influences outcomes, decided that race-conscious school integration and reduction of racial isolation are important goals (while a different 5-4 majority rejected two voluntary school plans that achieved these goals by giving preference to individual students on the basis of their race).

PRRAC's Small Grants program supported part of my work in compiling hundreds of scholarly articles on the effects of school and classroom composition on educational outcomes and translating the findings from this compilation for public access and dissemination. This work allowed me to contribute to the amicus brief of 553 social scientists submitted by the Harvard Civil Rights Project, as well as the amicus briefs filed by the American Educational Research Association, the Swann Fellowship and the NAACP.

THE LARGER RESEARCH PROJECT

The work supported by PRRAC is part of a larger project I began in late 2005 with support from the American Sociological Association's Spivack Program in Applied

Social Research and Social Policy. The Spivack Project is a survey and synthesis of research about the effects of school and classroom composition on educational outcomes. Currently, this work continues with support from the National Science Foundation's REESE program.

During the last few decades, the social science evidence on the educational benefits of integrated education for all students has become more definitive. Social science research methods have improved our ability to investigate the complexity of the real world in which students learn. For example, we all know that a "3.8 GPA" from one high school is not necessarily the same as a "3.8 GPA" at another high school. Schools differ in ways that matter for achievement.

These new research tools model the fact that students are nested in schools. They allow us to examine the interrelationships amongst the student, family, classroom and school factors that shape achievement. One of the most valuable of these statistical tools is called multilevel modeling (or hierarchical linear modeling). Multilevel modeling offers a clearer interpretation of the relative effects of school characteristics (including racial composition) and family background (including race/ethnicity and social class) on students' academic outcomes. The preponderance of findings from this newer social science, behavioral and educational research indicates racial composition matters for educational outcomes in the following ways:

- Desegregated schools and classrooms have positive effects on achievement. Critical thinking and problem-solving skills of all students are likely to improve in racially diverse classrooms.
- Positive effects can occur at the elementary, middle and high school levels.
- Desegregated learning environments can have positive effects on mathematics and language achievement.
- Students from all racial and social class backgrounds are likely to demonstrate higher achievement in racially balanced schools. To be sure, there are variations in the size of the effects by state, by subject matter, school level and ethnic group.
- Racial isolation has harmful effects on the achievement of African-American and many Latino students. Research is less clear about harmful effects of racial isolation on Whites and Asian Americans, although there are some studies that indicate racially isolated White schools may not be optimal for Whites either.
- The ways that schools and classrooms are organized contribute to the opportunities to learn within them. Compared to racially isolated minority schools, diverse schools and classrooms are more likely to offer higher quality and greater equity in opportunities to learn in terms of:
  - Teacher quality and material resources.
  - Depth and breadth of curricular coverage, including more AP courses and other forms of enrichment.
  - A positive academic climate in terms of higher expectations from teachers and peers.
  - Stability of teaching staff and student populations.

- Academic tracking, ability grouping and special education programs (including those for gifted children) often resegregate desegregated schools. Tracking within desegregated schools can dilute the effects of school integration on achievement because African-American and Latino students are more likely to be found in lower tracks than their White and Asian-American peers with comparable prior achievement, family background and other characteristics.
- A school's racial composition is related to but not equivalent to its socioeconomic composition. Both the racial and socioeconomic composition of a school affect achievement outcomes.
- In the long term, diverse schools and classrooms reduce prejudice and fears while they foster interracial friendships and understanding. Integrated schooling inhibits the intergenerational perpetuation of racial hatred, prejudice and fear.
- Adults, especially members of disadvantaged minority groups, who attended desegregated K-12 schools are more likely to attain higher education, to have higher status jobs, and to live and work in racially diverse settings compared to their counterparts who attended racially isolated minority schools.

THE SOCIAL SCIENTISTS' STATEMENT\

The findings summarized above are presented in great detail in the social science statement signed by 553 scholars whose expertise covers the issues of race, education and life course opportunities. The social science statement concluded:

- Racially integrated student bodies are essential if K-12 public schools are to prepare children to be global citizens in our increasingly diverse society.
- Racially integrated schools enhance students' learning, expand their future opportunities and benefit society at large.
- Racially integrated schools promote social cohesion and reduce prejudice.
- School districts that have not been able to implement race-conscious policies have not achieved the racial integration necessary to obtain the short-term and long-term benefits of integrated education.

As part of my work for PRRAC, I developed several PowerPoint presentations on the benefits of school and classroom diversity and the harms of racial isolation. These can be used by local researchers and trainers to help spread the word on the continuing importance of school and classroom diversity. The PowerPoint presentations include resources for school leaders seeking to implement diversity programs.

THE SPIVACK ARCHIVE

When the Spivack Project is completed in 2008, a searchable electronic database— called the Spivack Archive—with detailed summaries of all the social, behavioral and educational research surveyed will be available at the American Sociological Association's website, www.asanet. org. The Spivack Archive will serve as a resource for people who wish to use social science evidence in efforts to foster diverse, integrated schools.

The Supreme Court has given a green light to school districts to continue to support racial diversity in education. Justice Kennedy's controlling opinion in the Louisville and Seattle cases means the majority of the Justices accepted the vital principle that overcoming racial isolation in public schools is a compelling interest. Local communities and their school district leaders should respond to the invitation from Justice Kennedy and take the actions necessary to foster diversity in their schools and the classrooms within them.

How Colleges and Universities Can Promote K-12 Diversity: A Modest Proposal

Julius Chambers, John Charles Boger & William Tobin

Today, court-supervised desegregation at the K-12 level is encountering an array of serious impediments. Indeed, some 50 years after *Brown*, very few legal or compulsory means remain to ensure that our nation's schools remain racially and economically diverse. Unless school boards can be shown to be acting intentionally to promote segregation by race, federal courts have no constitutional tools to compel school authorities to provide racially diverse educational environments. Freed from judicial oversight, many local school boards and districts are currently opting for student assignment policies that lead inexorably to racial and economic isolation. And while the portion of the Supreme Court's recent majority opinion in *Parents Involved in Community Schools v. Seattle School District No. 1* authored by Justice Kennedy suggests that challenging racial and economic isolation at the K-12 level may constitute a compelling interest, the Court's closely divided ruling likely will discourage most school districts from using race and ethnicity in current and future student assignment programs.

The developing consequences of these new legal and institutional patterns are clear: According to a report by the Civil Rights Project at Harvard University, in 2006 51 percent of all African-American students in the Northeast, 46 percent in Border states, 42 percent in the Midwest and 30 percent in the South now attend schools that are 90–100 percent minority. Ironically, in districts like Jefferson County, Kentucky and Seattle, Washington, where school boards opted for integrated pubic schools, disgruntled white parents have alleged that these choices designed to maintain public school integration violate the Fourteenth Amendment.

In this environment, it is not surprising that parents of school-age children are increasingly raising questions about the benefits of integrated public schools at the K-12 level. Many parents whose prime concern is helping their children gain admission to our nation's best colleges have made secondary school choices largely on the basis of what they perceive these colleges want. Convinced that colleges and universities are primarily concerned about high academic achievement and that diversity and high academic standards are incompatible, many families have spurned diverse high schools. Parents who appreciate the value of diversity would gladly send their children to an inclusive high school if they believed their child's access to the college of their choice would be "protected." Many African-American parents find themselves in a different kind of dilemma: Their children are frequently trapped in grossly inferior segregated schools. In most cases, high-achieving schools that are racially and economically diverse are simply not available for their children.

AN OPPORTUNITY FOR ELITE COLLEGES AND UNIVERSITIES

As interest in integration has waned within our federal courts, few voices in American civil society have emerged to champion the cause of integrated public schools. In the *Grutter* and *Gratz* cases in 2003, however, the nation's elite colleges and universities came forward in numerous friend-of-the-Court briefs to assert their ongoing interest in racially diverse learning environments. We are convinced that these schools have not only the knowledge, but the tools, the self-interest and the moral authority to help ensure that America's public secondary schools remain economically and racially integrated.

Our selective universities have an extraordinary, implicit power, in their own admissions policies, to influence the kinds of educational choices parents demand for their children. For the past two years, we have been working with college administrators, scholars, university general counsels and higher-education organizations to explore the viability and promise of awarding an admissions advantage to academically qualified college applicants who have attended a high school with demonstrated capacity to prepare a racially inclusive student body for college and who have personally demonstrated the ability to compete, cooperate in this diverse educational setting. Over the long term, we believe that providing an admissions advantage to such high schools and students can critically shift the current calculus of millions of parents, and can encourage the creation of more high schools that are both inclusive and academically rigorous high schools capable of producing graduates who may be thought of as agents of diversity, first in our college communities and later in our nation's communities.

The higher-education community knows well that diversity and excellence can coexist. Indeed, the amici curiae briefs submitted by colleges and universities in *Grutter v. Bollinger*, the University of Michigan case, indicate that diversity is an appropriate goal in the field of higher education. The Supreme Court's decision in *Grutter* illustrates how authoritative the higher-education community can be on questions of diversity. Justice O'Connor explained in her majority decision in *Grutter* that the university's "educational judgment that such diversity is essential to its educational mission is one to which we defer."

Colleges and universities can help parents appreciate the value of individual accomplishments achieved in an environment that mirrors and does not elide the diverse character of our society. For parents who wish to send their children to diverse high schools, but are afraid that racially mixed schools might have lower statewide testing results, colleges and universities can help address these fears by making it clear that they too attach great value to schools that reflect the make-up of present-day America. For parents in failing schools that are racially and economically segregated, colleges and universities can send the message that their children have not been forgotten. If those parents who acquiesce in racially isolated public schools are motivated largely by their desire to improve the chances of their children to attend the colleges of their choice, and if they now believe that a homogeneous secondary education is likely to be more rigorous and/or safe for their children, America's elite colleges and universities have a unique opportunity, by acting upon their own deepest values, to abate those tensions and re-order parental priorities.

OUR APPROACH

We have used Justice Powell's holding in *Bakke*—which the *Grutter* Court recognized as the "touchstone for constitutional analysis of race admissions policies"—as a starting point for our efforts to move this initiative forward. Powell wrote that "race or ethnic background may be deemed a 'plus' factor in the context of a flexible and individualized consideration of each college applicant." Looking to the future, Powell urged adoption of admissions criteria that are "often individual qualities or experiences not dependent on race, but sometimes associated with it."

Our approach emphasizes collaboration. In an era in which top-down, judicially-mandated desegregation at the K-12 level is largely over, we are convinced that the greatest challenge—even for attorneys—is to develop voluntary and creative ways to ensure racial and economic integration at that level. Our first challenge was to devise a collaborative strategy that would energize and mobilize the higher-education community. We grappled with the challenge of building a social movement within the higher-education community and how best to bring about institutional change, both within individual institutions and across the higher-education community at large. While we realized that the participation of college presidents and chancellors would be critical, we also recognized that much preliminary work and relationship-building would be required before we approached these leaders. So we began close to home. We first talked with administrative officials at Duke University and the University of North Carolina-Chapel Hill—universities with which we are affiliated.

These conversations persuaded us that we should pursue a strategy that is simultaneously "bottom-up" and "top-down." We should first build relationships with middle-level actors within universities, including undergraduate deans of arts and sciences, chief university diversity officers, university general counsels, education scholars and, of course, admissions directors. We believed these actors would have an institutional interest in this initiative, would be able to advocate for it within their institutions, and would ultimately be responsible for its implementation. Second, we focused on engaging university presidents/chancellors who—we hoped—would then publicly explore the viability of this initiative. We further believed that there would be productive synergy between these two approaches.

FOUR RELATED TRAJECTORIES

We began to implement this strategy in September of 2006 when Julius Chambers formally introduced the initiative at the Politics of Inclusion Conference, a national gathering of college and university administrators held in Chapel Hill. We built on the momentum of his address by forging individual relationships with admissions directors, diversity officers, general counsels, deans and provosts from colleges across the country. From these conversations we learned that (in addition to the moral appeal we were making) it was critical to emphasize how the presence of high school students with diverse experiences would directly benefit colleges and universities. In addition, these conversations convinced us that our strategy would be most effective if we targeted four communities within the university world: admissions officials, who would implement this initiative; scholars—who could test the empirical assumptions that animate the initiative; university general counsels and other relevant attorneys—to consider the initiative's legal viability and the limits of race-neutral programs; and, most importantly, presidents/chancellors, who would commit their institutions to this idea. Over the past months, we have coalesced four related and ongoing trajectories involving these groups. For this chapter, we focus on our work with college and university admissions directors across the country and, more briefly, efforts to engage college leaders.

NEW IDEAS IN UNDERGRADUATE ADMISSIONS

After discussions with more than a dozen admissions directors in the Fall of 2006, in January of 2007 we convened a group of seven admissions directors representing selective private and public institutions to discuss the viability of our initiative. Soon after this meeting, the College Board—best known for the SAT, but which also sponsors meetings and colloquia that attract college officials throughout the country—expressed interest in co-sponsoring (with the UNC Center for Civil Rights) a meeting that would further develop the concept. More than 20 admissions officials from around the country—including those representing large public universities that are grappling with new state laws that limit the use of race in the admissions process—met in June of 2007.

Together, these meetings helped us refine our original idea, which was an "admissions plus" for simply attending a racially and economically diverse high school. The admissions officials encouraged us to focus on identifying: 1) qualities that would enable students to adeptly negotiate and enrich an inclusive educational setting, and 2) the characteristics of the environments where students would likely acquire these qualities—in most, but not all cases, high schools.

These insights led us to develop the concept of "diversity capital." Diversity capital is an alternative way to conceptualize diversity in both high school and college settings. Diversity capital is analogous to "human capital" or "cultural capital." It denotes the qualities, skills and life experiences that enable a student to communicate, cooperate, compete and achieve in a truly inclusive setting. While diversity capital is an attribute of individuals, it is experientially acquired, not ascriptively given. Students develop diversity capital. Put differently, diversity capital might be considered one form of cultural competence necessary to be successful in our contemporary democracy and globalized world.

From a social scientific perspective we would anticipate clear benefits of diversity capital at both the individual and collective levels. Individual students who possess diversity capital and the qualities associated with it may display a range of improved outcomes both within and outside the classroom. Students with diversity capital might be expected to do better in a range of areas, both in high school and college. And the presence of a critical mass of students who possess this capital may advance the general educational mission of our colleges by serving as agents of engagement and inclusion. These, of course, are merely assumptions. We are now in the process of testing these assumptions with relevant national data.

There are a number of advantages to this focus on diversity capital. First, unlike many other admissions criteria—legacy status, for example—the ability to work cooperatively in an inclusive educational setting is a skill that is directly transferable to the college setting. Second, unlike athletic prowess, diversity capital would be an admissions criterion that would be relevant to all applicants. Potentially, all applicants could develop diversity capital. (Of course, the development of bridge-building skills—like the development of special music skills—would not be a requirement for all applicants in the type of individualized, holistic review that most of our selective colleges now undertake.) Third, a focus on diversity capital would make this initiative race-neutral, even as its introduction would be undertaken with the knowledge that at present few white students who apply to our selective colleges and universities attend diverse high schools. Indeed, while the language is certainly race-neutral, the intent is also race-neutral. Conversations with a broad range of attorneys have convinced us that the knowledge that at present historically underrepresented minority students are more likely to have these qualities—precisely because they are more likely to have attended a diverse school—does not make this merely a "proxy for race" and, thus, a policy requiring strict scrutiny by the courts. Finally, diversity capital might be used to complement quantitative data collected at the individual, school and, increasingly, at the neighborhood level (i.e., GPA, class rank and quantitative measures of the socioeconomic make-up of the neighborhoods and high schools from which applicants are drawn).

How would diversity capital actually operate in the undergraduate admissions process? At one of our national meetings, an admissions director provided one vision of how this concept might be operationalized. He began by noting that every admissions initiative his college had designed to attract students who could enrich an inclusive educational environment on his campus had been "gamed"—mostly by parents, advisors and personal coaches. Typically, the family's week-long vacation to the Dominican Republic or Costa Rica, or Mexico had enabled the applicant to develop at once an appreciation for and familiarity with difference. He said that the idea of diversity capital would create a different set of incentives. Indeed, he went on to say that his college was prepared to give an admissions advantage—"a thumb on the scale"—to that student who: 1) attended a high-performing, inclusive diverse secondary school—a school, for example, in which the demographic profile of the college track resembled the profile of the overall student body, and 2) demonstrated leadership or bridge-building qualities—one form of diversity capital. Under this policy, "gaming the system" would both produce more of the kinds of applicants this college desired as it challenged the increasing racial and economic isolation in our country. Indeed, according to another admissions director, our challenge is to proceed in a manner that links individual private gain with long-term public good.

ENGAGING UNIVERSITY LEADERS

A related trajectory centers on our efforts to involve university leaders in our work. This past April, Chancellor James Moeser at UNC-Chapel Hill led a discussion at the American Association of Universities that focused on this initiative. He began the conversation by asking his fellow presidents and chancellors if our nation's finest universities had a collective—as distinct from an institutional—responsibility to challenge increasing racial and economic isolation at the K-12 level.

The conversation that followed was far-ranging and passionate. Four critical points emerged. First, there was general agreement that this issue was directly relevant to the mission of our greatest public and private universities. The assembled presidents assumed that at a meeting of university presidents it was important to talk about racial and economic isolation at the K-12 level. Second, there was great pessimism about the future of integrated schooling, not only at K-12—and this was before the Supreme Court's ruling in the Jefferson County and Seattle cases—but also at the higher-education level. One president predicted that "in the very near term the only integrated schools left will be the private academies that are very intentional in their admissions policies." He was convinced that "we have lost integration altogether in the public schools." Several presidents who are also law school graduates believed that the Supreme Court would soon reverse *Grutter*, given how quickly they are reversing elements of the *Roe* decision. Third, many of the assembled presidents stressed the necessity of developing new ideas. "We are losing affirmative action," one Ivy League president noted. He continued: "It is soon going to be completely shut down in this country, either by the Supreme Court in a reversal of *Grutter*, or through a series of statewide initiatives. We have to figure out how to work in a totally new environment." Fourth, several presidents believed that an admissions "plus" for simply attending a diverse high school was not a sufficiently nuanced instrument to address this problem. This reaction (along with our conversations with admissions officials) led to our present focus on individual qualities and school characteristics and development of the concept of diversity capital. We are actively engaged in finding ways to continue this conversation among the leaders of the higher-education community.

NEXT STEPS

In addition to continuing work on these trajectories, we intend to focus on extending this conversation to the K-12 sector. We began this work trying to gauge the interest of the higher-education community in our concept. We are now convinced that there is ample evidence of such interest. We now seek to engage leaders at the K-12 level. Indeed, the project cannot move forward without the active participation of these leaders. Specifically, in the coming months we seek to explore how to define a genuinely inclusive and high-performing high school; what individual qualities—and these presumably would vary depending on the mission, geography and make-up of the school—should be privileged; and how the relationship between school characteristics and individual qualities should be conceptualized.

* * * * *

COMMENTARIES

* * * * *

IT MIGHT ACTUALLY WORK

PEDRO NOGUERA

Since the Supreme Court's ruling in *Parents v. Seattle Schools*, I have heard little more than anguish and frustration about this decision and its long-term implications. In fact, most of the legal analysis I have read describes it as the death knell for serious efforts to promote racial integration in our nation's schools. In an attempt at positive spin, one colleague at NYU Law School suggested that the conservative majority on the Supreme Court view matters pertaining to race in a manner that is not dissimilar to their stance on gays in the military: As long as districts don't say they are using race as a factor in school enrollment, the courts will not intervene. Such a strategy is hardly encouraging, given that the forces in opposition to affirmative action and school desegregation (i.e., Ward Connerly and the Pacific Legal Foundation, to cite just two of the better-known opponents) appear to be closely monitoring the actions and policies of schools and universities on matters pertaining to racial inclusion.

It is against the backdrop of growing pessimism that I read and became genuinely excited about the strategy described by Chambers, Boger and Tobin. The article offers one of the few creative ideas on how to bring about racial diversity in higher education that I have encountered in recent years. What sets their proposal apart from the others is that it might actually work. As the authors point out, several leaders in higher education (and in many elite prep schools) filed amici curiae briefs in *Grutter v. Bollinger*, and, unlike many public universities, most have not allowed the number of minority students they enroll to drop. Pushing them to go a step further by sending a clear signal to secondary schools (and to parents of high-school seniors) that they not only value diversity but will give extra credit in the admissions process to students who attended diverse high schools may actually result in greater willingness to support racial inclusion in secondary schools. We know from past trends that the admissions policies of colleges and universities have had a trickledown effect on high schools in other areas (e.g., AP enrollment, service learning, advanced math enrollment, etc.) Now the question is, can a similar approach be taken to further efforts to promote diversity in secondary schools? I think there is reason to believe it can.

Even before affirmative action policies and practices were challenged by the courts, and in some cases state propositions, colleges and universities across the country were faced with declining minority enrollments due to a "pipeline crisis." For several years, the number of highachieving minority students eligible for admission to top universities has been decreasing. Many factors have contributed to this decline, but perhaps the most important is the fact that African-American and Latino students are disproportionately concentrated in the lowest-performing schools. In many cases, such schools serve the poorest students with the greatest needs, and typically lack the resources (i.e., books, technology, certified teachers, advanced placement courses, etc.) to prepare these students adequately for college. In the absence of a plan to address gross inequity and de facto segregation in many of our nation's secondary schools, there is little hope that the trend toward declining minority enrollments will be reversed.

This is why the ideas put forward by Chambers, Boger and Tobin are so appealing. In the absence of legal mandates that protect the rights of school districts to promote racial inclusion, it may be that the only recourse available is to rely upon the leadership of elite universities to assert that greater diversity is a public good that should be valued and recognized in the admissions process. Of course, the main weakness with this idea is that it relies almost exclusively upon the goodwill and commitment of university and college presidents to remain supportive of efforts to retain some degree of diversity among their student populations. That may not comfort those who want more—legal mandates, busing orders, consent decrees, etc. However, it doesn't seem likely that these strategies will return any time soon. In the meantime, the kind of creativity captured in the Chambers et al. proposal may be our best bet.

* * * * *

SOME POSSIBLE CHANGES, CRITICS AND CAUTIONS

JOHN A. POWELL

The effort of Julius Chambers, Dean Jack Boger and William Tobin should be applauded. They are looking for a creative way to change the trajectory that has pointed toward both restricting diversity in higher education and increased racial isolation in K-12. Their effort should be engaged and experimented with on several fronts. I would like to use this response to suggest some possible changes, critics and cautions. There is some conflating of ideas in the chapter that is not useful. The chapter talks about diversity, integration and inclusion interchangeably. These concepts have related but important differences at a conceptual level and a pedagogical level. The chapter too quickly acquiesces to the most narrow view of where the country is and where it is going on issues of racial inclusion and integration. For example, their concept of diversity capital attempts to be race-neutral both in word and content in order to shield it from attacks by the Court and other detractors. As far as the Court is concerned, their effort is to adopt a plan that will not be subject to strict scrutiny. There are a number of problems with this approach, as the Court made clear in *Bakke* and reaffirmed with greater clarity and strength in *Grutter*. Using race can pass constitutional muster under strict scrutiny, acceptable under *Grutter*.

It is not clear why there should be an effort to avoid race. In *Parents Involved . . .*, Justice Kennedy in his controlling opinion was clear that there is a compelling government interest in addressing racial isolation. In supporting these race-conscious approaches, Kennedy noted that in many efforts where racial goals are the aim, that does not automatically trigger strict scrutiny. He went on to say that, when not using the individual race of the student, "Executive and legislative branches . . . should be permitted to employ them with candor and with confidence that a constitutional violation does not occur whenever a decisionmaker considers the impact a given approach might have on students of different races."

In their effort to come up with a safe alternative, the authors concede too much too quickly. Of course, they could be right as to where the Court and the country are headed, but it is not clear. Remember that democratically elected school boards in Seattle and Louisville opted for integration.

Diversity is important, but it does not do the same work as integration. The authors will need to be clear about when the goal is diversity and when it is integration or inclusion. The authors at times refer to the importance of democracy, as Justice

O'Connor did in *Grutter* and Chief Justice Warren did in *Brown*. I would like to see some version of what they are suggesting more closely tied to democracy and the role of colleges. This does not detract from the importance of diversity, but, again, it is a related but different valence. Finally, the role of the university in its relationship to the general public is not just individualistic. When the authors speak of doing something from the bottom up, tied to the mission of universities, I expected something about the public good and the community to show up in their work.

The country is both very conflicted and at times confused about the role of race and the importance of concepts like diversity, inclusion and integration. I believe it would help to clarify the use of these concepts, tying them to both our vision of our democracy and the mission of the university. Their admissions policies should be informed by their respective missions. The country may continue to retreat on the commitment to racial integration and inclusion. Four members of the Supreme Court clearly would restrict not only the use of race but also its consideration. However, there also are four members of the Court who would not only embrace the use of race but also tie it strongly to the value of inclusion and our democratic ideals. Justice Kennedy embraces aspects of both the more narrow plurality and the more expansive dissent, and there is reason to believe he is in transition. There is also reason to believe that as a society we are in transition. How these important alternatives that the authors suggest are put forth, debated and hopefully adopted will have implications not just for the schools and the students but also which way the Court and the country are likely to break. The idea of creating incentives to support diversity, and, by suggestion, democracy, should be explored. I welcome the conversation started by the authors.

* * * * *

AN IMPORTANT STEP

WILLIAM L. TAYLOR

Out of the promising ferment about national policy emerging from the current Presidential campaign, there may come a couple of ideas that will be useful in advancing the goal of a diverse and racially inclusive society. One such is the Chambers/Boger/Tobin proposal to make attendance at diverse high schools a plus factor in college admissions.

Paradoxically, the most recent Supreme Court decisions in the Seattle and Louisville cases leave less room for voluntary race-conscious admissions policies at the K-12 level than the earlier University of Michigan decisions did at the university level—a difference largely due to the Court's change in membership, The Chambers et al. proposal will give colleges the discretion to adopt policies that recognize the value of diversity at earlier stages in education and will encourage the voluntary adoption of diversity policies in elementary and high schools.

The proposed policy should draw the support of the college presidents, business leaders and military officials who argued forcefully as friends of the Court in the Michigan case that an increasingly diverse society requires well-prepared, diverse leadership. It should help persuade advantaged parents that enrollment at diverse schools will not penalize their children in their quest for an elite education.

As the lawyer for schoolchildren in St. Louis who helped develop the largest and most successful interdistrict desegregation program in the nation more than 20 years ago, I have seen how the experience helps youngsters of all races not only in their academic performance but in developing those noncognitive skills that prepare them for leadership and effective citizenship. The Chambers et al. proposal could take another important step in this direction.

* * * * *

A MORE THAN MODEST PROPOSAL

WENDY PURIEFOY

As far as we may believe we have come since the *Brown v Board of Education* decision regarding racial justice in public education, the sad truth is that too many of our schools remain racially segregated. (In the Northeast, for example, 51 percent of African-American students attend schools that are composed of 90–100 percent minority students.) And the recent U.S. Supreme Court decision to reject voluntary public school assignment plans based on race in Seattle and Jefferson County, Kentucky marked another sad point in our democracy's history.

Still, in the more than 50 years that have passed since *Brown*, we have seen countless benefits accrue to generations of children as a result of conscious racial diversity policies. Racially diverse educational settings provide sound environments for children of all races to achieve academically, develop socially, and live and work on a diverse planet. Most Americans believe in racial diversity in their public schools, K-12 as well as colleges and universities.

The ideas put forth by Chambers, Boger and Tobin in their "modest proposal" for colleges and universities to promote K-12 diversity are more than modest. They are brilliant. "Diversity capital" should rank in the same legions as human or financial capital. Institutions of higher education prepare people for the world, a world that becomes more diverse every day. As such, we must promote further diversity in these institutions.

* * * * *

AN EXCELLENT IDEA

RICHARD D. KAHLENBERG

Chambers, Boger and Tobin have offered an important and constructive proposal, exploiting the competition for selective colleges to promote more equitable K-12 schooling. The authors are right to emphasize high school diversity by both race and class. Racial integration is important for building social cohesion and tolerance, while economic integration is important for promoting academic achievement. And the authors are right to seek "bridge builders." Higher education needs integration (seeking common ground) as much as diversity (emphasizing difference).

In further defining the proposal, the authors should encourage colleges to set clear parameters of what constitutes a diverse high school (percentage free or reduced lunch, and racial and ethnic make-up). If left ambiguous, upper-middle-class parents may not take the perceived "risk" of sending their child to an economically and racially diverse school. Likewise, more research should explore the extent to which the Texas 10 percent plan—providing automatic admissions to the Univ. of Texas-Austin for those in the top 10 percent of every high school class—encouraged more affluent families to relocate. The Texas plan is an important precedent worth studying.

* * * * *

REWARDING STUDENTS BY NUDGING ADULTS

JENICE L. VIEW

Professors Chambers, Boger and Tobin propose the fascinating idea that colleges and universities can promote K-12 racial/ethnic diversity by privileging those college applicants who demonstrate significant amounts of "diversity capital"—life experiences, behaviors and perspectives gained from attending a high-performing, inclusive, diverse secondary school. This is a noble goal, given the recent legal and political reversals that create a greater number of segregated public schools. We have come to understand that enforced racial isolation does not serve our children well in a world where global consciousness is a highly valued commodity.

The authors concede that the concept of diversity capital requires refinement. Indeed, the core idea assumes that schools with a high degree of racial/ethnic diversity will offer experiences and conditions that generate diversity capital among students. However, racial/ethnic integration in a school (let's say one with at least 30–40 percent students of color) is only as good as the educational opportunities offered to all students within the high-performing, inclusive school. But we need to ask: Is there academic tracking? What is the proportional representation of students of color and poor students in Advanced Placement, International Baccalaureate, and honors courses? What is the rate of suspension/expulsion of students of color? Are student athletes expected to perform at a high academic level? If the secondary schools can claim that there is diversity in their body count but the social pyramid replicates the inequities of the larger society, then it is questionable whether students will accrue diversity capital simply by breathing the air.

The authors indicate that "at present few white students who apply to our selective colleges and universities attend diverse high schools." So, too, for students of color. As stated at the outset of their chapter, increasing numbers of students of color attend schools that are 90–100 percent minority. So, those students would not be credited with diversity capital. A more likely scenario is that students of color at "diverse schools" are in the numeric minority at predominantly white schools. Yet, this does not equate to having experienced an "inclusive school." The experiences of these students may be sufficiently negative that they would bring to college anxieties (or "liabilities") that are contrary to the concept of diversity capital. Viewed from another angle, the diversity capital that a successful and eager student of color brings to college—having been a numeric minority in a predominantly white school—may be very similar to the characteristics and perspectives that currently make such students attractive to selective colleges and universities. In other words, there might not be a net gain in the number of students of color with diversity capital.

The white student with genuine diversity capital (as opposed to the student whose family vacation to Latin America is presented as cultural exchange/community service/diversity awareness) might demonstrate school-based experiences as an antiracist ally with people of color. This is very different from saying, "Some of my best friends from high school were [people of color]." Let's assume that such exemplary secondary schools exist where students can gain this experience and perspective. Are they more likely to be in urban areas on the East and West coasts? If so, there may be implications for geographic diversity in current college admissions.

Again, the authors propose a very interesting idea that may well shape the composition and tenor of college classrooms in 2028. For colleges and universities to take the leadership in rewarding talented students from schools and school districts that invest in racial equity—this can only be regarded as a social good.

When the Feds Won't Act: School Desegregation, State Courts, and Minnesota's The Choice is Yours Program

Myron Orfield & Baris Gumus-Dawes

New strategies are needed to fight school segregation, which continues to undermine equality of opportunity in the U.S. Since the early 1990s, federal courts have been more unwilling to mandate desegregation under the Constitution's Equal Protection clause. Plaintiffs therefore are increasingly turning to state courts, seeking remedies under state constitutional Equal Protection clauses and/or by invoking the fundamental right to education in state constitutions.

In one seminal Connecticut case—*Sheff v. O'Neill*—the court recognized that a segregated education was a state constitutional violation and ordered Connecticut to desegregate its schools. In Minnesota, the state settled a somewhat similar claim by initiating a voluntary integration program, The Choice is Yours. This promising program shows the viability of state court desegregation remedies in the face of the waning federal commitment to desegregation. The success of The Choice is Yours also demonstrates that a voluntary school integration program can achieve acceptance in predominantly white communities if adequate financial incentives are put in place.

THE SETTLEMENT

The Choice is Yours Program was created in 2000 in response to a lawsuit filed on behalf of the children enrolled in Minneapolis public schools. The plaintiffs argued that a segregated education violates the Minnesota State Constitution's Education and Equal Protection clauses. The plaintiffs alleged that the State of Minnesota had not taken effective action to desegregate Minneapolis schools and that the state reinforced racial and economic inequality through its school construction policies. A major part of the settlement agreement was creation of The Choice is Yours Program.

288

THE CHOICE IS YOURS PROGRAM

The program has an interdistrict student transfer component, which greatly expanded educational opportunities for low-income children in Minneapolis. Under this component, children of Minneapolis residents who qualify for free or reduced-cost lunch programs are eligible for priority placement in participating schools in eight suburban school districts. Almost all of the sending Minneapolis schools were predominantly nonwhite, with high percentages of children receiving free and reduced-cost lunch. Receiving school districts ranged from 41 percent white to 87 percent white, with much lower rates of school poverty.

The program allocated a minimum of 500 priority placement slots per year, starting with the 2001–2002 school year, eventually setting aside an estimated 2,000 slots over four years. While the legal settlement that resulted in The Choice is Yours Program expired in June 2005, the program's interdistrict transfer component continues to operate under the West Metro Education Program's comprehensive desegregation plan, thanks to ongoing support from the receiving districts.

At the beginning of the 2005–2006 school year, approximately 1,680 children were enrolled in The Choice is Yours Program; 1,090 of these students were returning from the previous year. The majority of the participants had previously attended overwhelmingly poor Minneapolis schools. African-American and Asian students participated in the program at rates higher than their respective shares in the student population. Because the program was designed to target students by income, and not by race, it was not completely efficient in achieving racial desegregation. Nonetheless, 81 percent of the participating students were students of color. Geographically, North Minneapolis neighborhoods were the largest contributors to the program. Not surprisingly, suburban districts immediately adjacent to these neighborhoods received more students under the program than any other district.

A PROMISING PUBLIC SCHOOL
CHOICE MODEL FOR SCHOOL INTEGRATION

Students who participated in The Choice is Yours Program experienced significant achievement gains. Averaged across all demographics, students from grades 3 through 7 made consistent and significant improvements in reading and mathematics. In comparison with the program-eligible but nonparticipating students, The Choice is Yours suburban students made annual gains that were nearly a third higher.

Ideally, one needs to compare the test scores of program participants with the scores of eligible students who were not accepted into the program in order to control for the self-selection bias of highly motivated students and parents who seek public choice programs. However, such a comparison is impossible since enrollment capacity limits for The Choice is Yours have not yet been reached and no applicants have yet been rejected.

Instead, the Minnesota Department of Education attempted to correct for this self-selection bias by studying students who began in the program with a wide range of achievement levels. Students who scored below the 50th percentile initially made gains similar to other Program participants. In both reading and mathematics, low-performing participants scored 19 percentile points higher in mathematics progress than nonparticipants and 13–22 percentile points higher in reading. These findings show that The Choice is Yours Program holds promise for its academic quality.

The program has been favorably regarded by parents, students, the Minnesota Office of the Legislative Auditor and even the Bush administration. One of the nine choice programs nationwide to receive a federal grant while those monies were still available, the program was considered the best among these programs.

Interviews with parents of the students who participated in the program revealed great satisfaction with it. Ninety-eight percent of all the parents whose children participated claimed they would recommend the program to others. During the 2005–2006 school year, 70 percent of the parents reported that they had actually recommended the program to other parents. Parents rated the schools well on a variety of factors, including setting high standards for achievement, creating community and making students feel welcome. Academic quality and school safety were the main reasons parents enrolled their children in suburban school districts.

Suburban school districts participating in the program have been receptive to incoming students for two reasons. Many of these districts have been facing declining or stagnating enrollments and as a result have been losing state revenues. The program fills these empty seats and not only brings needed diversity but also the per-pupil state revenues the suburban districts need to maintain their level of service. Moreover, these school districts are given additional financial incentives for receiving students. Minnesota's school finance law rewards suburban districts for receiving students who participate in The Choice is Yours Program because these students bring with them what is known as "compensatory revenue" in addition to the base amount of state aid allocated to all students. Compensatory revenue is awarded under a state formula based on the number of low-income children in each district. This means that suburban districts receive more state aid for The Choice is Yours participants than they do for other students. In addition, these districts receive state desegregation transportation aid funds to finance the transport of Program participants.

STRENGTHENING THE PROGRAM

While The Choice is Yours Program's interdistrict choice model is a promising approach and has been proven beneficial to the students involved, its limited geographic scope has been counter-productive. Because of neighborhood transition in inner-ring suburbs participating in the program, increased racial segregation and poverty concentration have become growing issues in some participating schools. Two changes to the program are necessary for its continuing success in the short run.

Instituting poverty caps on individual schools would limit the number of program participants any individual school could enroll. This would prevent future concentrations of poverty in individual schools. Ensuring a wider distribution of program participants across districts would also prevent any school district from becoming racially and economically segregated.

In order to implement its original goal of integrating disadvantaged students into opportunity-rich, well-performing schools in the long run, however, the program should be significantly expanded to encompass many more school districts. Increasing the number of participating suburban school districts could help distribute poverty enrollments over a larger set of schools and school districts, and ensure that all participating schools remain economically and racially integrated. The program's continuing success depends on avoiding future concentrations of poverty and racial segregation in participating schools and school districts.

Reaffirming the Role of School Integration in K-12 Education Policy

Post-Conference Statement: An Urgent Need for Federal Support

National Coalition on School Diversity

The November 13, 2009 Conference of the National Coalition on School Diversity brought together more than 300 people from across the nation. This included parents, teachers, school administrators, local and state elected leaders, long-time civil rights advocates, community organizers, and government officials. We engaged in a substantive, compelling dialogue with representatives from the U.S. Department of Education (USDOE), the Justice Department, the Department of Housing & Urban Development (HUD), congressional staff, and the White House Domestic Policy Council. We expressed our collective concerns about the slow pace of support for voluntary school integration in the new administration. We feel that our concerns were heard. Now, we must work together to ensure that the new leadership at USDOE goes beyond a mere rejection of the prior administration's hostile approach toward racial and economic integration, affirmatively expanding support for policies that directly ensure that educational and social benefits reach all racial groups.

This statement summarizes the most important steps we believe the federal government must take in the next two years to support voluntary school integration in American public schools. It is not intended as an exhaustive recap of all the research and policy proposals presented.

1. Rescind the August 2008 Guidance Issued by the Previous Administration

The goals of promoting integration and avoiding racial isolation were recently reaffirmed as compelling government interests by five justices of the U.S. Supreme Court in *Parents Involved in Community Schools v. Seattle School District #1*. The decision did strike down specific elements of voluntary plans in Seattle and Louisville. However, a majority of the Court indicated support for a wide range of race-conscious measures to promote school integration that do not assign individual students based on their race.

In August 2008, the USDOE issued a misleading "Guidance" to local districts suggesting that race-conscious plans were no longer permissible, and advising districts to adopt "race-neutral" policies. Needless to say, the Department's 2008 Guidance caused confusion among school administrators. We urge the USDOE, in consultation with the Department of Justice, to rescind the 2008 Guidance and replace it with an affirmative statement that accurately reflects the law.

2. Expand Funding for the Magnet Schools Assistance Act

The Magnet Schools Assistance Program (MSAP) is the primary source of federal funding for innovative school integration programs. As set out in the No Child Left Behind Act, "[i]t is in the best interests of the United States. . . . to continue to desegregate and diversify schools by supporting magnet schools, recognizing that segregation exists between minority and nonminority students as well as among students of different minority groups." 20 U.S.C. § 7231(a)(4). However, as we heard at the conference, the president's FY 2010 budget for MSAP has been flat-funded since FY 08, and the number of school districts served has steadily decreased. The current budget level funds the program at $104.83 million, supporting approximately 41 MSAP grantees in 17 states. Without funding increases or adjustments for inflation, MSAP is unable to meet the demand for more magnet school programs. We urge the USDOE to double funding for the MSAP to at least $210 million in 2011–2012, and to include much stronger integration goals in the funding application process, along with other equity measures (including protection against within-school segregation and tracking).

3. Provide Support for Interdistrict Transfer Programs

Some of the most successful school integration programs now operating involve the voluntary transfer of students in high-poverty urban districts across district lines to attend higher-performing (and racially integrated) suburban public schools. These programs have been studied exhaustively, and it is clear that they provide important benefits to both city and suburban students. They need the full support of the federal government, and could serve as models for other highly segregated metropolitan areas. This should include support for parent education and organizing, and transportation costs, as well as staff development and training to ensure that incoming students receive the best possible education when they arrive. Additional efforts should be made to avoid in-school segregation and address the needs of low-income Latino students, students with disabilities, and students with limited English proficiency.

4. Open up the New Stimulus Education Funds
to Voluntary School Integration Programs

The "Race to the Top Fund" and the "Investing in Innovation Fund," adopted pursuant to the American Recovery and Reinvestment Act of 2009 (ARRA), both have the potential to expand quality, integrated educational options for low-income children in low-performing schools. We again urge the USDOE to consider its mandate to promote racial and economic integration in its administration of these funds.

5. Promote School Integration in the Reauthorization of
the Elementary and Secondary Education Act (ESEA)

The upcoming reauthorization of the ESEA (which includes most of the current elements of "No Child Left Behind") is an important opportunity to restructure the delivery of Title I funding to states and local districts in a way that incentivizes integration. Specifically, the USDOE should consider strong incentives to states to require cross-district transfers to permit low-income students to move from high-poverty schools to lower-poverty schools, with funds appropriately following the students to their new districts. The USDOE should also support revisions in the basic Title I funding formula to more strongly encourage racial and economic integration, expansion of funding for parent involvement, and inclusion of a "private right of action" to permit parents to enforce their children's rights under the act.

6. Incorporate Civil Rights Requirements in the Charter School System

The growing charter school system should not be exempt from the obligation to promote racial and economic integration. These schools have great potential for diversity, because they are usually not restricted by school district boundaries. Yet in practice these schools tend to be more segregated than nearby conventional public schools. The USDOE should require all charter schools receiving federal funding to take affirmative steps to promote racial and economic integration – including active recruitment of children of color, lower-income families, English language learners and students with disabilities under the IDEA, as well as other appropriate prointegration measures consistent with the *Parents Involved* decision. Similarly, consistent with Title VI, the department should also refrain from funding new racially isolated schools unless such funding is necessary to prevent imminent educational harm.

7. Better Coordinate Housing and School Policy
in Support of School Integration

HUD and the U.S. Department of Treasury, through their extensive low-income housing programs, exert significant control over where low-income families are permitted to live. However, in spite of a clear mandate to promote integration, these agencies have generally not considered the educational impacts of their policies—

often steering children of low-income families and children of color into high-poverty, segregated schools. It is time for the USDOE to work collaboratively with HUD and Treasury to better link federal housing and school policy, including civil rights siting requirements for the Low Income Housing Tax Credit Program, strong affirmative marketing of all federally funded housing assets in high-performing school districts, and expansion of mobility counseling in the portable Housing Choice Voucher Program to allow families with young children to move into higher-performing schools.

8. Support Strong Civil Rights–Related Research at the Department of Education

The federal government should engage in and fund research designed to assist racially integrated schools both to improve and sustain their diversity. Similarly, studies of successful, integrated schools need to be disseminated and understood. For example, teachers in diverse and racially changing schools could benefit from research on strategies that confront and resolve racial tension, teaching strategies that include and affirm children from a variety of cultural backgrounds, and strategies that help educators devise effective and fair alternatives to "tracking" systems that often disproportionately place students of color in lower-level classes. The USDOE should also explore joint research efforts with HUD on combined housing and education strategies to reduce school segregation.

9. Increase Civil Rights Monitoring and Enforcement

The USDOE, through its Office of Civil Rights, should visibly increase its monitoring and enforcement of civil rights laws, including such issues as parental concerns of racially segregated students in re-established school boundaries and "neighborhood" schools, unnecessary clustering of English language learner students, access to special programs such as gifted and talented programs, and ongoing active review of existing enforcement agreements.

10. Use the Secretary's National Leadership Role to Endorse Racial Integration in Schools and Inspire Integration Efforts

In speeches and other public comments, the secretary of education could emphasize that integrated public schools are important training grounds as our nation becomes more diverse. Such schools, the Secretary should emphasize, are critical elements in the health of our democracy. Visits to racially integrated magnet schools, that are also high-performing, for example, would provide public examples of such models and further endorse the goal of racial integration in public schools. Officials can stress that prodiversity efforts are voluntary measures that provide families expanded educational choices.

Middle-Income Peers As Educational Resources and the Constitutional Right to Equal Access

Derek W. Black

Integrating our nation's public schools continues to be one of the most important and daunting challenges to delivering equal education opportunities. Decades of research confirms that the socioeconomic composition of a school is one of the, if not the most, important factors in individual students' achievement. Yet policies and realistic legal strategies supporting the expansion of voluntary desegregation are few and far between. Mandatory racial desegregation has all but run its course. Voluntary desegregation, while still possible, is subject to significant constitutional limitations that can make it difficult for school districts to devise workable plans. See, e.g., *Parents Involved in Community Schools v. Seattle School District No. 1, 551 U.S. 701* (2007). School finance litigation has attempted to force states to more fairly distribute resources so as to compensate for the effects of student disadvantage and poverty concentration, but has rarely lodged direct challenges at the problem of segregation. As of late, school finance litigation has even been tepid about challenging resource inequality, conceding to the reality that the recession has emptied state coffers and undermined public services in general.

The inability to defend integration over the past two decades has allowed schools to resegregate to levels similar to those that existed when desegregation first began in earnest in the late 1960s and early 1970s. The inability to fundamentally alter the way schools are funded results in predominantly poor and minority schools routinely receiving thousands of dollars less per pupil than their suburban counterparts. In short, today's schools are both segregated and unequal. Given the severity of today's segregation and inequality, a racial achievement gap between whites and minorities equivalent to two years of learning by the eighth grade is not entirely surprising. What is surprising is the dearth of policy and legal solutions to the problem.

One solution may lie in re-envisioning school finance litigation. For over a decade, scholars have called for a "fourth wave" of school finance litigation that would combine racial desegregation and school finance into a single movement. The idea has been that racial and/or socioeconomic isolation deprives students of their state constitutional right to an equal or adequate education. With the exception of an opinion by the Connecticut Supreme Court in *Sheff v O'Neill*, 678 A.2d 1267 (1996), this theory has yet to take firm root. Only a few advocates have even attempted to pursue integration through school finance claims. The benefit of litigating segregation through school finance is that it avoids various doctrinal limitations that exist in the federal courts. Yet current theories of desegregation through school finance would require significant expansion of current state precedent and also pose many of the same practical problems that the federal desegregation posed: interdistrict desegregation, judicial capacity and judicial authority.

Integrative approaches to school finance, however, need not confront these practical limitations or require significant expansions of precedent. A careful examination of current school finance precedent indicates that a constitutional right to equal access to middle-income peers at the school district level should already exist. The theory is not that students can compel a state or school district to create racially or socioeconomically integrated environments where they would not otherwise exist, but that past school finance decisions provide a basis on which to constrain the distribution of middle-income students within individual school districts. A constitutional right to equal access to middle-income peers within individual school districts flows from four basic principles, three of which already find solid support.

THE RIGHT TO EQUITABLE AND QUALITY EDUCATIONAL OPPORTUNITIES, NOT JUST MONEY

Although routinely dubbed school finance litigation because additional funding has been the primary remedy litigants have requested, the core holdings in school finance litigation establish constitutional guarantees of equal and quality educational opportunity that are about far more than money. In fact, the constitutional violation in most cases is not funding inequity itself, but the substantive and outcome-based inequities that can result from funding inequity. Funding is relevant only because it can purchase critical inputs, such as teachers and curricula, that are necessary to offer students an equal educational opportunity or some qualitative level of education. The ultimate issue is whether students are receiving the appropriate constitutional education, which can be jeopardized through any number of state and local school policies, only one of which is financing.

EDUCATIONAL RESPONSIBILITY AT THE LOCAL LEVEL

Constitutional duties to deliver a quality or an equal education extend to districts in addition to states. Most states bear the ultimate responsibility for educational failures, but local school districts are also responsible for supporting and delivering a constitutional education. To reason otherwise would afford districts wider constitutional latitude than states, when the primary constitutional power and duty itself is vested with the state. States are responsible for setting up an educational structure and monitoring local activities. They then delegate extensive responsibilities to school districts, including financial, staffing and implementation issues, leaving the daily and practical aspects of delivering a constitutional education to the discretion of school districts. When school districts exercise this discretion poorly, they can just as easily create inadequate and unequal educational opportunities as the state when it fails to provide sufficient funding or establish appropriate policies. In short, districts, like states, have a constitutional duty to deliver appropriate educational opportunities.

THE RESOURCE DISTRIBUTION PRINCIPLE

Educational constitutional duties include an obligation of strategic and equitable resource distribution. Courts have recognized that an abundance of resources will not guarantee equitable or quality education opportunities without a careful and fair distribution of those resources. For instance, states and school districts with abundant funds and resources can still fail to provide equal or adequate opportunities if those funds are spent on the wrong services or distributed to the wrong places. See *Abbott v. Burke*, 575 A.2d 359, 377 (N.J. 1990), discussing the role of variances in how efficiently districts use their funds as a problem in determining whether money matters. Likewise, a district might have just enough resources to deliver a constitutional education but still fail to do so because it does not make the best strategic choices in deploying the resources. In effect, the state may have done its part to make a constitutional education possible, but the district takes action that inhibits the delivery of appropriate education. Even though the state might have the ultimate responsibility to correct such a district, the constitutional failure occurs at the district level and the solution is not more funding for the district, but better allocation of existing resources. Of course, it is also possible that failures occur at both the state and district level. The state might provide inadequate funds and a district might make matters worse by poorly allocating those resources. Either way, constitutional rights to education require that educational systems adhere to effective distributional mechanisms and principles.

This concept is embedded in the very language of several state constitutions. Nineteen state constitutions mandate an "efficient" education. At the most basic level, dictionary definitions of efficient offer straightforward meanings that include "performing or functioning in the best possible manner with the least waste of time and effort"; and "satisfactory and economical to use." Courts have interpreted their constitutional language consistent with such definitions. For instance, the West Virginia Supreme Court found that the constitutional phrase "efficient" commanded that "the education system be absolutely complete, attentive to every detail, . . . [and] produce results without waste." *Pauley v. Kelly*, 255 S.E.2d 859, 874 (1979). Likewise, the state must deliver a quality education "economically." Id. at 877. This duty also encompasses local school district actions. The court noted that many other courts "have required specific actions by local boards to bring them to compliance with the constitutional mandate" and state action that failed to ensure local compliance has likewise "been declared unconstitutional." Id. at 874. Thus, in addition to quality instruction and facilities, "state and local monitoring for waste and incompetency [are] implicit in the definition of 'a thorough and efficient system.'" Id. at 877.

This constitutional mandate of strategic distribution even extends to states whose constitution does not explicitly mandate "efficiency." For instance, the North Carolina Supreme Court was more prescriptive on this principle than states with "efficiency" clauses. The court indicated "'that neither the State nor . . . [the Hoke County School System] are strategically allocating the available resources to see that at-risk children have the equal opportunity to obtain a sound basic education," *Hoke Cnty. Bd. of Educ. v. State*, 599 S.E.2d 365, 388 (N.C. 2004). It then directed both the state and school districts to "conduct self-examinations of the present allocation of resources and . . . produce a rational, comprehensive plan which strategically focuses available resources and funds towards meeting the needs of all children, including at-risk children to obtain a sound basic education." Id. at 389. In short, the manner in which state and local school districts allocate their resources is as important as the amount of resources they have. Thus, courts have found that their constitutions require that states and districts strategically distribute their resources in ways that minimize waste and maximize equal opportunity.

MIDDLE-INCOME PEERS AS EDUCATIONAL RESOURCES

The final conceptual step in a constitutional right to middle-income peers is not as simple as the first three. It requires a reorientation in thinking about educational resources. Legally relevant educational resources tend to be conceptualized as those things that schools can buy, develop or create that have positive impacts on educational outcomes. This conceptualization, however, is overly narrow and ignores reality. Schools enjoy any number of important resources that they do not and cannot buy, such as the communities, public services, partnerships and private industries surrounding them that support the educational environment. The more important, obvious and direct noneconomic resource is a school district's middle-income students. Common sense, as well as decades of social science, indicates that students learn not only from their teachers, but also their peers. Middle-income peers (and their parents) bring a host of experiences, outside learning and high expectations to schools that positively impact other students in their schools. In fact, the percentage of middle-income students in a school can be more important to the educational achievement of all students in that school than any other resource. Students, regardless of their individual socioeconomic status or race, achieve at higher levels in predominantly middle-class schools and achieve at lower levels in predominantly poor schools. In short, while not a traditional resource that schools can buy, middle-income students are an invaluable resource that exerts significant effects on the achievement of all students.

EMPIRICAL FINDINGS ON RACIALLY UNEQUAL ACCESS TO MIDDLE-INCOME PEERS

Reconceptualizing educational resources to include middle-income students by itself is not enough. Courts must also reorient their perception of poverty and racial segregation. Poverty and racial segregation today are perceived as inevitable, beyond the control of states and districts, and natural. Of course, it is true that school districts have almost no control over the total number of middle-income and poor students in their districts, but they have complete control over the assignment of those middle-income and poor students who are, in fact, enrolled in their districts. Conventional wisdom over the past two decades, however, has been to ignore this basic fact and the problem of segregation within districts because the most extreme and extensive segregation exists between districts. While conventional wisdom may be correct in its assessment of interdistrict segregation, interdistrict segregation has proven largely impenetrable thus far. In any event, it does not follow that segregation within districts is not occurring or serious.

To the contrary, my recently published empirical study of access to middle-income peers reveals that many school districts have the capacity to expose all students to middle-income environments, but instead deny minorities of the experience. See 53 *Boston College Law Review* 373 (2012) available at http://ssrn.com/abstract=2008731. A serious problem with racially unequal access to middle-income peers within districts stretched across all eleven states included in the study. Some districts were providing access that was so unequal it was shocking. In four of the states, some districts provided whites twice as much access to middle-income peers as minorities. This is the difference between whites attending a solidly middle-income school, with 70 percent middle-income peers, and minorities attending a solidly poor school with only 35 percent middle-income peers. A few districts even provided whites access that was three to five times that of minorities. The data also revealed that in several states a quarter of the districts were providing access that, although not shockingly unequal, was disparate enough to create qualitatively different experiences for white and minority students. And on the basic question of rough equality, in some states, only about half the districts provided equal access. In short, far too many school districts have student assignment policies that place minority students at educational risk in comparison to whites and thus raise serious constitutional concerns.

Interestingly, the study also uncovered a pattern of many other school districts doing the opposite by providing minority students equal access to middle-income environments. The fact that this inequality of access is occurring within the confines of individual school districts, but not others, demonstrates that the current racially and socioeconomically isolated nature of many districts is not inevitable. Rather, districts are making choices about how they distribute valuable resources—too often to the disadvantage of minorities.

UNEQUAL ACCESS AND ACHIEVEMENT GAPS

Consistent with the literature, this unequal access appeared to have consequences for minority students' academic achievement. After identifying the varying levels of equitable and inequitable access, the study analyzed whether racial inequality in access to middle-income peers corresponded with any change in the racial achievement gap. It found that, in general, those districts with the most inequitable access for minorities also had the highest achievement gaps, whereas districts that provided minorities the most equitable access had the lowest achievement gaps. Moreover, the difference in achievement gaps between these unequal and equal access districts was drastic. In seven of eleven states, the achievement gap drop between inequitable-access districts and equitable-access districts was more than 50 percent, cutting the achievement gap in half. And in all the remaining states but one, the drop in the achievement gap was still large. These empirical findings not only force a reorientation of how one perceives racial inequality in student assignments, but suggest that a widespread pattern of segregative student assignments and wide achievement gaps persists that would otherwise be inconsistent with a constitutional right to equal access to middle-income peers.

CONCLUSION

The failure of an integration movement to emerge in state courts may be more a result of perception and strategy than doctrine and reality. While not as broad as prior theories, this chapter's theory offers a strategy for school integration that has strong conceptual grounds in school finance precedent. Once one understands that middle-income students are one of the many resources districts distribute, the equitable and strategic distribution of resources that school finance precedent has forced on schools and districts is directly implicated. Of course, no court has yet explicitly conceptualized middle-income students as resources, but a review of social science literature, as well as the differing academic achievement that students produce based on their exposure to middle-income peers, renders the concept undeniable. Courts already intuit this notion and heavily scrutinize and condemn the prevailing poor performance of districts with concentrated poverty. And parents already act on it, often flocking to schools based more on the socioeconomic status of the students who attend them than the characteristics of the school facility or the particular staff who teach in them. Once legal analysis catches up to reality and intuition, state constitutional education precedent will squarely apply.

Community-Based Accountability: Best Practices for School Officials

Jason Langberg, Taiyyaba Qureshi & Eldrin Deas

Accountability in education must include the idea that school systems have certain obligations to their stakeholders. Traditional notions of accountability are mostly focused on measuring performance outputs of students, teachers and principals, and fail to identify metrics by which elected and appointed policymakers can be held accountable for their actions. Unfortunately, this trend has become even more prevalent as so-called market-based reforms (e.g., expanded high-stakes testing, merit pay, privatization) are adopted on the federal, state and local levels. These policy changes in fact "de-form" democratic principles of good governance and fairness, which require that school system leaders be held accountable to the community. Over the past four years, education policymakers and community advocates in Wake County, North Carolina demonstrated that such accountability is essential to creating a healthy relationship between the school district and the community it serves, and to producing high-quality, equitable outcomes for students.

To promote diversity and student achievement, the Wake County Public School System (WCPSS) implemented a student assignment plan in 2000 which minimized concentrations of low-wealth or low-performing students by limiting each school in the district to a maximum of 40 percent of students eligible for free and reduced lunch and no more than 25 percent of students performing below grade level. Along with the district's award-winning magnet schools, the policy made the WCPSS a nationally acclaimed leader in high-quality education. However, the WCPSS also faced significant challenges, including huge achievement gaps, a massive school-to-prison pipeline, inadequate funding, rapid growth and instability in school assignment.

In 2009, a staunchly conservative majority took over the WCPSS Board of Education. The new board removed the diversity mandate from the student assignment policy and began moving the district to a "neighborhood schools" model that increased racial and socioeconomic segregation. Moreover, new members' campaign promises to higher-income and predominantly White neighborhoods to dismantle the diversity-conscious student assignment policy gave the public the impression that the board only sought to please its electoral base instead of engaging in research-based decision-making that serves the interests of all the district's students. The board also failed to adequately address repeated concerns about excessive suspension rates and severe racial disparities in student discipline. The board's regressive actions and its reluctance to meaningfully engage with advocates soured prospects for amicable political and policy solutions.

In 2010, the first interim student reassignments produced predictable segregative outcomes. Advocates quickly formed a coalition of student and parent activists, education experts and civil rights attorneys who shared a commitment to diversity in education, eliminating the school-to-prison pipeline, narrowing achievement gaps, and holding the board publicly and legally responsible. This diverse coalition of advocates pushed to hold the board accountable through several means, including: (1) direct action, such as marches, rallies, pickets and civil disobedience; (2) lobbying by testifying at school board meetings and communicating regularly with staff and policymakers; (3) public education through media, workshops, publications and regular community meetings; and (4) electoral advocacy.

Further, as the board continued to resist mounting public pressure to address resegregation and the school-to-prison pipeline, the coalition initiated legal actions, including Title VI complaints to the Office for Civil Rights of the U.S. Department of Education; complaints about special education to the North Carolina Department of Public Instruction; an AdvancED accreditation complaint; and individual representation to students for suspension and special education matters. By filing a lawsuit over the district's violation of North Carolina open meetings laws, the coalition also challenged the board's undemocratic, nontransparent governance that made community-based accountability more difficult.

Committed advocates slowly succeeded in making the board more accountable and responsive to public demand for an integrated and equitable system with fair discipline policies. Strong electoral advocacy resulted in the most conservative board member—the chairperson—being replaced and the election of more moderate members willing to engage broader community concerns. The WCPSS also responded to pressure from advocates for more public input by conducting online surveys, holding community hearings and forming special committees. In July 2012, WCPSS passed a resolution supporting diversity in school assignment, thereby demonstrating a commitment to reversing the system's regression towards high-poverty, racially isolated schools (masquerading as "school choice"). Additionally, over the last three years, suspensions declined, the Student Code of Conduct was revised, and alternative education expanded.

Wake County's education advocates learned several lessons from this experience. When community concerns first arose, the board had the opportunity to gain allies through meaningful engagement with stakeholders. Instead, the board spent years and precious human and financial resources in media and legal battles, rather than working with the community toward a high-quality, equitable education for all students. As education law attorneys and researchers who assisted advocates in the push for community-driven, democratic accountability, the authors offer the following suggestions as best practices for elected and appointed school officials:

1. Commit to honest and comprehensive engagement by reaching out to all segments of the community. Take the initiative to involve stakeholders early in policy development and implementation processes to create trust and buy-in.

- Solicit diverse viewpoints by engaging with the whole community—across geographic, age, socioeconomic and racial groups. Even in systems with district-based elections (rather than districtwide elections), each board member should be conscious of needs across the whole district. Avoiding the impression that the board serves particular interest groups creates trust in the board as a body with the best interests of all children at heart.
- Provide regular, open, diverse forums (e.g., online and phone surveys, public hearings, community meetings and task forces) to solicit feedback from stakeholders, rather than relying only on time-constrained public comments at regularly scheduled meetings. Short time limits may increase meeting efficiency, but more importantly, they frustrate advocates and prevent the board from hearing the whole story.
- Involve students, parents, knowledgeable community members and trained educators in both the creation and implementation of policies and practices, including significant financial decisions. This will help the board create evidence-based policies, promote community buy-in and avoid the impression that the board is making political decisions without adequate consideration of or to the detriment of students.

2. Act with transparency and ensure due process for discipline, employment and all other grievances.

- Develop and implement transparency policies, including requirements for open meetings, adequate notice, publicly available and timely copies of board materials, thorough and quickly released minutes, and prompt and easy access to public records.
- Be sensitive about scheduling important meetings during times and places where stakeholders can attend. Some boards rotate meeting times and locations and repeat important hearings to attract parents and students with inflexible work or transportation schedules. Anticipate interest in issues and choose venues that have size and sound capacity to allow everyone to attend and hear. Provide daycare and translation to facilitate full engagement.
- Enact and comply with policies for fair dispute resolution and appeals for employees and students, including grievances, suspension and expulsion

appeals, misconduct by law enforcement officers and security officers assigned to schools, and special education.

3. Enact prospective policies to promote equitable student assignment and discipline at the district, school and classroom level for students and teachers.

- Implement policies that position a district to succeed with a high-quality, racially and socioeconomically diverse educational experience at every school. Setting up schools, teachers and students to succeed in this way enriches the educational experience, reinforces community engagement and prevents legal confrontations.
- Implement policies and practices that prevent the push-out of students, such as positive behavior interventions and supports, ample support services (e.g., psychologists, social workers and mentors), restorative justice and high-quality alternative education.
- Employment policies, including recruitment, benefits and fair grievance procedures, must be tailored to attract and retain highly effective and culturally sensitive teachers and administrators.
- Seek advice from law firms or organizations qualified to objectively advise the Board on legally sound, equity-based policies, not just risk management. Given the Supportive School Discipline Initiative (a joint effort of the U.S. Departments of Education and Justice), voluminous research from civil rights organizations, recent Title VI findings, and the December 2011 "Guidance on the Voluntary Use of Race to Achieve Diversity and Avoid Racial Isolation in Elementary and Secondary Schools," school districts have clear legal and policy paths to create diverse, fair and safe educational environments.

4. Speak up! Fulfill ethical and professional obligations to promote transparency and equity in the system.

- Even if representing minority viewpoints, board members and administrative staff should not be afraid to voice their opinions and "blow the whistle" when necessary, including when budget cuts and resource starvation force them into a position of violating the law. Courage, integrity and honesty are essential to accountability and to the struggle for equity.

The Role of Teacher Union Locals in Advancing Racial Justice and Improving the Quality of Schooling in the United States

Mark Simon

In 2005, a dozen or so progressive teacher union leaders created the Mooney Institute for Teacher and Union Leadership (MITUL), an outgrowth of the ten-year-old Teacher Union Reform Network (TURN). We created MITUL out of a deep understanding of just how difficult it is to lead a teacher union local in a progressive direction. We wanted to define what progressive unionism is, develop a curriculum through which our fellow unionists would deepen their understanding of the approach, and then institutionalize coaching and support for next-generation unionists to take their locals and the national unions in that direction. We wanted to cultivate bold, creative, reform-oriented union leaders and locals.

The institute convinced a handful of foundations to support our effort and began work with our first cohort of nine major urban union locals. We developed tools to communicate about the approach, a website and blog (http://www.mitul.org/), and got the attention of the leadership of both the National Education Association and the American Federation of Teachers, who were cautiously supportive.

Tom Mooney, AFT vice-president from Ohio, and a great reform leader as president of the Cincinnati Federation of Teachers (CFT) was one of our MITUL founders. When he passed away unexpectedly in 2006, we re-named the institute after him. The MITUL website includes descriptions of Tom's life and work and why his view of teacher unionism has been a guiding light to many of us.

DEFINING PROGRESSIVE UNIONISM

Progressive unionism, as we defined it, included an equal emphasis on three frames: 1) traditional (industrial) unionism; 2) professional unionism; and 3) social justice unionism. The locals in our first cohort acknowledged right off the bat that their existing local activity fell almost entirely in the industrial frame, and that both the professional and social justice frames were underdeveloped. The work undertaken then was to develop plans for building community alliances, taking up strategies for improving teacher quality, and helping teachers to adopt approaches to teaching that enabled them to empower and be more successful with disadvantaged students. MI-TUL took up the need to re-think seniority rights, the need for the union to invest in peer review and other innovations to teacher evaluation. We viewed collaboration with management, not as a goal, but a strategy for exerting teacher influence over the important decisions in our members' work lives, those related to curriculum, assessment and instruction. We also discussed the need for the union to be connected with other movements for social justice and economic change to further what became known as the "broader, bolder approach" to education reform. The Mooney Institute authored two opinion columns in *Ed Week*, and we looked forward to the change in the president in the White House but also the ones in both the NEA and the AFT, all in 2008.

The most well-meaning of elected local union leaders come into the job and feel immediately overwhelmed. It is an awesome responsibility to speak for thousands of hard-working teachers. The language, work styles and daily patterns of teacher unionism since the late 1960s have been defined by industrial unionism. Teacher unions are frequently largely reactive. They handle individual teacher complaints and grievances. They serve on management committees as the teacher voice. They periodically bargain pay rates, hours and working conditions. The daily routines of most union leaders are defined by others. We were trying through the institute to help union leaders see that their mission needed to be to define the public education reform agenda—to fight for equity and justice through changes in curriculum, authentic assessment tools, improvements in instruction and teacher quality control. We wanted to change the community face and role of the union.

We found tremendous receptivity to our ideas among teacher unionists, but the main impediment to the work of the institute has been the growing sense of crisis and being under siege that has become the norm in public education. The crisis is both fiscal and political. The sense of being embattled frequently brings out the worst of the industrial instincts and training of teacher unionists.

Now, more than two years into the Obama presidency—with the failure of the education jobs bill in Congress under the then-Democratic majority in both houses, the end of a brief foray into an attempt at economic stimulus, and then a devastating election in which Republicans gained a majority in the House of Representatives and the whole idea of government having a role in economic downturns was replaced by a new goal of deficit reduction—things have dramatically taken a turn for the worse. From the beginning of its term in office, the Obama administration looked to some of the same foundations and think tanks that had brought corporate-style reform strategies to Bush administration education policy development—the Gates Foundation, the New Schools Venture Fund, the Broad Foundation and the Ed

Trust. As Diane Ravitch argues, we have a tsunami that has put teacher unions in the crosshairs. The economic downturn put pressure on state and district revenues, forcing districts to make massive cuts, which led many to target teacher pensions, health benefits and class sizes. The new Obama strategies have doubled down on Bush strategies—School Improvement Grants and Race to the Top funding conditioned on promoting charter schools; labeling schools in high-poverty neighborhoods as failures and closing them; evaluating teachers based on student test scores; firing half the teachers in low-performing schools as a condition of getting federal funds, and in some cases letting the whole teaching staff go when test scores are low. These "quick fix" prescriptions create a collision course with teachers and their unions, but avoid the tough work of improving schools in urban, high-poverty neighborhoods.

A PIVOTAL MOMENT

This is a pivotal moment for teacher unions in the United States. And it is a pivotal moment for community groups and organizers for racial justice to understand the role and potential of teacher unions.

There is a powerful, richly funded and well-orchestrated campaign afoot to fundamentally restructure public education on a corporate efficiency and privatization model. It uses the rhetoric of civil rights to intensify the sense of urgency for change that all parents feel, particularly the families of low-income students of color. The reform movement has attracted surprising spokespeople in the likes of Newt Gingrich, Al Sharpton, Joel Klein, Cory Booker and Michelle Rhee, none of whom had run a school or a school system or much of anything that involved teaching or learning when they jumped in as the enablers for these neoliberal reform strategies. It also seems to have captured the Obama administration's Education Department. Funding for these reforms and the propagation of this powerful narrative comes from some of the largest education foundations, including Gates, Broad, hedge fund managers who bankroll Democrats for Education Reform, and from the federal government.

A primary purpose of this campaign is to disempower teacher unions and make public education cheaper by accelerating turnover in the teacher workforce—getting rid of older teachers, hiring younger ones who don't plan to stay long, reducing legacy costs in the form of cutting pensions and teacher healthcare. The goal also seems to be to teacher-proof the curriculum, centralize the content and instructional methodologies in line with high-stakes assessments, and to de-professionalize teaching. To make these changes possible, editorial boards and foundation-supported think tanks have waged a tremendous PR effort to undermine teacher unions and label them the cause of what ails public education. In a sense, the frontal attacks by Wisconsin's Scott Walker and Republican governors in Ohio and Michigan have been able to build on the fertile ground left by liberal corporate reformers.

A FALSE NARRATIVE

The dominant narrative that underlies the federal reform agenda goes something like this: Public education has failed to provide disadvantaged children with the opportunity for upward mobility, and has left middle-class children without the technological skills they need to compete in a world economy. Plenty of money has been spent on improving teaching and learning conditions, training teachers and ensuring that students are ready for school, which should have enabled the educational system to overcome differences in student background and preparation. The solution lies in high-stakes and test-based accountability and serious sanctions for failure, as measured by standardized exams. The stakes will be dramatically increased when teachers are evaluated not by their qualifications, experience, or overall competence and effectiveness, but by the basic-skills test score gains of their students. This view holds that schools and school systems need to be shaken up and required to compete with alternatives that include charter schools operated by private entities not bound by the restrictions that purportedly impede regular public schools. The status quo is so obviously broken, the purveyors of this narrative maintain, that any change, no matter how radical, can't possibly make things worse.

The problem is that this simple narrative is false. From the perspective of students, parents and teachers, things can get worse. Community groups are rising up spontaneously in New York, Los Angeles, Boston, Chicago, Philadelphia, Cleveland and elsewhere against school closings and consolidations in their neighborhoods. The common analysis by those community groups is that school closings and consolidations have more to do with opening new schools in gentrifying neighborhoods and closing schools in poor neighborhoods, furthering gentrification strategies of the banks and developers, than it does with real school improvement. In Chicago, Washington DC and Philadelphia, school consolidations led to gang violence predicted by community leaders. Research by the Consortium for Chicago School Research now shows that low-income students forced to attend new schools in other neighborhoods did no better, or even a little worse. It turns out that improving schools is more complicated than the promoters of Chicago's Renaissance 2010 and other quick turnaround efforts advertised. By and large, those efforts failed to deliver.

While individual charter schools sometimes offer a good education, the only large, national data-set study of charter schools, by Stanford University's Margaret Raymond, showed that 83 percent of charter schools have produced no better results than the neighborhood schools those students would have attended. Notwithstanding the fictionalized but emotionally gripping accounts like "Waiting for Superman," the success of some charters depends on selecting and attracting more highly motivated kids. In and of themselves, charters represent no reform strategy whatsoever. In fact, *NY Daily News* columnist Juan Gonzales warns of a coming avalanche of scandals of corruption and conflicts of interest by the corporate boards of loosely regulated, unaccountable charter schools.

We've had over a decade of No Child Left Behind and the achievement gap has not at all narrowed. NAEP scores have not improved over the past decade of NCLB, but were improving, it turns out, in the previous decades under different strategies. Test-driven reform is leading to epidemics of cheating, wasteful test-prep, narrowing of the curriculum, and educationally unsound practices in response to the high-stakes attached to standardized test scores. What test-driven reform has done is increase top-down management control, while narrowing and dumbing-down what is taught to what is tested in many schools and districts.

One reason the dominant narrative and thoughtless reforms have caught hold is that educators, unions and community-based organizations never developed an alternative reform narrative that would have empowered teachers, parents and students. All was not right in many of this nation's schools, but educators and even parents had become complacent. Indeed, local teacher unions did not help their cause by too often living the stereotype as obstructionists and defenders of the status quo. The response of NEA and AFT to the corporate reform models has been slow, complicated and a bit like deer-in-the-headlights over the past couple of years, and the national unions have had little impact on helping their locals to step up to lead alternatives to the dominant reforms.

RECLAIMING THE AGENDA

Although we are now playing catch-up, teacher unions, parent and community groups, and progressive education researchers and activists must reclaim the agenda for school and public education improvement. Our focus must be on real education reform. That means serious support for teachers to teach better. Teaching better has very little to do with getting test scores up, although test score results do provide a marker for how far we have to go. It rather has to do with supports for teachers to expand our repertoire of strategies for making learning engaging and effective. It means broadening and enriching the curriculum. It means engaging families and building neighborhood communities of support around schools. It could mean parent visitation programs like that developed in Sacramento, CA. It certainly means helping communities resist simple-minded school turnaround and closing strategies in favor of programs that better address the real causes of low student achievement in poor communities.

A body of research is beginning to unfold from the work of the Chicago Consortium for Chicago Schools Research in their book, *Organizing Schools for Improvement, and the Syracuse "Say Yes to Education" project*, in the Promise Neighborhood strategies emerging in NY, NJ and elsewhere, and the work in developing Teacher Residencies that actually serve to build the profession of teaching. Teacher unions can be at the forefront of pushing for peer assistance and review programs and other supports for new teachers. We have to get school districts to do justice to the complexity of the craft of teaching. We have to work with families and communities to identify strategies to ready students for learning.

Unions and community groups together can blow the whistle when ambitious superintendents or chancellors choose strategies that jeopardize the integrity of high-quality teaching and real learning, or when the real needs of communities are being ignored. Whether educators, parents and communities are going to have anything to say about the nature of public education depends on our ability to build alliances around a common vision of quality public education.

In this overview, I have attempted to present my sense of the challenges facing educators and community activists attempting to carve out a progressive agenda and perspective. I continue to think that the two national teacher unions, NEA and AFT, are sleeping giants with tremendous potential as allies of both teacher empowerment and grassroots community-led support for better reforms. Given the severity of the economic attacks on working-class communities, the attacks on public education itself, and the more and more brazen attacks on teacher unions, nothing is more important than building those alliances.

American Indian Boarding Schools

The following is a Feb. 2008 Shadow Report (lightly edited) submitted as a response to the Periodic Report of the United States to the United Nations Committee on the Elimination of Racial Discrimination. The full report can be found at http://www.ushrnetwork.org/fhere. See also the 2-part NPR series, May 12, 2008 ("American Indian School a Far Cry from the Past") and May 13, 2008 ("American Indian Boarding Schools Haunt Many"). See also "On the Reservation and Off, Schools See a Changing Tide," New York Times, *May 25, 2008.*

* * * * *

BRIEF HISTORY

During the 19th century and into the 20th century, American Indian children were forcibly abducted from their homes to attend Christian and U.S. government-run boarding schools as a matter of state policy. This system had its beginnings in the 1600s when John Eliot erected praying towns for American Indians, where he separated them out from their communities to receive Christian civilizing instruction.

However, colonists soon concluded that such practices should be targeted towards children, because they believed adults were too set in their ways to become Christianized. Jesuit priests began developing schools for Indian children along the St. Lawrence River in the 1600s.

However, the boarding school system became more formalized under the Grants Peace Policy of 1869/1870. The goal of this policy was to turn over the administration of Indian reservations to Christian denominations. As part of this policy, Congress set aside funds to erect school facilities to be run by churches and missionary societies. These facilities were a combination of day and boarding schools erected on Indian reservations.

Then, in 1879, the first off-reservation boarding school, Carlisle, was founded by Richard Pratt. He argued that as long as boarding schools were primarily situated on reservations: 1) It was too easy for children to run away from school; and 2) The efforts to assimilate Indian children into boarding schools would be reversed when children went back home to their families during the summer. He proposed a policy where children would be taken far from their homes at an early age and not returned to their homes until they were young adults. By 1909, there were 25 off-reservation boarding schools, 157 on-reservation boarding schools, and 307 day schools in operation. The stated rationale of the policy was to "Kill the Indian and save the man." Children in these schools were not allowed to speak Native languages or practice Native traditions. . . .

[The goal of the program was to] [s]eparate children from their parents, inculcate Christianity and white cultural values into them, and encourage/force them to assimilate into the dominant society. Of course, because of the racism in the U.S., Native peoples could never really assimilate into the dominant society. Hence, the consequence of this policy was to assimilate them into the bottom of the socioeconomic ladder of the larger society. For the most part, schools primarily prepared Native boys for manual labor or farming and Native girls for domestic work.

The rationale for choosing cultural rather than physical genocide was often economic. Carl Schurz [a former Commissioner of Indian Affairs] concluded that it would cost a million dollars to kill an Indian in warfare, whereas it cost only $1,200 to school an Indian child for eight years. Secretary of the Interior Henry Teller argued that it would cost $22 million to wage war against Indians over a ten-year period, but would cost less than a quarter of that amount to educate 30,000 children for a year. Consequently, administrators of these schools ran them as inexpensively as possible. Children were given inadequate food and medical care, and were overcrowded in these schools. As a result, children routinely died in mass numbers of starvation and disease. In addition, children were often forced to do grueling work in order to raise monies for the schools and salaries for the teachers and administrators. Overcrowding within schools contributed to widespread disease and death.

Attendance at these boarding schools was mandatory, and children were forcibly taken from their homes for the majority of the year. They were forced to worship as Christians and speak English (Native traditions and languages were prohibited). Sexual/physical/emotional violence was rampant. While not all Native peoples see their boarding school experiences as negative, it is generally the case that much if not most of the current dysfunctionality in Native communities can be traced to the boarding school era.

Today, most of the schools have closed down. Nevertheless, some boarding schools still remain. While the same level of abuse has not continued, there are still continuing charges of physical and sexual abuses in currently operating schools.

Because these schools target American Indians specifically, they are in violation of CERD.

THE CONTINUING EFFECTS
OF HUMAN RIGHTS VIOLATIONS

Human Rights Violations: A number of human rights violations have occurred and continue to occur in these schools. The U.S. has provided no recompense for victims of boarding schools, nor have they attended to the continuing effects of human rights violations. The Boarding School Healing Project (303/513-5922, 605/200-0164) has begun documenting some of these abuses in South Dakota. Below are some of the violations that have targeted American Indians, constituting racial discrimination:

Religious/Cultural Suppression: [Because] Native children were generally not allowed to speak their Native languages or practice their spiritual traditions, many Native peoples can no longer speak their Native languages. Survivors widely report being punished severely if they spoke Native languages. However, the U.S. has grossly underfunded language revitalization programs.

Because boarding schools were run cheaply, children generally received inadequate food. Survivors testify that the best food was saved for school administrators and teachers.

[And] according to one former BIA school administrator in Arizona: "I will say this. . .

[C]hild molestation at BIA schools is a dirty little secret and has been for years. I can't speak for other reservations, but I have talked to a lot of other BIA administrators who make the same kind of charges." Despite the epidemic of sexual abuse in boarding schools, the Bureau of Indian Affairs did not issue a policy on reporting sexual abuse until 1987, and did not issue a policy to strengthen the background checks of potential teachers until 1989. The Indian Child Protection Act in 1990 was passed to provide a registry for sexual offenders in Indian Country, mandate a reporting system, provide rigid guidelines for BIA and IHS [Indian Health Services] for doing background checks on prospective employees, and provide education to parents, school officials and law enforcement on how to recognize sexual abuse. However, this law was never sufficiently funded or implemented, and child sexual abuse rates are dramatically increasing in Indian Country while they are remaining stable for the general population. Sexual predators know they can abuse Indian children with impunity.

As a result of all this abuse, Native communities now are suffering the continuing effects through increased physical and sexual violence that was largely absent prior to colonization. However, the U.S. fails to redress these effects by not providing adequate healing services for boarding school survivors.

Forced Labor: Children were also involuntarily leased out to white homes as menial labor during the summers rather than sent back to their homes. In addition, they had to do hard labor for the schools, often forced to do very dangerous chores. Some survivors report children being killed because they were forced to operate dangerous machinery. Children were never compensated for their labor.

Deaths in Schools: Thousands of children have died in these schools, through beatings, medical neglect and malnutrition. The cemetery at Haskell Indian School alone has 102 student graves, and at least 500 students died and were buried elsewhere. These deaths continue today. On December 6, 2004, Cindy Sohappy was found dead in a holding cell in Chemawa Boarding School (Oregon), where she had been placed after she became intoxicated. She was supposed to be checked every fifteen minutes, but no one checked on her for over three hours. At that point, she was found not breathing, and declared dead a few minutes later. The U.S. Attorney declined to charge the staff with involuntary manslaughter. Sohappy's mother is planning to sue the school. A videotape showed that no one checked on her when she started convulsing or stopped moving. The school has been warned for the past fifteen years from federal health officials in Indian Health Services about the dangers of holding cells, but these warnings were ignored. Particularly troubling was that she and other young women who had histories of sexual assault, abuse and suicide attempts were put in these cells of solitary confinement.

Affirmative Furthering of Fair Housing: The 21st Century Challenge

Rob Breymaier

> *We're going to make this an open city, because it's right. We're going to make it an open city, because it's practical. We're going to make it an open city, because it's sound economics. We're going to make it an open city, because we're tired of being humiliated.*

—Rev. Dr. Martin Luther King, Jr., Chicago 1966

Since passage of the Fair Housing Act in 1968, the fair housing community has had a number of important accomplishments. First among these would be the relief provided to hundreds of thousands of victims of discrimination. This enforcement of the Fair Housing Act has provided housing and monetary relief for complainants as well as required training and monitoring of respondents. Through litigation, private fair housing organizations (with limited assistance from government agencies) have also provided systemic reform in the insurance industry and continue to serve as an important part of the movement to reform unscrupulous lending practices.

In addition, the fair housing movement has encouraged the housing industry to comply with fair housing law. This effort has had its most apparent impact on the real estate sales industry. For instance, in Illinois, real estate agents are required to take a continuing education course on fair housing every other year throughout their careers.

NO OPEN CITY OR REGION

Unfortunately, these efforts have not resulted in an open city or region. Despite their success in providing relief to victims of discrimination, enforcement efforts have been extremely limited in overcoming or preventing segregation in our metropolitan areas. Segregation continues be a dominant factor in the formation of American urban geographies. One-third of our 331 metropolitan areas have a high Index of Dissimilarity. Only 15 (almost exclusively small MSAs in the Rocky Mountains) have a low index. Furthermore, this structure of segregation continues to reinforce other forms of inequality, as I will detail below.

The small integration gains that have occurred owe much to the affirmative furthering of fair housing. While enforcement efforts have been invaluable on an individual basis and industry basis, it is efforts to affirmatively further fair housing that are responsible for improving integration. The relative progress in enforcement and affirmative furthering is reflected in the enforcement through the Fair Housing Assistance Program (FHAP) and the Private Enforcement Initiative (PEI) of the Fair Housing Initiatives Program (FHIP). Meanwhile, HUD allocated only $4.2 million to the FHIP Education and Outreach Initiative (EOI). Yet even this is misleading, as the bulk of FHIP-EOI grants are spent on consumer and housing industry education, not on projects attempting structural reform.

Affirmative furthering should at least include actively encouraging affirmative moves by all people (including whites); challenging government agencies to implement their programs in a way that balances housing and community development needs; and promoting predominantly white communities to market themselves as open to minorities.

Chicago serves as a good example of continuing segregation and how segregation continues to reduce the opportunities available to minorities, as well as a good example of remedies to segregation. Chicago has the advantage of being home to vibrant nonprofit and academic institutions that have spent time addressing segregation and inequality. The Chicago region is also the nation's fifth most segregated.

Shortly before its closing in June 2006, the Leadership Council for Metropolitan Open Communities published the definitive report "The Segregation of Opportunities," on the extremely high correlation between race and opportunity in the Chicago region. It reported that, despite minor improvements in minorities' access to housing in area communities and reduced instances of housing discrimination reported in HUD's Housing Discrimination Survey, stark racial and economic disparities persist in the distribution of access to opportunities across the Chicago region. According to the executive summary: "The study measured a variety of opportunity factors at the municipal level, including strength of the local tax base, quality of schools, access to jobs and transportation, and other quality of life issues, as compared to regionwide averages and the extent to which opportunities are accessible to people from various socioeconomic groups, specifically by race and income. All of the municipalities in the region were placed into one of five classes, from highest to lowest opportunities. 94 percent of Black residents and 83 percent of Latino residents lived in either the low- or lowest-opportunity areas."

This followed "Empty Promises," a report (which I co-wrote) a few months earlier showing how little local suburban governments were doing to enforce fair housing or promote their communities affirmatively. Of the 271 suburban municipalities, fewer than a dozen made strong efforts to maintain an open and inclusive community. Over half of those communities had predominantly African-American populations.

Neither of these reports provided any surprises. People in Chicagoland know they live in a segregated place and that little is being done to change that. However, the reports did provide, for the first time, peer-reviewed documentation of how segregation harms people of color directly and every person indirectly.

Despite these reports, opposing viewpoints primarily cited a will to self-segregate on the part of minorities while ignoring the fact that predominantly Black and racially diverse communities were doing the most to foster integration. This argument has gained in popularity in the Chicago region because new immigrant populations with language barriers do find some advantage to locating near one another. However, this argument does not hold true for second-generation minorities and especially not for African Americans who have lived in the region for decades.

In December 2006, Maria Krysan and Tyrone Foreman of the University of Illinois at Chicago presented data from the Chicago Area Survey that provided evidence that African Americans and Latinos usually do not seek out communities where they are in the majority. On the contrary, the Survey found that whites were very likely to only consider communities where they were in the majority.

In Chicago, one could also argue that the issue of housing choice is more about individual perceptions and governmental efforts than about housing industry practices. While discriminatory acts have decreased, research shows discrimination by real estate agents, landlords, lenders and insurance agents still occurs in 20–40 percent of all minority housing transactions. Thus, enforcement is still necessary. However, an important, yet largely unaddressed factor in the perpetuation of segregation is the absence of affirmative measures by municipalities in the region. The dearth of affirmative programs is evidence that municipalities are either promoting or ignoring prevailing perceptions of exclusivity in the region. If a suburb that is 95 percent white does nothing to promote itself affirmatively, it is essentially maintaining regional segregation patterns.

These perceptions are important because they affect which communities minorities will even consider. Most people do not want a hassle. And, finding a place to live is a stressful undertaking in the best of circumstances. So, when people at risk for discrimination think about buying or renting a home, they either consciously or subconsciously steer clear of places that they feel will involve anything from discouragement to harassment. The most effective way to counter this problem is to persuade (or force if necessary) municipalities to affirmatively further fair housing in their communities. Until this occurs, choices will continue to be limited from the start.

Race and Public Housing: Revisiting the Federal Role

Richard Rothstein

Residential racial segregation, accompanied by social and economic hardship, burdens the learning of many urban children. But school reformers often express hope that, harsh though these obstacles may be, children in high-poverty, racially isolated neighborhoods could typically still be successful if only they had better teachers, more orderly schools and more hours of instruction.

To support this hope, advocates seek examples of disadvantaged children who succeeded, overcoming great socioeconomic handicaps. Some such cases exist, of course—there is a range of outcomes for any human condition—but the reality that some who grew up in "truly disadvantaged" neighborhoods beat the odds does not mean that many can. Frequently cited examples of such success usually turn out, upon examination, to be chimeras.

A claim by U.S. Secretary of Education Arne Duncan, referring to former New York City Schools Chancellor Joel Klein, is one. Mr. Duncan said: "Klein knows, as I do, that great teachers can transform a child's life chances—and that poverty is not destiny. It's a belief deeply rooted in his childhood, as a kid growing up in public housing in Queens. . . . He understands that education is . . . the force that lifts children from public housing projects to first-generation college students. . . ."

Our credulity about Duncan's well-intentioned observation reveals a shocking loss of collective memory about how public policy created and remains responsible for the hopeless segregated ghettos in which too many children live today.

True, Joel Klein grew up in public housing. But from the Depression into the early 1950s, faced with housing shortages compounded by a flood of returning war veterans, cities constructed public housing for white working- and middle-class families. These projects, for stable white families like Joel Klein's, became highly prized treasures, the most desirable housing available, their lucky residents the object of envy. The projects were located in mostly all-white neighborhoods, and admitted only a token few black residents, if any.

NYC'S SUBSIDIZED HOUSING

Meanwhile, cities also built projects for low-income African Americans in ghetto neighborhoods, or sometimes in neighborhoods to which planners wanted to relocate a ghetto. Unlike projects for middle-class whites who paid market rents that fully covered construction and operating costs, projects for low-income blacks were heavily subsidized with federal and sometimes state and local funds.

There were also privately built and owned developments that were subsidized by public land clearance and tax breaks—such as the whites-only Stuyvesant Town in New York City. These remain today as middle-class urban islands, but forgotten have been the truly public projects—built, owned and operated by government—for working- and middle-class whites. The Woodside Houses in Queens, New York, where Joel Klein lived as a boy, was one of these.

The New York City Housing Authority carefully screened applicants for projects like Woodside. Preference was given to war veterans. Only two-parent families were accepted, and applicants had to produce marriage licenses to prove their status. Investigators visited potential tenants to verify they had good furniture and housekeeping habits, and well-behaved children. Stable post-war employment records, good credit, no teenage pregnant daughters and no alcohol or drug problems were also required. Tenants typically had civil service jobs (like Klein's father, a postal worker) or worked in trades or manufacturing. Some were small business owners.

When the unsubsidized Woodside project opened in 1949, its tenants were 92 percent white. In the surrounding neighborhood was nary a black face. Across the borough in South Jamaica, the Authority built a project for low-income tenants: 30 percent white when it opened pre-war and down to 12 percent white by the mid-1950s. Citywide, the Authority respected applicants' preferences regarding which project they wished to occupy, guided by a rule established during the New Deal by Harold Ickes, head of the Public Works Administration: Public projects could not alter neighborhood racial composition.

As applied by New York City, the rule ensured that few low-income whites would live in South Jamaica, and few middle-income blacks would live in Woodside. Housing Authority board minutes explain that the South Jamaica project should house minorities because it was "located in a neighborhood having a preponderance of colored people." The project had lower income limits than Woodside, and rental rates were subsidized with federal funds, but not all projects designed for African Americans were low-income: A project the Housing Authority built contemporaneously with Woodside, also designed for stable higher-income working families where rents covered the full housing cost, was the Colonial Park Houses in Harlem—it was 92 percent black, 7 percent Puerto Rican, and 1 percent white.

But as projects like Woodside filled up with middle-class whites, other federal policies lured these families out of projects into even whiter suburbs. These were the mortgage insurance programs of the Federal Housing Administration (FHA) and the Veterans Administration (VA), from which black families were mostly excluded. In the 1950s, as single-family home construction accelerated, the housing shortage eased and white families took advantage of these guarantees to decamp from Woodside and similar projects for the suburbs. FHA- and VA-guaranteed mortgages were so favorable that monthly carrying charges were often less, for comparable rooms and square footage, than rents in the public projects.

Whether in the city or suburbs, the FHA required developers seeking its financing to include restrictive covenants in their homeowner deeds, prohibiting sales or re-sales to African Americans. For example, Levittown, a suburb just east of Queens, was built in 1947 with 17,500 mass-produced two-bedroom houses, requiring veterans to put nothing down and make monthly payments of only $56. (Compare this to the $75 unsubsidized charge in Woodside Houses for apartments of comparable size.) At the FHA's insistence, developer William Levitt did not sell homes to blacks, and each deed included a prohibition of such re-sales in the future.

Of 300 large private subdivisions built from 1935 to 1947 in New York's Queens, Nassau, and Westchester counties, 83 percent had racially restrictive deeds, with preambles like, "Whereas the Federal Housing Administration requires that the existing mortgages on the said premises be subject and subordinated to the said [racial] restrictions . . . [except for] domestic servants of a different race domiciled with an owner or tenant. . . ."

As whites fled cities, public housing units were filled with lower-income African Americans. In 1968, New York City abandoned its middle-class public housing program, accepting federal subsidies for Woodside Houses and several other such projects. Long-term tenants with middle-class incomes who did not leave voluntarily were evicted. The Authority announced that it would abandon previous requirements of employment, stability and orderliness and would no longer consider "morals of the applicants." Many economically and socially distressed minority tenants, some with unruly teenagers, were funneled into once-middle-class projects. Changed population characteristics were accompanied by a deterioration in project upkeep. Students attending neighborhood schools now had drastically different, and greater, needs.

As public housing nationwide became racially identifiable and associated solely with poverty, public and media stereotypes of public housing changed. By 1973,

President Richard Nixon could describe many public housing projects as "monstrous, depressing places—rundown, overcrowded, crime-ridden."

These patterns were not unique to New York, but were repeated nationwide.

St. Louis

In the 1960s, Pruitt-Igoe homes became a national symbol of dysfunctional public housing—high-rise towers packed with welfare-dependent families, many of which were headed by barely literate single parents. Youth gang activity became more frequent. A combination of deteriorating social conditions and public disinvestment made life in the projects so untenable that the federal government evicted all residents and dynamited the 33 towers in 1972.

But few knew another side of St. Louis history. When federal housing funds became available during the New Deal, St. Louis proposed to raze a racially integrated low-income neighborhood whose population was about 75 percent white and 25 percent black, to construct on that land a whites-only low-rise project for two-parent families with steady employment. When Washington objected, St. Louis proposed an additional blacks-only project removed from the white one, but also in a previously integrated area. This met the federal government's conditions, insisted upon by liberals and civil rights leaders, for nondiscriminatory funding. The segregated projects were opened in 1945 with preference for veterans. The white project remained predominantly so until the late 1950s, when most early residents had relocated to suburbs, many with FHA- and VA- guaranteed mortgages and restrictive covenants.

Cleveland

Public housing constructed during WW II was open only to white workers, at the insistence of the Ohio Congressional delegation. Towards the war's end, a few African Americans were admitted to previously white-only projects, in token compliance with nominal (but unenforced) federal nondiscrimination policy. By 1945, black presence in Cleveland's four designated-for-whites projects ranged from 0.3 percent to 3 percent.

Detroit

In 1941, the government built the Ford Willow Run bomber plant in a previously undeveloped suburb without pre-existing racial housing patterns. The Federal Public Housing Agency then built housing for white workers only. Thus, the workforce necessarily was overwhelmingly white, in contrast to Ford's city operations. By 1944, as whites left public housing for FHA-subsidized single-family suburban homes, three thousand Detroit public housing units were vacant, while black workers in desperate need of housing were barred from occupancy in the city as well as from employment opportunities in the suburbs.

As the post-war housing shortage eased, whites' opposition to public housing grew. In 1948–1949, the Detroit City Council proposed twelve projects in white areas. The mayor vetoed them all; only housing in predominantly black areas was approved.

Los Angeles

Over 10,000 African-American families migrated during WW II for work in shipyards, aircraft plants and other war industries that, desperately in need of labor, hired blacks for the first time. But little or no adequate housing was open to blacks. Public housing was built in white neighborhoods, and the city's Housing Authority did not permit blacks to reside there. African Americans eligible for public housing remained homeless while units set aside for whites remained vacant. The Housing Authority chairman explained in 1943 that "the Authority selects its residents by following the previous racial pattern of the neighborhoods in which [projects] are located."

But faced with a growing housing crisis and civil rights protests, the Los Angeles Housing Authority soon reversed itself and adopted a nondiscrimination policy for all projects. It even adopted a lease clause that promised eviction for those who contributed to a disturbance based on "racial intolerance." The new policy was swiftly implemented, and by 1947 Los Angeles public housing was extensively integrated. But this was only temporary. As white tenants left the projects for homes in more solidly middle-class suburbs, blacks—for whom housing elsewhere was barred—disproportionately remained. Whereas in 1947 Los Angeles public housing tenants were 55 percent white and 30 percent black, by 1959, they were only 14 percent white and 65 percent black, with Mexican-origin tenants another 19 percent. Los Angeles public housing came to be perceived as "Negro housing," and whites began to protest the location of new projects in their neighborhoods. Public officials caved in, and projects initially designated for white areas were relocated to Watts. A project designated on the Santa Monica border, for example, was cancelled after such protests and relocated to Watts. Three new projects were built in Watts between 1953 and 1955 alone, turning Watts from an area where some blacks were already residing to an impoverished and racially isolated ghetto.

But best known in Los Angeles' public housing history was an attempt to build a racially integrated project in Chavez Ravine, northwest of downtown and far from Watts. By the end of 1951, land had been cleared and construction begun. But the City Council called an emergency meeting and cancelled the project. The California Supreme Court voided the cancellation, but the Council sponsored a 1952 referendum and voters overwhelmingly rejected the public housing. The

City then sold the land that had been cleared to the Dodgers baseball team for its stadium.

Boston

In the late 1930s, the city razed a dilapidated, overcrowded and low-cost neighborhood, to replace it with public housing for white middle-class families. Slum dwellers whose homes were demolished could not afford to live in the new public units with their relatively high rents. When the first project, Old Harbor, was opened in 1938, median monthly rent of $26 was only $3 below the citywide median. In 1940, only 9 percent of project residents were unemployed, compared to 30 percent in the surrounding neighborhood who were either unemployed or on public work relief; neighborhood median rent was $15. The project accepted families whose income was five times the citywide median rent (six times for families with three or more children). Another nearby development, the D Street Project, opened in 1949, mostly for veterans; tenants' median education level included some college, considerably higher than typical levels at the time.

As in New York, Boston disqualified prospective tenants for cohabitation, out-of-wedlock children, excessive drinking and unsanitary housekeeping. Inspectors entered prospective tenants' apartments without notice (or permission) to evaluate their household habits. Applicants had to provide references from previous landlords and prove stable employment histories. After WW II, veterans were given preference.

Also like New York, Boston assigned a token number of African Americans to Old Harbor and D Street, while maintaining other projects where few whites resided. But a 1962 discrimination complaint forced the city to assign additional black tenants to the middle-class projects. Initially, only middle-class families were assigned, but as more whites took advantage of FHA and VA subsidies to move, earlier residents were gradually replaced by much lower-income minorities.

D Street had initially accepted only two-parent families, but by 1960, there were 50 percent more adult females than males. It had opened with higher rents than those in the surrounding distressed area, but by 1970, rents were below those in any nearby community. Early tenants had more than high school education, but by 1975 the median adult level was 10th grade.

And Elsewhere

Examples nationwide abound of how public housing was used by federal, state and local governments to create the segregated metropolitan areas we know today. In 1960, Savannah (Georgia) evicted all white residents from its Francis Bartow Place project, creating an all-black neighborhood where integration previously existed. The Housing Authority asserted that with national (and local) housing shortages abating, whites could easily find housing elsewhere and blacks needed the housing more. In Miami, where black tenants had been assigned to segregated projects while whites were given vouchers to subsidize private apartment rentals, it was not until 1998 that a legal settlement required that vouchers also be offered to blacks. The remedy was insufficient to undo the segregation that public policy had created and abetted.

In 1984, The Dallas Morning News investigated federally funded projects in forty-seven cities, reporting that the nation's nearly 10 million public housing residents were still almost always segregated by race. The few remaining predominantly white projects had superior facilities, amenities, services and maintenance in comparison to predominantly black ones.

In 1976, the Supreme Court found that the Chicago Housing Authority, collaborating with federal agencies, had unconstitutionally selected sites to maintain segregation. Mayor Richard Daley had stated, in rejecting projects for predominantly white neighborhoods, that public housing should only go "where this kind of housing is most needed and accepted." President Richard Nixon told a news conference: "I believe that forced integration of the suburbs is not in the national interest," and then followed up with a formal policy pledging not to require any suburb to accept public housing over the suburb's protest. In the Chicago case, President Gerald Ford's Solicitor General Robert Bork stated the government's opposition to public housing in white communities: "There will be an enormous practical impact on innocent communities who have to bear the burden of the housing, who will have to house a plaintiff class from Chicago, which they wronged in no way." The federal government thus defined nondiscriminatory housing as punishment visited on innocent suburbanites.

Other court decisions, for example in Baltimore, Yonkers and Dallas, have also confirmed that the federal government created or perpetuated ghettos with its public housing site location and tenant assignment policies.

THE GOVERNMENT'S ONE-TWO PUNCH

The result has been a one-two punch. With public housing, federal and local government increased African Americans' isolation in urban ghettos. And with mortgage guarantees, the government subsidized whites to abandon urban areas for suburbs. The combination contributed heavily to creation of the segregated neighborhoods and schools we know today, with truly disadvantaged minority students isolated in poverty-concentrated schools where teachers struggle unsuccessfully to overcome families' multiple needs. Without these public policies, the racial achievement gap that has been so daunting to educators would be a very different, and lesser, challenge. That gap can't be addressed by nostalgia for a fanciful past when whites grew up in public housing and succeeded solely by benefiting from good teachers.

The conventional idea that we now suffer from "de facto" segregation, created by vague market and demographic forces (Justice Potter Stewart once termed them "unknown and perhaps unknowable") is urban mythology. Residential segregation was as much the product of purposeful public policy as was "de jure" school segregation. The legacy of both endures.

*Citations and sources can be found in the online version of this chapter at http://prrac.org/newsletters/novdec2012.pdf or obtained from the author at rrothstein@epi.org.

Integration and Housing Choice: A Dialogue

This year [2008], PRRAC has had the honor of supporting the work of the National Commission on Fair Housing and Equal Opportunity, an independent Commission co-chaired by former HUD Secretaries Henry Cisneros and Jack Kemp, and sponsored by the Leadership Conference on Human and Civil Rights, the Lawyers Committee for Civil Rights, the National Fair Housing Alliance and the NAACP Legal Defense Fund. Over the course of hearings in five cities, the Commission heard testimony on serious problems in fair housing enforcement, the need for stronger fair housing oversight of HUD grantees, origins and solutions to the foreclosure crisis, the relation between school and housing segregation, and the structural impediments to fair housing in federal and state housing programs. Several of the Commission witnesses also spoke to the complex question of personal choice in a housing market that has been distorted by discrimination and public policy decisions—exploring the meaning of choice in such a market, the extent to which choice is influenced by racial perceptions, and what policymakers can do to support integrative choices. The three witnesses excerpted here (Camille Zubrinsky Charles, Ingrid Gould Ellen and Maria Krysan) provide different and complementary perspectives on this question.

* * * * *

WHO WILL LIVE NEAR WHOM?

CAMILLE ZUBRINSKY CHARLES

Scholars and policymakers have long viewed residential segregation by race as a core aspect of racial inequality, implicated in both intergroup relations and in larger processes of individual and group social mobility.

328

Whether by choice or by constraint, persisting racial residential segregation has serious implications for both present and future mobility opportunities. Where we live affects our proximity to good jobs, educational quality and safety from crime, as well as the quality of our social networks and our physical and mental health.

As one of the most racially, ethnically and culturally diverse cities in the world, Los Angeles offers important lessons for understanding patterns of residential segregation by race as well as the factors—both individual and structural—that influence aggregate-level neighborhood patterns. There is a long history of African-American settlement there. Moreover, as a top destination for new immigrants, the school system there offers instruction in nearly 100 languages, boasts the largest Latino/a and Korean populations in the country and is home to the first majority-Chinese suburb (Monterey Park). As one of nearly 40 majority-minority metros, Los Angeles offers a glimpse of the future of America.

Rapid changes in population composition associated with massive immigration from Latin America and Asia (e.g., in 2000, about one-third of LA County residents were foreign-born, up from 22 percent in 1980); economic restructuring and persistent economic inequality along racial-ethnic lines (e.g., in 2000, nearly one-quarter of blacks and Latinos lived in poverty, compared to less than 10 percent of whites and 14 percent of Asians); and patterns of intergroup tensions and often negative racial attitudes (e.g., uprisings in 1965 and 1992, increasing black-brown tensions) all contribute to—and are consequences of—persisting residential segregation by race.

In terms of trends in racial residential segregation, since 1980, Los Angeles is one of a very few large metros that embodies several national trends. Like many older cities of the Midwest and Northeast, blacks are hypersegregated—exhibiting extreme isolation on at least four of five standard measures of residential distribution. And, in a new twist, Los Angeles is one of only two cities (New York is the other), as of the 2000 Census, to see its Latino population become hypersegregated. Equally important, despite reports of declining black-white segregation since 1980, there has been virtually no increase in blacks' exposure to whites in their neighborhoods; both Latinos and Asians have experienced substantial declines in their exposure to whites since 1980 as well. To the extent that racial residential segregation is deeply implicated in persisting racial economic inequality and tenuous intergroup relations, and inasmuch as trends in Los Angeles point to our national future, it is an optimal location for a consideration of the future of fair housing.

In general, social scientists debate the relative importance of three factors—real and/or perceived social class disadvantage, neighborhood racial composition preferences, and housing market discrimination—as primary contributors to persisting racial residential segregation. While economic inequality between racial/ethnic groups remains a pressing problem, objective differences in social class status cannot account for persisting racial residential segregation. Analyses of the housing market also reveal persisting discrimination against African Americans, Latinos and Asians in both the owner and rental markets. Here, I focus on the role of neighborhood racial composition preferences—and in particular the factors that motivate preferences—as critical for understanding not only aggregate housing patterns, but the role fair housing legislation can play in creating and maintaining stable, racially/ethnically integrated communities, in light of current patterns and trends in racial attitudes (including preferences).

Neighborhood Racial Composition Preferences: A Brief Summary

Over the last two and a half decades, there has been meaningful change in the neighborhood racial composition preferences of whites, shifting toward increased tolerance for sharing neighborhoods with more than token numbers of blacks and other minorities. At the same time, a clear majority of blacks remain willing to live in areas where their group is in the minority, and show a clear preference for 50/50 neighborhoods. Nonetheless, substantial differences remain in both the meaning and preferred levels of racial integration across racial categories. For many whites, a racially integrated neighborhood is one that is majority-white. To put it plainly, whites are willing to live with small numbers of blacks, Latinos and/or Asians, but prefer to live in predominantly same-race neighborhoods. Nonwhites, on the other hand, all prefer substantially more racial integration and are more comfortable as a numerical minority compared to whites. Still, the same-race preferences of nonwhites exceed whites' preferences for integration. Moreover, patterns of neighborhood racial composition preferences follow a predictable racial hierarchy: Whites are always the most-preferred out-group and blacks the least-preferred; Asians and Latinos, usually in that order, are located in between these two extremes.

What Drives Preferences—Classism, Ethnocentrism or Prejudice?

A variety of factors shape residential decision making: cost and affordability, the quality of the housing stock, preferences for particular dwelling amenities, proximity to work or other important destinations, stage in the life course, the quality of the public schools. Consequently, aggregate-level residential outcomes are the result of a multitude of individual-level attitudes and behaviors. In analyses of patterns of racial residential preferences, however, three hypotheses are typically considered:

Classism: Perceived differences in socioeconomic status that heavily coincide with racial-ethnic boundaries contribute to racial residential preferences.
Ethnocentrism: Members of all social groups tend to be ethnocentric—that is, prefer to associate with co-ethnics.
Prejudice: More active out-group avoidance is at the root of neighborhood racial composition preferences.

The expression of prejudice can take a variety of forms, including negative racial stereotypes, perceptions of social distance and the belief that one or more groups pose a competitive threat to one's own group. Also important, though not typically considered, are minority-group beliefs about the prevalence of discrimination; these beliefs may influence the preferences of minority-group members for whites or for same-race neighbors. To understand what drives neighborhood racial composition preferences requires systematic testing of the various hypotheses, preferably the simultaneous examination of said explanations.

Three items capture variants of prejudice. Racial stereotyping is an important aspect of traditional prejudice or simple out-group hostility. The measure used here is a summary of four traits—intelligence, preference for welfare dependence, English-language ability, and involvement in drugs and gangs. Social distance is the degree to which respondents believe that an out-group is "difficult to get along with socially" relative to his or her own group. Rather than simple out-group hostility, this form of prejudice is fueled by a commitment to a specific group status or relative group position, as opposed to simple out-group hostility. What matters most is the magnitude or degree of difference from particular out-groups that in-group members have socially learned to expect and maintain. Beliefs about racial-group threat or competition offer another lens through which to examine feelings of racial hostility—the degree to which an individual believes that more opportunities (economic and/or political) for an out-group results in fewer opportunities for one's own group. Finally, minority-group members' beliefs about whites' attitudes toward them and/or the prevalence of racial discrimination is captured in a general perception of whites as "tending to discriminate" against minority groups. Results of my research indicate that classism and ethnocentrism play, at best, marginal roles in individuals' residential decision making—with the clear exception of Asians, but even for this group class concerns appear to be much more salient for immigrants than for the native-born. In most cases, any evidence that supports these explanations pales in comparison to evidence that supports explanations rooted in the various forms of racial prejudice. Simply put, whites' preferences for neighborhood racial integration are best understood as motivated by prejudice, not classism or ethnocentrism.

The most powerful predictors of blacks' neighborhood racial composition preferences is racial prejudice—whether negative racial stereotypes, the perception of whites and Asians as socially distant, the perception of whites as tending to discriminate against them, or the fear that more jobs and political power for Asians means less for them. Neither concerns about avoiding poverty nor some "innate" desire to stay "with my own kind" are influential.

Latinos' neighborhood racial composition preferences are motivated primarily by prejudice and perceptions of whites as discriminatory; perceptions of blacks as economically disadvantaged play a very minor role, as does ethnocentrism when potential neighbors are Asian or same-race.

In summary, neighborhood racial composition preferences are primarily a function of racial prejudice; for blacks, Latinos and, to a lesser extent, Asians, there is the added concern about hostility directed toward them by whites. Assertions that preferences are driven primarily by either "classism" or ethnocentrism are simply not supported by the evidence.

Where Do We Go From Here?

My goal is to elucidate patterns of neighborhood racial composition preferences and the forces that drive them, and to situate racial preferences within the broader context of historic and contemporary American race relations. The good news for the future of public policy related to housing opportunity, housing choice and inequality more broadly is that whites are increasingly willing to live in close proximity to racial minorities, and a sizable number of blacks, Latinos and Asians remain willing to live in predominantly white areas. To capitalize on this willingness, however, requires being always mindful of the way that race continues to shape both our day-to-day interactions and our overall worldview.

The bad news, both for public policy and the nation, is that most whites still prefer predominantly or overwhelmingly white neighborhoods, while most nonwhites prefer more same-race neighbors than most whites are willing to tolerate. Most Americans—irrespective of race, ethnicity or nativity status—continue to embrace anti-minority stereotypes, including many who are willing to share residential space with racial minorities. Conversely, most blacks, Latinos, and Asians have a keen sense of their subordinate positions relative to whites, and of whites' negative attitudes; this often leaves them suspicious of overwhelmingly white areas (a sort of "better safe than sorry" mentality).

Across racial groups, patterns of neighborhood racial composition preferences reveal a clear and consistent racial rank-ordering of out-groups as potential neighbors: Whites are always the most preferred out-group neighbors, and the most likely to prefer entirely same-race neighborhoods and/or only limited contact with nonwhites—especially blacks. Blacks are always the least-preferred out-group neighbors, and the most open to substantial integration with all other groups. Asians and Latinos, respectively, are in between these extremes. To varying degrees, all groups express preferences for both meaningful integration and a strong co-ethnic presence, yet preferences for the latter appear to depend on the race of potential neighbors, and are strongest when potential neighbors are black.

Available evidence indicates that active, present-day racial prejudice plays a particularly important role in driving preferences, always more important than either social class concerns or ethnocentrism. In many instances, neither of these factors matters at all. And, although the evidence supports both variants of racial prejudice, it is particularly persuasive with respect to the sense of group position hypothesis. This is especially true for whites, the group at the top of the status hierarchy: Maintaining their status advantages and privilege necessitates a certain amount of social distance from nonwhites—particularly blacks and Latinos, who occupy the lowest positions on the aforementioned hierarchies. More than token integration with these groups signals an unwelcome change in status relationships. Indeed, the racial pecking order is so widely known that Latinos and Asians—many of them unassimilated immigrants—mirror (and arguably exaggerate) it in their preferences for integration.

Conversely, with whites clearly in the most privileged positions of the economic, political and prestige hierarchies in American society, nonwhites have traditionally associated upward social mobility with proximity to them. That many nonwhites hold negative stereotypes of whites but are still interested in sharing residential space with them is indicative of this orientation. At the same time, nonwhites' beliefs about discrimination and hostility from whites, combined with an awareness that whites are not "on the same page" may cause some minority homeseekers to limit their housing searches to areas where they feel welcome, or to decide not to search at all. Thus, a neighborhood's racial composition acts as a signal for homeseekers: Areas with substantial co-ethnic representation are viewed as welcoming; overwhelmingly white neighborhoods can evoke concerns for nonwhites about hostility, isolation and discomfort—both psychological and, sometimes, physical; and, for whites, racially mixed or majority-minority neighborhoods signal at least a perceptual loss of relative status advantage, particularly when there is a sizable black and/or Latino community. Thus, for all groups, preferences for same-race neighbors have more to do with aversion to others than with in-group solidarity.

These clearly racial concerns cut across class lines. Indeed, studies of the attitudes and experiences of middle-class blacks suggest that, paradoxically, this subset of blacks may be: 1) most pessimistic about the future of race relations; 2) most likely to believe that whites have negative attitudes toward them; and 3) increasingly less interested in predominantly white neighborhoods. Thus, the most upwardly mobile blacks may be among the most suspicious of whites and least interested in sharing residential space with them. For this group, affordability is not nearly the obstacle that whites' racial prejudice is, and this is due, in no small measure, to the fact that most whites—irrespective of their own social class status—adhere to negative racial stereotypes, deny the persistence of pervasive racial prejudice and discrimination, and are quite likely to oppose race-targeted social policies.

Whites' racial prejudice—and minority responses to it—poses a more obvious, but equally difficult challenge for improving the housing options of the poor, including those who participate in public housing programs. For many, the obvious material benefits clearly outweigh concerns about and/or day-to-day experiences of prejudice and discrimination. For a nontrivial few, however, fears of isolation and hostility will prevail, and participants will return to the ghetto, and others will opt out entirely when confronted with the reality of moving to a potentially hostile environment. While not at the bottom of the status hierarchy, Asians and Latinos are also subordinate groups grappling with similar racial issues. As we increase our knowledge of Asian and Latino racial attitudes, a similar paradox may emerge within these groups as well.

As we move into the 21st century and continue to struggle with racial inequality in all areas of American life, we must be ever mindful that race still matters, and it matters over and above social class characteristics. In so doing, we must also be mindful of how and why race matters. White objections to race-targeted social policy point to the necessity for well-crafted, universal housing policies that will gain widespread public support but also manage to address issues more directly tied to race. Potentially useful strategies for encouraging whites and nonwhites to share residential space come from studies documenting the characteristics of stably integrated neighborhoods. Residents of these communities often work together on community betterment projects (e.g., building playground equipment for a park or working to have street lights installed) or general community-building efforts that bring people of varied racial backgrounds together, working toward a common goal. Such activities, particularly when they become part of the larger neighborhood culture, can fundamentally alter attitudes on both sides of the racial divide by highlighting what residents share in common, helping to build trust and potentially reducing stereotypes.

Another common strategy emphasizes aggressive public relations campaigns that sing the praises of particular communities. Some of these may stress the value added by diversity; others highlight desirable neighborhood amenities, services and community events that make the area generally attractive; those that do both might ultimately be the most successful. Aggressive marketing strategies seem particularly beneficial when neighborhoods can be advertised as among "the best" in a particular metropolitan area. Positive marketing might also help to attract blacks, Latinos and Asians to overwhelmingly white communities by informing these groups that they are open to and interested in creating stable, friendly and racially diverse communities.

Active, diligent enforcement of anti-discrimination laws is also both appropriate and necessary. This, however, is likely to be a far more difficult and potentially less rewarding task. As it stands, the burden of proving discrimination is placed on the victim, yet empirical evidence suggests that present-day discrimination is often so subtle that few victims are likely to suspect that their housing choices are being constrained. Add to this the gulf of racial misunderstanding separating whites and racial minorities: Where blacks see "a racist moment," whites see "an isolated incident" or a "misinterpretation of events" or, even worse, they argue that blacks are "overreacting." In response, blacks become increasingly distrustful of a system that is supposed to protect them, pessimistic about the future of race relations, and increasingly less inclined to incur the psychic costs associated with filing a complaint.

To give teeth to anti-discrimination enforcement, we need a new enforcement strategy that builds the capacity of local, state and federal civil rights agencies to conduct widespread, ongoing audit studies as a credible deterrent. Tests could be undertaken of randomly selected real estate agencies and of those suspected of discrimination. Those agencies found to consistently evince fair treatment could be publicly rewarded, while those shown to discriminate could be sanctioned, both publicly and financially. In the lending market, where audit studies are more difficult, regular analysis of Home Mortgage Disclosure Act data presents a method for charting the practices of lenders. Such strategies have the potential to create meaningful deterrents. Furthermore, with regular monitoring, there are published records of documented discrimination that could: 1) help to alter whites' beliefs about inequality and discrimination; and 2) be used by victims as evidence in complaints, documenting systematic mistreatment. Together, these benefits could help move us toward better racial understanding as whites have the "proof" they need to believe what blacks and other racial minorities "just know."

Without such efforts, and given the state of race relations more generally, it seems unlikely that we can "live together" in the near future. It has been argued that increasing racial diversity might create a "buffer" for blacks, creating opportunities for residential mobility and contact with whites. Yet Latinos and Asians are at least as likely to hold negative stereotypes of blacks as whites are, and more likely to object to the prospect of sharing residential space with them. Furthermore, while whites hold negative stereotypes of both Latinos and Asians, they tend to be less severe than their stereotypes of blacks. Thus, whites are likely to view blacks as culturally deficient, while perceiving largely immigrant Latino and Asian populations as culturally distinct. Similarly, stereotypes of immigrants working hard at menial jobs and complaining less may further fuel anti-black sentiment, fostering the belief that blacks "push too hard" or "are always looking for a handout." Hence, rather than operating as a "buffer" or source of greater options and acceptance for blacks, increasing racial diversity may simply add to the climate of resistance to blacks as neighbors, and further complicate efforts at achieving either greater racial understanding or more equitable housing outcomes.

* * * * *

SUPPORTING INTEGRATIVE CHOICES

INGRID GOULD ELLEN

I have been asked to draw on my research on racially integrated neighborhoods—and in particular neighborhoods shared by white and black households—in order to suggest a few policies that might help to promote racial integration. I am focusing on policies other than anti-discrimination efforts in the housing market, but this should not imply in any way that I believe that housing market discrimination does not exist or is unimportant to address. Indeed, it's critical.

That said, much of the policy discussion about racial segregation has focused *solely* on housing market discrimination. As I argued in my 2000 book, *Sharing America's Neighborhoods: The Prospects for Stable, Racial Integration,* I believe the causes of the current ongoing levels of segregation are complex and involve more than housing market discrimination. Accordingly, any effective policy response should be multifaceted as well, supplementing anti-discrimination efforts with other prointegrative policies.

One key cause of ongoing segregation, besides the failure to adequately combat housing market discrimination, is the fact that white households, when moving in the ordinary course, tend to avoid moving into integrated neighborhoods. The question is why. My research suggests that white households' motivation to avoid sharing neighborhoods with blacks often does not stem from a desire to live exclusively among other whites or from the fact that their taste for local public services differs from that of blacks. White resistance to integrated living appears to be much more the result of negative racial attitudes, and in particular, race-based neighborhood stereotyping. Specifically, white households tend to believe that: (1) black-white integrated neighborhoods, even if they are currently appealing places to live, will soon enough become all-black; and (2) all-black neighborhoods are bad places to live, with poor schools and high rates of dilapidation and crime. Based as they are on negative stereotypes about partly or largely black neighborhoods, white decisions to avoid integrated neighborhoods seem objectionable in a way that decisions to cluster voluntarily with other members of one's own ethnic group are not.

What is more, there are social costs to this ongoing perpetuation of racial segregation. There's considerable research suggesting that neighborhood segregation contributes to racial differences in education, health, housing and labor market outcomes. And while evidence is inconclusive, several studies suggest that white households typically become more racially tolerant as a result of living among and being exposed to others from different racial groups. Finally, the collective consequences of individual residential choices may result in fewer integrated neighborhoods than is socially optimal. Many white and black households, that is, may in fact prefer to live in racially mixed environments, but because of a widespread lack of faith in the stability of these areas, these environments are relatively rare.

In short, there are reasons to believe that racial segregation is harmful not only to minority households (because separate is still unequal in so many respects) but also to society as a whole. Thus, in my view, there is justification for some carefully tailored, noncoercive government policies to promote integration—policies that go beyond combating discrimination. As noted, white households do not typically make their residential choices based on some innate preferences or tastes for racial composition; rather, neighborhood preferences are mutable and profoundly shaped by circumstances, context and the set of alternatives. Put simply, neighborhood stereotypes can be chipped away at.

In the spirit of Cass Sunstein's and Richard Thaler's book, *Nudge* (Yale Univ. Press, 2008), I'd like to push us all to think about ways that we can "nudge" households to make residential choices that might promote racial integration and ultimately prove to be better matches for them, too. I am not suggesting that we force households to live in particular neighborhoods—any policies that restrict people's freedom to live where they want should be avoided—but I believe there are ways we can encourage households to broaden their horizons and consider a wider set of communities in making their residential choices.

My policy suggestions fall into three categories: (1) providing accurate information; (2) making the choice of a mixed neighborhood more appealing in low-cost ways; and (3) changing the "architecture of choice," to borrow the words of Sunstein and Thaler.

The Need for Information

First, in terms of information, perhaps most critically, we can let households know that while a majority of neighborhoods are racially segregated, a substantial and growing minority are well integrated and not just fleetingly, but typically over many years. My own empirical research has demonstrated this. Yet the stubborn belief on the part of many that rapid racial transition is inevitable has helped, by its self-fulfilling nature, to undermine racial mixing. The more we can do to break the chain of assumptions that white households reflexively hold about integrated neighborhoods, the more likely those neighborhoods will remain stable.

Many households make their residential choices based on very limited information and consider only a small set of alternatives. Thus, we might also invest in web-based neighborhood information systems that would make it easy for people to gather information about a broad set of neighborhoods when making their residential choices—about school quality, crime and the like. There will no doubt be some integrated neighborhoods that, in terms of these legitimate quality-of-life indicators, score low in peoples' minds, just as there are all-white neighborhoods that score low; but there will be plenty of mixed neighborhoods that score relatively high.

Making Integrated Neighborhoods More Appealing

A second set of policies would try to make the choice of an integrated neighborhood more appealing in relatively low-cost ways. My research suggests that when white households have more secure expectations about the future quality of life in a community, they are more likely to tolerate racial integration. The implication is that racial mixing is more stable in communities in which school quality, property values and other neighborhood attributes seem particularly secure. To the extent this is true, aggressively attacking any superficial signs of decline—"fixing the broken windows" that James Q. Wilson and George Kelling (in their March 1982 *Atlantic Monthly* article) pointed to as a signal of social disorder—may be critical in encouraging white households to consider integrated communities they might otherwise avoid. Another possibility would be to invest in specialized magnet schools and to introduce school choice, at least within the public school system. For if it is true, as my research suggests, that much of white resistance to integrated neighborhoods is rooted in fears about the quality of integrated schools, then breaking the link between residence and school should encourage white households to be more open to living in racially diverse environments.

Altering the "Architecture" of Choice

Finally, I'd like to push us to think about ways to change the "architecture" of residential choices. Can we come up with ways to present neighborhood choices in a manner that will encourage—though not force—households to make prointegrative choices? One relatively modest possibility is for government to undertake affirmative marketing strategies to encourage white and minority households to consider neighborhoods where they are racially underrepresented—through a traditional television advertising campaign, for example, that promotes the benefits of mixed neighborhoods. In order to get realtors involved in these efforts, too, which is critical, we might consider something more novel. Specifically, in combination with a significant crackdown on unlawful racial steering by realtors (which research suggests remains a significant issue), we might consider offering a legal safe-harbor from the crackdown to those realtors who show clients a certain number of homes in a neighborhood in which the clients are racially underrepresented. Obviously, there would be lots of issues to work through before something like this could and should be tried, but I hope it's illustrative of the kind of policy brainstorming I think we need in this area.

Using Section 8 As a Tool

There's also considerable room to change the architecture of choice among one set of households—Section 8 recipients. Experience in other policy areas suggests that changing the default option for choices can lead to profoundly different outcomes. Thus, why not reform the Section 8 voucher program so it is administered at a regional level? Why not introduce more widespread counseling? And why not incorporate a default option that voucher holders use their vouchers in low-poverty neighborhoods? Households could of course opt out of this default choice if they had a strong reason to prefer to live in higher-poverty areas. But in the process of opting out, they would be pushed to reflect on their decision, rather than simply reflexively choosing a high-poverty community, which for most voucher recipients is the status quo.

In summary, I would argue that there are many noncoercive policies we could adopt that would encourage households to consider a wider set of residential choices and foster racial integration in the process. I have suggested a few. While the optimism of many people during the civil rights era that integration was just around the corner now seems hopelessly naïve, I remain hopeful that in conjunction with stepped-up antidiscrimination efforts, these policies can help to broaden people's residential choice sets and nudge us all towards a more integrated world.

* * * * *

CONFRONTING RACIAL "BLIND SPOTS"

MARIA KRYSAN

Segregation is caused by a complicated set of interrelated processes. I focus on just one part of this complicated process. But that should not be taken to mean that it is the only one, or even the most important one. However, I believe it has not received the attention it deserves.

I have spent more than a decade investigating the attitudes people hold about sharing neighborhoods with people of different races/ethnicities. My research on these racial residential preferences, however, tends to complicate what is too often construed as a "personal choice" explanation for segregation. The argument often goes: If preferences cause segregation, then policy has no role, since we are segregated because people "want" it that way. In short, the preferences explanation is often pitted against the idea that there is housing discrimination, and the two are seen as independent and in competition with each other as explanations of segregation.

My work tends to show that discrimination and preferences are not independent and that preferences are not "neutral" and "unproblematic," but rather constrained and complicated. For example, I show that to describe African-American racial residential preferences as favoring "50-50" or majority-minority neighborhoods and to then conclude, as some have, that segregation is caused by minority preferences, is problematic. Indeed, if we look more in-depth at African-American preferences, using different methods, we find that African-American preferences are far from "segregation-promoting." Or, by asking why African Americans hold the preferences they do, we discover that it is less because of a "neutral" in-group preference, and more because of a desire to avoid discrimination in largely white communities.

Racial Blind Spots

I want to discuss a new concept—racial blind spots—that I have been developing with my colleagues in Detroit and Chicago. Much of our understanding of racial residential preferences comes from asking people in surveys about hypothetical neighborhoods with imaginary racial compositions. By gauging preferences in this way, we sidestep the really important point that people don't buy imaginary homes in hypothetical neighborhoods. People buy and rent real homes in actual communities. And if peoples' knowledge of the metropolitan area and of the neighborhoods they might live in is racialized—and by that I mean if residents of different racial/ ethnic backgrounds know about different communities in the metropolitan area in which they live—and if that knowledge is shaped by the racial/ethnic composition of the community, then these patterns of knowledge—or the lack of knowledge—may constitute an important barrier to integrated living, since it is difficult to move into a neighborhood if you don't know anything about it.

In a recent large-scale survey in Chicago and Detroit, we showed people maps that identified many communities in the Chicago or Detroit metropolitan area and asked, among other things, which of them they "didn't know anything about."

For the most part, we found that whites, blacks and Latinos all tend to know more about communities their co-ethnics live in. But it is also the case that African Americans and Latinos, relative to whites, know about a broader range of different kinds of communities—racially mixed and racially segregated alike. For African Americans and Latinos, the few blind spots are communities that are both predominantly white and geographically distant from the city, thus creating a barrier to the possible integration of communities like this. But there are plenty of predominantly white communities about which African Americans do not have blind spots relative to whites; as such, there are clearly other barriers—perhaps discrimination, or perhaps "negative" knowledge about how African Americans are treated in these communities.

For their part, whites are far less likely than Latinos or African Americans to know about heavily African American communities, perhaps not surprisingly. But what is troubling, from the standpoint of encouraging integration, is that whites' blind spots also include communities that are racially mixed (either with Latinos or African Americans)—even those where whites are in the majority. To remain stably integrated, of course, communities like this must have housing demand from all racial/ethnic groups. And our study shows whites have a blind spot for these kinds of communities.

In sum, to move to a place, a person must have knowledge of it. Of course, those who consult with real estate agents may be introduced to communities they never considered, but it is likely that many people approach an agent with a particular geography already in mind. Moreover, in another question on our survey, we learned that there is substantial racial matching between client and agent: The great majority of whites (98 percent), blacks (70 percent) and Latinos (70 percent) are assisted by a real estate agent of their same racial/ethnic background. Thus, although agents' blind spots are likely to be fewer than those of their clients, this race-matching of agent and client may further aggravate the barrier of community knowledge or at the least minimizes the improvements a real estate agent might offer.

Our study of racial blind spots suggests that affirmative marketing—educating residents about the variety of housing options available—is a critical step in the goal for integrated living. There are substantial racial blind spots in community knowledge that must be overcome. The kinds of work currently being done by places like the Oak Park Regional Housing Center or to be done in the future by the start-up, MoveSmart.org, are two examples of organizations seeking to reduce these kinds of blind spots. Policies and programs like this, in concert with critical enforcement work, can be one part of the solution needed to help dismantle the pernicious pattern of segregation in many of our nation's cities.

What Are We Holding Our Public Schools Accountable For? The Gap Between What is Measured and What is Needed to Prepare Children for an Increasingly Diverse Society

Amy Stuart Wells

In 2011, for the first time, less than half of the babies born in the U.S. were white and non-Hispanic. Instead, the majority of newborns were Latino, African-American, Asian and/or Native American, a sign that the identity of our nation is changing, as are the social and cultural skills needed to succeed here. In the coming years, when these babies go to school, a public educational system that is now about 54 percent white, non-Hispanic will be demographically very different from what it was only 35 years ago, when 78 percent of the students were white, non-Hispanic. How we prepare our children for the society they will inherit needs to be rethought.

The good news is that we know much more today about how best to educate children to thrive in a racially, ethnically and culturally diverse society than ever before. The bad news is that the policymakers who set the legislative and legal agenda in education appear to be paying little, if any, attention to either our new demographic reality or the knowledge base on what to do about it. In fact, for the last few decades, when these policymakers have addressed educational issues, they have mostly focused on testing and school choice—the two primary methods for holding the public schools accountable for better results. But the question that voters, advocates and, most importantly, parents need to ask is whether the current accountability system reflects the values and needs of our rapidly changing society, not to mention the educational needs of our children.

EVIDENCE THAT WE NEED A BROADER FOCUS IN EDUCATIONAL POLICY

A growing body of social science research explains why racial/ethnic diversity should be an important factor we consider when we are thinking about education policy.

First of all, decades of research has shown the positive academic and long-term mobility outcomes for students of color who attend racially diverse, as opposed to segregated, schools, in part because of the likelihood that they will have access to a more challenging curriculum, better prepared teachers, and more resources in schools that enroll affluent and white students.

Secondly, robust evidence suggests there are multiple short- and long-term benefits for students of all racial and ethnic backgrounds who attend racially diverse schools. In particular, both survey- and interview-based research finds that attending an integrated school has a strong positive effect on students' racial attitudes, cross-racial understanding and comfort levels in diverse settings. Furthermore, this research suggests that such effects are not fully realized until well after the students graduate and enter the workforce, where they are most likely to interact with people of different cultural backgrounds, races and ethnicities as adults.

Another area of research suggests that racially diverse schools provide the contexts in which educators and students can and often do grapple with cultural differences in a way that will assist all students in grappling with complex issues and exploring deeper meanings. In sync with this research on "sociocultural" issues in education is an expanding knowledge base among educational professionals who work in diverse schools and classrooms. If this professional knowledge were more widely disseminated, it would be clear that we have many more answers to questions about how to better teach students from diverse backgrounds, drawing on the strengths and insights each brings to the classroom. We also know from the evidence, common sense and parents' intuition that it is essential for the future of our democracy to create racially and ethnically diverse schools and classrooms in which this type of learning may occur.

POLICYMAKERS, OUR DEMOGRAPHIC FUTURE AND EVIDENCE ON WHAT WE SHOULD DO ABOUT IT

Despite significant demographic changes in the U.S. and the mounting evidence about how we might address them in the K-12 public schools, most policymakers, on both sides of the political aisle, are focused elsewhere. They argue that the best way to improve the educational system and close the achievement gap (as defined by standardized tests alone) between white students and students of color is to hold schools accountable for "outcomes" (namely test scores) and offer parents the option to "vote with their feet" if the schools are not performing. That we have been trying these reforms with little measured success for almost 30 years is rarely mentioned. Also ignored is the mounting evidence that newer "school choice" plans, including charter schools and voucher plans, that rarely include transportation for students tend to lead to greater racial segregation. Add to that important research on the negative impact of test-based accountability systems on racially diverse schools. This scholarship shows that as schools are increasingly judged primarily based on narrow outcome data, more diverse schools are regularly deemed to be "worse" than more affluent and predominantly white or Asian schools with higher test scores, despite any dynamic teaching and learning that could be occurring in the more diverse environment.

Indeed, it appears that not only are policymakers ignoring the evidence about how and why they should support creation of more racially diverse schools, many policies they are advocating are, as currently constructed, pushing us in the opposite direction. Rarely—if ever—do current policymakers ponder whether they should be holding public schools accountable for preparing our next multiethnic, multiracial and multicultural generation of children to navigate the complexity of an increasingly diverse society.

CHANGE FROM THE BOTTOM UP?

Ironically, if you listen to many parents of school-age children—those who were born and raised in a post-civil rights era—they seem to know intuitively and intellectually that learning to get along with others of different backgrounds is an important life skill they would like their children to have. They also know that the current educational system, with its mostly racially and ethnically segregated schools and multitude of standardized tests, is not providing them with many options to achieve this goal.

In fact, a growing number of parents of school-age children in a U.S. public school are bemoaning the number of standardized tests their children take as they travel through different grade levels, developmental stages and subjects of our educational system. There is no escaping standardized tests in U.S. public schools, making our students some of the most "tested" students on the planet.

Meanwhile, our research on parents of school-age children suggests that many are conflicted between doing whatever they can to get their children in schools with high scores (and thus high status) and finding schools that better reflect their values and beliefs about education in a diverse society. Indeed, our center at Teachers College, Columbia University, the Center for Understanding Race and Education (CURE), is conducting cutting-edge research into these issues as they play out in demographically changing communities in both suburban and urban contexts. What we have learned is that today's parents feel caught between an accountability system that is being imposed on them and their children by policymakers and their own understanding of what matters to them as parents as they see the society become increasingly racially and ethnically diverse.

For instance, I recently published with Allison Roda in the *American Journal of Education,* "School Choice Policies and Racial Segregation: Where White Parents' Good Intentions, Anxiety, and Privilege Collide," examining one New York City community school district—called "District Q"—that is racially diverse overall but extremely racially divided either at the school or classroom level. At the school level, neighborhood schools are divided by attendance zones that circumscribe racially divided pockets of private apartment buildings and public housing units. Despite the geographic proximity of the public and private housing in this district, the school boundaries, in most cases, lead to more separation between the children who live in the two different types of homes. As a result, almost all of District Q's white elementary school students were enrolled in only 6 of the 18 elementary schools.

At the classroom level, students enrolled in the few public schools that are more diverse overall tend to be divided into special "gifted and talented" (G&T) versus "general education" classrooms based on testing and an application process that occurs when they are in pre-school. In these more "diverse" schools, G&T and general education classes are remarkably distinct racially and ethnically, with all the white and Asian students in the G&T classrooms and virtually all the black and Latino students in the general education classes. Of the six District Q elementary schools with student bodies that are 22 percent or more white, three house G&T programs that separate their students in this way.

Walking down the hallways of these schools evokes in researchers and parents alike a sense of racial apartheid. All of the parents we studied were uncomfortable with this within-school segregation. Many parents of school-age children today grew up believing that such stark racial segregation was a thing of the past, and many moved to New York City so that they could raise their children in a more diverse and cosmopolitan city. They did not anticipate choosing among public school programs that resemble those in the deep South prior to the *Brown* decision and the Civil Rights Act of 1964.

Yet what was painfully clear about the findings to emerge from our study of mostly white and middle- or upper-middle-class parents who were choosing elementary schools for their children in this district is that giving parents only the choice of racially and socioeconomically separate and unequal schools and programs despite overall district demographics that are very diverse is basically no choice at all. In other words, the way in which the school choice policies are written, regulated and implemented had huge implications for the kinds of outcomes they foster—both in terms of their short-term effects on school-level racial diversity and their long-term effects on political support for public education. Thus, despite the history of NYC's public school system, to use the separate and unequal G&T programs to keep white, middle-class families from leaving the public schools, our interview data strongly suggest that more diverse and undivided options would ultimately help keep more of these parents in public, as opposed to private, schools for kindergarten. In fact, there was a waitlist of such parents for the only elementary school in the district that is far more racially and ethnically diverse at both the school and the classroom level than the other schools in the district.

We believe that public school officials in New York City and elsewhere could learn from our analysis of how white parents in District Q make sense of their school choices. For instance, our findings suggest that it's not surprising, given the lack of racially diverse schools and programs available in District Q, that these parents struggle with the choices they make. Given their lousy options of putting their children in segregated almost all-white or segregated almost all-African-American and/ or all-Latino classrooms, they usually end up making the choice to be with other families like theirs, a choice that reinforces the segregation and inequality.

Given the lack of other options, these race-driven parental choices are logical at some level, especially for white and more affluent parents, given what we know about the relationship between racial segregation, educational inequality and concentrated poverty. If the burden of ending racial apartheid in District Q schools and classrooms is left entirely up to them, it will most likely never happen. Yet when we examine this sense-making in progress, on the ground, we see the missed opportunities in school choice policies that could have tapped into parents' interest and demand for more diverse, equal and challenging educational environments for their children.

Even small amendments to school choice policies could appeal to white parents' intuition about the importance of school-level diversity and work against some of the forces that continue to push the system toward more segregation. But those with the power to make change within District Q and thousands of school districts across this country with racially segregated schools and G&T programs within schools must be open to learning from the parents we studied and their understandings of the missed opportunities for providing better choices for all children within an increasingly diverse society.

QUESTIONS OUR POLICYMAKERS SHOULD ANSWER: HOLDING THOSE IN POWER ACCOUNTABLE

How did we end up with an increasingly diverse society and increasingly racially and ethnically homogeneous public schools? How did our system become one in which students, educators and communities are not held accountable for teaching and learning life skills that a silent majority of Americans know matter in the day-to-day reality of our increasingly diverse society? Why do we have an educational system in which so much time, energy and resources are spent on achieving narrow educational outcomes—e.g., those measured by standardized tests—while ignoring key goals that are important to our children and our future?

While testing students in reading and math skills is not necessarily a bad idea, we need to question whether or not we have gone overboard in terms of the amount of time, energy and resources currently spent on testing, test prep and organizing an educational system around the consequences of test scores. It could well be that the more time our children spend on tests—which only measure some of knowledge we want them to gain by going to school—the less they learn about how to make their way in the real world with the diverse mix of people who will be their future co-workers and fellow citizens. Thus, the central question we should be asking is whether we can hold our policymakers accountable for a different set of results to better meet the challenge and promise of our increasing diversity.

The Goal of Inclusive, Diverse Communities: Introduction to the Final Report of the National Commission on Fair Housing and Equal Opportunity

The National Commission on Fair Housing and Equal Opportunity's recently released final report includes significant new recommendations for reforming fair housing enforcement and federal housing policy to promote housing choice and reverse continuing trends of residential segregation. The commission, co-chaired by former HUD Secretaries Henry Cisneros and Jack Kemp, was created through the partnership of four leading national civil rights organizations: the Leadership Conference on Civil and Human Rights Education Fund (LCCR/EF); the Lawyers' Committee for Civil Rights under Law (LCCRUL); the National Fair Housing Alliance (NFHA); and the NAACP Legal Defense and Educational Fund (LDF). PRRAC served as one of the consultants to the Commission.

The key recommendations in the final report include:

- Moving fair housing enforcement (investigation and prosecution of discrimination complaints) from HUD to a new independent agency, advised by a commission appointed by the President, with day-to-day operations overseen by a career staff (in the near term, while this structural change is being implemented, the Commission also recommends separating HUD's current Office of Fair Housing and Equal Opportunity into two offices, the Office of Fair Housing and the Office of Civil Rights in order to prioritize and strengthen both fair housing enforcement and internal agency compliance).
- Revitalizing the President's Fair Housing Council to coordinate fair housing activities throughout the federal government, as provided by Executive Order 12892.
- Strengthening the Fair Housing Initiatives Program by increased funding to $52 million immediately, with a longer-term goal of supporting a private fair housing group in every metropolitan region in the country.

346

- A renewed commitment to *affirmatively furthering fair housing* among HUD grantees that includes enforceable time frames, comprehensive agency review of community plans and sanctions for noncompliance.
- Incorporating a fair housing analysis in the response to the foreclosure crisis, requiring HUD and Treasury to affirmatively further fair housing in mortgage rescue activities and marketing foreclosed properties.
- Restoring the central role of fair housing in the design and implementation of federal housing programs, including major HUD housing programs (Section 8, public housing, HOME, CDBG), the Low Income Housing Tax Credit and USDA housing programs.
- Providing a renewed emphasis on the value of diverse, inclusive communities in national media campaigns.

Commission members in addition to former Secretaries Cisneros and Kemp included Okianer Christian Dark, Associate Dean for Academic Affairs at the Howard University College of Law; Gordon Quan, Houston, Former Mayor Pro Tem and Chair of the Housing Committee for the City of Houston; Pat Combs, past President of the National Association of Realtors; Myron Orfield, Professor at the University of Minnesota School of Law; and I. King Jordan, President-Emeritus of Gallaudet University. A copy of the full Commission report is available at www.prrac.org and on the websites of each of the sponsoring civil rights organizations.

The following excerpt (notes omitted) sets out the Commission's vision for inclusive, diverse communities:

Forty years after the passage of the Fair Housing Act in 1968 and 20 years after the Fair Housing Amendments Act of 1988, the National Commission on Fair Housing and Equal Opportunity (Commission) was convened to address the significant and ongoing national crisis of housing discrimination and residential segregation. The commission conducted regional hearings in Chicago, Los Angeles, Boston, Atlanta, and Houston, to collect information and hear testimony about the nature and extent of illegal housing discrimination and its origins, its connection with government policy and practice, and its effect on American communities. In this report, the commission calls for renewed efforts to end both old and new patterns of housing discrimination through better enforcement, better education, and systemic change.

When the Fair Housing Act was first passed, racially and ethnically diverse neighborhoods were generally discussed only in terms of benefits to racial or ethnic minorities. Today, many recognize that diverse neighborhoods have tangible benefits for all people who live in them and that true diversity is more than just racial integration. Rather, a diverse community is one where all residents are included, where no group is privileged above any other group, and where everyone has equal access to opportunity.

The goal of the fair housing movement is to support and promote these inclusive, diverse communities of choice: communities and neighborhoods where families choose to live; where housing and schools are stable and well supported; where employment is accessible; and where all racial and ethnic groups, and persons with disabilities, are an integral part of the larger community.

What are some of the characteristics of these communities?

- Inclusive, diverse communities have quality schools with diverse student bodies that enhance outcomes for all children.
- Inclusive, diverse communities have a healthy, robust housing market that competes for buyers and renters from all racial and ethnic groups in a region and cannot be easily targeted by predatory lenders.
- Inclusive, diverse communities contribute to the regional economy with a range of housing choices for workers of all income ranges, and help to prevent the harmful concentration of racially isolated poverty at the core of the metropolitan region.
- Inclusive, diverse communities incorporate accessible design and housing options that maximize inclusion of persons with disabilities in the built environment and in communications.
- Inclusive, diverse communities successfully resist sprawl and its negative social and environmental impacts by consolidating growth for a mixed-income, diverse population along efficient transportation corridors and by bringing workers closer to regional job centers.

We also recognize that these inclusive and diverse communities can be formed in different ways. They may include predominantly White suburban towns that are becoming more economically and racially diverse; or integrated older inner-ring suburbs facing high rates of foreclosure, which may need infrastructure and marketing support to maintain a stable, diverse population over time; or lower-income urban neighborhoods experiencing gentrification and the accompanying influx of new money and community services that brings both benefits and threats to existing residents. Each of these community contexts demands different types of support in order to maintain a stable, inclusive, diverse character.

Congress passed the Fair Housing Act in 1968 to guarantee the right to choose where to live without facing discrimination or legally imposed obstacles. This is a core value that needs no additional justification. But it is also important to recognize the other benefits and values that are promoted by inclusive and diverse communities:

Diversity in communities leads to diversity in schools.

A diverse, inclusive learning environment is one of the most important benefits of fair housing. In most parts of the country, housing and school segregation are closely linked. Most school districts rely on geography to assign students, resulting in school demographic patterns tracking residential patterns. School diversity has been shown to reduce racial prejudice, increase racial tolerance, and even improve critical thinking skills. Minority students who attend diverse schools are more likely to graduate from high school, attend and graduate from college, and connect to social and labor networks that lead to higher earning potential as adults.

Inclusive and diverse communities can break down social divisions.

The deep geographic racial divide in the United States feeds a sense of fear, suspicion, and alienation. In his testimony, Professor john powell highlighted the impacts of this racial divide on economic inequality, and the sense of unfairness and resentment that geographic separation can foster:

> [I]n many regions, we are polarizing into socially, economically and racially isolated enclaves of extreme high and low opportunity. A range of high- and low-opportunity areas is to be expected; people and places are diverse. The challenge for us, for our democracy, and for our children is not that a range of communities exist, but that the gulf between the high- and low-opportunity areas today is often so wide as to hardly be transcended. Often, the highest performing schools, the healthiest air and groceries, the most active social networks critical to finding sustainable employment are concentrated together and removed from the vast majority of residents. These "favored quarters" dot our regions and threaten to undermine a sense of shared community.

Just as school integration can reduce racial prejudice among children, we can expect a similar result in shared communities and neighborhoods. For example, recent research shows that sustained cross-racial contact lowers stereotyping and prejudice, even on a subconscious level.

Inclusive and diverse communities provide a base for family economic success.

A home is the major asset for the vast majority of American families and the primary means of building equity and passing wealth from one generation to the next. Yet segregation has made minority families more vulnerable to predatory lending practices as well as to the devastating social and depreciation impacts associated with foreclosures concentrated in a community.

Inclusive, diverse communities attract a wider range of potential buyers from throughout the metropolitan area, which sustains housing prices and leads to more balanced appreciation in home value. Diverse communities are also less likely to be targeted for predatory or subprime loan products.

Inclusive and diverse communities provide access to opportunity for lower-income families.

Racial segregation separates lower-income African-American and Latino families from opportunity in metropolitan areas, which predictably leads to depressed outcomes in education, employment, health, and other measures.

In the 1980s, the Gautreaux Assisted Housing Program demonstrated that families benefited by moving from high-poverty, racially isolated neighborhoods to very low-poverty, racially integrated suburban communities. These new areas also happened to be areas of high opportunity, with high-quality schools and richer employment offerings, which led to positive results for many Gautreaux movers and their children (including higher rates of employment for mothers and academic benefits for children). There was also evidence that these moves to higher-opportunity areas gave residents a new sense of efficacy and control and more interracial contact, leading to a reduction in racial stereotypes.

Inclusive and diverse communities support smart growth and environmental values.

Smart growth planning emphasizes mixed-use, mixed-income, higher-density, pedestrian-friendly communities that are accessible to public transportation, enjoy ample open space and recreational opportunities, and reduce traffic congestion, energy consumption, concentrated poverty and sprawl. Many smart growth advocates have rejected a no-growth approach to limiting sprawl and have embraced affordable housing as a key element of socially equitable smart growth planning. Affordable housing development distributed equitably across communities in a region furthers smart growth goals by increasing housing densities, encouraging transit-oriented development, bringing low-wage workers closer to jobs, and shifting land use planning from the local to the regional level.

Inclusive and diverse communities support regional and global competitiveness.

America's economy is now centered in metropolitan areas that encompass large cities, old and new suburbs, and even exurban and rural areas that, by virtue of their interwoven labor and housing markets, share common economic destinies. But segregation has a detrimental impact on the competitiveness of metropolitan areas in our increasingly global economy. A true rebirth of distressed areas (and the cities in which they are located) will only occur if we make these places "neighborhoods of connection that are fully linked to metropolitan opportunities" for individuals and families with a broad range of incomes.

A recent report about Minneapolis/St. Paul explains the consequences of our nation's current course that is reflective of the situation throughout the nation: Without serious attention to the next generation of workers, who are more likely to be minority, and more likely to be poor, the Twin Cities workforce will be smaller and less skilled than currently, presenting the possibility of a less competitive future. Reducing disparities between individuals of different backgrounds and socioeconomic statuses is critical to economic competitiveness and "can promote a strong future workforce, improve the region's fiscal situation, and build a healthier region."

All over America, thoughtful advocates, community organizers, and families are working to find ways to build equal opportunity in housing. In this report, we build upon that innovation, those ideas, and the spirit of change, offering concrete recommendations for actions that we believe are critical to move us forward toward our vision of creating and sustaining stable, diverse, inclusive neighborhoods across America.

Lessons from Mount Laurel: The Benefits of Affordable Housing for All Concerned

Douglas S. Massey

In 1983, the New Jersey Supreme Court handed down a landmark decision in the case of *South Burlington County NAACP v. Mount Laurel Township*. Commonly known as Mount Laurel II, the ruling held that all municipalities in New Jersey had an affirmative obligation, under the state constitution, to house their fair share of affordable housing in the region. The decision effectively forbade the use of zoning to prevent the construction of affordable housing units in affluent suburban communities. According to the official state estimate, the "'Mount Laurel doctrine" and the implementation of the decision through the Council on Affordable Housing has led to the creation of 60,000 affordable housing units statewide.

In Mount Laurel Township itself, although the township officials and the original plaintiffs entered into a consent decree in 1985, the affordable development, which came to be known as Ethel Lawrence Homes (ELH), did not open its doors until late 2000, when 100 affordable units were allocated to low- and moderate-income families on a first-come, first-served basis. Another 40 units were completed and filled in the same way in 2004. Because these units were designed as affordable rental housing and marketed to low-income families, and because we were able to obtain access to marketing data and invited to meet with residents, the ELH development provided us with an ideal site to assess the impacts of Mount Laurel on the community and the families who moved in.

In 2009–2010, I joined with a team of colleagues to undertake a systematic evaluation of the effect that ELH had on the township and surrounding neighborhoods, as well as on the lives of the people who were able to take advantage of access to affordable housing in an affluent suburb of Philadelphia. Both evaluations followed a quasi-experimental design.

IMPACTS OF THE AFFORDABLE DEVELOPMENT
ON THE TOWNSHIP AND NEIGHBORHOOD

To assess the effect of ELH on the township itself, we undertook a multiple time series study that compared trends in home values, tax burdens and crime rates in Mount Laurel before and after 2001, with trends in a matched set of nearby townships before and after the same date. Performing a statistical analysis of "differences in differences" before and after the opening of ELH, we found no detectable effects of the project's opening on any outcome. Trends in home values, crime rates and taxes were the same in Mount Laurel as in similar townships nearby.

Even in neighborhoods immediately adjacent to the project, we found no effect of ELH on crime, property values or taxes. Indeed, in a survey we conducted among neighbors, one-third didn't know affordable housing even existed in the neighborhood, and among those who did know, only 40 percent could successfully name the project. Despite dire predictions and outsized fears expressed before the fact, when ELH finally opened, it was not with a bang, but a whimper.

OUTCOMES FOR RESIDENTS

The manner by which units in ELH were allocated to tenants also afforded a quasi-experimental research design. After a period of regional advertising, aspiring tenants were instructed to come into the developer's office to complete and hand in an application form. All applications received during the application period were placed on a list and assigned a sequence number indicating the order in which they were submitted. The applications were then evaluated in order received, and if they met income and other eligibility criteria determined from the form, they were offered a unit in the development.

Applicants still on the waiting list at the time of our study constitute a good comparison group with which to assess the effects of ELH residence. Since applicants admitted and still waiting were both self-selected into the population of people wishing to take advantage of affordable housing, selection bias is effectively controlled. We therefore interviewed all project residents along with a sample selected from the waiting list. In order to further ensure comparability between the two groups, we coded up all of the information on the application form and from it estimated equations predicting the likelihood of being offered a unit. These were then used to generate propensity scores, and each ELH resident was matched with a nonresident from the waiting list with a similar propensity score.

Our comparison of matched ELH residents and nonresidents revealed a dramatic reduction in exposure to neighborhood disorder and violence as a result of moving into the development, which in turn yielded a significantly lower frequency of negative life events and improved mental health. Owing in part to these improvements, along with other advantages associated with suburban residence, ELH residents displayed higher rates of employment, larger share of income from work, greater total incomes, and lower rates of welfare dependency.

As for the children living in ELH, school quality also improved dramatically relative to the comparison group, while exposure to school disorder and violence declined steeply. ELH children also reported greater access to a quiet place to study, more time spent studying and more educationally engaged parents. Although we found no significant direct effect of ELH residence on the grades earned by students, we did find significant indirect effects through hours studied, school quality and school disorder, which on net improved grades.

CONCLUSIONS

These findings have both policy and scholarly importance. In terms of policy, they suggest that ELH and the underlying Mount Laurel Doctrine (when implemented to produce affordable rental housing) are both unequivocal successes. The construction of affordable units in an affluent suburb using tax credits and low-interest loans produced a self-supporting housing development that dramatically improved the lives of low- and moderate-income residents and greatly advanced the mobility prospects of their children while imposing no negative externalities on neighbors or township residents. However, it is important to emphasize that these kinds of results are a direct result of the affirmative marketing efforts made by Fair Share Housing Development—attracting applicants to the development from more disadvantaged neighborhoods. This type of affirmative marketing is also consistent with the fair housing goals underlying the Mount Laurel doctrine, but it has not always been implemented by developers and managers.

In terms of scholarship, our findings confirm the importance of neighborhoods in determining individual and family outcomes, and demonstrate the validity and power of neighborhood effects in conditioning human well-being.

Housing America's Native People

Wendy L. Helgemo

The sun shines most days of the year on the adobe homes of a Pueblo outside of Albuquerque, New Mexico. Some have no running water. Some have foundation falling away, letting daylight in through the cracks. Some are bright, sprawling "ramblers," all new construction.

A thunderstorm rolls in over a green valley in southeastern Montana. A modern, but modest, house stands across from a small church. It is made from straw bale technology and is heated by solar energy. Another home has cold wind blowing through plastic sheeting over where the glass window panes should be. An old wood burning stove is used for heat.

Each of these places someone calls home. While there is a supply of safe, sanitary and adequate housing stock in Indian Country, housing in Native American communities is still far more substandard than for the rest of the country. Things are changing, but some say Third World conditions exist right here in America.

HOUSING IN INDIAN COUNTRY

After two centuries of U.S. federal policy, Indian Country is comparatively underdeveloped to an alarming degree. An estimated 200,000 housing units are needed immediately in Indian Country, and approximately 90,000 Native families are homeless or underhoused. Overcrowding on tribal lands is almost 15 percent, and 11 percent of Indian homes lack complete plumbing and kitchen facilities; less than half of all reservation homes are connected to a public sewer. Unemployment rates in Native American communities average 15 percent, and in some areas it is as high as 80 percent. Because most American Indian reservations and Alaska Native communities are in geographically remote and rural areas, building homes is an extremely costly endeavor and one reason for the high cost of housing development in Native communities. A well-built and maintained road system, housing, electricity, wastewater and land improvements all contribute the necessary foundation for economic growth, increased safety and improved quality of life for Native people.

OVERVIEW OF FEDERAL HOUSING PROGRAMS FOR NATIVE AMERICANS

What has become the leading source of capital for housing in Indian Country is the Native American Housing Assistance and Self-Determination Act of 1996 (NAHASDA), the major federal law relating to Native American housing and community development. NAHASDA has opened the door for American Indian tribes and Alaska Natives to improve tribal capacity and increase tribal decision-making in the housing arena. NAHASDA also has enabled greater tribal participation in the development of federal regulations through the negotiated rule-making process and has spurred housing development through the leveraging of federal dollars.

Federal housing programs for American Indians, Alaska Natives and Native Hawaiians ("Native Americans") are administered by the U.S. Department of Housing and Urban Development (HUD). Within HUD, the secretary, operating through the Office of Native American Programs (ONAP), carries out the United States' trust responsibility to Indian tribes and Indian people by improving their housing conditions and socioeconomic status.

Other federal programs in the Departments of Agriculture, Veterans Affairs, Health, and Interior also have components that serve tribal housing needs.

The Native American Housing Assistance and Self-Determination Act

The Native American Housing Assistance and Self-Determination Act of 1996 (as amended, Pub. L. 104-330), as noted above, is the main source of legal authority under which the United States provides housing and housing-related programs for Native Americans. Enacted in 1996, NAHASDA combined scattered federal public housing programs into a consolidated block grant to better serve the unique needs of Native American communities. NAHASDA established the Indian Housing Block Grant (IHBG) to provide direct federal assistance to Indian tribes to carry out affordable housing activities. Prior to NAHASDA, tribes, through tribal housing authorities or departments, operated housing programs under the 1937 Housing Act, the first law in which Congress addressed the housing needs of low-income Americans. Notably, tribes had to wait until 1961 to become eligible for assistance and housing programs administered by HUD. Currently, almost 300 tribal housing authorities manage anywhere from a few hundred homes to thousands of homes in Indian Country.

The Indian Housing Block Grant

The Indian Housing Block Grant (IHBG) is the single largest source of capital made available by the United States for housing development, housing-related infrastructure, and home repair and maintenance in Indian Country. Since FY 1998, more than $7 billion in federal housing assistance has been invested in Native American communities for purposes of making downpayments on homes, making monthly rents, helping with rehabilitation and building new housing units. Prior to NAHASDA implementation, an estimated 2,000 units a year were being built, whereas over 6,000 units were built in NAHASDA's first year alone.

Indian Community Development Block Grant

The Indian Community Development Block Grant (ICDBG) is a direct grant program for community development in Indian and Alaska Native Communities. Community development includes decent housing, a suitable living environment and economic opportunities, primarily for low- and moderate-income persons. Eligible grantees are any Indian tribe, band, group or nation or Alaska Native village. Specifically, ICDBG funding can be used for housing (new construction and rehabilitation), community facilities and economic development. Ninety-five percent of the grant funds are awarded on a competitive basis. The remaining 5 percent is awarded on a noncompetitive, first-come/first-served basis to eliminate problems that pose an imminent threat to public health or safety.

Title VI Tribal Housing Activities Loan Guarantee Program

The Title VI Tribal Housing Activities Loan Guarantee Program (Title VI) provides the backing of a federal guarantee on loans to Indian tribes from private lenders or investors. Title VI loans finance eligible affordable housing activities such as housing assistance, housing development, housing services, housing management services, crime prevention and safety activities, and model activities. Indian tribes pledge future IHBG funds as security for repayment of Title VI loan obligations.

An amendment to Title VI established in 2009 a demonstration program to guarantee the notes and obligations issued by Indian tribes to finance activities that are eligible for financing under the Housing and Community Development Act of 1974, including economic development, housing rehabilitation, public facilities and large-scale physical development projects.

Section 184 Indian Housing Loan Guarantee Program

The Section 184 Indian Housing Loan Guarantee Program was established to serve the Native American homeownership market, which is underserved due to the trust status of Indian lands. Indian tribes and individual Native Americans are eligible for Section 184 loans. Loans can be for new construction, rehabilitation of an existing home and refinancing. The default rate is less than 1 percent.

Training and Technical Assistance

NAHASDA authorizes appropriations for assistance to a national organization representing Native American housing interests in order to provide training and technical assistance to Indian housing authorities and tribally designated housing entities. Tribal housing authorities rely on training and technical assistance to effectively implement their housing programs. Training and technical assistance has proven to be an effective and invaluable tool for capacity-building for tribes and their housing authorities.

Since the 1996 enactment of NAHASDA, the National American Indian Housing Council (NAIHC) has served as the lead training and technical assistance provider in Indian Country. For nearly 35 years, NAIHC has assisted tribes with their primary goal of providing housing and community development for Native American communities. NAIHC consists of 270 members, representing 463 tribes and the Department of Hawaiian Home Lands.

This assistance has come in the form of on-site technical assistance; tuition-free training classes provided by housing professionals in the employ of NAIHC; scholarship programs that help offset the cost to tribal-designated housing entity employees to attend professional training sessions; and NAIHC's Leadership Institute, a low-cost professional certification course for housing professionals who work in Indian housing development.

The Native American Veterans Home Loan Program

Within the U.S. Department of Veterans Affairs, the Native American Veterans Home Loan Program serves eligible Native-American veterans who wish to purchase, improve or construct a home on tribal lands. VA direct loans are generally limited to the cost of the home, or the Federal Home Loan Mortgage Corporation single-family conforming loan unit, whichever is less. The maximum loan amount may not exceed VA's estimate of the reasonable value of the property to be purchased.

Indian Health Service Sanitation Facilities

Within the Department of Health and Human Services, the Indian Health Service (IHS) Division of Sanitation Facilities Construction is charged with providing Native American homes and communities with essential water supply, sewage disposal and solid waste disposal facilities.

Housing development in Native American communities involves more than simply building dwelling units. Community development often starts with the design and construction of basic physical infrastructure and amenities that most Americans take for granted. This includes water and wastewater infrastructure, electricity, heat and cooling systems, and a host of other elements. Recurring challenges to the physical infrastructure issue involve access to capital and financing, conflicting statutory and regulatory provisions, and a need for comprehensive planning.

Therefore, this IHS program is extremely taxed. Current appropriations language prevents IHS sanitation funds to be used in conjunction with NAHASDA funds to connect water and wastewater infrastructure to the new homes.

HUD Rural Housing and Economic Development

While not a specific Indian program, tribes are eligible to participate in HUD's Rural Housing and Economic Development programs (RHED). RHED is another tool Native-American communities use to help build homes on isolated Indian lands. These programs serve to assist in capacity-building, fund innovative activities and provide support for new programs. Funds are awarded on a competitive basis. The maximum award under capacity-building is $150,000. The maximum amount awarded for housing development and economic development activities is $400,000.

USDA Rural Housing

Within the U.S. Department of Agriculture (USDA), rural housing programs serve the housing needs of low-income and very low-income Americans, including Native Americans. Indian tribes can participate in the Direct Home Loan Program (Section 502) and the Rental Housing Direct Loan Program (Section 538). Section 502 loans are primarily used to help low-income individuals or households purchase homes in rural areas. Section 502 funds can be used to build, repair, renovate or relocate a home, or to purchase and prepare sites, including providing water and sewage facilities. Section 538 loans are for new rental housing and acquisition with rehabilitation of existing properties. The purpose of the Section 538 program is to increase the supply of affordable rural rental housing, through the use of loan guarantees that encourage partnerships between the Rural Development Program, private lenders and public agencies. Indian tribes can use these programs for housing and related infrastructure development in conjunction with HUD and Bureau of Indian Affairs funding.

The Housing Improvement Program (HIP)

Within the U.S. Department of the Interior, the Bureau of Indians Affairs (BIA) is authorized to assist Indian tribes with housing improvement. In 1965, the Housing Improvement Program (HIP) was established pursuant to the Snyder Act of 1924 (25 U.S.C. Â§13) to provide grants of modest amounts (often not more than $1,500) for home rehabilitation, renovation and repair. As the waiting lists for new homes continue to grow and housing stock becomes older and dilapidated, HIP strives to ensure that existing housing stock remain safe, healthy and habitable. According to the BIA, HIP assists 375 Indian families annually. The HIP serves a valuable role in keeping existing housing stock in habitable conditions for the neediest within the Indian communities: Indian elders and low-income people.

Low-Income Housing Tax Credits

One way tribes can spur new housing development is through leveraging the IHBG. In 1986, Congress changed the Internal Revenue Service Tax Code to encourage homeownership through the creation of low-income housing tax credits (LIHTC). Tribes can use IHBG funds for project-based or tenant-based rental assistance in LIHTC projects as an eligible affordable housing activity.

While word about LIHTC leveraging is getting around Indian Country, only a small number of tribes have undertaken LIHTC projects. Education and capacity-building of tribal housing authorities are key in increasing usage of the program. There is a clear need to increase the training opportunities for housing authorities in the area of LIHTC program development. This will open up more doors to opportunities to work with investors, program developers, compliance experts and consultants, and state housing finance agencies and housing departments.

Financial Education

Tribal economies can be strengthened through increased financial education programs and through the development and promotion of asset-building rather than asset-stripping in Native communities. Since access to capital is an ongoing obstacle to housing and community development in Indian Country, the pervasiveness and impact of predatory lending in all its iterations has destructive consequences in Native communities. Development of credit programs and increasing borrowing opportunities through Tribal Community Development Financial Institutions (CDFIs) will reduce the demand for predatory lending in tribal communities. Financial education is also a key to combating predatory lending and needs to be culturally-specific and tailored to Native communities. Asset development, including tribal individual development accounts and other forms of matched savings accounts, should be emphasized to change the landscape from asset-stripping to asset-building.

Recommendations for a New Congress and Administration

- Restore the focus of federal housing and housing-related programs and services to one respecting the hallmark of Indian self-determination;
- Ensure meaningful consultation with tribal governments and housing authorities in advance of the development of relevant regulations and policies;
- Restore to the federal agencies an appropriate role in terms of oversight and monitoring of tribal housing programs and services;

- Re-institute a vigorous negotiated rule-making procedure with tribal governments and housing authorities so that the impacts and consequences of proposed federal actions can be fully debated and agreed to prior to implementation;
- Improve housing development and leveraging capacity within Indian housing authorities, as distinguished from simply improving housing management skills according to federal guidelines;
- Increase federal funding levels for Native American housing, with a particular emphasis on achieving parity with jurisdictions of comparable size;
- Assist Indian tribes in the construction and maintenance of physical infrastructure, including methods of financing similar to those available to state and local governments;
- Ameliorate high energy and other costs of construction due in large part to isolated locations;
- Improve eGrant submission issues, particularly at HUD, as the current system negatively impacts tribal communities;
- Collaborate with tribal governments and housing authorities to initiate and develop comprehensive and effective risk management and other self-insurance programs and services related to Native American housing and related assets and property;
- Ensure a Native presence at White House and Cabinet-level positions - e.g., HUD's Assistant Secretary for Indian Housing and Community Development.

CONCLUSION

America's First Americans—Native Americans—have been experiencing their own housing and economic crises since the era of Treaty-making and have an immediate need for culturally relevant, decent, safe, sanitary and affordable housing. The lack of significant private investment, functioning housing markets and the dire economic conditions most Indian communities face mean that federal dollars make up a significant amount of total housing resources for Native people. We must continue to work to improve housing conditions in Indian Country by deconstructing remaining barriers to Indian tribes which endeavor to develop their communities and economies and improve the lives of their people.

No Home in Indian Country

Janeen Comenote

AMERICAN INDIANS AND ALASKA NATIVES: AN OVERVIEW

The United States is an immigrant nation to all but one population, American Indians and Alaska Natives. There are essentially two populations to examine. We have an on-reservation population (governed by tribal governments) and the off-reservation population of Native peoples. However, an added complexity to keep in mind is the notion of citizenship. Native people often hold triplicate citizenship, that of: a) the "home tribe" and "homeland"; b) a citizen of the United States; and c) for off-reservation populations, the city or town in which they reside.

While we can fairly assess that both populations suffer disproportionately from economic stress and lack of access to fair credit and housing, we need to realize that tribal governments operate under a dramatically different set of regulations, rules of law and constituent responsibilities. A simple way of thinking about tribal populations in the United States is to consider that both tribal nations and the U.S. Congress observe a sovereign government-to-government relationship between tribes and the United States government formalized in American law in the 1832 case *Worcester v. Georgia*. Simply put, when the U.S. was forming, legally binding treaties were made to the tribes who relinquished millions of acres of lands and numerous age-old freedoms. In exchange, the federal government is legally bound to the provision of service, including the provision of housing, to Native people in perpetuity.

THE TRUST RESPONSIBILITIES OF CONGRESS
AND THE EXECUTIVE BRANCH

The federal trust responsibility to Indian nations can be divided into three components.

1. The protection of Indian trust lands and Indian rights to use those lands;
2. The protection of tribal sovereignty and rights of self-governance;
3. The provision of basic social, medical and educational services for tribal members.

Often considered an "invisible minority," American Indians and Alaska Natives are often left out or relegated into the category of "other" within the racial equity framework in the United States. The racial equity framework must be adapted and explicitly expanded to include an indigenous lens. American Indian communities often adopt a stance of "measured separatism" that legal writer R.A. Williams describes as "much different from the types of minority rights that were and remain at the center of the continuing struggle for racial equality." J.E. Nielsen, citing T. Biolsi, notes: "It may be appropriate for Native communities to adopt a racial equity perspective in some situations/geopolitical spaces—other circumstances/spaces require that we operate from a stance of sovereignty and self-determination—an indigenous lens. Opportunity is specialized and may look different in tribal space than in nontribal space."

Geography and Demographics: In Census 2000, 4.3 million people, or 1.5 percent of the total U.S. population, reported that they were American Indian or Alaska Native, representing over 500 individual tribal nations. This number included 2.4 million people, or 1 percent of the U.S. total, who reported AI/AN as their only race.

The geography of the AI/AN population is widely distributed in the United States, with a majority of Native people residing off-reservation. Slightly over 64 percent live outside tribal areas; 33.5 percent live in American Indian Areas (which includes federal reservations and/or off-reservation trust lands, Oklahoma tribal statistical areas, tribal-designated statistical areas, state reservations, and state-designated American Indian statistical areas); and slightly over 2 percent live in Alaska Native Villages.

Poverty: Regardless of geographic location, poverty remains the singularly most challenging aspect of contemporary AI/AN experience. There is considerable indicative information that Native Americans are disproportionably affected by monetary or economic poverty. The following examples point out some of these disparities:

- 25.3 percent is the 2007 poverty rate of people who reported they were AI/AN and no other race. However, this does not reflect the poverty rate of those individuals reporting AI/AN in combination with another race.

- Residents of reservations experience deep poverty, meaning they live at less than 75 percent of the poverty level, and do so at twice the rate of the total U.S. population (26 percent for American Indians versus 12 percent nationally).
- Unemployment in some reservations can be several times the national average.
- Off-reservation and urban AI/AN people also experience disproportionate levels of poverty, three times that of whites.

Housing

- 14.7 percent of homes are overcrowded, compared to 5.7 percent of homes of the general U.S. population.
- Indian Country has a denial rate for conventional home purchase loans of 23 percent—twice that of Caucasians.
- The percentage of Indian Country without adequate plumbing facilities is 10 times the general U.S. population.
- 11 percent of Indian Country lacks kitchen facilities, compared to 1 percent of the U.S.
- In an 8-state (MN, IA, ND, SD, MT, ID, WA, OR) study of housing needs in 30 Metropolitan Statistical Areas, the 2000 U.S. Census reports that 46 percent of Indian renters pay more than 30 percent of their total income for rent. The census also reveals that 2 percent of renters are forced to pay at least a half of their monthly income for rent.
- In looking at the disparities within the poverty and housing indicators cited above, it becomes clear that there is an interdependence between accessibility to fair credit and housing for AI/AN people regardless of their geographic location on or off the reservation. As such, coordinated national strategies are needed to address these barriers.

Fair Housing: The U.S. Department of Housing and Urban Development (HUD) defines housing affordability by asserting that no more than 30 percent of a household's income should be dedicated to housing (rent and utilities). The lack of affordable housing is a significant hardship for low-income households, preventing them from meeting their other basic needs such as nutrition and healthcare, or saving for their future and that of their families. While this holds true for all disadvantaged communities in the United States, it has significant differences when examined from AI/AN perspectives, with a key point being that the federal government has a legal and trust responsibility to provide adequate housing for Native people.

On-Reservation Populations: HUD is charged with housing construction and maintenance on Native American trust lands and reservations. Under the Native American Housing Assistance and Self-Determination Act (NAHASDA) of 1996, the federal government makes block grants to tribes and tribally designated housing entities. While the block grant program has led to greater local control, its success has been undercut by lack of funding. At its current level, NAHASDA funding will only meet 5 percent of the total need for housing in Native communities.

NAHASDA separated Native-American housing from general public housing, both administratively and financially. The act, recognizing tribal rights to self-governance and self-determination, was designed to permit tribal recipients to manage and monitor housing assistance programs. It is structured to provide flexibility in tribal planning, implementation and administration of housing programs. Given the unique housing challenges Native Americans face—including impoverished economic conditions, restrictions on individual land rights, lack of homeownership, and substandard housing—greater and immediate federal financial support is imperative.

Off-Reservation Populations: In an 8-state community-based research project, over 1,200 urban-dwelling Native people were interviewed in 4 major metropolitan areas regarding a number of poverty indicators, including access to housing. Respondents cited the following barriers to getting into housing: credit checks, low income, lack of affordable housing stock, background checks, and deposits/downpayment requirements. It is likely that these outcomes do not vary significantly nationwide.

Nearly every city represented in the National Urban Indian Family Coalition reports a disproportionate number of Natives in shelter care but very few transitional housing projects serving the Native community. This points to the need for capacity in the Native nonprofit sector and for the will and ability of tribal governments to develop collaborative national strategies to impact this on a policy and practice level. It is important to note that this remains merely anecdotal information until a research agenda is developed to quantify this experience.

RECOMMENDATIONS

Provide opportunities and resources, both on and off the reservation, for Native people to become more financially literate in order to improve both their credit scores and access to homeownership:

- Fund and support the continued development of Native community development financial institutions (CDFIs). There are presently 48 U.S. Treasury-certified Native CDFIs, with another 50+ in various stages of emergence, up from just 6 such at the end of 2000. These locally based, Native institutions have become economic engines for communities, providing homebuyer education, financial education, entrepreneurship, individual development account (IDA) matched savings programs, credit counseling, anti-predatory lending, mortgages and small business loans.
- Explore policies regarding requiring predatory lending institutions and banks to contribute to a general fund designated specifically for financial literacy education. Within this, specify that a percentage of the fund go to tribal governments

and Native nonprofit organizations to provide financial literacy and relevant economic enhancement services in their communities.

- Fund an Indian community development block grant through HUD or the Administration for Native Americans for tribal governments and Native nonprofits to build economic capacity and literacy in their communities. Specific language must be included for off-reservation populations.

Establish a Research Agenda: AI/AN communities need more research to fully understand the conditions our people are experiencing in tribal and urban settings. We are not interested in merely being the "subjects" of research, however; what we need is the resources that will enable us to build our own capacity to define research questions, gather data, and draw our own conclusions based on those data. Specifically, the National Congress of American Indians Policy Research Center, the Harvard Project on American Indian Economic Development, or other culturally relevant scholars and research institutions should be engaged to conduct the needed research:

- *Access to Fair Housing:* While there exists some research and analysis on housing as it relates to on-reservation housing and access to housing, there exists a clear need to examine this from the standpoint of off-reservation Native populations who now comprise a majority of the AI/AN people in the United States. A comprehensive examination of the current housing crisis for this population needs exploration, with a focus on the equitable distribution of resources compared to the disproportionate local representation in their homeless populations.
- *Access to Fair Credit:* There is very little current information on best practices and strategies for increasing access to credit by AI/AN populations either on- or off-reservation. We need to develop a research agenda to explore this aspect of the AI/AN experience. The 2000 Native American Lending Study was an important first step and led to the creation of the present Expanding Native Opportunity Initiatives of the U.S. Treasury CDFI Fund. More detailed and current information is now required.

Collaborate with the Native Financial Education Coalition (NFEC) to enact policy recommendations: NFEC is a group of local, regional and national organizations and government agencies that have joined together for one purpose: to promote financial education in Native communities. Each year, the NFEC develops a comprehensive set of policy recommendations relating to Financial Education in Native communities:

Support the development and growth of the newly formed Native CDFI Network: Help to create a policy platform that addresses the broader issues of asset-building and community development in Native communities.

Expand Tribal Housing Authority: Expand the capacity of tribal governments and/or Tribal Designated Housing Entities (TDHE) to develop fair market housing with

Indian preference in off-reservation locations. This policy recommendation needs to be crafted in conjunction with appropriate tribal governmental bodies, advocacy and off-reservation organizations.

Explore and enact policy recommendations as laid out in the 2003 U.S. Civil Rights Commission report, "A Quiet Crisis in Indian Country": The report focused on the adequacy of federal funding for programs and services targeting American Indians, Federally Recognized Indian Tribal Governments and Native American Organizations. Attention was directed at unmet needs, the portion of basic needs among Native Americans that the government is supposed to supply but does not. For the purposes of this overview, we are concentrating on the segments of the report focusing on housing.

The report details 11 recommendations with regard to the distribution of federal resources in Indian Country—while each recommendation made by the U.S. Civil Rights Commission deserves and requires additional attention by the federal government, two come to the forefront that might bear fruit when applied towards issues of fair housing and fair credit:

- *Recommendation 2:* All agencies that distribute funds for Native American programs should be required to regularly assess unmet needs for both urban and rural Native individuals. Such an assessment would compare community needs with available resources and identify gaps in service delivery. Agencies should establish benchmarks for the elevation of Native-American living conditions to those of other Americans, and in doing so create attainable resource-driven goals.

  In addition, each federal agency that administers Native-American programs should specifically and accurately document Native American participation in its programs and account for all projects and initiatives. This inventory will provide tribal governments and Native individuals with up-to-date information on the services and programs available and will enable agencies to identify and reduce program redundancies.

- *Recommendation 8:* Federal appropriations must account for costs that are unique to Indian tribes, such as those required to build necessary infrastructure, those associated with geographic remoteness, and those required for training and technical assistance. Overall, more money is needed to support independent enterprise, such as through guaranteed loans that facilitate home and business ownership, and to provide incentives for lending institutions, builders, educators and health management companies to conduct business on Indian lands. The federal government should develop widespread incentives to facilitate education and to promote the return of services to Indian communities. In doing so, it will promote economic development in Indian Country, which will eventually reduce reliance on government services.

In addition, the unique needs of nonreservation and urban Native Americans must be assessed, and adequate funding must be provided for programs to serve these individuals. Native Americans are increasingly leaving reservations and their way of life, not always by choice but due to economic hardships. Yet funding for health, education, housing, job training and other critical needs of urban Native Americans is a low priority.

OTHER CONSIDERATIONS

Tribal Sovereignty

The United States government has a unique legal relationship with Native American tribal governments, as set forth in the Constitution of the United States, treaties, statutes and court decisions. As executive departments and agencies undertake activities affecting Native American tribal rights or trust resources, such activities should be implemented in a knowledgeable, sensitive manner respectful of tribal sovereignty. As such, when examining policy and research within the context of Indian Country, this political aspect must be taken into consideration, and any actionable policy recommendations need to be developed in consultation with tribal governments.

Programs that are funded in Indian Country must be enacted under tribal sovereignty and self-determination. Julie Nielsen noted: "There is ample evidence that in Native nations, the best outcomes of federally funded programs emerge when tribal governments are able to exercise their inherent sovereignty and to exercise self-determination. In fact, according to Stephen Cornell and Jonathan Taylor, over 12 years of research and evaluation from both the Harvard Project on American Indian Economic Development and the Udall Center for Public Policy at the University of Arizona indicate that the only successful public development strategies in Indian Country are those that have been enacted under tribal control. They also suggest that state goals, as well, have been advanced through successful tribal control over publicly funded development."

CONSULTATION

Indian Country has developed infrastructure and experts in the field of housing and credit. The following institutions should be included in future policy development:

Financial Empowerment: First Nations Development Institute, Oweesta, Native Financial Education Coalition

Housing: National American Indian Housing Council, National Congress of American Indians, National Urban Indian Family Coalition

Mossville, Louisiana: A Community's Fight for the Human Right to a Healthy Environment

Michele Roberts

Mossville is not located on most U.S. maps. Yet some of America's largest industrial corporations have found this unincorporated African-American community and exploit its natural resources and proximity to the Gulf of Mexico. Near Mossville, homes, churches and playgrounds, there are 14 industrial facilities and an extensive network of underground and elevated pipelines that carry flammable and hazardous materials. The fact that African Americans have lived in Mossville for the last three centuries is of no moment to the industrial corporations. Nor is it relevant to our government, which has approved environmental permitting, zoning and significant tax subsidies that allow millions of pounds of toxic pollution to engulf Mossville residents. More egregious is that our government has enacted environmental laws that deny Mossville residents the legal right to a remedy.

Mossville residents suffer, and some have died from severe health problems associated with industrial pollution that includes elevated levels of dioxins in their blood. The fertile land and rich biodiversity in Mossville have been replaced with contaminated soil, fish kills, as well as unhealthy levels of carcinogenic chemicals in the air and water. However, there is no court in the United States where Mossville residents can go to find a remedy. The significant industrial pollution in Mossville is not prohibited by the Constitution or federal and state law. It is legal for the environmental-permitted industrial facilities to harm the Mossville community.

"We have been told over and over again by the Environmental Protection Agency that the facilities have a right to the environmental permits. But what about our rights?," asked Dorothy Felix, a resident of Mossville, who along with her neighbors organized Mossville Environmental Action Now.

PETITIONING THE OAS

On behalf of the Mossville group and residents, Advocates for Environmental Human Rights filed a petition with the Inter-American Commission on Human Rights of the Organization of American States (OAS). The petition seeks nonmonetary remedies—healthcare, residential relocation, environmental restoration and regulatory reform—from the U.S. government for establishing a deeply flawed system for environmental protection that violates the human rights of Mossville residents. As a member of the OAS, the United States has the legal obligation to protect human rights.

In March 2010, the commission issued a ruling that the Mossville petition is admissible for a review on the merits, which marked the first time for an international human rights body to take jurisdiction over a case of environmental racism in the United States. The admissibility ruling is based on the finding that the U.S. legal system provides no remedy for the racially disproportionate pollution burdens and unequal environmental protection suffered by Mossville residents. The commission's decision opens the door to a human rights trial of the U.S. environmental regulatory system that not only condemns the historic African-American community of Mossville to industrial hazards, but systematically subjects people of color and poor communities across the country to unhealthy and unsafe environmental conditions.

For years, environmental justice communities have advocated for remedies. Governmental agencies have responded inadequately by issuing vague guidelines that do not have the force of law and by hosting dialogue sessions with community advocates, science and health experts, as well as representatives of industrial companies. The governmental response, however well-intentioned, shifts the focus away from developing a legal remedy for the injustice of racially disparate toxic health threats and recognizing a legal right to a healthy environment.

The Mossville human rights case compels a departure from the inadequate governmental response to environmental racism and injustice. This one community that is omitted from most U.S. maps is the place where people are pushing our country toward embracing a new vision for environmental protection that is based on human rights.

Understanding Health Impact Assessment: A Tool for Addressing Health Disparities

Saneta DeVuono-powell & Jonathan Heller

Health is a big topic of concern these days. Despite outspending all other developed nations on healthcare, our nation ranks 26th in life expectancy. In recent years, we have witnessed growing obesity, diabetes and asthma rates, in addition to numerous other health problems. Not surprisingly, these health problems have a disparate impact on vulnerable communities, with people of color and those in poverty bearing a disproportionate health burden. For example, infant mortality rates for African Americans are more than twice the national average, and the life expectancy gap between poor African-American men and affluent white women is more than 14 years. For advocates who work with these communities, health disparities are not new. What is new is the emerging consensus that health outcomes will not improve unless we address social and environmental factors traditionally understood as unrelated to health. Improving access to healthcare and trying to change behaviors are not enough; we must address the decisions and policies that are not traditionally thought of as associated with health.

For the past few decades, public health agencies focused on trying to improve health by addressing individual behavior related to poor health outcomes. At the same time, social and economic inequalities continued to increase and we witnessed growing and persistent health disparities. Today, the life expectancy gap between the most and least affluent is increasing, and the areas with the greatest social and economic inequalities have the worst life expectancy and mortality rates. Studies repeatedly show that even when you control for individual variables, external factors like where people live, the quality of their housing and education, income attainment and stress levels correlate with depression, chronic disease, mortality and health risk behaviors. Given this knowledge, health advocates have begun to realize that they cannot improve health conditions without addressing these factors, which are known in public health circles as the social determinants of health. Health Impact Assessment (HIA) is a tool that can help highlight these links and mitigate health disparities because HIA addresses these determinants of health. Although HIA has been practiced outside of the United States for many years, its use here is just beginning to gain traction. In 2007, a study found just 27 HIAs had been conducted in the U.S. In the subsequent four years, an additional 92 HIAs have begun or been completed.

A Health Impact Assessment is defined as "a combination of procedures, methods and tools that systematically judges the potential, and sometimes unintended, effects of a proposed project, plan or policy on the health of a population and the distribution of those effects within the population." HIA aims to increase the consideration of health in decision-making arenas that typically do not consider health. HIA also identifies appropriate actions to manage those effects. There are two desired outcomes of an HIA. One is to influence plans, policies and projects in a way that improves health and diminishes health disparities. The other is to engage community members and other stakeholders so they understand what is impacting community health and how to advocate for improving health using a transparent and evidence-based process.

A typical HIA includes six steps:

1. Screening—Determines the need, value and feasibility of an HIA;
2. Scoping—Determines which health impacts to evaluate, the methods for analysis, and the workplan for completing the assessment;
3. Assessment—Provides: a) a profile of existing health conditions; b) evaluation of potential health impacts;
4. Recommendations—Provides strategies to manage identified adverse health impacts or enhance positive health impacts;
5. Reporting—Includes development of the HIA report and communication of findings and recommendations; and
6. Monitoring—Tracks impacts on decision-making processes and the decision, as well as impacts of the decision on health determinants.

Within this general framework, approaches to HIA vary as HIAs are tailored to work with the specific needs, timeline and resources of each particular project. This chapter briefly describes two HIAs as examples of how and when an HIA can be conducted and then discusses strategies for using HIA to address health disparities.

CASE 1: LONG BEACH DOWNTOWN DEVELOPMENT PLAN

In 2010, the City of Long Beach in Southern California proposed plans for extensive new development in their downtown area. The Long Beach Downtown Plan proposed including 5,000 new residential units, 1.5 million square feet of office, civic and cultural spaces, 384,000 square feet of new retail space, and 5,200 new jobs. The plan, however, did not mention affordable housing or job creation for the current residents of the area. This oversight was particularly troublesome, given the demographics of downtown Long Beach, an area that is currently populated by an ethnically diverse and predominantly low-income population whose current employment and housing needs are not being met (the list for Section 8 housing is currently closed and has a ten-year wait).

Concern about the potentially adverse impacts this plan would have for local residents led local organizations to decide to conduct a rapid Health Impact Assessment. The HIA, conducted by East Yard Communities for Environmental Justice, Californians for Justice, and Human Impact Partners (HIP—an Oakland-based nonprofit) in early 2011, focused on measuring what impacts the proposed plan would have on housing and employment and how these changes would affect the health of residents. Because the advocates wanted to be able to use the HIA to respond to the Draft Environmental Impact Report (EIR), there was a short timeline. This necessarily limited the scope of the HIA, but it was still a useful tool for concerned community advocates and local organizations. Fortunately, there was a proposed Community Benefits Agreement, which allowed the HIA to focus its recommendations as well as point to a specific and feasible alternative course of action. Over a three-month period, staff worked together to gather data on: (1) existing health, housing and employment conditions in downtown Long Beach; (2) the potential impacts of the proposed plan; and (3) the potential impacts of proposed community benefits.

The availability of affordable, quality housing and adequate employment opportunities has direct health impacts. The Long Beach HIA cited studies showing that the nature and stability of housing and employment impact a variety of health indicators, including mortality rates, infectious disease, depression and substance abuse. Based on the analysis of the existing demographics and conditions in downtown Long Beach, the HIA found that the diverse residents (Long Beach is the most ethnically diverse city in California) were already facing a shortage of quality affordable housing and adequate employment opportunities and suffering from associated health problems. For example, the HIA found that 46 percent of renters were spending more than the recommended 30 percent of their income on rent and 25 percent were spending more than 50 percent of their incomes on rent, and that overcrowding was already a problem in Long Beach. Not surprisingly, the rates of asthma, heart disease and other health issues (which can be related back to housing cost and quality and to jobs) in Long Beach are significantly higher than the county average.

The HIA findings indicated that, as proposed, the Downtown Plan was likely to have negative impacts on a variety of health-related indicators, including: overcrowding, population displacement and unemployment. The HIA also found that adoption of the proposed Community Benefits Agreement would mitigate some of the negative impacts resulting from the proposed Downtown Plan by providing additional very-low-income and moderate-income housing units and increasing employment opportunities. The HIA recommended that the plan adopt these benefits. The HIA in Long Beach was in response to a city development plan, was submitted as a comment on a Draft Environmental Impact Report, and was limited in scope to impacts on housing and jobs. Findings from the rapid HIA were highlighted in local media campaigns focused on the proposed Downtown Plan. The City of Long Beach is expected to respond to comments on the EIR in the coming months.

CASE 2: PAID SICK DAYS POLICIES

In most developed countries, paid sick days are a given. In the U.S., however, there is no federal law mandating paid sick days and about 4 out of every 10 workers do not have paid sick days. Not surprisingly, low-wage workers, mothers and those who work in the food service industry are much less likely to have paid sick days than most white-collar workers. In 2007, San Francisco became the first jurisdiction in the U.S. to mandate paid sick days for employees. Subsequently, various jurisdictions have introduced legislation that would do the same, including California in 2008 and Congress in 2009—neither of which passed. Surprisingly, although access to paid sick days has clear health implications, initially health was not part of the discussion surrounding efforts to mandate paid sick days. The main frame through which decision makers viewed this legislation was that of economic impact of requiring employers to provide paid sick days.

From 2008–2010, a series of Health Impact Assessments that looked at paid sick day requirements were conducted. In 2008, an HIA of the California Healthy Families, Healthy Workplaces Act (AB 2716, entitling employees to accrue one hour of paid sick time for every 30 hours worked) was completed by Human Impact Partners and the San Francisco Department of Public Health (SFDPH) at the request of the Labor Project for Working Families. The following year, HIP and SFDPH conducted an HIA of the federal Healthy Families Act of 2009. The California and Federal Paid Sick Days HIAs looked at the potential health outcomes for workers, families and communities, including impacts on recovery from illness, use of preventive healthcare services versus emergency rooms, as well the transmission of infectious disease in restaurants, schools and workplaces. The HIAs found that paid sick days has many positive health outcomes, including: improved food safety in restaurants; reduced transmission of the flu in childcare settings and nursing homes; and reduced emergency room usage. The HIAs showed that legislation that would entitle more workers to paid sick days would be good for everyone's health—workers themselves, as well as people whose lives are touched by the same workers.

Paid Sick Day HIAs were used by coalitions of proponents of the various paid sick days legislation. Although neither the California nor federal legislation passed, the HIA helped advocates articulate a public health rationale for the policy, thereby changing the public discourse about the issue from a question of labor rights or employer costs to the issue of improving the health of all people. At the same time, the HIA offered a rationale for public health officials to support paid sick days, a policy they may not have previously engaged. This health framing was picked up in other jurisdictions, and Milwaukee advocates used the California HIA along with

Milwaukee-specific data to inform public opinion on a local 2008 paid sick day ballot measure. Legislative advocates publicized health facts through the local media,
and the initiative passed with the support of two-thirds of the votes of Milwaukee
residents. More recently, Connecticut became the first state to pass paid sick days
legislation. In making their argument, advocates in Connecticut focused on the
health benefits the bill would provide.

STRATEGIES FOR USING HIA TO ADDRESS HEALTH

There are a wide variety of projects, policies and plans where an HIA can be useful, and the first step of any HIA helps determine whether it is an appropriate tool.
Conducting an HIA requires six steps (as outlined above). During the first two steps
(screening and scoping), those involved assess the need for an HIA as well as which
health measures to evaluate. HIAs start with hypotheses that are informed by scientific review as well as by lived experience of communities and stakeholders, and then
research informs whether the hypotheses are true. This process allows those involved
to think about the health of a particular community and understand the variety of
ways that social factors are implicated in heath.

The HIA on the Downtown Plan in Long Beach and the HIA on paid sick days
highlight how advocates can use a health lens. Framing the issue of equity around
health can be a very powerful tool. Because HIA addresses social determinants of
health, advocates and communities may find that the use of an HIA can create headway around a social issue. Often a health lens makes it more difficult for opponents
to argue against addressing the real needs of a community. Using an HIA as a strategy
for developing a health lens can be particularly effective because HIA is a research-
based tool that provides scientific data in addition to assessing mitigation strategies.

The differences between the two above case studies highlight two complementary
strategies for using HIA to address health disparities: focus on process, and focus on
outcomes. Ideally, an HIA utilizes a robust process of multistakeholder participation, and also uses robust data analysis to influence the outcome of the project it is
assessing in a manner that produces good health outcomes. However, HIA can have
powerful impact even if it ends up being more outcome- than process-driven, or
vice versa.

In Long Beach, advocates were concerned about a land use plan and wanted a
tool they could use to weigh in on an existing, fast-moving process. Although the
HIA process was important, given the short timelines, what mattered most was to
have an impact on the proposed plan. HIA was appealing because it could produce
an evidence-based report, highlighting potential health consequences, to submit as
a comment on the Draft Environmental Impact Report that was being prepared. In
this case, this created a time constraint, which limited and therefore deemphasized
the HIA process. HIAs provide stakeholders with multiple ways to weigh in at various stages in a decision-making process, almost always with the goal of influencing

the final decision. The HIA can be used to legitimize or assuage concerns, and can offer a mechanism to introduce recommendations or alternatives.

Although HIAs are typically set up in a way that allows them to have some impact on outcomes, there are also reasons for conducting an HIA that focuses more on process. Through conducting an HIA, structured opportunities for capacity-building, relationship-building, transparent and democratic process (e.g., stakeholder participation), community organizing, and developing messages are available. Regardless of outcome, an HIA can be useful and impactful because of these opportunities.

Often, the process of engaging multiple stakeholders in HIA actually brings about change in the decision. In addition to quantitative data, HIAs often include community surveys or focus groups, which help lend a voice and credibility to concerns about the issue. In the Paid Sick Days HIAs, the material gathered from focus groups was useful for highlighting the health concerns of workers, giving a personal voice to the issue, and for engaging more people in the policy-making process. The process of gathering these narratives and combining them with more quantitative (e.g., statistical) data creates a story about the people impacted by the proposed plan, project or policy. As this story emerges, powerful messages that can be used for advocacy also emerge, as HIA can build capacity and relationships. Although the HIAs on paid sick days did not lead to the immediate passage of new legislation mandating paid sick days, their impact was felt through the narratives that emerged during the process. The health frame that was established through the data and personal stories has been picked up by other paid sick days advocates and was used in recent legislative victories.

Because HIA is a collaborative process, when effectively executed it can build capacity and relationships. HIA is a tool in which multiple stakeholders have an opportunity to engage, allowing for deepening relationships but also building the capacity of these stakeholders to engage meaningfully. The process of the HIA can be so important that the skills and opportunities for advocacy it provides become primary goals and are as important as outcome-related goals. When a group of community organizations in West Oakland decided to learn about HIA, they decided to conduct a rapid HIA on a proposed neighborhood development. Although they were initially more interested in the HIA process than in any specific outcome, during the HIA they began to work with the developer and as a result the project ended up adopting many of the HIA recommendations to protect future residents from air pollution and pedestrian injury from traffic.

In another HIA conducted in Los Angeles, a community organizing group successfully engaged community members in data collection as well as advocacy. The HIA, conducted on a development project in South Central Los Angeles, involved multiple stakeholders, including the developer, the public health agency and the redevelopment agency, from the beginning, which led the stakeholders to agree to changes based on the community findings. Here, the process and outcome were both considered important, and the success of the outcome depended on the success of the process.

Another potential use of HIA is as a litigation tool or as a tool to prevent litigation. For a plaintiff, an HIA can serve to: (1) provide notice of potential harm, and (2) show the feasibility of alternatives. Alternatively, where steps have been taken to address concerns raised in an HIA and recommendations are adopted, the HIA could insulate projects from subsequent litigation by showing that health was seriously considered and that necessary steps were taken to address legitimate concerns. After adopting mitigations to address environmental health concerns for low-income housing raised in an HIA in Pittsburg, California, city agencies then used the HIA to defeat NIMBY [Not In My Back Yard] efforts to eliminate that housing.

CONCLUSION

Regardless of what type of project, plan or policy decision is being considered, a Health Impact Assessment may be a strategic tool for a variety of reasons. In addition to providing a health lens and health analysis, an HIA can contribute a robust participatory process and a structure for communities and other stakeholders to collaborate and provide input on decisions being made. HIAs may be appropriate on a wide variety of subjects. The value of an HIA can be determined by the magnitude and likelihood of potential health impacts, the distribution of those impacts, an accurate assessment of the likelihood of achieving the process and/or outcome objectives of the HIA, and a realistic evaluation of resources, capacity and stakeholder interest.

Health Equity for Asian American, Native Hawaiian, and Pacific Islander Children and Youth: What's Racism Got to Do With It?

Laurin Mayeno, Joseph Keawe'aimoku Kaholokula, David MKI Liu, Lloyd Y. Asato & Winston Tseng

- Since entering high school, Kekoa, a 16-year-old obese Native Hawaiian male with type 2 diabetes, has become depressed and taken up cigarette smoking and drinking on a daily basis.
- In 2007, Seung-Hui Cho, a 23-year-old Korean American college student with mental illness, killed 32 people and wounded many more, before committing suicide.

These are two individual examples of health inequities that threaten the well-being of Asian American (AA) and Native Hawaiian and Pacific Islander (NHPI) children and youth. In this chapter, we highlight these health inequities and pose the question: "What's racism got to do with it?" We begin by presenting data on health inequities and briefly discuss existing investigation and theory. We then explore, through the stories of Kekoa and Seung-Hui, how the health of children and youth of AA and NHPI communities is shaped by pervasive racism in our society. While focusing on the fundamental problems that contribute to health inequities among AA and NHPI children and youth, we also discuss the supportive role that family, community and culture can play in fostering their health and well-being.

DISAGGREGATING AA AND NHPI

NHPI and AA communities have distinct histories, cultures, experiences and health challenges. The arbitrary grouping together of NHPI and AA for data collection and funding purposes creates barriers to understanding and addressing their health issues. Within both the NHPI and AA categories, there are numerous communities whose acculturation experiences, socioeconomic status and health issues are very different.

Therefore, when possible, we will make distinctions between different ethnic groups that fall under these broader classifications and respect each group's cultural and classification preferences.

RECOGNIZING HEALTH INEQUITIES

Before we can address AA and NHPI health inequities, they must be acknowledged. Over the past few decades, AA and NHPI advocates and researchers have increased visibility for health inequities that impact their communities. NHPI communities have worked to have their health issues become visible and recognized as distinct from those impacting AAs. AA communities have worked to dispel the myth of the model minority and, with the use of disaggregated data, have demonstrated that not all AAs are healthy, particularly recent immigrant and low-income AAs. (Native Hawaiians and other Pacific Islanders are people whose origins are from three main groups of Islands in the Pacific: Polynesia, Micronesia and Melanesia. Native Hawaiians are the largest group of Pacific Islanders in the U.S. Other major Pacific Islander groups in the U.S. include Samoans, Guamanians (Chamorro) and other Micronesian groups (Federated State of Micronesia, Republic of the Marshall Islands and Republic of Palau). Asian Americans are persons with ancestry from Asian countries and islands in the Pacific Rim who live in the United States. The largest Asian-American populations are Chinese, Filipino, Asian Indian, Vietnamese, Korean and Japanese, each of which number over 1 million. Cambodian, Laotian, Pakistani and Hmong number over 200,000 each.)

Although much of the data is focused on adults, there is recently a growing body of evidence that health inequities do indeed exist for AA and NHPI children and youth. Here are some examples:

NATIVE HAWAIIAN AND PACIFIC ISLANDER CHILDREN AND YOUTH

- From 2003–2005, NHPI mothers in California and Hawaii had higher rates of low birth weight and pre-term birth than Whites (4.1 percent LBW and 7.5 percent pre-term birth), with rates for Marshallese mothers among the highest: low birth weight 8.4 percent and pre-term birth 18.8 percent.
- 54 percent of Samoan children (5th graders) in California followed by "Other" Pacific Islander (42 percent), Guamanian (35 percent), Native Hawaiian (35 percent) and Tahitian (34 percent) children are not within the Healthy Fitness Zone, according to their body mass index, compared to the state average (32 percent) and Whites.
- Native Hawaiian youth are also more likely to be obese and smoke cigarettes, compared to youth of other ethnic groups.

- 30 percent of NHPI adolescents (ages 12–17) in California were diagnosed with asthma in 2003–2005, compared with the state average (20 percent).

ASIAN-AMERICAN CHILDREN AND YOUTH

- From 2003–2005, Cambodian and Laotian mothers in California and Hawaii had higher rates of both low birth weight (8.8 percent and 9.2 percent, respectively) and pre-term birth (14.0 percent and 13.7 percent, respectively), compared to Whites (4.1 percent LBW and 7.5 percent pre-term birth). 28 percent of South Asian adolescents (ages 12–17) in California were diagnosed with asthma in 2003–2005, compared with the state average (20 percent).
- 30 percent of Filipino and 29 percent of Laotian children (5th graders) in California are not within the Healthy Fitness Zone according to their body mass index, compared to Whites (23 percent).
- 36 percent of sexually active Chinese adolescents or their partner in California, followed by Filipino (49 percent), Korean (50 percent) and South Asian (51 percent) adolescents or their partner, used any type of birth control the last time they had sex, compared to the state average (72 percent) and Whites (79 percent).

In order to address these health inequities, there is a need to understand the broader social framework that shapes children's lives and health. Some researchers have articulated that racial constructions, exposures to racism, and other environmental and psychosocial stressors interact with biological systems to increase health risks and problems among adults.

We next discuss existing frameworks that explore the impact of racism on children's health. There have been few studies investigating the role of racism in children's health, including a few focused on racism and mental health among AA adolescents. Huge gaps exist in research on racism and children's health for both AA and NHPI communities. There is a dire need for more work on this topic in order to document community assets and needs, and develop effective intervention strategies and policies.

THEORETICAL FRAMEWORK

To conceptualize the role of racism in child health, K. Sanders-Phillips and colleagues propose a general framework that draws from different theoretical models. From ecological theory, they discuss the role of a child's immediate environment (microsystem) and larger social environment (macrosystem). They suggest that institutional racism at the macrosystem level, such as educational and housing policies that put a particular racial/ethnic group at a disadvantage, can impact variables at the microsystem, such as family functioning and neighborhood health conditions that increase behavioral and biological health risks for children of color. From social stratification theory, they suggest that a group's historical and current place in the social hierarchy can impact experiences and exposure to risk factors. From theories of racial inequality and social integration, they posit that racial discrimination has an impact on individuals' judgments, decisions and behaviors. There are multiple resulting consequences for children and their parents, which ultimately lead to inequities in biological, behavioral and social functioning. Protective factors mentioned in the model include racial awareness, racial socialization and certain parenting styles that protect against the negative impact of discrimination.

In the Sanders-Phillips model, exposure to racial discrimination at both the microsystem and macro-system levels creates psychological responses, such as decreased self-efficacy and depression, and biological responses through changes in chronic stress and allostatic load, which in turn may produce decreased immune function and higher, or paradoxically blunted, cortisol levels. This, in turn, results in disparities or inequities in child health outcomes.

In the section that follows, we explore two case examples of health inequities among NHPI and AA youth, using Sanders-Phillips' framework as a point of reference.

CASE STUDIES

The stories of Kekoa and Seung-Hui give us a window into how racism interacts with other social and cultural factors to impact the health of some AA and NHPI children and youth. These two examples do not represent the full spectrum of the AA or NHPI experience. However, they do bear witness to health issues and social dynamics that we cannot afford to ignore.

Kekoa's Story

Kekoa, a 16-year-old Native Hawaiian male, lives in a Hawaiian homestead community with his parents and three siblings and attends a nearby public high school in urban Honolulu.

Exposure to Racial Discrimination. Racism and colonialism are difficult to disentangle in the Pacific, as racism can be considered the ideology that has informed and justified the contagion of colonialism across the Pacific. Kekoa's story illustrates how present-day colonialism continues to structure the distribution of power, resources and money largely along racial and ethnic lines. His ancestors were dispossessed of their land and resources and became second-class citizens in Hawaii's ethnic/racial hierarchy—a social ranking that continues today. The Hawaiian homestead he and his family reside in is the result of a settlement to return Native Hawaiians back to their lands after the occupation of Hawaii by the U.S. However, many Hawaiian homesteads are among the most impoverished and obesiogenic neighborhoods in Hawai'i.

Kekoa often hears his parents' wish for Native Hawaiians to regain political autonomy from the U.S. so they can improve their quality of life. He also learns from his parents of how the U.S. illegally took over Hawai'i and made Native Hawaiians second-class citizens in their own homeland. Most neighbors in his homestead community share similar thoughts and frustrations and struggle to make ends meet. Ironically, most or all of this communication occurs not in the Hawaiian language, but in English, a further result of colonization.

Kekoa's family has an annual household income of $35,000, which is barely enough to pay the bills and provide for the four children, in a state with one of the highest costs of living. He experiences the frustration and sense of helplessness of his parents in trying to make ends meet. Because of their economic hardship and resulting stressors, his father often turns to alcohol to deal with the stress and frustration. After drinking, his father sometimes physically abuses his mother.

Kekoa's social environment at home and in his homestead community, where a majority is Native Hawaiian, is in sharp contrast to his school environment. Although a large number of students are Native Hawaiian and other Pacific Islanders (35 percent), the faculty of the school is predominantly of Asian descent (50 percent), with only a small minority (8 percent) being Native Hawaiian and other Pacific Islanders. At school, Kekoa does not feel comfortable or accepted by his teachers and peers, who are of other ethnic groups. He prefers hanging out with other Native Hawaiian students whom he can better relate to.

As a result of these and other factors, the public school system in Hawai'i has been accused of inadvertently maintaining the poor social and economic condition of Native Hawaiians and other Pacific Islanders.

Psychological and Biological Response. Since entering high school, Kekoa has become depressed. He does not feel valued as a Native Hawaiian and believes society does not have much to offer him in the way of a bright future. When asked what is going on with him, he just responds by saying, "I Hawaiian so no moa [more] much for me. No make sense. I not going college so no need get good grades. Mo bettah I get one job and help my 'ohana [family]." Although Kekoa has always been overweight, he has gained a significant amount of excess weight since starting high school and is now obese, which has markedly decreased his physical functioning.

Resulting Health Inequities. Kekoa has taken up cigarette smoking and drinking on a daily basis, his grades have dropped, and he is frequently absent from school. He was recently diagnosed with Type 2 diabetes. However, his retinal exam showed early signs of eye disease, suggesting that he has had diabetes for some time. Coupled with his smoking and drinking, he is at risk for other diabetes-related complications, such as cardiovascular and kidney disease.

For NHPI children in the U.S., racism has both direct and indirect effects, experienced both in immediate health outcomes and through shaping the social determinants of health. Many believe the compulsory acculturation process due to U.S. occupation of Hawaii has had direct adverse effects on the health of Native Hawaiians through increased chronic stress, allostatic load, historical/cultural trauma, and impoverished, damaged environments. These effects may be directly implicated in the higher suicide attempt rates for Native Hawaiian youth, compared to youth of other ethnic groups in Hawai'i (12.9 percent vs. 9.6 percent).

Eliminating Health Inequities. The resilience and fortitude of Native Hawaiians have allowed them to withstand many adversities and remain steadfast in their cultural beliefs, practices and aspirations. These cultural practices and beliefs are being revived to uplift Native Hawaiian youth and their families. For example, Hawaiian language immersion schools and cultural-based public charter schools in Hawai'i (open to students of all races and ethnicities) are building a stronger Hawaiian identity and providing the educational milieu necessary to improve the social and self-image of Native Hawaiian youth. Many substance abuse interventions involve reconnecting Native Hawaiian youth to land- and sea-based activities, such as Kalo farming, aquaculture and canoeing, as the venue for building the personal, cultural and social assets and supports needed to overcome their addiction. Cultural-based programs such as these offer the promise of addressing the social determinants of Native Hawaiian health inequities. On a larger scale, there are a multitude of Native Hawaiian efforts to increase self-governance.

Ultimately, addressing the effects of racism and U.S. occupation on Native Hawaiian children requires deconstructing the genealogy of the "sick" islander child, whether from attention deficit disorder, anxiety, depression, obesity or diabetes. The deconstruction of the "sick" child can provide a historical context to shift the discourse away from one of "blame the victim" to one of restoring the agency of resistance, persistence and reclamation among NHPI children and families.

Seung-Hui's Story

On April 16, 2007, Seung-Hui Cho, a 23-year-old Korean college senior, killed 32 people and wounded many others in what has been known as the "Virginia Tech massacre" before committing suicide. The national coverage labeled Seung-Hui as primarily responsible for his rampage and for not seeking help sooner. Blame was placed on this mentally ill Korean immigrant student instead of examining and addressing the root causes and solutions to youth violence among our growing diverse populations.

Exposure to Racial Discrimination. A closer examination of Seung-Hui Cho's personal history and mental health trajectory suggests that the chain of events leading to the shooting rampage and suicide started in childhood. Racism, closely connected with xenophobia, played a large part in his immigrant experiences, which included social alienation, generational and cultural gaps, bullying and inadequate services. Seung-Hui came to the U.S. from Korea when he was 8 years old. His father worked as a presser at a dry cleaner to help pay for his children's education. Seung-Hui was labeled as a shy boy with an accent who did not speak much. His classmates in junior high and high school made fun of him and occasionally called out to him "go back to China." He was also bullied by affluent Korean youth through Korean church groups. At home, he was shy and not talkative, and often misunderstood by his immigrant parents due to their traditional Korean expectations of his American academic and social life.

Psychological Response. Lack of adequate, culturally competent mental health services also played a role in the chain of events. In 8th grade, he was diagnosed with selective-mutism, a symptom of schizophrenia. He often refused or avoided taking medication when it was prescribed. Throughout his youth, his family sought help for him through Korean churches, but avoided mental health services. In college, he was labeled "question-mark kid" by classmates. Seung-Hui's mental condition progressively worsened over the years, without adequate care or support, and led to increasing social alienation and humiliation at school and at home. He underwent basic psychiatric assessments in college, but continued to fall through the cracks of the school and mental health systems. His mental health condition was not fully diagnosed before he committed suicide.

Resulting Health Inequities. Although the level of violence and tragedy in Seung-Hui's case is unprecedented, it would be a mistake to view his mental illness as an isolated case. The lack of awareness and understanding by family members, schools and healthcare providers about the experiences of Seung-Hui and other Korean and Asian immigrant youth with mild and severe mental health challenges pose major barriers to ensuring the provision of needed support and care.

The leading causes of death among Asian-American youth are unintentional injuries, suicide and homicide, but little is known about their root causes in Asian communities, such as the potential roles of racism and youth violence, and the impact of violent death at an early age on the neighborhood, behavioral and mental health of Asian families and communities across America.

Eliminating Health Inequities. Seung-Hui's story points to the importance of ensuring that Asian immigrant youth with mild and severe mental health conditions are fully supported at home, school, in the communities and by service providers. In Korean communities, for example, school teachers and service providers need to ensure they are culturally sensitive and engage family members, friends and churches who play central roles to care for Korean youth in everyday life. Reducing racism and youth violence across Asian-American communities also requires more data and research, prevention programs, community engagement and advocacy.

Currently, few or no data exist about racism, youth violence and mental health among Asian American children and youth. More data are needed to identify the causes of these issues, their interconnections, and to develop strategies for prevention. Data collection should be culturally appropriate and ensure disaggregation of Asian ethnic subgroups.

Prevention strategies must be aimed at addressing root causes, such as racial discrimination and the culture of violence in American schools and communities, while also building on community and cultural strengths, educating Asian immigrant youth and their parents to access and navigate American social and mental health services in their neighborhoods and schools, and fostering youth resilience.

It is essential to place our efforts in historical context.

Asian-American youth programs that build a sense of belonging and self-esteem can facilitate the prevention of violence, reduce risk factors and strengthen protective factors in the community. Such youth programs can mobilize families and communities, conduct research projects, implement prevention programs and lead advocacy efforts. In addition, cultural competency training is critical for all service providers and should include respect and understanding about Asian mental health beliefs and practices, particularly about "face"; the importance of culturally appropriate mental health services to ensure accurate diagnosis and treatment; the importance of ensuring family member involvement in all aspects of mental healthcare; and the provision of social support and health education for family caregivers.

Finally, partnerships of broad community collaborations across Asian youth, family members, schools, mental health providers, advocates and law enforcement in undoing racism and strengthening youth violence prevention initiatives, and working together in caring and advocating for Asian youth with behavioral and mental health conditions across our nation are more critical than ever in preventing youth violence and building healthy families and safe communities for Asian youth.

CONCLUSION

AA and NHPI children and youth are impacted by a wide spectrum of interconnected social and health inequities, including those that seriously threaten their quality of life and life itself. Understanding and addressing these inequities requires that we look beyond the surface and confront difficult social issues that are embedded in history and current realities. We need to disaggregate our data and ethnic community experiences to seek a richer understanding of the cultural contexts and gaps facing different ethnic communities.

There is an urgent need for further exploration of social, physical and mental health inequities. The theoretical model proposed by Sanders-Phillips and her colleagues shows promise as a framework for understanding and addressing the role of racism. Further work to build an evidence base will be needed to confirm the relevance of this framework among AA and NHPI communities. While empirical studies may help us understand the direct role of racism as a determinant of health, it is crucial that we also examine the indirect, invisible role racism plays in shaping other social determinants. In this regard, it is essential to place our efforts in historical context and explore the role that racism has played in colonial devastation and displacement of indigenous people as well as xenophobia and anti-immigrant discrimination, and their effects in shaping contemporary institutions and policies. This exploration can be effective only if we deconstruct narratives of victim-blaming and "sick" children, and work to restore agency in resisting oppression and building community health.

In this context, it is essential to acknowledge the role that family, culture and community can play in fostering health equity in developing strategies at the micro-system and macro-system levels. There are rich opportunities to learn from existing cultural and community-based programs to discover and build upon promising practices.

Neighborhood—The Smallest Unit of Health: A Health Center Model for Pacific Islander and Asian Health

Jamila Jarmon

"Neighbors being Neighborly to Neighbors." This is how Kokua Kalihi Valley Comprehensive Family Services (KKV) approaches neighborhood health in Kalihi Valley, a mostly immigrant community of 30,000 residents on the edge of urban Honolulu. KKV is a federally-qualified community health center, serving about 10,000 residents, primarily Pacific Islander and Asian-American, a year, fostering neighborly values to ensure health for all. Through the years, KKV has grown and currently operates at seven separate locations in the community, including the largest public housing complex in the State of Hawai`i. With growth, KKV retains an original grassroots vision of health and well-being developed together with the community.

KKV has humble roots, beginning in 1972 with four outreach workers operating out of a trailer, going door-to-door getting to know their neighbors: their immediate needs, their hopes, dreams and individual talents, too. The four spoke three different languages and were able to assist community members with agency resources. From their trailer-offices, workers interacted with the community. Soon, physicians and dentists volunteered their time, broadening KKV's community participation. Standing by its motto, KKV continues to expand, maintaining an active and ongoing conversation with the growing community that includes Hawaiians, Filipinos, Samoans and Micronesians, to name a few. The traditional services associated with community health centers are present at KKV, including primary care physicians, dental, nutrition, behavioral health, elderly care, and maternal-child health services. These services help KKV to retain its identity as a traditional community healthcenter. In addition, KKV staff speak 21 different languages, supporting language access and cultural competency for limited-English-proficient speakers. KKV staff diversity enables it to develop innovative programs that support neighborhood health in culturally competent ways.

Adapting a community-based health model pioneered by Dr. Jack Geiger and others on the mainland U.S., KKV understands that communities want to be active participants in developing solutions and strategies that benefit neighborhood health. KKV addresses ongoing human resource needs by hiring from the community, building lasting relationships and thinking programmatically. Hiring workers from the community allows KKV to have a continued connection with the community. The employee is able to listen and work to develop programs within the community that are sustainable. The policy also provides paying jobs to the community, yielding not only health impacts, but also economic impact. By building relationships and working on an equalized plane, KKV is able to not only recognize strength and leadership within the community, it also builds trust as an institution in the community. This helps KKV fulfill its mission of "serving communities, families and individuals through strong relationships that foster health and harmony."

KKV focuses on its internal capacity to continue providing services to the community. The bottom line for KKV is the neighborhood's health and well-being; all programs that begin out of this community dialogue are designed for sustainability. As a community participant, KKV seeks to develop the internal capacity of its partners and clients so that programs can last beyond individual project funding. The neighborhood is an integral part driving programming based on need. For KKV, it is important to keep up the organization's side of the partnership and retain continuity of the programs offered, regardless of funding challenges.

KKV embraces an expanded meaning of "healthcare" by having a broad view of neighborhood health. It has developed a variety of innovative neighborhood health partnerships that serve its diverse ethnic community, which includes many new Pacific-Islander and Asian-American immigrant communities. This chapter highlights four programs at KKV: Lei Hipu`u o Kalihi; Kalihi Valley Instructional Bike Exchange; Medical-Legal Partnership for Children in Hawai`i; and Ho`oulu `Aina. Focusing on culture and family, these programs are guided and led by the community.

LEI HIPU`U O KALIHI

KKV's Lei Hipu`u o Kalihi (Lei Hipu`u) is a grantee of the Health Through Action Grant from the Asian & Pacific Islander American Health Forum sponsored by the W.K. Kellogg Foundation. Lei Hipu`u's purpose it to work on capacity-building in the area of early childhood health within the Kalihi Valley community. Because KKV serves various ethnic groups, Lei Hipu`u conducts focus groups with each around early childhood health issues, identifying cultural similarities and differences. These focus groups produce qualitative data that help Lei Hipu`u, as a representative of KKV, understand how the community raises their children. Many of these focus groups are assembled by the community outreach specialist for Lei Hipu`u, who is a leader in the Chuukese (Micronesian) community. Hiring from the community for this position provides Lei Hipu'u continuous opportunities to work in partnership with the community and understand neighborhood priorities. The Micronesian community is the newest and fastest growing immigrant community in Hawai'i and a large consumer of KKV services. Hiring from the community not only created the opportunity to build a relationship with a new and growing immigrant population, it built the community outreach specialists' capacity and provided economic opportunity for work previously done without pay.

Relationships are built through Lei Hipu'u, which serves as a connector in the neighborhood. Lei Hipu'u created a "Leadership Council" that comes together monthly as a cohort of Kalihi-based service providers, including social workers, librarians, school staff and officials, community leaders, doctors, lawyers and more. The relationships developed have resulted in increased trust, support and collaboration among the community of service providers. The prevailing culture of the Leadership Council remains focused on the ever-shifting needs and hopes of the communities served.

Lei Hipu'u fosters a notable community relationship with the Kuhio Park Terrace Residents Association (KPTRA). Kuhio Park Terrace (KPT) is the largest public housing complex in the State of Hawai'i, and many residents receive services from KKV. KPTRA, in partnership with Lei Hipu'u, created monthly "talk story" meetings. "Talking story" is a custom of dialoguing about community and family issues or events. These talk stories have resulted in committees forming to address issues within the community, such as tackling fire safety with the Honolulu Fire Department and discussion of traditional health practices amongst the different cultures in housing led by residents of KPT. Lei Hipu'u builds the capacity and confidence of the KPTRA to continue a dialogue in the community in order to recognize needs of their neighbors. Lei Hipu'u contributes greatly to neighborhood health and the equalization of resources to benefit all participants in the Kalihi Valley community. Lei Hipu'u's goal is for community residents to take ownership of their neighborhood's health.

KALIHI VALLEY INSTRUCTIONAL BIKE EXCHANGE

The Kalihi Valley Instructional Bike Exchange (KVIBE) is a program of KKV that lives by the motto "If you build it they will come." KVIBE is a nonprofit bicycle shop that began in 2005 and promotes bicycle-related activities for at-risk youth in Kalihi Valley. KVIBE stocks about 100 bikes at a time and relies on steady donations. Two neighborhood residents who previously volunteered with the program currently staff KVIBE. One had previous bicycle repair expertise and the other was a youth participant who developed skills over time. Personal relationships help to foster trust in KVIBE. This trust engages Kalihi Valley youth to come and either buy, build or repair bikes there. Those who choose to build do so with the help of KVIBE staff and other youth who have gained skills from their time at KVIBE. This program exists because it recognizes that a bike shop is one method to affect or understand community health.

KKV acknowledges that through knowledge of building a bike, KVIBE is able to build the capacity of the Kalihi Valley youth. Not only do they redeem a bike after building it, they learn responsibility, hard work, and gain mentors to help guide them. KVIBE staff are trained to discuss healthy relationships and foster a safe environment where no gang colors are allowed, targeting youth to build a sustained neighborhood health capacity for the future of Kalihi Valley. KVIBE is a true innovation in neighborhood health, providing youth a viable alternative to learn, grow and make healthy choices from positive experiences.

MEDICAL-LEGAL PARTNERSHIP FOR CHILDREN IN HAWAIʻI

The Medical-Legal Partnership for Children in Hawaiʻi (MLPC Hawaiʻi) is a project of the Health Law Policy Center of the William S. Richardson School of Law (University of Hawaiʻi at Manoa). Medical-legal partnerships follow a model established by Dr. Barry Zuckerman of the Boston Medical Clinic, who hired an attorney to "address the social determinants that negatively impact the health of vulnerable populations." Recognizing KKV's unique relationship with the Kalihi Valley community, the co-director of the Health Law Policy Center partnered with a pediatrician at KKV to construct a program that allowed legal interventions and advocacy to improve healthcare and access. This particular doctor and lawyer saw that there were instances when medical conditions could be alleviated through legal intervention, such as when a child with chronic asthma and eye infections needs a landlord to fix a leaky pipe that has caused mold to develop in his bedroom. MLPC Hawaiʻi approached its partnership with KKV by engaging with the community first. To begin, the MLPC Hawaiʻi legal director and law student interns accompanied KKV public housing outreach workers on a door-to-door survey to introduce KKV services and to hear about public housing residents' needs, including the lack of accessible legal services. After listening to the neighborhood, MLPC Hawaiʻi built on the trust families have with their children's doctors and began providing direct legal services to families at KKV to address the social/legal problems that negatively impact their health. MLPC Hawaiʻi runs its legal clinics to coincide with the KKV pediatric clinics, allowing legal advocates to meet with families alongside pediatricians in the exam rooms during well-child medical visits. KKV generously provided office space to MLPC Hawaiʻi in their office located in the KPT Resource Center, giving MLPC Hawaiʻi a central and constant presence in the neighborhood to continue garnering trust.

MLPC Hawaiʻi also works to build the capacity of the community to advocate for themselves. Clients are taught about their legal rights, recognize the effect on health, and are empowered with the understanding that those rights are enforceable. For example, the right to have habitable housing is reinforced with law for clients because many health ailments are exacerbated or persist from uninhabitable living conditions.

Also, MLPC Hawai`i has engaged in language access advocacy on both individual and systemic levels. They enlist the help of interpreters from KKV staff to ensure open dialogue with their many limited-English-proficient clients. They even look to the community for translation services to produce legal resources and information in native languages. In addition, MLPC Hawai`i advocates provide clients with "language access rights" cards so they can enforce their state and federal right to an interpreter at state agencies, federal agencies and hospitals. Knowledge is power and can galvanize people to act; providing these resources gives the community this power and experience to effectively advocate for themselves. Working closely with the community, service providers and health professionals foster the goals of MLPC Hawai`i to value and respect collaboration in real-life settings. Taking the time to build and foster these valuable relationships also helps legal advocates to stay in touch with the ever-shifting needs and hopes of the neighborhood. MLPC Hawaii's partnership with KKV has contributed to building resources and advocacy opportunities for the neighborhood.

HO`OULU `AINA

Ho`oulu `Aina is a part of KKV located on a 99-acre land preserve in Kalihi Valley to engage communities in nurturing their land. Hawaiians for generations and until today honor this area as sacred to the creation gods, and this land in the past was very fertile, providing sustenance for the people of Kalihi Valley and beyond. Ho`oulu `Aina recognizes land as a community member. In partnership with the community, Ho`oulu `Aina uses a land-based program to improve overall neighborhood health. When people come to Ho`oulu `Aina to work, they nurture the land, which in turn nurtures them: "O ka ha o ka `aina ke ola o ka po`e: the breath of the land is the life of the people."

Most of the staff at Ho`oulu `Aina live in Kalihi Valley and bring valuable relationships to enrich accessibility to this unique neighborhood experience. These opportunities are, like other KKV programs, fostered through community dialogue. For example, KKV's nutrition program's diabetes group has utilized this access for exercise and nutrition purposes. For a year, the nutrition program was unable to influence members of the Chuukese diabetes group to exercise. In a meeting, the interpreter explained that there was no word for "exercise" in Chuukese. They tried "Take a walk"—to which the participants said—"To where?" It is not in their culture to "take a walk" or "exercise" without a purpose or destination. Also, highly urban areas like Kalihi are sometimes difficult or dangerous for walking. Farming was mentioned as an option and hands shot up! This led to weekly trips to Ho`oulu `Aina, to begin clearing land so that gardens could be planted, harvested, cooked and shared with family and neighbors, for their "exercise." In addition, other programs at

Ho`oulu `Aina enforce health through story-telling, native reforestation and learning the history of Kalihi Valley.

Ho`oulu `Aina recognizes the community as experts in their health and values their expertise in understanding the social forces that affect neighborhood health. During an open dialogue with the community, they discussed how difficult it was to find or afford healthy food in Kalihi Valley. In addition, the large immigrant population is unfamiliar with Western foods and their nutritional value. Ho`oulu `Aina and partners are now embarking on the "Roots Project," with the goal of building community capital by providing more education and opportunity to enjoy and prepare healthy foods as neighbors. Ho`oulu `Aina will increase food production with the neighborhood and utilize the new commercial kitchen being built at KKV's main clinic. Neighbors will have the opportunity to work the land, grow food, learn how to prepare that food in new ways, and then share the fruits of their labor, coming together as neighbors. Ho`oulu `Aina, in partnership with the community, is directly impacting neighborhood health through food production and consumption.

"NEIGHBORS BEING NEIGHBORLY TO NEIGHBORS"

KKV is an innovative community health center because it understands that the community is a neighbor and collaborator. Direct services are grounded in the various cultural traditions of patients and residents working together to provide resources necessary for health access. KKV understands that language access goes hand-in-hand with cultural competency, creating a trusting environment. Language access and cultural competency does not stop there, however; hiring from the community creates more cultural context and gives economic incentive to retain language and culture. KKV recognizes that when working with a diverse community of new immigrants, Pacific Islanders and Asian Americans, community dialogue and support create sustainable programs to serve the neighborhood. KKV is a community health center with place-based focus and a health justice mission. This neighborhood health model's use has broad application for any institution or individual working to affect neighborhood health. Health is not only medical health; it is holistic. Health is community. Health is legal advocacy. Health is self-advocacy. Health is a bike shop. Health is reconnecting with culture and land. By being a neighbor, KKV creates programs that foster a healthy community. Institutions and individuals have the ability to be neighborly. As a neighbor, KKV is a vital part of revitalizing and sustaining the Kalihi Valley community now and for future generations.

Healthcare and Indigenous Peoples in the United States

Michael Yellow Bird

The health disparities of Indigenous Peoples in the United States are numerous and pressing, and offer a significant policy challenge to the next Congress and presidential administration. Both must be committed to honoring the long-standing treaty obligations that the United States has to provide adequate healthcare services to Indigenous tribal nations. The United States has a legal responsibility to provide healthcare to Indigenous Peoples. In fulfilling this obligation, it must ensure that there is sufficient funding for tribal and Indian Health Service programs, staffing, technology, research and facility construction, modernizing and maintenance.

WHO ARE INDIGENOUS PEOPLES?

In the contiguous 48 United States and Alaska, many Indigenous Peoples are mistakenly called Indians, American Indians or Native Americans. They are not Indians or American Indians, because they are not from India. They are not Native Americans, because Indigenous Peoples did not refer to these lands as America until Europeans arrived and imposed this name. Indian, American Indian and Native American are colonized and inaccurate labels that subjugate the identities of Indigenous Peoples. While many Indigenous Peoples still prefer to use these former labels. a growing number want to be identified according to their own tribal nation or affiliation.

Indigenous Peoples are diverse populations who reside on ancestral lands, share an ancestry with the original inhabitants of these lands, have distinct cultures and languages, and regard themselves as different from those who have colonized and now control their lands and lives. As of July 1, 2007, the U.S. Census Bureau estimated the population of Indigenous Peoples, including those of more than one race, to be 4.5 million, or 1.5 percent of the total U.S. population. Of this group, 2.9 million identified themselves only as "American Indian" or "Alaska Native." There are more than 560 federally recognized Indigenous tribes in the United States. Approximately half of the Indigenous population resides on or near federal "Indian" reservations, while the remaining half reside in urban areas.

Not much is known about the health circumstances of urban natives. One major study completed by the Urban Indian Health Commission in 2005 reported that cardiovascular diseases, diabetes and depression afflict urban Indigenous Peoples in disproportionate numbers.

THE LEGAL BASIS FOR INDIGENOUS HEALTHCARE

From 1778 to 1871, the Indigenous nations, of what is now referred to as the United States of America, negotiated and signed nearly 400 treaties with this nation. During this century of treaty-making, the U.S. government agreed to provide, among other things, health services to Indian tribes in exchange for billions of acres of land, natural resources, friendship and peace. In a confirmation of the treaty process, the legal basis to provide healthcare was accepted by the U.S. and first articulated in The Snyder Act of 1921. This legislation enabled the U.S. Congress to authorize the Bureau of Indian Affairs (BIA) to "expend such moneys as Congress may from time to time appropriate" for the relief of distress and conservation of health. In 1955, health services for Indigenous Peoples were transferred from the BIA to the Indian Health Service (IHS). which became part of the Public Health Service (PHS). The Indian Health Service is now a program within the U.S. Department of Health and Human Services that is responsible for providing health services to Indigenous Peoples who are members of federally recognized tribes in the United States.

The Indian Health Care Improvement Act, P.L. 94-437 (IHCIA) was first enacted in 1976 as the next legal provision of healthcare services to Indigenous Peoples to address long-standing healthcare disparities. The major aims of this legislation were to increase the number of health professionals serving Indigenous communities; allow services to urban populations; remedy health facility problems; and ensure access to other federal healthcare such as Medicaid and Medicare. The IHCIA has been reauthorized five times, adding a number of amendments each time. In the original findings of this legislation, the U.S. Congress agreed that:

Federal health services to maintain and improve the health of the Indians are consonant with and required by the Federal government's historical and unique legal relationship with, and resulting responsibility to, the American Indian people.

A major national goal of the United States is to provide the quantity and quality of health services which will permit the health status of Indians to be raised to the highest possible level and to encourage the maximum participation of Indians in the planning and management of those services.

The unmet health needs of the American Indian people are severe, and the health status of Indians is far below that of the general population of the United States.

ANOTHER REALITY

Some progress has been made in upgrading the health of Indigenous Peoples that can be attributed to the actions of U.S. federal government. However, much remains to be done. Despite the compelling and binding language in the IHCIA, the U.S. has rarely lived up to its promises to provide sufficient, proper and necessary healthcare to Indigenous communities. Once the U.S. got all the lands and resources it needed from Indigenous Peoples, it has maintained a steady path of insufficient, marginally effective assistance in raising the health status of Indigenous Peoples to the highest possible level. This negligence, self-serving behavior and dishonesty are transparent and have taken an enormous toll on the health of our peoples.

The health of Indigenous Peoples seriously lags behind the rest of the U.S. population in several critical areas. This is especially true for those who reside on or near "Indian" reservations and depend on the U.S. federal government to provide health services to them through the Indian Health Service. Indeed, for many of us who grew up on our reservations, we have had an up-close view of the struggles, hardships and suffering that have gripped lives of our friends, relatives and members of our tribes due to insufficient health services. While many have been able to overcome challenging health circumstances, many have experienced more than their share of difficulties in achieving and maintaining a sufficient level of health. While health statistics show that various groups of Indigenous Peoples carry an enormous burden of illness, statistics rarely give true insights into the pain, hopelessness and distress that is felt and shared by those who live in this reality.

For many years, I witnessed the sorrow of death and the despair of disability within my own tribal community. Many needlessly succumbed to numerous preventable diseases, such as diabetes, alcoholism, suicide, homicide, depression, obesity, substance abuse, hypertension, heart disease and cancer, to name a few. Because of the significant loss of life among my tribe, I've learned to appreciate the "Years of Potential Life Lost" (YPLL) statistical measure that is used to calculate the total number of years lost in a community from premature death from a certain cause. While this computation yields important data, I believe that the subsequent stress and grief that lingers among our communities, due to high morbidity and mortality, is a major contributor to the continuing poor health of Indigenous Peoples.

When I was the health director for my tribe more than 20 years ago, we faced many daunting challenges. Chronic illnesses and behavioral disorders were widespread and, in many instances, deadly. Shortages in funding to deliver health services were common and often compromised the care of many of our most vulnerable citizens. The lack of competent medical personnel, substandard healthcare facilities, traveling long distances to reach medical services under difficult conditions, and the absence of advanced, life-saving technologies also produced a daily hardship for our reservation communities. While some studies report that progress has been made to reduce or eliminate gaps in Indigenous Peoples' health, many communities and individuals continue to be confronted by many of the challenges we faced more than two decades ago.

THE FACTS

At present, there are numerous and appalling health disparities among Indigenous Peoples that require immediate attention and resolution. A press release sent out on September 8, 2003 by the U.S. Department of Health and Human Services, titled, "Eliminating Health Disparities in the American Indian and Alaska Native Community," underscores this reality. The statement reported that death rates, due to a number of specific illnesses and disorders, were significantly higher for Indigenous Peoples than for other Americans:

- Alcoholism 770 percent higher
- Tuberculosis 750 percent higher
- Diabetes 420 percent higher
- Accidents 280 percent higher
- Homicide 210 percent higher
- Suicide 190 percent higher

In 1994, when I completed the writing of my Ph.D. dissertation, "The Use of Health Services by American Indians on Federal Indian Lands," I referred to several of these same mortality health statistics to show the poor health of Indigenous Peoples. The data that I reported came from 1987 statistics that were collected by the Indian Health Service:

- Tuberculosis 400 percent higher
- Alcoholism 322 percent higher
- Diabetes 139 percent higher
- Accidents 139 percent higher
- Homicide 64 percent higher
- Suicide 28 percent higher

In 2002, the National Center for Health Statistics reported that Indigenous Peoples have higher mortality rates than whites in all age categories up to age 64. The largest gap is in the 25-44 years age category: There are 227.4 deaths among Indigenous People per 100,000, versus 141.7 for whites—a 62 percent higher rate of death. However, in certain geographical areas, life expectancy for Indigenous men is dismal. In an investigation of mortality disparities by race and counties in the United States covering the period 1982–2001, Christopher J.L. Murray found that the lowest life expectancy for men in the United States was in South Dakota counties that had large populations of Indigenous Peoples. Those living in these areas can expect to live 66.6 years, well short of the 79 years for low-income rural white people in the Northern Plains. Focusing only on Indigenous men in these counties, life expectancy plummets to 58 years.

There are lapses and severely inadequate levels of funding to pay for the health needs of Indigenous Peoples. For instance, a 2003 study by the U.S. Commission on Civil Rights, titled "A Quiet Crisis," found that the unmet healthcare needs of Native Americans remain among the most severe of any group in the United States. Despite their need for healthcare and although there are designated health services, the monetary value of Native American care is significantly less than the average health expenditure for all Americans. The federal government's rate of spending on healthcare for Native Americans is 50 percent less than for prisoners or Medicaid recipients, and 60 percent less than is spent annually on healthcare for the average American. IHS real spending per Native American, after adjusting for inflation and population growth, has fallen over time, despite funding increases.

There are very troubling epidemics of substance abuse and dependence among Indigenous Peoples. On September 8, 2003, the U.S. Department of Health and Human Services issued a press release that identified a number of disparities within the Indigenous population:

- Rates of substance dependence and abuse among persons age 12 and older is highest among American Indians and Alaska Natives (14.1 percent).
- Rates of illicit drug use (10.1 percent), alcohol (44.7 percent).
- Binge alcohol use (27.9 percent) is among the highest in the nation.

Death due to alcohol abuse among Indigenous Peoples is overwhelming. Examining death certificates from 2001 to 2005, the Centers for Disease Control and Prevention released a report on August 28, 2008 that found the rate of alcohol-related deaths among Indigenous Peoples was close to four times higher than that of the overall U.S. population. During this period, 11.7 percent of deaths, or 1,514 deaths, were alcohol-related, compared with 3.3 percent for the U.S. as a whole. The findings showed that 68 percent of the deaths were men and 66 percent were younger than 50 years old, and 7 percent were less than 20 years old.

The fact that two-thirds of the deaths involve people younger than age 50 is very troubling. Many in this group represent the next generation of elders that will not be lending their knowledge, presence and experience to those younger age groups who might have depended on them for learning their tribal language, culture and critical aspects of traditional leadership. The fact that such a large number are men means that many children will grow up without fathers, uncles, brothers and grandfathers who, in most tribal communities, serve as important supports and mentors.

For every 100,000 American Indian deaths, 55 involved excessive alcohol use. In the general population, excessive alcohol consumption figured in 27 of every 100,000 deaths. The leading causes cited in alcohol-related deaths among Native Americans:

- Motor vehicle crashes - 27.5 percent
- Liver disease - 25.2 percent
- Alcohol dependence - 6.8 percent
- Homicide - 6.6 percent
- Liver cirrhosis - 6.2 percent
- Suicide - 5.2 percent

Among different age groups and tribal communities, there exist widespread epidemics of depression, anxiety and other mood disorders. Psychologists refer to depression as a whole body illness. It causes intense emotional pain, helplessness, hopelessness, loss of sleep and interest in life. It is strongly associated with suicide, thoughts of death, and chronic fatigue, sadness and negative emotions. In a 2005 report titled, "Invisible Tribes: Urban Indians and their Health in a Changing World," it was reported that depression afflicts Indigenous Peoples in disproportionate numbers. About 30 percent of this population suffers with depression. Those most affected live in cities. In a national study titled, "Prevalence of Depression among U.S. Adults with Diabetes: Findings from the 2006 Behavioral Risk Factor Surveillance System," which examined depression and diabetes, Indigenous Peoples were identified as the ethnic group having the highest prevalence rates of depression (27.8 percent).

Of course, diabetes presents a major problem for many communities. On a personal level, I know the disease quite well. Of my 11 brothers and 4 sisters in my family, only 5 of us are not burdened by this illness. My father died from diabetes-related complications, and my mother has lived with it for nearly 40 years. Numerous studies show that Indigenous Peoples have the highest prevalence of Type 2 diabetes in the world. The incidence of Type 2 diabetes is rising faster among Indigenous children and young adults than in any other ethnic population, 2.6 times the national average. In a report titled, "The Diabetes Epidemic Among American Indians and Alaska Natives," the National Diabetes Education Program, National Institutes of Health, U.S. Department of Health and Human Services documented that about 16.5 percent of American Indians and Alaska Natives age 20 years and older who are served by the Indian Health Service have diagnosed diabetes.

WHAT IS THE FUTURE OF INDIGENOUS HEALTH?

On March 12, 2008, a U.S. House of Representatives subcommittee held a hearing on President Bush's proposed 2009 Indian Health Service budget, which presented a $21 million decrease from the 2008 budget. The chairman of the committee, Rep. Norm Dicks (D-WA), met with 30 tribal representatives who expressed concern over the budget proposal. Chairman Dicks quoted the governor of the Pueblo of Acoma, Chandler Sanchez, stating that, "The Indian Health Service is dying a slow death from a 1,000 budget cuts." During the hearing, IHS Acting Director Robert

McSwain acknowledged that the Bush cuts would severely restrict the agency's ability to meet the needs of many of its patients and would result in:

- 218,000 fewer outpatient visits
- 9,000 fewer patients receiving services from diabetes programs
- 12,465 fewer patients receiving dental services
- 1,500 fewer patients receiving mammogram screenings
- 3,000 fewer patients receiving cancer screenings

Despite numerous health disparities faced by Indigenous Peoples and a legal responsibility agreed to by the United States to meet the healthcare needs of these groups, the funding that has been provided to the Indian Health Service has never been adequate. Services are fragmented and mediocre; medical personnel are in short supply; facilities are outdated; technology and research are limited; and the patients who use this system have substantial needs, often beyond the capacity of the healthcare system. Long ago, Indigenous nations exchanged their lands, freedom and resources for federal promises of providing for the health of the people. However, the United States has insufficiently delivered on its promise. As a result, the health of Indigenous Peoples has suffered, especially when compared to the rest of America. Let's demand that the next Congress and occupant of the White House will honor the obligations that this nation has to the health of Indigenous Peoples.

Race, Poverty and Incarceration

Donald Braman

Londa and her three children live in a small row house that is part of a Section 8 housing project in central Washington, DC. Inside her home, surrounded by the debris of family life—toys, a few empty kid-sized boxes of juice, dishes on the table from a lunch just finished, bottles and baby blankets strewn over the couch—she is apologetic for the mess. "But," she says, "I've got three kids, a broken leg and a husband who's locked up." She's been struggling against her husband's crack addiction and struggling to keep her family together for 15 years. Gesturing out the window, she says: "I don't want to end up like everyone else. I guess I'm halfway there. But my kids need a father. I look around here and none of these kids have fathers. It's a mess what's happened."

What has happened—to her family, to her community, to our criminal justice system and to our society as a whole—truly is a mess. If the massive expansion of the criminal justice system is intended to make people safer, why can a person buy crack cocaine on any corner in Londa's neighborhood at any time of the day or night? Why can't she walk alone to or from public transportation after dark? Like most inner-city residents living in areas where incarceration rates are highest, just about no one feels safe or protected. We spend over $40 billion a year on incarceration, locking up over 2 million Americans on any given day and far more than that over the course of any given year. And, while incarceration does temporarily incapacitate some criminal offenders, something is clearly going wrong. The more researchers find out about the rapid and massive expansion of the criminal justice system over the last three decades, the more troubling our public policies appear. It turns out that mass incarceration is not only a bad way to go about protecting the public, it goes a fair distance towards draining low-income communities of wealth, trust and intact families.

How can incarceration, our principal response to crime and ostensibly a boon to public safety, be so destructive? To understand this, one has to understand the social nature of incarceration. Incarceration, as a growing body of research details, doesn't just affect those who break the law. Most inmates, like Londa's husband Derrick, are fathers, and most incarcerated fathers, like Derrick, lived with their children prior to incarceration and remain in contact with them during their incarceration. Most who spend time behind bars were also gainfully employed prior to being incarcerated, but earn close to nothing while in prison and, when released, face significantly diminished earning potential. The vast majority are also nonviolent offenders. And most drug offenders, like Derrick, are not required to complete a drug treatment program.

Indeed, far from holding them accountable in any meaningful way, incarceration effectively holds offenders unaccountable to everyone who matters: their victims, their families and their communities. Forcibly removed from their social networks, they are excused from all meaningful social obligations for extended periods of time, then dumped back into their families and communities with lower job prospects and damaged relationships. The cumulative effect on family life, local economies and social norms regarding responsible behavior are, these studies show, a policy disaster. By holding offenders unaccountable to their families and communities, incarceration—at least as it is currently practiced—is creating the kind of concentrated intergenerational poverty in historically disadvantaged communities that we spend billions of public dollars trying to combat. Indeed, of all the social institutions that contribute to racial disparities in the United States today, it may well be our criminal justice system that is making the most significant contribution.

The lack of attention to the families and communities affected by incarceration can help to explain the historical willingness of states to accept mass incarceration as a default response to social disorder. Thankfully, policymakers are beginning to take note. Congress recently held hearings on the costs, both social and material, associated with mass incarceration, and most states are in the process of reviewing and revising their criminal codes with an eye to reducing the number of offenders sentenced to prison. It's a wake-up call that is long overdue.

A TYPICAL CYCLE

To grasp the basic problem, consider the story that Londa tells about the cycle of incarceration followed by relapse and re-incarceration—one that is all too familiar to those living in disadvantaged communities. Perhaps the most obvious effects of current criminal practices are material. Reviewing Londa's income and expenses, it becomes clear that her financial problems are directly related to the loss of Derrick's income and the additional costs that accompany his incarceration. She lives on a fixed income of $463 a month from the welfare system. After $100 for rent and another $300 for groceries (which works out to less than $3 for food per day, per person), there isn't enough to pay for electricity, the phone and transportation. She is far from lazy, but with two children and one infant, she doesn't have the resources to care for them herself. "Oh, I can't stand to ask anybody to help me with anything. So I really hate asking my mother now, but I can't walk, I can't get around. So it's just really, really hard right now."

Londa's mother helps care for the children, buys groceries and even pays Londa's rent when things are tight. But her assistance is limited to what she herself can afford, and that is not much. Already, Londa feels she has asked for far too much far too often from her mother. "I know that she doesn't have a lot, too, so that's something I have to think about." Derrick's sisters also try to help when they can, but they have families of their own and are struggling just to get by. Derrick's sister, Brenda, describes her surprise at how "it just all adds up." "The phone bills—the phone bill is something else!" One of the more unpleasant surprises to many families is the high cost of phone calls from prison. Inmates can only call collect, and additional charges for monitoring and recording by the prison phone company add up quickly; indeed, many families have their phones disconnected within two months of an incarceration.

Indeed, the most costly regular expense for many families are prison phone charges. Most correctional facilities contract out phone services and actually receive money from the phone company for doing so. Phone companies thus compete with each other for the service, but not by providing lower prices: The key issue phone companies compete on is how much revenue the service will return to the Department of Corrections in each state. Because phone conversations are often time-limited, many families are required to accept several calls to complete a single conversation, with connection charges applying to each call. As a result, collect calls from prisons can be as much as 20 times as expensive as standard collect calls. Families with loved ones incarcerated out of state have shown me years of phone records that average well over $200 a month. Many families in this study, including Londa's, have had their phone or electricity cut off for lack of payment.

After having her phone cut off for high unpaid bills the last time Derrick was incarcerated, Londa realized she had trouble refusing calls she couldn't afford and had a "block" placed on her phone, preventing collect calls. In an arrangement that is not unusual, Derrick's sisters now serve as a conduit to his extended family; because no one else will accept the expense of collect calls from prison, they try to patch him through to whomever he needs to talk to, using three-way calling. While it further increases the overall price of the call, it is another way for Derrick's family to spread the cost of his incarceration.

While Londa is fortunate to have family willing to help her in Derrick's absence, her family doesn't have much to help her with. By spreading the costs of raising Derrick's children and maintaining ties with him, Londa's and Derrick's families have enabled Londa to keep and care for her children. While this is undoubtedly desirable, the cost has simply been spread to other low-income households with few resources, lessening the impact on any one person, but creating a steady drain on the extended family.

Londa, for example, can no longer afford her own car—an issue that became quite serious when her mother's car broke down and, largely as a result of helping Londa, her mother was unable to afford the repair costs. Derrick's sister, Brenda, has also struggled with the sacrifices that she makes to keep her brother in touch with his family:

> I'm gonna be there regardless of what. And his wife, well, she's having it rough, her and her kids, because she don't have anything, which I don't have anything either, but a lot of times I [still help out]. My kids don't like it, because I try to give to [Derrick's family], because, you know . . . I . . . I feel for them and for him in that jail. [And] when school comes it's like, do my kids, do they get new shoes or does he get to talk to his kids. And, you know, I just think he needs to talk to them.

Families can be tremendous resources, but they are not limitless funds of wealth and generosity. The costs of Derrick's repeated incarcerations have been dear in both material and emotional terms.

Indeed, despite the emphasis on accountability when policymakers talk about the criminal justice system, Londa's story shows us how, in an attempt to punish criminality, policymakers have effectively held offenders like Derrick almost entirely not accountable in ways that matter a great deal. His enforced withdrawal from the economic responsibilities of family life has pushed both his and Londa's extended family more deeply into poverty. Given that they started with little, that loss has been all the more keenly felt.

RACE AND POVERTY

While most accounts relating poverty and crime generally describe poverty as driving criminal activity and thus involvement in the criminal justice system, the relationship runs both ways and is arguably cyclical. Many inner-city families not only experience incarceration because they are poor, they are also poor because they experience incarceration. In light of their experiences, standard correlations, such as those shown above, take on a very different meaning.

One way—the traditional way—of interpreting these data would be to infer that people who are unemployed or have less money are more likely to engage in criminal activity. This is one of the main findings of William Julius Wilson's book, *When Work Disappears*: "As many studies have revealed, the decline in legitimate employment opportunities among inner-city residents has increased incentives to sell drugs." But the experiences of families like Londa's tell us that the reverse is also true: Incarceration can significantly lower the income and increase the expenses of prisoners' families.

Like Derrick, over two-thirds of the incarcerated population was gainfully employed prior to arrest. Even though family members sent to prison make, on average, poverty wages, the median household income is still lowered by the elimination of these wages. And, because many prisoners are often a source of income in households prior to their arrest, the per-capita income in that household, including unemployed, children and elderly, is also lowered when they are removed. Further, many ex-offenders find it difficult to obtain employment after release, and when they do, their earning potential is significantly lowered compared with that of nonoffenders. The decreased family income is thus due not only to the removal of a wage-earning family member to prison, but also to the lowered lifetime earning potential of that family member after return from prison.

The effects of this tax are profound. A recent study by Mark Joseph (in Waldo Johnson, Jr., ed., *Social Work and Social Welfare Responses to African American Males*) estimated the effects of incarceration on the lifetime earnings of offenders at over $300 billion—and that is limited to the age cohort that is 16 years old today. The full impact across the generations, while far larger, is also far harder to estimate. These are costs not borne solely, or even predominantly, by offenders themselves. We know, for example, that, as noted above, phone companies and departments of corrections draw hundreds of millions of dollars each year from prisoners' families. We also know that a broad array of other costs—from childcare and eldercare, to services to replace household help, to travel and legal expenses—are borne by families. But because these costs are more diffuse and difficult to estimate, they are rarely discussed.

IMPACT ON WEALTH ACCUMULATION

More subtle than the immediate and direct material effects of incarceration on these families, but perhaps more serious, is the cumulative impact they can have on familial wealth across generations. By depleting the savings of offenders' families, incarceration inhibits capital accumulation and reduces the ability of parents to pass wealth on to their children and grandchildren through inheritance and gifts. Indeed, incarceration's draining of the resources of extended family members in the Joseph study—particularly from older family members—helps explain why there has been so little capital accumulation and inheritance among inner-city families in general and minority families in particular.

This becomes apparent when we see Derrick's family struggling to save enough to buy their children school supplies, let alone provide for their inheritance. The disproportionate incarceration of men like Derrick helps to explain why black families are less able to save money and why each successive generation inherits less wealth than their white counterparts. Criminal sanctions—at least in their current form— act like a hidden tax, one that is visited disproportionately on poor and minority families and communities, and while the costs are most directly felt by the adults closest to the incarcerated family member, the full effect is eventually felt by the next generation as well.

Viewed in this light, the racial disparities in arrests, sentencing and parole described by many researchers take on a broader significance. For example, Census data show that blacks typically possess only one-third the assets of whites with similar incomes. While this pattern is generally attributed to lower savings and inheritance, this explanation begs the question of why savings and inheritance are lower—something that the concentration of incarceration in minority communities and its effect on capital accumulation help to explain.

Finally, it is worth noting that familial costs can also decrease investments in what is often called "human capital," as moving to a better school district, purchasing an up-to-date computer and attending college all become less affordable. Educational attainment is one of the best predictors we have for avoiding the criminal justice system; but the benefits of investing in (and the costs of neglecting) human capital extend well beyond crime rates. As the stock of resources that a family possesses diminishes, and as members are prevented from caring for one another, more than money and objects are lost. Indeed, the material losses these families face may, in the end, be the least significant concern.

IMPACT ON FATHER ABSENCE

An examination of the relationship between incarceration and father absence in different income groups illustrates the extent to which income may mediate the impact of incarceration on family organization.

For all three income groups, where incarceration rates are at their lowest, father absence is fairly similar, occurring in fewer than 25 percent of households with children. As the incarceration rate increases among lower-income families, father absence increases at a far greater rate than it does among middle-income families, among whom father absence increases at a greater rate than among upper-income families. So, as the incarceration rate increases to 2 percent, the percentage of families absent fathers in upper-income neighborhoods climbs about 5 percent; in middle-income neighborhoods, it climbs about 15 percent; and, in lower-income neighborhoods, it climbs over 25 percent. The common-sense implication of this is that poor families are not only exposed to incarceration more often, they are far more likely to be broken by it.

A PROBLEM AND AN OPPORTUNITY

While it is commonly assumed that the rise of incarceration reflects a peculiarly punitive attitude among Americans, in fact just about no one is happy with the status quo. Indeed, when asked to rank their satisfaction with the various parts of the criminal justice system, Americans put prisons at the bottom of the list. Rather than more incarceration, most Americans favor a thoughtful and socially constructive response to crime. For example, by a margin of nearly two-to-one, Americans favor fighting crime through reforms that feature spending money on "social and economic problems" over spending money on "police, prisons and judges."

The question is whether the state can meet the public's preferred response to crime, help push offenders back into a cooperative, prosocial stance, and thus strengthen the norm of cooperation and responsibility-taking in their families and communities. If the state can do this, a natural outcome will be increased participation in the social networks essential to healthy family and community life. Recall that in Londa's neighborhood this would not be an effect at the margins; it would alter the behavior of a substantial majority of the young men.

The answer to the question is a resounding yes. The best programs—like New York's La Bodega de la Familia, for example—aren't blunt attempts to replace failing social networks with the heavy hand of incarceration, but thoughtful preventative programs that make the most of the social networks already in place in families and communities. By reassuring individuals in a community that the state will push offenders back into responsible behavior rather than remove them from it, prosocial interventions can help increase the likelihood that others in the community will also behave responsibly—which, in turn, makes it more likely that individuals will enter into and remain in the prosocial relationships that sustain and are sustained by that behavior. These are the networks that truly hold offenders accountable.

We should be encouraged by the increased willingness of state and federal legislators, both liberal and conservative, to take a fresh look at their sentencing laws and correctional programs. Mass incarceration, some are coming to see, is far too costly to be sustained in the long run, and works against the values they want to see the law promote.

This renewed interest in sentencing reform is apparent in the substantial interest state legislators, judges and administrators have shown, for example, in the Vera Institute's State Sentencing and Corrections Program, which brings these parties together to discuss and share ideas about the substantive needs and political realities that often make sentencing and corrections reform difficult to achieve. A number of programs (including the Family Justice Program) are also talking across state borders to help each other better understand what is working and what could use improvement. What is encouraging here is state officials' increased interest in what community corrections professionals have to offer them in terms of cost savings and public safety—an interest that has brought them into a broader dialogue about healthy families and communities.

While we should be chastened by the immense cost that our criminal justice system has needlessly imposed on disadvantaged families and communities, it seems the time is ripe for change. It should be inspiring to know that, if we work hard enough and smart enough, Londa's daughter and the millions of children growing in families and communities like hers can have a brighter future.

A Strategy for Dismantling Structural Racism in the Juvenile Justice System

Edgar S. Cahn, Keri A. Nash & Cynthia Robbins

Juveniles of color are more likely than their white counterparts to be arrested, referred to juvenile court rather than diversion programs, waived to adult court, detained pre-trial and locked up at disposition.

In 2008, the Racial Justice Initiative (RJI) of TimeBanks USA—www.RacialJusticeInitiative.org—developed a new social advocacy and litigation strategy focused on dismantling structural racism in the juvenile justice and child welfare systems as well as other public systems that affect vulnerable youth.

The data on the depth of the racial disparity and the resulting negative outcomes for youth of color have been well documented for years. This chapter provides some of the national data that underscore the extensive racial disparity that persists in the juvenile justice system. Second, the chapter will narrow the focus to Washington, DC, where the RJI is working more intensively in 2011 and beyond. Finally, the chapter sets forth how this strategy could be implemented to break through more than three decades of logjam on legal challenges to racial disparity in juvenile justice. Although Congress annually appropriates hundreds of millions of dollars to reduce the racial disparity in juvenile justice, more than 35 years after enactment of the seminal juvenile delinquency prevention act, results in most jurisdictions are barely discernible.

NATIONAL ARREST, PROSECUTION AND INCARCERATION RATES REVEAL SUBSTANTIAL DISPROPORTIONALITY

While young people of all races commit delinquent acts, some receive treatment while others are arrested, funneled into the delinquency system, and too often eventually incarcerated. According to the National Council on Crime and Delinquency, from 2002 to 2004, African Americans comprised only 16 percent of all youth in the United States, but constituted 28 percent of juvenile arrests; 30 percent of referrals to juvenile court; 37 percent of the detained population; 34 percent of youth formally processed by the juvenile court; 30 percent of adjudicated youth; 35 percent of youth judicially waived to adult criminal court; 38 percent of youth in residential placement; and 58 percent of youth admitted to state adult prison. There is incontrovertible evidence that race bias affects critical decisions leading to confinement, and that the consequences of this disparate treatment are devastating to juveniles of color.

Over the last 30 years, multiple studies have shown that disproportionate minority contact (DMC) afflicts nearly every processing point in nearly every juvenile justice system in the country. In Michael J. Leiber's article, "Disproportionate Minority Confinement of Youth: An Analysis of State and Federal Efforts to Address the Issue," he noted that 32 of 46 studies conducted by 40 states reported "race effects"—defined as "the presence of a statistically significant race relationship, with a case outcome that remains once controls for legal factors have been considered." Whereas African Americans, Latinos, Native Americans, Asian and Pacific Islanders constituted only 35 percent of the U.S. youth population, they comprised 65 percent of all youth who were securely detained pre-adjudication. Youth of color are four times more likely to be arrested for a drug trafficking offense, even though white teens' self-reported experiences of using and selling drugs are at rates greater than that of African-American teens. The length of incarceration compounds both the disparity and the injury inflicted; on average, African-American and Latino juveniles are confined, respectively, 61 and 112 days longer than white youth. Additionally, as noted in a previous (2010) RJI publication—"An Offer They Can't Refuse: Racial Disparities in Juvenile Justice and Deliberate Indifference Meet Alternatives That Work"—"minorities account for more than 58 percent of youth admitted to state adult prisons."

In an attempt to eliminate DMC, federal law requires states that receive federal juvenile delinquency prevention funding to measure the rate of DMC at ten different decision points in the juvenile justice system: juvenile arrests; referral to juvenile court; cases diverted; cases involving secure detention; cases petitioned (charges filed); cases resulting in delinquent findings; cases resulting in probation placement; cases resulting in confinement in secure juvenile facilities; and, cases transferred to adult court.

WASHINGTON, DC

Washington, DC is, like many cities, a majority-minority city. However, that alone does not explain the depth of the racial disparity in the juvenile justice system. The RJI's strategy can be implemented in any public system in this nation, but we focus on jurisdictions where the disparity is stark and the outcomes for youth of color are even starker. A brief display of some basic statistics of the disproportionate rate of system engagement for youth of color in DC provides a snapshot of the inequities manifest throughout the country.

In 2007, the youth population in the District of Columbia ages 10 to 17 was 49,394. It was comprised of: 38,131 (77 percent) African Americans, 9,848 (20 percent) Whites, and 1,415 (3 percent) Latinos/Hispanics. There were 3,410 (7 percent) classified as Latino/Hispanic, which overlaps with other racial categories because Latino/Hispanic was classified as ethnicity and not a race, according to U.S. Census Bureau statistics. Indeed, youth of color constitute the majority, but we find an overrepresentation of youth of color at every decision point in the delinquency system, except for the most important decision at the outset: to avert involvement through diversion. In 2007, 3,279 juveniles were arrested, and African-American youth made up the majority, with 3,051 (93 percent) arrests. An African-American youth is approximately 19 times more likely to be arrested than a White youth in the district.

Data for Juvenile Delinquency Involvement in Washington, DC

In addition to the juvenile arrests, there was disproportionate representation at almost every other major decision point in the juvenile justice system. In 2007, 3,364 youths were referred to juvenile court, with 2,624 (78 percent) referrals for African-American youth; 637 (19 percent) referrals for Other/ Mixed youth, 81 (2 percent) referrals for Hispanic youth, 17 (1 percent) referrals for White youth, and 5 (0.1 percent) referrals for Asian youth. The decision to divert youth from the system is the only decision point where the 582 youth arrested who were diverted was proportionate because the majority of youth diverted were youth of color.

There were 1,212 total cases involving secure detention, of which 1,173 (97 percent) were African-American, 29 (2 percent) were Hispanic, and 5 (.04 percent) were White. And 2,478 youth had cases petitioned: 1,940 (78 percent) were African-American, 458 (18 percent) were Other/Mixed, 63 (3 percent) were Hispanic, 12 (0.48 percent) were White, and, 5 (0.2 percent) were Asian. Also, 616 youth had cases that resulted in delinquent findings, with 589 (96 percent) African-American, 22 (4 percent) Hispanic. In addition, there was 1 White and 1 Asian youth who each had cases that resulted in delinquent findings.

At the deeper end of the spectrum of juvenile justice system involvement, the statistics show the same story of disproportionality. In 2007, 369 cases resulted in probation in placement, with 349 (95 percent) African-American youth, 16 (4 percent) Hispanic youth, 2 (0.54 percent) White youth, and 1 (0.27 percent) Asian youth. There were 247 cases that resulted in confinement, with 240 (97 percent) African-American, 6 (2 percent) Hispanic and 1 (0.4 percent) Asian. There were no White youth sent to correctional facilities. Additionally, there were 80 juvenile cases transferred to adult court, of which 61 cases (76 percent) were African-American, 17 cases (21 percent) were Other/Mixed, 2 cases (3 percent) were Hispanic. Again, there were no cases of white youth transferred to adult court.

HELPING TO MOVE PUBLIC OFFICIALS
TO USE EFFECTIVE ALTERNATIVES TO
JUVENILE DELINQUENCY SYSTEM INVOLVEMENT

As noted, the RJI is a combination social advocacy and litigation strategy designed to combat structural racism in the juvenile justice system. In an earlier article by the RJI team in *The Clearinghouse Review* (Vol. 44, "Public Notice Forums: Choosing Among Alternatives to Confront the Intent Requirement"), we acknowledged that, "[l]itigation is not necessarily the best—or the only—way to create awareness of alternatives to prevailing practice, community engagement, support for leaders who seek change, or oversight of its implementation." Litigation has heretofore not been an effective tool to combat structural racism because challengers have found it almost impossible to meet the obligation to prove intent to discriminate. However, in the social advocacy strategy developed by the RJI, we advocate use of Public Notice Forums, to mobilize the community and challenge the interpretation of the law on structural racism and raise the principle that public officials should be obligated to use what we know works.

Public officials seem to be the only category of people who are under no obligation to make use of knowledge in order to avoid injury to others. If doctors or lawyers fail to remain current on developments in their fields, they can be charged with malpractice. If plumbers or electricians fail to use known effective strategies to respond to a problem, they can be sued for negligence. Ever since 1932, there has been a widespread understanding that the obligation to exercise reasonable care includes the obligation to utilize new knowledge of how to avoid injury.

In fact, there is a famous case that stands for this proposition, *The T.J. Hooper*, 60 F. 2d 737 (2d Cir. 1932). Justice Learned Hand's opinion remains gospel except when it comes to the obligation for public officials to stay abreast of innovations in the field and to implement them. In the Hooper case, the court upheld the trial court's finding that the tugboat was unseaworthy because it did not have a radio set with which to receive weather reports even though such radio sets were not yet standard industry practice. Case briefs summarize *The T.J. Hooper* as standing for the proposition that there are precautions that are so imperative that even their universal disregard by the industry will not excuse their omission.

Public officials appear exempt from that obligation; they can and regularly do invoke official discretion and immunity from challenge when their actions and practices persist in ignoring the state of knowledge. Accordingly, public officials, such as those making the decisions to overinvolve youth of color in the delinquency system, remain free to fail to use what we know works. These delinquency system officials persist in subjecting the public to wasteful expenditures and to predictable increases in crime based on their overreliance on involving youth of color in the juvenile delinquency system, despite overwhelming evidence that doing so increases recidivism while imposing a great fiscal burden on the jurisdiction.

The RJI is founded on the premise that there is a possible exception to public officials' immunity from an obligation to use known, effective practices, when it comes to violations of basic civil rights. In the past, judicial relief from racial disparity has not been forthcoming because the injured parties have been required to prove that the disparity was the result of discriminatory intent. That burden of proof has thwarted efforts to challenge structural racism stemming from the systematic practices and policies of governmental agencies. We propose to meet the intent requirement by shifting the focus from past to future.

In the United States Supreme Court case *City of Canton v. Harris,* 489 U.S. 387 (1989), the Court's decision said that intent can be inferred when government policymakers choose among alternatives to follow an injurious course of action, demonstrating a "deliberate indifference" to rights protected by the U.S. Constitution and federal laws. Under the RJI theory, based, in part, on the *City of Canton* case, when official decision makers have formal notice of alternatives that are less costly and yield significant, sustained effects which have been replicated or which experts regard as promising or exemplary, the failure to use these alternatives constitutes "deliberate indifference" to injury to the fundamental Constitutional rights of youths of color in the juvenile justice system. We believe that this strategy would at least shift the burden of proof from plaintiffs alleging discrimination to the institutional actors denying intent.

PUBLIC NOTICE FORUM

The first step for communities seeking to employ the RJI strategy is to hold a Public Notice Forum or process. These forums provide formal notice to the public officials of the structural racism embedded in the decisions to disproportionately engage youth of color in the delinquency system. As important, the Public Notice process presents an opportunity for stakeholders to give public officials formal notice about "state of the art" alternative practices that are cheaper and more effective than present practice. Various stakeholders in the juvenile justice system, such as executive branch officials, judges, frontline workers at community-based programs, attorneys, and youth and families who have had entanglement in the delinquency system, can all share their unique knowledge and experiences on best practices to limit juvenile delinquency system involvement. Finally, this process also creates the record of public officials choosing from among alternatives, should it become necessary to file a lawsuit.

The Public Notice Forum strategy as a precursor to potential litigation changes the odds in challenging racial disparity in two ways. First, the strategy converts the "intent" requirement into a weapon to be used by those seeking to dismantle structural racism; it shifts the burden of proof to defendants to prove that their decision not to use alternatives that save lives and public resources does not violate the Constitution or federal law. Following a Public Notice Forum process, the public officials will bear the burden of explaining how this persistent disproportionality does not constitute intentional racism. Second, the strategy changes the forum and shifts the odds by giving legislators and other interested stakeholders the initiative to ask of public officials: "Why aren't you using more effective and less expensive alternatives to delinquency system engagement?" Public Notice Forum processes also offer a sympathetic forum for system change advocates and the community, particularly the affected youth and their families, to put the system on trial before the very decision makers who control the budget and define the authority within which the system must operate.

HOW DO WE KNOW WHAT WORKS?

An extensive body of knowledge has emerged over the past 35 years that would save vast amounts of money, reduce DMC and mitigate its most injurious manifestations: 1) the failure to use diversion, and 2) the overuse of detention and confinement of minority youth. This information can clearly, succinctly and formally be shared with officials through a Public Notice Forum process so that there is a record of putting the officials on notice that existing practices have a disproportionately injurious impact on youth of color.

First, recent research literature now distinguishes two types of programs: External Control Programs and Therapeutic Programs. The Georgetown University Center for Juvenile Justice Reform has recently released "A New Perspective on Evidence-Based Practice" (http://cjjr. georgetown.edu/pdfs/ebp/ebppaper.pdf), which provides a useful overview developed by a team headed by Mark Lipsey at Vanderbilt University. They include in the first category the following illustrations:

- Programs oriented toward instilling discipline (e.g., paramilitary regimens in boot camps)
- Programs aimed at deterrence through fear of the consequences of bad behavior (e.g., prison visitation programs such as Scared Straight)
- Programs emphasizing surveillance to detect delinquent behavior (e.g., intensive probation or parole supervision)

Therapeutic programs include the following categories:

- Restorative (e.g., restitution, victim-offender mediation)
- Skill-building (e.g., cognitive-behavioral techniques, social skills, academic and vocational skill- building)
- Counseling (e.g., individual, group, family, mentoring)
- Multiple coordinated services (e.g., case management and service brokering)

Their conclusion is specific: "Programs with a therapeutic philosophy were notably more effective than those with a control philosophy." They note that many intensive probation programs often include intensive counseling components and thus "represent a mix of control and therapeutic strategies."

Second, there is increased demand for evidence-based programs and practices—with some important caveats and distinctions. Experts caution against equating "evidence-based" practices with "brand-name" model programs. They stress that while such programs generally show positive effects, they do not show notably better effects than the no-name programs that incorporate the same evidence-based practices.

Third, these experts in the field call for increased use of programs that have established a track record of success, but are careful to avoid stifling innovation or limiting funding to only those that have met a standard called "evidence-based." Evidence-based programs tend to refer to programs governed by a specific manual or protocol, and have been demonstrated on separate client samples. There are also "research-based groups," "theory-based groups," and pilot programs which may become evidence-based.

Fourth, there is a general consensus that detention should be used only as a last resort and that, in general, it is now overused. Only a small fraction of youth confined in juvenile facilities have histories that actually warrant confinement.

Fifth, two national foundations, among many others, the Juvenile Detentions Alternatives Initiative of Annie E. Casey Foundation (http://www.aecf.org/MajorInitiatives/Juvenile DetentionAlternativesInitiative.aspx) and the Models for Change of the John D. and Catherine T. MacArthur Foundation (http://www.modelsforchange.net/index.html), have made major multiyear investments in efforts to develop knowledge about what works and what does not work and also to support efforts to create alternatives that are less costly and more effective than prevailing practice. They each provide extensive bodies of documentation about those initiatives. In addition, the Office of Juvenile Justice and Delinquency Prevention of the U.S. Department of Justice (http://www. ojjdp.gov/) provides extensive analysis of programs and offers a web-based directory of alternatives for every stage of the process to assist states in shaping their juvenile justice systems.

Finally, TimeBanks USA (http:// www.timebanks.org/) and the RJI would single out one element of effective programs that needs more specific emphasis and articulation: programs that provide an opportunity for youth to contribute and to gain self-esteem by efforts that make a difference for others. Two programs that have achieved great outcomes for youth while enabling them to give back are the Time Dollar Youth Court of Washington, DC (http://www.tdyc. org/) and the Youth Advocate Program, Inc. (http://www. yapinc.org)

The Time Dollar Youth Court is a diversion program where first-time juvenile offenders go before a jury of teenagers vested with authority by the DC Superior Court to impose sentences that may include an apology, restitution, writing an essay, participating in LifeSkills training, or jury duty for the Time Dollar Youth Court.

After ten years, the program has handled 65–70 percent of nonviolent misdemeanors by DC youngsters at a per person cost of less than $500, as compared with a cost of more than $2,250 for youth to go through the delinquency system even if eventually placed on probation in the community. Some 80 percent or more of the jurors are former offenders. Recidivism rates are below 10 percent and created a new cadre of youth leaders with exceptional capability and authenticity.

The Youth Advocate Program (YAP) focuses on youth contribution and youth as assets. YAP hires local residents and trains them as Advocates who become part of the extended family for youth who have a record of re-offending and who otherwise would be subject to involuntary institutional detention. With a 40-year success rate of over 80 percent, the YAP program starts with identifying the youth's strengths and creating a program for that youth that defines him or her as a contribuitor with capacity to give back.

CONCLUSION

We are a nation that arrests and incarcerates a higher percentage of its citizenry than any other country. We do so in ways that undermine our national commitment to equality and justice. The RJI urges that we undertake to dismantle structural racism in the juvenile delinquency system by seeking ways to compel public officials to use what we know works. Wouldn't it be wonderful if our public officials, responsible for disbursing scarce public resources and managing systems, such as the delinquency system that can make or break the future of vulnerable youth, and consequently of the community, were obligated to use the strategies and alternatives to system involvement that work? We know what works, we think it is about time for public officials to be compelled to use what we know works and to stop the use of practices that will lead to failure for young people and ultimately for the community as a whole.

* * * * *

JJDPA

First enacted in 1974, the Juvenile Justice and Delinquency Prevention Act (JJDPA) incentivizes states to adhere to four core protections designed to protect court-involved youth across the nation.

Among these is the Disproportionate Minority Contact (DMC) core protection, which directs states to "address juvenile delinquency prevention efforts and system improvement efforts designed to reduce . . . the disproportionate number of juvenile members of minority groups who come into contact with the juvenile justice system."

Since 2007, the Act 4 Juvenile Justice Campaign (Act4JJ) has advocated for a number of improvements to the JJDPA, including one that would strengthen the DMC core protection to require states and localities to take more concrete steps to achieve measurable reductions in DMC more effectively, and provide the supports they need to do so. This improvement, and other needed amendments to the JJDPA, has twice been approved by the U.S. Senate Judiciary Committee in the 110th and 111th Congresses.

Since its addition to the JJDPA in 1988, the DMC core protection has led jurisdictions to pay much more attention to this issue. Of the 55 states and territories that participate with the JJDPA, better than 90 percent of them have state-level committees dedicated to addressing DMC within their borders. A key feature of these efforts is data-gathering; states are required to report their disparities, and many jurisdictions are beginning to learn how to interpret that information and to consider ways to implement meaningful interventions. The challenge is that involving the community, accurate gathering of data, meaningful interpretation of such data, finding and implementing solutions indicated by the data, and engaging in transparent assessment of success are what jurisdictions need to do in order to create meaningful change. The strengthening amendments to the DMC provision of the JJDPA are designed to guide and support states in achieving these next steps.

Reauthorization of the JJDPA is now four years overdue. The Act4JJ Campaign continues to gain momentum to reauthorize a strong and forward-thinking JJDPA that is grounded in more than 30 years of research about "what works" and aligns with emerging practices proven to reduce delinquency, protect youth and improve public safety. To learn more, visit www.act4jj.org.

—Courtesy of Tara Andrews, Deputy Exec. Dir., Policy & Programs, Coalition for Juvenile Justice

Native Americans and Juvenile Justice: A Hidden Tragedy

Terry L. Cross

In the United States in 2008, there are more than 560 federally recognized American Indian tribes comprising an American Indian/Alaska Native (AI/AN) population of approximately 4 million individuals. About half this population lives on reservations, and the others live off-reservation, primarily in urban communities. The AI/AN population is young: 42 percent—"almost 2 million"—are under 19 years of age. Twenty percent (800,000) are at risk—60,000 suffer abuse or neglect each year. According to the Youth Violence Research Bulletin, the suicide rate for American Indian juveniles (57 per 1 million) was almost twice the rate for white juveniles and the highest for any race. In addition, 200,000 are believed to suffer from serious emotional disturbances.

American Indian youth are grossly overrepresented in state and federal juvenile justice systems and secure confinement. Incarcerated Indian youth are much more likely to be subjected to the harshest treatment in the most restrictive environments and less likely to have received the help they need from other systems. AI/AN youth are 50 percent more likely than whites to receive the most punitive measures. Pepper spray, restraint and isolation appear to be grossly and disproportionately applied to Indian youth, who have no recourse, no alternatives and few advocates.

In 2003, litigation over conditions in a South Dakota state training school revealed horrible abuses in the use of restraints and isolation, yet little in the way of education or mental health services. Findings also showed that Native youth were significantly overrepresented in the lockdown unit and thus subject to the worst abuses. For example, one young girl from the Pine Ridge Reservation had been held in a secure unit within the facility for almost two years, during which time she was placed in four-point restraints while spread-eagled on a cement slab for hours at a time, kept in isolation for days and even weeks, and pepper-sprayed numerous times. This young girl, like many of the females confined at the facility, suffered from significant mental health and substance abuse issues. Due to the lack of appropriate

415

mental health treatment and the harsh conditions in the facility, she resorted to self-harming behavior as a way to draw attention to herself, and like many of the other girls now has scars up and down her arms from cutting herself. Finally, the facility also instituted a rule that penalized Native youth for speaking in their Native language, and several were placed on lockdown status for speaking Lakota to each other.

There is a growing awareness that many tribes' children and youth are being taken outside the care, custody and control of their families, communities and tribal government, and that many are suffering from extreme physical, mental and emotional abuse in the process.

EXPLORATORY QUALITATIVE RESEARCH RESULTS

Beginning in 2003, the National Indian Child Welfare Association (NICWA) has conducted exploratory research to identify and highlight the issues of American Indian children and youth with regard to juvenile rights and justice. What we have learned can be best summarized in the words of some of the focus group participants:

American Indian youth are ending up in adult facilities because there are no separate facilities for young people in some communities, despite laws forbidding contact between minors and adults in correction facilities; sometimes even parents are not notified when young people are taken into custody. (2002 NICWA leader focus group)

Indian status offenders are often treated as if they were violent offenders; a young woman (under 16 years of age) was charged with fourth degree assault for spitting on a nurse.

State and county workers act discriminatorily to both tribal social service workers and young Indian clients.

Children are often placed in correctional facilities for inappropriate reasons (truancy, parents' behavior and overdoses).

I'm proud and sad to be Indian at the same time. It feels really bad seeing people drinking and dying. I blaze home to Browning for a funeral every other month.

Participants felt that the kids who most needed help, the kids who made bad choices already ("bad kids"), were likely to be left out. One participant succinctly captured the essence of this concern: Yeah, half the people have problems from the life they chose, but what challenges you to change if no one gives you a chance?

Children are often taken out of the community and offered nonculturally specific/relevant services as individuals (not services in conjunction with their family) even when tribal services are available.

DISPARATE RATES AND AT-RISK YOUTH: SPARSE DATA

In addition to qualitative research, NICWA has also conducted reviews of the literature to determine the level of attention these issues are receiving in research and in the literature. Sparse data exist, but the data that are available point to a serious problem that is not currently being addressed.

- The Bureau of Justice Statistics publication, *American Indian Crime*, reported: On a given day, 1 in 25 American Indians age 18 or older is under the jurisdiction of the criminal justice system, 2.4 times the per capita rate of Whites, and that nearly a third of all American Indian victims of violence are between ages 18 and 24. This group of American Indians experienced the highest per capita rate of violence of any racial group considered by age—about 1 violent crime for every 4 persons of this age.
- Native American youth represent 1 percent of the U.S. population, yet they constitute 2–3 percent of the youth arrested for such offenses as larceny-theft and liquor law violations.
- In 26 states, Native American youth are disproportionately placed in secure confinement in comparison to their population. For example, in four states (South Dakota, Alaska, North Dakota, Montana), Native youth account for anywhere from 29–42 percent of youth in secure confinement.
- Nationwide, the average rate of new commitments to adult state prison for Native American youth is almost twice (1.84 times) that of White youth. In the states with enough Native Americans to facilitate comparisons, Native American youth were committed to adult prison from 1.3 to 18.1 times the rate of Whites.
- Of the youth in custody of the Federal Bureau of Prisons, 79 percent were Native American as of October 2000, an increase of 50 percent since 1994.
- Alcohol-related deaths among Native Americans ages 15-24 are 17 times higher than the national averages. The suicide rate for Native American youth is three times the national average. Forty-four percent of all American Indian students drop out of high school, more than any other group in the country, the rate varies between 25 percent and 93 percent, depending on region.

FEDERAL MANDATES

The Juvenile Justice Delinquency Prevention Act (JJDPA) of 1974 was amended in 1989 to include a provision addressing the needs of federally recognized Indian tribes. The JJDPA stipulates that states in their three-year plans must include the juvenile justice needs of Indian tribes.

States with a minority representing 1 percent or more in the general population are required by the Act to have a Disproportionate Minority Contact (DMC) plan that addressed the issues, concerns and problems of their overrepresentation. More proactive alternatives to the use of secure confinement for the Native youth are needed, and collaborative relations between Indian tribes and states could be strengthened. Our efforts and findings are intended to assist states in their strategic planning to reduce Native overrepresentation and disparate treatment.

Native American youth who have committed one of 16 major federal crimes on Indian lands with exclusive federal jurisdiction are prosecuted by the U.S. Attorney's Office. Of all youth in the nation who are prosecuted federally, 32 percent are placed in a secure facility for juvenile offenders, and 74 percent of these are Native-American. As there are no federal correctional facilities nationwide specifically for juvenile offenders, the Federal Bureau of Prisons contracts beds in state or private facilities for these youth in their custody. Such facilities must be within proximity to the youths' homes and have culturally appropriate services.

WHAT WE DO NOT KNOW: KEY ELEMENTS

Unfortunately, there is too much that is unknown about American Indian children and youth and the juvenile justice system. Without reliable knowledge, attempts at mobilizing advocacy efforts have gone without funding and have failed to gain traction. Research is needed to raise awareness of the issues and to justify the need for funding to begin to address the issues. Things that we do not know and research must address include the following:

About the Youth

What is the true nature and character of Indian youth in the juvenile justice system (demographics, nature of offenses, victims of abuse and neglect, drug and alcohol involvement, gang membership, emotional problems, risk of suicide, educational attainment and special needs, degree to which youth experienced detention, etc.)?

How many American Indian youth are held in: (a) adult jails, (b) juvenile detention facilities, (c) juvenile commitment facilities or training schools, and (d) adult prisons? Are American Indian youth overrepresented at each stage of the justice system: arrest, detention, transfer to adult court, adjudication, disposition, and incarceration in juvenile or adult facilities?

What is the experience of American Indian youth in the juvenile justice system? Are their special needs being met? Are they treated differently than other youth?

What is the experience of the parents of American Indian youth in the juvenile justice system? In what ways are they involved?

About the Systems

What is the nature and character of current juvenile justice systems and services that serve American Indian youth and families? Are there culturally authentic support, treatment and rehabilitation services? What are the current recidivism rates of Native youth?

To what degree are juvenile justice interventions being used in lieu of mental health, child welfare and educational services that are unavailable?

Are tribal religious leaders and Native healers gaining frequent access to juvenile correctional facilities to work with and counsel Native youth? Are tribal religions and ceremonial practices included in these facilities?

What is the nature and character of current tribal juvenile justice systems and services? In what ways are they involved with tribal youth in the custody of the state or the Federal Bureau of Prisons?

RECOMMENDATIONS

The NICWA Board of Directors identified the issue of juvenile rights as an area of concern in 2002, when it became apparent that Indian children and youth were being maltreated in juvenile detention facilities and that many of the youth being confined in those facilities were there, not because they committed a crime, but because there were not appropriate mental health or child welfare resources available to meet their needs. Through our examination of these issues over a five-year period, we arrived at several recommendations.

It is recommended that the Department of Justice (DOJ) or private funders conduct or sponsor formative research in states that are known to have particularly high levels of overrepresentation or have documented harsh treatment of Indian youth in juvenile justice systems or juvenile facilities and that have already begun to engage in some dialogue with tribes to explore solutions. Such formative research should address the following questions:

- What is the nature and character of current juvenile justice systems and services that serve American Indian youth and families?
- To what degree are there data, research or literature regarding American Indian youth in the juvenile justice system?
- To what degree does an advocacy movement, network or voice exist for American Indian youth in the juvenile justice system?
- To what degree are tribal government officials having influence in the treatment, rehabilitation and disposition regarding their tribal members in state or federal juvenile justice systems and facilities?

It is further recommended that DOJ engage leaders in planning for strategic activities that will lead to clear identification of related problems in Native communities, including what might be effective alternatives and strategies to address the problems. Finally, it is recommended that the Juvenile Justice and Delinquency Prevention Act be amended to ensure the rights of tribal youth and to begin to provide resources to correct this hidden problem.

CONCLUSION

Currently, Indian children and youth who are identified as delinquent have few protections and even fewer advocates. Parents of these children who are served in this system often experience a sense of powerlessness and report being discriminated against. Tribes that might be resources for positive change are without resources or the right to intervene on their citizens' behalf. This chapter is a call to action aimed at stimulating dialogue about this little-discussed topic.

National Statement to Support Human and Civil Rights for All Immigrants and to Oppose Compromise Immigration Reform Proposal

The National Network for Immigrant and Refugee Rights, headed by PRRAC Board member Catherine Tactaquin, convened a series of discussions among members and partners around the current [2006] immigration proposals before Congress; the following Statement is the product of those meetings.

FAIR AND JUST IMMIGRATION REFORM FOR ALL

We stand together as immigrant, faith, social justice, labor, peace, human and civil rights organizations and other concerned communities to support human and civil rights for all immigrants and to oppose the immigration "reform" proposals presently in the U.S. Senate. We oppose H.R. 4437, the immigration bill passed in the House of Representatives in December, as well as all of the compromise bills presented in the Senate.

We call upon members of Congress and the Administration to stop masquerading these proposals as immigration reform. We demand nothing less than immigration policies that are fair and just, and that respect the rights and dignity of all immigrants and other members of our society.

The rush to reach a bipartisan accord on immigration legislation has led to a compromise that would create deep divisions within the immigrant community and leave millions of undocumented immigrants in the shadows of our country. We oppose the behind-the-scenes brokering currently playing out in the legislative process. These trade-offs and deals are based on election-year campaigning and demands by business lobbyists, rather than on the best interests and voices of immigrant communities. We say, "No deal!"

In a re-ignited Civil Rights Movement, millions of immigrants, their families, neighbors and co-workers, along with faith and labor leaders, peace and justice advocates, have marched and rallied in cities across the U.S. The mobilizations have served as a wake-up call for the whole country to acknowledge the vital role of immigrants as co-workers, neighbors and members of our broad society. And, as details of the current legislative compromise have become known, the voices of immigrant communities are rejecting the proposals for a so-called legalization program, and are denouncing the further erosion of human and civil rights through the enforcement and criminalization provisions. The stakes are considerable, and affect all of us.

This year is the 20th anniversary of the 1986 legalization and employer sanctions law, and the 10th anniversary of the restrictive Illegal Immigration Reform and Immigrant Responsibility Act. We cannot allow the current proposals to be enacted as this generation's flawed immigration reform legacy.

WHAT WE WANT: FAIR AND JUST IMMIGRATION REFORM

Fair and just immigration reform means:

- Genuine legalization and opportunities to adjust status for all undocumented immigrants, including youth and farmworkers
- Preservation of due process, including restoration of access to the courts and meaningful judicial review for immigrants
- No indefinite detention or expansion of mandatory detention
- No expansion of guest worker programs
- No more wasted resources allocated to further militarize our borders and to contribute to the crisis of human rights and lives in the border regions
- An end to employer sanctions and electronic worker verification systems
- The strengthening and enforcement of labor law protections for all workers, native and foreign-born
- No use of city, state or other government agencies in the enforcement of immigration law
- No more criminalization of immigrants, or their service providers
- Expansion of legal immigration opportunities, support for family reunification and immediate processing of the backlog of pending visa applications
- Elimination of harsh obstacles to immigrating, including the HIV ban, "3 and 10 year bars," and high income requirements for immigrant sponsors

THE CURRENT "LEGALIZATION" PROPOSAL IS UNACCEPTABLE

The proposed 3-tiered temporary worker program offers little hope for broad, inclusive legalization of undocumented immigrants. What some are calling a "path to citizenship" in the last Senate bill is merely a massive temporary worker program without worker protections, and contains numerous hurdles that will drastically limit the number of undocumented immigrants who can actually legalize. Such a program would divide communities, including mixed-status families, erode wage and benefits standards, and place a greater burden on safety-net services.

THE ENFORCEMENT PROPOSALS
UNDERMINE ALL OF OUR RIGHTS

Significant provisions in the current Senate proposals would dramatically undermine a broad array of rights, increase the criminalization of all immigrants, result in mass deportations, and unfairly exclude millions from eligibility for any legalization opportunity. The expansion of expedited removal would eliminate the right to a court hearing, while the broadened definition of "aggravated felony" to include many minor offenses would result in mandatory detention and mass deportations. The proposals also seek to reinstate indefinite detention and increase detention facilities, including the use of closed military bases. Encouraging local police to enforce immigration law would not only add an additional burden that detracts from current responsibilities, but would discourage immigrant access to public safety institutions.

Moreover, the increased resources to militarize the border, which has already cost over $30 billion in the past 12 years, has not deterred unauthorized border crossings and instead has caused a humanitarian crisis with the deaths of some 4,000 people in the desert. Current border enforcement policies, without provision for safe and legal entry, have resulted in the detention and criminalization of tens of thousands of people at a significant daily cost to taxpayers.

THE PROPOSALS FAIL TO PROTECT WORKERS

The current proposals would further erode already weak labor protections and rights for immigrants and other workers. Immigrant workers have historically been used as "cheap labor" by employers and industries unwilling to pay decent wages or to maintain reasonable working conditions. These proposals continue in that same shameful vein, and are designed to force and keep wages down to compete with cheap labor suppliers globally.

Workers need more, not less, rights. A real legalization proposal needs to be coupled with the repeal of employer sanctions, the provision of the landmark 1986 Immigration Reform and Control Act that has led to the criminalization of immigrant workers, and which would be deepened through an expansion of an employment verification system. This program has done nothing in the last 20 years but increase discrimination and abuse of immigrant workers. Employers have had greater leverage to threaten and intimidate immigrant workers, break organizing efforts, carry out unjust firings, and lower wages and work conditions for all working people. These abuses impact the entire American workforce, particularly the most vulnerable toiling in low-wage jobs such as farmworkers, day laborers and domestic workers.

NO EXPANSION OF GUEST WORKER PROGRAMS

A key concern is the significant expansion of guest worker programs found in almost all Senate proposals and supported by the Administration. We oppose these programs both when they are tied to legalization for undocumented immigrants already living and working here, and as a means for managing future flows of immigrants into the United States. The U.S. does not have a shortage of workers; what we have is a shortage of employers willing to pay a living wage and maintain decent working conditions.

Guest worker programs have been condemned by labor and immigrant communities for their long record of violations of labor rights and standards, including blacklists and deportations of workers who protest. In 1964, Ernesto Galarza, Cesar Chavez and other defenders of workplace rights won the abolition of the old Bracero guest worker program. The purpose of that program, they said, was the creation a vulnerable workforce in order to drive down wages and break union organizing efforts among immigrants and nonimmigrants alike. The purpose of current proposals is the same. Temporary, contract workers are prevented the option of putting down roots and becoming full and equal members of our communities.

Future migrants should not be forced to accept a second-class status, violating our country's most basic commitments to equality. They should be given permanent residence status, allowing them to work and travel freely, to exercise their labor rights, and to live as any other member of our society.

NO COMPROMISE, NO DEAL ON
FAIR AND JUST IMMIGRATION REFORM

In recent years, immigrant community members, including youth and students, farmworkers and others, have effectively organized and rallied in support of legislative proposals to strengthen their rights and opportunities to be equal members of this society. Despite the loud and determined voice of immigrant communities, advocates and supporters for fair and just immigration reform this year, we have yet to see an acceptable proposal from Congress. And with H.R. 4437 already passed by the House, we are very aware that any proposal from the Senate would be subject to further compromise in a Senate-House reconciliation process, and would likely produce laws that would detrimentally affect current and future immigrants for years to come.

Increased enforcement does not address the complex issue of global migration. Employer sanctions and beefed-up border security have been in place for decades as deterrents to migration, and yet the number of undocumented continues to grow. The sources of migration rest in the problems of economic and political instability, poverty and war in migrant-sending countries. Despite the urgency of the immigration issue in this country, it is clearly not just a "domestic" issue, and our policies need to consider support for economic stability, fair trade agreements and peace as vital to addressing the migration of people in search of work, survival, and safety.

We will continue to raise our voices for genuine immigration reform that respects the rights and dignity of all immigrants, and is fair and just. Immigrant workers, students and families are making incredible sacrifices to raise their voices for themselves and future generations, in the face of recriminations and disciplinary actions from employers and schools. As immigrant communities continue to mobilize for their rights, on May 1 and beyond, we will support their right and choice to express themselves.

We pledge to increase public education efforts and the building and mobilization of meaningful alliances, and we will encourage and support immigrant community leadership to advance real immigration reform. We call upon Congress and the Administration to heed the voices of immigrant communities demanding genuine immigration reforms: real legalization, equitable inclusion in our society, justice, and respect for human rights.

21st Century Gateways: Immigrants in Suburban America

Audrey Singer, Susan W. Hardwick & Caroline B. Brettell

New trends in immigrant settlement patterns are changing communities across the United States. The traditional American story of immigrant enclaves in the heart of major cities has been fundamentally altered with the restructuring of the U.S. economy, the decentralization of cities, and the growth of the suburbs as major employment centers.

Prior to the 1990s, immigrant settlement had a predictable pattern and was limited to mostly Southwestern and coastal states and metropolitan New York, Los Angeles, Miami and Chicago.

By the last century's end, due to shifts in labor markets, immigrants, both legal and illegal, were increasingly settling outside well-established immigrant gateways in a new group of cities and suburbs. The swiftness of the influx has often been accompanied by social and economic stress. In many rural areas, small towns and suburban areas, the institutional structures that could assist in integrating immigrants—both community and governmental—are insufficient or nonexistent.

Many of the newest, largest destinations, such as Atlanta, Las Vegas and Charlotte, are places with no history or identity of immigration. Other metropolitan areas, such as Sacramento, Minneapolis-St. Paul and Seattle, once important gateways in the early part of the 20th century, have recently re-emerged as major new destinations.

Taken together, the fastest growing "second-tier" metropolitan areas, including Atlanta, Austin, Charlotte, Dallas, Minneapolis-St. Paul, Phoenix, Portland (OR), Sacramento and Washington, DC, along with 11 other metropolitan areas, house one-fifth of all immigrants in the United States today. We have named this class of metropolitan areas the 21st century gateways. These 20 metropolitan areas are largely characterized by post-World War II urban development, very recent growth of their immigrant populations, and predominantly suburban settlement.

In contrast to more established central-city destinations and patterns of settlement, trends in 21st century gateways constitute a new context for the social, economic and political incorporation of immigrants. All of these places are confronting fast-paced change that has wide-reaching effects on neighborhoods, schools, workplaces and local public coffers.

IDENTIFYING THE 21ST CENTURY GATEWAYS

Our identification of 21st century gateways is based on a historical typology of urban immigrant settlement in the United States developed by co-author demographer Audrey Singer. Based on trends in the size and growth of the immigrant population over the course of the 20th century, this typology includes seven immigrant gateway types:

- Former gateways, such as Buffalo and Pittsburgh, attracted considerable numbers of immigrants in the early 1900s, but no longer do.
- Continuous gateways, such as New York and Chicago, are long-established destinations for immigrants and continue to receive large numbers of the foreign-born.
- Post–World War II gateways, such as Houston, Los Angeles and Miami, began attracting immigrants in large numbers only during the past 50 years or less.
- Together, the continuous and the post-World War II gateways will be referred to as established immigrant gateways here.
- Emerging gateways are those places that have had rapidly growing immigrant populations during the past 25 years alone. Atlanta, Dallas-Ft. Worth and Washington, DC are prime examples.
- Re-emerging gateways, such as Minneapolis-St. Paul and Seattle, began the 20th Century with a strong attraction for immigrants, waned as destinations during the middle of the century, but are now re-emerging as immigrant gateways.
- Pre-emerging gateways are those places, such as Raleigh-Durham and Austin, where immigrant populations have grown very rapidly starting in the 1990s and are likely to continue to grow as immigrant destinations.

IMMIGRANT GATEWAY
GROWTH IN COMPARATIVE PERSPECTIVE

Some of the fastest immigrant growth rates during the 1990s registered in metropolitan areas with very small immigrant populations to begin with. Nonetheless, many large metropolitan areas saw a doubling or more of their foreign-born populations in the 1990s alone, including Atlanta, Dallas-Ft. Worth, Portland (OR), Minneapolis-St. Paul and Las Vegas.

At the same time, in the more established immigrant gateways, growth rates registered smaller percentage change: an average of 45 percent in the continuous gateways and 39 percent in the post-World War II gateways.

Likewise, it is not unexpected that some of the largest established gateways have seen minor percentage growth recently. This is due in part simply to the absolute size of the immigrant populations in places such as Los Angeles, where the immigrant population grew only 3.1 percent (but grew exceptionally fast in nearby Riverside-San Bernardino), and New York, which had only 9 percent growth between 2000 and 2006.

Other metros that registered strong growth in their immigrant populations in the 1990s due to the technology boom, such as San Francisco and San Jose, have seen the pace of foreign-born growth dramatically slow since 2000, when the technology bubble burst.

In contrast, during the same 2000–2006 period, the greatest percentage increases in foreign-born populations among metropolitan areas were in emerging Orlando, Atlanta and Las Vegas and pre-emerging Charlotte and Raleigh (all between 53–62 percent).

In absolute terms, Dallas-Ft. Worth, Atlanta, Washington, DC and Phoenix saw the largest gains among the 21st century immigrant gateways. However, established New York topped the list with an estimated 450,000 immigrant newcomers settling since 2000. Post-World War II gateways Houston, Riverside-San Bernardino and Miami followed, each with more than 250,000 new immigrants in the most recent period.

IMMIGRANTS IN SUBURBAN METROPOLISES

Another new immigrant settlement trend—one taking place wholly within metropolitan areas—was the dramatic increase in suburban settlement of immigrants, beginning in the 1990s. As the urban economy has shifted from manufacturing to new economy services, the suburbs have become the preferred location for dispersed commercial and office space.

Immigrants have followed the suburban job and housing opportunities in great numbers. By doing so, they have broken with historical patterns of immigrants moving to central cities where housing and jobs were plentiful, and where they found others from their own background. Now many immigrants move directly to suburban areas from abroad.

While the more established gateways have seen suburban settlement taking place over a protracted period of time, one of the most prominent—and complicating—features of 21st century gateways is that they are, for the most part, metropolitan areas that are fairly suburban in form. They tend to be metropolitan areas that grew after World War II and feature large, lower-density, sprawling, automobile-oriented areas.

Although several of them, such as Charlotte, Phoenix and Austin, have large central cities stemming from annexation, those cities are suburban-like in the way they function, especially when contrasted with the dense cores in more established cities along the East Coast, in the Midwest and dotting the West Coast that received earlier waves of immigrants. This is not to say that some of the more established immigrant gateways are not suburban in form (think Los Angeles) or that immigrants are not living in suburbs in metro areas with a high proportion residing in central cities (think suburban New York, which runs through at least three neighboring states).

To explore some of the most recent trends, and the most recent challenges, we turn to a few examples of 21st century gateways. Although these metropolitan areas share many defining characteristics, such as the sudden influx of immigrants, the lack of recent history of immigration, and heavily suburban form of development, each has distinctive features.

We focus on two case examples that do not usually top the list of typical immigrant destinations: Atlanta and Sacramento.

Atlanta typifies immigration in metropolitan areas in "New South," a geography historically outside the trajectory of most immigrants that has become increasingly cosmopolitan, in part through immigration in the past few decades, and in part through domestic in-migration.

Sacramento, although it is the capital of California and located in a traditional settlement state, had been largely bypassed by immigrants during the mid-20th century, but began to see a rise in its foreign-born population during the 1980s and 1990s. Refugee resettlement has heavily impacted Sacramento's foreign-born.

ATLANTA: UNSETTLED IN THE SUBURBS

Atlanta offers an excellent example of an emerging gateway in the "New South." During the past few decades, many from within the United States and from abroad flocked to Atlanta as the metropolitan area's economy rapidly expanded with the acquisition of major national and multinational corporations. Atlanta is also home to one of the busiest airports in the world and is a major destination for conventions.

The work of historian Mary Odem shows that the racial and ethnic landscape of this traditionally black/white region began to change in the 1980s as Southeast Asian refugees were resettled in the area.

The foreign-born population comprised only 2 percent of the metro-area population in 1980, but by 1990 it had doubled to 4 percent. During the 1990s, Mexicans were drawn to the area by employment opportunities. With the exception of Dallas, another emerging gateway, Atlanta added more jobs than any other metropolitan area in the United States.

By 2000, the foreign-born were 10 percent of the population of metropolitan Atlanta, and by 2006 immigrants comprised more than 11 percent of the total population; a slight majority are Latin-American immigrants.

The city of Atlanta is a relatively small jurisdiction at the core of a sprawling metropolis. Thus, most of the population lives outside the city where, in 2005, 96 percent of metropolitan Atlanta's immigrants lived as well.

Atlanta is a region divided by race: Predominantly white residential areas are in the north and predominantly black neighborhoods in the south.

According to Odem's analysis, the foreign-born have not moved into areas in southwestern Atlanta and southern DeKalb County where the neighborhoods of the highest concentration of black residents are located. By contrast, however, clusters of immigrants have settled in central DeKalb County and northeastern Clayton County where African Americans comprise one-third of the population.

What has happened at the local suburban level is perhaps best represented by the recent histories of two mature suburban cities in northern DeKalb County, Chamblee and Doraville. Prior to 1970, these two places were largely white, blue-collar communities whose residents worked in nearby factories.

As the economy slowed down in the 1970s and factories closed, many residents began to leave the area, leaving vacant many commercial, industrial and residential properties lining major highways. At the same time, Atlanta began to resettle refugees in the region, and this area became a prime location for low-cost housing for refugee newcomers, with property managers eager to rent their properties.

By the 1980s, two rail stops on the regional train line made this an attractive area for other immigrants, particularly those from China, Korea and Latin America. By 1990, the Chamblee-Doraville area had become one of the most ethnically diverse in the Southeastern United States.

Non-Hispanic whites were almost 90 percent of Chamblee's population in 1980 but only 24 percent in 2000, while Latinos comprised 54 percent and Asians almost 15 percent. Numerous strip shopping malls along the major thoroughfare, the Buford Highway, are now lined with immigrant and ethnic enterprises.

Recently, Latin American and Asian immigrants, such as those from Vietnam and Korea, have been leaving the low-cost apartment complexes in Chamblee and Doraville as their economic situations have improved. They head north to more remote counties to purchase single-family homes. The formerly all-white suburbs of Gwinnett, northern Fulton and Cobb counties have also become increasingly diverse (home to immigrants and native-born blacks) and are equally characterized by clusters of ethnic business that have cropped up along major arteries.

Chamblee has responded to increasing diversity by embracing it as a means to attract developers, businesses and tourists, passing new zoning to create an International Village. But, in contrast, Chamblee passed an ordinance in 1996 forbidding people to "assemble on private property for the purpose of soliciting work as a day laborer without the permission of the property owner."

A host of local suburban areas have passed additional restrictive ordinances that affect everything from educational access to housing to law enforcement. For example, the County Board of Commissioners of Cherokee County, an area that has been attractive to increasing numbers of Latinos, passed legislation in 2006 that declared

English the official language of the county and that will penalize landlords who rent housing to undocumented immigrants. This reflects similar legislation that passed in Farmers Branch, an inner-ring suburb of the city of Dallas, but was recently struck down as unconstitutional by a federal judge.

At the state level, Georgia legislators have rejected bilingual education, placing their emphasis instead on programs that emphasize learning English quickly. In 2006, Georgia was one of the first states to pass legislation to address immigration issues, with the sweeping Georgia Security and Immigration Compliance Act.

This act instituted a range of restrictive measures related to unauthorized immigration, including denying tax-supported benefits to adults without status; requiring police to check status of anyone arrested for a felony and reporting those without status to federal authorities; and requiring proof of legal authorization to work on all state contracts. Since then, other states, such as Arizona and Oklahoma, have passed legislation in the absence of federal immigration reform.

While Atlanta, Dallas, Washington, DC and Phoenix offer good examples of what has been happening in emerging gateways, Portland (OR), Minneapolis-St. Paul and Sacramento offer case studies of what has been happening in re-emerging gateways. These metropolitan areas have something in common—a significant number of the foreign-born are refugees from Southeast Asia and Eastern Europe. The suburban patterns of settlement are equally characteristic of these metropolitan areas.

SACRAMENTO'S CHANGING SUBURBAN LANDSCAPE

Geographers Robin Datel and Dennis Dingemans identify a host of forces that have led to the re-emergence of Sacramento as a gateway of immigration. These include a history of immigrant settlement, the region's role as a refugee magnet, the availability of inexpensive suburban housing, and the demand for both "brain" and "brawn" migrants.

Sacramento had about 250,000 foreign-born residents in 2000, and it gained another 100,000 by 2006, making it 17.6 percent foreign-born. Forty-one percent of this population is from Asia; 33 percent from Latin America; and 11 percent from Eastern Europe. Furthermore, Sacramento ranked tenth among all U.S. metropolitan areas in the absolute number of refugees that were resettled between 1983 and 2004.

Immigrants have had an impact on the commercial and religious geography of suburban Sacramento communities, as well as on schools that have become increasingly diverse. Notably, Eastern European refugees have been attracted to Sacramento northeast of downtown, as well as to West Sacramento, where a previous generation of Russian immigrants made their home and where religious institutions (Baptist as well as Orthodox) are well established.

The other large refugee population settling in Sacramento is from Southeast Asia, particularly Vietnam and Laos, including many Hmong. Churches on the south side of Sacramento played an instrumental role in sponsoring refugees. Refugee service organizations, such as Sacramento Lao Family Community, Inc. and the Hmong Women's Heritage Association, sprang up in this area.

Southeast Asian refugees settled not only in the south side of the city but also in the adjacent, unincorporated and more suburban area of Sacramento County.

Since Hmong tend to have the lowest incomes among Asian immigrants, they have moved into less-expensive housing, either in the city or in the older inner suburbs.

The impact of the foreign-born on the suburban commercial landscape of Sacramento is significant. A Little Saigon has emerged along Stockton Boulevard, with 350 Asian businesses.

In another area of the city, along six miles of Franklin Boulevard, a Latino commercial strip has developed. Elsewhere in the city there are Korean and Slavic entrepreneurial clusters.

In addition to commercial enterprises, the foreign-born in Sacramento have made their mark on the suburban landscape through their houses of worship—Buddhist, Hindu, Sikh and Tao temples; mosques; Korean and Vietnamese Catholic churches; and Protestant iglesias. Fifty-eight churches in the region, most located in the suburbs, are associated with ex-Soviet immigrants.

In Sacramento, as in many other emerging, re-emerging and pre-emerging suburban gateways, the rapid increase in the foreign-born population is most dramatically felt in the schools. In the local media, several Sacramento radio stations sell air time to ethnic broadcasters, and newspapers in Vietnamese, Lao and Ukrainian are readily available.

The foreign-born also have an impact on the public landscape through their ethnic festivals and their sports activities. Major soccer tournaments are held in the suburbs, and cricket matches take place in the more prosperous suburban communities where South Asians have settled.

LOOKING AHEAD

Local places, whether cities, suburban communities or states, have responded in different ways to the presence of the foreign-born, particularly unauthorized immigrants. These responses have ranged from accommodating and inclusionary to hostile and exclusionary.

When these responses have been legislated through passing local or state ordinances, they reflect the frustrations that many public officials at the state and local level feel about the absence of federal movement on reforming federal immigration policy.

Many of these proposals and new laws affect access to jobs, housing, drivers' licenses and education. Some communities are passing laws that allow local law enforcement to work with federal immigration authorities; others are forbidding this kind of action.

In the inner-ring Dallas suburb of Farmers Branch, as noted above, the population voted to make it illegal for landlords to rent to unauthorized immigrants. In several suburban communities outside Washington, DC, measures regulating immigrant day labor sites, as well as those denying services to unauthorized immigrants, have been put into place. And several Atlanta suburbs have tightened housing occupancy codes, as well as passed English-language ordinances.

But it is equally important to note that in other local communities—often within the same metropolitan areas—programs and policies have been implemented to reach out to immigrants.

Another Dallas area community, Plano, has a number of outreach programs run by the library system, which offers popular language and literacy programs.

Austin and various other municipalities, including Prince George's County in suburban Washington, have joint police-bank programs to bring immigrants into mainstream banking practices as a way of reducing street crime targeted at immigrants. Many local areas use public money for formal day labor centers.

And mayors and other local elected officials have declared their jurisdictions as places of "sanctuary" that forbid local police to work with immigration authorities. Sanctuary cities include long-standing large gateways such as Los Angeles, San Francisco, Houston and New York. But the list also includes many 21st century gateways, such as Austin, Minneapolis, Portland (OR), Seattle and Washington, DC.

Although many of the more restrictive laws may eventually be struck down, they have fostered such intense debate that immigration has become an issue of major social significance in numerous local communities nationwide.

With national debate focused on border enforcement and legal status of immigrants, it's easy to overlook the fact that immigrants are local actors. They work in local firms, shops and factories, their children attend local schools, they join local religious congregations, they interact with municipal institutions. The locus of immigrant integration is the local community. This is where social, economic and civic integration happens.

Natural Allies or Irreconcilable Foes? Reflections on African-American/ Immigrant Relations

Andrew Grant-Thomas, Yusuf Sarfati & Cheryl Staats

For better and worse, attention to relations between African Americans and immigrants is sharply on the rise. In 2006, the Minutemen Civil Defense Corps chose to begin their national caravan against undocumented immigration from a park in an African-American neighborhood in Los Angeles. That same year, the Center for New Community in Chicago launched its national Which Way Forward campaign, hoping to nurture an informed debate among black Americans about the impact of immigration and the anti-immigration movement on their communities. Recent years have seen a spate of books and articles with such titles as *Help or Hindrance? The Economic Implications of Immigration for African Americans*, "The Real Face of the Immigration Debate? Explaining Attitudes toward Immigration among African Americans," and *On the Back of Blacks? Immigrants and the Fortunes of African Americans*.

In terms of dialogue, writing and programming, concern with "Black-Brown" relations is rampant. Of course, many immigrants are not Latino, and many Latinos are not immigrants. However, in light of the fact that fully two in five Latinos in the United States were born elsewhere, and that immigrants and their children comprise the majority of Latinos in this country, it is clear that immigrants are deeply implicated in the "Brown" part of the "Black-Brown" phenomenon. Why this surge of interest in African-American/immigrant relations?

Demographic trends provide a partial answer. One century after W.E.B. DuBois foretold that the problem of the 20th century would be the problem of the color line, our nation looks astoundingly different. In 1950, the United States was 90 percent white, and African Americans, heavily concentrated in the rural South and urban North, were the country's only significant minority population. Today, the country is 66 percent white, while Latinos and Asians living in metropolitan areas in the West and Southwest, their numbers fuelled by immigration, represent our fastest growing populations. Latinos now outnumber blacks nationally, and several states, and many of our largest cities, are already minority-majority. To some degree, then, sheer force of numbers itself compels interest.

Tensions and perceived tensions between the groups also draw attention. From gang violence to political representation, from labor concerns to negative stereotypes, black Americans and immigrants are contesting a range of issues. A pervasive media storyline that underscores instances of conflict while all but ignoring signs of cooperation only exacerbates the difficulties. In many communities, including some in the South, Midwest and Northeast previously characterized almost exclusively by black-white interactions, relations among people of color are more politically prominent than relations between whites and nonwhites.

Many progressives also note that during this generation-long era of deepening inequality between the most affluent Americans and everyone else, African Americans and immigrants number disproportionately among our nation's truly disadvantaged. The point could be made with respect to virtually any dimension of well-being, including poverty, health, wealth, education, criminal justice and civic engagement. Consider the present housing foreclosure crisis. United for a Fair Economy (UFE) reports that people of color are three times more likely than whites (55 percent vs.17 percent) to receive high-cost, subprime loans, with black and Latino neighborhoods being the hardest hit. UFE predicts that Latino and African-American households each stand to lose upwards of $100 billion over the next few years, largely eviscerating modest reductions in the racial wealth gap made over the last generation.

Increasingly, we hear nonprofit leaders, scholars, advocates, community members and even elected officials pushing the observation about the communities' common challenges a step further. Rather than succumb to largely structural inducements to regard each other as rivals, they argue, the interests of black Americans and immigrants would be well served by strategic collaboration between them. Echoing Dr. Martin Luther King, Jr.'s support for Cesar Chavez and the farm-workers four decades earlier, Reverend Jesse Jackson, Jr. wrote in the August 13, 2006 edition of *Motion Magazine* that the "new immigrant freedom movement must and is being embraced by African Americans and today's movement for peace and social justice . . . [T]he hands that picked the cotton are joining with the hands that picked the lettuce, connecting barrios and ghettos, fields and plantations."

The stakes involved in the course of African-American/immigrant relations extend beyond the groups themselves. Many progressives regard the communities as core constituents within any viable, broad-based movement for expanded social justice in the United States. In that light, the current tension tragically recapitulates the conflict between blacks and working-class whites that has long hampered the development of a multiracial, class-based social justice movement in the United States. If nothing else, that history underlines the error behind the presumption that alliances between black Americans and immigrants are either natural or inevitable. Indeed, the obstacles to the emergence of a robust partnership are almost as daunting as its possible benefits are attractive.

BUILDING EFFECTIVE ALLIANCES

Building effective alliances typically involves time, money, strong organizations and a measure of expertise, among other resources. Among people subject to the double jeopardy of living in poor families and neighborhoods, as blacks and Latinos disproportionately are, these resources are scarce. Political, economic and social conflicts of interest, coupled with a ragged history of power-sharing in places where one group has predominated and broad ignorance of each other's historical and current struggles, create a potentially volatile mix. Members of both groups too often interpret sociopolitical realities in positional, zero-sum terms, whereby gains for one side imply losses for the other.

In this context, cultural differences too readily become cultural clashes. Mutual mistrust, negative stereotyping and language barriers hinder attempts at communication. Institutional segregation—in workplaces and places of worship, for example— can reinforce cultural distance even when members of the two communities share neighborhoods. In that regard, the cynical manipulations of an aggressive nativist movement, built substantially on the leadership and organizational foundations of former white power activists, hardly help.

Differences in racial sensibilities add to these problems. Whereas many Latino and African immigrants do not embrace race as a primary identity marker, African Americans typically do. These differing perceptions about the salience and meaning of race can also create significant hurdles to constructive dialogue and joint action.

OBSERVATIONS FROM THE FIELD: OPPORTUNITIES AND STRATEGIES OF COMMUNITY ORGANIZING

With financial support from Public Interest Projects (the collaborative of funds that supported this project), we recently spoke to a number of African-American and immigrant activists and organizers to solicit their wisdom into the status of relations between their respective constituencies. While acknowledging the challenges, most were firm in their conviction that a robust set of opportunities for meaningful partnerships exists.

Alongside the admitted vulnerabilities of their communities, they see numerous strengths. They see that both groups command meaningful political, economic and social assets. They welcome the rapid emergence of whole categories of potential bridge-building leaders, including African, Caribbean and Afro-Latino immigrants, and multicultural youth. They celebrate the increasing number of promising venues for collaboration—worker centers, unions, schools and multiracial churches among them. Above all, the community leaders and organizers who shared their strategies and visions with us believe that the fates of Latinos, African Americans and immigrants in the United States are linked, and that it is past time that the advocacy and activism emanating from both communities better reflect that reality.

From our conversations, we identified a set of approaches based on alternative logics around which African-American/immigrant alliances are formed: intercultural relationship-building, issue-based organizing, and workplace-based organizing. These three do not exhaust the range of alliance-building efforts in the field; nor are they mutually exclusive. Some organizations employ multiple or hybrid strategies. Our descriptions refer to ideal types that may or may not correspond to the practices of particular initiatives on the ground.

Intercultural Relationship-building

Community organizers who use this approach aspire to build strong multicultural communities. For them, establishing healthy relationships among people of color is an important value in itself. Insofar as relationship-building reshapes identities and interests, it is also seen as a prerequisite for effective issue campaigns. These organizers suggest that interpersonal trust between the communities needs to be established first, and this can be done only by speaking to commonly held misconceptions through deliberate re-education. Without the trust born of solid relationships, racial and xenophobic tensions invariably emerge and partnership development becomes episodic at best. In sum, relationship-building measures must be central to the alliance and should precede any efforts at political or grassroots mobilization. Such measures can range from preparing simple cultural exchange events to engaging in specialized curriculums and trainings.

The Bay Area's Black Alliance for Just Immigration (BAJI), which grew out of the Priority Africa Network, is a prominent example of an organization that uses a relationship-building approach. BAJI's *African Diaspora Dialogues* program aims to forge closer relations between African immigrants and African Americans. In these informal conversations, activists create spaces for participants to tell their personal stories. These individual narratives help to expose the misconceptions each group harbors about the other. Reverend Kelvin Sauls, a BAJI co-founder, says that "the biggest tool that folks use to divide is ignorance." Nunu Kidane, network coordinator for the Priority Africa Network, affirms that dialogues have effectively challenged prejudicial frames and myths. She believes that "it has been phenomenally transformative in changing the way African Americans and African immigrants look at one another."

The Southeast Regional Economic Justice Network uses a similar relationship-first approach. Its *Resisting Rivalry* project is an effort to build intentional relationships among youth, women and low-wage workers of African-American and Latino immigrant communities. *Resisting Rivalry* provides extensive education through focus groups and workshops, among other methods. Another promising program, *South by Southwest*, was launched through the partnership among Southern Echo, Southwest Organizing Project and Southwest Workers' Union. These organizations use historical narratives and art as a way to transform the identities of their constituents and create cultural bridges. The program "brings together African-American and Latino communities from three states—New Mexico, Texas and Mississippi—to share histories and current realities in each state from the perspective of grassroots struggles, and at the same time develop trust between all of the participants." In this program, participants learn about the shared histories of Mexico and the United States. Leroy Johnson, executive director of Southern Echo, asserts that "we have to start with the historical and cultural perspectives of the different communities and how these histories come together." Art, including poetry, writing and photography, is utilized to explicate the cultural-historical linkages.

Lastly, some organizers use toolkits and curricular materials to dissolve barriers and create inclusive, empathetic space for participants. The *Crossing Borders* curriculum, developed by the Center for Community Change, Fair Immigration Reform Movement, and CASA de Maryland, is one important example. This curriculum includes activities that inform African Americans about the global forces that propel immigration to the United States and the relation between racism and the immigration debate. For immigrants, it provides important information about the history of the civil rights struggle in the U.S., the centrality of African Americans in the struggle, and the structures that constrain black American communities today.

The National Network for Immigrant and Refugee Rights and the Highlander Research Center have prepared a similar toolkit, *Building a Race and Immigration Dialogue in the Global Era (BRIDGE)*. The curriculum includes "a set of popular educational tools and exercises designed to engage the immigrant and refugee community members in a dialogue about racism, labor, migration and global economic structures in relation to migration."

Issue-based Organizing

Some community activists place a premium on collaboration around issues of mutual concern rather than on trust-building. As noted above, immigrant and African-American communities share many important concerns. Both suffer the racialization of the criminal justice system, racial profiling and police brutality. In many low-opportunity neighborhoods, immigrant and African-American children have low academic performances and high dropout rates in underresourced public schools. Thus, funding for public education emerges as a common cause. These shared concerns turn into opportunities to the extent that advocates act on the recognition that progressive policy reform in these areas would benefit all communities of color.

Issue-based organizing acknowledges the importance of relationship-building. However, the community organizers who embrace this approach argue that the best way to build solidarity across lines of race, ethnicity and nativity is through appeals to shared "bread and butter" interests. Trust develops most surely as a byproduct of common struggle, preferably one that yields tangible successes. With reference to immigrants, Bill Chandler, executive director of the Mississippi Immigrants' Rights Alliance, suggested that the "first step is to connect with the African-American community because you're dealing with common issues, including racism, which here in the South, particularly in Mississippi, but also in Alabama and Georgia, is driving the attack on immigrants." In contrast, these organizers claim, intergroup relationship challenges, as such, provide uncertain motivation for partnerships, especially among poor and working-class people likely to have more pressing concerns. "Issue-first" alliances are typically formed between organizations, rather than within particular organizations.

The 2006 campaign against racial profiling in Portland, Oregon by the Center for Intercultural Organizing, Oregon Action, the Latino Network, and Northwest Constitutional Rights Center, exemplified this kind of organizing. This issue was salient for all of the organizations. As noted by Jo Ann Bowman, Executive Director of Oregon Action, "We realized at that time that this was a severe community problem and challenge that we needed to take some formal action on." The organizations approached the mayor to request a series of listening sessions between the public and the police. After these sessions, the organizations wrote a report in December 2006 that was presented to the police chief and City Council. Since that time, a community organization has been established to track complaints about the police. In addition, the City Council created a racial profiling committee that includes representatives from a range of community groups whose constituencies are most affected by racial profiling.

Workplace-based Organizing

In some sectors of the economy, especially in low-paying jobs, African Americans and immigrants work side-by-side, making workplaces, along with schools, the frontlines of de facto negotiations between the groups. These sectors include construction work, the hotel industry, restaurants and the meatpacking industry. Some workplaces are home to initiatives that operate in the absence of formal coalitions. Unlike initiatives shaped by the first two approaches, these initiatives mobilize constituents not around their identities as "African Americans," "immigrants," or people of color, but around their common identity as workers. In other words, the goal of the organization is not to support immigrant or African-American issues, as such, but to promote worker issues. Organizers tend to emphasize the salience of associational rather than communal identities.

Perhaps the most visible of these initiatives is the "Justice at Smithfield" campaign, which began in 1994 at the biggest hog-processing plant in the United States, in Tar Heel, North Carolina. This initiative is based on the attempt of workers to unionize, to improve health and safety conditions in the plant, and to democratize their job environment. Latinos, mostly immigrants, constitute 60 percent of the workforce of the plant; 30 percent of the workers are African Americans. A 2007 report prepared for the Chief Justice Earl Warren Institute at the University of California-Berkeley details different grassroots solidarity initiatives emerging between Latino immigrants and African-American laborers similar to the "Justice at Smithfield" campaign.

Another successful mobilization occurred in the restaurant industry in New York City, when the Restaurant Opportunities Center of New York (ROC-NY) was formed in the aftermath of 9/11 with the workers who lost their jobs at the famous Windows on the World restaurant in the World Trade Center. The organization, composed of Latino, African-American, African immigrant, Arab, Asian and white restaurant workers, has enjoyed solid successes, winning over $1,000,000 for restaurant workers from employers, following charges of discrimination and unpaid wages.

The organization also opened COLORS, a cooperatively owned restaurant that serves dinners featuring global cuisine in the evenings and serves as the location for the COLORS Hospitality Opportunities for Workers training institute during the day. Saru Jayaraman, one of ROC-NY's co-founders, reported that members of ROC-NY are mobilized as restaurant workers, rather than as Blacks, Latinos or Arabs. She believes that "people absolutely feel a lot more identity as a restaurant worker, in my experience, than they do as an immigrant worker."

CONCLUDING OBSERVATIONS

African Americans and immigrants are neither natural allies nor irreconcilable foes. The potential benefits of greater collaboration between them are real, but so, too, are the challenges to realizing those benefits. After talking to dozens of advocates and activists across the country engaged in this critical work, we find reasons for optimism. From the worlds of advocacy and philanthropy, and from the communities themselves, more people are calling for and supportive of strong, sustained partnerships. Groups such as the Applied Research Center, Highlander Education and Research Center, the Center for Community Change, the Center for New Community, and our own Kirwan Institute for the Study of Race and Ethnicity promote powerful analyses that discern the roots of intergroup tension in macro-economic dynamics such as globalization and policy developments like NAFTA. These analyses recognize that our fates are linked across lines of race, ethnicity and class.

While each geographic region of the country generates its own dynamic, organizers identified several common needs. These include a comprehensive mapping of alliance-building efforts across the country; the collection and dissemination of existing educational and relationship-building curricular materials; the development of new materials adaptable to regional and local contexts; the identification, commissioning and dissemination of applied research studies and instructive case studies of African-American/immigrant alliances and other forms of "joint action"; the creation of curricular materials targeted to community organizations and residents who wish to guard against African-American/immigrant divides in their communities; and the development of fact-based media frames and talking points for local, state and federal policymakers that go beyond mere "myth-busting."

Ongoing efforts and evident opportunities for collaboration are grounds for hope about the future of African-American/immigrant alliance-building work, but more support is needed to bring these opportunities to fruition. Creating alliances that endure and prosper is a challenging task that requires considerable resources. Organizers also highlighted the need for more grassroots leadership training and institutional capacity-building so that the viability of partnerships does not rely on the health of particular interpersonal relationships alone. The importance of building the field and sharing knowledge and resources among the community organizers undertaking this work cannot be overstated. The prospects are promising but will only be fully realized with additional support and continued dedication.

Transportation and Civil Rights

Thomas W. Sanchez & Marc Brenman

This article is the authors' updated version of their Introduction to their 2007 book The Right to Transportation: Moving to Equity. *We then asked several transportation-knowledgeable commentators to respond—that Forum appears directly following the article—CH*

Transportation is vital. The Supreme Court has recognized the right to travel as one of the fundamental rights guaranteed by the Fourteenth Amendment to the U.S. Constitution. The Universal Declaration of Human Rights, at Article 13, states, "Everyone has the right to freedom of movement and residence within the borders of each state." Given this important role, it is expected that policymakers, advocates and users battle over transportation policy and its implementation. Too often, however, those battles are over specific project funding and construction in particular states, congressional districts, towns and neighborhoods, and scant attention is paid to larger social and economic effects.

The history of the Civil Rights Movement shows the importance of transportation to people of color. In the slavery-era South, African Americans had to possess passes to travel off their plantations. The Underground Railroad, while symbolic and not a real mode of transportation, signified escape to freedom. In 1955, the arrest of Rosa Parks for refusing to give her seat on a bus to a white rider sparked the Montgomery bus boycott. Freedom Riders faced violent attacks to assert the rights of African Americans to ride on integrated buses traveling interstate. Today, we have recurrent issues of racial profiling and police stops for "driving while black and brown." Many past and current transportation policies have limited the life chances of minorities and other traditionally discriminated against people by preventing timely access to places and opportunities at an acceptable level of accessibility, service, quality and safety.

442

Americans have become increasingly mobile and reliant on automobiles to meet their travel needs, due largely to transportation policies adopted after World War II that emphasized highway development over public transportation. According to recent Census estimates, less than 5 percent of urban work trips were made by public transit; however, this varies significantly by race and location. Minorities are less likely to own cars than whites and are more often dependent on public transportation. Cold numbers are brought to life by examples like Hurricane Katrina, where many African Americans could not evacuate due to lack of transportation. The "transit-dependent" rely on public transportation not only to travel to work but also to get to school, obtain medical care, attend religious services, and shop for basic necessities such as groceries. These needs intertwine, often for the worse. For example, lack of accessibility to fresh and healthy food leads to health problems, such as obesity and high blood pressure. The transit-dependent are often people with low incomes, and face economic inequities because transportation policies, and enormous subsidies of public funds, are oriented toward travel by car.

Through the years, a number of key Supreme Court civil rights decisions hinged on transportation issues, including ones concerning the right of owners to pursue fleeing slaves across state lines (*Dred Scott v. Sandford*, 1857), and creating the "separate but equal" concept of provision of services to African Americans (*Plessy v. Ferguson*, 1896).

THE MODERN CIVIL RIGHTS MOVEMENT AND TRANSPORTATION

Nearly 100 years after the *Dred Scott* decision, civil rights and transportation issues persisted. As alluded to above, on December 1, 1955, Rosa Parks, a black seamstress and civil rights activist, was arrested for refusing to obey a Montgomery, Alabama, bus driver's order to give her seat up for a boarding white passenger as required by city ordinance. Such municipal and state laws designed to separate the races were common in the South at the time. Outrage in Montgomery's black community over the arrest sparked a boycott against the city's bus line—the Montgomery bus boycott, one crucial incident igniting the modern Civil Rights Movement. The Rev. Dr. Martin Luther King, Jr. emerged as the president of the Montgomery Improvement Association (MIA), which organized the boycott. As the MIA's demands expanded beyond open bus seating to include more equal access to other municipal services, white opposition increased. Preaching nonviolence, Dr. King was convinced that the cause could be won through a combination of dignified behavior and economic pressure on the part of the protesters.

The boycott ended in December 1956, over a year after it began. The U.S. Supreme Court ruled that segregation on city buses was unconstitutional. Desegregation of buses took place on December 20, 1956, after federal injunctions were served on the City and bus company officials, forcing them to follow the ruling. There was also a little-known six-month bus boycott in Tallahassee, Florida, in 1956, which was not successful in desegregating local bus service.

Another famous challenge to racial discrimination and transportation took place when a mixed group of whites and blacks, called Freedom Riders, was sent by the Congress Of Racial Equality (CORE) in May 1961 to lead a campaign forcing integration in bus terminals and challenging segregation in local interstate travel. Congressman John Lewis, a pioneer of the modern Civil Rights Movement and one of the original 13 Freedom Riders, has said: "It was almost impossible for blacks and whites to travel together from Washington, DC through the South to New Orleans . . . you had signs saying, 'White Waiting,' 'Colored Waiting,' 'White Men,' 'Colored Men,' 'White Women,' 'Colored Women.' Segregation was the order of the day. There was a tremendous amount of fear . . . the Ride was going to test this decision, try to desegregate these places, but also . . . take the Civil Rights Movement into the heart of deep South."

At bus terminals, the black Freedom Riders would go to the white dining areas and waiting rooms, while the white Freedom Riders would go to the area reserved for blacks. The buses were attacked by mobs in Anniston, Alabama, where one bus was destroyed by a firebomb. There were riots in Birmingham and Montgomery, Alabama, when blacks attempted to use facilities reserved for whites; federal marshals and the National Guard were called out to restore order and escort the Freedom Riders to Mississippi. Many were arrested in Jackson, Mississippi, for violating the state's segregation laws, and a long series of court battles began. These protests led in 1961 to an Interstate Commerce Commission ban on segregation in all interstate transportation facilities.

TITLE VI OF THE CIVIL RIGHTS ACT OF 1964

Title VI of the Civil Rights Act of 1964 prohibits discrimination on the basis of race, color or national origin by recipients of federal financial assistance. It applies to all recipients of federal aid, such as state departments of transportation, metropolitan planning organizations (MPOs) and transit agencies. It also applies to all programs run by federal aid recipients, regardless of whether the specific program is federally funded. Prohibited discrimination includes denial of benefits or services, provision of inferior benefits or services, segregation, and any other treatment of an individual or a group differently and adversely because of race, color or national origin. The federal courts have defined these criteria to include limited English proficiency and accent based on national origin or race. For example, a Title VI violation would occur if a state transportation agency decided to furnish replacement housing to whites but not to people of color being displaced because of a highway project.

In 2001, the U.S. Supreme Court in *Alexander v. Sandoval* ended the ability of private individuals to bring suit to enforce Title VI regulations. Federal regulations under Title VI prohibit recipients of federal funds from conducting activities that have a less favorable effect or "disparate impact" on members of one racial or ethnic group than on another. Disparate impact is discrimination that results from methods of program administration or facially neutral practices that, though uniformly applied to all persons, nonetheless have the effect of disproportionately excluding members of a protected class; denying them an aid, benefit or service; or providing them a lower level of service than others. Now individuals may bring lawsuits charging a violation of Title VI only when they can prove that an action was taken intentionally to discriminate. It is much harder to prove discrimination by intent than by disparate impact. Individuals can no longer rely solely on statistical evidence to show that an action had a disparate impact on persons of a specific race, color or national origin.

Federal agencies still can and must enforce these regulations. Individuals and groups can still file administrative complaints with federal agencies. These are supposed to be investigated and findings made. Federal agencies may suspend or terminate funding to obtain compliance with Title VI or may seek equitable relief, such as an injunction. However, this is rarely done, and there are allegations that federal agencies are not sufficiently vigorous in their enforcement of the law. Today, an agency like the Environmental Protection Agency has a backlog of approximately 300 Title VI complaints that it has not investigated or made findings on. The *Sandoval* decision argues for the federal government to more rigorously enforce Title VI because private lawsuits are now severely limited.

Federal agencies such as the Federal Highway Administration and the Federal Transit Administration have issued guidance on Title VI and environmental justice. In addition, Executive Order 12898 requires federal agencies to achieve environmental justice by "identifying and addressing disproportionately high and adverse human health or environmental effects of its programs, policies, and activities on minority populations and low-income populations." The adverse impacts the Executive Order speaks of include "the denial of, reduction in, or significant delay in the receipt of, benefits of DOT programs, policies, or activities." (DOT Order, 62 Fed. Reg. at 18381) The duty to "identify and address" these adverse impacts falls not just on the federal agencies, but also on their funding recipients. But the guidance has failed to address the concerns most often raised by community groups about the accumulation of negative economic and environmental impacts caused by transportation projects, their location, and the distribution of resources and services across metropolitan communities. The guidance called for processes to review potential Title VI or environmental justice issues, but established no thresholds, expectations or standards. There is still debate as to what exactly is required, though a recent administrative complaint finding in 2010, in *Urban Habitat Program et al. v. Bay Area Rapid Transit* (BART) has indicated the need for a federal funding recipient to conduct an equity analysis of the impact of major service changes and fare increases on minority and low-income populations. In this case, BART wanted to extend a transit line to the Oakland Airport using stimulus funds provided by the American Reinvestment and Recovery Act. The line would have replaced existing bus shuttle service, but at double the fare; the complaint also challenged the elimination from the half-billion dollar, 3.2 mile project of intermediate stops that would have provided low-income and minority residents of the surrounding East Oakland neighborhood with access to retail and hotel jobs along the way. Finding that BART had failed to conduct the required equity analysis, FTA withdrew $70 million in stimulus funds from the project.

BART had initially claimed that it met the requirement in its environmental impact study for the project. But attempts to graft transportation equity onto environmental review requirements have not been notably successful. An example of this failure is the construction in 2004 of a site for building a highway bridge parts on the site of a large Native American burial ground in Port Angeles, Washington. Although an extensive environmental impact statement was prepared, it failed to notice the burial site.

THE BROADER FRAMEWORK

In a broader sense, transportation equity is also about environmental justice, metropolitan equity and the just distribution of resources. These concepts represent an evolution in how civil rights and transportation are interrelated—especially when we look back on the early cases involving slave transport and the events precipitating the Montgomery bus boycott. These debates involve difficult and unsettled issues of what constitutes equity, justice and opportunity. A further debate involves looking forward versus repairing the errors and injustices of the past. The concept of affirmative action never took hold in transportation equity, and now, as the federal courts have largely discarded affirmative action, that window of opportunity may be gone. The current economic crisis in the U.S. means that transportation-disadvantaged people are stuck with the vestiges of a crumbling transportation infrastructure that never did serve them well. Instead, resources are put into dreamy and expensive projects like high-speed rail that will be prohibitively expensive for them to ride, and will cut through their communities one more time. Strong enforcement of a robust equity analysis requirement, on the other hand, could inject some meaningful "affirmative" requirements into the process of allocating billions of dollars for transportation projects. U.S. DOT's environmental justice order, for instance, requires an analysis "to identify, early in the development of the program, policy or activity, the risk of discrimination so that positive corrective action can be taken."

MORE RECENT CASES

One of the major breakthroughs of the transportation equity movement came when the Los Angeles Metropolitan Transportation Authority (LAMTA) and the Los Angeles Bus Riders Union, a project of the Labor/Community Strategy Center, negotiated a consent decree as part of a court settlement in 1996. In the case, *Labor/Community Strategy Center and Los Angeles Bus Riders Union v. Los Angeles Metropolitan Transportation Authority*, the court was asked to find that LAMTA had provided inferior services to Los Angeles's largely minority and low-income bus riders. Furthermore, LAMTA was directing resources to its commuter rail lines, which served a more affluent and primarily white population, at the expense of its bus users. Prior to trial, the judge directed that the parties work to settle the case. This settlement included hundreds of millions of dollars for new buses, which are ridden primarily by people of color and low-income people.

The economic downturn has caused many transit providers across the country to consider or institute cutbacks in services or fare hikes. Since a high percent of bus riders are people of color and low-income, these cutbacks disproportionately affect those who are already transportation-disadvantaged. For example, in the Washington, DC area, the Washington Metropolitan Area Transportation Authority increased fares by 20 percent for buses, and 15 percent for Metrorail. Metrorail is a heavy-rail system ridden primarily by suburban commuters and tourists. The Transportation Equity Network (TEN) and the Gamaliel Foundation are monitoring such impacts and advocating for greater attention toward public transportation needs.

Other civil rights cases are working their way through the courts, including a suit filed in 2010 by Arlington, Virginia, alleging that state and federal transportation officials violated Title VI in proposing to build high-occupancy toll lanes along a major highway that cuts through minority areas. It alleges that services to people of color along the corridor would be decreased, in favor of whiter and higher-income commuters from the outer suburbs. Once again, the realities of separated housing both drive transportation issues and are their effect. The U.S. District Court in the case, *County Board of Arlington v. Department of Transportation, et al.*, has permitted it to go forward. As noted above, however, it is notoriously difficult for civil rights intent cases to be proved.

Debate over the new surface transportation funding bill continues, with the bill on hold as of this writing. One element of the debate is how to fund surface transportation. The current method, based on a fuel tax paid by users, is drying up. We hope that it is replaced with a more equitable system, because currently it constitutes a flat tax that has economically regressive effects on low-income people. Economic issues inevitably intercede in transportation debates. Another example is the current popularity of tolling of roads, bridges and tunnels. If instituted simply, such tolls also have economically regressive effects. The long-term implications for declining social mobility in the U.S. are disturbing. There are methods around the problem, such as using some of the new tolling revenues to purchase more public transportation. But in the current poisonous partisan atmosphere, will there be room for such rational debate and solutions?

Another critical equity issue before Congress in the funding bill is the restoration of federal operating assistance for transit. Until it was eliminated by the Gingrich Congress, federal subsidies had supported not just transit capital projects, but also operations. The lack of adequate operating revenue often hits the local bus systems used by minority and low-income riders the hardest, since those systems are unable to recover the same farebox revenues as deluxe commuter rail systems that cater to a more affluent ridership. An early victory in restoring operating assistance was an amendment to the stimulus bill in Spring 2009 that allowed up to 10 percent of ARRA transit funds to be used for operating purposes. Many eyes are currently on a bill that would authorize $2 billion for emergency transit operating assistance for transit systems across the country.

In May 2010, the State of Arizona passed controversial anti-immigrant legislation, SB 1070, with provisions that many social justice advocates regard as discriminatory and punitive against Latinos. The American Civil Liberties Union, the Mexican American Legal Defense and Education Fund, and the National Immigrant Law Center have filed suit in federal court to challenge the legality of the statute. One of the causes of action in the suit concerns the constitutionally protected right to travel. It states that the Privileges and Immunities Clause of the U.S. Constitution, art. IV, § 2, cl. 1 and the Fourteenth Amendment prevent states from infringing upon the right to travel, including the right to be treated as a welcome visitor rather than an unfriendly alien when temporarily present in another state, without a rational or compelling justification. The suit states that SB 1070 interferes with the rights of out-of-state citizens to travel freely through the State of Arizona without being stopped, interrogated and detained. This resonates with the Freedom Rider cases, and shows how transportation concepts continue to be viable in the pursuit of civil rights.

WHAT IS TRANSPORTATION EQUITY?

Transportation mobility is a hallmark of full membership in American society. The early challenges related to racial discrimination and segregation involved discriminatory practices that directly limited transportation access and mobility of people of color. The effects of limited transportation mobility persist. The lack of mobility helped create ghettos, de facto segregated schools and housing, and social and community isolation and lack of cohesion. Opportunities for civic participation and public involvement were physically cut off. Promises made by the leadership of the dominant society, such as housing to replace that destroyed in "blight clearing" projects, are often unfulfilled. Whites in suburbs have forgone physical mobility for social cohesion, while destroyed inner-city neighborhoods have been left with neither mobility nor social cohesion.

Efforts to challenge discrimination, segregation and inequitable transportation policies have become increasingly sophisticated, encompassing a broad range of related social impacts. The term transportation equity refers to a range of strategies and policies that address inequities in the nation's transportation planning and project delivery system. Community-based organizations of low-income and minority residents, with the important involvement and leadership of faith-based organizations, are recognizing transportation's significant role in shaping local opportunities and disinvestment. Though the definition of transportation equity varies from place to place, most of these community residents would agree that an equitable transportation system should:

- Ensure opportunities for meaningful public involvement in the transportation planning process, particularly for those communities that most directly feel the impact of projects or funding choices.
- Be held to a high standard of public accountability and financial transparency.
- Distribute the benefits and burdens from transportation projects equally across all income levels and communities.
- Provide high-quality services—emphasizing access to economic opportunity and basic mobility—to all communities, but with an emphasis on transit-dependent populations.
- Equally prioritize efforts both to revitalize poor and minority communities and to expand transportation infrastructure.
- Repair some of the damage caused by previous policies that fueled urban disinvestment and suburban sprawl.

CONCLUSION

Transportation infrastructure can displace residents and permanently damage community structure and integrity. Both the construction and operation of infrastructure can impair (or benefit) walkability and livability. Use of motor vehicles and rail cause air pollution, noise and pedestrian hazards, disproportionately affecting people living near them. Preferential investments in auto-centered transport have generated a transit-dependent subclass that has substantial barriers to access. Transportation systems facilitate race-, ethnic- and class-based segregation, contributing to environmental injustice.

On-road mobile sources contribute to the highest health risks near major roadways. Land use decisions should be made with an attempt to protect sensitive individuals where air pollution is expected. There are lessons to be learned from environmental law and process. At the scoping stage in the National Environmental Policy Act (NEPA) process, there should be adequate consideration of Title VI and environmental justice. Minority and low-income populations should be identified early and their concerns examined and addressed, at the planning stage. Cumulative impacts need to be considered. The precautionary principle should be invoked. As the recent massive and catastrophic oil leaks in the Gulf of Mexico have shown, categorical exclusions to the need for a proper environmental impact statement (EIS) cannot be lightly granted by federal agencies. But even an EIS is not a solution if social needs and cultural history are not properly considered, as was shown in the

Port Angeles case. The responsibilities of planners are more than legal, because a conservative federal judiciary has undercut legal requirements. Planners' responsibilities are also moral and ethical. Just as a number of faith-based organizations have undertaken environmental concerns due to a sense of responsibility for stewardship of God's creation, planners need to get back to their roots of responsibility.

Solutions need to be sought, not just by advocates and not just in faith, but also in legislatures and Congress. Fixing the *Sandoval* decision, returning the "private attorney general" provision for private right of suit under Title VI, and incorporating environmental justice concepts into statute would be important steps. Also important is avoiding panic-driven decisions to cut public transportation services to those who most need them. The ARRA "shovel-ready project" concept has led to funding too many pothole-filling efforts. The larger American polity needs to be considered, with a return to the American creed of social mobility and opportunity.

* * * * *

COMMENTARIES

GUILLERMO MAYER, ANGELA GLOVER BLACKWELL, EUGENE B. BENSON, WADE HENDERSON, DAVID RUSK & LAURA BARRETT

Guillermo Mayer

To combat structural racism in transportation, federal statutory and regulatory reforms are needed. Existing legal frameworks exclude communities of color and low-income populations from an equitable share in the benefits of transportation investments. Some of these barriers come in the guise of seemingly innocuous and "race-neutral" policies that so far have largely escaped Title VI and environmental justice scrutiny. One significant example is the capital-only restriction imposed by Congress on the use of federal transit dollars. This restriction has the effect of starving urban transit systems of the funding they need to operate existing and expanded transit service for their large transit-dependent and minority populations. Instead, the restriction favors the construction of expensive, mostly rail, capital projects that generally benefit disproportionately white and affluent "choice riders." The biases inherent in these policies have been slowly unmasked over the years by advocates in places like the San Francisco Bay Area, and are now being exposed nationally by a timely convergence of environmental justice, labor, transit and equity advocates pursuing federal legislation to fund transit operations.

Other legal barriers, such as the *Alexander v. Sandoval* case that Sanchez and Brenman refer to, will require an even greater political "lift" to undo. A concerted effort in Congress to legislatively override *Sandoval* was in the works last year, but the legislation was not introduced. In the meantime, a parallel effort by the Transit Riders for Public Transportation campaign—a national coalition of grassroots groups representing transit riders in cities such as Los Angeles, New York, Chicago, Atlanta and New Orleans—has generated awareness and support for a partial *Sandoval* fix in the upcoming transportation reauthorization bill.

As the debate over the transportation reauthorization continues into next year, advocates appear to be well poised to pursue an array of legislative proposals to advance transportation equity.

Angela Glover Blackwell

Transportation is back as a major civil rights issue. Today's focus is not on getting a seat at the front of the bus but on making sure the bus takes us where we need to go.

As Sanchez and Brenman point out, stark and persistent inequities exist in our nation's transportation system. Past transportation practices have resulted in skewed patterns of regional growth; destabilized neighborhoods; increased air pollution; contributed to the rise of obesity and other chronic conditions; and cut off many communities from meaningful work opportunities. All these consequences are worse for low-income people and communities of color.

Yet transportation investments have enormous potential to catalyze the development of communities of opportunity. Sanchez and Brenman describe several community organizations that have achieved admirable transportation equity victories. If such success stories guide federal policy, communities across the United States will benefit.

The authorization of our nation's surface transportation program will fundamentally shape our communities for years to come. With up to $500 billion at stake, social equity advocates must show Congress and the Obama administration a full picture of the benefits of an equitable, reformed transportation system—one that ensures access, mobility, and economic and social opportunity for all people and communities.

PolicyLink and Transportation for America recently convened leaders from transportation, civil rights, health, community development, environmental justice, labor and faith organizations to advance four principles for the federal transportation authorization:

1. Create affordable transportation options for all people.
2. Ensure access to quality jobs, workforce development and contracting opportunities in the transportation industry.
3. Promote healthy, safe and inclusive communities.
4. Invest equitably and focus on results.

Charting a new course for our transportation system will not be easy. But like winning the right to sit anywhere on a bus, it takes us closer toward creating a stronger, more inclusive nation.

Eugene B. Benson

Sanchez and Brenman do a good job setting forth equity problems caused by a national, state and local transportation system that all too often shortchanges lower-income people and people of color. The Boston area is one example. In metropolitan Boston, government subsidizes the commutes of higher-income suburban white riders six times as much as it subsidizes the commutes of lower-income urban riders of color—and has spent more than two decades extending rail to distant suburbs, underfunding public transit, and allowing subways to deteriorate to the point that delays are commonplace; and a 2009 study reported that parts of the subway system are unsafe to ride.

In Boston, the T Riders Union and On the Move: The Greater Boston Transportation Justice Coalition have been organizing transit riders and groups to fight for first-class service and transit equity—and they have achieved victories but not yet the systemic change that is required. On the Move has adopted this transportation justice agenda: 1) A public transit system that is reliable, affordable and safe, works for all riders, is equitable across transit types, and recognizes the special importance of public transit to people who cannot afford automobiles; 2) A transportation system in which clean air, environmental protection, environmental justice and protection of the public health are top priorities and in which no community is overburdened with pollution or other adverse impacts of transportation; 3) A transportation funding system that provides adequate funds for reliable, affordable and safe urban transit and safe bicycle and pedestrian spaces on all our streets; 4) A transportation planning system in which transportation improvements further the creation of diverse livable communities with housing affordable to all income levels; and 5) A transportation decision-making system that is democratic, open, transparent and accountable to transit riders, and in which transit-dependent riders have a seat at the table.

It is time for the federal government to require transportation justice, insist that transit riders be at the decision-making table, and no longer accept a meaningless equity check-off box on funding forms.

Wade Henderson

The American Dream is premised on the bedrock of equal opportunity—the ideal that those who live in the United States should have equal access to quality education, employment, housing, and certainly transportation, which most directly affects access to all of those things. That's why The Leadership Conference on Civil and Human Rights is committed to seeking greater equity in transportation policy and mobility for all people.

When decisions are made about transportation resources and funding, those decisions are rarely made in consultation with or in consideration of low-income people who tend to rely heavily on public transportation as their main access to services. Not surprisingly, transportation spending programs do not benefit all populations equally; and the negative impacts of some transportation decisions—dissecting neighborhoods of low-income families and people of color, physically isolating them from needed services and businesses, and disrupting once-stable communities, among other things—are broadly felt and have lasting effects.

In many ways, the current fight to end these injustices is a continuation of the struggle that an earlier generation of civil rights champions fought to end segregated transportation policies. Rosa Parks' refusal to give up her seat and her subsequent arrest sparked the Montgomery Bus Boycott. Likewise, the Freedom Riders helped bring an end to segregated bus terminals in interstate travel. Over the years, the fight has expanded to seek greater access for minority and disadvantaged communities to transportation-related jobs.

Notwithstanding the heroic efforts and the monumental social and economic gains made over the decades, transportation equity remains a key civil rights priority. Transportation provides access to opportunity and serves as a key component in addressing poverty, unemployment and equal opportunity goals. Now is the time to ensure transportation equity for all people.

David Rusk

Assessing his 25 years as local Urban League executive, Rochester Mayor Bill Johnson memorably observed: "For years we prepared ourselves to walk through doors opened by the Civil Rights Revolution . . . but all that time, we failed to realize that real opportunity was being relentlessly relocated beyond our grasp."

"Transportation drives development," author/developer Chris Leinberger writes, and the highway-driven relocation of good jobs—"job sprawl"—ever farther from where the great majority of African Americans and Hispanics live has been federal/ state transportation policies' worst anti-civil rights impact.

By 2006, the Brookings Institution reports, 45 percent of jobs in our 98 largest metro areas were located more than 10 miles from the urban core. With job losses hitting city and inner-suburban employers hardest, the next post-recession survey will probably show over half of all jobs beyond the 10-mile zone.

Building One America, a coalition of grassroots regional equity organizations and fair housing groups (including PRRAC) forcefully advocates that the next surface transportation authorization act must make creating racially and economically integrated communities an essential condition of any federal transportation assistance wherever development occurs—whether in outer suburban "greenfields" or older suburban and inner-city "brownfields" (especially in transit-oriented developments). Our policy proposals for reforming a wide range of federal programs are set forth in "Building Sustainable, Inclusive Communities," accessible at http://www. prrac.org/ pdf/SustainableInclusiveCommunities.pdf.

Laura Barrett

Tom Sanchez's and Marc Brenman's "Transportation and Civil Rights" provides important context for the struggles the Transportation Equity Network is engaged in every day. Our many members across 41 states—especially people of color and low-income people—are living out the civil rights struggle for equitable transportation access in their work.

TEN is building leaders in our 350 member organizations who are working to transform the next surface transportation authorization act. As the chapter's authors point out, the bill is a crucial one. It will determine how half a trillion dollars in federal transportation funds will be spent in the coming years—and they must be spent differently than in the past. Among TEN's priorities for the bill are restoring the civil rights protections that have been eroded in recent years; instituting meaningful workforce equity requirements for federally funded transportation construction projects; and shifting the overwhelming focus on highway construction toward a fairer balance with the transit systems that low-income people and people of color disproportionately rely on.

With the bill's timing uncertain, the question is what Americans can do right now. Again, the authors point to a crucial battleground: the shortfalls in transit operating funds that are leading to service cuts and fare hikes in 84 percent of our nation's transit systems. TEN is working to build support for bills by Rep. Russ Carnahan (D-MO) and Sen. Sherrod Brown (D-OH) that would let states use more federal funds for operating costs to keep these systems running.

If emergency transit operating funds do become available—and when a comprehensive transportation spending bill is passed—the work of local groups will be crucial to make sure that state departments of transportation and metropolitan planning organizations allocate money in ways that produce equitable results.

Right to the City:
Social Movement and Theory

Jacqueline Leavitt, Tony Roshan Samara & Marnie Brady

THE CITY AS A CENTRAL FRAME

The city as a contested place is not a new concept, but in 2007 grassroots organizers in the United States chose to make it the central frame in the struggle for social justice and human rights. They formed the U.S. Right to the City (RTTC) Alliance as a means of taking their cities back from the coalitions of affluence that had formed during the 1980s, and reframing the central scale of social struggle from the global to the urban. RTTC is one of the first mass formations to emerge from the previous era of sustained anti-globalization struggle stretching from the end of the Cold War through the election of George Bush, the attacks of September 11, 2001, and the war on Iraq. The issues, analysis and resistance that marked the anti-globalization movements are still vital, but it is also clear we are transitioning to a period when the city is also becoming a primary terrain of social conflict.

At the January 2007 founding meeting of RTTC in Los Angeles, California, organizers from around the country adopted a set of core principles and agreed that just as the backward nature of urban development policies are the result of capital operating at multiple scales simultaneously, so too must the RTTC movement be local, regional, national and transnational. RTTC organizations articulated a need to integrate with ongoing struggles taking place across the cities of the United States and beyond. This was not organizing as usual.

The RTTC developed out of dialogue and organizing among three organizations: the Miami Workers Center, Strategic Actions for a Just Economy (Los Angeles) and Tenants and Workers United (Alexandria, VA). Today, the RTTC Alliance is composed of over 40 core and allied members, across seven states, nine major cities and eight metro regions: Boston, Providence, DC metro, Los Angeles, Miami, New Orleans, New York, and San Francisco/Oakland. Since 2007, the RTTC Alliance has developed a national governance structure, regional networks and thematic working groups that collaborate with allied researchers, lawyers, academics, movement strategists and funders. In its own words, Right to the City "is a national alliance of membership-based organizations and allies organizing to build a united response to gentrification and displacement in our cities. Our goal is to build a national urban movement for housing, education, health, racial justice and democracy. We are building our power through strengthening local organizing; cross-regional collaboration; developing a national platform; and supporting community reclamation in New Orleans and the Gulf Coast."

In its first two years, the volunteer Steering Committee hired two staff people and organizational development consultants. A representative from each region is on the Steering Committee, and there is staggered replacement of its members. Annual national meetings take place, where members from organizations participate in workshops, subcommittees have face-to-face meetings, networking is done formally and informally, and organizational objectives are debated – e.g., a campaign in which all members agree to participate. Other national events, in Miami and Providence, were both planned to take advantage of the U.S. Conference of Mayors meeting in these cities and for Right to the City to issue its own demands. Critically, these meetings help regional and local groups press their campaigns as well. An elaborate communication system is still under development that will take greater advantage of telecommuting via webinars and conference calls. Establishing a new organization that is committed to modeling democratic practices, as is RTTC, will take some time, and the organization is bound to make some mistakes. Developing a horizontal exchange of ideas that is analogous to peer-to-peer dialogues and refining principles that cover a broad scope will also take time.

The view that community-based organizing is frequently engaged in small actions misreads what is happening at the local level. Grassroots groups have in fact demonstrated a capacity to scale up their struggles. For example, immigrant organizing among day laborers in multiple urban areas across the country was the catalyst for forming a National Day Laborer Organizing Network (NDLON). The various struggles RTTC organizations are engaged in, individually and collectively, may at present be less noticeable than the Civil Rights Movement of the 1960s, but their significance should not be underestimated. Indeed, it is important to recall that the work of women in Birmingham, Alabama in the 1950s laid the groundwork for Rosa Parks' refusal to move to the back of the bus in Montgomery and signaled the visibility of an emerging mass movement. Furthermore, across the globe, some of the most vibrant social movements to emerge in recent years are community-based movements that situate their local struggles in national and global contexts. Immigrant communities with global roots are organizing across borders, such as in Los Angeles and New York, where the GABRIELA Network organizes for the human rights of Filipino women workers in their cities and the Philippines.

Our goal here is to briefly introduce the RTTC Alliance by discussing some of the campaigns in which members are engaged. From this, we attempt to draw out some of the key principles and issues that unite these organizations, inform efforts to develop national expressions, and link these groups to others across the country and globe. Right to the City as a concept has captured the imagination of many involved with urban social struggles, but it remains an underdeveloped social movement ideology. Our data are drawn from interviews with RTTC members, participant observation, and review of movement documents and campaigns.

WHY THE CITY?

The city has rapidly become a central battleground in the new global configurations of power and wealth. This shift is linked to increased urbanization and the relative emptying of the countryside, as economic migrants stream into the cities in search of work. Cities have also grown to such an extent that in many cases urban birth-rates are themselves a cause of the planet's urban expansion. Furthermore, as urban scholars have documented, major cities have become regional and global command and control centers for transnational finance capital. The emergence of the city as a central site of social struggle is linked closely to the unprecedented growth of urban populations alongside an equally dramatic increase in urban inequality and poverty.

The implications of this shift for poor people of color concentrated in cities have become all too clear: Whereas once they were segregated and ignored in abandoned downtowns while whites fled to the suburbs, now low-income residents are expected to disperse as cities are reconfigured by global capital, national real estate markets, local political elites and the consumer classes. Their presence in the urban core in any capacity other than as cheap labor is unwelcome, a blight on the landscape of the new environment as cities compete for status as world cities by attracting entertainment, sports and the "creative class." To understand the intense conflicts breaking out in cities around the world, we need to pay close attention to the contradiction between valuable land and "surplus" people, and the logic that generates it.

But just as the new urban economy produces new forms of oppression, it is also producing new theories and practices of resistance. RTTC organizers see Right to the City as an ideological framework to help urban residents make sense of the varied challenges thrown their way on a daily basis and, at the same time, as a theory through which individuals and communities can formulate and articulate their collective interests and wage struggles for their collective liberation. For many organizations, the concept of Right to the City reveals the limitations of small-scale struggles, places the focus on the colonization of entire communities, and highlights the national and international dimensions of local challenges.

THE CITY AS BATTLEGROUND: RTTC CAMPAIGNS

What unites these various organizations, each formed in response to local events at different times, is a sense of urgency in defending urban neighborhoods from encroaching developers; gentrifiers; apathetic, negligent or antagonistic officials; and deeper national and global forces attempting to radically redraw the urban social, economic and cultural topography. Our goal here is not to provide a systematic analysis of campaigns nor to identify all of the current campaigns by all members, but to introduce some that are representative of the struggles with which RTTC members are engaged.

City Life/Vida Urbana, based in the Jamaica Plain neighborhood of Boston, was founded in 1973 to fight disinvestment and over time expanded tenant organizing to other parts of Boston. They pioneered the idea of an Eviction Free Zone and a Community Controlled Housing Zone to forestall evictions, make visible existing ownership patterns and identify where power was situated. As gentrification in Jamaica Plain expanded, City Life/Vida Urbana collaborated with the Jamaica Plain Neighborhood Development Corporation and mounted a highly visible campaign to have landlords pledge publicly to maintain affordable rents. Since 2007, they have been mounting eviction blockades, invoking the principle of the right to stay just as the foreclosure crisis hit and began to depopulate many communities. This successful campaign has prevented 12 evictions out of 15 blockades as of this writing; even the 3 evictions that were carried out helped to spur a broader movement against the banks and financial institutions behind the crisis in Boston.

Other Right to the City organizations were founded in response to more recent neoliberal policies that saw the public sector support investment-driven real estate development, first by ignoring their own planning departments, which identified ways to sustain existing housing, and second by moving ahead on "glamorous" projects such as entertainment complexes that demolished buildings and displaced tenants. In 1996, two organizations formed in Boyle Heights, across the Los Angeles River from downtown. One formed initially to fight against the HOPE VI public housing redevelopment program when the Housing Authority slipped eviction notices under the doors of tenants who wanted to stay where they were. A second became a community developer of affordable housing and subsequently added an organizing division to challenge gentrification. Both groups—Union de Vecinos and East Los Angeles Community Corporation—belong to the L.A. Right to the City region. Union de Vecinos continues to mount actions to take back the streets and alleyways, forcing the city to pay attention to safety and survival issues of existing residents even as a new mass transit line led to demolishing existing dwellings.

In Koreatown, west of downtown Los Angeles, overseas investment had turned commercial areas into a hot market, and this was followed by the construction of luxury condominiums and mixed-use development. Although the financial crisis has led to a slowdown, the Koreatown Immigrant Workers Alliance (KIWA) continues to fight to protect the mainly immigrant tenant population from being displaced and losing jobs. Over the past six months, the tenant leaders from these organizations have been waging a joint campaign to preserve affordable housing, using participatory action research and training tenant leaders who have been surveying their neighbors in order to document deteriorating conditions. Women and men from the Latino, Korean and South Asian communities have been exchanging ideas and are moving towards issuing their own housing report, as distinguished from the mayor's, which they feel will underserve poor people.

New York City's Right to the City regional formation emerged in 2007 from an existing coalition of anti-gentrification community-based organizing groups. The chapter's membership-based groups are working on individual and interconnected campaigns, and each shares a strong focus on the leadership development of their respective and collective membership base. For example, Fabulous Independent Educated Radicals for Community Empowerment (FIERCE), an LGBTQ youth of color member-group, is organizing for the right to public space by opposing the privatization of NYC's waterfront and campaigning for a youth-led community center on Pier 40 in the West Village. FIERCE has played a key role in organizing youth-led forums to promote and support youth leadership in RTTC at both the local NYC and national levels.

Picture the Homeless is also one of RTTC-NYC's nearly 20 base-building groups. It was founded in 1999 by homeless people, in the midst of New York City's war on poor and working-class people of color. Seeking justice and respect, the organization is led by the homeless and is intent on stopping the criminalization of homeless people. They organized a series of direct actions in 2009, including the occupation of a vacant building and the orchestration of a tent city on a vacant land parcel in East Harlem. The land is owned by JP Morgan Chase, a firm that received billions of dollars in public TARP funding. The organization's "housing, not warehousing" campaign calls for the conversion of vacant buildings to affordable housing for homeless and low-income NYC residents.

This year, RTTC-NYC issued a platform directed at upcoming citywide elections. Through a participatory and unifying process involving member organizations and allies, the local Alliance identified six issue areas and related demands: Federal Stimulus Funds; Community Decision-Making Power; Low-Income Housing; Environmental Justice & Public Health; Jobs & Workforce Development; and Public Space. The document not only articulates key policy opportunities, it also lays out an historical and political analysis questioning the commodification of basic human needs such as housing. The platform also grounds policy concerns within a set of principles for each issue area and maps out public space accessibility, stimulus funding sources, environmental health indicators, and poverty statistics for the city. In addition to promoting the platform, the regional chapter has taken on a united citywide campaign to convert empty or stalled luxury condominium developments to affordable housing for the low-income and homeless population. This summer, RTTC-NYC demonstrated its growing membership capacity in coordinating the groundwork for the campaign launch. Members and leaders created a detailed mass census of condominium development projects by conducting neighborhood-by-neighborhood walk-throughs in several boroughs.

WHAT IS RIGHT TO THE CITY?

What theory of Right to the City emerges from looking at the actual struggles and campaigns being waged by RTTC organizations, and the analyses they are developing? At the 2007 RTTC founding conference, people acknowledged that there was no consensus on a definition of RTTC, either in social movements or academic circles, and that beginning to formulate one was one of the primary tasks of the conference. We should first stress that today Right to the City remains very much a work in progress, as a movement and a theory. Within and beyond the RTTC, individuals and organizations are involved with the difficult political work of generating a theory that is both rooted in day-to-day struggles and realities of people, and capable of creating opportunities for radical, long-lasting social change. While the debate will continue, looking at RTTC campaigns allows us to begin to identify some emergent principles. Right to the City at its most elementary concerns the relationship between people and place. It is from here, arguably, that all other rights derive and, in turn, ground them. Drawing from Henri Lefebvre's original 1968 work, *Le Droit a La Ville* (Right to the City). Right to the City is a political feature of the urban inhabitant, a new form of political belonging that is not rooted in national citizenship; inhabitance implies residence, it implies this relationship and draws its political power from it. These issues have surfaced recently in immigrant struggles to get the vote in local and municipal elections, and there is a history of undocumented immigrants gaining voting rights in school elections.

Anti-eviction blockades; the right to return to New Orleans; resistance to gentrification; confronting police harassment of homeless men, women and youth; and ICE harassment of immigrant communities—these struggles are all grounded in the right of communities and individuals to be and to remain where they are (or were), to be there free of violence and fear, and free to determine the destinies of the places they call home. As the emphasis on affordable housing and gentrification suggests, the organizations in RTTC are all confronting sustained, well-funded and often violent efforts to break the relationship of their members to place.

From this central principle, we can see in the actions and analyses of RTTC members and the Alliance as a whole a sub-set of rights that give a more defined form to the Rights to the City. These are neither written in stone, nor do they necessarily apply to all communities in all places, but they do allow us to move the process of defining the Right to the City forward as grounded in actual struggle. Engagement with an ever-widening circle of social movements committed to deep transformation will only strengthen the frame.

Within this:

1) Right to Participate

Within the context of a right to stay, perhaps the most important right is the right to participate in all levels of decision making and planning regarding the community.

As University of Washington-Seattle scholar Mark Purcell points out, for Lefebvre inhabitance can serve as a proxy for citizenship rooted in the national state. More recently, scholars across many disciplines have begun to study changing notions of citizenship being generated by transnational migrations, a re-scaling of politics and the work of social movements and activists. While national citizenship remains the central frame for membership in a formal political community and rights claims, this dominance is being challenged by developments on the ground. Chicago, San Francisco and Takoma Park (MD) already allow noncitizen voting for school boards. As a result, we have an opportunity to redraw existing political maps and create new forms of citizenship through social struggle. This opportunity is central to Right to the City, as movement and theory. In this frame, democratic rights, rather than being based on formal political membership in a national community, are based on physical presence in the city, participating in its economic, social and political life. This is of obvious value for RTTC organizations from immigrant communities, but the value extends far beyond these communities as well. The guiding principle in this new citizenship is to legitimate and institutionalize the participation of marginalized individuals, groups and communities from all levels of the political process.

2) Right to Security

Insecurity marks the lives of many people living in urban areas across the world. Being present in a place and having a right to participate are only meaningful if people are secure. Unlike the militarized understanding of security that reigned during the Cold War and gained new life post-September 11, 2001, security in the context of Right to the City is both broader and deeper, mirroring at the local level the global movement for human security. Human security refers to the full spectrum of security, addressing issues ranging from sexual assault and lack of food, to armed conflict and environmental destruction. At the level of the city, human security issues are apparent in the terror sowed by ICE raids and racial profiling by police, to electricity cutoffs and evictions driven by poverty, and the commodification of basic human needs. Human security also extends to housing. Rachel G. Bratt, Michael E. Stone and Chester Hartman, in their book, *A Right to Housing: Foundation of a New Social Agenda*, respond to the question of why a right to housing is needed by referring to Franklin D. Roosevelt's 1944 State of the Union address, where FDR suggested a second Bill of Rights that would offer security for jobs, healthcare, a good education and a right to a home. The right to security, though its content will have to be determined by communities themselves, asserts that in principle people have the right to demand urban policies and practices that support, rather than undermine, the security of people.

3) Right to Resist

Faced with the real threat of community breakdown and displacement, whether by gentrification, foreclosure, systematic discrimination by immigration or criminal justice authorities, malign neglect, or any of the other myriad ways in which communities are broken, Right to the City means a right to resist. Resistance here means more than permitted marches and other overregulated forms of "free speech." Instead, the principle of a right to resist draws inspiration from ideals, such as those articulated in the Declaration of Independence and the Declaration of the Rights of Man and of the Citizen; from the living memories of resistance by colonized and oppressed peoples around the world; and from liberation struggles being waged today. It is a right that can be claimed by people marginalized from formal political processes, or for whom these processes have proven to be ineffective or, at times, weapons of the powerful. It is a right that questions the fundamental legality and morality of existing institutions and practices, and therefore takes as its primary goal their reform or abolition

CONCLUSION

It is impossible to disentangle the discussion of rights from that of democracy, and perhaps Right to the City is best understood as one of this generation's attempts to breathe new life into government by the people. as the struggle for radical democracy. This formulation allows us to connect the movement to its historical ancestry and to acknowledge its contemporary urgency. At the same time, the movement and theory must be grounded in the lives of real people and the concrete conditions of urban communities. Categories such citizen and worker, while still relevant, are insufficient to contain and represent the multifaceted struggles of urban inhabitants who are women, documented and undocumented immigrants, LGBTQ, people of color, and who may exist at the peripheries or even outside of the formal economy. New struggles for democracy, inside the city and beyond, will need to create political subjects and agendas that transcend these categories, but without losing sight of the particularities that shape their lives.

Central to RTTC campaigns and analyses is the idea that the struggle for democracy today requires a return to the concept of rights. Along with academic, policy and other movement allies, RTTC is engaged in the process of revitalizing the rights struggle and re-raising unsettled questions in the context of new political challenges. Questions of inclusion, for example, are far from new, yet the attack on immigrant communities forces us to acknowledge we still lack powerful rights movements and institutions that can adequately protect them. Similarly, market-driven displacement, criminalization and unresponsive elected officials reveal the inability of even citizenship to safeguard peoples' civil rights. Finally, existing rights, those guaranteed to citizens and for which many documented and undocumented immigrants strive, fail to even address basic issues of human security, including housing, medical care and employment. In all these instances, communities are once again coming up against the limits of the individualistic and formal political rights that mark the liberal democracies.

RTTC and other movements like it across the globe have their work cut out for them. In addition to day-to-day demands, they face a vast sea of challenges as they seek to create, articulate and implement new and powerful conceptions of rights and inclusion that connect the everyday to long-term struggle. But there are encouraging signs of momentum. In addition to ongoing regional and national work within the Alliance, RTTC recently co-convened the Inter-Alliance Dialogue, a process of discussion and joint activity between National Jobs with Justice, National Day Laborer Organizing Network, National Domestic Workers Alliance, the Right to the City Alliance, and Grassroots Global Justice. Beyond the U.S. border, the 2010 World Urban Forum V, to be held this coming March in Rio de Janeiro, Brazil, has taken as its theme Right to the City. This is certainly encouraging. While much remains to be done, we must also acknowledge that much has been accomplished.

IV

CIVIL RIGHTS HISTORY

Bayard Rustin and
the Civil Rights Movement

Daniel Levine

Bayard Rustin is most remembered as the organizer who made the 1963 March on Washington happen. He organized or did himself the day-to-day grunt work like arranging transportation and renting facilities. He also worked on grand plans and vision for that day. But he was much more than that. He had been one of the very few to adapt the theory and practice of Non-Violent Direct Action (NVDA) to race relations in the United States. NVDA was created for quite different circumstances and was counter to American traditional culture, so the process was a slow one. After 1965, Rustin favored moving "From Protest to Politics," the title of his most famous article. He was always an integrationist who stood strongly against ideas of separatism or black nationalism. He tried, and only partly succeeded, to unite the labor movement with the drive for racial justice, because he believed both were primarily issues of economic class. His is also the story of a man finding out that moral crusades, no matter how righteous, are futile unless combined with actual power, political power.

Rustin came to the Civil Rights Movement from the international pacifist movement, where he had intimate knowledge and experience of nonviolent direct action. As a member of the pacifist Fellowship of Reconciliation (FOR) in the 1930s and 1940s, he ran NVDA workshops all over the country, sometimes actually trying out the method by challenging racism in department stores or restaurants. Throughout the Civil Rights Movement, Bayard Rustin was always there. He was there in the 1940s, when the struggle for black equality seemed discouragingly small. He was there as the movement accelerated in the 1950s. He was with King in Montgomery and with the students when they revitalized the movement in the 1960s. When he was not physically at the center, people who were would be constantly on the telephone with him.

RUSTIN'S BACKGROUND

Rustin was born in 1912 in West Chester, Pennsylvania, but lived most of his life in New York, only briefly in Harlem. Since his mother was only 16 and unmarried when he was born, he was raised by his grandparents, whom he always thought of as "ma and pa." His circle of friends, as a child and adult, always included blacks and whites. He was a superb student in high school, a talented singer and athlete. He went for a year or two to several colleges, but did not graduate from any. At City College of New York, he was, for about a year and a half, a member of the Young Communist League, because the YCL opposed American entry into World War II. Rustin was a pacifist who had joined the Society of Friends (the church of his great-grandmother) in 1936. When Hitler attacked Russia and the Communist Party abandoned pacifism, Rustin abandoned the Party.

He would not serve in the military nor co-operate in any way with Selective Service, although in later years he said that if he had known about the Holocaust, he would have served in some noncombat capacity. In the 1940s, he and other "noncooperators" went to prison. Bayard Rustin was a difficult prisoner. He was constantly challenging racial segregation, and he was an active homosexual. He had discovered his homosexuality as a teenager, and was for decades tortured about it. He considered homosexuality wrong, in religious terms, a sin. In prison, he was punished for it by isolation. His isolation was in the prison library, which in fact was a wonderful opportunity, given his passion for learning. In 1945, Rustin and other pacifists were stunned by news of the atomic bomb. They felt that all other crusades had to be suspended in the face of this threat to all life. He became a model prisoner, and was released in March of 1947.

The half dozen years after his release were ones of whirlwind activity. He moved into an apartment on Mott Street in New York City, a building filled with reformers and activists. He began talking with George Houser, who was also thinking about how NVDA could be applied to race relations, about a "Journey of Reconciliation," a bus trip through the segregated South by an interracial group. The Supreme Court had outlawed segregation on interstate travel in 1946, but the decision was not enforced. A "Journey of Reconciliation" would challenge state segregation laws and perhaps bring the whole question of segregation to national attention. The Journey began in Washington in April of 1947, going not into the deep South, but in the border states. There was a bit of violence in Chapel Hill, North Carolina. Bayard and others were arrested, and the Journey went on, but no further south than Tennessee, then back to Washington. If Rustin, Houser and the others hoped to bring segregation to national attention, they failed. The Journey was only noticed by the Afro-American press, but it became the model for the "Freedom Rides" of 1961.

Rustin's trial was a year later. After a 15-minute deliberation, he and another rider were convicted and given a sentence of 30 days on a chain gang. The verdict was of course appealed.

Also in 1947, Rustin ran, and A. Philip Randolph chaired, League for Nonviolent Civil Disobedience Against Military Segregation. In March of 1948, President Truman met with a number of "Negro" leaders, including Randolph, and issued a somewhat ambiguous order desegregating the military. Randolph thought the order was adequate, and the League disbanded.

While the appeal of his North Carolina conviction was going on, Rustin traveled to India, via London, to a world peace conference. This was the first of many trips to London, and he developed an English accent, which he could turn off and on. When and why he spoke with that accent is not clear. In India, Rustin traveled and spoke widely, becoming a much admired figure, and met the major Indian leaders. A few weeks later, he was on the chain gang in North Carolina. He served, with "good time," 22 days. His account of those days, as reported in the *New York Post*, August 22–26, 1949, was one factor which led to abolition of the chain gang in the state.

During the Summer of 1951, a black family rented an apartment in Cicero, Illinois, and was greeted by a white mob. Walter White from the NAACP was there, and FOR sent Houser and Rustin. The latter two drew up a sensible practical proposal for the Cicero Committee of the Chicago Council Against Racial and Religious Discrimination, a private group, saying that mob violence must not be allowed to prevail. The proposal was ignored, and the black family felt they had to move out. Mob violence prevailed. Later, however, the police chief and several town officials were convicted under federal law for not doing their duty.

NVDA had failed on the Journey of Reconciliation, but the threat of civil disobedience succeeded in the campaign to end segregation in the military. NVDA had failed in Cicero, but eventually there was progress with federal help. Rustin was gradually coming to the conclusion that NVDA needed the aid of political power to make any progress.

NVDA had been developed in an anti-colonial campaign. Perhaps it could be further developed in other anti-colonial battles, perhaps Africa. In 1952, under the auspices of the American Friends Service Committee (AFSC) and FOR, Bayard attended another world peace conference in England, then a quick stop in Paris, then to Africa, particularly the Gold Coast (later renamed Ghana), to meet Kwame Nkrumah and other African leaders. But it would be hard to find any effect on the anti-colonial process from the American NVDA effort.

Rustin returned to the United States and resumed his writing and lecturing all over the country. He was by now the leading theorist and practitioner of Non-Violent Direct Action in the country, was in fact "Mr. NVDA." He was an obvious choice for a leadership position in FOR or some organization in the growing Civil Rights Movement.

Then he was arrested in Los Angeles, not for any pacifist or civil rights activity, but on a "morals" (that is, homosexuality) charge. In January of 1953, he was convicted and sentenced to prison. He was devastated; again overcome by guilt. His friends and associates, far from being supportive, added their criticism to his own sense of distress. "I know now," he wrote in 1953, "that for me sex must be sublimated if I am to live with myself." On his release, he resigned from FOR (or was asked to), but with the support of FOR's chairman, A.J. Muste, sought a "cure" with the help of a psychiatrist. The psychiatrist, Robert Ascher, concluded that Rustin would not change, and the two ended up discussing simply how Rustin might be more discreet. He was now unacceptable to FOR, and even to the theoretically tolerant Society of Friends. He eventually found a home with another tiny pacifist organization, the War Resisters League. During the next few years, Bayard Rustin came more to accept himself without guilt.

MARTIN LUTHER KING AND A. PHILIP RANDOLPH

At about the same time, a then unknown young minister in Montgomery, Alabama was chairing a bus boycott and something called the Montgomery Improvement Association. A. Philip Randolph, long-time activist and head of the largest "Negro" union, The Brotherhood of Sleeping Car Porters, and some other Northern activists thought there ought to be some way to help. Since the boycott was a nonviolent action, it was obvious that "Mr. NVDA" might be helpful. Rustin went to Alabama. In Montgomery, Rustin and King hit it off immediately, and the two talked for many hours about the theory, theology and practice of Non-Violent Direct Action. Rustin always denied that he taught King about NVDA, but King admitted he had not thought deeply about it before. Soon Rustin had to leave, as local authorities and the Montgomery newspaper began to find out about this outsider, this ex-Communist and homosexual who was helping the boycott. So Rustin returned to New York and with others created "In Friendship," a Northern group supporting King. Gradually, Martin Luther King became better known, and also NVDA, four initials hitherto virtually unknown to most Americans.

On a subsequent visit to Montgomery, Rustin suggested to King that organizing in one Southern city was not enough. There needed to be a South-wide organization protesting against segregation in its many forms and in many places. Probably other people were thinking along the same lines, and after various meetings and conferences, the Southern Christian Leadership Conference was founded in 1957. No one paid much attention, and virtually no one realized that SCLC would become perhaps the best known of the direct action organizations of the Civil Rights Movement. While the boycott was still going on, Rustin wrote a series of working papers. In one of these, he analyzed why the movement was succeeding and suggested that these rules applied to other actions: The protest must be related to the objective; the participants must be those actually aggrieved; the participants must constantly talk about methods and rededicate themselves to the theory and practice of NVDA. If these principles were ignored, as they frequently were, particularly in the North, the protest action often failed.

When, in 1963, A. Philip Randolph chose Bayard Rustin as deputy director of the March on Washington, he chose the person who had the ability and experience to carry out a successful demonstration. Randolph had threatened such a march in 1941 in order to get "Negro" workers into the defense industries, and Rustin had been the "Youth Organizers" for that march. That march did not have to take place, because President Roosevelt issued an Executive Order (8802) which officially prohibited racial discrimination in defense plants, but the "March on Washington Movement" continued formally to exist, and Randolph became known as "Mr. March." This "nonmarch" was the beginning of Rustin's experience organizing demonstrations.

In one of Rustin's working papers for what became the Southern Christian Leadership Conference, he recommended that the emerging organization should stress the need for increased Negro voting, which would require federal support. The first action of the SCLC was therefore a "Prayer Pilgrimage" in May of 1957. Randolph, Roy Wilkins and Martin Luther King were co-chairs, and Bayard Rustin and Ella Baker, a vigorous long-time NAACP organizer, in fact organized it. The Prayer Pilgrimage took place on May 17, 1957, with perhaps 15,000 people attending. Martin Luther King delivered the most memorable speech. "Give us the right to vote," he cried. National media took almost no notice of the pilgrimage, and the right to vote was not guaranteed by federal action until 1965.

ORGANIZING MARCHES

As the Civil Rights Movement gathered momentum, as Southern opposition to school integration mounted, Randolph, as official chairman, but again with Bayard doing the actual planning, organized a Youth March for Integrated Schools in 1958. It was essentially a Northern operation, with strong support from labor unions. Bayard would always continue to believe that the labor movement and Civil Rights Movement could be allies. The march on October 15 had about 10,000 participants. There were stirring speeches, including one by Martin Luther King, read by Coretta Scott King, because her husband was in the hospital recovering from an assassination attempt in Harlem by a deranged black woman. Harry Belafonte, who, along with Roy Wilkins and Jackie Robinson, had also delivered rousing speeches, led a delegation to the White House. President Eisenhower did not receive them, nor even send a staff member. They left a message with a guard at the gate.

Rustin organized a second Youth March for Integrated Schools for April 1959. This time, there were over 300 buses and perhaps 25,000 people. Again, the event was hardly noticed by the national media. Again, Martin Luther King gave a rousing speech. Again, Harry Belafonte led a delegation to the White House. This time they were received by Gerald P. Morgan, the only black member of Eisenhower's staff, who assured the delegation that the president was sympathetic to ending discrimination. Rustin told the crowd, "When we come back with 50,000, I promise you, the President will be in town. And when we bring 100,000, Congress will sit in special session."

Beside SCLC, other civil rights organizations were springing up or getting renewed energy, based on the ideas and methods of NVDA. There was the Student
Nonviolent Coordinating Committee in the Spring of 1960, inspired by Rustin's
friend Ella Baker, and the 1961 Freedom Rides, spearheaded by a revived Congress
of Racial Equality (CORE), based explicitly on the Journey of Reconciliation. SCLC
was no longer just a few Baptist ministers, but was a presence in the national consciousness. There was the confrontation in Birmingham, with police dogs and water
cannon directed against the demonstrators. President Kennedy introduced what
became the Civil Rights Act of 1964. The Civil Rights Movement had become the
most important series of events on the national scene.

By 1963, Randolph, Rustin and others were considering a new march, with more
general support, for racial justice, to be part of this burgeoning stream. And Bayard
Rustin was the obvious man to make the march happen. Randolph's original idea
had been a march to protest widespread "Negro" unemployment. In June, President
Kennedy introduced the Civil Rights Act of 1964, and the aims of the march broadened. Randolph again was the titular head, but Rustin would do the actual work.

This was to be the big one, the one Rustin had talked about four years before. The
headquarters on West 130th Street in Harlem was a beehive of activity: arranging
bus schedules, renting the public address system, being sure there were enough portable toilets, and, probably the most time-consuming, raising the money. Of course
the NAACP contributed, but most of the civil rights organizations had no money.
Contributions came in from the United Auto Workers, the International Ladies
Garment Workers Union, and the largest single donation was from the Archdiocese
of Washington, DC.

The march was tightly controlled. Other groups could not blur the message. All
placards had to be approved by the central office: "We march for Jobs and Freedom,"
"End Segregation Now," and the like. The marchers were to come, march, hear music and the speeches, and then leave the city. Rustin knew that any potential white
disruptions would come from outside the city, so he arranged with the Washington
police department to have white officers on the periphery of the downtown.

There was also great fun at headquarters. Rustin was a great joker, high-spirited.
He once joked that what he wanted on his tombstone was, "This Nigger Had Fun,"
and he did.

There was opposition to the march and of course to Rustin himself, mostly but
not entirely from Southerners. President Kennedy at first opposed the march, but
then tried to capture it. Roy Wilkins came to the headquarters one day and said that
Kennedy wanted to speak. But the march was supposed to be the people speaking
to the president, not the other way around. After a brief pause, during which Rustin
pretended to go to the restroom, he told Wilkins that some Negroes might stone
the president, a point Rustin invented on the spot, and the request from Kennedy
disappeared.

Early on the day of the march, Rustin, in fact full of doubts, was interviewed
on the Washington Mall. The reporters pointed out that not many people were

there yet. Rustin consulted papers on a clipboard and said in his best English accent, "Everything is precisely on schedule." In fact, the paper was a blank sheet. But soon the people began to come. We know now that the march was a triumph. There were perhaps 250,000 people there, black and white. And yet, what really changed? There was the longest congressional filibuster in American history against Kennedy's bill; there was the bombing of the girls attending Sunday school in Birmingham. The civil rights demonstrators in Selma, Alabama were beaten. "It proved," said Rustin, "that we were capable of being one people." But was anything else accomplished?

With the success of the march, Rustin became a national figure. He spoke to many groups, often colleges. His talks were moving, but rationally moving. With his six-foot two height, he might lean over the podium and might say, "There are three points we have to remember," then would raise one finger, then after a sentence or two get to point two, two fingers; a few more words, then three fingers. He would never have to pause to say "umm" or to find a word. After the talk, he would often stay up late talking with the students, perhaps sitting in the student union, smoking, with his long legs stretched out in front of him.

POST-MARCH ON WASHINGTON

In the Spring and Summer of 1964, civil rights activists, mostly black but with some white participation, organized the Mississippi Freedom Democratic Party. The MFDP's aim was to challenge the all-white segregated Mississippi delegation to the National Democratic Convention in Atlantic City that August. The MFDP appeared before the Credentials Committee, and Fannie Lou Hamer made an eloquent "case." Lyndon Johnson, worried about a Southern walk-out, offered, through subordinates, two seats "at large"—that is, not representing any state. The question was, should the MFDP accept? Rustin, Martin Luther King and other national leaders urged acceptance at a meeting of the MFDP on August 26 in the basement of a nearby Baptist Church. While Rustin was making his case, someone from the delegation shouted, "You're a traitor, Bayard, a traitor. Sit down!" The MFDP turned down the "compromise" and went home. But the national Democratic Party resolved that in the future they would not recognize any delegation chosen on a segregated basis. This was the beginning of Rustin and the Civil Rights Movement diverging.

In the Summer of 1964, Harlem exploded with fires, smashing store windows, looting. Rustin, walking around the streets, realized he did not know anyone. His work had been with other parts of society. Noting racism in the North, Martin Luther King wanted to move SCLC north, say to Chicago. Bayard was against it, and the attempt proved futile. In fact, while King's international reputation was growing, he was awarded the Nobel Peace Prize in 1964, and Bayard accompanied him to Oslo. His stature in the United States, as well as the whole NVDA phase of the Civil Rights Movement, was in decline. In 1965, King, against Rustin's advice, went out to Los Angeles after the Watts riot. Rustin went with him, and the two found that they were regarded as irrelevant by the young people in the streets.

What was in ascendance was some form of nationalism or separatism. Rustin understood how frustration might lead that way, but called the Black Power Movement "frustration, stupidity." Rustin was convinced that much of that frustration stemmed from economic as well as racial injustice. With Leon Keyserling, formerly chair of the President's Council of Economic Advisors, he worked out a large program of public works which they called the "Freedom Budget for All Americans." [See Chester Hartman's chapter in this volume.] Thousands of copies of a pamphlet detailing the program were sent out, but the Freedom Budget got nowhere.

Kennedy came to support the Civil Rights Movement both tactically and, as he said, as a moral issue. Lyndon Johnson looked into the TV camera and announced, "We shall overcome." The Civil Rights Movement was now part of the Democratic Party. Bayard Rustin understood that the realities of American politics had changed, and the Civil Rights Movement had to change too, as he wrote in "From Protest to Politics" (*Commentary* 39: February 1965, 25–31). Rustin, the former pacifist, was even ambiguous about the Vietnam War. We were now part of the process, he argued, and we should no longer act as outsiders. When his pacifist friends were outraged at his support of a man waging a war in Vietnam, he responded, "You don't understand power. You guys"—and he meant the whole pacifist movement—"cannot deliver a single pint of milk to the kids in Harlem, and Lyndon Johnson can." Many of his former allies thought he had been seduced by power and gone over to the other side, the establishment side. Rustin was always interested in actual results more than moral purity. And in fact, the "establishment," in the person of J. Edgar Hoover, thought he was enough of a radical threat that the F.B.I. tapped his telephone.

Rustin was a vigorous anti-communist, but he still had a basically class-based view of social issues. A. Philip Randolph, the AFL-CIO and others, in the hopes of uniting the civil rights and labor movements, founded the A. Philip Randolph Institute in 1965. The aim of the APRI was to train young blacks to pass the apprenticeship exams of various unions, particularly the construction trades. These unions had been obstinate in resisting enrollment of black members. The program proved so successful that soon it became a separate organization and received aid from the U.S. Department of Labor. But Rustin was perceived by members of the civil rights groups as being prolabor—that is, supportive of a group antagonistic to racial justice. They would have preferred quotas mandated by the federal government. Rustin argued that working with the unions would, in the long run, be more productive than creating the sort of antagonism that quotas would bring. He knew that means and ends were inextricably intertwined. The training program was ended when Ronald Reagan became president.

Rustin was further alienated from the new Civil Rights Movement by the controversy in Ocean Hill-Brownsville, a black neighborhood in Brooklyn. The city tried to "decentralize" the schools by establishing local school boards with somewhat ill-defined power. In May of 1968, the school board for Ocean Hill-Brownsville fired (or "reassigned") several teachers without the due process required by the contract with the United Federation of Teachers. To Randolph and Rustin, the issue was clear: Union members had been fired illegally. Also, Rustin pointed out, community control could become the equivalent of states' rights, whereby white communities could conspire against black teachers. To black activists, the Ocean Hill-Brownsville board had exercised their right, a case of Black Power manifest. The issue was further complicated by the fact that most teachers in New York City were Jewish. There were clear anti-Jewish statements from supporters of the local school board. Rustin supported the union, and that assured his permanent schism with what seemed to be the Northern version of the civil rights organization.

In fact, Bayard Rustin no longer had a place in racial politics. He turned again to the international realm. He loved to travel anyway, and joined the International Rescue Committee. The IRC had been originally established to aid Jewish refugees from Nazi Germany, but now concentrated on refugees all over the world, particularly Southeast Asia. He was often in Thailand, for example, bringing attention and aid to Vietnamese refugees. He was also a frequent election observer as democracy, or at least elections, spread around the world. Rustin was now a celebrity, perhaps, but no longer an engaged participant in social change.

In 1987, he traveled to Haiti as an election observer. On his return, he seemed to sicken, and not improve. He was taken to the hospital, where, early in the morning of August 24, he died of cardiac arrest.

Looking back on the civil rights era, one is tempted to say, "If only. . . ." If only the March on Washington coalition could have held together; if only integration had been more real and less token; if only NVDA could have been successfully modified to suit Northern conditions; if only the War on Poverty could have been expanded; if only loud black voices for separatism had been more quickly rejected; if only conservative politicians had not exploited racial fears. And yet there has been slow progress, mostly on the basis that Bayard Rustin was predicting. He could not have foreseen the election of Barack Obama, but he would have been in Grant Park that night, with tears in his eyes.

A Civil Right to Organize

Richard D. Kahlenberg & Moshe Z. Marvit

On April 4, 1968, when Dr. Martin Luther King, Jr. was tragically gunned down in Memphis, Tennessee, he stood at the intersection of two great forces for greater human dignity: the Civil Rights Movement and the labor movement. King was in Memphis, it should be remembered, to support striking black sanitation workers who marched with King carrying posters with the iconic message, "I AM A MAN."

The signs had resonance in part because, as black Americans, the sanitation workers were sick of being derisively referred to by racist whites as "boy." But in addition, as garbage collectors, they were tired of being poorly treated by management and by fellow citizens, who looked down upon them. Because their employer would not provide them with a place to shower after work, garbage collectors were shunned by bus drivers and fellow passengers and often had to walk home. Managers, failing to fully recognize the basic humanity of sanitation workers, refused to install safety features on garbage trucks. After two sanitation workers were accidentally crushed to death by a defective packing mechanism on a garbage truck, 1,300 workers went on strike. Their message, "I AM A MAN," contained a powerful demand for better treatment.

King rallied with sanitation workers and affirmed their dual message of racial and economic justice. "Whenever you are engaged in work that serves humanity and is for the building of humanity, it has dignity and it has worth," King told American Federation of State, County and Municipal Employees (AFSCME) workers in March 1968. He told them, "All labor has dignity."

King had long seen the connection between the labor and Civil Rights Movements as engines for human equality for men and women alike. While some racist union locals famously resisted progress for blacks, most were far more progressive on issues of civil rights than society as a whole. The massive labor federation, the American Federation of Labor and the Congress of Industrial Organizations (AFL-

CIO), became a critical supporter of civil rights legislation, including the 1964 Civil Rights Act, which, in Title VII, forbade racial discrimination in employment. In a 1961 speech to the AFL-CIO, King declared, "Our needs are identical with labor's needs: decent wages, fair working conditions, livable housing, old age security, health and welfare measures, conditions in which families can grow, have education for their children, and respect in the community. . . . The duality of interests of labor and Negroes makes any crisis which lacerates you a crisis from which we bleed."

In the last year of his life, King had begun a multiracial Poor People's Campaign, and in his final Sunday sermon, delivered at the National Cathedral in Washington, DC, he called his vision of economic justice nothing less than his "last, greatest dream." In Memphis, King recounted the great victories for civil rights in Montgomery and Selma, and suggested, "You are going beyond purely civil rights questions to questions of human rights," raising "the economic issue." People must not only have the right to sit at a lunch counter, but also the right to afford a hamburger, he told the audience.

WHAT CAME OF KING'S TWIN DREAMS?

In the years since King was struck down, enormous improvements have been made in racial attitudes and in the life chances of African Americans. The black middle class has grown significantly, the number of black professionals has increased, and the black/white educational gap on such matters as high school graduation rates has shrunk dramatically. While far more progress needs to be made, we have since 1968 witnessed a sea change in racial attitudes, culminating in the once inconceivable idea of a black American president being elected. As Harvard law professor Randall Kennedy has written in his 2011 book, *The Persistence of the Color Line: Racial Politics and the Obama Presidency*: "One of the great achievements of the Civil Rights Revolution was its delegitimization of racial prejudice." In that sense, the 1964 Civil Rights Act has proven a tremendous success. Among the broader public in America and internationally, the Civil Rights Movement is rightly regarded as iconic in the struggle for human dignity and inclusion. While more work surely needs to be done, the trajectory on race is generally pointed in the right direction.

By contrast, since the 1960s, the American labor movement has seen enormous setbacks. Labor once dreamed that, with the vanquishing of Jim Crow, the racism that had kept working-class whites in the South from uniting with blacks would diminish and Southern states could be unionized. But organized labor did not conquer the South; instead, to a significant degree, Southern anti-union practices have spread through much of the country. From its peak in the mid-1950s, organized labor has declined from more than one-third of private sector workers (and one-half of the industrial workforce) to less than one-tenth. Today, even public sector unionism is under attack in several states. Meanwhile, economic inequality has skyrocketed to the point that the top 1 percent of Americans own more than the bottom 90 percent, and income from productivity gains has gone almost exclusively to the top 10 percent. Economists agree the two phenomena are connected, and that rising economic inequality in America is due in some significant measure to the weakness of the American labor movement.

THE CIVIL RIGHTS AND NATIONAL LABOR RELATIONS ACTS

There are many factors that help explain why the nation has progressed on King's vision for civil rights while it has moved backward on his emphasis on the importance of economic equality and union strength. However, among the most important—and the easiest to remedy—is the substantial difference between the strength of our laws on civil rights and on labor. Seventy-five years of experience with the National Labor Relations Act of 1935 (NLRA) and 45 years of experience with Title VII of the Civil Rights Act of 1964 suggest that the former has proven largely ineffectual in protecting workers, while the latter has been quite successful in diminishing discrimination and changing social attitudes.

The 1964 Civil Rights Act, subsequently amended in 1991, provides powerful penalties for employers who discriminate on the basis of race, sex, national origin or religion. Under the 1991 amendments, employment discrimination remedies have been expanded to include not only back pay but compensatory and punitive damages up to $300,000. Civil rights laws also provide plaintiffs with the opportunity to pursue legal discovery, something that employers assiduously seek to avoid. Furthermore, plaintiffs are given access to jury trials; and when plaintiffs prevail, defendants are liable for up to double the hourly rate for plaintiffs' attorneys' fees.

Under the NLRA, it is likewise illegal to discriminate against employees for trying to organize a union, because lawmakers recognized that firms should not be allowed to use their disproportionate power to intimidate workers. But the penalties and processes under the NLRA are far weaker. If employers are found to have violated the law, they must reinstate any terminated employees and provide them with back pay, normally after a lengthy and arduous process of enforcement. And under the NLRA, there is extremely limited opportunity for discovery and no jury trial. Faced with the prospect of having to negotiate substantial wage and benefit increases with a union, businesses have a strong financial incentive to fire organizing employees and risk paying the penalties as a cost of doing business. Labor lawyer Thomas Geoghegan writes in his 1991 book, *Which Side Are You On?*: "An employer who didn't break the law would have to be what economists call an 'irrational firm.'"

AMENDING THE CIVIL RIGHTS ACT
FOR LABOR ORGANIZING

The central thesis of our new book, *Why Labor Organizing Should Be a Civil Right*, is that the Civil Rights Act should be amended to add protection for employees seeking to organize a union. Just as it is illegal to fire someone for race or gender or national origin or religion, it would be illegal under the Civil Rights Act to fire someone for trying to organize or join a union.

Title VII of the 1964 Civil Rights Act (which now prohibits discrimination based on race, gender, religion and other factors from wrongful termination and other forms of employment discrimination) would be amended to prohibit discrimination against workers who are attempting to organize a labor union, making them eligible not only for back pay but for compensatory and punitive damages as well. (Alternatively, a stand-alone bill could be offered that would have the effect of adding Title VII-type protections for labor organizing without literally amending the Civil Rights Act.)

We argue that for labor suits under the Civil Rights Act, procedures similar to those of the Equal Employment Opportunity Commission (EEOC) should be followed, but the National Labor Relations Board should continue to administer disputes. This approach would combine a process that has proved effective with an agency that is finely attuned to the nuances of labor law through its more than 75 years of experience handling labor disputes.

Significantly, Title VII remedies for unlawful discharge of unionizing workers would likely be an even more effective deterrent than they have been for racial and gender discrimination, because unlawfully discharged workers trying to form a union would have an important financial reservoir not available to victims of race and gender bias. American labor unions have a total annual income that runs in the billions of dollars. By contrast, civil rights and women's organizations have much smaller financial bases on which to draw, so most women and people of color must rely on contingency lawyers.

Conceivably, writing labor organizing protections into the Civil Rights Act could also spawn a cultural shift in employer behavior. Employers who are found guilty of racial or gender discrimination are today seen to have done something shameful, a seismic shift from the days when business routinely espoused racist and chauvinistic attitudes. Today, there is no lucrative industry to aid employers in thwarting civil rights laws, as there is to keep unions out. Instead, the opposite is found, where employers spend billions of dollars a year on human resource departments in part to ensure that all employees understand the requirements of Title VII.

By contrast, managers are unapologetic about wanting to silence the voice of workers. Wal-Mart CEO Lee Scott, for example, famously said—as quoted by Thomas Frank in the Nov. 19, 2008 *Wall Street Journal:* "We like driving the car and we're not going to give the steering wheel to anybody but us." Shifting labor organizing protections to civil rights legislation could, over time, bring about a cultural shift in which the country sees corporations that fire employees for trying to form a union, join the middle class, and have a say in the workplace, as morally suspect—as they already are seen in Europe.

ADVANTAGES TO THE CIVIL RIGHTS APPROACH

Conceptually, an amendment to the Civil Rights Act would not break new ground, as it is already illegal under the NLRA to fire someone for organizing. But amending the Civil Rights Act to protect union organizing would offer two fundamental advantages. First, it would put teeth into the existing NLRA prohibition by applying the full force of Civil Rights penalties and procedures to businesses that break the law. Today, labor leaders note, "the right to form a union is the only legally guaranteed right that Americans are afraid to exercise" (Steven Greenhouse in the June 25, 1998 *New York Times*). Amending the Civil Rights Act would provide a far more effective deterrent to lawbreaking than the current statute recognizing the theoretical right to organize as authentic.

The second advantage to this approach lies in its potential to break a long-standing political logjam surrounding labor law reform. Amending the Civil Rights Act rather than the NLRA would, for the broader American public, help elevate the debate from the obscure confines of labor law to the higher arena of civil rights, which Americans readily understand. Whereas labor law is seen by many as a body of technical rules governing relations between two sets of "special interests"—business and labor—Americans understand the principle of nondiscrimination as an issue of fundamental fairness. Employment rights have long been considered civil rights, and there is no reason to exclude labor rights from this formulation. Framing labor organizing as a civil right could provide a new paradigm that might fundamentally alter the political landscape, breaking the deadlock over reform.

Since passage of the anti-labor Labor–Management Relations Act in the 1940s (known as the Taft-Hartley Act), organized labor has had four major chances to reform labor laws in order to level the playing field for workers. Each time that Democrats have controlled the presidency and both houses in Congress they have sought to alter labor law, and each time they have failed. Under Lyndon Johnson, Democrats fell short in a Senate effort to modify Taft-Hartley. Under Jimmy Carter, labor law reform that would have enhanced penalties for unfair labor practices failed by two votes in a Democratically controlled Senate. During Bill Clinton's first term, legislation to outlaw the permanent replacement of strikers stalled. And under Barack Obama, the Employee Free Choice Act (EFCA) to stiffen penalties for employer abuses and allow a majority of employees to authorize union representation through "card check" procedures was not even put to a formal vote in the Senate.

The fundamental problem with these efforts was that labor is caught in a political box. In order to achieve reform, labor needs political power, which requires expanding union membership; but in order to grow, unions need labor law reform. As Harvard law professor Paul C. Weiler noted more than a decade ago, in the Sept. 4, 1999 *Wall Street Journal*, "No part of American law in the last 50 years has been less amenable to reform than labor law." The Civil Rights strategy would offer a fresh approach. Republican-controlled bodies of Congress are unlikely to support efforts to strengthen labor under any circumstances, but progressives need to begin developing a new strategy now so that when they do regain full political power, they do not miss a fifth chance to revitalize labor.

Recent developments suggest that labor may have the public on its side. Following the 2010 elections, Republican governors in Wisconsin, Ohio, Indiana and elsewhere took what had primarily been an assault on private sector collective bargaining rights to the public sector, which had previously faced a more favorable climate. These attacks on public sector collective bargaining prominently raised fundamental issues about the role of labor in American society and energized many progressives who had taken the right of employees to band together collectively for granted. Indeed, recent polling suggests that while the opinions of Americans are mixed on unions, they strongly believe, by margins of two to one, and even three to one, in the basic right of collective bargaining. In November 2011, the people of Ohio overwhelmingly voted to repeal an anti-union law that restricted public employee collective bargaining rights.

Moreover, the attack on public sector unions for receiving more generous pension and health benefits than private sector workers raises the possibility of a different discussion: Rather than pursuing a race to the bottom, where the diminishing benefits of nonunionized private employees are used as a club against unionized public employees, why not take steps to strengthen private sector unionization, so that private sector employees can enjoy the same level of benefits as those enjoyed by those employed in the public sector?

THE CIVIL RIGHTS ACT AS THE APPROPRIATE VEHICLE

When we outlined our proposal in an op-ed in the February 29, 2012 *New York Times*, the AFL-CIO's president Richard Trumka endorsed the idea and conservative pundit Ann Coulter denounced it on Fox News on March 12, 2012. In a classic divide-and-conquer strategy, Coulter argued that "Civil rights is for blacks. . . . Now they [Democrats] want to call everything a civil right, whether it's women or immigrants, and now, labor unions?!"

We believe that the Civil Rights Act is the right vehicle for protecting those trying to organize a union, for three distinct reasons: (1) labor organizing is a basic human right, which is bound up with an important democratic right of association; (2) strengthening labor advances the values and interests of the Civil Rights Movement by promoting dignity and equality, particularly for people of color; (3) stronger unions can enhance existing protections against discrimination by race, gender, national origin and religion by reducing employer discretion and enhancing processes for redress.

Labor organizing is connected to the fundamental constitutional right of association that is recognized as part of the First Amendment. In a democracy, individuals have a right to join together with others to promote their interests and values. Just as the original Civil Rights Act extended the Fourteenth Amendment's prohibition against government discrimination to apply to private-sector employers, adding anti-discrimination protection for labor organizing extends a First Amendment right against government restraint of free association to apply to private-sector employers. Of course, Congress already extended association rights to the private sector when it passed the 1935 NLRA recognizing the "right to self-organization." Including labor protections in the Civil Rights Act, therefore, does not break new ground conceptually, but it does provide workers with a much better way to hold accountable employers who violate their rights.

Some may believe that civil rights laws should only protect individuals from discrimination based on immutable factors such as race, national origin and gender. However, the Civil Rights Act was never limited to these immutable characteristics. The 1964 act itself included protection against discrimination based on religion, which is a mutable characteristic. A Christian who converts to Islam, for example, is protected against an employer's religious discrimination; the employer cannot defend discrimination on the basis that the employee chose to convert. A survey of civil rights legislation shows that such laws have incrementally been extended to prohibit discrimination based on behavioral factors such as pregnancy, prior criminal conviction, whistle-blowing, indebtedness or bankruptcy.

Significantly, anti-discrimination laws apply even when they could hurt the profitability of a company. In the early days of civil rights law, for example, law firms were not allowed to justify discrimination against black attorneys based on evidence that white clients would not want to work with them. The principle already established under the NLRA and UN Declaration of Human Rights suggests that, even if unions cut into corporate profits, employers cannot abuse their economic power by firing employees for trying to organize.

Moreover, strengthening labor can advance the larger objectives of the Civil Rights Act itself: promoting greater dignity and equality, particularly for people of color. The labor and civil rights movements, while not always allied, are fundamentally bound by similar values, interests, tactics and enemies. Labor recognizes that individuals should be treated with decency, a core belief of the Civil Rights Movement; their emphasis on a shared humanity explains why labor leaders and civil rights advocates refer to one another as brothers and sisters.

Not only do the movements share similar values, King recognized that they have common interests. As a predominantly working people, blacks had much to gain from a stronger union movement. Julian Bond, as chairman of the National Association for the Advancement of Colored People, noted in a 2005 address that minorities are disproportionately represented in organized labor; that African Americans who are members of unions earn 35 percent more than nonunionized black people; and that black Americans are more likely than whites to want to join unions. In this way, amending the Civil Rights Act to protect workers trying to organize a union would not diminish the Act's commitment to racial equality; it would extend and affirm that commitment in new ways.

The civil rights and labor movements have also used similar tactics, like civil disobedience, sit-ins and picket lines. And both movements faced a common source of resistance. It is no accident that the eleven states that today are most resistant to unions and have the lowest union density rates are all states that were previously governed by Jim Crow. Historical evidence is clear that the anti-union "right to work" movement was originally aimed at weakening labor's ability to fight against racial segregation.

Finally, stronger unions, by protecting employees against arbitrary dismissals in general, provide an additional shield against the type of racial and gender discrimination that is forbidden by the Civil Rights Act. Most employees currently work "at-will": They can be fired for "good cause, bad cause, or no cause" (the standard definition of "at-will employment"). Unions work to remove arbitrary terminations and the at-will employment system from the workplace, and limit the type of employer discretion that allows discrimination to take place. Unions also put procedures in place to address grievances, providing an employee with the possibility of faster relief should she suffer from discrimination. In this way, adding the right to organize to the Civil Rights Act does not distract from the original focus of the Act, but rather enhances it through internal nongovernmental procedures that can remedy racial discrimination in the workplace in a faster and more efficient manner than litigation.

A POLITICALLY VIABLE IDEA?

Labor law reform has been a very tough sell in the United States, but there are considerable political advantages to framing the right to organize as a matter of moral values rather than a battle of raw "interests" (labor versus management); plus the advantages of having a fight over "anti-discrimination law" rather than "labor law."

The rhetoric of "rights" is very powerful in American political discourse. Indeed, when asked to identify government's most important role, 59 percent say it is to protect individual rights and liberty. "Civil rights" are already a part of the conversation about labor, but, unfortunately, it has been anti-labor forces who employ the rhetoric and symbols of civil rights against workers. The Employee Free Choice Act to improve labor laws failed in part on the argument that workers had a right to a secret ballot. Likewise, for years, business has appropriated the slogan "right to work" to signify state legislation that allows employees to benefit from collective bargaining agreements without paying their fair share of dues—a tactic that prevailed recently even in the labor stronghold of Michigan. And the "Employee Rights Act," which is the Republican version of labor law reform, uses the language of civil rights against workers.

Belatedly, union leaders are beginning to take back the rhetoric of rights, and the AFL-CIO has sponsored rallies to protest illegal firings, likening the campaign, as reported by Steven Greenhouse in his *New York Times* article cited above, to "a new civil rights movement." Connecting labor to the Civil Rights Movement is especially vital to making the issue easier to understand for young people, who may not personally know any friends or family members who are part of organized labor.

Labor law has become increasingly complex and technical, and is understood by few beyond its practitioners. As a civil right, labor law becomes almost intuitively understandable, and its importance becomes easy to communicate to those outside the field. Whereas labor law reform does not excite people, civil rights do. Thomas Geoghegan writes in *Which Side Are You On?*: "If we only thought of the [NLRA] as a civil rights law, instead of a labor law, then maybe liberals would wake up and do something."

Americans long to be part of something larger than themselves, and just as promoters of equal educational opportunity and a cleaner environment have characterized their causes as part of this generation's Civil Rights Movement, so labor organizing—which shares with the Civil Rights Movement the basic quest for human dignity—has a very strong claim to that mantle. In Memphis, Martin Luther King understood that the fate of the labor movement and the civil rights community were inextricably bound. Now is the time to write the protection of organized labor into the Civil Rights Act itself.

* * * * *

COMMENTARIES ON THE KAHLENBERG-MARVIT ARTICLE

Theodore M. Shaw

Richard Kahlenberg's and Moshe Marvit's précis of their book left me with deeply conflicted feelings and reactions. It is provocative and thought-worthy in a manner that requires more time and greater reflection. Consequentially, my initial reactions may not survive further reflection; still, they are strong enough that they demand articulation, if only because I cannot get to where Kahlenberg and Marvit (K&M) are without jumping significant hurdles and reordering long-held principles and beliefs. My own views of class and race invite a "gut rush" acceptance of K&M's thesis; yet I am left with a profound discomfort that defies my ability to organize adequately into thoughts.

The invocation of Dr. Martin Luther King's last campaign, grounded in an understanding of historical and contemporary relationship between class and race, and of the need to adopt the politics of a movement for racial and economic justice, exerts a powerfully seductive force on progressives. Dr. King did not want to go to Memphis, but the strike by black sanitation workers appealed to his core beliefs in a way that coincided with his development as a leader that took him beyond the struggle against racial segregation and discrimination. By 1968, King could no longer stay silent about the Vietnam War and American militarism. Nor could he pursue his dream of a just society without addressing economic inequality, not only for black

Americans whose struggle against racial discrimination had left them economically disadvantaged, but for *all* Americans. King was charting new territory, not because no American had challenged economic injustice before him, or even because no African-American leader had done so. King's position as the pre-eminent and eloquent Civil Rights Movement spokesperson, as Nobel Peace Prize laureate, and as an international human rights advocate, uniquely positioned him to challenge the conscience of America, even if it was by no means certain that if he had lived his campaign against poverty would have succeeded. Indeed, it is the unfinished nature of his life's work that invites 21st century advocates and activists from varying ideological backgrounds to claim him. Right-wing conservatives embrace their version of Dr. King in support of a color-blind paradigm that would render illegal all conscious efforts to voluntarily address systemic vestiges of slavery and Jim Crow segregation. Progressives invoke King in their quest to awaken the Nation to the dangers and the injustice of the yawning chasm between "the 99 percent" and working- and middle-class Americans.

K&M correctly point to the complex role of labor unions during the era of the Civil Rights Movement. Labor unions were, in some instances, some of the biggest obstacles to equal employment opportunity. On the national level, however, labor became some of the staunchest allies of the Civil Rights Movement. Today, public employee unions represent a disproportionate number of black and brown people in the labor force, and unions in general have largely aligned their interests with those of people of color. This alignment is clearly visible in partisan politics at the state and local level, with the Republican Party seen as the party of white people and the wealthy, and the Democrats viewed as the party of "minorities" and labor. And of course, regardless of how much of 21st century economic polarization is attributable to the weakened position of American labor unions, K&M correctly point to the assault on labor and the right to organize as an important battleground between conservatives and progressives. The right of workers to unionize is as old as the labor movement in America; late 19th and early 20th century America far surpasses the bitter political debates that characterize our time. Nonetheless, contemporary assaults on the right to organize pose profound threats to the well-being of working- and middle-class people in the United States, and raise important civil and human rights issues.

My discomfort with K&M is not with their belief that the right of labor to organize should be recognized as a civil right. My discomfort stems from a sense that while K&M pay lip service to the fact that "more work surely needs to be done," their sense that "the trajectory on race is generally pointed in the right direction" may give more ground to those who are arguing that in the age of Obama we have entered into a "post-racial" America. At a time when conscious efforts to address stubborn, intractable and systemic racial inequality for many African Americans and other people of color are under assault from the forces of "color-blindness," we cannot let up. Kahlenberg for some time has promoted the notion of class-conscious affirmative action or diversity efforts as a response to the assault on race-conscious affirmative action and diversity efforts. While I suffer no illusions about the fact that many, if not most, progressives have abandoned and fled the terminology of "affirmative action," or the facts about the direction of the Supreme Court as presently constituted, and while as a matter of principle I independently believe in the importance and the correctness of addressing class-based inequality, I refuse to surrender to the intellectual or legal equation of race-conscious affirmative action and racism. I support, as does Kahlenberg, class-based affirmative action, but I refuse to cede the ground he has ceded on issues of race. Nor do I believe that the tremendous progress to which he and Marvit rightly point is reason to think that we need to shift our focus to a greater degree on issues of economic inequality. We are presently facing an assault on diversity efforts in admission to selective institutions of higher education, an avenue that has desegregated leadership and governance in America for the last 35 years. We face an assault on the constitutionality of the Voting Rights Act. The Fair Housing Act is under assault, and indeed the underpinnings of Title VII of the Civil Rights Act of 1964, which K&M venerate so dearly, are in the crosshairs of radical conservatives whose race project since the days of the Warren Court has been to undo its jurisprudence.

It is this reality that leads me to my core concern with K&M's proposal. Civil rights legislation has been successful, and many Americans have come to an understanding of its importance they once did not have. Nonetheless, since the enactment of Title VII, which K&M propose to amend, and of the Voting Rights Act of 1965, and of the Fair Housing Act of 1968 (which shares the standard known as "the effects test" with Title VII, despised by radical conservatives), these statutes have never been completely safe. They have been under assault by the progenitors of the radical right-wing race project. They have been opened for amendment only when necessity demanded it and when the politics of the moment allowed or demanded it. Opening Title VII for amendment two years after the Supreme Court's decision in *Ricci*, with a House of Representatives in control of radical conservatives, is a risky proposition at best.

Moreover, the amendment to Title VII proposed by K&M would change the nature of a long-existing statute. Even granting their "religion" retort to the "immutable characteristics" argument some might pose to K&M, there is another distinction their proposal would create. Whether it is race, gender, national origin or religion, these are all aspects of who and what we are. (Yes, arguably one can change religion, but I doubt that takes religion out of the "who or what we are" category.) Organizing is "what we do." In other words, to borrow terminology from a Supreme Court decision, the protected class to be added to Title VII is arguably "analytically distinct" from those already in the statute. That does not mean the classification could not be protected in independent legislation; it may pose a question of "fit."

In sum, I support the effort to create the right of labor to organize as a civil right. I support the effort to bring human rights norms to the United States that would, among other things, protect the right of labor to organize. For tactical as well as conceptual reasons, I do not support opening Title VII at this time to rest protection of the right of labor to organize there. I believe that independent legislation is a better path toward the ends K&M seek.

Julius Getman

It is time to amend the National Labor Relations Act. It has failed to meet the stated statutory goal of "encouraging the practice and procedure of collective bargaining," and it has failed to protect the right of employees to unionize. Kahlenberg and Marvit recognize the law's weakness and suggest strengthening it by bringing the right to organize under the Civil Rights Act. This would have the beneficial effect of increasing penalties imposed on employers who discharge or otherwise penalize union supporters. They suggest that the National Labor Relations Board administer the new approach, describing the Board as "an agency that is finely attuned to the nuances of labor law through its more than 75 years of experience handling labor disputes."

Kahlenberg and Marvit anticipate a cultural change occurring once this new approach is tried. They see their proposed change in the law as a step towards making anti-union discrimination as culturally despised as racism. If this occurs, employers might stop opposing unions so fiercely. "Conceivably, writing labor organizing protections into the Civil Rights Act could also spawn a cultural shift in employer behavior. Employers who are found guilty of racial or gender discrimination are today seen to have done something shameful," they write.

I favor their proposal because it would grant significant protection to employees who are now legally vulnerable to economic devastation. I do not, however, see this as something likely to have a major effect on organizing. It would not eliminate the advantages that employers now have in campaigning against unions, such as the right to make captive audience speeches and to keep union organizers off their premises. It is unlikely to alter the proemployer bias of the courts. Nor would it be wise for unions and their supporters to anticipate this law leading to "a cultural shift in employer behavior."

I think that the authors are too kind to the NLRB. It would, for example, have been extremely difficult for observers to note any deep understanding of nuances in the decisions of the Bush Board. If Romney had won, there is reason to believe that the Board would have become openly and consistently anti-union and anti-worker. Finding a way to make the Board less of a political battleground would itself be a significant reform.

A cultural shift in attitudes towards unions would be highly desirable. I do not believe that it can be achieved to any significant extent by using the language or applying the law of employment discrimination. It will require more sweeping changes in the law, such as prohibiting the hiring of permanent replacements in strikes and eliminating or reducing the secondary boycott prohibitions. It will also require changes in the labor movement, such as more consistent mobilizing of the rank-and-file, continuing aggressive struggle against the "malefactors of great wealth" (think

Walmart and Sheldon Adelson), and making common cause with other progressive movements. There is reason to be hopeful that needed changes are in fact taking place, but the process is slow and the obstacles formidable.

Despite my criticisms, the authors are to be commended for stimulating discussion about needed changes in our dysfunctional labor laws.

Leo W. Gerard

Unions put power in the hands of working people, just as the vote put power in the hands of black people. Immediately after President Abraham Lincoln emancipated the slaves, former slaveholders—that is, the wealthy of the Confederacy—conspired to prevent black people from exercising their franchise, to prevent them from wielding the power of the vote to improve their lives. Immediately after the Wagner Act was passed in 1935, right-wing politicians, at the behest of robber barons, conspired to prevent working people from exercising the right to organize enshrined in the law, a right that enabled working people to improve their lives.

Over the years, those intent on denying black people their human rights devised numerous ways to obstruct them from voting, including poll taxes, literacy tests and terrorization by the KKK. They lynched black people to repress an entire race. They lynched union organizers to repress a powerful idea. The great Rev. Martin Luther King embraced unionization as a method for all working people to ensure that they received a just portion of the profits derived from the fruit of their labor. On the day he died, he had supported striking Memphis sanitation workers who carried signs that said, "I AM A MAN."

Inherent in manhood—in personhood—is self-determination. For self-determination, a person must have the ability to exercise the right to vote. And for self-determination, people must have the ability to support themselves and their families. In recent years, right-wingers have once again openly and actively sought to deny the vote to whole categories of people, including the poor and black people, by demanding specific photo identification at polling places. And they've passed union suppression laws in state after state.

In 1944, President Franklin Delano Roosevelt proposed a second Bill of Rights, what he called an Economic Bill of Rights. He said: "We cannot be content, no matter how high that general standard of living may be, if some fraction of our people—whether it be one-third or one-fifth or one-tenth—is ill-fed, ill-clothed, ill-housed, and insecure." Unfortunately, this great proposal was one he did not live to achieve. Now, collective bargaining is among the only methods working people can use to assure their economic rights. Like voting rights, the right to unionize should be strengthened, not weakened.

Sheryll Cashin

I will leave it to others more expert than me to comment on the substantive merits of the proposal to amend the Civil Rights Act put forth by Richard Kahlenberg and

Moshe Marvit. I will say this: They are surely on to something important, perhaps transformative. I agree with them and Dr. King that there is a profound congruence between the goals of the labor movement and the demand for universal human dignity that animated the Civil Rights Movement. The forgotten march, The Poor People's Campaign of 1968, which King envisioned but did not live to see to fruition, embodied this convergence. The campaign would bring blacks, Chicanos, Native Americans and rural whites from invisible hamlets of poverty to occupy the National Mall in a tent city that lasted six weeks. As King imagined it, this multiracial coalition united by economic oppression would kick-start the second phase of the Movement. Mere civil rights, the ability to sit at any lunch counter, were irrelevant without economic means, and so he conceived of a civilly disobedient campaign to put pressure on national leaders to adopt an "economic bill of rights."

The Campaign is forgotten largely because it was unsuccessful and ended badly, with a forced eviction by police. Sound familiar? It is ironic that Kahlenberg and Marvit seek to leverage the success of the Civil Rights Act in order to improve the political saliency of the labor movement. They acknowledge, as they must, that politics is currently set against their proposal, just as politics is currently set against common sense. What is missing from most progressive issue briefs is a strategic plan for altering the political landscape in order to make progressive policy choices possible. The real unfinished business of the Civil Rights Movement is completing the Beloved Community that King imagined. In 1956, when the movement was in its infancy, King delivered a speech entitled, "Facing the Challenge of a New Age." He expounded on the ultimate ends of the civil rights revolution that Rosa Parks had ignited a year before. The end of the movement was not the rights of Negroes per se but reconciliation and the creation of the Beloved Community.

In pragmatic terms for progressives today, that means bringing more working-class whites into their multiracial tent. While pundits and armchair analysts lecture Republicans about demographics and its Latino problem, the GOP is able to adopt "right-to-work" laws in states like Michigan and Indiana in part because the party has become a cultural home for blue-collar workingmen. Without a multracial majority that consistently gets to 55 percent in elections and policy battles, there is little chance of enacting sound policies that might promote collective bargaining, much less correct the underlying structures that create racial and economic inequality. In the case of anti-democratic measures like super-majority requirements to break a filibuster in the U.S., even more cross-racial political cohesion is required. We can begin to reconcile, to move past racial resentments, and create a politics of economic fairness by being quite intentional in our choice of policies and language. Our best hope for a saner politics is a language based upon common harms and the common weal. The best place to start in building multiracial, multiclass coalitions for the common good is with numerous faith-based coalitions that are already working in scores of communities, often in a bipartisan manner. Elsewhere, I have written about this wonderful, righteous work. (See Cashin, "Shall We Overcome? Transcending Race, Class and Ideology Through Interest Convergence," 79 *St. John's L. Rev.* 253–91, 2005).

Throughout American history, economic elites used racial categories and racism to drive a wedge between working-class whites and people of color they might ally with. In the colonial era, indentured servitude gave way to white freedom and black slavery, so that white servants no longer had incentive to join blacks in revolt, as they did in Bacon's Rebellion. In the late-19th century, Jim Crow laws proliferated when a bi-racial farmers' alliance threatened to change unfair financial policies imposed by elites. And the GOP devised a cynical, race-coded Southern strategy that broke up the multiracial alliance that made the New Deal possible. Given this history and its current manifestations, intentional efforts are sorely needed to begin to rebuild trust among "we the people" and to fully realize the Beloved Community.

Larry Cohen

Using Dr. King as their vehicle, Kahlenberg and Marvit write on how Labor and Civil Rights are intertwined, and they note the ascension of civil rights and decline of labor rights since the 1960s.

On a tactical level, our partners in the Civil Rights Movement tell me that they would be opposed to opening the Civil Rights Act, but would be supportive of adding private right of action to their existing support for collective action in the workplace.

Any such initiative will be the target of the same sustained U.S. Chamber of Commerce campaign which has rolled back worker rights, our standard of living and the U.S. economy. In the U.S., our collective bargaining framework has been systematically destroyed by the Chamber's 40-year campaign, resulting in flat real wages for 30 years.

This frame is correct for the United States, but not globally. In Brazil, South Korea and South Africa, we've seen the rise of strong labor movements linked to political movements from the ashes of military dictatorships or even worse, apartheid. Their success should embolden us to see the possibilities of a resurgent movement linking workers' rights to other economic justice and democracy issues.

Let's note that the U.S. House of Representatives, led by Speaker Pelosi, over-whelmingly passed the Employee Free Choice Act. In the U.S. Senate, we had a majority as well, but the expansion of filibuster rules prevented even debate not only on Employee Free Choice but nearly every major piece of legislation passed by the House in the last Congress. Richard and Moshe dismiss Free Choice too quickly and incorrectly.

Yes, in 2013 we must broaden our approach to workers' rights in many ways, and speak to 100 million U.S. working women and men, currently with no effective bargaining or organizing rights. We should include encouragement for new forms of collective action as well as the private right of action.

Our democracy is corrupted. Money is not speech. Corporations are not people. Our path to change must rely on massive movement-building, uniting economic justice and democracy.

[Pls., at Cohen's request, if you have feedback you'd like to get to him, send it to me— chartman@prrac.org—and I'll pass all such on to him—CH]

Randi Weingarten

We've always been a nation built on the simple belief that everyone deserves equal access to economic opportunity and a path to the American dream. That no matter who you are or where you are from—immigrant or native-born—each of us should have a fair shot to achieve our dreams and care for our families. Today, that fair shot, that path to economic opportunity, is under attack by a group of elites seeking to enrich themselves at the expense of the rest of us.

And one of the biggest threats to economic opportunity is the coordinated effort to strip Americans of their right to collectively bargain for fair wages and benefits and a better life for their families and communities. Consider this: Between 1973 and 2007, union membership in the private sector dropped from more than 34 percent to 8 percent. During that time, wage inequality in the private sector increased by more than 40 percent. As we saw in Michigan, extremist politicians continue to ram through policies dubbed "right-to-work" which instead choke the ability of unions to act effectively. These so-called "right-to-work" laws have depressed wages and sup- pressed the ability of workers to collectively bargain. Today, when workers seek to join unions, 25 percent of employers fire at least one prounion worker. And workers are routinely harassed, intimidated and threatened for trying to form or join a union.

We know that workers who belong to unions earn 28 percent more than non- union workers; nearly 87 percent of union workers have guaranteed pensions; and 84 percent of union workers have jobs that provide health insurance benefits. Back when more than one-third of Americans belonged to unions, we were able to set wage-and- benefit standards for entire industries—for union and nonunion workers alike.

This attack on the fundamental right of workers to freely join unions not only threatens economic opportunity but also the strength of our democracy by taking out the only true way—at either the bargaining table or the ballot box—that work- ing families can have a say in their own destiny. Collective bargaining is a necessary part of a capitalist democracy; it ensures economic fairness and reduces income inequality. Given how the scales have tipped against working families, and that economic inequality is at the highest level since the Great Depression, it is time to amend the Civil Rights Act to make it illegal to fire or discriminate against workers who are trying to form a union and to better their lives and their communities.

* * * * *

KAHLENBERG & MARVIT RESPOND

We are grateful that such eminent scholars, labor and civil rights leaders have taken the time to consider our argument and offered such thoughtful responses. Though we cannot address all the important issues the commentators raise in the depth they deserve, we will address here some of their central concerns, and look forward to continuing this conversation as the debates over labor law reform develop.

Each of the commentators agrees that stronger legal protections must be afforded labor rights, and several general themes stand out in the responses. Julius Getman, Larry Cohen and Theodore Shaw each make political arguments concerning the viability of our proposal, the tactic of opening up the Civil Rights Act, and additional political changes that must accompany any successful labor law reform effort. Shaw extends this critique to also question whether our proposal marks a premature shift from focusing on race to focusing on class. He also questions whether protections for activity belong in legislation designed to protect identity. Randi Weingarten argues that collective action by workers can help them enhance their economic positions and political voices. Sheryll Cashin suggests that in addition to looking to King's Poor People's Campaign, we must look towards his idea of the Beloved Community, especially with regard to building multiclass, multiracial coalitions. Leo Gerard, using a civil rights frame, looks at the historical parallels between the opponents of labor and opponents of voting rights for African Americans, arguing that both forms of suppression constitute power grabs.

The conferral of legal rights has created norms in America that would have been unimaginable in America 50 years ago. This shift, however incomplete it is, is a positive development that would not have been possible without legislation. Labor is in need of a similar shift, and if our proposal aids in a change in attitudes towards labor, it will open the door for the additional reforms proposed by Julius Getman. Indeed, as Leo Gerard notes, joining a union and bargaining collectively are "among the only methods working people can use to assure their economic rights." As such, the economic goals of the Civil Rights Act will be further achieved by making labor organizing a civil right.

Larry Cohen and Theodore Shaw each support passing legislation to make labor organizing a civil right, but believe that the Civil Rights Act should not be opened at this time. As Shaw correctly notes, civil rights laws "have never been completely safe," and there is a danger in opening up the Act when both the Supreme Court and the House of Representatives are dominated by radical conservatives. These concerns are reasonable, and the problems associated are easily avoided in a manner that does not significantly alter our proposal. Several pieces of civil rights reform, including the Age Discrimination in Employment Act (ADEA), which created civil rights protections for age discrimination, were accomplished through stand-alone legislation. Similarly, a stand-alone bill, which tracks the language of the Civil Rights Act and writes civil rights into our labor law, would have the same practical benefit as opening up the Civil Rights Act. By pursuing stand-alone labor reform legislation, we can avoid any potential dangers associated with amending the vital protections of the Civil Rights Act.

Julius Getman agrees that the protections offered by civil rights legislation would benefit workers and unions, but remains skeptical that the law would lead to any significant change in conduct by employers. He points to the extreme advantages employers currently enjoy with respect to organizing campaigns, and suggests focusing also on legislation prohibiting the hiring of permanent replacements and eliminating prohibitions on secondary boycotts.

Our proposal to make labor organizing a civil right would do much to protect workers from the high levels of discrimination and retaliation they currently face. Furthermore, it would help shift the debate from one over the private interests of employers and unions to one of basic rights of workers. We do not view our proposal as the singular answer to revitalize labor, nor do we think there is such a silver bullet. Getman is indeed correct that repealing Taft-Hartley and limiting or banning the permanent replacement of strikers is necessary to have a robust labor movement in America. However, such bills have repeatedly failed to make it through Congress under the best political conditions. The current climate in Washington and weakness of labor mean that direct labor law reform is likely impossible in the near future. Part of the political problem is the result of filibuster, as Cohen suggests, but even prior to the modern expansion of the filibuster, prolabor legal reform proved elusive.

In order to pass these more traditional forms of labor law reform, a higher percentage of employees would need to benefit from union coverage, and labor would need to be stronger. Our proposal attempts to get around this Catch-22—where labor must be strengthened in order to effectuate significant reform but significant reform is necessary in order to strengthen labor. Randi Weingarten raises precisely this point when she discusses how the political positions of workers are diminished by low union density. She writes that "the attack on the fundamental right of workers to freely join unions not only threatens economic opportunity but also the strength of our democracy, by taking out the only true way—at either the bargaining table or the ballot box—that working families can have a say in their own destiny." Similarly, Leo Gerard argues that essential components of self-determination are economic security and the right to a free vote. Opponents of labor have shown a propensity to attack both, and the response should be to strengthen the right to vote and the right to act collectively. Strengthening the right to join a union and bargain collectively holds the hope of creating a political environment under which workers can achieve further progressive reforms. With the increasing difficulty of passing traditional labor law reform, we propose that the debate should be centered around the civil rights of workers to associate and have a voice in the workplace. Civil and individual rights present a far more powerful and compelling argument to most Americans than the technical and often obscure confines of labor law.

As Sheryll Cashin argues in her response, in order for progressive politics to advance, coalitions must be built that defy traditional boundaries. Cashin makes the important argument that in addition to King's Poor People's Campaign, labor should also look to the principles of his Beloved Community. Central to King's Beloved Community is the building of multiracial, multiclass coalitions around common principles. Though labor fights for the dignity and voice of workers, it is too often politically, legally and socially isolated. Opponents make the incorrect charge that unions fight only for their own members, often at the expense of other workers. We believe that building a movement around labor organizing as a civil right universalizes the cause in important respects. Learning from the Civil Rights Movement, and partnering more closely with civil rights organizations, will help labor build the community and interfaith coalitions that were central to the Civil Rights Movement.

Though the protections of the Civil Rights Act would not eliminate the advantages employers have, it would do much to change their behavior by changing the employer calculus of violating workers' rights. In addition to the increased penalties available under the Civil Rights Act, employees and unions would gain meaningful access to the courts. Getman rightly acknowledges the "proemployer bias of the courts" and suggests that our proposal would do nothing to change that. However, workers need not win in court in order to enjoy the significant benefits of a private right of action. The courts, as Arthur Kinoy made clear in the labor battles of the 1950s, are a political institution in which labor should seek a voice. Using the liberal rules of pre-trial discovery, discriminated-against workers and unions would be able to depose management under penalty of perjury, examine the employer's books, read e-mails and memos with anti-union consultants, and have access to the inner workings of the company. In short, this would allow workers and unions to disrupt employers in a manner currently unavailable. Furthermore, workers and unions need not win in court in order to succeed in a lawsuit. Because of the costs and uncertainty of litigation, the majority of employment discrimination cases settle well before trial. In this context, such settlement negotiations can be fruitful venues for securing important concessions in organizing campaigns, such as a card check or neutrality agreement.

Getman also suggests that "finding a way to make the Board less of a political battleground would itself be a significant reform." Though not the primary purpose, our proposal may lead to this shift. One of the reasons the Board finds itself in the middle of political battles is that it has exclusive jurisdiction over labor disputes. Reducing funding for the Board or appointing members who are openly hostile to labor are effective tactics because workers must proceed through the Board process. However, if workers have a private right of action, the Board loses its place as the sole labor battleground.

Shaw writes that although he is supportive of the idea of making labor organizing a civil right, he is concerned that our proposal may give ground to those who argue we are in a "post-racial America." He argues that any legislation making organizing a civil right should not shift the focus from race to class, and points out that one of us (Kahlenberg) is a long-time proponent of replacing race-based with class-based affirmative action in education. There are principled reasons to favor or oppose Kahlenberg's position on affirmative action in education, but our argument on labor organizing as a civil right is different. We do not call for replacing one kind of approach with another, as in the debates on race-based or class-based affirmative action. Rather, here we suggest supplementing the protected categories in the Civil Rights Act with an additional category that would help advance some of the original goals of the Act. Our intent is not to shift the focus away from race and towards class, but rather to address some of the intractable issues of class with some of the legal tools that have helped change attitudes and culture on race.

Additionally, Shaw characterizes the protections of civil rights legislation as protecting "who or what we are" (even when mutable), rather than "what we do." He argues that conduct-based protections are analytically distinct from identity-based protections, and that the two may not fit in the same legislation. However, stand-alone legislation, as discussed above, does not require the two to co-exist in the same legislation. The deeper point here is well-taken: that going beyond the original categories of the Civil Rights Act is a conceptual leap. However, federal and state civil rights legislation has already made this leap by including as protected categories pregnancy, past criminal conviction, bankruptcy, unemployment and the like. The civil rights framework has already been extended beyond identity categories to cover conduct. The question of whether conduct is appropriate for civil rights protections should hinge on two issues: whether the additional category would help promote the original purpose of the Civil Rights Act, and whether the conduct is linked to a fundamental or constitutional right. As described in our chapter above, our proposal meets both of these criteria.

Each of the commentators discusses the poison of our current politics, describing it as "corrupted" and "set against common sense." However desperate this political situation may be, the one positive benefit to this reality is that it forces progressives to build broad-based coalitions rather than individually proceeding along narrow political interests. Our proposal of making labor organizing a civil right is premised on the importance of such coalitions. This alone will not revitalize labor, but it will help workers vindicate long-held rights and help labor promote other progressive policies.

Local People as Law Shapers: Lessons from Atlanta's Civil Rights Movement

Tomiko Brown-Nagin

Many of those who profess to want change "don't care nothing about poor people. . . . If they had poor people at heart, they could make it better." Ethel Mae Mathews, president of the Atlanta chapter of the National Welfare Rights Organization, made this statement in 2000, after decades of community-based activism in Atlanta. Five decades after passage of the Civil Rights and Voting Rights Acts, Mathews criticized policymakers who ignored the poor. The African-American woman directed special contempt at other African-American leaders, elected and self-appointed: "They forget about you, they forget about who they are and where they come from, and who helped them get where they is."

Years of work in Atlanta's impoverished neighborhoods informed Mathews' assessment of civil rights and anti-poverty activism at the dawn of the 21st century. The daughter of Alabama sharecroppers, Mathews had arrived in Atlanta penniless during the 1950s. She had a sixth-grade education. She found work as a housekeeper and lived in public housing, where she struggled to raise her children. Mathews found her political voice in the welfare rights movement. Budget cuts by federal and state legislators to programs to aid the poor angered her. Moreover, Congress had enacted the Civil Rights Act of 1964 and the 1965 Voting Rights Act—legislative landmarks—but neither law had cured her ills. Formal equality under the law had not changed her daily life; and the right to vote, alone, had not brought about a responsive government.

Mathews, together with Eva Davis, Emma Armour and other occupants of Atlanta's housing projects, organized. They protested budget cuts and other policies that undermined the poor—in the streets, in the legislature, in the courts. The women demanded concrete changes for themselves and their children. They sought an adequate income, affordable housing and desegregated schools.

Ethel Mae Mathews and the searing critiques of the legal and social orders that she and fellow activists lodged during the late 1960s feature prominently in my book, *Courage to Dissent: Atlanta and the Long History of the Civil Rights Movement.* Mathews is just one of the book's figures who answer the central question posed: What would the story of black Americans' struggle for civil rights look like if legal historians shifted the focus from the work of the national NAACP, the legendary Thurgood Marshall and the U.S. Supreme Court, to local agents of change?

The book answers the question by shining a spotlight on unsung lawyers and activists who fought for equality in Atlanta from the 1940s through 1980. It shows that courageous local lawyers, organizers, negotiators, students and working-class men and women shook up the nation—and frequently clashed with the mandates of the national black leadership.

Courage to Dissent discusses three distinct waves of dissenters from the racial status quo at three different historical moments. All of the dissenters sought "equality," but each wave of lawyers and activists imputed different meaning to the word and had different priorities and tactics for achieving equality.

The book discusses "pragmatists," dominant beginning in the late 1940s, "movement lawyers and demonstrators" who burst onto the scene during the 1960s, and "welfare rights activists," prominent during the 1970s. Each wave of civil rights activists insisted on defining equality and the paths toward it in its own way, and each group gave rise to a new wave of activists with different priorities, strategies and tactics. The book discusses debates among these waves of dissenters over politics, housing, education and economic disparities—issues that continue to incite debate among activists.

THE PRAGMATISTS

The pragmatists sought to challenge Jim Crow laws incrementally, without destroying the social and economic capital the black middle class built during segregation. One of the South's first African-American lawyers, Austin Thomas ("A.T.") Walden, numbered among this group. Walden valued voting rights over litigation and rejected the idea that integration equaled equality—a cornerstone of the NAACP's court battles. Like Walden, black college presidents, ministers, teachers and contractors also championed racial reform through voting rights. But these professionals shied away from legal challenges to school and housing segregation. Both sorts of litigation posed financial threats to the pragmatists. Black teachers might lose their jobs if school desegregation occurred. Black builders, who enjoyed a captive market under segregation, would compete in a larger environment if Jim Crow fell in housing. The pragmatists also could cite community-interested rationales to support their choices. Pragmatists argued that black students might meet hostility in desegregated schools. And they noted that blacks prospered in same-race neighborhoods where they maintained cultural ties. If pragmatists accommodated segregation, they did so for good reasons, they believed.

THE MOVEMENT LAWYERS

Movement lawyers and the demonstrators challenged the incrementalism of the pragmatists, whom they dismissed as "Uncle Toms." The demonstrators sought "Freedom Now." They protested segregated public accommodations in the streets, staged rent strikes and demanded the right to vote. The students found allies in a new generation of the civil rights bar—trailblazing lawyers Len Holt and Howard Moore, Jr. Holt introduced the Student Non-violent Coordinating Committee (SNCC) to "movement lawyering"—a style of civil rights litigation supportive of direct action. Moore, SNCC's general counsel, litigated across a wide variety of cases—criminal, school desegregation and draft resistance actions, among others.

Moore eventually represented some of his clients when they took advantage of new opportunities created by the Voting Rights Act. In a bid to transition from "protest to politics," student radicals ran for public office, and some won. By the early 1970s, Atlanta had elected a black mayor, a black Board of Education chairman, a black Congressman, and blacks held half the seats on the school board.

WELFARE RIGHTS ACTIVISTS

These changes, however symbolically significant, did not satisfy the third wave of dissenters—welfare rights activists such as Ethel Mae Mathews, who emerged during the late 1960s and 1970s. This final wave of dissidents attacked economic and structural inequality in society—the same world that some middle-class blacks had helped to build and fought to preserve. Mathews and other anti-poverty activists also criticized the political structure—the same structure that some of the 1960s demonstrators had now embraced.

Thus, the disappointments that Mathews expressed in 2000 had deep roots; they rested in the unfinished struggles of the 1960s. Her critique persisted because the legacy of Jim Crow that she had identified—racialized poverty—remained.

Courage to Dissent illuminates the relationship between the past and the present. The story it tells about Atlanta and its evolution over the post-war era is unique, but Atlanta's post-war history is, in many ways, representative of urban America. And Ethel Mae Mathews stands in for many Americans, forgotten citizens who still seek a political voice and political power.

LESSONS LEARNED

What lessons, then, does *Courage to Dissent* offer for today? Each reader can find something in the book that relates to his or her movement of choice—whether it is the continuing struggle for racial justice, women's rights, environmental justice or gay rights. Above all else, this bottom-up history of legal activism teaches that people from all walks of life can be law shapers—if given the chance. The gift the array of featured dissenters pass along to contemporary change agents is, as the conclusion notes, "a tradition of protest itself, the will to object to injustice, in some way."

This lesson—about the power of human agency—sometimes seems lost on lawyers who favor court-based forms of advocacy. Yet the most beloved lawyers in *Courage to Dissent,* Len Holt and Howard Moore, Jr., embraced the grassroots. During the movement's finest hours, community-based protest and ideas from below shaped legal and political agendas. The imperatives of the poor mattered.

Freedom Riders

Raymond Arsenault

Freedom Riders: 1961 and the Struggle for Racial Justice, *published by Oxford University Press, is an extraordinary study, by Raymond Arsenault, the appropriately named John Hope Franklin Professor of Southern History at the Univ. of South Florida, St. Petersburg (rarsenau@stpt.usf.edu). The product of 10 years of research, this 690-page book details the courage and tenacity of a remarkable, diverse group of racial justice activists and their success in tearing down unconstitutional Southern segregation practices regarding interstate travel. Buttressed by 73 pages of endnotes, a 27-page bibliography and, most amazingly, a Roster of Riders Appendix listing 64 Freedom Rides and their 436 Freedom Riders (with race, age, gender, occupation and, where available, information about their later lives and careers), this engagingly written account is an important piece of our nation's history. We reprint here the book's (slightly shortened) Introduction (minus its endnotes, deleted due to space limitations; see the book for proper source attributions).*

> The plan . . . was simplicity itself. In any sane, even half-civilized society it would have been completely innocuous, hardly worth a second thought or meriting any comment at all. CORE would be sending an integrated team—black and white together—from the nation's capital to New Orleans on public transportation. That's all. Except, of course, that they would sit randomly on the buses in integrated pairs and in the stations they would use waiting room facilities casually, ignoring the white/colored signs. What could be more harmless . . . in any even marginally healthy society?
> —Stokely Carmichael

May 21, 1961. It was Sunday night on the New Frontier, and freedom was on the line in Montgomery, Alabama. Earlier in the evening, more than a thousand black Americans, including the Reverend Martin Luther King Jr. and several other nationally prominent civil rights leaders, had gathered at the First Baptist Church (Colored) to show their support for a visiting band of activists known as Freedom Riders.

Located just a few blocks from the state capitol where President Jefferson Davis had sworn allegiance to the Confederate cause in 1861, First Baptist had been the setting for a number of dramatic events over the years, but the historic church had never witnessed anything quite like the situation unfolding both inside and outside its red-brick walls. For several hours, the Freedom Riders and the congregation sang hymns and freedom songs and listened to testimonials about courage and commitment. But as the spirit of hope and justice rose inside the crowded sanctuary, a wholly different mood of defiance and outrage developed outside.

By nightfall the church was surrounded and besieged by a swelling mob of white protesters determined to defend a time-honored system of racial segregation. Screaming racial epithets and hurling rocks and Molotov cocktails, the protesters threatened to overwhelm a beleaguered group of federal marshals who feared that some members of the mob were intent on burning the church to the ground. When it became obvious that the marshals were overmatched, the governor of Alabama deployed a battalion of National Guardsmen to disperse the crowd, and tragedy was averted. But it would be early morning before the surrounding streets were secure enough for the Freedom Riders and their supporters to leave the church. Loaded into a convoy of military trucks and looking much like wartime refugees, the troublesome visitors and their hosts were escorted back to a black community that must have wondered what other indignities and challenges lay ahead. The battle of May 21 was over, but the centuries-old struggle for racial justice would continue.

How the Freedom Riders came to be at First Baptist, why they inspired so much hope and fear, and what happened to them—and the hundreds of other Americans who joined their ranks—are the questions that drive this book. As the epigraph from Stokely Carmichael suggests, these are important and perplexing questions that should engage anyone concerned with freedom, justice, and the realization of America's democratic ideals. With characters and plot lines rivaling those of the most imaginative fiction, the saga of the Freedom Rides is an improbable, almost unbelievable story. In 1961, during the first year of John F. Kennedy's presidency, more than four hundred Americans participated in a dangerous experiment designed to awaken the conscience of a complacent nation. Inspired by visions of social revolution and moral regeneration, these self-proclaimed "Freedom Riders" challenged the mores of a racially segregated society by performing a disarmingly simple act. Traveling together in small interracial groups, they sat where they pleased on buses and trains and demanded unrestricted access to terminal restaurants and waiting rooms, even in areas of the Deep South where such behavior was forbidden by law and custom.

Patterned after a 1947 Congress of Racial Equality (CORE) project known as the Journey of Reconciliation, the Freedom Rides began in early May with a single group of thirteen Riders recruited and trained by CORE's national staff. By early summer the Rides had evolved into a broad-based movement involving hundreds of activists representing a number of allied local, regional, and national civil rights organizations. Attracting a diverse assortment of volunteers—black and white, young and old, male and female, religious and secular, Northern and Southern—the Freedom

Rider movement transcended the traditional legalistic approach to civil rights, taking the struggle out of the courtroom and into the streets and jails of the Jim Crow South. Empowered by two U.S. Supreme Court decisions mandating the desegregation of interstate travel facilities, the Freedom Riders brazenly flouted state and local segregation statutes, all but daring Southern officials to arrest them.

Deliberately provoking a crisis of authority, the Riders challenged federal officials to enforce the law and uphold the constitutional right to travel without being subjected to degrading and humiliating racial restrictions. Most amazingly, they did so knowing that their actions would almost certainly provoke a savage and violent response from militant white supremacists. Invoking the philosophy of nonviolent direct action, they willingly put their bodies on the line for the cause of racial justice. Openly defying the social conventions of a security-conscious society, they appeared to court martyrdom with a reckless disregard for personal safety or civic order. None of the obstacles placed in their path—not widespread censure, not political and financial pressure, not arrest and imprisonment, not even the threat of death—seemed to weaken their commitment to nonviolent struggle. On the contrary, the hardships and suffering imposed upon them appeared to stiffen their resolve, confounding their white supremacist antagonists and testing the patience of even those who sympathized with their cause.

Time and again, the Riders seemed on the verge of defeat, but in every instance they found a way to sustain and expand their challenge to Jim Crow segregation. After marauding Alabama Klansmen used bombs and mob violence to disrupt and disband the original CORE Freedom Ride, student activists from Nashville stepped forward to organize a Ride of their own, eventually forcing federal officials to intervene on their behalf. Later, when Mississippi officials placed hundreds of Freedom Riders in prison and imposed bond payments that threatened the financial solvency of CORE, the net effect was to strengthen rather than to weaken the nonviolent movement. On a number of other occasions, too, attempts to intimidate the Freedom Riders and their supporters backfired, reinvigorating and prolonging a crisis that would not go away.

It is little wonder, then, that the Freedom Rides sent shock waves through American society, evoking fears of widespread social disorder, racial polarization, and a messy constitutional crisis. In the mid-1950s the Montgomery Bus Boycott and its leader Martin Luther King, Jr. had familiarized Americans with the tactics and philosophy of Gandhian nonviolent resistance, and in 1960 the sit-in movement conducted by black college students in Greensboro, North Carolina, and scores of other Southern cities had introduced direct action on a mass scale. But nothing in the recent past had fully prepared the American public for the Freedom Riders' interracial "invasion" of the segregated South. With the Freedom Rides, the civil rights struggle reached a level of intensity that even the sit-ins, potentially the most disruptive episode of the pre-1961 era, had managed to avoid. Loosely organized by local student activists and only tangentially connected to federal court mandates, the sit-in movement had skirted the potentially explosive issues of states' rights and outside agitation by Northern-based civil rights organizations.

The closest thing to a national civil rights crisis prior to the Freedom Rides was the school desegregation fight following the *Brown v. Board of Education* implementation decision of 1955, but the refusal of the Eisenhower administration to press for anything more than token integration had seemingly defused the crisis by the end of the decade. Even in Little Rock, Arkansas, where Eisenhower had dispatched troops to enforce a court order in 1957, the spirit of intense confrontation had largely subsided by the time of the Freedom Rides. By then John Kennedy's New Frontier was in full swing, but there was no indication that the new Administration was willing to sacrifice civic peace or political capital in the interests of school desegregation or any other civil rights issue, despite periodic pledges to abide by the Supreme Court's "with all deliberate speed" implementation order. Indeed, with public opinion polls showing little interest in civil rights among white Americans, there was no compelling reason, other than a personal commitment to abstract principles of freedom and justice, for any national political leader to challenge the racial orthodoxies and mores of Jim Crow culture.

During and after the fall campaign, Kennedy proclaimed that his New Frontier policies would transcend the stolid conservatism of the Eisenhower era; and in a stirring inaugural address he declared that the United States would "pay any price, bear any burden, meet any hardship, support any friend, oppose any foe to assure the survival and success of liberty." In the Winter and early Spring of 1961, however, the New Frontier manifested itself primarily in an assertive presence abroad, not in enhanced social justice at home. As civil rights leaders waited for the first sign of a bold initiative on the domestic front, superheated rhetoric about "missile gaps" and Soviet expansionism heightened Cold War tensions, fostering a crisis mentality that led to the ill-fated Bay of Pigs invasion in April. Marginalizing all other issues, including civil rights, the military and diplomatic fiasco in Cuba only served to sharpen the administration's focus on international affairs.

The president himself set the tone, and by early May there was no longer any doubt, as the journalist Richard Reeves later observed, that the Cold Warrior in the White House regarded civil rights matters as an unwelcome "diversion from the priority business of promoting and winning freedom around the world." Father Theodore Hesburgh, the chairman of the U.S. Civil Rights Commission, was one of the first to learn this sobering truth. During an early briefing held two weeks after the inauguration, Kennedy made it clear that he considered white supremacist transgressions such as the Alabama National Guard's illegal exclusion of black soldiers to be a trivial matter in the grand scheme of world affairs. "Look, Father," he explained, "I may have to send the Alabama National Guard to Berlin tomorrow and I don't want to have to do it in the middle of a revolution at home." Neither he nor Hesburgh had the faintest suspicion that in three months' time these same Alabama Guardsmen would be called not to Berlin but rather to a besieged black church in Montgomery where Freedom Riders required protection from a white supremacist mob. In early February, neither man had any reason to believe that a group of American citizens would deliberately place themselves in jeopardy by traveling to Alabama, counting "upon the racists of the South to create a crisis, so that the federal government would be compelled to enforce federal law," as CORE's national director Jim Farmer put it.

To many Americans, including the president, the rationale behind the Freedom Rides bordered on madness. But Farmer and other proponents of direct action reasoned that they could turn the President's passion for Cold War politics to their advantage by exposing and dramatizing the hypocrisy of promoting freedom abroad while maintaining Jim Crow in places like Alabama and Mississippi. With the onset of decolonization, the "colored" nations of Africa and Asia had emerged as important players in the escalating struggle between the United States and the Soviet Union, and it was no secret that America's long and continuing association with racial discrimination posed a potential threat to the State Department's continuing efforts to secure the loyalty and respect of the so-called Third World. If movement leaders could find some means of highlighting the diplomatic costs of Jim Crow, the administration would be forced to address civil rights issues as a function of national security.

Putting this strategy into practice, however, was extremely risky in a nation still conditioned by a decade of McCarthyism. To embarrass the nation on the world stage, for whatever reason, was to invite charges of disloyalty and collusion with Communist enemies. Even though a growing number of Americans acknowledged the connection between civil rights and the legitimacy of America's claims to democratic virtue and moral authority, very few, even among self-professed liberals, were willing to place the nation's international stature at risk for the purpose of accelerating the pace of social change. Such considerations extended to the Civil Rights Movement itself, where internecine Red-baiting and periodic purges had been common since the late 1940s. In varying degrees, every civil rights organization, from the NAACP to CORE, had to guard against charges of subversion and "fellow-traveling," and even the most cautious advocates of racial justice were sometimes subject to Cold War suspicions.

Civil rights activists of all persuasions faced an uphill struggle in the Cold War context of 1961. For the Freedom Riders, however, the challenge of mounting an effective protest movement was compounded by the fundamental conservatism of a nation wedded to consensus politics. As earlier generations of radical activists had discovered, enlisting support for direct action, economic boycotts, and other disruptive tactics was a difficult task in a society infused with the mythology of superior national virtue and equal access to legal redress. While a majority of Americans endorsed the goal of desegregating interstate transportation, a much smaller proportion supported the use of direct action, nonviolent or otherwise. According to a Gallup Poll conducted in late May and early June 1961, 66 percent of Americans agreed with the Supreme Court's recent ruling "that racial segregation on trains, buses, and in public waiting rooms must end," but only 24 percent approved "of what the 'freedom riders' are doing." When asked if sit-ins, Freedom Rides, and "other demonstrations by Negroes" would "hurt or help the Negros' chances of being integrated in the South," only 27 percent of the respondents thought they would help.

In many communities, public opposition to the Rides was reinforced by negative press coverage. Editorial condemnation of CORE's intrusive direct action campaign was almost universal in the white South, but negative characterizations of the Freedom Rides as foolhardy and unnecessarily confrontational were also common in the national press. Although most of the nation's leading editors and commentators embraced the ideal of desegregation, very few acknowledged that Freedom Rides and other disruptive tactics were a necessary catalyst for timely social change. Indeed, many journalists, like many of their readers and listeners, seemed to accept the moral equivalency of pro- and anti-civil-rights demonstrators, blaming one side as much as the other for the social disorder surrounding the Rides. In later years it would become fashionable to hail the Freedom Riders as courageous visionaries, but in 1961 they were more often criticized as misguided, if not dangerous, radicals.

The Freedom Riders' negative public image was the product of many factors, but two of their most obvious problems were bad timing and a deeply rooted suspicion of radical agitation by "outsiders." Set against the backdrop of the Civil War Centennial celebration, which began in April 1961, the Freedom Rides evoked vivid memories of meddling abolitionists and invading armies. This was especially true in the white South, where a resurgent "siege mentality" was in full force during the post-*Brown* era. But "outside agitators" were also unpopular in the North, where Cold War anxieties mingled with the ambiguous legacy of Reconstruction. When trying to comprehend the motivations behind the Freedom Rides, Americans of all regions and of all political leanings drew upon the one historical example that had influenced national life for nearly a century: the allegedly misguided attempt to bring about a Radical Reconstruction of the Confederate South. While some Americans appreciated the moral and political imperatives of Reconstruction, the dominant image of the tumultuous decade following the Civil War was that of a "tragic era" sullied by corruption and opportunism.

Among black Americans and white liberals the *Brown* decision had given rise to the idea of a long-overdue Second Reconstruction, but even in the civil rights community there was some reluctance to embrace a neoabolitionist approach to social change. Some civil rights advocates, including Thurgood Marshall and Roy Wilkins of the NAACP, feared that Freedom Riders and other proponents of direct action would actually slow the process of change by needlessly provoking a white backlash and squandering the movement's financial and legal resources. To Wilkins, who admired the Riders' courage but questioned their sanity, the CORE project represented "a desperately brave, reckless strategy," a judgment seconded by Leslie Dunbar, the executive director of the Southern Regional Council. "When I heard about all those Northerners heading south I was sure they were going to catch hell and maybe even get themselves killed," Dunbar recalled many years later.

Dunbar had good reason to be concerned. In a nation where the mystique of states' rights and local control enjoyed considerable popularity, crossing state lines for the purpose of challenging parochial mores was a highly provocative act. The notion that Freedom Riders were outside agitators and provocateurs cast serious doubt on their legitimacy, eliminating most of the moral capital that normally accompanied nonviolent struggle. Freedom Rides, by their very nature, involved physical mobility and a measure of outside involvement, if only in the form of traveling from one place to another. But the discovery—or in some cases, the assumption—that most of the Freedom Riders were Northerners deepened the sense of public anxiety surrounding the Rides. Judging by the national press and contemporary public commentary, the archetypal Freedom Rider was an idealistic but naive white activist from the North, probably a college student but possibly an older religious or labor leader. In actuality, while many Freedom Riders resembled that description, many others did not. The Freedom Riders were much more diverse than most Americans realized. Black activists born and raised in the South accounted for six of the original 13 Freedom Riders and approximately 40 percent of the 400+ Riders who later joined the movement. The Freedom Rider movement was as interregional as it was interracial, but for some reason the indigenous contribution to the Rides did not seem to register in the public consciousness, then or later. Part of the explanation undoubtedly resides in the conventional wisdom that Southern blacks were too beaten down to become involved in their own liberation. Even after the Montgomery Bus Boycott and the 1960 sit-ins suggested otherwise, this misconception plagued popular and even scholarly explanations of the civil rights struggle, including accounts of the Freedom Rides.

Redressing this misconception is reason enough to write a revisionist history of the Freedom Rides. But there are a number of other issues, both interpretative and factual, that merit attention. Chief among them is the tendency to treat the Freedom Rides as little more than a dramatic prelude to the climactic events of the mid- and late 1960s. In the rush to tell the stories of Birmingham, Freedom Summer, the Civil Rights Acts of 1964 and 1965, the Black Power movement, and the urban riots, assassinations, and political and cultural crises that have come to define a decade of breathless change, the Freedom Rides have often gotten lost. Occupying the midpoint between the 1954 *Brown* decision and the 1968 assassination of Martin Luther King, the events of 1961 would seem to be a likely choice as the pivot of a pivotal era in civil rights history. But that is not the way the Rides are generally depicted in civil rights historiography. While virtually every historical survey of the Civil Rights Movement includes a brief section on the Freedom Rides, they have not attracted the attention that they deserve. The first scholarly monograph on the subject was published in 2003, and amazingly the present volume represents the first attempt by a professional historian to write a book-length account of the Freedom Rides.

As the first historical study of this remarkable group of activists, *Freedom Riders* attempts to reconstruct the text and context of a pivotal moment in American history. At the mythic level, the saga of the Freedom Riders is a fairly simple tale of collective engagement and empowerment, of the pursuit and realization of democratic ideals, and of good triumphing over evil. But a carefully reconstructed history reveals a much more interesting story. Lying just below the surface, encased in memory and long-overlooked documents, is the real story of the Freedom Rides, a complicated mesh of commitment and indecision, cooperation and conflict, triumph and disappointment. In an attempt to recapture the meaning and significance of the Freedom Rides without sacrificing the drama of personal experience and historical contingency, I have written a book that is chronological and narrative in form. From the outset my goal has been to produce a "braided narrative" that addresses major analytical questions related to cause and consequence, but I have done so in a way that allows the art of storytelling to dominate the structure of the work.

Whenever possible, I have let the historical actors speak for themselves, and much of the book relies on interviews with former Freedom Riders, journalists, and government officials. Focusing on individual stories, I have tried to be faithful to the complexity of human experience, to treat the Freedom Riders and their contemporaries as flesh-and-blood human beings capable of inconsistency, confusion, and varying modes of behavior and belief. The Freedom Riders, no less than the other civil rights activists who transformed American life in the decades following World War II, were dynamic figures. Indeed, the ability to adapt and to learn from their experiences, both good and bad, was an essential element of their success. Early on, they learned that pushing a reluctant nation into action required nimble minds and subtle judgments, not to mention a measure of luck.

While they sometimes characterized the Civil Rights Movement as an irrepressible force, the Freedom Riders knew all too well that they faced powerful and resilient enemies backed by regional and national institutions and traditions. Fortunately, the men and women who participated in the Freedom Rides had access to institutions and traditions of their own. When they boarded the "freedom buses" in 1961, they knew that others had gone before them, figuratively in the case of crusading abolitionists and the black and white soldiers who marched into the South during the Civil War and Reconstruction, and literally in the case of the CORE veterans who participated in the 1947 Journey of Reconciliation. In the early 20th century, local black activists in several Southern cities had staged successful boycotts of segregated streetcars; in the 1930s and 1940s, labor and peace activists had employed sit-ins and other forms of direct action; and more recently the Gandhian liberation of India and the unexpected mass movements in Montgomery, Tallahassee, Greensboro, Nashville, and other centers of insurgency had demonstrated that the power of nonviolence was more than a philosophical chimera. At the same time, the legal successes of the NAACP and the gathering strength of the Civil Rights Movement in the years since the Second World War, not to mention the emerging decolonization of the Third World, infused Freedom Riders with the belief that the arc of history was finally bending in the right direction. Racial progress, if not inevitable, was at least possible, and the Riders were determined to do all they could to accelerate the pace of change.

Convincing their fellow Americans, black or white, that nonviolent struggle was a reliable and acceptable means of combating racial discrimination would not be easy. Indeed, even getting the nation's leaders to acknowledge that such discrimination required immediate and sustained attention was a major challenge. Notwithstanding the empowering and instructive legacy left by earlier generations of freedom fighters, the Freedom Riders knew that the road to racial equality remained long and hard, and that advancing down that road would test their composure and fortitude.

The Riders' dangerous passage through the bus terminals and jails of the Jim Crow South represented only one part of an extended journey for justice that stretched back to the dawn of American history and beyond. But once that passage was completed, there was renewed hope that the nation would eventually find its way to a true and inclusive democracy. For the brave activists who led the way, and for those of us who can only marvel at their courage and determination, this link to a brighter future was a great victory. Yet, as we shall see, it came with the sobering reminder that "power concedes nothing without a demand," as the abolitionist and former slave Frederick Douglass wrote in 1857. . .

The Chicago Freedom Movement
40 Years Later: A Symposium

ASSESSING THE CHICAGAO FREEDOM MOVEMENT

JAMES RALPH

The Chicago Freedom Movement was the most ambitious civil rights mobilization ever launched in the North. The product of an alliance of the Southern Christian Leadership Conference (SCLC) and the Coordinating Council of Community Organizations (CCCO—a coalition of Chicago civil rights groups), the Chicago Freedom Movement lasted from 1965 to 1967. It built upon the hard work of the CCCO in contesting racial inequality in Chicago, especially in its public schools. And it attracted national attention in the Summer of 1966 when it launched a series of marches to expose persistent housing discrimination in metropolitan Chicago. On one open-housing march, Martin Luther King, Jr. was struck on the head by a rock. "Frankly," he said, "I have never seen as much hatred and hostility on the part of so many people."

Faintly Remembered Today

What is striking, on the occasion of its 40th anniversary, is how faintly the Chicago Freedom Movement is remembered today. While there are museums devoted to the famous civil rights campaigns in Montgomery, Birmingham and Selma, Alabama, there is no museum commemorating the Chicago Freedom Movement. In fact, the city of Chicago lacks even historic markers acknowledging the important sites of the Chicago movement. In Atlanta, the National Park Service maintains the childhood home of Martin Luther King. In Memphis, the Lorraine Motel, where King was assassinated in 1968, is the centerpiece of an impressive civil rights museum. In Chicago, by contrast, the North Lawndale apartment building where King lived for a time in order to be close to African Americans confined to Chicago's West Side ghetto was torn down many years ago and remained a vacant lot. (In 2011, the Lawndale Christian Development Corporation opened the 45-unit Dr. King Legacy Apartments on the corner of 16th Street and South Hamlin Avenue, and it now includes a Fair Housing Museum.)

The custodians of that which is deemed important in American history—the textbooks and the surveys—second this lack of public acknowledgment of the Chicago Freedom Movement. The fifth edition of *America's History* does not mention it. Nor does a recent edition of *American Journey*. The same is true for the second edition of *American Destiny: Narrative of a Nation* and the fifth edition of *Out of Many*. In each of these textbooks, Martin Luther King's and SCLC's earlier Birmingham and Selma campaigns are discussed. Even James Patterson's prizewinning history of America from 1945 to 1974, *Grand Expectations*, is silent on the Chicago Movement.

A critical question, then, is how can this discrepancy in the public memory of the Chicago Freedom Movement and King's and SCLC's other campaigns be explained.

The explanation stems in part from the popular judgment that the Chicago Freedom Movement was a defeat, especially compared to the Birmingham and Selma initiatives. The verdict of failure circled the Chicago movement even before it came to an end. Dissatisfied activists helped to fuel such a reading when in the wake of the Summit Agreement—a pact reached in late August 1966 between Martin Luther King, Al Raby (convenor of the CCCO) and other civil rights leaders, and Mayor Richard J. Daley and civic, business and religious elites to bring a halt to the open-housing marches and to take concrete steps to end the racial divide in the region—they decided to stage a march in Cicero, long known for its hostility toward blacks.

As Robert Lucas, who led the march in Cicero in September 1966, has stated, "King went up against Richard J. Daley, and he lost." Over the decades, this assessment has been the dominant one in Chicago. Surveying the state of the city's West Side 20 years after the Chicago Freedom Movement, one African-American resident concluded, "Nothing really happened." And recently, Leon Despres, a supporter of civil rights who opposed the Daley Administration during the 1960s, has said that results of the Chicago campaign were "not much of a victory for Martin Luther King, Jr."

This bleak reading of the Chicago Freedom Movement shaped the perspective of the first major biography of King, written by David Levering Lewis in 1970. "The Chicago debacle" was how Lewis categorized its outcome. Many later scholars arrived at the same conclusion. *In America in Our Time,* published in 1976, Godfrey Hodgson stated that "Martin Luther King went to Chicago and was routed . . ." Nearly a decade later, Alonzo Hamby, in *Liberalism and its Challengers,* concluded that the Chicago Freedom Movement "undeniably was more failure than success." In the early 1990s, in his survey of the Civil Rights Movement, *Freedom Bound,* Robert Weisbrot argued that "In many respects, the Chicago freedom movement had emerged as a debacle to rival the Albany [GA] movement."

The assessment of the Chicago Freedom Movement as a defeat is not the only reason for its diminished place in the country's public memory. That the Chicago Movement was more focused on changing local conditions than were the Birmingham campaign and especially the Selma campaign also accounts for its modest national standing. During their initiatives in the South, King and SCLC were much more attentive to the national response (and corrective federal legislation) than they were in Chicago. The Chicago campaign, they hoped, would inspire similar nonviolent movements in other Northern cities.

The Summit Agreement, which marked the end of the most active phase of the Chicago Freedom Movement, was in fact the strongest local agreement King and SCLC had ever negotiated in any of their city projects. The settlement that ended the Birmingham campaign was fuzzier than the Summit Agreement. But, as Taylor Branch has recently noted in his new book, *At Canaan's Edge*, its weaknesses "disappeared in a rippling tide that dissolved formal segregation by comprehensive national law." Though the Chicago Freedom Movement was part of the constellation of forces that led to the passage of a federal fair housing law in 1968, housing discrimination, residential segregation and inner-city slums have not disappeared the way that segregated lunch counters and blatantly racist voting registrars have.

Even a recent outpouring of scholarship focusing on the Civil Rights Movement in the North is unlikely to boost the reputation of the Chicago Freedom Movement. (For a sweeping survey of that broader struggle, see Thomas J. Sugrue, *Sweet Land of Liberty: The Forgotten Struggle for Civil Rights in the North*, Random House, 2008.) New books like Matthew Countryman's *Up South: Civil Rights and Black Power in Philadelphia* and Martha Biondi's *To Stand and Fight: The Struggle for Civil Rights in Postwar New York City* point to a growing recognition of the importance and complexity of the fight for racial equality in the North. So rich is Jeanne Theoharis and Komozi Woodard's *Freedom North*, a new collection of essays about Northern activism, that the conventional view of the Civil Rights Movement as confined to the South in the 1950s and 1960s is destined for revision. But the place of the Chicago Freedom Movement in this new scholarship is ambiguous. Putting a spotlight on the Chicago campaign deflects attention from the wide array of local movements in the North and suggests that Northern protest relied on the influence of Martin Luther King and Southern-based civil rights organizations.

An Alternative Reading

The prevailing wisdom, then, is that the Chicago Freedom Movement was not one of the most noteworthy or significant episodes of recent history. Yet looking back after 40 years, there is a strong case for an alternative reading.

First, there is the overwhelming evidence that the Chicago project—whose motto was "End Slums"—was decisive to Martin Luther King's evolution as a national leader for social justice. As his leading biographers, David Garrow and Taylor Branch, have shown, King's encounter with the slums and racial inequality in Chicago propelled him to agitate for more searching reform and to focus on the need to eliminate poverty throughout the country.

There is also a strong argument to be made for the centrality of the Chicago Freedom Movement in the overall trajectory of the broader Civil Rights Movement and contemporary American race relations. Over 20 years ago, Allen Matusow placed the Chicago Freedom Movement at the center of his history of the 1960s. In *The Unraveling of America*, Matusow pointed to the uneven record of accomplishment of the Chicago Movement, but, more significantly, he viewed its unfolding as illustrative of the challenge of confronting Northern racial inequality. "Civil Rights in the North," he wrote, "was a drama in three parts—schools, housing, and jobs—played out in Chicago and featuring Mayor Richard J. Daley, Lyndon Johnson, and Martin Luther King."

The Chicago Freedom Movement was more, however, than an illuminating transitional episode. It also produced substantial achievements, achievements that have become more evident with the passage of time. The focus of the movement's direct action campaign—housing discrimination—was an eleventh-hour decision and was initially questioned by many activists and observers. But over time, the prescience of this focus has become clearer. As Douglas Massey and Nancy Denton have argued in *American Apartheid*, housing segregation is at the heart of inequality in contemporary America. Where one lives is highly determinative of one's quality of life. The poor in America—especially those of color—too often find themselves confined to bleak settings, isolated from the country's currents of opportunity and prosperity.

The Leadership Council for Metropolitan Open Communities, the one long-lasting product of the Summit Agreement, was a pioneer for four decades in developing new strategies to open up housing opportunities for all. Because of its work and that of other fair housing groups, residential segregation—while still severe—is not as rigid as it might have been if housing discrimination had not been challenged over the past 40 years.

The Chicago Freedom Movement also recognized that good jobs were essential to the fortunes of all Chicagoans. The Chicago chapter of Operation Breadbasket, established in 1966 with Jesse Jackson at its helm, turned to selective buying campaigns in order to break racial barriers in employment. For the past four decades, Jackson and his supporters—subsequently as Operation PUSH and today as the Rainbow/PUSH Coalition—have fought to open up the American economy to minorities.

Nonviolence

The Chicago Freedom Movement is increasingly seen as a critical stage in the application of nonviolent direct action to promoting social change. The Chicago movement represented the first time a nonviolent campaign was launched in a sprawling metropolis. The city of Selma, Alabama, consisted of roughly 30,000 residents in 1965; Birmingham, Alabama, in 1963 numbered only about 300,000.

Chicago, with 3 million residents in the city proper, dwarfed them. To this day, two of the leading architects of the Chicago Freedom Movement, James Bevel and Bernard LaFayette, view the Chicago campaign as a decisive episode in the history of nonviolence. Bill Moyer, a member of the staff of the American Friends Service Committee and the original formulator of the open-housing strategy in 1966, and David Jehnsen, a staffer with the West Side Christian Parish in the mid-1960s, drew from the lessons learned during the Chicago Freedom Movement in spreading the message of the power of nonviolent movements in subsequent years. And there are others—veterans of the Chicago campaign—who have continued to promote the nonviolent way. Any contemporary history of non-violence should acknowledge the radiating influence of the Chicago Freedom Movement.

Finally, the Chicago Freedom Movement—more than any Southern civil rights campaign—speaks directly to the importance of developing a broad coalition in confronting injustice. The Chicago open-housing marches, which were contemporaneous with the rising influence of Black Power, were interracial and represented a wide range of social classes. Moreover, the Chicago movement saw the limitations of viewing race relations through a binary lens. In its demands, it sought equal opportunities for "whites, Negroes, and Latin Americans." In this sense, it prefigured Martin Luther King's Poor People's Campaign and Jesse Jackson's "Rainbow Coalition." The Chicago Freedom Movement, then, went beyond the black/white orientation of Southern campaigns for civil rights. It envisioned a multicultural future.

* * * * *

SUCCESS AND THE CHICAGO FREEDOM MOVEMENT

MARY LOU FINLEY

Housing segregation still persists in Chicago, and by some measures poverty has even worsened in the 40 years since Martin Luther King, Jr. moved into a slum apartment on Chicago's West Side in January 1966 as a profound statement of support for the poor. Yet to conclude that the movement was, as one historian characterized it, "defeat in Chicago" is to miss much about the significance of this movement.

To see that significance, we need to trace the forces of change set in motion by the Chicago Freedom Movement and follow those energies forward through the years, even decades, to see what changes emerged over time. In this, its 40th anniversary year, we can begin to do just that.

The Chicago Freedom Movement was multifaceted. However, it can largely be characterized as two interwoven movements: first, the concluding chapter of a decade-long nonviolent movement against racial segregation which began with the 1955 Montgomery bus boycott and concluded with the open housing marches opposing housing segregation in Chicago in the Summer of 1966; and secondly, the beginning stages of an anti-poverty/economic justice movement. We need to follow the threads of both of these efforts if we are to understand the outcomes of the Chicago movement.

Activist Bill Moyer's Movement Action Plan (MAP) model of social movements, developed to help organizers better understand their movements and strategize more effectively, can provide a useful framework in our efforts to assess the impact of the Chicago Freedom Movement.

The MAP model suggests that successful social movements pass through eight stages: (1) Normal Times; (2) Proving the Failure of Existing Institutions; (3) Ripening Conditions; (4) Movement Take-off; (5) Perception of Failure—a movement detour; (6) Building Majority Public Support; (7) Success; and (8) Continuing the Struggle. Moyer also suggests that when victories have been won on many issues within a larger movement, it is easier to win on the next issue within that frame, as both the public and powerholders have already made commitments to change and the movement's message has begun to resonate widely. (For example, it was easier to win the integration of swimming pools and theaters in a town after the integration of restaurants had already been won.)

The Open Housing Campaign

Using the MAP lens, I would suggest that by the Spring of 1966, the open housing issue was ripe for movement take-off. Earlier successes in Southern desegregation campaigns had brought segregation into the public spotlight and convinced many—although far from everyone—that segregation was wrong. Significant groundwork had been done in fair housing organizing in Chicago during the previous decade, largely by the American Friends Service Committee. Chicago had passed a fair housing ordinance in 1963, but tests of real estate offices by black and white prospective buyers had proved the ordinance ineffective (propelling this movement through Stage 2, Proving the Failure of Existing Institutions). Nonviolent tactics for confronting the real estate industry, such as picketing real estate offices known to discriminate against black homebuyers or renters, had been developed and tried on a small scale.

The open housing marches served as the "trigger event" that sparked a Stage 4 take-off of the movement against housing segregation. The drama of the nonviolent marches themselves, the violent neighborhood response and the presence of Martin Luther King, Jr. prompted a citywide crisis in Chicago and brought national and international attention. Housing segregation was placed in the national spotlight, and the clear violation of the rights of African Americans to equal treatment was made startlingly visible. A fair housing bill was introduced in Congress. The Summit Agreement reached by negotiations between the movement and Mayor Richard J. Daley ended the marches and committed Chicago institutions to make changes. However, it was viewed by many—both then and now—as weak.

If we view the open housing marches through the lens of the MAP model, we see that movement victories are seldom won at the end of Stage 4, Movement Take-off. Rather, they come later, as the forces set in motion by the movement engage a wide range of community members in the sometimes slow and deliberate work of propelling each movement issue forward to victory over time. Political scientist Sidney Tarrow, in his book *Power in Movement: Social Movements and Contentious Politics*, noted a similar pattern: "Cycles of contention are a season for sowing, but the reaping is often done in periods of demobilization that follow, by latecomers to the cause, by elites and authorities." While Tarrow seemed to view this process as rather mysterious, the MAP model provides clues as to how this next chapter of a movement's life unfolds.

In Stage 6, Building Majority Public Support, movement work shifts from protest to quieter, protracted struggle, utilizing educational efforts to deepen and broaden public support, and, as public support grows, to work through legislative, legal and community channels to institutionalize change, propelling the movement, issue by issue, to Stage 7, Success. Protests may also occur, but they tend to be smaller and localized, either directed at specific local targets or prompted by "re-trigger events" which again pull movement issues into the public spotlight. (Cindy Sheehan's decision to camp out in Crawford, Texas outside President Bush's home in August 2005 was such an event in the movement against the Iraq war. Multitudinous vigils supporting her sprung up across the U.S. in less than a week.)

How did this Stage 6 work, Building Majority Public Support, unfold, then, in the months and years following the Summer 1966 open housing marches? This story is yet to be fully told, but I can at least cite a few examples, many of which address the original 1966 demands posted by Martin Luther King, Jr. on the door of Chicago's City Hall.

The Civil Rights Act of 1968, with provisions for fair housing, was passed by Congress in April 1968, shortly after Martin Luther King, Jr.'s assassination. It was further strengthened in 1988. The Leadership Council for Metropolitan Open Communities, established by the 1966 Summit Agreement, for 40 years continued to support thousands of African Americans moving into predominantly white neighborhoods in the city and its suburbs. The noisy, virulent and sometimes violent opposition to these move-ins which had been a characteristic of race relations in Chicago since the early 20th century were, by the mid-1990s, virtually ended. An anti-redlining movement against discrimination in mortgage-lending, which spread across the country in the late 1960s and early 1970s, was rooted in Chicago and led by Chicagoans such as Gail Cincotta, director of National Peoples Action. The Community Reinvestment Act passed by Congress in 1977 guaranteed equality in bank-lending and required bank investment in communities with bank branches. The *Gautreaux* case against the Chicago Housing Authority, led by Alex Polikoff and described in his compelling new book, *Waiting for Gautreaux*, won a 1976 Supreme Court ruling that required CHA to house African Americans in predominantly white neighborhoods. This case was intertwined with the Chicago Freedom

Movement's work in significant ways: Dorothy Gautreaux was active in the Coordinating Council of Community Organizations, and others in the American Civil Liberties Union—which engaged Polikoff in this project—were quietly supporting the Chicago Freedom Movement. The Contract Buyers League, which emerged from organizing out of Presentation Catholic Church on the West Side in the late 1960s, fought for the rights of homeowners who had been unable to get conventional bank mortgages.

Moyer's MAP model suggests that "reformers" who carry Movement issues on to victory through legislative and legal channels and patient community work in the later stages of a movement, as described above, are often different individuals or groups from the "rebels" who organized the initial protests and brought the issue to public attention. Activists involved in these different roles may even be unaware of each other's contributions to the overall movement effort. Yet, Moyer contends, all are critical for a movement's ultimate success, and all of this work needs to be seen as a part of the larger movement whole.

The "End the Slums" and Economic Justice Campaigns

The "End the Slums" campaign had a dual focus: organizing tenants around improved housing conditions; and secondly, a more general anti-poverty effort to bring to public consciousness the indignities of poverty, the systemic, institutionalized nature of poverty, and the immorality of a society which allows poverty to persist in the midst of wealth. Operation Breadbasket, led by Rev. Jesse Jackson and a group of black ministers, conducted a focused economic justice campaign aimed at more jobs and economic empowerment for African Americans.

Both the tenants' rights movement and the general anti-poverty movement were in their very early stages in 1965–1967. It was a time for experimenting with ways of framing issues and developing organizing strategies, but the MAP model suggests that we would not expect massive mobilizations during these early stages.

Jesse Gray's organizing of tenant councils and rent strikes in New York City was known to Freedom Movement organizers and served as an inspiration. Martin Luther King's decision to move into a slum apartment himself brought widespread public attention to poor housing conditions in the black community. Bernard Lafayette's work on a lead poisoning campaign with neighborhood youth highlighted the very real health dangers of slum housing while teaching youth strategies for bringing change in their community. Southern Christian Leadership Conference Project Director Rev. James Bevel proposed the development of tenant unions, in which tenants would seek collective bargaining agreements with landlords; this formed the basis of the tenant organizing work.

Tenant union organizing efforts brought an important victory a few days after the rally at Soldier's Field kicking off the summer campaign. On July 13, 1966, East Garfield Park slumlords John Condor and Louis Costallis agreed to sign a collective bargaining agreement with their tenants allowing rent withholding if buildings were in dangerous states of disrepair. The importance of this work was swallowed up at the time in preparations for the open housing marches, and its innovative potential seems to have been overlooked by many movement observers. Yet it is the type of victory the MAP model would lead us to anticipate when a movement is in its early stages; it is small and local and, at the same time, a creative new approach, full of potential.

Tenant organizing continued in Chicago, but it was not until the 1980s that the tenants' rights movement reached take-off. In the mid-1980s, the 40-group Coalition for Tenants Rights formed and in 1986 won a Chicago city ordinance offering new tenant protections, including a "repair and deduct" provision which, according to Gregory Squires and his colleagues, "allows tenants to make repairs that are necessary for health or safety reasons and deduct the cost from the rent," paralleling the Freedom Movement's original tenant-landlord collective bargaining agreement. Meanwhile, the National Low Income Housing Coalition was formed in 1974, "dedicated to ending America's affordable housing crisis," and tenant organizations emerged in other cities to protect tenants' rights.

Operation Breadbasket won its first victory in April 1966, gaining commitments for jobs for African Americans in companies through its strategy of selective buying campaigns, taking on one dairy, soft drink company, grocery chain at a time. This approach to improving job opportunities—which itself paralleled earlier "don't shop where you can't work" campaigns in Chicago dating back to the 1930s—provided early practical and conceptual support for affirmative action, with its goals and time-tables for hiring minorities, ordered by the Supreme Court in 1971.

Breadbasket also expanded rapidly in its first year to include broader economic empowerment goals, winning campaigns for increased deposits in black-owned banks, marketing assistance for black businessmen and other efforts to strengthen the black community's economic base. Rev. Jesse Jackson and others have continued this highly successful work for the last 40 years, continuing to organize in support of new economic opportunities for African Americans and for African-American-owned businesses. This organization became independent of SCLC in 1971 and now operates as Rainbow/PUSH.

As Paul Street's new report for the Chicago Urban League documents, there has been a very substantial expansion of the black middle class, upper middle class and upper class since the 1970s. For example, he notes: "Between 1970 and 2000 the number of African American Chicagoans receiving an income . . . of $75,000 and above [according to]..the 2000 census increased by 13 percent," while "the comparable increase for all Chicagoans was only 1 percent." The efforts of Breadbasket/PUSH, combined with nationally mandated anti-discrimination and affirmative action programs in colleges and universities as well as workplaces, have no doubt contributed significantly to this expansion of the African-American middle and upper classes. These are important victories.

Anti-Poverty Efforts

The same cannot be said, however, of anti-poverty efforts. The Chicago Freedom Movement developed an analysis of the slum as an exploited community, a community from which resources were drained, a victim of an "internal colonialism"; the Union to End Slums was an effort to organize around this analysis. Yet it did not go far. Specific anti-poverty provisions were included in the Summer 1966 demands, such as a call for an increase in the minimum wage and improvements in the administration of the welfare system, as well as institution of fair employment practices. The movement did not—at this point—succeed in developing viable strategies and tactics for tackling the issue of poverty. However, Martin Luther King's speeches framing poverty as an issue of economic justice are an important legacy of that time.

After Chicago, anti-poverty movements were increasingly Dr. King's focus, and, when he was assassinated in April of 1968, he was deeply engaged in two such campaigns: the Poor Peoples Campaign, a multiracial nonviolent action campaign to bring poor people from across the country to the seat of power in the nation's capital to demand that poverty be abolished; and the Memphis garbage workers' strike. Both of these campaigns represented strategic innovations that provided more powerful vehicles for raising the issue of poverty in the public arena. Yet this work was cut short by Dr. King's tragic assassination.

Former SCLC staffers Dorothy Wright Tillman—now alderman for a Chicago South Side ward—and Rev. Al Sampson, pastor of a South Side church, have continued to address the needs of the poor in Chicago over the intervening decades. When Rev. Jesse Jackson ran for president in 1984 and 1988, he brought the issues of economic justice and poverty to national political debates.

While the other issues raised by the Chicago movement are by no means completely resolved, I would suggest that the battle against poverty is the great unfinished work of that time.

Yet this cannot be seen just as a movement failure. Anti-poverty movements in Chicago and other Northern cities continued to build in the late 1960s and early 1970s. But with the election of Ronald Reagan in 1980 a great backlash took hold. Reagan cut social spending, refused to raise the minimum wage, reduced taxes for the rich and, with his attack on mythical "welfare queens," began a decades-long ideological battle to label the poor as "unworthy," and undercut the framing of poverty as an issue of justice. The deindustrialization begun in the 1970s and the continued outsourcing of well-paying jobs have also made the escape from poverty ever more difficult.

Only in the last decade have we begun to see the serious revival of an economic justice movement. Living-wage ordinances have been adopted by over 100 cities and counties, and there have been successful state-level initiatives to raise the minimum wage, most recently in Florida and Nevada. Labor efforts to organize the unorganized, particularly in the service industry, are revitalizing the labor movement and bringing hope to workers. Hurricane Katrina brought persistent poverty back into the public spotlight and broke through the Reaganesque caricatures of the poor, reviving widespread empathy for mothers with hungry children and others who are suffering.

Perhaps the anti-poverty/economic justice movement will, finally, take off and we will begin to work together as a nation to address this painful legacy of untended public business.

In conclusion, I would suggest that the Chicago Freedom Movement did its work, the work that could be done at that moment in history. It brought the housing segregation movement to take-off and succeeded in framing anti-poverty efforts as a matter of economic justice. Its tenant union organizing helped the nascent tenant movement to grow. The economic empowerment work begun by Operation Breadbasket has borne fruit for the last 40 years. All of these undertakings were furthered, often by others, in the decades that followed, and, over the years, there were many successes. Yet there is still much to be done.

As we commemorate the Chicago Freedom Movement's 40th anniversary this year, a call will be issued inviting everyone to join in the unfinished work.

* * * * *

THE END-THE-SLUMS MOVEMENT

BERNARD LAFAYETTE, JR.

Although the most well-publicized focus of the Chicago Freedom Movement was the Open Housing Campaign, a parallel "End-the-Slums" campaign raised the issue of housing and health in a combined research and advocacy campaign.

This campaign focused on the condition of slum housing in the area where people of color lived. In addition to the lack of trash pick-up and unswept streets, the physical housing was in disrepair: broken windows, busted door locks, unpainted surfaces, crumbling steps, and of most concern was the lead-based paint peeling from the walls.

Tony Henry, who directed the American Friends Service Committee's (AFSC) Pre-Adolescent Enrichment Program, initiated the idea of organizing a union of the tenants that would include dues check-off and formal representatives for the tenants. In the process of organizing the tenants, we discovered that young children were experiencing severe health problems. Young children suffered from swollen stomachs, blindness, damaged internal organs, vomiting and paralysis due to ingestion of peeling lead-based paint chips from the interior walls of the slum housing. The peeling paint chips fell from the interior walls of the ceiling onto the floors and sometimes even in the babies' cribs. The walking toddlers sometimes gnawed on the window sills as they peered out the windows. The lead from the paint caused irreversible damage to the children's brain cells, which led to a permanent physiological impairment.

Rather than organize a protest march to address the problem, which is always an appropriate method after gathering the information, educating the constituents, and preparing oneself for the campaign, we decided to address the problem directly.

While we were organizing the tenants, we were organizing the youth in the community under the leadership of Clarence James, a local high school student. The organization was named SOUL (Students Organization for Urban Leadership).

Dr. David Elwyn, a university chemistry professor, developed a litmus test to detect high contents of elements in the urine, which is an indicator of disproportional presence of lead in the body. The high school students were trained to properly collect urine samples from the small children who lived in housing where peeling paint was discovered. These samples were taken to a make-shift laboratory in the basement of the AFSC Project House on the west side of Chicago.

Once the test results showed that a high content of elements existed in a urine sample—which indicated a high presence of lead in the child's body—the parents were notified and the child was taken to Presbyterian St. Luke Hospital for a more precise blood level test. The child was consequently hospitalized for treatment.

This model served as an example of how the human resources of a community can be used to address the problem directly, which strengthened our demand that the city and state take responsibility to properly address the problem in a systematic way. The high school students who participated consequently saw improvement in their grades, specifically in the areas of science. Some of these students even went on to become medical professionals.

The City of Chicago consequently employed service workers to implement our Lead Poisoning Project. We were able to show the relationship between slum housing and environmental health problems in children.

* * * * *

FORTY YEARS OF THE CIVIL RIGHTS MOVEMENT IN CHICAGO

DICK SIMPSON

Forty years ago, the civil rights marches burst upon the scene in Chicago. Within a year, there was a summit agreement of sorts between Martin Luther King, Jr. and Mayor Richard J. Daley. Many at the time saw the agreement as a sham and simply a way for Dr. King to leave town and take the movement other places where there would be more success. Others note today that the gap between poor Blacks and rich Whites in the Chicago Metropolitan region is greater than in Dr. King's time. Yet, to claim that nothing was gained then or now is to miss significant changes that have occurred.

For most of the 1960s, African Americans were represented in the City Council of Chicago by the "Silent Six" Black aldermen. In this period, African Americans were best represented by a White alderman, 5th Ward Alderman Leon Despres, who was described by novelist Ronald Fair as the "only 'Negro' in city government" and by David Llorens in the *Negro Digest* in 1966 as the "lone 'Negro' spokesman in Chicago's City Council."

In 1967, demographer Pierre de Vise wrote *The Widening Color Gap*, in which he contrasted the 10 richest White areas of the metropolitan region and the 10 poorest Black communities. Unfortunately, the "color gap" between rich Whites and poor Blacks continued to grow even after the Civil Rights Act and the War on Poverty were implemented by the national government. William Julius Wilson, when studying some of the same Black ghettoes, declared that the ghettoes grew only worse and were the breeding ground of a "permanent underclass."

Sixty years ago, the law in the South and the practice in the North was segregation. In Chicago, progress has been slow but steady. It may not seem like much to have gone from a segregation index of 94 percent to 86 percent (the percent of people who would have to move to have each community have the same racial profile as the metropolitan region as a whole). But despite itself, Chicago is moving toward more integration and shared power and wealth between the races.

Since the 1960s, there have been advances in racial justice and power-sharing. The Chicago City Council has replaced the "Silent Six" Black aldermen with 20 African-American aldermen who are prepared, at least on clear racial issues, to vote the views and needs of their constituents. Unfortunately, they are also part of a White, Black, and Latino rubber stamp City Council which goes along with Mayor Richard M. Daley far too often. They don't have Dr. King's courage or vision (with a few notable exceptions). Even so, they are a manifestation of Black power in practice—as are the Black state legislators, judges and Congressmen Chicago voters regularly elect. In social science language, Blacks have been incorporated into the ruling elite governing the city.

The high water mark of Black Power, of course, was Harold Washington's mayoralty from 1983–1987. He began programs of affirmative action in city jobs and contracts which have brought thousands of government jobs and millions of dollars in city contracts to the Black community. He not only empowered Blacks, but also Latinos, Asians, women, gays and progressive Whites. As his supporters like to say, with justification, he raised the floor of city government. Since his death, the programs of affirmative action in jobs and contracts, minorities in key cabinet positions and city leadership roles have continued. But this was a plateau from which Blacks have not advanced further, even as other minorities have made significant gains in the Richard M. Daley era.

Mayor Richard M. Daley's cabinet contains seven African Americans (17 percent), 24 Whites (59 percent), 7 Hispanics (17 percent) and 3 Asians (7 percent). So Whites continue to vastly outnumber everyone else, but Blacks and Latinos are represented in the highest positions.

More telling are city jobs and contracts. During Mayor Richard M. Daley's reign, despite having roughly 36 percent of the population and 40 percent City Council membership, and providing an increasing level of electoral support for the mayor, African Americans have averaged only 12 percent of the city contracts throughout his term, and in the last year, dropped to an all-time low since 1987 of 9 percent. While Blacks have increased their vote for Daley from 10 percent in 1989 to 57 percent in 2003, Black jobs have dropped slightly, from 33.25 percent to 32 percent.

So in city jobs and contracts Blacks have stood still, while by contrast Latinos have made substantial gains. Although with 28 percent of Chicago' population, Latinos are underrepresented in the Chicago City Council with eight Latino aldermen (16 percent), they have made remarkable gains in jobs and contracts. Under Mayor Washington, they received for the first time 4 percent of city contracts and 5 percent of city jobs by 1987. They have increased under Mayor Richard M. Daley to 14 percent of contracts and 11 percent of jobs. Partially, this is a reward for the more than 80 percent of their votes which they give Mayor Daley every election. A White/Latino coalition now governs the city, although Latinos are distinctly the junior partners in the arrangement.

To make any final assessment of the impact of the Civil Rights Movement in Chicago, it is critical to realize that it has gone beyond the bounds of the African-American community. Women, Latinos, gays and Asians have all benefitted from the Civil Rights Movement of the 1960s and all the years since. Immigrants are the newest members of the movement. As civil rights leader Reverend Jesse Jackson wrote in his *Sun-Times* op-ed column on May 2, 2006, the day after 700,000 immigrants and their supporters marched to demand their rights in Chicago, "immigrants and their human rights supporters took to the streets, reigniting this era's civil rights struggle. . . . As I see it, their rally cry—'Si se puede'—is Spanish for 'We shall overcome'." Civil rights is now the rallying cry not just of Blacks, but of all groups that are oppressed and mistreated in our society.

Have we made it to the promised land since the marches began in Chicago 40 years ago? No, we haven't. There have been many setbacks and many failings. With a conservative president and Congress, progress is slower than many of us would like.

But there are still clear signs of progress. Overt discrimination is against the law, and Blacks, like other minorities, have been incorporated into the mainstream of corporate Chicago and political Chicago. To make further progress requires rebuilding a rainbow coalition of Blacks, Whites, Latinos and Asians; of women and men; of straights and gays; and of new immigrants and American-born. The strongest force for change is in fact new movements, rightful successors of the decades-old civil rights marches—the Anti-Iraq War Movement, the Women Rights, the Gay Rights and the brand-new Immigrant Rights Movement. Only together can we make further progress towards social justice.

* * * * *

OVERALL, THINGS ARE NOT GOOD

SALIM MUWAKKIL

Martin Luther King's publicity-savvy Southern Christian Leadership Conference arrived in Chicago with a campaign to attack racial biases and improve the quality of life in the city's notoriously squalid black ghettos. The SCLC-Coordinating Council of Community Organizations collaboration was particularly focused on housing discrimination, but it targeted an array of race-based urban ills. After the Southern campaign's success prodding the passage of the Civil Rights Act of 1964 and the Voting Rights Act of 1965, movement strategists thought a Northern strategy could also prompt legislative action.

The flagrantly racist resistance of Southern whites to the SCLC's Southern campaigns garnered national sympathy. But the Chicago demonstrations for open housing and education equality attracted much less national support. What's more, the violent uprisings in Harlem, New York in 1964 and Watts, California in 1965 had triggered a growing white backlash.

Chicago was an urban area with easily identified ills: Housing and job discrimination were among the most pressing problems for the city's African-American population. But the issue of education generated the most street heat among blacks in the Windy City. The failure to address school overcrowding and other issues of educational neglect in the city's black communities sparked many angry protests. Al Raby, the man who led CCCO and importuned King and company to come to Chicago, was himself a former teacher drawn into the movement through the education issue.

During the Summer of 1965, the city experienced one of the most sustained periods of protests in Chicago history. This protest infuriated the administration of Mayor Richard J. Daley, which denied it could do much to address educational issues, even as it offered conciliatory rhetoric. His response presaged the administration's reaction to the Chicago Freedom Movement's later charges of housing discrimination and slum-like conditions. During 1966, the movement organized several large marches dedicated to housing issues. King was hit with a rock during a march through one of the city's most racially hostile neighborhoods, and that incident came to symbolize the movement's failure. King's foray into the wilds of the Windy City is retrospectively judged as an overreach that mistakenly applied Southern-born tactics to Northern realities.

There is some truth to that assessment, but there's more. The Chicago Freedom Movement certainly failed to end slums; that was only a rhetorical goal. But it also failed to revitalize any single neighborhood. In fact, with its focus on open housing in other neighborhoods, it may have helped devitalize the very communities King hoped to save. Some research (especially that of William Julius Wilson) suggests many black neighborhoods were hurt by the exodus of middle-class African Americans who had served as stabilizing factors. Ultimately, even those fleeing middle-class blacks wound up in racially segregated neighborhoods.

Changes in the City's Racial Landscape

However, the Chicago Freedom Movement did provoke some serious changes in the city's racial landscape; it shot some adrenalin into the city's activist community. Al Raby and other movement leaders intentionally employed some gang members as protection on marches through dangerous neighborhoods. Many youths were radicalized by that contact, and they helped form the basis of a vital Black Panther chapter in the city. Chronic police harassment of militant black organizations and the brazen assassination of Black Panther leaders Fred Hampton and Mark Clark help spark an independent political movement that led eventually to the 1983 election of Harold Washington as the city's first African-American mayor.

Signs of Success Are Rare

But 40 years after that promising attempt to connect the Southern Civil Rights Movement to the Northern freedom struggle, signs of success are rare. The "slums" that King targeted evolved into "ghettos," and now those "inner-city" neighborhoods offer graphic testimony that semantics make little difference to residents' quality of life. The state of black Chicago in 2006 displays little of what was promised 40 years ago.

There have been some bright spots. The electoral realm, for example, has seen an explosion of African-American representation, including the mayoral elections of Harold Washington in 1983 and 1987; the 1992 election of Carol Moseley Braun as the first black female U.S. Senator; the 2004 election and growing prominence of U.S. Senator Barack Obama, only the third black U.S. Senator since Reconstruction. The Rev. Jesse Jackson, who was one of King's lieutenants, is now leader of the Rainbow/PUSH organization and the father of Cong. Jesse Jackson, Jr. (D-IL). And there are many other tales of black political triumph in the city.

But overall things are not good. According to a recent Urban League study, "Still Separate, Unequal: Race, Place, Policy and the State of Black Chicago," the city remains "deeply in the thrall of racial separation and racial inequality." Among the figures noted in the 2005 report is that the average black Chicagoan lives in a census tract where about four of every five residents are African-American; the average white lives in a tract where less than 1 of every 10 residents is black. Within Chicago, the average black K-12 public school student attends a school that is 86 percent African-American. Black students are less exposed to other groups than any other ethnic/racial group in the city. This state of virtual apartheid has not changed in any significant way since King's movement left town, and the other racial disparities remain largely unchanged.

These imbalances are in income, education, employment, poverty rates, economic vitality, etc. In income, for example, black households are disproportionately low earners. The median income of the average black neighborhood was $36,298 in 2004 (the latest year for which there are figures—many experts estimate that figure dropped a bit in 2006), $61,952 in predominantly white neighborhoods.

Education has remained a potent issue as study after study confirms the dismal state of schools in the city's black communities. Drop-out rates remain high. In fact, the Urban League study reveals that only 38 percent of black males have graduated high school since 1995. An analyses of jobless data found that in 2004, more than 50 percent of so-called "unattached youth" ages 16–24 were dangerously disconnected from both the labor market and the educational system. Of the city's 15 poorest neighborhoods, 14 were disproportionately black and 11 were more that 94 percent black. In 15 of the city's 77 community areas in 2004, more than 28 percent of the children lived in "deep poverty," and 14 of these neighborhoods were in predominantly black areas of Chicago's south and west sides.

And this is where inadequate education and poverty connect: Of the city's 293 predominantly black schools, fully two-thirds (170) report 90 percent or more of their students as "low-income," and low-income has been closely correlated with poor academic performance. Nearly six in ten African-American ninth graders do not graduate with a regular high school degree within four years. Black males are significantly absent in the Chicago region's institutions of higher education. They have very little presence at the area's most competitive colleges and universities. In fact, black males are becoming less visible in many aspects of American life (but that's another problem, perhaps for another time).

One of the fallouts from this educational failure is the destructive incarceration epidemic that found nearly 23,000 more black males in the Illinois state prison system than enrolled in the state's public universities in 2004. Sixty-six percent of the state's roughly 45,000 prisoners and 63 percent of its 34,000 parolees in 2004 were African-American. In 2004, the state's incarceration rate for African Americans was more than ten times the rate for whites.

Forty years since the Chicago Freedom Movement, there are signs of progress as well: Black poverty rates fell, black employment rose, black median family income and college enrollment also rose. As in the rest of America, there is a "best of times, worst of times" quality to black life in Chicago. Unfortunately, the worst times are getting even worse, and the best are declining.

The Student Nonviolent Coordinating Committee Gathers 50 Years After It Started: A Report on the Reunion

Mike Miller

Held April 15–18, 2010, at Shaw University, the nation's oldest historically Black institution of higher education, SNCC's 50th Anniversary Reunion Program notes on its cover page, "This conference was planned in strict accordance with SNCC's principles of decision-making. Therefore, we don't really know what will happen when until it does. An attitude of flexibility mixed with humor will help a lot." In fact, the reunion was tightly organized and ran on time. That was all the more remarkable because more than 1,000 attended an event that many of its planners originally anticipated to be attended by a maximum of 500. Indeed, it was an earlier myth about SNCC that it was disorganized . . . though it became that in its later years.

SNCC'S HISTORY

For those who don't remember, or don't know, SNCC was born in April, 1960 when leaders of the sit-in movement convened at Shaw University at the invitation of legendary African-American organizer Ella Baker, then the Southern Christian Leadership Conference's acting executive director. SCLC hoped the student movement would become its youth arm. Baker advised the students to form an independent organization. They did, and wrote a major chapter of the Deep South Civil Rights Movement history from 1960–1965, then opened the debate over black power when SNCC chairman Stokely Carmichael made the slogan popular beginning in 1966.

In 1961, after the Southern Black student movement exploded with sit-ins and Freedom Rides, a small group left their college campuses to become full-time "Field Secretaries," using community organizing tools to attempt registration of Black voters in places where racist power depended on its exclusion. When SNCC threatened to self-destruct in an internal debate over direct action versus voter registration, Ella Baker's wisdom came to the rescue, and the organization decided to do both.

Working with the most marginalized low-income Black people in counties where they were as much as 85 percent of the population, SNCC's patient door-to-door canvassing led to the formation of grassroots organizations across the "Black Belt." In Albany and rural Southwest Georgia; Selma and Lowndes County, Alabama; Cambridge, Maryland; Danville, Virginia; the Mississippi and Arkansas Deltas, and more, SNCC organizers built or strengthened local movements for racial and economic justice and voting rights. The best known of these efforts resulted in the Mississippi Freedom Democratic Party and its 1964 challenge to the seating of the all-white delegation at the Democratic Party National Convention, and rejection of a so-called "compromise" that offered MFDP two at-large delegates. While the rest of the Civil Rights Movement urged acceptance of the compromise, MFDP's delegation, with SNCC support, overwhelmingly rejected it.

Mississippi's 1964 visibility resulted from a summer project that invited 800+ Northern volunteers into the state and the state murder of three people—a local black, a newly arrived volunteer, and another Northerner who was already working in the state. Within SNCC, the Project was controversial because it threatened to overwhelm the still-fragile grassroots relationships SNCC had been cultivating, and because the mostly white volunteers would replicate historic patterns of deference to whites. COINTELPRO infiltration, and bitter internal debates on Black Power and its meaning, the role of whites in the organization, the nature of the U.S. government, and more all combined to unravel SNCC; it disbanded in 1970.

THE REUNION

The reunion held within it all the elements of SNCC's history: deep feelings of comradeship ("a band of brothers ['and sisters' was later added], a circle of trust"), humor, rich music of the gospel tradition, creative singing and song-writing of SNCC's Freedom Singers, bonds between Black and white SNCC workers that remain strong today, militant nationalism, Pan African Marxism, anger at what remains undone in the struggle for racial and economic justice. And there are people who still don't talk to one another because of struggles 50 years ago or conflicts in planning this gathering. The SNCC experience was an intense one. As I reflect on it, it was an extraordinary privilege to work for five years in a Black-led organization dedicated to racial and economic justice and democratic participation by poor and illiterate Southern African Americans.

SNCC's accomplishments were celebrated in speeches and panels. Former SNCC Field Secretaries, who are now nationally and internationally recognized leaders, spoke, as did other notables—the best-known of them: John Lewis, member of Congress and a Majority Party Whip. Rev. James Lawson, nonviolence teacher of the Nashville Movement; Julian Bond, past Chairman of the NAACP Board; Bob

Moses, initiator of the Algebra Project, which uses experiential learning methods to teach math to low-performing middle- and high-school students; Bernice Johnson Reagon, scholar and founder of Sweet Honey in the Rock. Each was greeted with thundering applause.

The 1964 Civil Rights and 1965 Voting Rights Acts resulted from the combination of earlier NAACP legal and local action, and CORE (Congress Of Racial Equality), SCLC and SNCC direct action and voting rights work in the South. SNCC added two crucial ingredients: When others were willing to compromise or were intimidated by violence, SNCC was not. CORE stopped Freedom Rides because of violence in Alabama; SNCC picked up the banner and continued the Rides into Jackson, MS, where the Riders were all jailed. SCLC did short-term mobilizations designed to arouse white support in the North and put pressure on Congress and the President. SNCC dug deep roots in the Black Belt counties and stayed over the long haul. During the 1960s, SNCC was denounced by the Kennedy and Johnson administrations, and by many liberals and mainstream media (including the *New York Times*). At the reunion, Attorney General Eric Holder, representing the Obama administration, paid homage to SNCC's courage and intelligence, saying, "There is a direct line between the sit-ins and President Obama in The White House." The City of Raleigh, State of North Carolina and President of Shaw University all gave greetings, and Shaw donated its facilities for the reunion.

One of the purposes of the reunion was to pass on experience to a younger generation. Student leaders and activists from Black and other colleges and universities in the South were present, as were the children of SNCC activists. The Young People's Project, an outgrowth of the Algebra Project, had a strong presence. A number of children of SNCC veterans spoke, expressed respect and love for their parents' generation, and demonstrated their own commitment to activism.

More than 20 panels and other sessions examined a multitude of questions, including: nonviolent philosophy; the shift from campus activism to full-time fieldwork; organization-building; national response to SNCC; Northern support work; the larger vision beyond civil rights; black power; Pan African Marxism; the role of whites; the role of women; SNCC's political impact; how SNCC evolved; the role of the Mississippi Freedom Democratic Party (MFDP) in reshaping the Democratic Party; why SNCC ceased to exist; organizing poor whites; SNCC's influence on Black art; current imprisonment of substantial numbers of young Black men; and more.

Additional plenary and general sessions included Harry Belafonte, Dick Gregory, Danny Glover, SNCC photography and SNCC music. A book party included 35 authors, most of them former SNCC staff. And a film festival featured documentaries and docudramas telling SNCC's story.

REVIVING SNCC?

Harry Belafonte's lunch talk, 45 minutes without a single note, took SNCC to task for indulging in self-congratulation. His remarks were well received, and he got several standing ovations. But conference planners rejected any idea of reviving SNCC and decided young activists in attendance would draw whatever they found useful from the reflections on the past. Some informal talk in the hallways and hotel bar expressed dissatisfaction at the lack of focused attention on past mistakes, why they were made and how today's activists and organizers might avoid them. SNCC's veteran field secretary Charlie Cobb once said to me, "We never figured out how to be an organization of organizers." Two clear and competing views might have been resolved, had SNCC remained rooted in the communities where it worked. By 1965, that rootedness began to erode. An early 1967 Executive Committee meeting debated what organizing was and could not resolve the question.

My view is that with the first group to drop out of school to become full-time workers in the Black Belt, SNCC's core mission became building Black people's power, guided by justice values. It lost sight of that mission and lost its rootedness in local people. The two losses are deeply intertwined; I think they were a result of deepening despair at the pace of change in the South, and the murders of Martin Luther King, Malcolm X and dozens of lesser-known Black leaders.

For me, the SNCC experience was one of the most meaningful of my life. It, and my subsequent work directing an organizing project for Saul Alinsky, infused my subsequent 45 years as a community organizer. As it was a privilege to be part of SNCC, so it was a privilege to be part of the reunion. One would have to travel far and wide to be in the presence of such a smart, joyful, committed and talented group of people.

The Other Side of Immigration: Humane, Sensible and Replicable Responses in a Changing Nation

Susan E. Eaton

Xenophobia may still grab the headlines and reliably fuel the scorn of conservative talk radio. It may even this year advance more state legislative proposals that would criminalize immigrants, make life difficult for them and make it easier to deport them.

With immigrant enforcement bills passing first in Arizona in 2010 and in Georgia, Alabama, South Carolina, Utah and Indiana in 2011, human and civil rights organizations have had no trouble identifying who and what to fight against. But amid the nativist noise and the legislative rancor, a comparably quiet movement is giving immigrants and their supporters something concrete to fight *for*.

The relatively newly branded, but long-standing "immigrant integration" initiative provides a powerful framework for articulating and implementing humane, constructive and practical alternatives to marginalizing and excluding immigrants. This impulse plays out in programs, policies and practices in communities all across the country, and in most cases, extends to immigrants who are both legally present and not. On-the-ground examples have taken hold in a wide range of communities across the country.

A BETTER WAY TO LIVE

In the city of Dalton in north Georgia, local health officials train women from the growing Latino population as *promotoras*. A common public health practice in Latin-American countries, the *promotoras* bring to more Spanish speakers proper care and information, reducing fear and increasing comfort with and access to the American healthcare system.

Public education officials in Utah have invested in a growing system of dual immersion schools through which native English speakers and the growing number of native Spanish speakers come together to learn in both languages.

In 2000, the then-mayor of Indianapolis, Bart Peterson, faced minimal opposition in development of a cohesive immigrant integration agenda to welcome and assist immigrants from around the world. The programs in operation include policies and training designed to improve public safety in immigrant communities, increase immigrants' access to loans and banks, and establishment of an Immigrant Welcoming Center that provides coordinated services. City officials credit the immigrant integration initiatives with increases in business investment, new international trade relationships, and a reduction in crime. Other city governments that have taken the lead in welcoming and integrating immigrants through English classes, language access, education, training and coordinated services include Philadelphia, Pittsburgh and Littleton, Colorado.

The town of Fremont, Nebraska gained notoriety in the Summer of 2010 when 57 percent of voters passed an ordinance that made it unlawful to rent apartments or houses to people who are in the country illegally. It also banned the hiring or "harboring" of people without documents. The local ordinance spurred a spate of what have become costly lawsuits. The ordinance has yet to be implemented because the ACLU won a court injunction against the law and local observers doubt it ever will. In the shadow of this national controversy, immigrants from Latin America, Africa and Southeast Asia began meeting with native-born Americans in towns across Nebraska for structured dialogue and social events designed to reduce stereotypes, enhance social cohesion and educate local reporters about the contributions immigrants make in their communities. It is one of dozens of efforts operated at the grassroots level but coordinated in part by the national organization Welcoming America.

"Ordinarily, we'd all be leading entirely separate lives," says Kristen Ostrom, who helped begin the Fremont branch of the organization, Nebraska is Home, with her acquaintance, Maria Ortiz. "We have each other now and we will be a force . . . for the future. But more importantly, I think, it's our relationships with each other, this sharing, that gives us power. We found a better way to live."

"A TWO-WAY PROCESS" THAT FILLS A GAP

The idea behind immigrant integration is simple and best expressed by The Migration Policy Institute, the national leader in immigrant integration research and policy analysis:

"We define integration broadly as the process by which immigrant newcomers achieve economic mobility and social inclusion in the larger society," MPI researchers write. This definition of integration goes much further than assimilation, MPI explains, and implies a "dynamic, two-way process" that involves changes on the part of not just immigrants but also of members of the receiving community." Since

2009, the Migration Policy Institute has recognized the best immigrant integration practices through its annual *E Pluribus Unum* prizes.

It is important to understand the immigrant integration movement as "proactive" as opposed to the largely "reactive" marches and protests in recent years, which usually responded to proposed measures designed to criminalize immigrants. Those highly publicized events enhanced coalition-building and provided important momentum, but the protest architects had yet to articulate a clear on-the-ground alternative to immigrant exclusion. Immigrant integration fills that gap.

Advocates and practitioners frame immigrant integration as a reflection of a few deeply held American values and common-sense principles:

- One: "Integration" reflects the United States' true, better self as an inclusive, welcoming nation built and enhanced by the contributions of immigrants.
- Two: Integrating immigrants—through education, self-sustaining work and in areas of health and social life—so that they become self-reliant stakeholders who identify with, care about and contribute to their communities helps immigrants and their families but is also in our collective economic and social interest.
- The third argument, advocating for increased opportunities for citizenship, is that a voting, engaged, enfranchised and invested public strengthens democracy and social cohesion at the local, state and national levels.

SETTING AN EXAMPLE IN INTEGRATION NATION

So then, what, exactly would immigrant integration look like in a community, a state legislature or expressed in a federal budget? How would it manifest itself in policy and practice?

In a school where educators are committed to "immigrant integration." counselors and teachers would create a safety net for vulnerable immigrant children and second-generation immigrant children through pre-school programs, after-school programs and the facilitation of multilingualism for all students.

In a community, every adult would have access to English classes and, if necessary, to job-training. People who are still learning English would have access to important information and government services in their native language through translation technology or interpreters. It would be easier to become a naturalized citizen of the United States because community agencies would provide classes that prepare immigrants for their naturalization tests and would also provide assistance with the legal process of becoming a citizen. Local law enforcement practice would encourage immigrants' trust of the police, rather than exacerbate fear of deportation and racial profiling. Immigrants and their families would have a place to go, such as Philadelphia's Welcoming Center for New Pennsylvanians or the 35-year-old Refugee and Immigrant Center in Salt Lake City, Utah, where new Americans can ask questions, get connected to services and become oriented to the community.

In the economic sphere, credentialing systems would allow immigrants and the larger society to benefit from the skills many immigrants arrive with. Safe working conditions and wage standards and freedom to organize would be in place for all workers. Healthcare institutions would be welcoming and safe, and develop culturally relevant practices for reaching out to immigrant communities. Credit unions, like those in Durham, North Carolina and Albuquerque, New Mexico, would provide safe places for immigrants, both legally present and not, to save money and to benefit from fair lending practices.

On the state level, more elected leaders, such as Massachusetts Gov. Deval Patrick and Washington Gov. Christine Gregoire, would encourage development of immigration integration agendas and use the "bully pulpit" to express support for immigrant communities, possibly through public welcoming campaigns. Perhaps a state office of "Immigrant Services," of the sort that operates in Illinois, would oversee and advance integration policies and funding and be a focal point for immigrants and their supporters to voice concerns and become engaged with civic life.

On the federal level, legislation would provide a path to citizenship for now undocumented immigrants and for legal permanent residents. The DREAM Act would allow young people who came with their parents to the U.S. without required documents to earn legal residency.

One challenge in development of a broad integration strategy is the inherently local, piecemeal nature of immigrant integration. The United States, unlike some countries that have large shares of immigrants—Israel or Canada, for example—has never engaged in an "immigrant integration" effort. As a result, federal policies and programs related to integration are, as Michael Fix of the Migration Policy Institute characterizes them: "ad hoc, underfunded and skeletal."

However, some state governments have pursued concerted, coherent integration efforts. Five states—Illinois, Washington, Massachusetts, Maryland and New Jersey—have taken the lead in crafting coherent integration agendas. In each, Democratic governors signed executive orders establishing an advisory council or task force on immigrant integration or "incorporation." The plans that resulted from these executive orders are in varying stages of implementation. In every state, efforts have been hampered by budget constraints and in some cases by leadership changes. Even so, these efforts are significant because they represent the first establishment of "immigrant integration" as an affirmative agenda. In so doing, they provide templates for other states.

"We are and we will continue to be a nation that depends and thrives on the contributions of immigrants and refugees," Massachusetts Gov. Deval Patrick said at a press conference where he expressed full support for the "New Americans Agenda" developed by a diverse committee of advocates, practitioners and government officials. "Our nation and our economy have been at their best when we welcome the ideas and the commitment of newcomers and when we help them integrate into our language and into our society."

WHY NOW? THE IMMIGRANT INTEGRATION IMPERATIVE

Experts offer four reasons why the traditional "hands off" approach to immigrant integration is no longer sensible.

First and most obviously is the substantial share composed of the immigrant population and their children. About 12 percent of the nation's population—or about 36.7 million people—are foreign-born, according to the U.S. Census. Another 33 million—or 11 percent of the population—are children of at least one foreign-born parent. Thus, 1 in 5 people in the United States is either a first- or second-generation immigrant. The foreign-born population is growing at a far faster rate than the native-born population. (From 2000-2008, the immigrant population increased by 22 percent, while the native-born population increased by just 6.3 percent.)

Second, over the last 20 years, immigrants have begun settling in new areas of the country (the South in particular) and in new types of communities, including smaller cities, rural areas and suburbs. These places tend not to be well-equipped to incorporate immigrants and have little experience with immigrants from Latin America, whose experiences and cultures differ from earlier European immigrants.

Third, historians explain that during previous major migration waves, integration was achieved by what the Migration Policy Institute terms "mediating" institutions, which no longer have a strong a presence in our society. This included large manufacturing companies, unions that welcomed immigrants into their ranks, and political party "machines" that vied for membership. Now, if anyone assists immigrants, it is usually small and underfunded community-based organizations, churches and schools. More funding would certainly increase these organizations' effectiveness. However, experts also stress that such organizations do not have capacity or skills to accomplish the enormous, multifaceted task of immigrant integration without coordination and guidance at other levels.

Finally, the "status" of immigrants has changed, with a larger share of the whole "undocumented" or "unauthorized" immigrants, who are vulnerable to deportation and exploitation and thus forced into a second-class membership. Undocumented "status" alone prevents people from integrating as full members of a community, except, of course, through their labor. This has negative implications not only for the undocumented but for growing numbers of children. The Pew Hispanic Center finds that of the 10.2 million undocumented immigrants in the United States, nearly half are parents of minor children. A parent's vulnerability and disenfranchisement makes these U.S. citizen children highly vulnerable, too, for a host of reasons. In the worst case, separation from a deported parent obviously negatively affects child well-being in numerous ways, as does persistent anxiety about the possibility of that separation.

Surveying immigrant integration initiatives across a country as vast and varied as ours, it becomes clear that people come to support such policies and programs and practices for a variety of reasons. Some of these reasons may be moral, even spiritual, and others grow from common-sense economics. On the national level, it is progressive organizations that are immigrant integration's most vocal advocates. But in local communities, immigrant integration supporters are quite often nonideological people who have traditionally kept low profiles. They often include business leaders, directors of English as a Second Language centers, mayors, practical-minded bureaucrats, elected leaders in government and heads of nonprofits. Perhaps this is why the movement—or, more accurately, the practice of immigrant integration—manages to find support from both liberal and conservative thinkers and academics. Immigrant integration advocates and practitioners come from a wide variety of fields and political persuasions but speak in unison about shared fate. They stick to a basic message: Economic prosperity and the integrity of our democracy depends upon immigrants finding their own success and in their committing to their communities and to the United States over the long term.

PRRAC Board of Directors and Social Science Advisory Board—Current and Former Members

Names in bold for current members. At the end of those entries is either a bolded B or bolded S, indicating which of the two bodies that person serves on.

Additional identification markings: BM-E= Board Member Emeritus; SSAB-E= Social Science Advisory Board Emeritus

The first-listed institutional identification is that at the time of the person's PRRAC appointment. If more than one institution is listed, the second is the person's present or recent location.

Darrell Armstrong: Shiloh Baptist Church, Trenton, NJ (BM-E)

Richard Berk: UCLA Dept. of Sociology (SSAB-E)

Angela Glover Blackwell: Urban Strategies Council; PolicyLink, Oakland (BM-E)

Maria Blanco: Lawyers' Committee for Civil Rights of the San Francisco Bay Area (BM-E)

John Charles Boger: Univ. of North Carolina Law School, Chapel Hill (**B**)

Frank Bonilla: Hunter College Center for Puerto Rican Studies (SSAB-E)

Gordon Bonnyman: Legal Services of Middle Tennessee; Tennessee Justice Center (BM-E)

Raphael Bostic: Univ. of Southern California (**S**)

Janis Bowdler: National Council of La Raza (BM-E)

Xavier de Souza Briggs: MIT Dept. of Urban Studies and Planning (SSAB-E)

536

Wade Henderson: NAACP; Leadership Conference on Civil & Human Rights, Washington, DC (BM-E)

Helen Hershkoff: American Civil Liberties Union; NYU School of Law (BM-E)

Damon Hewitt: Open Society Foundations; NAACP Legal Defense & Educational Fund, Inc.

Phyllis Holmen: Georgia Legal Services (BM-E)

Camille Holmes: Hewitt Legal Education Fund, Inc.; National Legal Aid & Defender Assn., Washington, DC (**B**)

Mary Ellen Hombs: Legal Services Homelessness Task Force; Massachusetts Housing and Shelter Alliance (BM-E)

Chung-Wha Hong: National Korean American Service & Educational Consortium, Flushing, NY (BM-E)

Alan Houseman: Center for Law & Social Policy, Washington, DC (BM-E)

Maria Jimenez: Immigration Law Enforcement Monitoring Project, Houston, TX (BM-E)

Judith Johnson: DeWitt Wallace-Readers Digest Fund, NYC (BM-E)

Olati Johnson: Columbia Univ. Law School (**B**)

Rucker Johnson: Univ. of California—Berkeley Public Policy (**S**)

Elizabeth Julian: Inclusive Communities Project, Dallas, TX (**B**)

Jerry Kang: UCLA Law School (**B**)

Kenneth Kimerling: Puerto Rican Legal Defense & Education Fund; Asian American Legal Defense & Education Fund, NYC (BM-E)

William Kornblum: CUNY Center for Social Research (**S**)

Robert Lehrer: Legal Assistance Foundation of Chicago; Lehrer & Redleaf (BM-E)

Harriette McAdoo: Michigan State School of Human Ecology (**S**)

Demetria McCain: Inclusive Communities Project, Dallas, TX (**B**)

Fernando Mendoza: Stanford Univ. Dept. of Pediatrics (**S**)

Roslyn Arlin Mickelson: Univ. No. Carolina-Charlotte (**S**)

S.M. Miller: Commonwealth Inst., Cambridge, MA (**B**)

Ronald Mincy: The Urban Inst.; The Ford Foundation (SSAB-E)

Don Nakanishi: UCLA Asian American Studies Center (**B**)

Pedro Noguera: NYU School of Education (**S**)

Index

The Contributors

Dolores Acevedo-Garcia, a member of PRRAC's Social Science Advisory Board, is the Samuel F. & Rose B. Gingold Prof. of Human Development & Social Policy at Brandeis Univ., where she heads the Inst. for Child, Youth & Family Policy. d.acevedo@brandeis.edu

Elizabeth Anderson is John Dewey Distinguished University Prof. of Philosophy and Women's Studies at the Univ. of Michigan, Ann Arbor. eandersn@umich.edu

Raymond Arsenault is the appropriately named John Hope Franklin Prof. of Southern History at the Univ. South Florida, St. Petersburg. arsenau@stpt.usf.edu

Lloyd Y. Asato is Deputy Director at the National Council of Asian Pacific Islander Physicians. lasato@ncapip.org

Ralph Richard Banks is the Jackson Eli Reynolds Prof. of Law at Stanford Law School. He is the author of *Is Marriage for White People? How the African American Marriage Decline Affects Everyone* (Penguin, 2012), which has been released in paperback. rbanks@stanford.edu

Laura Barrett is the director of the Transportation Equity Network and the National Policy Director of the Gamaliel Foundation, a diverse, faith-based organizing network in 22 states. TEN is on the web at www.transportationequity.org. laura@transporationequity.org

Eugene B. Benson is Executive Director of the Massachusetts Association of Conservation Commissions. Prior to that, he was Legal Counsel and Legal Services Program Director at Alternatives for Community & Environment (ACE) in Roxbury, MA and counsel to the T Riders Union and On the Move. He also served on the Transportation for America Executive Committee. eugene.benson@maccweb.org

Daina Ramey Berry is Associate Prof. of History at the Univ. of Texas Austin. drb@austin.utexas.edu

Deepak Bhargava is Executive Director of the Center for Community Change in Washington, DC, a national organization whose mission is to build the power and capacity of low-income people and people of color to change the policies and institutions that affect their lives. His chapter was originally prepared for a Univ. of Calif.-Berkeley gathering of its new Center for Diversity and Inclusion. dbhargava@communitychange.org

Derek W. Black is a Prof. of Law at the Univ. of South Carolina School of Law. He is the author of the casebook *Education Law: Equality, Fairness, and Reform* (Aspen, 2013). This chapter is a redacted version of a full article by the same title which was published at 53 *Boston College Law Review* 373 (2012) and is available online at http://ssrn.com/abstract=2008731. blackdw@mailbox.sc.edu

Sherry Salway Black, a member of the Oglala Lakota tribe, has worked more than 30 years on American Indian issues with the U.S. Congress, the federal government and non-profit organizations. Among the boards she sits on are the Policy Research Center of the National Congress of American Indians and Harvard Univ.'s Honoring Contributions in the Governance of American Indian Nations. ssblack53@cox.net

Angela Glover Blackwell is the founder and CEO of PolicyLink, a national research and action institute advancing economic and social equity, and co-author of *Uncommon Common Ground: Race and America's Future* (W.W. Norton, 2010). She currently serves on The President's Advisory Council on Faith-based and Neighborhood Partnerships. In 2013, PolicyLink partnered with the Center for American Progress to release, *All-In Nation: An America that Works for All*, a book that lays out a comprehensive policy agenda to build an equitable economy in which everyone can participate and thrive. agb@policylink.org

Maria Blanco, a former PRRAC Board member, is Executive Director of the Earl Warren Inst. on Race, Ethnicity & Diversity at the UC-Berkeley School of Law. mblanco@law.berkeley.edu

John Charles Boger is Dean and Wade Edwards Distinguished Prof. at the Univ. of North Carolina School of Law, where he teaches and researches in the areas of constitutional law, education law, and race and poverty law. Prior to joining the Univ. North Carolina Law faculty, he was director of the Capital Punishment Project and the Poverty and Justice Program at the NAACP Legal Defense & Educational Fund, Inc. He has been PRRAC Board Chair since 1989. jcboger@email.unc.edu

Marnie Brady is a PhD student in Sociology at the Graduate Center, City Univ. of New York. mbrady1@gc.cuny.edu

Donald Braman is Associate Prof. of Law at the George Washington Univ. Law School. His book, *Doing Time on the Outside: Incarceration and Family Life in Urban America*, is available from the Univ. of Michigan Press. dbraman@law.gwu.edu

Marc Brenman is a consultant, teacher, and former state and federal civil rights agency official. With Tom Sanchez, he is the co-author of *Planning as if People Matter: Governing for Social Equity* (Island Press, 2012). mbrenman001@comcast.net

Caroline B. Brettell is Univ. Distinguished Prof. of Anthropology and Ruth Collins Altshuler Director of the Dedman College Interdisciplinary Institute at Southern Methodist Univ. cbrettell@mail.smu.edu

Rob Breymaier is the Executive Director of the Oak Park Regional Housing Center. The Center has a mission to achieve lasting racial diversity in Oak Park and surrounding communities. He is also serving as the current President of the Chicago Area Fair Housing Alliance. rob.breymaier@gmail.com

Tomiko Brown-Nagin is Prof. of Constitutional Law and Prof. of History, Harvard Univ. She is the author of *Courage to Dissent: Atlanta and the Long History of the Civil Rights Movement* (Oxford Univ. Press, 2011), winner of the Bancroft Prize. tbrown-nagin@law.harvard.edu

Lonnie G. Bunch, III is Founding Director of the Smithsonian's National Museum of African American History and Culture. nmaahcinfo@si.edu

Cassandra Butts is a former Deputy White House Counsel and was Senior Vice President for Domestic Policy at the Center for American Progress. cbutts@americanprogress.org

Edgar S. Cahn is founder of Time Dollars and TimeBanks USA, co-founder of the Racial Justice Initiative of TimeBanks USA and co-founder of the National Legal Service Program and of the Antioch School of Law, predecessor to the UDC David A. Clarke School of Law, where he is presently Distinguished Prof. of Law. yeswecan @aol.com.

Vanessa Carter is Senior Data Analyst at Program for Environmental & Regional Equity (PERE), where she focuses on racial equity, movement-building and qualitative data analysis. vbcarter@dornsife.usc.edu

Julius Chambers (1936–2013) was Clinical Prof. of Law and Director of the Center for Civil Rights at the Univ. No. Carolina School of Law. He formerly was Director-Counsel of the NAACP Legal Defense and Educational Fund, Inc. He argued and won seminal cases before the U.S. Supreme Court in the areas of school desegregation, voting rights and employment discrimination. He also served as Chancellor of No. Carolina Central Univ. jchambe1@email.unc.edu

Camille Zubrinsky Charles, a member of PRRAC's Social Science Advisory Board, is the Edmund J. and Louise W. Kahn Term Prof. in the Social Sciences, Prof. of Sociology, Africana Studies, and Education at the Univ. Pennsylvania. She is the author of *Won't You Be My Neighbor? Race, Class and Residence in Los Angeles* (Russell Sage, 2006). ccharles@pop.upenn.edu

Victor Tan Chen is the founding editor of *In The Fray* magazine (www.inthefray. org) and the National Science Foundation and American Sociological Association postdoctoral fellow at the Univ. of California, Berkeley. victor_chen@inthefray.org

Sandy Ciske is the former Regional Health Officer for Public Health-Seattle & King County. sandra.ciske@kingcounty.gov

Richard Clarke is Human Rights Officer with the Office of the United Nations High Commissioner for Human Rights and Secretary of the United Nations Working Group of Experts on People of African Descent. RClarke@ohchr.org

Janeen Comenote is Executive Director of the National Urban Indian Family Coalition in Seattle and an enrolled member of the Quinault Indian Nation. jcomenote@nuifc.org

Terry L. Cross is an enrolled member of the Seneca Nation of Indians and is the developer, founder and Executive Director of the National Indian Child Welfare Association. He is the author of *Heritage and Helping, Positive Indian Parenting,* and *Cross-Cultural Skills in Indian Child Welfare* (NICWA, 1995). terry@nicwa.org

Jill Cunningham is a long-term Volunteer Corps member serving as Director of the U.S. branch of the anti-poverty organization, ATD Fourth World. She acknowledges Janet Nelson, International Board member and former UNICEF Regional Deputy Director in Geneva, for help with this commentary. jillc@4thworldmovement.org

Eldrin Deas is a PhD student in Education; Culture, Curriculum and Change at UNC-Chapel Hill. EDeas1@live.unc.edu

Saneta DeVuono-powell is currently in Spain as a Fulbright researcher. sanetadp@gmail.com

John Dossett is the General Counsel for the National Congress of American Indians. jdossett@ncai.org

Susan E. Eaton is Research Director at the Charles Hamilton Houston Inst. at Harvard Law School and Co-Director of One Nation Indivisible, which documents inclusive community-based responses to our society's increasing racial, ethnic and linguistic diversity. www.onenationindivisible.org; seaton@law.harvard.edu

Peter Edelman is a Prof. of Law at Georgetown Law Center. He was Counselor to HHS Secretary Donna Shalala and then Assistant HHS Secretary for Planning and Evaluation in the Clinton Administration and was a Legislative Assistant to Senator Robert F. Kennedy. His most recent book is *So Rich, So Poor: Why It's So Hard to End Poverty in America* (The New Press, 2012). edelman@law.georgetown.edu

Robin Einhorn is Prof. of History at the Univ. of California-Berkeley. She is the author of *American Taxation, American Slavery* (Univ. of Chicago Press, 2006), about the impact of slavery on early American tax policy, and *Property Rules: Political Economy in Chicago, 1833–1872* (Univ. of Chicago Press, 1991), about the politics of public works financing. einhorn@berkeley.edu

Ingrid Gould Ellen, a member of PRRAC's Social Science Advisory Board, is Prof. of Urban Planning and Public Policy at New York Univ.'s Wagner School and Co-Director of the Furman Center for Real Estate and Urban Policy. She is author of *Sharing America's Neighborhoods: The Prospects for Stable Racial Integration* (Harvard Univ. Press, 2000) and numerous journal articles relating to the segregation of neighborhoods and schools. ige2@nyu.edu

Mary Lou Finley was on Martin Luther King's staff in Chicago in 1965–1966, where she served as secretary for Project Director Reverend James Bevel. She is a retired core faculty member from Antioch Univ. Seattle and a co-author of *Doing Democracy: the MAP Model for Organizing Social Movements* (New Society, 2001), with primary author Bill Moyer (now deceased), who was a collaborator in the initial thinking on the issues discussed in the chapter published here. mfinley@antioch.edu

Richard Thompson Ford is the George E. Osborne Prof. Law at Stanford Law School. He is author of *Rights Gone Wrong: How Law Corrupts the Struggle for Equality* (Farrar, Straus, Giroux, 2011). rford@stanford.edu

Herbert J. Gans is Robert S. Lynd Prof. of Sociology Emeritus at Columbia Univ. and a past president of the American Sociological Association. He is the author of over a dozen books, including *War Against the Poor* (Basic Books, 1995). hjg1@columbia.edu

Julius G. Getman occupies the Earl E. Sheffield Regents Chair at the Univ. of Texas School of Law. JGetman@law.utexas.edu

John I. Gilderbloom is a Prof. of Urban and Public Affairs at the Univ. of Louisville. john.gilderbloom@louisville.edu

Tiffany M. Gill is Assistant Prof. in the Department of History at Univ. of Texas Austin. tmgill@austin.utexas.edu

Rachel Godsil, a PRRAC Board Member, is the Eleanor Bontecou Prof. of Law at Seton Hall Univ. Law School and the Director of Research for the American Values Inst. rachel.godsil@shu.edu

Andrew Grant-Thomas is Deputy Director of the Kirwan Inst. for the Study of Race and Ethnicity, Ohio State Univ. agrantth@yahoo.com

Mark Greenberg is Acting Asst. Secretary for Children and Family, US Dept. of Health and Human Services, and formerly was the Center for American Progress' Task Force on Poverty Executive Director. mark.greenberg@ACF.hhs.gov

Kali Nicole Gross is Associate Chair and Associate Prof. of the African and African Diaspora Studies Department at the Univ. of Texas Austin. kngross@mail.utexas.edu

Justin Guilder is a Managing Director at MG3 Group, LLC and was co-counsel for the *Cobell* plaintiff class. jguilder@mg3group.com

Baris Gumus-Dawes is a Senior Researcher at the Metropolitan Council. She was formerly a Research Fellow at the Institute on Race and Poverty, Univ. of Minnesota and a researcher at the Kirwan Institute for the Study of Race and Ethnicity, Ohio State Univ. Baris.Dawes@metc.state.mn.us

Kaaryn Gustafson is a Prof. at the Univ. of Connecticut School of Law. This chapter is reprinted with permission from the American Constitution Society. kaaryn.gustafson@law.uconn.edu

Luis V. Gutiérrez is an 11-term Congressman representing Illinois' 4th CD (the heart of Chicago). He chairs the Democratic Caucus Immigration Task Force and recently (2013) published *Still Dreaming: My Journey from the Barrio to Capitol Hill* (W.W. Norton). www.gutierrez.house.gov

LeeAnn Hall is Executive Director of the Alliance for a Just Society. leeanne@allianceforajustsociety.org

Susan W. Hardwick is Prof. Emerita of Human Geography at the Univ. of Oregon. She is the author or co-author of more than a dozen books on immigration, the geography of North America, and geographic education. susanh@uoregon.edu

Glenn Harris is the manager of the Seattle Race and Social Justice Initiative. Glenn. Harris@seattle.gov

Chester Hartman is PRRAC's Director of Research and editor of *Mandate for Change: Policies and Leadership for 2009 and Beyond* (Lexington Books, 2009). chartman@prrac.org

Wendy L. Helgemo is a member of the Ho-Chunk Nation, a federally recognized Indian tribe in Wisconsin. She has served as the Director of Governmental Affairs at the National American Indian Housing Council in Washington, DC since 2006. whelgemo@NAIHC.net

Jonathan Heller co-founded Human Impact Partners in 2006. jch@humanimpact. org

Wade Henderson, a former PRRAC Board member, is President and CEO of the Leadership Conference on Civil and Human Rights, and Joseph L. Rauh, Jr. Prof. of Public Interest Law at the David A. Clarke School of Law, Univ. of the District of Columbia. Henderson@civilrights.org

Danny HoSang is an Associate Prof. of Ethnic Studies and Political Science at the Univ. of Oregon in Eugene and a board member of the Alliance for a Just Society. dhosang@uoregon.edu

Christopher Howard is Prof. of Government at the College of William and Mary and author of *The Welfare State Nobody Knows: Debunking Myths about U.S. Social Policy* (Princeton Univ. Press, 2007). cdhowa@wm.edu

Jamila Jarmon is an Associate Attorney at Porter McGuire Kiakona & Chow, LLP. jjarmon@hawaiilegal.com

Olati Johnson, a current PRRAC Board member, is Prof. of Law at Columbia Law School. johnsonolati@yahoo.com

Ida E. Jones is Assistant Curator at Howard Univ.'s Moorland-Spingarn Research Center. iejones@Howard.edu

Richard D. Kahlenberg, a Senior Fellow at The Century Foundation, is author of *Tough Liberal: Albert Shanker and the Battles Over Schools, Unions, Race and Democracy* (2007). Kahlenberg@tcf.org

Ira Katznelson is Ruggles Prof. of Political Science and History at Columbia Univ. He is the author of *When Affirmative Action Was White: An Untold History of Racial Inequality in America* (W.W. Norton, 2005). iikl@columbia.edu

Joseph Keawe'aimoku Kaholokula is Associate Prof. & Chair, Dept. of Native Hawaiian Health, John A. Burns School of Medicine, Univ. of Hawaii at Manoa. kaholoku@hawaii.edu

Maria Krysan is a member of the Inst. for Government & Public Affairs faculty and Prof. of Sociology at the Univ. of Illinois at Chicago. She is co-author (with H. Schuman, L. Bobo and C. Steeh) of *Racial Attitudes in America: Trends and Interpretations* (Harvard Univ. Press, 1997) and is responsible for a website that updates the data from that book. (http://www.igpa.uillinois.edu/programs/racialattitudes). krysan@uic.edu

Bernard LaFayette, Jr., a leader of the Nashville Movement and Freedom Rider, co-founded the Student Nonviolent Coordinating Committee. He is currently Senior Scholar in Residence at Emory Univ. blafaye@emory.edu

Jason Langberg is an education justice attorney and activist in North Carolina. Langberg@gmail.com

Jacqueline Leavitt is Prof. of Urban Planning at the Univ. of California-Los Angeles who teaches and writes about housing and community development, women and rights to the city, and works on international issues about gender, housing, and land use with the Huairou Commission. jleavitt@ucla.edu

Daniel Levine is Prof. of History Emeritus at Bowdoin College, where he has taught since 1963. He drew his chapter from his 2000 book, *Bayard Rustin and the Civil Rights Movement* (Rutgers Univ. Press). Among his other books is *Poverty and Society: The Growth of the American Welfare State in International Comparison.* (Rutgers Univ. Press, 1988). dlevine@bowdoin.edu

David MKI Liu is a staff physician at Consolidated Tribal Health Project in Ukiah, California. kliumd@gmail.com

Gordon A. Martin, Jr. is a retired Massachusetts trial judge. After two years in the Civil Rights Division of the Department of Justice, he became First Assistant United States Attorney for Massachusetts and later a Commissioner of the Massachusetts Commission Against Discrimination. gamartinjr@comcast.net

Moshe Z. Marvit is a labor and civil rights attorney and a fellow at The Century Foundation. He is the co-author (with Richard Kahlenberg) of *Why Labor Organizing Should be a Civil Right.* marvit@tcf.org

Douglas S. Massey is Henry G. Bryant Prof. of Sociology & Public Affairs at Princeton Univ. dmassey@princeton.edu

Laurin Mayeno is an independent consultant dedicated to building healthy multicultural organizations and communities. www.mayenoconsulting.com. laurin@mayenoconsulting.com

Guillermo Mayer is a Senior Staff Attorney with Public Advocates Inc., a non-profit civil rights law firm and advocacy organization based in San Francisco. gmayer@publicadvocates.org

Nancy McArdle is Senior Research Analyst with diversitydata.org and has served as an expert witness in several school and housing segregation cases. nancymcardle@comcast.net

Stephen Menendian is the Assistant Director at the Haas Inst. for a Fair & Inclusive Society, Univ. of California-Berkeley. steve.menendian@gmail.com

Roslyn Arlin Mickelson, a member of PRRAC's Social Science Advisory Board, is Prof. of Sociology, Public Policy, Women and Gender Studies, and Information Technology at the Univ. of North Carolina at Charlotte. RoslynMickelson@uncc.edu

Mike Miller directs ORGANIZE Training Center. He was a SNCC Field Secretary mid-1962 through 1966, working in Mississippi, but mostly doing support work in the Bay Area; co-coordinator of UFW's Schenley Liquor boycott; and director of Saul Alinsky's Kansas City, MO community organizing project and subsequent organizing projects in California. He is author of *A Community Organizer's Tale: People and Power in San Francisco* (Heyday Books, 2009). mikeotcmiller@gmail.com

S.M. Miller, a PRRAC Board member, is a Senior Fellow at the Commonwealth Inst. in Cambridge, MA, and Prof. Emeritus of Sociology at Boston Univ. He is currently writing a book on a longer-run progressive politics and policy. fivegood@aol.com

Salim Muwakkil is a Senior Editor at *In These Times* magazine and a contributing Op-Ed columnist for *The Chicago Tribune*. He is a member of the editorial board of the Madison-based Progressive Media Project and a 2000 Media Fellow of the Soros Open Society Inst. Salim4X@aol.com

Don T. Nakanishi, a PRRAC Board member, is Director/Professor Emeritus, UCLA Asian American Studies Center. dtn@ucla.edu

Keri A. Nash is currently a staff attorney with the Center for Children's Law and Policy. Prior to joining CCLP, Keri was the Committee Counsel for the Council of the District of Columbia's Committee on Health and was the Counsel for the Racial Justice Initiative of TimeBanks USA. knash@cclp.org

Marty Nathan, MD is Executive Director of the Greensboro Justice Fund, and a survivor of the Greensboro Massacre, widowed in the incident. martygif@comcast.net

The National Coalition on School Diversity is a network of national civil rights organizations, university-based research institutions, school administrators, local educational advocacy groups, and academic researchers seeking a greater commitment to racial and economic diversity in state and federal K-12 education policy and funding. www.school-diversity.org

The National Law Center on Homelessness & Poverty headed by Maria Foscarinis is located in Washington, DC. www.nlchp.org

Julie Nelson is the director of the Seattle Office for Civil Rights. julie.nelson@seattle.gov

Katherine S. Newman, Ph.D. is the James B. Knapp Dean of The Zanvyl Krieger School of Arts and Sciences and Prof. of Sociology at Johns Hopkins Univ. knewman@jhu.edu

Pedro Noguera is a Prof. of Sociology at the Steinhardt School of Culture, Education and Development at NYU and Executive Director of the Metropolitan Center for Urban Education. pan6@nyu.edu

The Opportunity Agenda was founded in 2004 with the mission of building the national will to expand opportunity in America. More detailed information at www.opportunityagenda.org. Further information on the Opportunity Impact Statement is available from Juhu Thukral, jthukral@opportunityagenda.org

Myron Orfield is Director of the Inst. on Metropolitan Opportunity at the Univ. of Minnesota and a Prof. at its Law School. orfield@umn.edu

Theresa Osypuk is Associate Prof. at the Univ. of Minnesota School of Public Health, in the Division of Epidemiology & Community Health, and Research Director of diversitydata.org. tosypuk@umn.edu

Manuel Pastor is a Prof. of Sociology at the Univ. of Southern California and the Director of USC's Program for Environmental and Regional Equity (PERE). mpastor@dornsife.usc.edu

Eva Paterson is President of the Oakland, Calif.-based Equal Justice Society. She previously worked at the Lawyers' Committee for Civil Rights for 26 years, 13 of them as Executive Director. She is the co-founder and current Co-Chair of the California Civil Rights Coalition, as well as Co-Chair of the Civil Rights at 50 campaign in California. epaterson@equaljusticesociety.org Twitter: @evapaterson

Dawn Phillips is the Co-Director of Programs for Causa Justa :: Just Cause, a regional multi-racial membership organization based in the Bay Area, committed to supporting low-income African Americans and Latinos in organizing for racial and economic justice. dawn@cjjc.org

Kate Pickett is Prof. of Epidemiology at York Univ. and a National Inst. Heath Research Scientist. kate.pickett@york.ac.uk

Maria Poblet, the Executive Director of Causa Justa :: Just Cause, was formerly on the staff of St. Peter's Housing Committee and currently serves on the Coordinating Committee of the Grassroots Global Justice Alliance. maria@cjjc.org

john a. powell, a PRRAC Board member, is Director of the Haas Inst. for a Fair and Inclusive Society, Univ. of California-Berkeley. powel008@yahoo.com

Wendy Puriefoy is President of the Washington, DC-based Public Education Network. wpureifoy@publiceducation.org

Taiyyaba Qureshi is Educational Advancement and Fair Opportunities Attorney-Fellow, UNC Center for Civil Rights. tqureshi@gmail.com

James Ralph is Rehnquist Prof. of American History and Culture at Middlebury College. He is author of *Northern Protest: Martin Luther King, Jr., Chicago, and the Civil Rights Movement* (Harvard Univ. Press, 1993). ralph@middlebury.edu

Jason Reece is the Director of Research at The Kirwan Inst. for the Study of Race and Ethnicity, Ohio State Univ. reece.35@osu.edu

Cynthia Robbins is an independent consultant, expert in organizational, program and resource development; co-founder of the Racial Justice Initiative of Time-Banks USA; and former Chair of Public Defender Service of the District of Columbia, CRobDC@gmail.com

Michele Roberts is Campaign & Policy Coordinator for Advocates for Environmental Human Rights, a public interest law firm dedicated to upholding our human right to live in a healthy environment. mroberts@ehumanrights.org

Richard Rothstein is a Research Associate at the Economic Policy Inst. and a Senior Fellow at the Chief Justice Earl Warren Inst. on Law & Social Policy at the Univ. of Calif.-Berkeley School of Law. rrothstein@epi.org

David Rusk is president of the Metropolitan Area Research Corporation and a founding member of the Building One America coalition. davidrusk@verizon.net

Tony Roshan Samara is Associate Prof. of Sociology at George Mason Univ. tsamara@gmu.edu

Thomas W. Sanchez is Prof. of Urban Affairs and Planning at Virginia Tech. tom.sanchez@vt.edu

Mtangulizi Sanyika is Project Manager, African-American Leadership Project of New Orleans. WAZURI@aol.com

Yusuf Sarfati is an Assistant Prof. in the Dept. of Politics & Government at Illinois State Univ. ysarfat@ilstu.edu

Cliff Schrupp is Executive Director of the Fair Housing Center of Metropolitan Detroit. fhcdet@mail.com

Theodore M. Shaw, a PRRAC Board Member, is a Prof. at Columbia Univ. Law School. tshaw@law.columbia.edu

David K. Shipler, a former *New York Times* reporter, is the author of six books, including *The Working Poor: Invisible in America* (Knopf, 2004) and *A Country of Strangers: Blacks and Whites in America* (Knopf, 1997). http://shiplerreport.blogspot.com/

Mark Simon was a high school teacher for 16 years and president of the teachers union in Montgomery County, MD. He serves as National Coordinator of the Mooney Inst. for Teacher & Union Leadership and as Education Policy Analyst at the Economic Policy Inst. in Washington, DC. msimon@epi.org

Dick Simpson is a Univ. of Illinois at Chicago Prof. and former head of the school's Political Science Department. One of his latest books is *Twenty-First Century Chicago*. simpson@uic.edu

Audrey Singer is a Senior Fellow in Metropolitan Policy at the Brookings Institution. asinger@brookings.edu

William E. Spriggs is Prof. and former Chair of the Dept. of Economics at Howard Univ. and the Chief Economist of the AFL-CIO. wspriggs@howard.edu

Gregory D. Squires is a member of PRRAC's Social Science Advisory Board, as well as a Prof. of Sociology and Public Policy and Public Administration at George Washington Univ. squires@gwu.edu

Cheryl Staats is a Research Associate at the Kirwan Inst. for the Study of Race & Ethnicity, Ohio State Univ. staats.23@osu.edu

Philippa Strum is Senior Scholar and former Director of U.S. Studies at the Woodrow Wilson International Center for Scholars in Washington, DC, as well as the Broeklundian Prof. of Political Science Emerita at the City Univ. of New York. Her previous books include *When The Nazis Came to Skokie: Freedom for the Speech We Hate* (Univ. Press of Kansas, 1999). Philippa.Strum@wilsoncenter.org

Janice Sumler-Edmond is the Director of the Honors Program and a Prof. of History at Huston-Tillotson Univ. jsedmond@htu.edu

William L. Taylor (1931–2010) was a PRRAC Board member, and chaired the Citizens Commission on Civil Rights.

Philip Tegeler is Executive Director of the Poverty & Race Research Action Council. He was previously involved as counsel for the plaintiffs in one of the public housing cases discussed in his chapter. ptegeler@prrac.org

Bruce R. Thomas lives and works in Chicago as a writer, researcher and activist in public education. He recently co-created a project called the Vulnerable Student Initiative to help schools improve their ability to work with challenging students. boom2@ameritech.net

William Tobin is a Research Fellow at the Social Science Research Institute at Duke Univ. He co-directs DukeEngage Dublin, a summer research and civic engagement program focused on migrants and refugees for select undergraduates and has published on education and topics in the social sciences. tobin@soc.duke.edu

Winston Tseng is Senior Research Associate at the Asian & Pacific Islander American Health Forum. wtseng@apiahf.org

Matias Valenzuela is the Manager for King County Equity & Social Justice and manages Community Engagement and Partnerships for Public Health - Seattle & King County. matias.valenzuela@kingcounty.gov

Jenice L. View is Associate Prof. in the College of Education and Human Development at George Mason Univ. jview@gmu.edu

Margy Waller is senior fellow at Topos Partnership and founding director of The Mobility Agenda. She served as a domestic policy advisor in the Clinton-Gore White House and a visiting fellow at the Brookings Institution. More about The Mobility Agenda's alternative to the poverty framework can be found at http://www.mobilityagenda.org. margywaller@mobilityagenda.org

Signe Waller is a survivor of and was widowed by the Nov. 3, 1979 Klan-Nazi attack; a member of the former Greensboro Truth and Community Reconciliation Project's Local Task Force; and author of *Love and Revolution, A Political Memoir: People's History of the Greensboro Massacre, Its Setting and Aftermath* (Rowman & Littlefield, 2002). signewaller@earthlink.net

Mark R. Warren is Associate Prof. of Public Policy and Public Affairs in the McCormack School of Policy and Global Affairs at the Univ. of Massachusetts Boston. He has published extensively on community organizing efforts to revitalize urban communities, transform public schools, and expand civic and political participation. He is the author of *Dry Bones Rattling: Community Building to Revitalize American Democracy* (Princeton Univ. Press, 2001) and *Fire in the Heart: How White Activists Embrace Racial Justice* (Oxford Univ. Press, 2010). mark.warren@umb.edu

Amy Stuart Wells is Prof. of Sociology and Education and the Director of the Center for Understanding Race and Education (CURE) at Teachers College, Columbia Univ. Wells@exchange.tc.columbia.edu

Michael R. Wenger is a Senior Fellow at the Joint Center for Political and Economic Studies, former Deputy Director for Outreach and Program Development for President Clinton's Initiative on Race, and the author of a memoir entitled *My Black Family, My White Privilege: A White Man's Journey Through the Nation's Racial Minefield* (iUniverse, 2012) mwenger@jointcenter.org

Maya Wiley is the Founder and President of the Center for Social Inclusion (CSI), a national policy strategy organization that works to transform structural inequity and exclusion into structural fairness and inclusion. www.centerforsocialinclusion.org; info@thecsi.org

Richard Wilkinson is Emeritus Prof. of Social Epidemiology, Univ. of Nottingham Medical School and co-founder of The Equality Trust. richard.wilkinson@equalitytrust.org.uk

William Julius Wilson is the Lewis P. and Linda L. Geyser University Professor at Harvard Univ. and the author of several award-winning books, including *The Declining Significance of Race: Blacks and Changing American Institutions* (Univ. Chi. Press, 2012); *The Truly Disadvantaged: The Inner City, The Underclass and Public Policy*

(Univ. Chi. Press, 1990); and *When Work Disappears: The World of the New Urban Poor* (Vintage, 1997). bill_wilson@harvard.edu

Howard Winant is Prof. of Sociology at UC-Santa Barbara and Founding Director of the Univ. of California Center for New Racial Studies. He is the author of *The World Is a Ghetto: Race and Democracy Since World War II* (Basic Books, 2001) and co-author (with Michael Omi) of *Racial Formation in the United States* (Routledge, 1994). hwinant@soc.ucsb.edu

Michael Yellow Bird is a citizen of the Sahnish and Hidatsa Nations, Associate Prof. of Indigenous Nations Studies at the Univ. of Kansas, and co-editor of *For Indigenous Eyes Only: The Decolonization Handbook* (Santa Fe: SAR Press, 2005). mybird@ku.edu